Costume Society of America Series

PHYLLIS A. SPECHT, SERIES EDITOR

American Menswear

American Menswear

FROM THE CIVIL WAR TO THE
TWENTY-FIRST CENTURY

Daniel Delis Hill

TEXAS TECH UNIVERSITY PRESS

The paper used in this book meets the minimum requirements of
ANSI/NISO Z39.48-1992 (R1997).

Library of Congress Cataloging-in-Publication Data
Hill, Daniel Delis, 1952–
American menswear : from the Civil War to the twenty-first century / Daniel Delis Hill.
pages cm. — (Costume Society of America)
Includes bibliographical references and index.
Summary: "A chronology of men's fashion and masculine style in the United States from the Civil War era through the beginning of the twenty-first century. Also demonstrates the democratization of men's fashion by mass production, distribution, and marketing. Includes illustrations"—
Provided by publisher.
ISBN 978-0-89672-722-9 (hardcover : alk. paper)
1. Men's clothing—United States—History. 2. Clothing and dress—Social aspects—United States—History. I. Title.
GT605.H55 2011
391'.10973—dc22   2010043200

Printed in the United States of America
11 12 13 14 15 16 17 18 19 / 9 8 7 6 5 4 3 2 1

Texas Tech University Press | Box 41037 | Lubbock, Texas 79409-1037 USA
800.832.4042 | ttup@ttu.edu
www.ttupress.org

[Contents]

Relatively few comprehensive books on the history of American menswear exist. Fashion survey texts are limited by space and consequently treat the topic only in the most general terms, usually focusing on suits and sportswear, but omitting categories such as outerwear, sleepwear, underwear, swimwear, headgear, neckwear, footwear, and accessories. One exception is the definitive *Esquire's Encyclopedia of Twentieth Century Men's Fashions* by Bill Gale and Oscar Schoeffler (1973), but the text concludes at the beginning of the 1970s, leaving a substantial gap of four decades. Even if a researcher can find a copy of that volume in a used books store, he can expect to pay a few hundred dollars for it. Equally rare is William Harlan Shaw's *American Men's Wear 1861–1982* (1982), one of the "series of theatre-related volumes published by Oracle Press"[1] primarily as a picture reference book with little substantive text. Other important texts on menswear focus on European perspectives. Farid Chenoune's *A History of Men's Fashions* (1993) is an excellent study of French and British styles with a few American pop culture references (and is also an expensive rarity when available). Vittoria de Buzzaccarini's *Elegance and Style: Two Hundred Years of Men's Fashions* (1992) covers Italian menswear into the 1960s. Maria Constantino's *Men's Fashion in the Twentieth Century* (1997) and Diana de Marly's *Fashion for Men* (1985) are both short but well-detailed histories of British menswear. Cally Blackman's *One Hundred Years of Menswear* (2009) is predominantly a pop culture picture book with captions, also with a British emphasis.

Other texts on the subject of menswear carve up the topic into categories that are hard to navigate when researching a chronology of men's dress and style. Colin McDowell's *The Man of Fashion: Peacock Males and Perfect Gentlemen* (1997) separates British men's dress into assorted garment types mixed with identity themes. Similarly, *Jocks and Nerds: Men's Style in the Twentieth Century* by Richard Martin and Harold Koda

(1989), examines the dress styles of a dozen masculine types. In 2009, Robert Bryan and the Council of Fashion Designers of America produced *American Fashion Menswear,* which is likewise divided into categories that make a chronology difficult to follow.

Thus, this book on American menswear undertakes three objectives. Foremost is the compilation of a detailed, well-illustrated chronology of men's fashion and masculine style in the United States from the Civil War era through the first decade of the twenty-first century. Second is an overview of the democratization of men's fashion by mass production, mass distribution, and mass marketing. Third is a historical and sociocultural introduction to each era with an assessment of the evolving and shifting ideas and ideals of masculinity in America during each period.

Although this study also includes an abbreviated look at American menswear in the first half of the nineteenth century, its primary focus is fashions and styles since the Civil War for several reasons. During the 1850s and 1860s, a number of innovative advances in apparel manufacturing methods, technology, distribution, and marketing converged at the cusp of the Second Industrial Revolution in America. Most important of all was the introduction of the foot treadle sewing machine of the 1850s, which revolutionized ready-to-wear manufacturing by cutting garment production time up to 90% over handsewn methods. In addition, refinements in the power loom and its conversion from water power to steam and then electricity made possible the high-speed production of a huge array of cheap woven and knit textiles to feed the growing ready-to-wear industry. Another key advance at the time was the Union Army's development of proportional tables for standardized garment sizes that were quickly adapted by civilian clothing makers, ensuring a more accurate fit for consumers.

With such an abundance of mass-produced clothing came new concepts of mass distribution and mass merchandising. In the 1850s and 1860s, large department stores were established in many U.S. cities, bringing under one roof the complete range of ready-to-wear and accessories for the entire family. At the same time, the earliest mail-order services were established, first by magazines in the 1850s and then by specialty catalog retailers soon after the war.

In tandem with the growth of department stores and mail-order businesses emerged new strategies of fashion marketing and mass media. Catalogs became profusely illustrated, some in color, with plates that showed men not only what the current styles of fashion were, but also how the clothes should fit and which accessories were appropriate for the well-dressed man. (Color Plate 1.) Similarly, retailers set up lavish window and counter displays to demonstrate the newest styles and the correct way in which to dress. In addition to the illustrated mail-order catalogs, mass distribution magazines of the time like *Godey's Lady's Book* (1830–98), *Vogue* (1892 to present), and *Harper's Bazaar* (1867 to present) often included fashion reports and illustrated style editorials on men's fashions. Also complementing the fashion guidance of catalogs and store displays was a barrage of illustrated advertising by ready-to-wear makers and retailers in magazines and newspapers, on posters and handbills, and stuffed into mailers.

Coinciding with these developments in manufacturing, commerce, and mass media was the emergence of a new form of men's fashion in the 1850s. The sack coat suit introduced from England quickly became the

Figure 1. Since the mid-nineteenth century, American ready-to-wear makers and retailers have continually inspired, urged, and coaxed men into a fashion awareness through mass marketing. Some advertising messages served as style guides for the unsure male, others appealed to certain masculine lifestyles, and still others, such as this 1965 color ad for Mohara suits, made their point through humor. (Color-blind men would not be able to see the "65" in the green and pink dots.)

Only 1 out of 25 men is color-blind.
The other 24 just dress that way.

And please don't give us that old song and dance about there not being any good colors to choose from. Haven't you seen the new J&F Mohara' suits? Pacific Mills wove the fabric for us in all the right colors for Spring '65. And we added all the right fashion details. Because J&F dates their suits. Like cars. Just look for the suits with the 1965 tag on the sleeve. Twenty-four out of twenty-five men will be able to spot them in a minute.

MOHARA SUITS

ubiquitous and standardized style of masculine dress throughout America. The sack coat suit was comfortable, practical, and fashionable for all socioeconomic classes as well as easy to manufacture for ready-to-wear makers. (Color Plate 2.)

From these mid-nineteenth-century developments of ready-to-wear mass styling, mass production, and mass distribution, coupled with mass advertising and mass media, emerged a democratization of fashion across the country. Fashionable clothing was no longer solely the purview of the social or economic elite. The factory worker could dress as smartly in the most current clothing styles as the factory owner. The American male was inculcated with the notion of fashion aspiration. He learned from these many marketing channel sources about fashion cycles and style obsolescence. By the end of the 1800s, most average working men could afford at least one ready-to-wear suit for Sundays and special occasions that had been mass manufactured in America and sold through a local retailer or by mail order. Remarkably, these symbiotic principles of the American ready-to-wear industry are still the formula with the same success as 150 years ago: inspiring, urging, and coaxing men into a fashion awareness and mass consumption. (Figure 1.)

In addition to the well-illustrated chronology of menswear categories and the historical and cultural introductions to each era, this study also examines ideas and ideals of masculinity and identity as expressed in dress. As many researchers and scholars have assessed in recent decades, dress is more than simply the clothes on our backs. In *Dress and Gender: Making and Meaning* (1992), Joanne B. Eicher defines dress as "an assemblage of body modifications and/or supplements displayed by a person in communicating with other human beings."[2] That communication through our choices in dress, says writer John Harvey, is the "persona we perform." "Styles of clothing carry feelings and trusts, investments, faiths and formalized fears," asserts Harvey. "Styles exert a social force, they enroll us in armies—moral armies, political armies, gendered armies, social armies."[3] And for the widely assorted armies of average American men over the past 150 years, a continuum of dress and masculine identity has expressed and demonstrated the collective persona of each generation. Key to that continuum has been conformity—a conformity to standardized tenets of behavior and conformity expressed visually in dress, which for each man and the society in which he lived gave clarity to the meaning of masculine identity in ways beyond a mere representation of gender. The blue serge sack suit of the Victorian man communicated a masculine identity of bourgeois authoritarianism in a brotherhood of familial patriarchs. The bulky sack suit of the Edwardian man conveyed his identification with the robust leadership of America—husky Teddy Roosevelt and ponderous William Taft. The trim drape cut suits of the years between the two World Wars projected the powerful athleticism of the youthful warrior who did battle against foreign aggressors and against economic calamities. The gray flannel suit of the 1950s Ivy Leaguer reflected the gray conformity and complacency of American men in the post-World War II years. Even in our postmodern era when individuality and self-expression have prevailed in men's fashion, the rigidly padded suit of the 1960s and 1970s was a unifying identity against the frightening style melee of the Peacock Revolution. The broad-shouldered power suit of the 1980s Greed Decade proclaimed the chauvinism and success of the yuppie. And the skinny look suit of the 2000s has been an assertive differentiation of the millennial masculine identity for Gen X'ers and Gen Y'ers.

The legacy of this linearity of American men's dress and masculine identity has been commented on by every generation since Victorian times. (Figure 2.) Typical was the assessment by a contributing editor to *Printer's Ink* in 1922 who complained, "The American [male] is very conservative in dress. He hates like the deuce to look different from other men, even to look better dressed. There is a monotony about men's dress in this country that is comical."[4] However, contrary to the often-voiced complaint that men's clothing styles hardly change, regular and significant changes have obviously occurred. Sometimes the shifts evolved so glacially that only in looking back over several years was the distinction apparent to the men who had experienced it such as the sack coat phases described above; other times, change was tectonic like the startling suddenness of the 1960s youthquake that overturned comfortable, decades-old conventions of masculine style and identity such as short hair and inconspicuousness in appearance and demeanor.

Moreover, there are important reasons for focusing on *American* men's dress and identity. Not only are there significant differences in the sociopolitical meanings of masculinity between the Latin-Mediterranean and Anglo-Germanic cultures of Europe and that of pluralistic America, but we also have distinctive forms of dress and identity that are relatively meaningless elsewhere in the world. The dress and accoutrement of American cowboys, for instance, might be adaptable to the outbacks of Australia or the Argentine pampas, but in London and Paris, the look would appear like an incongruous American movie costume. Yet on the streets of Manhattan or Chicago or Los Angeles, the tribal dress of an urban cowboy would garner little if any attention. Likewise, grunge, the Seattle youth look of the early nineties, was popularized in the United States by rock bands such as Pearl Jam and Nirvana, but where the music of grunge bands achieved international fame, the look did not. Even body modifications differ, as in the case of circumcision wherein two of every three American males are circumcised for cultural, aesthetic, and hygienic reasons as compared to fewer than one in ten in the rest of the world (excluding Judeo-Islamic regions).

By contrast, some distinctive tribal styles of European subcultures

Figure 2. The common complaint that men's fashions hardly changed was used for an ad campaign in the 1950s promoting a new look, ironically, for a menswear commodity product that actually had not changed in a hundred years. Ad 1958.

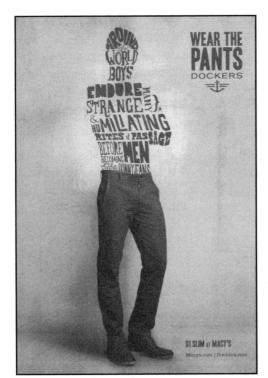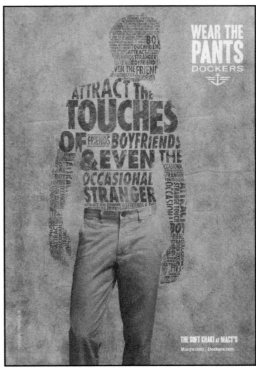

Figure 3. "Advertisements more truthfully reflect the customs, manners, and ideals of a nation than any other one thing," noted a marketing trade journal in 1927. By the end of the first decade of the twenty-first century, the pluralism of American masculinity was reflected in targeted niche marketing such as the Dockers "Wear the Pants" campaign of 2009–10. The "call of manhood" messages included having to "endure strange and humiliating rites of passage...like wearing skinny jeans" for heterosexuals, and dressing to "attract the touches of friends, boyfriends, and even the occasional stranger" for gay men." Left ad for *GQ*; right version for *Out*.

that must be included in world (or EuroAmerican) fashion histories are irrelevant in this work. The dress of England's Teddy boys in the 1950s and the look of the *zazous* of France in the 1940s were peculiar to those times and places, and had no impact on American fashions. And even when the styles of European subcultures were appropriated by Americans, they were transformed into something different from the original context. The mods of England, for example, were impeccably groomed and custom-suited teens of the early 1960s, but with the "British invasion" of the Beatles, Rolling Stones, and the Who, mod instead became for American youth a Peacock Revolution of sexualized, flamboyant fashions and long hair. Similarly, the dress of the British punks of the mid-1970s emerged as a protest look (and abrasive, confrontational attitude) of lower-working-class teenagers against the restrictive British class system. But in America, the punk look was stylized and homogenized by urban, middle-class teens solely as a rebellious look to shock parents and other authority figures, without the abusive behavior of their English counterparts.

To illustrate both the historical clothing and the way in which masculine identity was visually communicated in society, this study has relied extensively on period images from popular culture, especially advertising. In 1927, an American marketing trade journal asserted, "Advertisements more truthfully reflect the customs, manners, and ideals of a nation than any other one thing."[5] (Figure 3.) Since the earliest development of advertising as an industry in the mid-nineteenth century, marketers have understood how best to give customers what they wanted. For ready-to-wear makers, that meant providing images and props in illustrations with which the American male consumer could readily identify. The masculine identities of men as husbands, fathers, breadwinners, protectors of home and hearth, sportsmen, and (heterosexual) lovers were commonly represented in the artwork and photos of magazine and newspaper ads, and later in the new media of movies, television, and the Internet. The Victorian man might just as easily recognize himself in many of the images of manly roles—and clothing—depicted in the ads and TV commercials of the new millennium as those of his own time.

American Menswear

Ready-to-Wear

The Democratization of Men's Fashion in America

From Slops to Mass Production

The concept of ready-made clothing was not new to the nineteenth-century Industrial Revolution. As early as the sixteenth century, a variety of ready-made apparel was an export commodity for many European nations with a dependent market in their colonies. England, for example, produced "Indian briches" and "Papoose coats" for the northern American colonies and slave clothing made of coarse gray "negro cloth" for the South.

Journeymen tailors often made these types of garments as part of their training. The apprentices cut the cloth to patterns supplied by the master tailor and practiced their needlework techniques by constructing the variety of garments to be sold as ready-made. In larger shops, some cut pieces were sent out to be sewn by seamstresses working from their homes, and the journeymen would assemble the sections into completed garments.

In the port cities of America, tailor shops that expanded their operations to include the sale of ready-made clothing became known as slop shops. Proprietors maintained inventories of ready-made clothing—either imported or made in the shop—primarily for sailors who often had an immediate need for inexpensive clothes after long voyages. The English term "sloppes" had been used for centuries as a generic description of a sailor's clothing. Among the types of ready-made clothes advertised by slop shops in colonial newspapers were shirts, trousers, great coats, and pea jackets.

Colonial consumers of ready-made clothing seldom enjoyed a proper fit or consistent, precision tailoring. The very hang of a coat and swing of its skirt proclaimed whose clothing was professionally made-to-measure

Figure 1-1. To differentiate the quality of their handcrafted apparel from that of manufactured ready-to-wear, tailoring organizations widely promoted their "scientifically accurate" methods of measuring for a proper fit. At the end of World War I, for example, the Edward V. Price chain advertised nationally its guarantee of a "satisfactory fit and style" through a "perfected anatomical system" of measuring. Ad 1921.

and whose was off the shelf.

The production of ready-made clothing in the colonial era, though, was not the beginning of the democratization of men's fashion in America. Indeed, ready-made apparel of the time was in the same league as homemade clothes, both of which denoted the lower classes. The first steps toward the democratization of men's clothing occurred during the first quarter of the nineteenth century when tailors began to modify their techniques of garment construction to better address size, fit, and even trends in fashion for ready-made clothing.

One of the first milestones was the introduction around 1820 of the inch measuring tape. Previously, tailors developed personalized systems of taking measurements, usually by marking strips of paper with the lengths and proportions of the customer's body. From years of experience with taking measurements, each tailor prepared his own general guidelines for producing ready-made garments. With the inch tape, standardized rules for measuring emerged. Throughout the 1820s, a profusion of handbooks and "tailors' compasses" were published containing instructions, tables, and illustrations for accurate methods of measurement. As one of these guides noted, such standardized methods of measurements were "not only for a coat but for all sorts of coats; not for all sorts of coats only, but [also] for vest jackets and pantaloons."[1] Over subsequent decades, as techniques for measurements became more sophisticated and standardized, tailors and tailoring organizations emphasized in their advertising the importance of scientific accuracy for the correct fit of clothing. (Figure 1-1.)

From the standardization of measurements developed innovative proportional systems that reduced measuring and cutting to a series of mathematical calculations. The basic principle was that men's bodies had set proportions and one measurement could obviate the need for the other dozen or so measurements. For a coat, for example, a tailor could use the measurement of a man's chest and, by consulting a table of proportions, gauge the measurements of the rest of the garment. These early proportional drafting systems were a critical step toward the development of standardized sizes, which would be key in making ready-made clothing more broadly acceptable to a diverse market.

In addition, proportional drafting systems minimized human error and fabric wastage. The faster and more accurately a tailor could draft and cut garment pieces, the lower his costs in producing volumes of ready-made clothing. Other incentives for expanding ready-made operations included the need to use up fabric stocks and to keep journeymen busy during slack periods between seasonal peaks. A considerable work force of cheap labor was also readily available for sewing tasks regarded as unskilled, such as stitching straight seams on coats and trousers. Women and children worked at home at less than a quarter of the wages paid to skilled journeymen.

One of the earliest large-volume manufacturers of ready-made clothing in America was the U.S. Army Clothing Establishment. (Figure 1-2.) It was organized as a centralized supplier of uniforms during the War of 1812. The goal of the Establishment was much the same as that of most commercial makers of ready-made clothing: quality through consistency. By bringing much of the manufacturing operations under one roof, the military could better control consistency.

Standardized patterns were drafted by a master tailor and provided to cutters. To ensure that the patterns did not significantly lose their dimensions and shape with use, cutters were required to take the first of every one hundred garments cut from the original pattern and use that as the pattern for the rest of the lot. Cutters also had to know how to maximize the use of materials by arranging the patterns efficiently on the fabric. After all the pieces of each garment had been cut, they were bundled with the necessary buttons, lining material, thread, and padding, and the packages were sent out to women under contract to sew for the Army. Government records of the period indicate that these women received specialized training to construct the various garments of the Army uniforms. Once the garments were sewn, an inspector approved each one before payment was authorized. About a dozen skilled tailors also were employed for some high-skill finishing tasks such as ornamental stitching on officers' uniforms.

This simple system of manufacturing ready-made clothing served as a model for many commercial wholesale as well as retail enterprises in the second quarter of the nineteenth century. Since little capital outlay was required except for the cost of fabric, manufacturers of ready-made clothing proliferated throughout the northeast. The efficiency of the

Figure 1-2. The U.S. Army Clothing Establishment was one of the earliest mass-production manufacturers of ready-to-wear. Since the design and materials of uniforms were standardized and styles remained constant for years, the process of pattern making, cutting, and sewing could be effectively organized and regulated. Illustration from *Gleason's Pictorial* of the newly approved uniforms of the U.S. Navy, 1852.

Figure 1-3. During the Industrial Revolution, increasingly more efficient methods of flow production were developed in factories making possible the mass production of goods such as clothing and accessories. The greater the production volume the lower the cost to consumers. Mass production ready-to-wear factories: top, 1875; bottom, 1895.

subdivision of labor into specializations also continued to evolve. With the introduction of the sewing machine, factory work was divided between workers such as a machine operator, a baster, and a finisher, each of whom was responsible for the task of completing a certain quota of garments each day. (Figure 1-3.) Some sewers specialized in only one part of a garment as it was assembled piece by piece down a chain of task teams.

Despite much improvement in the quality of ready-made apparel, fit remained a problem for many men purchasing off-the-shelf clothing until the 1870s. Although proportional drafting systems provided some

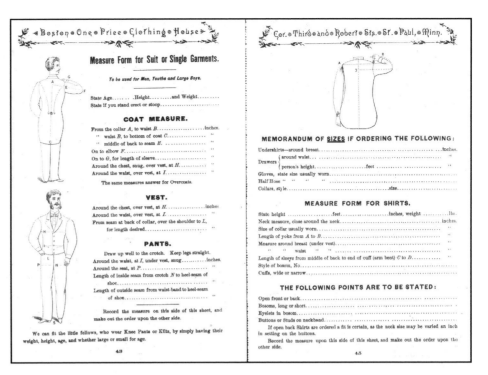

Figure 1-4. Early mail-order retailers provided guidelines to their customers for submitting their measurements to better ensure an accurate fit of ready-to-wear clothing. Pages from The Boston Store catalog 1887.

measuring calculation tables for body groups, clothing manufacturers continued to arrive at their own set of size measurements through trial and error.

During the Civil War, selected measurements of over a million conscripts were collected in a study by the U.S. Army and compiled into a proportional table of the form and build of the American male. When that report was later made available to civilian clothing manufacturers, the results reinforced what tailors already knew: certain sets of measurements were common throughout the population. For instance, for every chest size, there were average corresponding measurements for the waist and legs. Although the Army study was somewhat helpful, the statistical data used in preparing the tables was too incomplete to provide standardized sizes.

With the advent of the mail-order business in the 1870s, men, at last, were able to purchase ready-to-wear clothing that fit adequately. Catalogs included illustrated guides and instructions for submitting size measurements with orders. (Figure 1-4.) In earlier decades, ads from ready to wear retailers emphasized the multiplicity of clothing styles, quality fabrics, and the newest in fashion trends, but rarely was a proper fit promised. Mail-order businesses, though, could assure men of a fairly accurate fit by requiring a set of the customer's measurements. The Brown, King and Company of Boston noted in their 1893 catalog that "the matter of cutting has been reduced to an exact science, so that we are able to practically guarantee a fit."[2] By the early 1900s, catalog companies confidently offered money-back guarantees if the customer was not satisfied with the fit. (Figure 1-5.) In 1907, Sears promised in their annual big book catalog that their men's ready-to-wear suits were guaranteed to "fit you and please you in every way" or they would send a refund including reimbursement for return shipping.[3]

At the end of the nineteenth century, American men were well supplied with a huge array of affordable ready-to-wear clothing and furnish-

Figure 1-5. National mail order businesses usually carried a larger inventory of ready-to-wear apparel than local retailers. As a result, a customer was more likely to receive clothing that accurately fit the measurements he submitted with his order form. Examples of guarantees printed in menswear catalogs, 1910s.

Figure 1-6. The technological advances of the power loom in the nineteenth century allowed for high-speed production of textile weaving managed by fewer, less skilled workers. Left, Crompton & Knowles jacquard silk loom, 1918; right, George Crompton fancy loom with horizontal harness motion, 1865.

ings for all seasons and different social occasions. The stigma associated with wearing ready-made apparel from slop shops had been dispelled over the decades by the ever-improving quality of construction, fit, and style of mass-produced menswear. Many fashion editorials endorsed ready-to-wear by varying degrees. As early as 1875, *Harper's Bazar* asserted that "furnishing houses are providing ready-made suits at such reasonable prices and of such varied designs that something may be found to suit all tastes and purses."[4] In 1894, *Vogue's* elitist columnist for "As Seen by Him" conceded, "If I could not afford to have my things made by a first-class tailor I would rather purchase from a ready-make man. Some of them are very reputable."[5] Indeed, *Vogue* even addressed the "vexed question of English versus American clothes," and concluded, "It is hard to tell the difference between a suit of clothes cut by an English tailor and one supplied from Baker's or one of the other large ready-made clothiers."[6] In addition to the improved quality and construction of mass-produced clothing, mail-order catalogs made possible a wide distribution of affordable ready-to-wear, even to the most remote frontiers. This democratization of fashion through mass production and mass distribution meant that the farmer in Omaha or the dry goods clerk in Seattle could dress in clothing as current as that of *Vogue's* "As Seen by Him" editor in New York.

Industry and Technology

The evolution of ready-to-wear production methods from slop shops to mass manufacturing in the nineteenth century was only one factor in the democratization of men's fashions in America. Without inexpensive, high quality materials, ready-to-wear apparel would not have been affordable to the masses despite low costs in production and distribution.

During the Industrial Revolution of the eighteenth century, European and American inventors made enormous strides in mechanizing and improving textile production. In England, the fly shuttle, which literally flies through the warp threads to rapidly weave cloth, was perfected by John Kay in 1733. During the 1760s, James Hargreaves developed versions of the Spinning Jenny for the uniform drawing and twisting of yarns onto more than a hundred spindles simultaneously. In 1785, Edmund Cartwright patented the steam power loom, making possible the location of factories away from fast-flowing water sources. American inventor Samuel Slater brought out his Arkwright system of carding, drawing, and spinning cotton in 1789. A few years later, Eli Whitney solved the problem of removing seeds from cotton fibers with his cotton gin, ensuring a bountiful supply of raw cotton to the mills of both America and England.

In the nineteenth century, refinements in technology included the further automation of the power loom. For decades, the loom had to be stopped to refill the shuttle bobbins manually. When John Northrop introduced the automatic bobbin changer in 1891, mass production of textiles made a huge leap forward. One weaver could now manage dozens of looms that could produce more than two hundred yards of fabric per hour. (Figure 1-6.)

Other important advances in textile production in the eighteenth century were improvements in fabric printing. To compete with the abundant imports of cotton calicos from India and print silks from China, in the 1750s, the French developed a technique of one-color printing on fabric with engraved copper plates. In the 1780s, the Scotsman Thomas Bell adapted the engraved plate to a roller that could register up to six colors in a high-speed printing process. By the beginning of the nineteenth century, the beautifully patterned calicos that once had been a favorite of the affluent were now available to the masses in an endless variety of designs and colors.

Related to print fabrics was the production of fancy weaves. Although American textile mills could not match the better-grade fabrics such as broadcloths, brocades, satins, and silks made in Europe and Asia, they soon became competitive with the manufacture of figured woolens. In 1840, William Crompton modified the power loom to weave small-pattern fabrics. At first the technique was applied only to cotton textiles, but, by the 1850s, U.S. mills were mass producing figured woolens as well. Ready-to-wear makers now had an abundant supply of inexpensive richly textured fabrics for fashionable men's coats, jackets, vests, and trousers.

Equally important for the American ready-to-wear industry was the introduction of merino sheep in the early nineteenth century. The strong and resilient wool from this hearty breed of sheep was used in the manufacture of assorted medium-grade woolen cloths popularly used in men's suits, coats, and trousers. By the 1850s, inexpensive fabrics such as cassimere and cassinette, woven of cotton warp and wool weft, were ordered in the hundreds of thousands of yards each year by ready-to-wear makers. Retailers of the time advertised that these American woolens were warranted equal in quality to imported varieties and cost twenty percent less.

Of all the technological innovations that contributed to the success of the ready-to-wear industry, one of the most important was the sewing machine. Throughout the early nineteenth century, a number of individuals in both America and Europe explored mechanized methods of stitching. French inventor Barthelemy Thimmonier introduced a crude device in 1830 that could sew about two hundred stitches a minute—more than five times faster than the most skilled hand-sewer. He abandoned his invention, though, when his small ready-to-wear operation was destroyed by a mob of angry tailors. The following decade, American watchmaker Elias Howe developed a hand-cranked machine that featured a needle that moved horizontally with an underthread shuttle. At

Wilson shuttle sewing machine, 1872

Ladies' Home Journal treadle sewing machine, 1892

Figure 1-7. The single most important technological advance for the ready-to-wear industry was the invention of the sewing machine. In the years just before the Civil War, manufacturers replaced their armies of contract sewers with sewing machine operators, thereby cutting costs for production of some garments by as much as eighty percent.

Figure 1-8. For the Victorian housewife, the sewing machine eliminated the drudgery of hand sewing garments for herself and her family. If a woman could not afford a machine of her own, sewing machine makers encouraged the formation of ladies' sewing clubs in which each member would contribute a portion of the total cost and then share use of the machine. Illustration for a poem in *Peterson's Magazine,* 1883. Excerpt:

I stitch the never-ending seam,
Late into night my light burns low;
I hear the midnight striking slow:
With ev'ry stitch my heart-strings go![9]

about the same time, Isaac Singer produced a machine with a needle that functioned vertically, making curved seams easier to stitch. Equally important, Singer's machine was operated by a foot treadle, freeing both hands to manipulate the fabric. From about 1845 through 1895, more than 7,000 patents for sewing machines and components were registered, including numerous industrial versions that advanced the mass production of ready-to-wear. (Figure 1-7.) In 1860, *Godey's Lady's Book* rhapsodized about the sewing machine:

> The extreme facility with which garments are made by its help will enable thousands, ay, hundreds of thousands, to have new clothes...The very poor woman among servants and workpeople seldom have any ingenuity with the needle; they can often buy cheap and strong new fabrics, but they cannot make them up, and, heretofore, the making of the garment often cost more than the cloth. Now, the sewing machine, at a very small cost, sews up the seams; or, a ready-made garment can be purchased nearly as cheap as the cloth of which it is made.[7]

A table included in a follow-up editorial by *Godey's* that same year showed the time savings in producing men's garments with a sewing machine compared with hand sewing[8]:

	By Machine	By Hand
Men's shirt	1 hr/16 mins	14 hrs/26 mins
Frock coat	2 hrs/33 mins	16 hrs/35 mins
Satin vest	1 hr/14 mins	7 hrs/19 mins
Linen vest	0 hrs/48 mins	5 hrs/14 mins
Cloth pants	0 hrs/51 mins	5 hrs/10 mins
Summer pants	0 hrs/33 mins	2 hrs/50 mins

For housewives, the drudgery of garment sewing by hand was eliminated by the sewing machine. (Figure 1-8.) Either women acquired a home machine or settled for manufactured clothing for her and her family.

With amazing time-saving results such as those above, no clothing manufacturer could stay in business without the sewing machine. Costs to produce some garments were reduced by eighty percent. Between 1850 and 1860, capital investment in the clothing industry doubled while at the same time the number of establishments decreased by eleven percent as many small shops merged with larger manufacturers.[10]

Refinements and specialization in machine sewing continued to evolve in the early twentieth century. In 1902, blind stitch machines were introduced for padding collars and lapels. A few years later, a lock stitch machine was invented for finishing the bottoms of trousers that operated at about 600 stitches a minute. Even detailed finishing work, such as sewing buttons and button-holes, was commonly machine produced by World War I.

After the sewing machine, the next important technological advance that improved the efficiency of ready-to-wear production was the development of cutting machines. Until the last quarter of the nineteenth century, fabric cutting was a manual process that required strong, steady hands and sharp shears. A skilled worker could cut about three thicknesses at a time while preserving the integrity of the pattern. In 1872, a steam-powered cutting machine was introduced. The apparatus featured a long vertical blade that sliced through about eighteen layers of cloth. The massive tool was cumbersome, though, and inaccurate on curves and angles. Operators had to wear clumsy finger extensions made of tin to protect their hands. During the 1890s, various electrically powered cutters were developed. A high-speed rotary device that could cut about 100 layers of cloth replaced the vertical blade. As these machines became lighter and more manageable, the speed of the cutting operation became more aligned with the sewing operation.

Once the mass-produced garments were finished, they had to be pressed before packing and shipping. Through much of the nineteenth century, clothing was ironed by the tailor's goose, so called because the silhouette of early irons resembled the long-necked bird with its head turned backward. The cast iron goose was heated by hanging over a fire or sitting on a stove. Regulating the level required considerable judgment to ensure adequate heat for pressing but not so much that the fabric would be scorched. In the 1890s, gas-heated irons were introduced. (Figure 1-9.) The gas was piped in through a rubber hose providing a constant, even source of heat. Although electric irons were also developed at about the same time, the gas-heated versions were more widely used well into the first quarter of the twentieth century because gas was cheaper and more readily available.

The steam iron and pressing machines familiar to us today were developed in the 1910s. Pressing machines especially became indispensable for mass production. Garments were placed between pads, and a pressure of steam penetrated and moistened the fabric. Previously, garments had been dampened with a wet sponge or cloth—an insanitary process that contributed to the infection of the usual cuts and blisters on a pressman's hands. Clothing manufacturers took note of the advertised promises of cost savings and efficiencies from the makers of pressing machines. As one brochure declared in 1914: "Payrolls have been reduced more than 50 percent in many of the largest clothing factories in the world. Better creases, shaping, and a more uniform finish are the natural results from the use of this equipment."[11] By the 1920s, pressing machines, like sewing machines and cutting machines before them, had become specialized, each performing specific functions such as pressing sleeves, coat shoulders, or trouser legs, among others.

Distribution

The small slop shops and men's clothiers of the early nineteenth century usually offered the urban customer a range of apparel that included what was referred to as furnishings—neckwear, collars, handkerchiefs, suspenders and garters, hosiery and socks, sleepwear, underwear, and leather goods. In the country, general dry goods stores usually carried a more limited assortment of utilitarian garments and accessories. If a man wanted to be fashionably attired head-to-toe, he had to travel to a city for the menswear shops. However, by the second quarter of the nineteenth century, the increased volume and diversity of manufactured goods and the increasing demand from customers forced retailers to expand operations and rethink sales methods.

In Europe, the first department store was established in 1838. The concept spread rapidly as the innovation and technological advances of the Industrial Revolution made possible ever more varieties of manufactured goods. These new retail giants brought together under one roof a complete range of ready-to-wear clothing and accessories for the entire

Figure 1-9. Gas-heated irons were less expensive to operate than electrical versions although both types were introduced in the 1890s. From 1903: top, the Steward gas-heated flatiron was advertised to cost 4 cents for 10 hours of work; bottom, the American Electrical iron was promised as a "clean" alternative without the "odor of burned gas or sooty smell."

Bloomingdale's, New York, 1890

Stern Brothers, New York, 1897

Figure 1-10. With its extensive selections of ready-to-wear clothing and accessories, its alluring and educational displays of apparel, and its readily available consulting services, the nineteenth-century department store was a significant factor in the democratization of fashions for men.

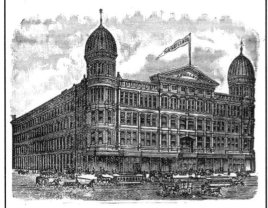

O'Neill's, New York, 1895

family as well as a wide assortment of mass-produced household goods. In the United States, the establishment of the department store was an urban phenomenon of the Civil War era, notably Marshall Field and Carson Pirie Scott in Chicago during the 1850s, Alexander T. Stewart in New York in 1862, and John Wanamaker in Philadelphia in 1862. By the last quarter of the nineteenth century, almost every city had at least one department store, and large metropolitan areas often had several. (Figure 1-10.) Some large operations even opened regional branches—a prelude to the chain store—which were continually supplied with fresh merchandise from centralized distribution centers.

The department stores led the way in the evolution of merchandising and selling to a sophisticated spectacle by the end of the nineteenth century. The 1890s was the "plate glass era" in retailing as new stores and remodeled stores were designed with huge display windows lining the streets. From the start these enormous showcases were filled with a dazzling array of fashions and goods. Eye-catching props and tableaus of mannequins were theatrically arranged to capture the public's attention. "Window shopping" entered the American vernacular. Store interiors became opulent palaces with marble flooring, gilded columns, bronze fixtures, and finely crafted furnishings. (Figure 1-11.) Marshall Field's in Chicago was famous for its 6,000-square-foot dome made of Tiffany stained glass. Wanamaker's in Philadelphia provided music to its shoppers from the largest organ in the world at the time. Department stores were also among the first public buildings in many cities to be lit electrically and to install elevators and escalators. The addition of restaurants and soda fountains enticed the customer to visit more often and stay longer. Some stores included barber shops, shoe shine stands, laundry services, and even Turkish baths. Most offered free delivery for any purchase.

Menswear departments became well-accoutred shops with greater inventories and conveniences than most haberdasheries. Displays and mannequins instilled an aspiration for fashion among the masses. Sales clerks were living models for how to dress appropriately—the newest styles, the proper fit, and the correct accessories. Management trained employees on the latest fashion trends and dress etiquette, which, in turn, was provided as a free consulting service to the public.

Most Americans, however, lived far beyond city limits and suburban trolley lines. For this vast market of small-town residents and rural farmers, merchants expanded on the idea of serving customers by mail, a service that many publishers had provided their subscribers for decades. For example, beginning in the early 1850s, *Godey's* offered a mail-order shopping service to readers "living at a distance" who wanted to purchase items featured in their fashion plates. As the editors noted in 1857, orders had to be prepaid by check, and the customer had to provide "instructions as minute as possible, accompanied by a note of the height, complexion, and general style of the person, on which much depends in choice."[12] These orders were then passed on to the retailers that had provided samples and information about the fashions used to illustrate the plates. By the 1860s, some ready-to-wear items such as shawls and wraps began to be offered for sale by mail in the pages of omnibus ads placed at the back of magazines. From these marketing precedents developed the mail-order catalog.

Aaron Montgomery Ward is credited with the first mail-order catalog, produced in 1872 as a one-page price list. His mail list came from the membership roster for the Grangers, a midwest farmer's organization. Ironically, this first Ward's catalog, "devoted to furnishing farmers and mechanics throughout the Northwest with all kinds of merchandise," listed fifty-five manufactured clothing and accessory items for women but no menswear. However, Ward's catalogs met with such success that, just three years later, the 1875 spring issue had seventy-two pages that included more than 200 men's garments and furnishings. By the beginning of the twentieth century, the Ward's "wish book" catalog—popularly named because between its covers was virtually everything the modern consumer could want—offered a volume weighing 6-1/2 pounds containing

Figure 1-11. The great mercantile palaces of nineteenth-century America invited everyone, regardless of socioeconomic status, to enter and marvel at the opulence of the surroundings and to peruse the magnificent variety of goods for sale. Postcards of department store interiors, c. 1895-1905.

AN INTERIOR DECORATION. MARSHALL FIELD & CO.'S RETAIL STORE, CHICAGO.

MARSHALL FIELD & COMPANY. STORE FOR MEN. MAIN AISLE. FIRST FLOOR.

THE "NEW WAY" CLOTHING STORE, BREINIG & BACHMAN CO., SIXTH AND HAMILTON STS. ALLENTOWN, PA.

Figure 1-12. The giant mail-order wish books of the mass merchandising retailers contained hundreds of pages filled with tens of thousands of mass-produced items for every household and every member of the family. Montgomery Ward ad, 1904.

85,000 items with 30,000 illustrations, many in full color.[13] (Figure 1-12.)

During the last quarter of the nineteenth century, the mail-order industry exploded across America. From coast to coast, almost all department stores set up mail-order operations and produced catalogs. Many retailers, such as Wanamaker's and Stern's, sold nationally. By the beginning of the twentieth century, mass merchandisers such as Sears, Roebuck and Company and J. C. Penney joined Ward's in mailing out tens of thousands of their wish books nationwide. Huge distribution centers were well stocked with the manufactured products of the burgeoning American Industrial Revolution. (Figure 1-13.) Chicago became a centralized hub for many of the largest mail-order firms.

Despite the broad and extensive marketing of the mass merchandisers, specialty stores such as men's clothiers found they could successfully compete through direct mail. (Color Plate 1.) Their competitive advantage included a broader range of clothing styles, fabrics, and sizes than was available from a mass merchandiser. In 1887, the menswear store, The Boston (St. Paul, Minnesota) asserted in their spring catalog that they stocked over fifty lines of ready-to-wear suits ranging from sack styles to frock suits, each "made, finished, and wearing as well as the best, and cheaper than the cheapest, custom work."[14]

In addition, menswear catalogs were fashion guides to the masses. In page after page, catalogs illustrated a profusion of the newest ready-to-wear fashions with details of how clothes were to be properly worn and accessorized. As with the lavish merchandising and displays of department stores, catalogs also fueled consumer aspirations for fashion, variety, and wardrobe diversity.

The buying, warehousing, stocking, and advertising of manufactured clothing by catalog firms were only part of the distribution processes that contributed to the success of mail-order retailing and, consequently, the enormous leap in ready-to-wear consumption. In 1864, the United States Post Office introduced the postal money order. Previously, customers risked sending cash, and retailers risked accepting personal checks or regional banknotes, both of which could be payable by an insolvent bank. Often, postage stamps were sent as payment, but merchants and buying services could find themselves with a surplus of stamps that were not redeemable for cash at the post office. Soon after the postal money order became widely available, private money transfer firms, such as Western Union, provided money order services as well.

Once payment had been reconciled, the cataloger had to ensure delivery of the merchandise. In cities, department stores maintained fleets of delivery wagons, and, later, trucks that promised free, same-day delivery of any goods from a spool of thread to a house full of furniture. For mail-order merchants shipping far and wide, options were limited until the end of the nineteenth century.

The mileage of railroads in America quadrupled between the end of the Civil War and the beginning of the twentieth century. In 1869, the transcontinental railroad was completed, linking both coasts with a rapid means of transportation. Freight services followed the expansion of the railroads and established terminals at strategic junctions. From these distribution depots, stagecoaches and wagon-express operations carried packages to remote post offices.

The delivery of mail-order goods, though, depended mostly on the extensive reach of the U.S. Post Office. In 1896, both catalogers and consumers benefited from the establishment of the Rural Free Delivery service. Before then, people who lived on remote farmsteads and ranches had to go the post office in the closest town, fort, or trading post to collect their mail. Another change in postal regulations that improved mail-order delivery was a change in the four-pound weight limitations of parcel post shipments. In 1912, the Post Office began to accept packages up to twelve pounds, and the following year that was increased to twenty pounds. (Figure 1-14.)

Throughout the second half of the nineteenth century, the distribution needs of ready-to-wear makers were met by technology and marketing ingenuity. Railroads continued to expand across the American landscape making possible the rapid delivery of huge volumes of mass-produced goods to wholesalers, retailers, and consumers. Department stores brought together under one roof a vast array of clothing and other factory-made merchandise, providing local consumers with a one-stop shopping experience. For those consumers living far from cities, the

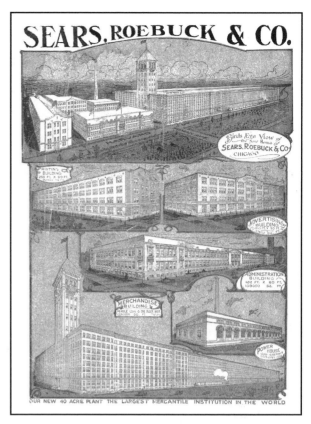

Figure 1-13. By the end of the nineteenth century, the massive enterprises of the major catalog retailers often included self-owned factories, massive distribution centers, and even in-house advertising agencies. Back cover of Sears catalog, 1907.

Figure 1-14. Mail-order businesses received a boost when the U.S. Post Office expanded services in 1912 and 1913 to include parcel post shipments up to twenty pounds in weight.

Figure 1-15. In the nineteenth century, mass marketing on a national scale was achieved through advertising in magazines. Mass media giants promoted their subscription numbers in marketing trade journals to encourage ad agencies to buy space in their publications for resale to clients. Magazine trade ads in *Printer's Ink,* 1897.

world of manufactured goods was made available through the pages of catalogs. Money orders made payment easy and safe, and the postal service conveniently delivered the merchandise to the home. As ever-increasing varieties of ready-to-wear became readily available to the masses and a consumer market responded voraciously to the marketing strategies of stores and catalogers, the democratization of fashion in America was relatively complete by the beginning of the twentieth century.

Fashion Marketing and Advertising

Concepts of marketing as a planned strategy of business evolved in tandem with the rapid advances in mass production, mass distribution, and mass merchandising during the Second Industrial Revolution of the late nineteenth century. For the ready-to-wear industry, three forces developed a symbiotic relationship that fueled a fashion consumerism across all socioeconomic strata in America. These three intertwining forces were mass production, fashion journalism, and national advertising—an inextricably linked combination that has remained critical to the marketing successes of the ready-to-wear industry ever since.

As mass production became faster, more efficient, and increasingly diverse, manufacturers and retailers explored ways of expanding their market. To broaden their consumer base, they had to add mass communication to their marketing efforts. Many urban newspaper chains offered large circulation numbers for regional markets. However, the principal form of mass communication on a national scale in the nineteenth century was magazines. (Figure 1-15.) By the end of the century, several thousand titles were published in the United States. Circulation numbers

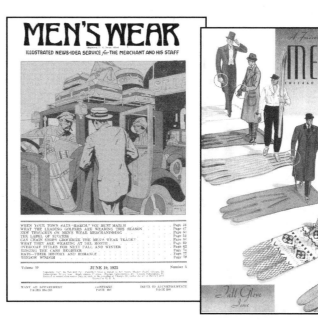

Figure 1-16. Fashion trade periodicals like *Men's Wear* provided information on style trends to retailers, tailors, and other industry professionals. Publications with an emphasis on style and fashion for men were products of the twentieth century: *Esquire* debuted in 1933, and *GQ* in 1957. *Men's Wear* issues from 1925 and 1935.

of some magazines demonstrated to marketers that an audience of hundreds of thousands of consumers was available coast to coast. According to *Printer's Ink* in 1897, the "strongest seven" magazine titles—*Munsey, McClure's, Harper's, Century, Scribner's, Cosmopolitan, Review of Reviews*—had a combined annual print run of more than 1 1/2 million copies.[15]

Although most magazines targeted a male readership, they seldom included much space for men's fashion editorials. A few menswear trade periodicals emerged in the nineteenth century such as *Tailor and Cutter, Haberdasher,* and *Men's Wear,* but consumers would only encounter the fashion advice of these publications if shared by the proprietors of men's clothiers or the clerks in department store menswear shops. (Figure 1-16.) On occasion, a fashion plate might be featured, but the accompanying text was rarely more than a brief description of fabrics, colors, or textile patterns. Details of how to wear the latest knot of the cravat or of the newest cut of the vest were usually absent.

Ironically, it was women's magazines that led the way for providing news and advice on menswear. In the decades before the Civil War, magazines such as *Godey's Lady's Book, Ladies' Repository,* and *Peterson's* included information and illustrations on men's clothing principally as guides for home sewing and embroidery projects. Shirts, sleepwear, lounging caps, and robes were the most commonly featured types of garments. Depictions of suits, riding habits, outerwear, and similar complex apparel were usually included only as a background accompaniment to women's styles in a fashion plate. As with men's trade publications, though, early women's magazines omitted comment on men's style; how and when to wear specific types of clothing were topics the editors avoided.

The first American magazine primarily devoted to fashion was *Harper's Bazar,* launched in 1867. (The title was changed to *Harper's Bazaar* in 1929.) Articles on menswear were much more detailed and style-oriented in *Bazar* than had been written previously. An example from 1883 featured details on the full masculine wardrobe by category including business suits, semiformal morning suits, day dress suits,

Figure 1-17. By the late nineteenth century, the variety of menswear, and the indefatigable promotion of new styles and trends by ready-to-wear makers, inspired many women's magazines to include in-depth reports on masculine dress. Pages from "As Seen by Him" in *Vogue*, 1895.

formal evening suits, overcoats, shirts and collars, scarves and neckties, hosiery, handkerchiefs, shoes, hats, gloves, and "varieties" such as canes, umbrellas, raincoats, cardigans, pajamas, and robes.[16] Prominent fashion retailers such as Lord and Taylor and Tiffany's were often credited in articles for contributing information and clothing samples for the articles and illustrations. In turn, the retailers enjoyed free advertising and the cachet of fashion experts.

By the 1890s, fashion journalists began to speak directly to men about style and changes in fashion through editorials in Sunday newspapers and even in issues of women's magazines. When *Vogue* made its debut in 1892, the format included a weekly column "As Seen by Him," in which men were advised on all varieties of masculine dress ranging from the correct cut of a suit for specific social events to the latest color of underwear seen in the "smart" shops. (Figure 1-17.) "Clothes are very necessary articles," wrote the "Him" columnist in 1894. "Everybody is interested in them."[17] Moreover, he asserted his credibility as an arbiter of men's style in another column: "'Him' finds out what a gentleman wears and not what a shopkeeper wishes to work off on unsuspecting customers and sell...This column is not a disguised advertising scheme."[18] It is evident that men read these fashion advice columns despite their placement in a women's magazine because *Vogue's* editor repeatedly commented on the number of letters he received from men.

Although fashion journalists for *Harper's Bazar*, *Vogue*, *McCall's*, *Delineator*, and numerous other women's magazines had increasingly included reports on men's clothing by the beginning of the twentieth century, men, as a target audience, did not have their own magazine that specifically focused on men's fashion and style until *Esquire* was published in 1933. Menswear makers and clothiers, at last, had a conduit to the fashion-minded American male. In turn, the abundance of men's fashion ads supplemented and complemented editorial content, each lending credibility to the other.

More critical to the marketing of menswear than fashion journalism, though, was consumer advertising. The earliest newspapers in colonial America commonly included columns of paid ad notices alerting the public to the availability of goods and services. Magazine editors, however, viewed advertising as a marginal, somewhat disreputable by-product of publishing. Until the last quarter of the nineteenth century, most magazines were reluctant to include much commercial advertising beyond simple booklists from the publisher. That concept changed during the depression of 1892–93 when *Munsey*, with its U.S. circulation of more than 600,000 subscribers, changed its business model to selling as much advertising space as possible based on circulation. This business practice allowed the magazine to be sold at a price below the cost of production, which helped increase subscription sales and renewals while still making considerable profits from advertising. This principle is still the formula of magazine publishing today.

As noted in the previous section of this chapter, mail order emerged

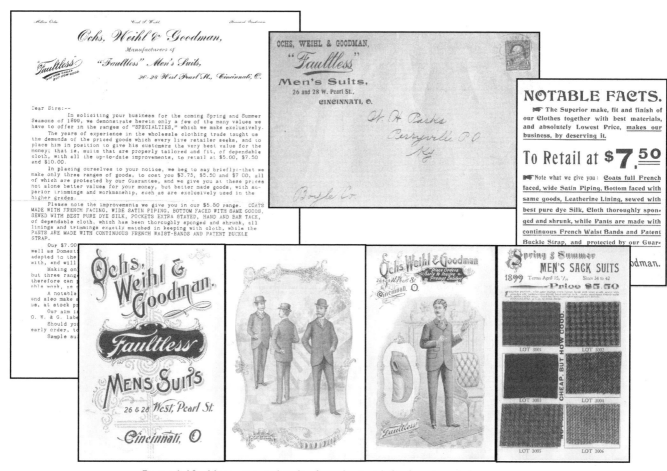

Figure 1-18. Menswear mail-order firms besieged the American male consumer relentlessly with catalogs and mailers stuffed with a variety of advertising materials that sometimes even included swatches of fabrics. Mailer and contents for Ochs, Weihl & Goodman, Cincinnati, 1899.

Posters, 1901

Billboard, 1923

Radio, 1925

TV, 1946

Internet, 2010

Figure 1-19. Throughout the twentieth century, advertisers exploited each new medium from its inception to get their marketing messages before an ever-expanding audience of consumers.

in the 1870s and quickly became a hugely successful distribution channel for ready-to-wear. Mail-order firms used print advertising such as the Ward's example shown in Figure 1-12 to accumulate mail lists, which, in turn, were used to reach target customers efficiently and cost effectively through direct mail. With the deployment of the Post Office's Rural Free Delivery service in the 1890s, menswear catalogs, postcards, and envelopes stuffed with flyers were delivered directly into the hands of male consumers nationwide. (Figure 1-18.)

By the end of the nineteenth century, American men faced at every turn, both in the home and outside, advertising about men's fashions and style. (Figure 1-19.) Catalogs and mailers filled the mailboxes. Magazines were full of illustrated, compelling ads. Yards of posters were plastered on the sides of buildings, fences, trees, and lamp posts. Countryside barn walls and roofs were painted with bold captions. Billboards lined the expanding rail lines and roadways. City trolley cars were wallpapered inside and out with advertising. Collectible tradecards with colorful depictions of sports figures and other images designed to appeal to men on one side and menswear trademarks on the other were handed out at tobacconists, barbershops, saloons, and other favorite men's haunts.

In the twentieth century, the electronic age opened new opportunities to menswear advertisers to reach even wider markets. Radio broadcasting was born in 1915. In less than a decade, radio stations dotted the U.S. landscape coast to coast, and radio became a mass medium—and advertising forum—for audiences numbering in the millions. Commercial television was introduced in the late 1930s, but only took off with consumers after World War II when technology improved and programming hours expanded. In the early 1990s, the Internet expanded marketing opportunities globally for menswear makers and retailers.

From the Civil War onward, the mass market of menswear consumers continually grew, aided by increasingly efficient modes of mass communication. Clothing manufacturers supported retailers with national campaigns about their labels. They also provided retailers with advertising material such as prepared newspaper and magazine ads to which retailers affixed their store name or logo before submitting the ad to the publication. In addition, lavishly illustrated window display posters and counter cards were available free to retailers. In 1908, co-op advertising was introduced, by which cash rebates were offered by manufacturers, usually 50% of the advertising costs, depending upon the size of the merchandise order placed by the retailer.

By the beginning of the twentieth century, some menswear advertisers began to change the focus of their message from product awareness to style persuasion. Illustrations in menswear catalogs and ads became more representative of men's actual lifestyles. Copy began to promote the importance of appearance, personal style, and correct dress. In 1922, an advertising journal advised men's ready-to-wear marketers that "if a man can be made conscious of the ugliness of the lamp on his table, the paper on his wall, or the paint on his house, or the beard on his chin, by advertising, surely it is possible to make him conscious by the same means of the ugliness and needlessness of bad dressing."[19] This challenge to the American male consumer has remained a theme in the advertising by menswear makers and retailers through today. (Figure 1-20.) "Learn the difference between style and fashion," chided *GQ* in 2007. "Style is about fit, proportion, and subtle details that will stand the test of time."[20]

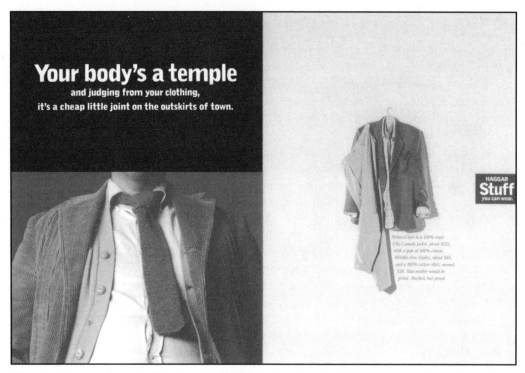

"Your body's a temple and judging from your clothing, it's a cheap little joint on the outskirts of town."
Haggar two-paged ad, 1995.

"Style counts. The want of it condemns."
Kuppenheimer ad, 1910.

"Identity theft is on the rise. Is yours worth stealing?"
Kenneth Cole ad, 2007.

Figure 1-20. Since the emergence of the ready-to-wear industry, the challenge of menswear makers has been to inculcate the male consumer with the idea of fashion and style.

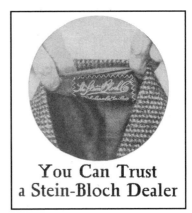

Figure 1-21. Menswear makers emphasized their branded labels in consumer ads as a guarantee of consistent quality. Details of men's clothing ads, 1907–10.

Once ready-to-wear makers had succeeded in establishing consumer confidence in their products, they needed to maintain that confidence to ensure future sales and sustain growth. One way to keep consumer confidence high was by building a brand recognition that was trusted by their customers. Branded trademarks became a promise of consistent quality—often backed with a money-back guarantee. Branding also provided differentiation of their products from those of the competition, particularly non-branded clothing that might look the same in an ad or in a store window, but was, in fact, inferior in manufacture or materials. In 1902, a *Men's Wear* article on clothing advertising suggested that, just five years earlier, not one consumer in a hundred could mention the name of a clothing manufacturer. But "today, we believe a good percentage of men would be able to name several among the fine clothing manufacturers who advertise liberally."[21] (Figure 1-21.) Over time, the equity that a business built up in its brand became a company asset of substantial value.

Conclusion

By the beginning of the twentieth century, all the elements necessary for the success of the American ready-to-wear industry were in place. Millions of yards of textiles were produced each year in every conceivable color, print, pattern, and texture. Efficient electrical machinery could uniformly cut all sorts of clothing patterns from hundreds of layers of fabric. Factory sewing machines could daily stitch miles of seams, attach buttons by the thousands, and affix collars, cuffs, pockets, and hundreds of similar fashion details. Specialty pressing machines could easily and effectively smooth wrinkled fabrics or permanently set creases, hemlines, and pleats.

Enormous volumes of mass-produced clothing were shipped from manufacturers to distributors by a continental railway system that eventually reached every American city and town coast to coast. Department stores and clothiers provided men with a full range of inexpensive ready-to-wear options including suits, outerwear, shirts, work clothes, active sports apparel, underwear, swimwear, neckwear, hats, shoes, and a wide assortment of complementary accessories. Mail-order businesses offered even the most remote citizens access to the latest styles of ready-to-wear, and the U.S. Post Office ensured the delivery of mountains of parcels even into rural areas.

To sustain their success, ready-to-wear makers and retailers aggressively adapted and refined marketing practices to fuel consumption. The masses were educated on what to wear and how to wear it through the displays in stores and shop windows and through the illustrations in catalogs, posters, and other forms of visual merchandising. Manufacturers developed branding strategies that promised consumers consistency in quality. National advertising campaigns promoted brand recognition and money-back guarantees that consumers came to trust.

Other marketing methods evolved to inculcate the American populace with the notion of changeable and cyclical style. Through mass communication, fashion journalism proclaimed the newest trends based on information from clothing industry leaders. Equally significant, the fashion reports also emphasized what was out of style. Hand-in-hand with fashion journalism, a constant barrage of ads by clothing manufacturers and retailers reinforced the notion of the obsolescence of style. To be out of style was to be ridiculous irrespective of one's socioeconomical status.

These successes of mass production, mass distribution, and mass marketing forged the democratization of men's fashion in America. The average working man of 1900 could afford at least one blue serge suit for Sundays at $5, mass manufactured in America, accessible from a local retailer or by mail-order, and delivered quickly and cheaply. He aspired to possess the newest patterned neckties, latest cable knit sweaters, or current types of print shirts, not only because they were readily available and affordable, but because they were fresh and modern. Through the variety and affordability of ready-to-wear, he was on an equal footing—at least in appearance—with other men. His new suit, shirt, and tie looked as good as those of society men featured in newspaper photos, the screen idols in Hollywood's movies, or any passerby on the main streets of his hometown.

Victorian

Fashions from the Civil War through the Fin de Siècle, 1860–1900

Expansionism to Imperial Power

America in the early nineteenth century was a vast, raw land that, throughout the period, inexorably expanded westward. In 1800, the United States consisted of the thirteen original colonies and three new states: Vermont (1791), Kentucky (1792), and Tennessee (1796). Enormous stretches of wilderness extended west to the Mississippi River, beckoning settlers by the thousands. In 1803, America doubled its size and westward extension with the Louisiana Purchase, luring the next generations of Americans across the Great Plains to the Pacific Ocean. By the 1840s, Americans had embraced the idea of a "manifest destiny," as newspaper editor John O'Sullivan wrote at the time, "to overspread and to possess the whole of the continent."[1] Spain had ceded Florida and the Gulf Coast in 1819. Following the Mexican War (1846–1848), the southwestern region from Texas to California was acquired by the United States—increasing the nation's total expanse by about one-third. Also in 1846, the Pacific Northwest was secured in a treaty with Britain, which granted the United States' claim to the Oregon territory.

The westward trickle of wagon trains bearing uncertain but resolute settlers suddenly became a rush when gold was discovered in California in 1848. As populations in the West rapidly increased, citizens began to petition for statehood. Throughout the 1850s, the sectionalism of the free-soil North versus the slave-holding South continually boiled over into political divisiveness as the balance of power shifted with the admission of free Western states. Consequently, the Union drifted toward dissolution.

When antislavery advocate Abraham Lincoln was elected president in 1860, Southern states reacted by seceding from the Union and forming the Confederate States of America. During the subsequent four years, from April 1861 through April 1865, the ravaging Civil War raged. When at last the South—outnumbered, exhausted, and devastated by the invading Northern forces—succumbed, the Union was preserved and slavery abolished.

In the decades following the Civil War, the United States continued its territorial expansion with the purchase of Alaska in 1867 from Russia. In 1898, the paradisiacal Hawaiian Islands were annexed. At the end of the century, the Spanish-American War gained the Philippines, Guam, and Puerto Rico for the United States. By the dawn of the twentieth century, America found itself a global imperial power.

The Second American Industrial Revolution

During the Civil War, the North enjoyed a burgeoning wartime economy with an abundance of capital for experimentation and testing of new technologies and industrial sciences. Continual improvements in machines were achieved within ever shorter generations of development. Many of these advances in machinery and production that had been applied to military purposes were quickly adapted to civilian use. The Bessemer-Kelly process of steel production made possible the rapid expansion of U.S. railroads and the building of skyscrapers, longer bridges, and other large-scale public works. Oil refinement techniques that emerged in the 1860s principally for the production of kerosene were expanded with the invention of the internal combustion machine in the 1880s, setting the stage for the auto industry at the beginning of the 1900s.

As the Second Industrial Revolution continued to gain momentum in the decades following the Civil War, more that 400,000 patents were issued.[2] The telephone was introduced by Alexander Graham Bell in 1876. The electric light was perfected by Thomas Edison in 1879. The portable typewriter, produced in numerous variations beginning in the 1870s, altered the structure of labor as more and more women left the home to work in offices. (Figure 2-1.) Business operations were facilitated by the cash register and the stock ticker. Public transportation systems replaced animal-drawn cars with electric railways. The transcontinental

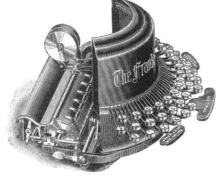

Figure 2-1. The first portable typewriters were invented in the 1870s. Male clerks found the task of typing too tedious, so women were increasingly hired for office work, further changing the structure of American labor. Franklin typewriter, 1893.

Figure 2-2. In the second half of the nineteenth century, the fastest methods of transportation and commercial shipping in the United States were by steamship and railway. Above, Hudson River steamboat, 1872; below, Baldwin narrow-gauge locomotive, 1875.

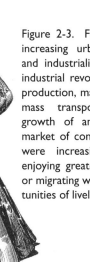

Figure 2-3. Following the Civil War, increasing urbanization, immigration, and industrialization fueled a second industrial revolution in America. Mass production, mass communication, and mass transportation spurred the growth of an ever-expanding mass market of consumers. Americans also were increasingly mobile whether enjoying greater leisure-time pursuits or migrating westward for new opportunities of livelihood and lifeways.

Silhouettes of women's fashions in the second half of the nineteenth century: left, crinoline era (1850s–1860s); center, bustle era (1870s–1880s); right, leg-of-mutton era (1890s)

Edison Phonograph, 1898

Windsor Kitchen Stove, 1895

American Gothic Revival house, 1860

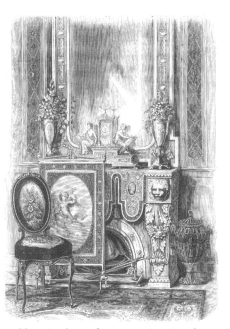

Victorian love of excessive interior decoration; middle-class parlor, 1875

Wickes Ice Box, 1898

Imperial Porcelain Bathtub, 1893

Varieties of buggies and wagons were the single family vehicles of the nineteenth century. Ad 1891

Palmer Cox's stories and illustrations of "Brownies" were a Victorian popular culture obsession. From *Brownies 'Round the World,* 1893

railroad was completed in 1869 linking the East with the West. More than 250,000 miles of rail crisscrossed America by the end of the century making possible the distribution of the vast quantities of mass-manufactured products nationwide.[3] (Figure 2-2.)

This convergence of advances in manufacturing technology, marketing, and distribution drove mass production and fueled a growing consumerism on a much broader scale than had evolved in the first half of the nineteenth century. Urbanization was boosted by the growth of factories built near the rail centers. City populations surged as families left the farm and immigrants flooded in to work for wages within manufacturing and service sectors. By 1900, New York, Chicago, and Philadelphia each had surpassed more than a million inhabitants. The national standard of living continued to rise. The well-fed American worker and middle classes enjoyed more physical comforts and leisure options than their counterparts in any other industrialized nation. (Figure 2-3.) Electric lighting, central heating, and indoor plumbing were increasingly accessible with affordable, mass-produced fixtures and equipment available by mail order from mass merchandisers like Montgomery Ward and Sears, Roebuck and Company.

Mass transit systems in cities and improved rural roadways encouraged mobility. Well-established wagon trails over the Great Plains guided many thousands of people westward in their quest for a better life. The first automobiles were built in the United States in 1893. The safety bicycle with its inflatable rubber tires, chain drive, and padded seat was introduced in 1889, transforming American society by making mobility accessible to a wide range of socioeconomic classes, even if only for weekend excursions to the city by rural folk or into the countryside by urbanites.

The Cultural and Social Shifts in America

The Union may have been preserved by the Civil War, but the states were not united. Reconstruction by bayonet in the South lasted until 1877. The abuses of the Blue Bellies and the Radical Republicans in Congress left an indelible scar upon the former Confederate states, setting in stone a pervasive cultural divide that endured for the next one hundred years.

Countless thousands of former slaves, wrenched from bondage to freedom overnight, migrated North to cities like Philadelphia and Washington, D.C., only to end up slaves to hunger, cold, and disease. Most ex-slaves who remained in the South came into the bondage of tenant farming and, with it, generations of poverty. Jim Crow laws forced blacks into a strictly segregated social structure and disenfranchisement. Despite such harsh adversities, though, black educators like Booker T. Washington and George Washington Carver led the way in improving education and economic opportunities for African Americans.

The dramatic social and economic changes in the second half of the nineteenth century enabled women to become increasingly independent. Women's rights advocates intensified their crusade for suffrage, particularly after the vote had been given to ex-slaves. Gradually, some states began to allow women to vote in local elections. Women also made inroads toward economic independence through greater employment opportunities. The many new factories of the Second Industrial Revolu-

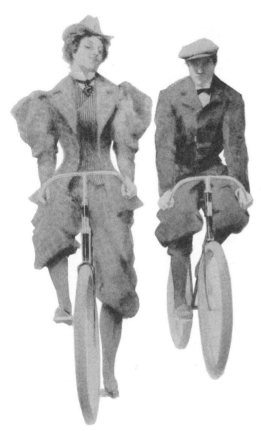

Figure 2-4. The bicycling craze of the 1890s provided women with greater independence. With the bicycle, women were freely mobile to explore new horizons. They discarded their constricting corsets and donned trousers to comfortably and safely enjoy riding. Editorial illustration from *Vogue*, 1895.

Figure 2-5. The iconic image of the New Woman was created by artist Charles Dana Gibson in the 1890s. The Gibson Girl was often depicted in nontraditional roles ranging from athlete to career woman. Pen and ink drawings by Charles Dana Gibson from *Life*, 1890s.

tion were insatiable for workers and hired thousands of women, especially in the textile and ready-to-wear industries. With the introduction of the typewriter in the 1870s, clerical work was restructured. Where once men handled handwritten correspondence and business records, instead, women were hired as typists—albeit at reduced wages—and male clerks became bookkeepers and office managers. As telephone lines stretched across the land, switchboards were managed and operated largely by women. Additionally, women found independence through mobility. The bicycling craze of the 1890s allowed women to escape the confines of Victorian domesticity and to explore new horizons. (Figure 2-4.) They experienced the freedom and confidence of maneuvering a mechanical device as it hurtled along on dual wheels over rugged country terrain or through urban traffic. Moreover, the bicycle led to clothing reform as women discarded constricting corsets and stepped into cycling suits with knee-length trousers called knickerbockers.

Social progressivism may have appeared broad through its perpetual representation in the mass media, but, in reality, it was not deep. The New Woman, as represented in the popular drawings by Charles Dana Gibson, was smart, athletic, independent, fashionable, and effortlessly beautiful. (Figure 2-5.) And as such, she was nontraditional, meaning she considered herself the equal of any man, and she likely indulged in radical new ideas like politics or birth control. But the Gibson Girl was the exception to the rule of the accepted norms of American womanhood. The social structures of separate spheres for men and women were natural law to most Americans. A man was the family breadwinner, protector, and patriarch; the woman's place was in the home as housewife and mother. Despite increasing opportunities in the workplace for women, less than twenty percent of women worked outside the home in 1900.[4]

Furthermore, Victorian America remained staunchly puritanical even at the end of the nineteenth century with all its advances in science and technology. Women's groups were far more unified by the anti-liquor movement than by women's rights issues. The Women's Christian Temperance Union (W.C.T.U.), organized in 1874, and the Anti-Saloon League, established in 1893, managed to force city, county, and, in some instances, statewide prohibition. Similarly, women's groups led the back-

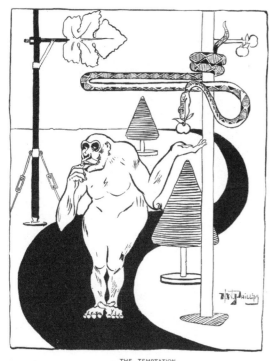

THE TEMPTATION.

A DRAWING IN THE PRESENT MODE, OF THE FAMOUS SCENE IN THE GARDEN
OF EDEN. (AFTER SUGGESTION BY PROF. DARWIN.)

Figure 2-6. Science and religion clashed repeatedly throughout the nineteenth century but seldom as tumultuously as when Charles Darwin published *On the Origin of Species* in 1859. Cartoon from *Life*, 1897.

lash against the idea of evolution, which included muzzling teachers and book censorship. When British naturalist Charles Darwin published his theories of evolution in *On the Origin of Species* (1859), science and religion collided as never before. (Figure 2-6.) The idea that humans evolved from lower life forms undermined the literal interpretation of the Bible as the infallible word of God, and fundamentalist Christians reacted by pressing local and state lawmakers to deny evolution and to restrict dissemination of the subject in schools or public forums.

As postwar America struggled with the social and economic changes of the era—industrialization, western expansion, immigration, and Reconstruction—a great international exposition was planned in 1876 to celebrate the nation's first 100 years. (Figure 2-7.) Philadelphia was chosen as the site for the event since it was there that the Declaration of Independence had been signed in 1776. President Grant opened the expo in May, and, over the following six months, more than eight million visitors viewed over 30,000 exhibitions from every state and twenty-five countries.[5] Every conceivable mechanized device was on display, ranging from the telephone and electric arc lighting to all the newest apparatuses of the clothing industries. Every U.S. manufacturer of sewing machines had models set up with young ladies demonstrating the operation of each. Numerous powerlooms clattered away rapidly weaving yards of American cotton, wool, and jute textiles. A new floor-covering "fabric" called "linoleum" made of cork and linseed oil promised to endure a dozen years of wear and scrubbing. American retailers such as Wanamaker's exhibited the latest ready-to-wear for the entire family. From England came Irish poplins, Balbriggan knit hose, and seamless oilcloths produced in 45-foot-wide panels. India sent sumptuously embroidered textiles and luxuriant gold and silver cloth. France displayed life-sized wax mannequins dressed in the newest Parisian couture fashions including several magnificent court dresses. Germany's mastery of chemical engineering was evident in their examples of brilliant-hued aniline dyes.

Figure 2-7. The United States celebrated its centennial in 1876 with an international exposition hosted by Philadelphia. In addition to displaying thousands of manufactured goods, many industries set up machinery and equipment to demonstrate the state-of-the-art technologies including power looms and home sewing machines. Interior of the Main Pavilion, Centennial Exposition, Philadelphia, 1876.

China presented 6,000 live silkworms industriously spinning the filaments used in weaving opulent Asian silks. In Machinery Hall, visitors could order a pair of shoes made of East Indian rubber and watch the molding process as they were made. In the end, the Centennial celebration was regarded as a huge success and a much-needed catharsis for the divisiveness and polarization that remained entrenched following the Civil War. Socioeconomic divides were checked at the expo gates as citizens from across the nation celebrated their pride and patriotism as Americans within the 180 buildings scattered across 450 acres.

Dress and Identity: Ideas and Ideals of Masculinity in Nineteenth-Century America

Over the past thirty years, researchers and scholars of men's studies have increasingly examined how dress has historically reflected and even transformed ideas and ideals of masculinity in America. The prevailing perspectives of what it meant to be a man in the formative decades of young America have traditionally been biased toward the white middle classes primarily for three reasons. First, the intelligentsia of that era—Thomas Carlyle, Thomas Jefferson, and William Cobbett, among others—viewed the New Man that emerged in postrevolutionary Europe and America as a self-determined individual who was free to shape his destiny as his talents, industry, and energy would allow. However, this emphasis on the freedom to make the choices for a self-determined life meant that many segments of men were excluded from this ideal: the African slave, the Native American, Asian immigrants, and even some ethnic whites from the Mediterranean area and Central Europe. Second, the New Man also was thought to possess an inherent gentility and (Protestant) moral principals that were viewed as beyond the grasp of the uncivilized native or European Catholic and Jewish peasantry. Third, from the earliest colonial era into the 1960s, men's dress in America was defined and dictated by London. Decade after decade, style decrees trickled from the venerable tailors of Savile Row to be eagerly adopted by all EuroAmerican clothiers and, later, by mass-market ready-to-wear makers. These unchallenged dictates of masculine style, in turn, altered the dress, and consequently the identity, of the African, Asian, Native American, and ethnic European living in America. As these ethnic segments modified or abandoned their traditional forms of dress—by demand of owners and overseers in the case of slaves, by economic expediency with Native Americans, and by assimilation necessity for immigrants—their ideas and ideals of masculine identity likewise began to shift toward the prevailing Anglo-Protestant concept of the postrevolution New Man.

In the aftermath of the French Revolution, the New Man emerged into the nineteenth century having rejected the old order, the *ancien régime*, and, with it, the tyrannies and injustices of aristocratic political authority, economic control, and hereditary class distinction. His world would be one in which the self-made man triumphed not by being to-the-manor-born but by hard work and quality of character.

To the New Man, sartorial splendor was considered one of the most visible identities of the corruption and decadence of the ruling elite. The luxuriousness of satins, laces, embroideries, and other such opulence of dress was an arrogant proclamation of the aristocrat's privileged socioeconomic status and an assertion of masculine power gained by birthright

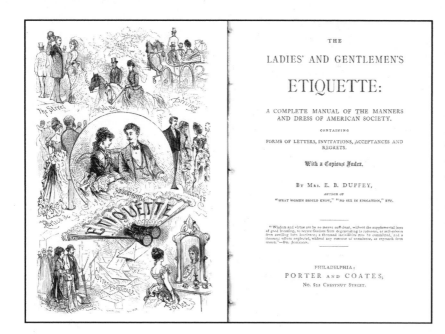

Figure 2-8. The age-old adage that manners make the man was a social tenet for Victorians. For the man who aspired to acceptance into polite society, etiquette books provided signposts for respectable masculine behavior. Title page spread of *Ladies' and Gentlemen's Etiquette*, 1877.

and sustained by jaded tradition and biased law. The New Man thus renounced not only the social order of the aristocrat but also most of his ideas of masculinity and its elitist trappings, adopting instead a concept of manhood rooted in middle-class values of thrift, duty, sobriety, and industriousness.

This self-made, genteel man led society by his moral example. His inherent good manners, propriety, and moral principles were the epitome of manliness. Gentility was no longer the exclusive domain of the aristocracy. Middle-class men of the nineteenth century appropriated and transformed these masculine qualities once exclusively associated with the gentry. Integrity, refinement, taste, and manners were masculine values adopted from the nobility by the self-made middle-classes, thus achieving a gentrified status while at the same time remaining anti-aristocratic.

Throughout the nineteenth century, the gentrification of American middle-class men was broadly perpetuated by etiquette manuals and courtesy advice columns in mass media. (Figure 2-8.) The old adage that "manners make the man" was a constant point of Victorian courtesy writers. "If manners do *not* make the man, what does?" asked *Gentlemen's Journal* in 1871. "Nothing;" concludes the editor, "for money and dress, which, at times stand out very prominently, are... far in the background; for a rogue or a fool may have both of these, and yet in character be not at all the better for them."[6]

Being the better was, indeed, at the heart of good manners and the very definition of a gentleman. As one Victorian etiquette manual asserted:

> A true gentleman is always himself at his best. He is inherently unselfish, thinking always of the needs and desires of others before his own....The manners of a gentleman are the index of his soul. His speech is innocent, because his life is pure; his thoughts are direct, because his actions are upright; his bearing gentle, because his blood and his impulses and his training are gentle too.[7]

Etiquette—that "regalia of civilization" by which "we may be recognized as belonging to the guild of ladies and gentlemen"—was perceived by the Victorians as a means to an end. Manners, like religion, if practiced assiduously, just might improve the inner man. "The true gentleman is rare," asserts Eliza Duffey, "but fortunately, there is no crime in counterfeiting his excellences. The best of it is that the counterfeit may, in course of time, develop into the real thing."[8]

The guides for the behavior of the nineteenth-century gentleman—etiquette manuals, medical journals, and magazines—were also important sources in conveying to men how they should look and dress the part. In tandem with the transformed ideal of masculinity evolved a complementary visual expression in dress based on modesty and plainness, which itself had been derived from the legacy of the dark, sober clothing of the Protestant Reformation with influences from the simplicity of the eighteenth-century Englishman's country dress. The nineteenth-century masculine wardrobe with its "studied plainness," as Ralph Waldo Emerson called it,[9] reflected the New Man with an emphatic distinction from the sumptuous exhibitionism of class in the Old World.

The renunciation of splendor in men's fashions meant not only a new idea of dress but also a new idea of consumption for men. As discussed in chapter 1, the emergence of the mass production of menswear in the nineteenth century, the mass distribution through department stores, and mass marketing through mail-order firms helped democratize fashion in America. Yet despite the simplicity and plainness of menswear, whether mass produced or custom tailored, the knowledge of what to wear and when to wear it became an indication of differentiation among the social classes. Knowledge was power, and clothing made masculine power evident to the public eye. In 1850, George Fox, stylist and tailor to the social elite of Washington, D.C., including President Millard Fillmore, wrote:

> We regard dress...as one of the most significant expressions of character, and sustaining an intimate relation with manners and morals. It is universally admitted that nothing marks the gentleman more than the style of his dress. The elegance, propriety and good taste which are conspicuous in that, at once create a presumption in his favor.[10]

The well-dressed man was accorded respect and deference since his fine wardrobe was presumed to express his fine inner qualities as a respectable gentleman.

The office clerk, whose income and education were often not much better than those of tradesmen, used his ready-to-wear business suit and starched shirt collar with a correctly knotted necktie to set himself apart and, in his mind, above the working classes. The semi-skilled, semi-empowered clerk, often not far away from having to join the laboring ranks, bolstered his respectability and masculine power through his dress. In turn, the business executives used their hand-tailored suits to differentiate themselves, and their power status, from the lower-paid clerks and junior managers of their offices. (Figure 2-9.)

Even an ambitious clerk, though, might have little opportunity to expand his experience and knowledge of correct dress into social arenas such as embassy balls, the opera, or travel abroad where an appropriate wardrobe was an important part of masculine identity. In those peer circles, dress was often a competition, not only in the subtle display of

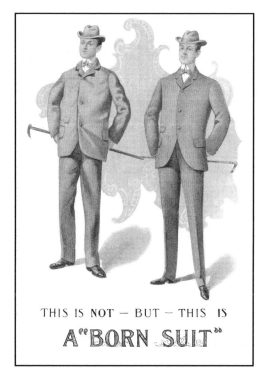

THIS IS NOT — BUT — THIS IS
A "BORN SUIT"

Figure 2-9. The outward expression of a respectable gentleman was his fine wardrobe. Pretenders and usurpers were evident by their lack of knowledge of proper dress and, by default, a lack of knowledge of gentlemanly behavior. Ready-to-wear makers extensively advertised the quality of their suits with an emphasis on the distinction of the man who wore their label. Ad for M. Born Company, 1901.

wealth, but in the exhibition of gentlemanly behavior. "We owe it to ourselves because others estimate us very naturally and very rightly by our outward appearance," emphasized the *Ladies' and Gentlemen's Etiquette* manual in 1877, "and we owe it to others because we have no right to put our friends to the blush by untidiness or uncouthness."[11] Correct attire was an expression of self-respect as well as a demonstration of respect for one's peers. "To be neatly and appropriately dressed is undoubtedly our duty as it is our interest," wrote Fox. "If we would seek the world's respect, provided we have the means, let the materials be the best of their kind."[12]

This concern for a correct and proper outward appearance was one of the ironies of the idea of the New Man. A display of wealth through dress still represented social leadership and worth in the New World just as it had for the prerevolution aristocrats of Europe. However, among the socioeconomic classes of men in America, the differences were far more subtle than they had been in the eighteenth century although still distinct. Hence, the anti-fashion of simple, plain clothing became itself fashion. The sartorial elegance of the nobility may have been rejected and masculinity may have been redefined as a natural modesty, but fashion continued to be "an exacting tyrant" conceded Fox. Even the "Doric simplicity" of American men's clothing was a "style commensurate with the growing importance and dignity of this national union," which could "cause Paris, London and Berlin to hide their diminished heads as arbiters of gentility."[13] Simplicity itself became the force of masculine fashion, a new tyrant to which virtually all men—particularly the middle-class masses—became enslaved.

The danger, though, for the aspiring middle-class American male who dressed above himself was being perceived as pretentious. In the nineteenth-century world of separate spheres discussed later in this section, pretension was a feminine trait. Among peers and before social superiors, a man whose dress exceeded his station ran the risk of the stigma of effeminacy. Equally significant, pretentious dress also carried with it the suspicion of fraud and mendacity. The honest simplicity of the sober three-piece suit was supposed to be the identity of a gentleman of honest and moral character. Men of virtuous quality and respectability could recognize each other by the visual symbol of the correct suit. For a man of poor character to disguise himself in the identity of a gentleman was deceitful, and deceit was simply bad manners.

Men on the lower economic scale of the middle classes, even those with talent and aspirations, particularly had to guard against crossing the line from appropriate attire to excess. As the quality and variety of mass-produced ready-to-wear continued to improve, men with limited means dressed ever better, especially with the guidance and inspiration from store displays, illustrated catalogs, and mass media. However, the middle classes had little need of some forms of attire, such as a top hat and tail coat. The standardized dark suit, worn to the office weekdays and to church on Sundays, was also sufficient for their dressy social occasions.

For the aspirational man, though, cautionary signposts for proper dress were readily available, notably in the style reports of social gazettes and in etiquette manuals. Courtesy writers especially often warned against dressing beyond one's station. In 1830, William Cobbett wrote in *Advice to Young Men,* "Dress should be suited to your rank and sta-

Figure 2-10. The nineteenth-century dandy was viewed as a vain man who was overly concerned with his appearance and with masculine decorum. His wardrobe and manners were a studied masculine identity lacking in the substantive sincerity of the natural gentleman. *Portrait of Rovert De Montesquiou* by Giovanni Boldoni, 1897.

tion:...there is no reason why a tradesman, a merchant's clerk, or clerk of any kind...should dress in an expensive manner."[14] Fox likewise stressed, "To be well dressed is to be dressed precisely as the occasion, place, weather, your height, figure, position, age—and remember it—your means, require."[15] Similarly, Duffey advised, "Gentlemen will always dress according to their age, their pecuniary circumstances, the hour of the day, the special occasion and their surroundings."[16] To do otherwise could mean being exposed as ungentlemanly. A social climber may temporarily disguise his lesser status with the camouflage of a superbly tailored wardrobe, but, when found out, the damage to his reputation and social standing could be irreversible. Utter ostracization could result.

But even more threatening and undermining for the brotherhood of genuine, natural gentlemen was the dandy, often disparagingly referred to as a fop: a vain man who is preoccupied with his appearance and manners to excess. (Figure 2-10.) In 1833, Thomas Carlyle wrote in *Sartor Resartus*, "A dandy is a clothes-wearing man, a man whose trade, office and existence consists in the wearing of clothes. Every faculty of his soul, spirit, purse and person is heroically consecrated to this one object, the wearing of clothes wisely and well: so that as others dress to live, he lives to dress."[17] Modern popular culture, especially Hollywood, has perpetuated the mincing caricature of the idle dandy whose dress and conduct were theatrical and ostentatious. Leslie Howard portrayed the quintessential fop in *The Scarlet Pimpernel* (1934). To the contrary of Hollywood's flamboyant depictions, though, the nineteenth-century dandy was actually among the most conservative and rigid adherents to the masculine ideas of the gentleman. In assessing the "beaux of olden time," John Doran wrote in 1865 of the most famous dandy of the era, Beau Brummell:

> Brummell saw that fame was to be achieved by simplicity....His chief aim was to avoid anything marked;...that the severest mortification a gentleman could incur was to attract observation in the street by his outward appearance. He exercised the most correct taste in the selection of each article of apparel of a form and color harmonious with all the rest for the purpose of producing a perfectly elegant general effect.[18]

The harmonies of form and color worn by Brummell were always subtle and subdued. As with all dandies, his conformity to the supreme concept of a gentleman's behavior and dress was unassailable regardless of the fanciful trends and fads of fashionable society. (Figure 2-11.) "He did not abandon the pursuit of beauty; he changed the kind of beauty that was admired," says Elizabeth Wilson.[19] The successful dandy, exemplified by Brummell, became an accomplished male mannequin. His studied masculine identity projected all the qualities of a gentleman, and his strict adherence to a sober plainness of dress projected the image of respectability.

It was, however, the very artifice of the dandy's calculated masculinity that was the undermining threat to the authentic natural gentleman. As noted previously, the studied plainness of Emerson's true gentleman could itself be studied and appropriated by deceitful men who would look the part but lack the character. This was the chief accusation so often leveled against dandies. Theirs was a self-absorbed pursuit of the aesthetic of correctness and personal discipline as expressed in constrained, severe dress and manners. Absent were the honorable masculine virtues of the genuine gentleman who was by nature modest, moral, and ever considerate of others. Instead, the dandy's manners were feigned and exaggerated, a contrived performance of masculinity.

A second threat the dandies posed to the nineteenth-century ideas of masculinity was effeminacy. This is not a reference to feminine flamboyance or to homosexuality. Indeed, unlike the eighteenth-century rake exemplified by Henry Fielding's Tom Jones, the dandy of the 1800s was largely regarded as sexually ambivalent and harmless. (Such demonstrative emotionalism as lust went against the reserved self-control of the dandy.) Brummell, for instance, was never known to have engaged in a liaison. Instead, effeminacy as viewed by men of the nineteenth century was derived from the concept of separate spheres: the prescribed roles for men and women, regardless of class, which formed the very basis of middle-class morality. In this sense, the term "sphere" commonly appears in women's magazines and courtesy manuals of the age. In 1870, Orson Fowler asserted in his book *Creative and Sexual Science* that "Nature leaves nothing unsettled or dubious, but has preadjusted all their minutiae...that the nature of each sex and its office at the creative altar, determine the status of each, and assign to each as regards the other its

Figure 2-11. The most famous dandy of the nineteenth century was Beau Brummell whose dogmatic approach to dress and manners was emulated even by the Prince of Wales. Portrait of Brummell, c. 1815.

respective rights, sphere, duties, social and political status...." Typical of the period, Fowler viewed the primary role for woman, after motherhood, as that of homemaker. Within the dominion of the household, her duty was to serve as the "head of its wardrobe, laundry, storeroom, and kitchen."[20] As such, she was also the chief consumer on behalf of the family. Shopping was a household chore, part of the division of labor within the separate spheres. Woman was the commissioner of supplies and services for the home whose purchasing power was well recognized by manufacturers and merchants of the Second Industrial Revolution in the nineteenth century. And upon the advent of mass marketing as a business discipline in the decades following the Civil War, women, far more often than men, were overwhelmingly the target of most advertising, even for many of the products made specifically for men.[21]

A significant part of equating consumerism with woman's sphere included fashion. If a man's sphere was utility—making a living, providing for a family, engaging in politics, protecting the home and nation—then a woman's sphere included ornament—decorating her home and herself—along with the homemaker tasks cited above. "It is the duty of every woman to make herself as beautiful as possible," chided Duffey. "As despotic as fashion may be," she continued, it is a woman's duty to "dress well and becomingly....A sensible woman will not go lank and hoopless when prevailing modes indicate great rotundity of the skirt."[22] Fowler echoed this duty of woman in lofty terms:

> Her beauties require to be shown to the best advantage. That which is best generally looks best, which fruits illustrate. Whatever is ornamental is therefore useful. Use is ornament, and ornament use, the world over. The two combine in nature and should in a wife....[23]

As with homemaking, the pursuit of fashion—the means for self-ornamentation—was an activity of consumption, one that American women of all classes accepted and exploited within their separate sphere. Although women of the middle and upper classes were the likely readers of *Godey's, Harper's Bazar,* and etiquette guides, shop girls and factory workers also had opportunities to dress in their Sunday best. Moreover, in the second half of the nineteenth century, the visual merchandising spectacles in urban department stores, particularly display windows, and the alluring style narratives contained in mail order catalogs that reached the most remote hinterlands encouraged feminine consumerism beyond the mere acquisition of practical necessities for home and hearth. Within woman's sphere, consumption went beyond the grocer, butcher, and bakery shop to include dressmakers, milliners, shoemakers, department stores, and mail order retailers. Consequently, a preoccupation with fashion and its consumption were outside the masculine sphere, and the very act of shopping became most associated with the feminine sphere.

Because the nineteenth-century ideas of masculinity were driven by an opposition to the luxuriousness, dissipation, and perceived effeminacy of the ancien régime, the dandies, were stigmatized by three transgressions. First, they were insincere posers who aped the manly qualities of authentic gentlemen but lacked the substance. Second, despite the dandy's conformity to the simple dress identity of the New Man, they, nonetheless, were guilty of effeminacy because of their preoccupation with, and consumption of, fashion—a particular vagary of woman's sphere. Third, their indulgence of luxuriousness was not in the display of rich fabrics, superfluous accessories, and other finery but in an excess of quantity. Brummell, for example, is noted for having spent a considerable effort each morning choosing and tying his cravat; visitors would find him before the mirror with a pile of cravats on the floor, to which the valet would lament: "These, sir, are our failures."[24] The dandies' variety and quantity of fashion were all too publicly evident.

By the end of the nineteenth century, a new generation of American men faced even more formidable challenges to the orthodoxy of masculinity than had their grandfathers and fathers. Of the two principal obsessions of the postrevolutionary new order of masculinity—the abandonment of luxuriousness and the rejection of the effeminacy of the aristocracy—only the renunciation of sumptuous excess had been consistently sustained. Less tangibly, though, effeminacy was a constant threat to the ideas and ideals of masculinity. New precepts regarding masculinity, and, consequently, effeminacy, gradually emerged during the last decades of the nineteenth century. Victorians had found comfort, for the most part, with the rigidity of the separate spheres of men's and women's domains and the accepted divisions of labor and power within each. Where the two spheres crossed, one or the other was undermined, and, by the late 1800s, the lines had eroded significantly.

During the decades between the Civil War and World War I, American society underwent a rapid transformation from rural to urban, from agrarian to industrial. The masculine training ground for boys—working the farm with their fathers—had been steadily disappearing. Industrialization had created labor needs that took men out of the fields and put them in offices or at the helm of some factory machine. As *Cosmopolitan* observed in 1899: "In well nigh a million new directions, forms of honored and remunerative social labor are opening up before the feet of modern man, which his ancestors never dreamed of." The mechanical marvels of the age insatiably required "a whole army of men of science, engineers, clerks and highly trained workmen for their invention, con-

Figure 2-12. During the last quarter of the nineteenth century, an increasing number of men left farmwork for jobs in industry and city businesses. As a result, boys were largely left in the care of women who were in control of the homes, schools, and religious institutions. Social theorists, religious leaders, and magazine publishers spread the alarm warning parents against the threat of the feminization of a generation of boys. Left, illustration from *Century*, 1888; right, illustration from *Youth's Companion*, 1892.

Figure 2-13. In the late nineteenth century, competitive sports became the recommended antidote against the perceived threat of the feminization of boys. New types of sports such as football, basketball, and volleyball were invented at this time to teach boys the masculine virtues of internal discipline, courage, and the ability to conform to strict rules. Ivory soap ad, 1892.

Do not restrain your boys in their instinctive desire for outdoor sports.

To achieve the full measure of strength, health and stature, boys should be encouraged early in life to frequent bathing, especially after perspiring and cooling, so that the skin-pores may be promptly opened and healthful reaction take place. The active boy who forms an affection for Ivory Soap will be the stronger for it, and "The stronger always succeeds."

struction and maintenance."[25]

As more and more men found employment away from the homestead twelve hours a day, six days a week, boys were increasingly left in the care of women for longer periods than earlier in the century. Mothers, sisters, teachers, and other female caregivers stepped in to fill the vacuum left by the absence of fathers and older brothers. (Figure 2-12.) Control of the homes, schools, and religious institutions was the purview of women. Consequently, a concern about the feminization of boys swept America during this transitional time.

Competitive sports became a solution to teach boys manly qualities and help preserve the polarized gender order of the separate spheres for subsequent generations. The first American national baseball league was established in 1871; intercollegiate football was organized in 1873; basketball was invented in 1891 followed by volleyball in 1895; the Olympics were revived in 1896. Intramural sports quickly became a part of school curriculums despite the concerns of many parents for the physical safety of their sons.

Advocates of sports for boys evangelized their enthusiasm through mass media. Such advocates proselytized parents and youngsters about the need and social value of sports in the development of a boy's masculinity. In 1892, a typical sports story in *Youth's Companion*, for example, presented a fictional tale about a football game in which were integrated many of the arguments for and against boys' sports that would ring familiar today. When the parents of a boy playing halfback hear horror stories about the severity of injuries in football, they forbid him to play any more. The captain of the team tries to persuade his much-needed halfback to go against the parent's decision, but the boy refuses. The team captain responds by calling him a "coward," "traitor," and "milksop," but the boy will not disobey his parents (a sub-moral to the story). Just before the "big game," the faculty sponsor convinces the father of the importance of football to his son's future as a man; as a player, the boy will become "keen to see, quick to understand, and strong to execute." The father relents, and the boy helps win the game by making the final touchdown. The boy's parents now realize that "in no other game is success more sure to breed success," and the father "received his full share of honor in the evening's celebrations."[26] The moral of the story, and of hundreds like it at the time, was two-fold. Sports were an important part of building masculine identity, and parents must support that development by encouraging boys to pursue sports. (Figure 2-13.)

Along with sports, boys' clubs and associations were organized to provide opportunities for boys to learn the masculine virtues of their forefathers. Before the Boy Scouts, which was founded in England in 1907 and America in 1910, national organizations such as the Woodcraft Indians and Sons of Daniel Boone existed. These male-only groups inculcated boys with the fundamentals of self-sufficiency and the pioneer spirit that had forged the American nation, qualities that had been lost in the liberal changes wrought by modern industrialism, social progressivism, and, worst of all, feminization.

In addition to the fear of feminization of boys by women caregivers and the dismantling of the doctrine of separate spheres by the emerging women's movement, a third social change contributed to the further redefining of modern masculinity, and, with it, a new view of effeminacy. During the late nineteenth century, science advanced propositions of human sexuality that had never even been conceived before, let alone articulated in a public forum. Although Sigmund Freud and Havelock Ellis are the two most famous researchers of human behavior and sexuality of the time, a number of other scientists preceded them in the 1870s and 1880s with revolutionary theories and clinical studies.

During these early years, the myth of the homosexual as the "third sex" originated and was widely studied. In fact, the term "homosexuality" did not exist before 1868 when it first appeared in the work of the Hungarian researcher Karoly Kertbeny. (The term "heterosexuality" followed shortly afterward.) By the 1890s, the topic of homosexuality had become commonplace in medical journals, scientific research papers, and books on sexuality. With book titles like *Sexual Psychopathy* (1886), *Perversions of the Sex Instinct* (1893), and *Sexual Inversion* (1897), it seemed clear to all that men of science largely agreed that homosexuality was a pathology, a mental disorder requiring treatment and conversion. Somehow acts of sodomy had been transposed into an expression of an essential being. "The sodomite had been a temporary aberration," wrote historian Michel Foucault, "the homosexual was now a species."[27] The polarization of homo- and heterosexualities was a cultural creation that evolved into an aspect of social control. "One was monstrous and the other virtuous," espoused Brian Pronger in his study of masculinity and sports. "The horror of homosexuality lay not so much in the homosexual acts as it did in the depravity of the creature that would perpetrate such acts."[28] Judeo-Christian traditions had long held that sodomy was a sin, and now legislatures across America, responding to the clamor over the discovery of a new classification of the mentally ill, expanded sodomy statutes to criminalize not only homosexual acts but the homosexual himself. Science wanted to cure the homosexual, and religion and the law wanted to punish him. The social stigma thus was set for generations to come, and the ideas and ideals of masculinity were significantly altered. Among the qualities of respectable, genuinely manly men, heterosexuality was at the top of the list.

In order to protect itself against the nefarious homosexual—to isolate and ostracize him—society needed to be able to recognize the deviants. Social scientists, once again, provided answers. Within many of the studies of homosexuality were analyses, descriptions, and case studies of men who exhibited feminine behavior ranging from a softened, high-

THE ROCK ON WHICH THEY SPLIT.

CHOLLEY TAPECOUNTER *(floorwalker at Lacy's)*.— I had a dwedful wow with young Richman, the millionaire's son, last night, at the Fried Cat table d'hôte.

GUSSIE YARDSTICK *(dress goods counter)*.— Deah me! I thought you and he weah *such* friends.

CHOLLEY TAPECOUNTER.—We weah. But when, flushed with his table claret, he said he was moah of a weal Bohemian than I was, I just could n't stand it !

"SHOVING THE QUEER."

Figure 2-14. In the late nineteenth century, a new dimension was added to the notion of effeminacy. The homosexual was invented by Victorian science and Western culture as a pathological entity whose perceived aberrant propensities were antithetical to masculine norms. Effeminacy had once primarily meant a trespass into the woman's sphere such as the indulgence of luxury or the consumption of fashion. Now, effeminacy was characterized by a display of feminine traits. By the end of the Victorian era, stereotypes of the homosexual were represented in the mass media as an effeminate man with dainty gestures, swishing walk, and softened voice. Left, cartoon from *Life*, 1890; right, cartoon from *Puck*, 1895. ("Shoving the queer" was Victorian street slang for passing counterfeit money.)

octave voice, dainty gestures, and a hip-swishing walk to varying degrees of transvestism. Hence, the limpwristed sissy became the obvious and most recognizable stereotype of the homosexual. (Figure 2-14.) By the beginning of the 1900s, the idea of effeminacy had shifted from a trespass into the woman's sphere—such as the fop's consumption of fashion—to a display of feminine traits. And according to science, effeminacy denoted homosexuality.

Straight men recognized that effeminacy in men or women signified a deference to masculine power. Effeminate men were professing their subordination, their willingness to yield to the authority or will of another man. "While such behavior is evident and somewhat acceptable in females in our culture, going under the name of feminine passivity...it is definitely antithetical to the masculine gender role," stresses Warren Steinberg.[29] The male gender role was characterized by power, self-control, and especially the control of others. By being submissive, effeminate men betrayed the power of male dominance. Every delicate gesture or sentiment that smacked of femininity or flamboyant nonconformity in dress was an affront to manhood, traits to be reviled in other men and to be guarded against in one's self. For true masculinity to maintain its power and control in modern American society, effeminacy must be held in contempt. Boys were taught to fear the humiliating consequences of effeminacy, and men who strayed, even by accident, suffered scorn and

ridicule from peers. The boy who did not dominate in the masculine arenas of childhood such as competitive sports, outdoor activities like hunting and fishing, and the mastery of tools and machinery was made to feel inferior. The man who was seen holding his wife's handbag or was discovered making purchases of feminine products for his wife was scorned and humiliated even by good friends.

On a more subtle level than the homophobia that developed at the fin de siècle was the projection of effeminacy into the racial divides in America. Following the publication of Charles Darwin's *On the Origin of Species* in 1859, social thinkers adapted his theories of natural selection to human societies. Survival of the fittest seemed logically evident to white men by their history of subjugation and dominance of other races and nationalities. Although blacks were no longer in servile bondage after the Civil War, they remained oppressed and dominated by whites on a national scale. Similarly, Native Americans had been forcibly removed from their homelands and consolidated onto reservations as dependents. Hispanic peoples had been on the losing sides of two American wars, one with Mexico in 1848 and the other with Spain in 1898. Chinese immigrants were disdained because they had allowed themselves not only to be tyrannized in their own country, but also endured further abuse by railroad and other labor contractors in America. Thus, at the opening of the modern era, among the new dimensions of effeminacy were race and national heritage. Straight, white, middle-class men preserved their masculine identity by excluding from power men of color or of non-Anglo heritage along with homosexuals and women.

Prelude: Suits of the Early Nineteenth Century

The New Man of postrevolutionary Europe and America experimented with expressions of an identity in dress that not only rejected the peacock flamboyance of the ancien régime but, at the same time, asserted his Protestant soberness, seriousness, and respectability. The immediate impact was easy and evident: Gone were sumptuous brocades, lavishly embroidered silks, frilly lace trimmings, and eye-catching vibrant hues. However, Neoclassicism still prevailed in the cut and fit of men's clothing. When artists and the intelligentsia became champions of the rediscovery of Antiquity during the third quarter of the eighteenth century, fashion was significantly impacted. The pear-shaped silhouette of the Rococo masculine form was transformed into the noble vision of the nude Greco-Roman hero. The jacket that had been designed to hang away from the body at the sides over a thigh-length vest was recut with a short, double-breasted front cropped at the waist. (Figure 2-15.) The contours were trim and narrow without the oversized cuffs and pocket flaps of earlier styles. The tails were simplified and the full, multiple fan pleats reduced to two. Vests, called waistcoats in England, were cropped high as well, extending to just a few inches below the jacket front at the waist. The result of the high, cropped front of the jacket and the short vest was a framing of the hips and legs. Breeches became skin tight to emphasize the youthful male anatomy and delineate the muscular shape of the legs. Men who lacked the requisite athletic build strapped on corsets and false calves. The waistband of the breeches was raised to be fully concealed beneath the vest creating a longer line of the legs. This tail coat, short vest, and trim breeches comprised the standardized suit of the

Figure 2-15. At the beginning of the nineteenth century, the masculine suit reflected the rejection of the aristocratic dress of the 1700s but retained the Neoclassical exhibitionism of the Antique nude hero. Coats and vests were cropped at the waist and knee breeches were formfitting. Fashion plates by Horace Vernet, 1810.

bourgeois male at the beginning of the nineteenth century.

Gradually, the knee breeches were replaced by ankle-length pantaloons for evening wear and trousers for daytime. Breeches lingered as a court costume into the 1840s and then survived in limited varieties as servant's livery to the end of the century. Although long trousers had been worn by boys and working class men since the mid-eighteenth century, the style was adopted by the bourgeois classes in the nineteenth century as a key element of their new egalitarian identity—a further statement of their rejection of the symbols of the old aristocracy. Pantaloons, from which we get "pants," fitted snugly, and some varieties were made of knit fabrics or with stirrup straps to fit under the instep of the shoe for a clinging, smooth definition of the thighs and calves. The "glued on" fit of pantaloons, as Honoré de Balzac described the look in *Lost Illusions* (1837), sustained the Neoclassical aesthetics of masculinity through the first quarter of the century. Older or portly men wore demi-pantaloons that were not so form fitting. Trousers, though, were loose, baggy tubes of fabric that ambiguously encased the legs, also often made with stirrups until the 1850s. In addition, a new construction of trousers with fly fronts became the standard form in the 1840s that replaced the antique fall front with a tab-covered button closure. Prior to that time, trousers were commonly made with a flap across the front called a "fall down" that concealed the opening of the fly. When the French military

Figure 2-16. The frock coat was revived in the late 1810s as a suit for business and daytime social events. The modesty of the full skirt better suited the sober, puritanical ideas of the New Man in postrevolutionary Europe and America. Left, frock coat, 1819; right, frock coats and tail coat from *Petite Courrier des Dames*, 1839.

adopted the fly-front trouser in 1842, the style became widespread.

The tail coat with vest and trousers became de rigueur formal wear for afternoon dress and evening events such as the theater, embassy receptions, or balls. Although tail coats of the early years of the century were often made of deep, rich colors such as midnight blue, pine green, garnet, sienna, and chocolate brown, the most prevalent choice was black. By the beginning of Victoria's reign at the end of the 1830s, black was the only acceptable color for a tail coat. At the same time, the cut became more uniform with a rolled collar, flat lapels, squared shoulders, smoothly inset sleeves, flapless pockets, and coffin-shaped swallow tails to the knees.

Most men wore the tail coat unbuttoned displaying the vest. Through about midcentury, the vest and neckwear were the two remaining garments with which men indulged in wearing vivid colors and bold textile patterns or prints. During the early decades, some men even donned double or triple vests of different cuts so that the layers of contrasting colors overlapped at the neckline and sometimes at the hem. But these were considered hidden garments, despite open coat fronts, and thus the distinction from the aristocrats of old who wore their richest fabrics on the outside surfaces of their dress. By the time the black silk tail coat had become the unquestionable masculine formalwear in the 1840s, the only acceptable type of accompanying vest was a single-breasted, white piqué version, usually with a shawl collar and deep V-cut front. The vest was so snugly fitted that it was often constructed to function as a corset. The trousers were of black vicuna or fine worsted and were sometimes trimmed with grosgrain ribbon or passementerie along the outside seams. Black silk hose and highly polished patent pumps completed the formal dress.

During the late 1810s, the frock coat reappeared after having been eclipsed by the cropped-front tail coat at the end of the previous century. (Figure 2-16.) The full-skirted frock coat better suited the sober Protestant puritanism of the American middle-class male than did the cropped tail coat that immodestly emphasized the form-fitting breeches or pantaloons. The original frock coat of the 1700s had been an English rustic jacket for outdoors, particularly hunting and riding. In France, the frock coat came to be known as a redingote from the English for riding coat. In England and America, the frock coat was worn as a daytime business suit and for making morning social calls. Through the first half of the century, the frock coat was trim and fitted with varying cuts of collars, lapels, and pocket treatments, and assorted lengths and fullness of the skirts. In the 1820s, frock coats were made with high standing collars, puffed sleeves, and full skirts attached to a seam at the waistline. From the 1830s through the 1840s, the skirts were less full but more bell shaped corresponding to the changing silhouettes of women's dresses. The bodice remained fitted and the waist cinched, but the rolled collar replaced the high-standing versions. During the following two decades, the frock coat skirt continued to narrow and the bodice became boxy, its cut aligning with the increasingly popular sack coat.

England's most famous dandy during the second quarter of the century was a French expatriate, Alfred de Grimaud, best known as Count d'Orsay. (Figure 2-17.) Although just twenty years old when he arrived in London, his exceptional good looks, six-foot-three stature, and trim, athletic build made him an instant sensation with the social set. He married

Figure 2-17. Count d'Orsay was England's most prominent style leader during the second quarter of the nineteenth century. Among the menswear trends he is credited with introducing was the loose-fitting, voluminous overcoat and the short, boxy sack coat. Drawing of Count d'Orsay by Daniel Maclise, 1834.

the daughter of Lord Blessington, one of England's wealthiest families and became society's preeminent arbiter of men's style for the next thirty years, including writing a newspaper column on fashion and style.

In the mid-1850s, d'Orsay is credited with introducing a short, boxy jacket that came to be called the sack coat (or lounge coat in England). In the 1860s, fashion journalists referred to the style as a d'Orsay coat.[30] Short jackets, though, were not new to the masculine wardrobe. Fashion lore holds that, in the 1790s, Lord George Spencer, having once too often singed the tails of his tail coat while standing before a fireplace, seized a pair of scissors and hacked off the burnt fabric appendages to the waist. He liked the results so much that he had a number of fitted, tailless jackets made, which became a trend for informal menswear and was quickly adapted to women's fashions. The sack coat, though, was an innovative look in the 1850s. It hung straight down from the shoulders without a seam at the waist and was cropped short at the hips. The first styles were single-breasted although in variations with three or four buttons. Vents were cut at the sides and back for sitting astride a horse. The collar was narrow with short lapels and a shallow V-front. The sack coat was worn with a contrasting vest and trousers of a lighter color or even checks or stripes. It was to be worn only in daytime, primarily mornings, and only in the most casual settings.

The new sack coat became an instant favorite of young men. It was regarded as scandalous by mature men who adhered to the lingering Regency styles. The press blasted the look as inelegant and vulgar. Tailors were appalled when asked to make one. Nevertheless, by the beginning of the Civil War, the practical and functional sack coat was ubiquitous all across America. Its simple lines and basic cut made the style easy to mass produce, and its loose, comfortable fit made it popular. In the early years of the twentieth century, even business executives and professional men began to abandon their dress of distinction, the frock coat, in favor of the comfortable and versatile sack coat.

Suits and Formal Dress 1860–1900

By the end of the 1850s, there were four principal variations of the three-piece suit: frock coat, dress coat, morning coat, and sack coat. The purpose and social protocol for each of these suits were exacting. The bourgeoisie and affluent classes continued to maintain distinctive social codes of dress, ever looking to the Old World, particularly London, for guidance. The correct attire depended upon the time of day, season, geography, and social circumstance. As a *Vogue* editor observed in 1899:

> A man must dress differently upon certain occasions, it is true; there are even slight shades and distinctions of dress which mark the differences of taste and individuality, and which may be indulged in if not carried to the extreme of becoming too noticeable upon all occasions, but the well-dressed man is always well dressed whether the day be bright and sunny, or the rain turning the streets into rivers of mud; whether you come across him with gun or rod in the heart of a forest or meet him in my lady's drawing room in the height of the season; whether you call upon him at his office upon some matter of business or bow to him across the boxes at the opera.[31]

Through these social conventions, the socioeconomic distinctions of class

Figure 2-18. The narrow, boxy frock coat called a Prince Albert was worn with a vest and trousers of contrasting colors and patterns. It was primarily a semi-dress suit worn only in daytime as business attire for executives and professional men or for social events. Photos, c. 1860–75.

in America were maintained. Those who could afford to keep up with the changing subtleties of men's fashion could also be informed of the social conventions of dress whether through their tailors or the many reports in the society columns of newspapers and gazettes. Men of the bourgeoisie knew, for example, never to wear a dress coat in daytime and never to wear a frock coat to an evening event. Even the finer points of etiquette governed not only what and how clothing was worn but also the decorum attached to the garment. For instance, among the more complex accouterments of masculine dress were hats. Choosing from among the vast array of shapes, textures, and colors for the correct accompaniment to a suit could be perplexing enough without the added uncertainty of when to remove a hat and what to do with it once in hand. Manipulating a hat could be a telltale sign of a man's social finesse or lack of polish, and a hat faux pas could be a scorching embarrassment for the socially ambitious.

For the masses, fashion became more democratized through mass production and mass distribution of ready-to-wear. The exigencies of the Civil War had prompted rapid improvements in the machinery and methods of clothing mass production, and distribution became broader and ever more expedient to market. One of the most significant steps in improving the quality of ready-to-wear was ensuring a proper fit. As noted in chapter 1, the Union Army collected the measurements of over a million soldiers from which proportional tables were compiled representing the typical form and build of the American male. From these statistics developed the first attempts at standardized sizes. Similarly, garment construction became more simplified and standardized. The fall-front cut of trousers was replaced with the fly front. The instep stirrups were abandoned. The sack coat, with its simple lines and uniform styling, was easy to pattern and cost effective to manufacture.

Despite the popularity of the sack coat throughout the second half of the nineteenth century, the most prevalent town suit for business executives and professional men was the frock coat with vest and trousers usually of contrasting materials. (Figure 2-18.) The tightly fitted bodices and full, bell-shaped skirts of the Regency frock coats disappeared in the 1850s when Prince Albert, consort to Queen Victoria, began wearing a style that was narrow, square, and looser fitting. The new form of frock coat came to be called the "Prince Albert" although sources are not clear on which Prince Albert to credit with the fashion sobriquet: the father, Prince Albert of Saxe-Coburg-Gotha or the Prince of Wales, Prince Albert Edward, later Edward VII. Most likely the nickname was derived from the latter since initially the fashion press referred to the style as the "Prince of Wales coat" following his official visit to America in 1860. By the 1870s, the frock coat was generally called a Prince Albert.

It was primarily a semi-dress suit worn only in daytime. As the sack coat became more popular, particularly as morning dress, the frock coat was largely worn for afternoon visits and fashionable events such as horse shows and society weddings. By the end of the century, fashion editorials began to predict the demise of the frock coat because the Prince of Wales and his circle began wearing variations of the sack coat into the afternoons. For certain professional men, though, such as bankers, professors, and politicians, the frock coat was a business uniform to be worn throughout the day.

The basic construction of the frock coat remained fairly consistent after 1860 with occasional variations in details such as lapel facings, collar notches, pocket treatments, and waist seam darts. (Figure 2-19.) Frock coats were made in both single- and double-breasted styles although the double-breasted version was the most common. The front closure was a straight vertical line intersecting with a straight horizontal hemline. The V-front opening was shallow and high on double-breasted styles, but deeper on single-breasted versions. The knee-length skirt was sewn to a waist seam that was variously darted to contour the masculine build without cinching the waist. In the 1880s, the Prince of Wales introduced the link closure, a gold chain that attached to the inside of each side just above the waist seam, allowing the coat to remain open without flapping about when walking. The girth of the Prince's waistline had expanded considerably in his middle years, and a trim frock coat was understandably uncomfortable when buttoned. Most frock coats were made of black or dark, blended colors such as forest green, deep blue, or brown. Diagonal worsted or corkscrew twills were the most common fabrics, particularly for ready-to-wear styles from mail-order retailers. Tailor-made frock coats were often of finely woven vicuna or lambswool.

Two variations of the frock coat were the cutaway frock coat and the morning coat. (Figure 2-20.) Both were cut with a skirt front that angled to the sides with rounded corners. The cutaway frock coat was daytime business attire that was regarded as dressier than the sack coat but less formal than the square-front frock. In 1895, *Vogue* described the popular business cutaway frocks as:

something between the sack and our old-time friend, the cut-

Figure 2-19. The double-breasted frock coat was a trim, rectilinear silhouette that featured a square cut front closure and a knee-length hemline. The knee-length skirt was attached to a waist seam and darts contoured the bodice without cinching the waist. Prince Albert suit from Work Brothers catalog, Chicago, 1892.

Cutaway frock suit in brown plaid from Work Brothers catalog, Chicago, 1892

Morning coat suit from J. Barter Company, 1894

Photo of a short cutaway frock coat, c. 1890

Figure 2-20. The cutaway frock coat was constructed with a skirt front that angled to the sides with rounded corners. Cutaway frocks with a short tail that somewhat resembled a sack coat when viewed from behind or versions made with patterned fabrics were regarded as less dressy than the square-front frock, but more formal than the sack coat. For formal daytime social events, the morning coat was a cutaway frock made of fine, dark fabrics and worn with contrasting gray or striped trousers.

away....The skirt is cut off from the hips in such a way as to suggest a bobtail garment. Others are a bit short behind, and are so cut that from the rear they look as if they were sack coats, while in front they present the characteristics of the cutaway. Trousers and waistcoats are the same material."[32]

The cutaway business frock suit—later to be differentiated as an "English walking coat" during the Edwardian era—came in a number of colorful and patterned fabrics that were especially popular with young men. Note that the man wearing the short business cutaway suit in Figure 2-20 holds a derby and he is without gloves, indicating he is dressed for the office, not a social engagement.

The morning coat was for daytime social events. *Harper's Bazar* observed in 1885 that the morning coat and the frock coat "are now considered equally correct as parts of day dress suits to be worn on any ceremonious occasion that takes place in the daytime, such as breakfast parties, luncheons, noon or afternoon weddings, day receptions, etc; they are also suitable for church, for day visits, walking in the city and for driving."[33] In essence, the morning coat was a cutaway frock made of a fine fabric like vicuna or diagonal worsteds in solid black, navy, or charcoal gray and worn with contrasting striped trousers usually in a light gray or sometimes "lavender" (a warm gray interwoven with red, pink, or russet.) In tailors' trade periodicals and photos of the era, a top hat and dove gray gloves were often shown as the correct complements to this form of the morning coat suit.

By the 1890s, though, the business cutaway frock came in such a variety of cuts, lengths, and fabrics that it diminished the formality of the morning coat. *Vogue* insisted that although the morning coat "in years gone by was considered almost as much full afternoon dress as the frock coat…[now,] garden parties, driving and informal receptions require the frock coat…." As for the short tail ditto versions, maintained *Vogue*, a gentleman "may not even pay informal calls in such a rig."[34]

Until the late 1880s, evening dress consisted of the cropped tail coat, a V- or U-front vest, and slim trousers. (Figure 2-21.) The tail coat suit changed so little that many men only bought a new one every ten years or so. The dress coat was cut with a four-button, double-breasted closure. The V-front opening was deep. The shapes and widths of lapels often varied year to year so that it was not uncommon to see peaked, notched, and shawl styles together at the same evening event. The facings of the lapels were made of satin, silk, or velvet, sometimes edged with cording or outlined with an inch of the same fabric as the coat. The front cropping was square and extended to slightly below the waist, aligning with the hemline of the vest. The coat was always worn unbuttoned, which was a test of a tailor's craftsmanship since the two sides tended to sag, creating an awkward profile or, worse, curled outward exposing too much of the vest. Fabrics were usually a fine diagonal twill or corkscrew weave, and, by the 1890s, smooth vicuna was especially popular. Dress suits made of heavier broadcloth were for men of mature years. Although black was overwhelmingly the predominant choice of most men for evening dress, colored coats periodically became a trend. In 1869, *Harper's Bazar* reported that "gay young gentlemen advocate the blue dress coat with gilt buttons, blue vest, and lavender pantaloons."[35] Similarly, George Fox wrote in his style book of 1871, "It is to be hoped that the beautiful blue coat, and gold or gold gilt buttons, with the buff vest, for evening costume, will be restored as the dress of Americans—colors so emblematic of those under which the independence of our country was won."[36] Even as late as 1894, *Vogue* noted the "strong leaning towards the colored dress coat," which was viewed as a curious revival of the fashions of the 1830s.[37]

The appropriate vest for evening dress was cut differently from daytime versions. The closure was usually a four- or six-button, double-breasted style although three-button, single-breasted closures were also popular. The form of the vest lapels matched that of the jacket; shawl collars were not to be worn with notched coats and vice-versa. The V-front opening of a dress suit vest followed the deep lines of the tail coat front opening, and U-fronts created a wide oval that displayed more of the bosom shirt. The vest was either black for dinner attire or brilliant white piqué for the ballroom. The white versions were sometimes hand embroidered in white by the gentleman's spouse or fiancée.

Dress trousers were of the same material as the tail coat. The cut was pegged with a slight fullness at the hips that tapered to a slim eighteen inches at the knees and sixteen and a half inches at the cuff.[38] A narrow stripe of black silk or satin concealed the outside seams of the legs. A white bow tie, white kid gloves, and silk top hat finished the dress suit.

In the 1880s, the sack-like dinner jacket was introduced as an alternative to the tail coat for evening dress in some limited social circumstances. The style likely originated from the British smoking jacket, called a cowes jacket, that was popular with the Prince of Wales as comfortable

Figure 2-21. The correct formalwear for men was the cropped tail coat in black with facings of the lapels in silk, satin, or velvet. The tail coat was worn over a U-front vest and brilliant white shirt. Trousers were of the same material as the jacket and were often trimmed along the side seams with grosgrain ribbon or braid. A white bow tie, white kid gloves, and a black silk top hat completed the evening ensemble. Dress suit from painting by A. B. Wenzell, 1899.

Figure 2-22. The short, boxy sack coat was developed in the mid-1850s as informal morning attire for the leisure classes who sometimes changed their dress two or more times a day. The style was widely adopted by all socioeconomic segments when American ready-to-wear makers began mass production of the style in the 1860s. From the end of the Civil War through today, ditto sack suits, made with a vest and trousers of the same material as the jacket, have been the ubiquitous masculine business uniform. Left, sack suits from *Harper's Bazar,* 1870; right and below, photos of sack suit variations, c. 1885–95.

after-dinner dress when gentlemen separated from their ladies and retired to a study or gamesroom for billiards and cigars. By the 1890s, the dinner jacket was increasingly accepted as a semi-formal dinner suit worn on voyages or in the dining rooms of the better hotels. Gradually, it appeared at dinner parties, the theater, and summer resorts. In France, the dinner jacket was called a smocking.[39] In America, it became known as the tuxedo because it made its debut in high society at the Tuxedo Park Club in New York in the 1880s.

The tuxedo jacket was initially cut like the short sack coat with a single-breasted closure. It hung straight from the shoulders with no seam or darts marking the waist. Most styles featured a shawl collar with silk facings. Black was the correct color although a white version for summer began to be seen at the end of the century. Vests were similar in cut to those of the dress tail coat suit—both single- and double-breasted in black, gray, or white. A black bow tie was worn with a dark vest and white bow tie with a white vest, never the opposite. (Some guides insisted that a white tie was only appropriate with a tail coat.) A derby or straw hat in summer was correct with a tuxedo but never a "topper."

The special appeal of the tuxedo was its comfort, especially when compared to the tightly fitted tail coat. A related development in the ease and comfort of men's evening dress was the introduction of the cummerbund as a replacement for the corset-like vest. This loose-fitting, decorative waist sash was an adaptation of the kamarband, a waist sash worn by the Mughal officers of India. British colonial officers brought the style to England in the last quarter of the nineteenth century where it was combined with the cowes jacket and later the dinner jacket in place of the vest. However, because the cummerbund was reviled in the fashion press and tailors denigrated the look, it took decades before the vest completely disappeared from the tuxedo suit.

In addition to providing a comfortable alternative to the constricting tail coat, the tuxedo jacket also solved another dress issue. Not only had the tail coat become the daytime suit of morticians and department store floor managers, but it was also the uniform of household servants. *Vogue* complained in 1895 that "fashion...is endeavoring to find a costume which shall be included in the wardrobe of a gentleman, but not that of a servant—it is sad that such a distinction should have to be marked—to prevent awkward mistakes."[40]

Although the sack coat was introduced in Europe as casual or "negligé" (also "negligée") dress for the leisure classes, it quickly became the sole choice of business attire for the American masses as well as their Sunday best for church and dressy social occasions. By the 1860s, innumerable variations of the sack coat were available from tailors and ready-to-wear makers. Among the sack coats shown in Figure 2-22 and Color Plate 2 are single- and double-breasted styles with squared and round-cornered hemlines. Double-breasted styles were sometimes referred to as pea jackets, named for the cut of the short outerwear coat.[41] Lapels include notched, peaked, and cloverleaf cuts, some with high, shallow openings and others with deep V-openings to the waist. Some suits are dittos, and others feature a matching vest with contrasting trousers or all three pieces of different materials. Mail-order catalogs of the era often list a huge assortment of fabrics available for the sack coat suit. Montgomery Ward's wishbook for 1895, for example, provided dozens of color

Figure 2-23. Men's shirts were regarded as a form of underwear, or negligé dress. Only in the presence of family or other men would the Victorian male feel at ease being seen in his shirt sleeves. Engraving from *Godey's,* 1861.

combinations and textile patterns in cheviot, cassimere, diagonal clay worsted, satinet, tricot long, flannel, and even cotton worsted and corduroy.[42] The swatch sample portfolios prepared by the mail-order retailers of the era are especially revealing in the variety and richness of the mass-produced textiles available for men's suits. Finely interwoven slubs of red or sienna warmed navys and blacks, and blue or green slubs cooled browns and grays. Pattern-on-pattern designs were sophisticated and complex such as hair-line stripes or subtle window-pane checks overlaying herringbone or houndstooth weaves. However, black and navy serge were by far the most common color choices for sack suits. The black and blue dittos were easy to mass-produce for manufacturers, and the three-piece ensembles resolved a lot of style questions for the masculine masses, most of whom cared little for the subtle dictates of fashion. By the end of the nineteenth century, virtually every American male owned at least one ditto sack coat suit.

Figure 2-24. Through most of the nineteenth century, men's shirts were designed as pullovers, often called "overshirts," that were made with a bosom or shield front and a low, banded collar to which an assortment of detachable collars could be buttoned. Bosom-front shirts from *Harper's Bazar* and *The Lady's Friend.*

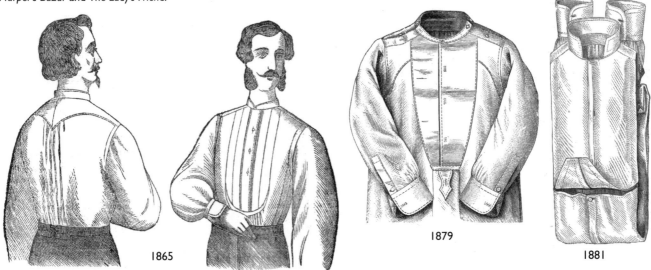

1865

1879

1881

Shirts 1860–1900

Until the end of the nineteenth century, men's shirts were regarded as underwear of sorts. For a man to be seen jacketless by a woman who was not family was highly embarrassing for both. One of the exceptions was laborers or tradesmen who might be seen on the streets and other public places in their shirt sleeves. In the presence of other men, such as on an outing in the woodlands or playing golf at an all-male club, men commonly discarded their jackets. (Figure 2-23.) Only toward the end of the century did it become more acceptable for men to remove their jackets in mixed company when playing lawn games such as tennis or croquet or participating in other strenuous activities like boating.

For centuries, men's shirts had been constructed as pullovers, usually with an opening for the neck and a keyhole front with laces or, later, buttons at the closure. Commonly called a bosom front, shield front, or breastplate front, the white dress shirt featured a reinforced panel over the chest that was variously shaped—some rectilinear with mitered corners and others shield-like, resembling an inverted Gothic arch. (Figure 2-24.) The bosom panel was made with a double layer of linen interfaced with cotton. The muslin shirt body was stitched to the panel with assorted tucks and pleats allowing for a fullness and loose fit. Bosom panels were often embellished with rows of tucks, pleats, or ruching arranged horizontally or vertically. The bosom fronts, collars, cuffs, and placket closures of eveningwear and wedding shirts were sometimes ornamented with white embroidered motifs like scrolling vine tendrils and geometric repeats. Ladies' magazines frequently illustrated embroidery patterns for bosom panels. However, by the 1890s, industrial sewing machines could produce yards of intricate embroidery in seconds that would take many hours to produce by hand. As a result, mass merchandisers offered lavishly embroidered ready-to-wear dress shirts priced from 60¢ to 85¢.

Shirt tails were either square cut or rounded with side slits. Through the 1860s, sleeves were wide with an abundance of gathers at the cuffs despite the close fit of coat sleeves. As the sack coat gained in popularity, shirt sleeves narrowed. Collars were widely varied ranging from stand-up bands called "stocks" to turn-down styles with pointed or rounded tips.

A REAL CALAMITY

Gus: "Pity Cholly is so awfully deformed, dontcherknow?"
Bertie: "Poor fellow! What's the matter with him?"
Gus: "Why—aw—his neck is so doocidly short that he always has to wear a turn-down collar."

Figure 2-25. Not to be in fashion, whether swallowed up within gigantic overcoats or strangled by 3-inch-high collars, was a calamity according to this cartoon from *Life* in 1897.

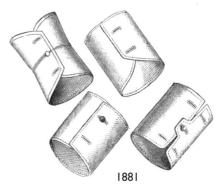

1881

1865

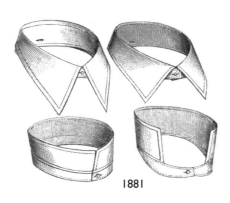

1881

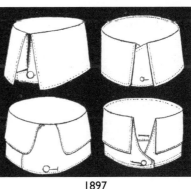

1897

Figure 2-26. Mass-produced detachable collars and cuffs not only provided men with different style options for their overshirts, but they were easier to launder than sewn versions. When collars and cuffs became frayed or stained, they were more economically replaced than an entire shirt. Detachable linen collars and cuffs from *Harper's Bazar* and *Vogue*.

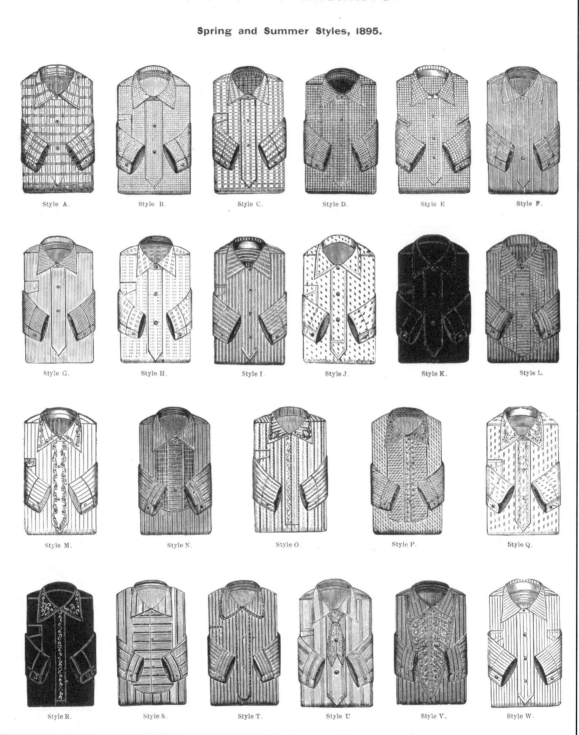

NEGLIGEE OVERSHIRTS.

Spring and Summer Styles, 1895.

Style A. Style B. Style C. Style D. Style E. Style F.

Style G. Style H. Style I. Style J. Style K. Style L.

Style M. Style N. Style O. Style P. Style Q.

Style R. Style S. Style T. Style U. Style V. Style W.

Figure 2-27. "Soft" shirts, commonly called "negligée" or "negligé" overshirts, were made with attached collars and cuffs. By the last quarter of the nineteenth century, mass production of textiles provided ready-to-wear makers with a constant, fresh supply of new colors, patterns, and prints for soft shirts. Page of fancy negligé (negligée) overshirts from Montgomery Ward, 1895.

From the 1860s until the 1890s, collars became increasingly taller until they were almost three inches high at the end of the century. (Figure 2-25.) Cuffs that were cut long enough to turn back were known as "French wrists" which were made with two button holes for cuff links. Since collars and cuffs soiled and frayed easily, ready-to-wear dress shirts were made with thin banded collars to which any number of collar types could be attached by a button at the back. The first commercially produced detachable collars were manufactured in Troy, New York, in 1827, and, by the 1890s, 30 million dozens were made annually.[43] Similarly, a variety of detachable cuffs could be buttoned over the self wrist band. (Figure 2-26.) In addition to being easier to launder, these detachable collars and cuffs also provided variety to the masculine wardrobe. The wealthier classes, though, had shirts custom made with the collars attached. It was not uncommon for men of the leisure classes to change shirts from a colorful negligé style worn with a morning sack coat to a plain white linen variety worn with a frock coat for afternoon occasions, and again in the evenings to a sleekly starched white dress shirt for tail coat.

Despite the general tenets of the sober masculine wardrobe, men's shirts offered some degree of youthful peacock expression. Palettes of vivid hues included lilac, heliotrope (purple), ecru, and, most popular of all, assorted pinks and blues. In addition, these colors were combined in an endless assortment of exuberant patterns such as tartan plaids, horizontal or vertical stripes, and all-over "fancies" like tiny polka dots, chevrons, diamonds, and crescents. However, colored and patterned shirts were only appropriate for daytime wear and then principally with the sack coat suit or sports jackets.

These forms of shirts were commonly called negligé shirts, overshirts, or "soft" shirts since they were not starched. Ready-to-wear makers produced huge quantities of soft shirts in varying degrees of quality. (Figure 2-27.) Those made of fine percales, usually in solid colors and subtle stripes, were worn with a suit and tie. Those of bolder colors and prints were the precursors of today's sports shirts. Some soft shirts were constructed with a banded collar for attaching a separate collar for which only turned-down collars were appropriate; a stand-up collar with a negligé shirt was considered gauche. Soft shirts were made with long sleeves that tapered to a narrow cuff, usually with a single button. Sleeves could be rolled up when engaging in a strenuous activity like bowling, tennis, or golf, but propriety had to be observed in mixed company.

The great leap from the pull-over style of shirts to the open front type of today occurred at the end of nineteenth century. Legend holds that, in the early 1890s, a famous stage actor accidentally tore open the front of his bosom shirt while changing for a performance. Upon examining the tattered garment, he exclaimed that this was the way shirts should be made, and he promptly placed an order with his tailor for a number of shirts with a center front button closure.[44] Originally called a "coat shirt" since it opened vertically down the center front like a sack coat suit, the convenient, comfortable style was an instant success. "No more of the unpleasant, unrefined and undignified over-the-head process," avowed the ad copy for QuickPutOn Shirts in 1894. "No more getting into or climbing out of or fighting your way through a shirt."[45] By the end of the century, most men's ready-to-wear makers were producing full lines of the new coat front shirt. (Figure 2-28.)

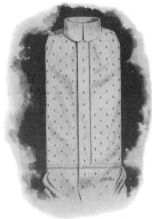

Figure 2-28. In the 1890s, a revolutionary concept in shirt styling was developed. The coat front shirt opened completely down the center front like a sack coat.

Work Clothes 1860–1900

The great majority of American men of the nineteenth century did not dress for work in a sack coat and tie. Ready-to-wear makers produced a wide array of work clothes for both the urban and rural working man. Some garments were specialized like the yellow oil cloth "sou'wester" hat and long coat of the fisherman, and others were uniforms specific to service sectors with large numbers of employees like the railroads, police department, and post office. The most common top for the working man was the long-sleeved soft shirt with a placket closure and turned down collar. Work shirts were made of heavy, 20-ounce twills, wool cassimere, or flannel. Basic woolen work pants were constructed with two front pockets, a button fly, and a button waistband for suspenders. (Figure 2-29.) In the 1890s, "cowboy pants" were advertised as "great wearing goods" made of heavy weight wool with "spring" cuffs reinforced with canvas.[46] Town workers such as grocers and bakers wore protective bib-aprons of heavy white or indigo cotton duck over a soft shirt and worsted trousers. Butchers and blacksmiths required more impermeable aprons of leather or rubber. Streetcar conductors, policemen, and postmen wore tunic uniforms of thick worsted. Factory workers, construction crews, dray drivers, and countless other semiskilled laborers wore flannel work shirts with pants or overalls made of heavy weight wool, cotton corduroy, blue or brown denim, or unbleached cotton duck. (Figure 2-30.)

Most ubiquitous of all work pants for farmers, ranchers, miners, and other rural workers were jeans. The story of jeans dates back to medieval France where a heavy twill fabric woven with white warp threads and a colored weft thread was first manufactured in Nimes.[47] This durable *serge de Nimes,* from which we get the term "denim," was especially favored for sailor's clothing. In the nineteenth century, the fabric—and later the pants—came to be called jeans named after the "genes" or Genoese sailors whose trousers were made of the material.

Many ready-to-wear makers produced jeans in blue or brown denim. In the 1870s, Jacob Davis, a Nevada tailor, hit on the idea of reinforcing jeans pockets and seams with metal rivets. The style was so popular that, in 1873, he arranged with a San Francisco dry goods retailer, Levi Strauss, to patent the idea and mass produce the riveted jeans.[48] From that partnership developed the iconic Levi's jeans.

Sportswear 1860–1900

Following the Civil War, sports and fitness became an obsession with many Americans. Increasingly, men left the physically demanding work on farms and ranches for sedentary jobs in offices or stationary, repetitive work in factories. Fearing generations of weak men, social scientists, physicians, and men's

Figure 2-29. Typical work clothes for urban, semiskilled workers were flannel overshirts paired with 20-ounce worsted "cowboy pants." Despite the itchy, hot wool, these garments were long-wearing for hard work in factories, loading docks, and similar town job sites. Cowboy pants from Work Brothers, 1892.

Figure 2-30. Durable jeans and denim overalls were preferred by laborers, ranchers, miners, and others whose work was particularly strenuous and dirty. Photo of farm boys, c. 1885.

Figure 2-31. Form-fitting athleticwear such as knit shirts, shorts, tights, leggings, and sweaters were mass produced and widely available from mass-market mail-order retailers. Photo of competitive cyclist (medal and ribbon on chest reads "100 Yard Dash") wearing knit top with cap sleeves and modesty skirt over matching knit shorts, c. 1895.

fraternal organizations began to advocate exercise and outdoor activities. The revival of the Olympics in 1896 inspired broad interest in a diversity of athletics. A myriad of new team ball games were devised in the last quarter of the nineteenth century including baseball, football, basketball, and volleyball. Publishers and travel agencies promoted wilderness excursions for camping, hiking, canoeing, sculling, fishing, hunting, and riding. In the 1890s, bicycling became a phenomenon all across America. Gyms opened in most towns providing men with opportunities for training and competitive masculine camaraderie in boxing, fencing, gymnastics, and calisthenics. Home fitness equipment ranging from simple free weights and hand instruments to adjustable pulley weight machines was available by mail order from mass merchandisers. "No home is complete without one," said Montgomery Ward of its portable gymnasium in 1895.[49] Magazines such as *Physical Culture* were established to provide information on fitness, health, and hygiene to the masses.

The average sports enthusiast could choose from a widely varied assortment of specialized clothing for almost every activity. Form-fitting, comfortable knits were particularly popular for vigorous exercise. (Figure 2-31.) Short-sleeve knit shirts, called quarter-sleeve or university shirts, with open, square or scoop necks, were worn under long-sleeved crew-neck sweaters that could be removed when the body warmed from exertion. Knit trunks, knee tights, and footed full-length tights were the most common gym clothes. Athletic supporters were cut like modern bikinis with lace-up fronts, and were made of cotton flannel rather than knits. Knit active sportswear was made of cotton for warm weather and lamb's wool or worsted for cool months.

The knit quarter-sleeve shirt and knee-length knit trunks were also adapted to swimwear. (Figure 2-32.) One-piece combination styles buttoned to the waist at the front like the union suit forms of underwear. For men who felt too exposed in a clinging, wet, one-piece suit, the two-piece

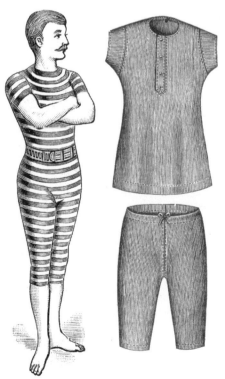

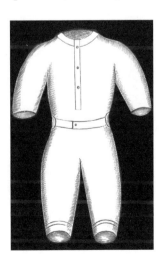

Figure 2-32. For the sports enthusiast of the late 1800s, comfortable stretch knit trunks, tops, and combination union suits were mass produced in a variety of forms for track and field, bicycling, and particularly swimming. Left, one-piece swimsuit from Jordan Marsh, 1883; center, two-piece swimsuit from Bloomingdale's, 1890; right, two-piece swimsuit from Butterick, 1897.

Figure 2-33. Among the sports clothes adopted into daytime wardrobes of Victorian men were sweaters and cardigans. High-speed knitting machines mass produced innumerable varieties of complex and sophisticated garments. Varsity cardigan from Georgetown University, c. 1895.

versions featured a long tunic top that extended to the thighs over separate drawstring trunks. Most men's swimwear was of cotton or worsted in black or navy although young men often preferred horizontal stripes.

Among the types of sports apparel that crossed over to general wear during the late nineteenth century were knit sweaters, so named for the obvious effect they had on the active wearer. Ready-to-wear makers developed high-speed knitting machines that mass produced a variety of complex knit stitches from different gauges of yarn. These sophisticated knits were combined to fashion intricate details and surface treatments for pullovers and cardigans like welt pockets, button holes, and ribbed collars and cuffs. (Figure 2-33.)

The most prevalent form of sports attire was the tweed knicker suit. Knee-length knickerbockers were cut as full, baggy trousers gathered at a knee band that was tucked into knee-high stockings. Knickers were ideally suited for outdoor activities when trouser cuffs could easily get tangled in brambles on hiking trails, wet on dewy golf courses, or stained by oiled bicycle chains. A mufti suit,[50] sometimes called a golf suit, included a jacket and vest that matched the knickers although various combinations of sweater or soft shirt and jacket were common. (Figure 2-34.) By the 1880s, the norfolk jacket had become the favored coat style worn with knickerbockers. The norfolk jacket was a variation of the sack coat with a self belt stitched at the waist, capacious patch pockets, and double box pleats from a shoulder yoke or seam to the hem in the front and back. (Figure 2-35.) The name of the style has been variously attributed to the Duke of Norfolk as the originator of the design and to the Prince of Wales who began wearing the style in the 1860s when on retreat at Sandringham Castle in Norfolk. In America, the style was also called a tourist jacket.

Although the ditto sack coat suit became the business and dress attire for most men, versions of the sack coat style were also adapted to casual dress, particularly for the middle classes whose leisure time and wages continued to increase as a benefit of the surging Second Industrial Revolution. In addition to the norfolk jacket, striped jackets were an alternative to the ditto sack coat for countryside outings and backyard lawn tennis. (Figure 2-36.) The vertical stripes ranged from fine-line pin stripes to one-inch awning stripes. The stripes were usually of one color from a broad palette of hues alternating with white, but some catalogs offered combinations such as orange and red together. Also in a wide range of solid colors were blazers that first became popular in the 1880s. The origin of the unusual name is unclear although two possibilities include the scarlet uniform jackets of the Cambridge College Boat Club or the jersey jacket tops worn by the crew of the ship H.M.S.

Figure 2-34. Belted knickerbockers, or knickers for short, were loose, baggy knee britches worn for outdoor activities and country holidays. Knickers usually came as part of a ditto suit although they were commonly combined with soft shirts, sweaters, and other casual sportswear. Belted knickers, pullover sweater, and sack coat, c. 1895.

Blazer.[51] Since the terms blazer, tennis jacket, and lounge coat were used interchangeably in the fashion press and catalogs, it is difficult to determine if any differentiations of cut or detailing existed between them. Each featured high, notched lapels, a three- or four-button closure, and patch pockets of various sizes and placement.

Besides the many innovative and derivative forms of casual wear that developed for the array of sports and outdoor activities of the late nineteenth century, an important design element was revived that changed menswear dramatically: belt loops. The belted waistband was not new to men's clothing. Depictions of trousers with belt loops are known from Roman frescoes, and a surviving example retrieved from the Thorsbjerg, Denmark, bogs dates to about 250 BCE.[52] Even jeans were made with suspender buttons rather than belt loops until the late 1890s. Sports such as golf and bicycling probably inspired the reintroduction of the belted trouser since golf swings and bicycle maneuverings were impeded by shifting suspenders. (Figure 2-37.) Even though working men often wore suspender trousers without the suspenders, for the middle-class sports enthusiast, that was not an option because such a look was considered an inappropriate state of undress in public where ladies might be present. Despite the convenience and comfort of the belted waistband, the style was primarily applied to sportswear including long trousers and knickers. The transition to suit trousers would begin in the early 1900s, when menswear makers combined the suspender button waistband with belt loops.

Two other elements of men's trouser styles developed in the late

Figure 2-35. The norfolk jacket was designed with a self belt or half belt and double box pleats in the front and back. Norfolk or tourist jacket from The Boston catalog, 1887.

Figure 2-36. The tennis jacket was an unlined variation of the sack coat, usually made of lightweight flannel in a variety of colorful vertical stripes. Left, Spalding tennis ad, 1887; right, awning striped blazer from Bloomingdales, 1890.

Figure 2-37. One of the most important design innovations of nineteenth-century menswear was the reintroduction of the belted waistband. As the Victorian male increasingly pursued sports and outdoor activities, he needed to be free of binding, shifting suspenders. Golf game illustrated in *Scribner's*, 1897.

nineteenth century—cuffs and creases. Pant cuffs were initially viewed with disdain, a carelessness of dress. They originated after the instep stirrup disappeared in the late 1850s. Men began to turn up the bottoms of their pant legs when dashing through muddy streets, but then turned them down again once indoors. In England, "roll-ups" or "turn-ups" became common with cricket and rowing clubs during the 1880s. The cuffs were tacked in place with a couple of stitches that could be clipped for laundering. During the 1890s, some young men began to experiment with versions of ditto suit trousers with prepressed cuffs, a look which was roundly criticized by sartorial purists and style guide writers. By the Edwardian era, though, trouser cuffs were widespread in America. Likewise, the pant leg crease was controversial when the look first appeared in England in the 1880s. There are numerous tales of how the pant leg crease came into being, most of which are linked to the Prince of Wales. As with cuffs, the pant crease developed after the instep stirrup was discarded, which had kept the long line of the trouser legs taut and straight. With the loose, hemmed bottom of trouser legs, the problem of baggy knees occurred when men sat for any length of time. The earliest pant leg creases were actually at the sides, along the seams. These are thought to have been the result of storing men's trousers flat in bureaus and wardrobe cabinets. The center crease began to emerge in the 1880s, initially to shape the trouser leg from the knee down, and then later, from the thigh down. Tailors recommended that the crease be lightly pressed to distinguish custom-made trousers from ready-to-wear with the razor-edge sharpness of their industrial steam-pressed creases.

One form of specialty sports attire associated exclusively with the elite was the equestrian habit. A weekday morning canter through the park was a luxury of the leisure classes who wished to greet and be seen by others of their social status. The morning coat with its cutaway front and vented tail was the preferred top, and trousers were often pegged with a particularly slim fit over the calves to easily fit into tall boots. By the late 1860s, the sack coat was increasingly worn for riding dress. (Figure 2-38.) As George Fox noted in his 1871 style book, "the dress or close-fitting habit [was] being almost superseded...by the loose negligé

Figure 2-38. Jodhpurs were introduced into England as riding britches by colonial officers who had adopted the design from East Indian military dress. The Jodhpur was full through the hips with flared thighs that tapered to a button closure at the knees. Top, equestrians dressed in morning suit and ditto riding habit, 1893; right, mixed riding costume, 1898.

garments of the period."[53] Unlike the long morning coat, the hip-length sack jacket did not get crushed while in a saddle, and the boxy fit was more comfortable than the constricting bodice of the morning coat.

In the 1880s, a new riding trouser was introduced into England from India. The jodhpur had been a form of trouser developed by the Mughal military for their hard-riding cavalry. The cut adapted by Westerners was full through the hips with flared thighs that tapered narrowly to the knees. The inner thighs and seat were reinforced with double-thick fabric against saddle rub. A fitted button closure just below the knees tucked into high riding boots. Matching gaiters were sometimes fastened over the boots.

Outerwear 1860–1900

Outerwear for men in the post-Civil War era was made in a wide assortment of styles based on just a few silhouettes. The names of these numerous types of coats as noted in mass media and apparel trade journals are often confusing to us today since some names were used broadly and generically, such as melton, which was actually a heavy twill fabric, and other names overlap with forms of daywear, such as pea coat, which was both a sack coat and an overcoat.

In the first half of the 1800s, there were two distinctive cuts of coats.

Figure 2-39. The capacious, cylindrical overcoat, cropped at the knees, and the longer ulster, extending to mid-shin, were the two most prevalent forms of outerwear for Victorian men. Both styles were made as single- and double-breasted with a wide assortment of pockets and collar treatments. Left, fly-front overcoat and velvet collared chesterfield, c. 1890; below, double-breasted ulster and knee-length overcoat from Work Brothers catalog, 1892.

One was fitted with a cinched waist and flared skirt, often attached at a waist seam. The other was a loose sack (sometimes written as "sacque" in texts of the time) or box coat called a paletot made without any horizontal seams. The former was the preferred style of the affluent, and the latter was outerwear for the working man.

During the 1840s, the box style became the preferred overcoat championed by England's most influential arbiter of men's fashions, Count d'Orsay. As the story goes, one day d'Orsay got caught in a sudden rain shower while riding in London's Hyde Park and bought a paletot from a passing sailor. The count liked the comfort of the capacious overcoat so much that he continued to wear the style, setting the trend for all others who followed his fashion cue. It is this boxy, easy fit of the paletot that is thought to have been the inspiration for the sack suit jacket in the 1850s also credited to d'Orsay.

By the second half of the nineteenth century, the basic contours of the overcoat were largely standardized. It was constructed to hang loosely from the shoulders in a cylindrical shape, democratically enveloping almost all masculine builds. Lengths varied from just below the knees to the ankles. The narrow, tubular sleeves were precision cut to set into the armscye forming a crisp angle to the shoulder line. Collars were rolled and lapels were high and narrow. Despite these standardizations, though, an infinite assortment of garment details, trim, and fabrics gave overcoats style variety year to year.

The two most widely available types of outerwear were the overcoat and the ulster, named for a belted style of topcoat common in Ulster, a region in northern Ireland. American mail-order catalogs and department store ads offered dozens of versions of both styles. The distinction between the two was length rather than cut or detailing. In catalog illustrations, both ulsters and overcoats were single- and double-breasted; both came with assorted arrangements of pockets and collar treatments; both included belts, half belts, or none; and both were made of the same materials. However, ulsters extended to midcalf, but overcoats were cropped just below the knees. (Figure 2-39.)

Among the numerous variations of the box overcoat that were introduced during the second half of the 1800s was the raglan sleeve coat. The raglan coat featured a shoulder and sleeve constructed from a single piece of fabric that attached to the coat body at the front and back with diagonal seams from the collar to side seams beneath the armscye. Most sources attribute the design to Lord James Somerset Fitzroy Raglan who had an arm amputated at the Battle of Waterloo, and for whom the soft shouldered coat was more manageable and comfortable. Another version of the raglan coat's origin dates to the Crimean War in the mid-1850s. When a British ship that was transporting winter supplies to the troops sank in a storm, the commander-in-chief, Lord Raglan, ordered the regiment tailors to make coats out of blankets until replacements could be sent. As an alternative to the time-consuming set-in sleeve, the tailors contrived the construction that was later named for their commander who died of cholera at the front.[54] Some later variations of the raglan sleeve coat were made with a set-in front shoulder seam but a raglan seam at the back.

Other forms of the basic overcoat included the Inverness cape coat, which was made with a fuller sleeve and an attached cape that extended to the wrists. The Inverness was made famous as the favored topcoat of Sherlock Holmes. The chesterfield was distinguished by a velvet collar that contrasted with the worsted lapels. A burnous was a box coat with influences from the Near East such as hoods, frog closures, and braid trimmed cuffs. The coachman's coat of the 1880s and 1890s was a revival of the fitted Regency greatcoat with a slightly cinched waist, a long skirt attached to a waist seam, and deep pleats at the back.

Raincoats were first developed in the 1820s when the Scottish chemist, Charles MacIntosh, patented a waterproof fabric made of thin sheets of India rubber cemented between woven textiles. The mackintosh, as the raincoat came to be called—a variation of the inventor's name—was not a commercial success at first because the coal-tar naphtha glue used to laminate the sheets of rubber reeked of a noxious chemical odor. In the 1830s, though, Thomas Burberry patented gabardine, a tightly woven twill fabric that repelled moisture. He later opened his own ready-to-wear shop and sold a wide variety of men's and women's rainwear made of his water-resistant gabardine. By the late nineteenth century, mass-produced rubber clothing and macks were available in all the mass merchandisers' wishbooks. In addition to rainwear for the masses, regulation styles were produced for firemen, featuring "an extra wide fly front with snaps and rings, and straps and buckles on the sleeves"; for policemen, regulation rainwear was designed with "ball and socket buttons," a special pocket for the "billy," and a protective "shield" for pinning the "star" badge.[55]

The unlined long coats made popular on the western prairies were called dusters. They were made of heavy linen or cotton duck that were easy to shake off the dust after a long ride. Dusters fitted loosely from the shoulders and were cut with a vent from the waist to the hemline to drape easily over a saddle. Huge patch pockets were necessary for the pioneer and cowboy to fill with a cargo of necessities while outdoors for long hours. As the horseless carriage gained in popularity at the end of the century, the long duster was a practical topcoat for touring in open automobiles over unpaved roads.

Outerwear jackets were not common for winter in the nineteenth century. During cool transitional months in autumn and spring, the many varieties of the wool sack coat were adequate. For active young men, though, the short, double-breasted pea coat was a favorite option. (Figure 2-40.) Most were fingertip length with deep collars and wide lapels that could be turned up against a frigid wind. The style was an

Figure 2-40. The short pea coat was a favorite style of outerwear for young men. Most pea coats were modeled after the British naval jacket with a double-breasted closure, deep collars, and wide lapels. Pea coats, c. 1885.

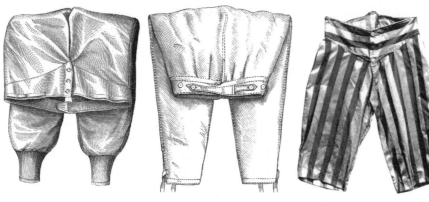

Figure 2-41. Men's drawers were constructed with a variety of waist treatments and button or tie closures. Styles were available in knit wool, linen, and silk, often in vivid colors and bold stripes. Left, wool knit drawers with ribbed cuffs, 1879; center, linen drawers with adjustable tab waist, 1881; right, striped silk drawers, 1898.

adaptation of a British naval jacket, which itself was possibly named for a Dutch version, the *piijekket* (also *pijekkat*). Other names for the nautical style were pilot coat and, in the 1890s, reefer.

Capes remained an alternative to coats. Full, sweeping styles that extended to midcalf or even to the ankles were preferred for traveling on horseback since they could be pulled over the legs in rain or cold. Capes were also an elegant covering for the dress suit since they would not crush starched linen collars, silk bow ties, and satin jacket lapels while en route to the opera or ball.

As a curious footnote to men's outerwear in the late nineteenth century, *Vogue* took issue with a trend they had observed in the mid-1890s—the "fashion prevailing to dispense with overcoats" even in the coldest weather. In more than one winter edition, the editors noted that, irrespective of the fashion decorum, the "non-wearing of overcoats" was a serious health concern. "An overcoat is a protection, not so much against the cold as against the changes of temperature one has to endure going into [an American] house from the open air. Here we have furnace or the hot air pipes...at full blast all winter, and many of our houses are like the hot room in a Turkish bath." In a time before rhinoviruses were understood, the Victorians feared that such shocks to the body caused pneumonia and the "dreaded *la grippe*" (influenza).[56]

Underwear 1860–1900

Men's unmentionables were actually mentioned often in public whether in the fashion editorials of mass publications or in countless underwear ads. Ready-to-wear makers developed cost effective methods of manufacturing underwear and continually expanded design lines to offer greater variety to a broader market. Department stores and menswear shops included "furnishings" counters where the latest cuts of undershirts and colors of drawers were presented in glass cases alongside suspenders, stockings, handkerchiefs, and other negligée clothing.

The basic forms of men's drawers and undershirts had been developed centuries earlier. Victorian versions, though, featured a number of construction improvements such as adjustable waist bands, fly fronts, button closures, and drop seats. (Figure 2-41.) The majority of men's underwear were made of wool knits—white merino, undyed natural, camel's hair, blue Balbriggan, and assorted "drab" colors including gray, brown, and tan. The red ensembles that were favorite costumes in color cartoons and comedy movies of the early twentieth century were listed in mass merchandise catalogs as "scarlet" underwear. Light "summer

Figure 2-42. The wool knit union suit was named for the uniting of the undershirt and drawers into a single garment. Mentor union suit, c. late 1890s.

weight" wools were preferred for warm months although linen was also available. Silk and silk-wool blends were imported from France. Fashion colors were often noted in the magazine editorials. In 1883, *Harper's Bazar* reported on the new lavender and pearl-gray silk drawers offered in New York stores.[57] Vertical stripes were common for men's drawers throughout the nineteenth century, but, by the 1890s, colorful prints and even personalized monogramming with initials and family crests were noted in some fashion reports.[58]

Matching wool knit undershirts were long-sleeved with placket-front button closures. Gauze and silk versions were made to complement the summer styles of drawers. Knit short-sleeved athletic tops were sometimes worn as undershirts as well.

In the second half of the 1800s, the knit undershirt and drop-seat drawers were combined into the union suit. Its name derived not from its mass production by union labor but rather from the union of the two pieces. (Figure 2-42.) A button-front placket extended from the collarless neckline to the crotch. Ankle-length union suits came to be known vernacularly as long johns because the famous boxing champion, John L. Sullivan, wore a form of knit sportswear tights during matches that resembled underwear.

Undergarments were a constant focus of clothing reform advocates throughout the nineteenth century. Fashionable men were chided by physicians, clergy, social scientists, and fraternal societies for indulging in the vanities of pernicious fashions. All sorts of maladies were attributed to choking collars, tight trousers, constricting shoes, cinched waists, and especially undergarments that were regarded as either poorly designed for the masculine anatomy or were made of the wrong materials. In the 1880s, Dr. Hans Gustav Jaeger, a German physician and zoologist, developed and promoted his theories of "hygienic dress" from which he generated a multimillion dollar ready-to-wear empire. Jaeger was critical of modern suit designs because the body was too exposed to damp, chilly drafts, the cause, he and most Victorians thought, of numerous preventable ailments. Trousers exposed the legs to harmful drafts sucked up from the cuffs, and cotton, linen, or silk drawers were ineffective protection. Sack coats were invariably worn open or, at best, buttoned only at the neck, allowing body heat to escape all around the torso. The panacea, Jaeger insisted, was a complete neck to ankle and wrist layer of "sanitary" underwear made of undyed virgin wool. Because wool next to the skin induced perspiration yet retained heat, the body was freed of malignant agents while staying properly warm. Jaeger developed not only new types of underwear but also sportswear, outerwear, blankets, and camping accouterment that he sold in his own retail establishments in America and Europe. His advertising and catalogs promoted his "Sanitary Woolen System" as "especially adapted to healthful enjoyment of outdoor life." (Figure 2-43.)

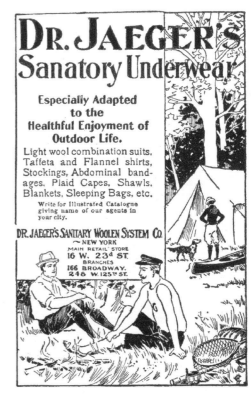

Figure 2-43. Beginning in the late 1880s, clothing reform advocate, Dr. Hans Gustav Jaeger. launched a "Sanitary Woolen System" whereby men were swaddled in wool clothing and underwear as a protection against drafts and chill. Ad, 1898.

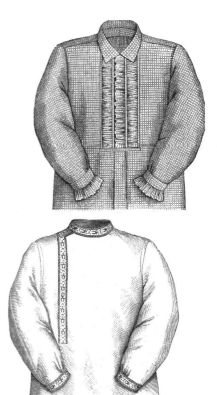

Figure 2-44. Until the late 1880s, most men slept in knee- or ankle-length nightgowns. Since sleepwear was among the most intimate of men's apparel, a man might ease his masculine guard and don nightshirts embellished with ruffles, embroidery, and other finery in the privacy of his bedroom. Nightshirts from *Harper's Bazar*, 1881.

Figure 2-45. Blanket bath robes were a negligé garment worn in the privacy of the bedroom or bathroom. The shorter dressing robe, though, was a substitute for a jacket that could be worn in the presence of family or the most intimate friends. Both were made of colorful, richly patterned fabrics accented with lavish trim and detailing. Dressing and bath robes from Stern's, 1897.

Sleepwear 1860–1900

For centuries, the most common form of men's sleepwear was the nightshirt cropped at the knees or nightgown extending to the ankles. Although nightshirts were basically another form of overshirt, the bosom fronts, necklines, collar treatments, and trimmings of sleepwear were much more decorative. (Figure 2-44.) A man who would eschew ruffled cuffs and bosoms or embroidered collars and plackets on his daytime shirts, where peer scrutiny might challenge his masculinity, was content to wear such finery to bed, especially if the garment had been made or embellished by his spouse. A soft cap and knee stockings completed the sleep attire.

In the 1870s, another influence from India (along with the cummerbund and jodhpurs) was introduced to England by returning colonial officers—the pajama suit. The loose pullover tunic top and baggy, drawstring trousers that were worn by the indigenous workers as day dress in the tropics of the Indian peninsula were adapted as comfortable, modest sleepwear for men. By the 1890s, the nightshirt was regarded as déclassé preferred by older men and traditionalists. In 1895, *Vogue* confirmed that "the pajama has been adopted as the night dress of civilization."[59] At the end of the century, as the coat front shirt became increasingly popular, pajama tops were also modified to include a full-length, button front closure.

Part of the negligé wardrobe for most men was an ankle-length bath robe to be worn while attending to morning grooming regimens or preparation for bed. (Figure 2-45.) The bath robe also accorded some degree of modesty for men as a covering over thin, clinging pajamas as

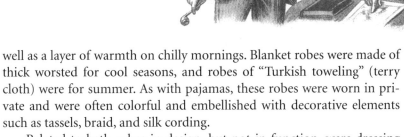

Figure 2-46. Smoking jackets, sometimes called cowes jackets, were an alternative to the dressing robe, worn only in the presence of family and male companions. These negligé sack jackets were the most opulent garments in the masculine wardrobe. Smoking jackets from Stern's, 1897.

well as a layer of warmth on chilly mornings. Blanket robes were made of thick worsted for cool seasons, and robes of "Turkish toweling" (terry cloth) were for summer. As with pajamas, these robes were worn in private and were often colorful and embellished with decorative elements such as tassels, braid, and silk cording.

Related to bath robes in design, but not in function, were dressing gowns. Strict protocol governed when and where a dressing gown might be worn. These were superfluous garments of the affluent worn in place of a suit coat during breakfast with the family or in evenings at home with intimate friends. "It is not correct to wear this garment at any other meal," attested George Fox in 1871, "and certainly not in the drawing rooms or parlors in presence of polite society."[60] Dressing robes were cut shorter than bath robes to about mid-shin, and they were made of finer materials with more sumptuous details. The two examples shown here were lined in satin and featured satin quilted lapels and cuffs, grosgrain ribbon edging, and V-front button closures.

An equally popular style of negligé dress was the smoking jacket, sometimes called a cowes jacket. (Figure 2-46.) These were worn as an alternative to the dressing robe and followed the same decorum. When the Prince of Wales was seen on the streets of Paris in 1895 wearing a smoking jacket in the daytime, it was widely reported in the press.[61] The smoking jacket was the most opulent external garment in the masculine wardrobe. Colors were rich jewel tones—garnet, sapphire, topaz—and sumptuous fabrics included silk matelassé, satin, velvet, and lavishly patterned jacquards.

Accessories 1860–1900

The most important men's fashion accessory of the nineteenth century, arguably, was the hat. No man ventured outdoors bareheaded. The sincere and pervasive belief held by Victorians that chilly air caused colds, influenza, pneumonia, and a host of other dreaded ailments ensured a broad market for the hat maker. In addition, the choice of hat style spoke volumes about its wearer from socioeconomic status to profession and even age range.

Moreover, no other single garment was imbued with such complex,

Derby

Homburg

Tall homburg

Crushers

Fedora

Silk top hat

Boss railroad

Straw boaters

Boating or yacht cap

Outing cap

Cowboys' sombreros

Figure 2-47. The Victorian man rarely went out-of-doors without a hat. His choice of head covering was a key expression of personal identity that conveyed a public image of socioeconomic status, profession, or even age range. Hats from various catalogs and ads, 1883–1898.

arcane social rituals. Etiquette manuals and courtesy editorials abounded with commentary on how to manipulate the hat decorously, and, even then, the arbiters of manners were frequently contradictory. "Certain rules of etiquette to the contrary," insisted a handbook in 1877, "a gentleman may keep his hat on when handing a lady to a carriage. Indeed, for him to do otherwise, and at the same time give proper assistance to the lady, he would find it necessary to have three hands."[62] However, common sense was seldom the standard in hat handling—and such social subtleties were noticed. In tipping a hat to a lady, it should be removed and held over the heart, not extended forward, bottom side up as a beggar soliciting a coin. When calling, a hat should be carried in hand or under the arm, never left on the hallway console. At balls, the flattened topper should be placed in the seat of one's partner, not held to her back like a great black insect.

For some men, which hat to wear with which type of attire, or color for the season, or fabric for the social event was as perplexing as the social graces required for handling one. Even the experts—from trendsetters and fashion journalists to hatters and tailors—often seemed to vary in opinion. "The hat which may be worn now," wrote stylist George Fox in 1871, "varies so much in shape and color, that all that can be said upon that subject is, that the wearer should select according to the season, fashion, and most suitable to his countenance."[63] (Figure 2-47.) Even the finest point of a hat design warranted scrutiny. In the 1890s, for instance, the ribbon bands of hats were popularly available in college colors, similar to baseball caps today, but *Vogue* regarded those men who wore colors of schools they had never attended as "cads."[64]

The most distinctive hat of the era was the top hat. Its predecessors date to the sixteenth century when brims were first added to tall, tapered toques. In the postrevolutionary years of the early 1800s, the stark shape of the plain top hat was the ideal antithesis to the furred, plumed,

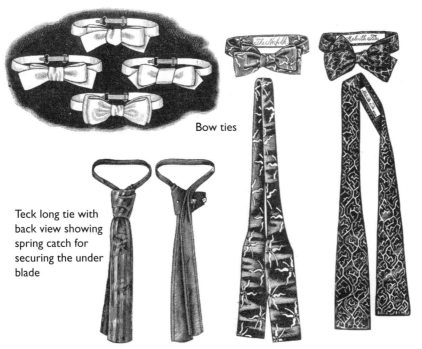

Bow ties

Scarf or De Joinville

Teck long tie with back view showing spring catch for securing the under blade

Ascot

Puff ascot

Tie ring

Four-in-hand knot

Sailor's knot

Figure 2-48. Neckwear for the nineteenth-century male was greatly varied, and provided men with colorful options of personal expression in their dress. For the man who could not master the innumerable versions of knots for each form of tie, ready-to-wear makers mass produced preknotted teck ties. Neckwear from various catalogs and ads, 1883–1898.

embroidered, and ribboned tricornes of the aristocracy. Throughout the nineteenth century, the top hat varied in contours and heights. Every grade schooler is familiar with the tall stovepipe hat of Abraham Lincoln. Through most of the nineteenth century, the top hat was a commodity head covering worn not only by presidents, bankers, and industry magnates, but also by coachmen, clerks, and school masters. Top hats were made in a variety of fabrics including beaver, rabbit or nutria fur, felt, plush, and, most famous of all, shiny black silk. Collapsible versions that flattened into a thin disk were for balls and the theater where seats were designed with a slotted shelf underneath for it to be deposited.

The most ubiquitous daytime hat of the century, though, was the round domed derby, or bowler as it was called in England. The shapes and dimensions of the derby, the width and roll of the brim, and the colors of the material and the hatband varied widely, even in the same season. As *Vogue* observed in 1899, "It would be quite impossible to devise any shape of derby equally becoming to all men, and therefore, slight differences in shape of crown and brim are not only permissible, but very desirable."[65] The derby was unequivocally the correct companion for the sack suit. Black was the preferred color, but derbies were also made in all shades of brown and gray and, periodically, navy or deep green.

The variety of hats available to the Victorian man was extensive. Fedoras were blocked with a deep crease front to back and could be cylindrical- or conical-shaped. In Britain, fedoras with a narrow, finished edge brim were popularized as homburgs, named for a hat factory in Homburg, Germany, that supplied several to the Prince of Wales. The crusher was a soft felt hat with a low, rounded or creased crown and a saucer-shaped brim. Because the crusher was only about three ounces—compared to a fourteen-ounce top hat—it was easily mashed and dented, hence its name. Sombreros were broad-brimmed hats for men of hot, sunny regions of America. They were also called planter's hats and were commonly listed in catalogs as the cowboy sombrero. In the summer months, men wore straw boaters made with low cylindrical crowns and flat brims. Panamas were straw fedoras, named for the tropical Central American nation. For leisure wear, soft caps were preferred to blocked hats. Versions of the modern baseball cap were variously called an engineer's cap, outing cap, or jockey cap. The tweed golf cap was made with a soft, sack-like crown affixed to a band with a narrow visor. The two caddies and the standing golfer in Figure 2-37 wear versions of the golf cap.

From the time of the Civil War, men's neckwear was largely standardized into four categories: bow tie, scarf, ascot, and long tie. (Figure 2-48.) Each style was worn with a specific type of shirt collar, and style guides commonly cautioned against incorrect combinations. There were a number of ways to knot each tie, which also bore a social penalty if not correct. Handbooks for tying neckwear were published as early as the 1810s. For the man who was less adept at the assorted folds, twists, and knots of neckwear, all four styles were available in ready-made forms labeled "teck" ties in catalogs of the era.

The necktie was one of the few garments with which men could still express individuality and peacock flair in spite of the sober plainness of ditto, frock, and penguin suits. The varieties of colors, textures, prints, and patterns were boundless. Ties could be punctuated with fanciful stickpins and jeweled rings. The tie was also a social pitfall if the color or print was too extreme or the knot and blades carelessly arranged. As *Vogue* judged severely in 1894:

> It is the tie which stamps the seal upon a man's individuality. You can almost read his character from his neckwear. It is only a sloven, a man badly turned out and disgracefully groomed, who will rush into a shop and take the very first tie which comes under his nose. A man who trusts the tradesman for guidance and advice shows want of firmness of character and complete lack of judgment. The man who allows a woman to select his ties for him is weak and of no possible account.[66]

Thus, most men delighted in the expressiveness of their neckwear, but, under such harsh public scrutiny, only with great care.

Besides the possibility of social opprobrium for bad taste in neckwear, Victorian men were cautious about the social meaning of certain types of ties. As Havelock Ellis recalled from his student days in the 1880s, a red necktie was a badge of "fairies"—"a visual symbol that served as a synonym for [homosexuality], not only in the minds of inverts themselves, but in the popular mind....Among my classmates at the medical school, few ever had the courage to wear a red tie; those who did never repeated the experiment."[67]

By the 1890s, two distinct shapes of the bow tie were prevalent. The butterfly bow was tied with a small, tight knot so that the two halves flared into wide, pointed ends resembling the colorful insect with wings outspread. The batwing was tied so that the ends separated slightly from the loops to form an "X" shape like a bat with its wings distended. Bow ties made of vibrant colors and sumptuous silks were for daytime only.

For evening dress, white was required for tail coats and black for tuxedos. To mix the latter two was bad form.

The scarf was a wide, oblong shape with squared ends. Some versions were up to six inches wide so that the two overlapping ends completely covered the shirt front at the neckline of the vest. Style guides and catalogs of the time usually refer to the scarf tie as a "De Joinville," named for Francois d'Orléans, Prince de Joinville, son of King Louis Philippe. While the prince lived in England in the 1840s, he popularized the wide scarf tie, which later bore his name.[68]

Similar to the scarf is the ascot, which also had squared ends and blades that crossed over the front, except it was only three inches wide. Puff ascots were tecks shaped with an interlining of wadding where the ends emerge from the sewn knot. Ascots were made of more subdued fabrics since they were often worn with the semiformal morning jacket.

The Victorian long tie originated from the various arrangements of cravats from the early part of the century. Long ties were square or oblong pieces of fabric folded to encircle the collar and tie in assorted knots at the front. By the end of the era, long ties were cut to shape on the bias and constructed with interfacings and linings. They were available in a variety of shapes, widths, and textiles. Some were cut with squared ends, but most were folded with a pointed tip. Unlike today's long ties that extend to the belt buckle, the Victorian long tie barely extended to mid-chest since it tucked into the vest or jacket. Only in the most casual circumstances would a man be seen jacketless, such as on the golf course or billiards room when no ladies were present. The most common knot was the four-in-hand, for which long ties were often named in catalogs and editorials. The name of the knot may have come from an English racing organization called the Four-in-Hand Club who adopted the knot from one used to tie the reins of carriage horses.[69]

The three principal types of shoes for men were ankle boot, oxford, and tall boot. (Figure 2-49.) The everyday shoe was the ankle boot, which came in a wide variety of styles. The most prevalent were lace-ups although button tops and pull ons were common. Pull ons became popular after the invention of rubberized textiles in the 1840s, which shoe makers inserted at one or both sides of the boot for greater comfort. Another new construction of the ankle boot that was introduced just after the Civil War was the gaiter boot, named for the spats-like fabric upper stitched to the leather last. Lace-up oxfords, also called low shoes, were primarily summer casual wear and were favorites of young men, particularly in contrasting two-tone leather. Other styles of low shoes included slip-on patent pumps for evening dress and a wide assortment of athletic shoes, notably the tennis shoe made with canvas uppers and rubber cleat soles. Tall boots were strictly functional footwear. The elegant, highly polished riding boot was for the equestrian while the opera cowboy boot with its ornate top stitching and high heels was for riding the range. Farmers opted for kip boots made of durable, untanned calf that required little care. Miners and fishermen wore hobnailed rubber boots lined with warm wool.

The shapes of toes were frequently a topic of editorials when assessing the most current fashions in footwear. Even then, the latest trends could be confusing as *Harper's Bazar* noted in 1883: "There is a tendency to broaden the toes of all shoes that have been worn nearly pointed on account of the closely fitted trousers, but sensible men have never fol-

Two-tone razor toe

Square toe with elastic inset

Kangaroo welt

Oxfords

Opera cowboy boot

Canvas and rubber tennis shoes

Figure 2-49. The everyday footwear for most Victorian men was the ankle boot made variously with laces, buttons, or elastic insets for pullons. Low shoes, or oxfords, were primarily worn by collegiate men. Tall boots were utilitarian footwear constructed distinctively for the urban equestrian, the prairie-roving cowboy, or the rural rancher. Shoes from ads and catalogs, 1889–95.

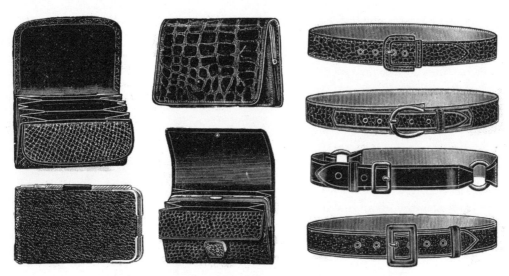

Figure 2-50. Among the small leather items a man wore or carried with him were belts, wallets, multi-compartment pocket books, change purses, spectacles and comb envelopes, card cases, and notepads. Small leather goods from ads and catalogs, 1883–95.

lowed either of these fashions to the extreme."[70] Extremes would range from the pinching razor tips to the wide, squared bluchers called "corn curers." But since catalogs of the time featured sharply pointed, rounded, and squared toe versions concurrently, the most current shapes of the toes were probably irrelevant to most men. Colors were only occasionally a subject for journalistic note since the majority of men's shoes were only available in black. Brown was regarded as a summer hue, and, when straw hats were put away for the season, so, too, were brown shoes. Besides assorted treatments of cowhide leather, a variety of exotic hides were also available for men's shoes including kangaroo, alligator, lizard, and sea porpoise.

With such a wide assortment of affordable shoes made available through mass production and mass distribution, and with mass advertising encouraging consumerism, men of the late nineteenth century likely owned a number of pairs. As *Vogue* avowed in 1895, "Boots and shoes are articles of which a man cannot have too many ."[71]

Other leather accessories of the Victorian male were wallets, change purses, notebooks, calling card cases, and spectacle and pocket comb envelopes. (Figure 2-50.) In addition to crushed calf and other textured leathers, men's pocket accessories were available in sheep, seal, reptile, and monkey skins. Many of these small leathers were trimmed in sterling silver or gold plate. For the man on a budget, simulated alligator, lizard, and snakeskin were mass produced from lesser grade cowhides.

Until the end of the century, men's trousers were held up by suspenders (called braces in England). (Figure 2-51.) Most were made of elastic web with leather tabs that attached to buttons on the front and back of the trouser waistband. The webs were vividly colored in solids, stripes, and richly patterned jacquards, and even embellished with machine embroidery. Women often hand embroidered suspenders as a gift to spouses or beaus, and women's magazines of the era frequently illustrated stitching patterns. The ad shown here outlines many of the complaints men had about ill-fitting suspenders including stress on

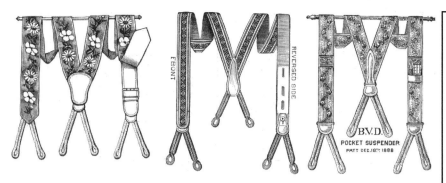

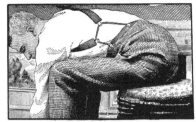

Figure 2-51. Suspenders were the singular method of supporting all varieties of trousers until the 1890s when belts were reintroduced for sportswear. Throughout the era, innumerable constructs of elasticized bands and cables were patented for suspenders, and webbing was mass produced in vibrant colors, bold stripes, and opulent patterns. Suspenders from ads and catalogs, 1883–95.

shoulders and waistband buttons, tugging of waistband and lifting of pants leg cuffs, and baggy fitting trousers. By the 1890s, when sports trousers and knickers were made with belt loops instead of suspender buttons, leather belts became a more comfortable and practical alternative to suspenders.

Gloves were one of the key differentiators between the socioeconomic classes in America. "Gloves should hold an important place in the wardrobe of a well-dressed man," advised *Vogue* in 1899. "A man must always wear gloves upon the street; he should in fact always wear gloves upon all possible occasions."[72] Kid and suede were the most common materials for gloves although some walking or promenade gloves were made of knit jersey and even silk taffeta. These were unlined to fit the hands snugly like a second skin. Gloves came in a surprising array of colors for men. Primrose, lavender, and fawn were cited in style guides of the 1870s.[73] By the end of the century, browns, tans, and grays were the most common colors of gloves for conservative men, but red and shades of yellow were favorites of young men. Only work gloves and heavy winter weather gloves came in black. White was worn with evening dress.

Despite the general austerity of the nineteenth-century masculine wardrobe, jewelry had not been completely abandoned. Magazines and style guides often cautioned men about flashy jewelry and nouveau riche exhibitionism. "As to the use of jewelry, it is difficult to decide how far its adoption is within good taste, but all ostentatious display should be studiously avoided," warned George Fox in 1871.[74] Nevertheless, a number of jewelry options remained for men. Signet rings, cuff links, tie pins and clips, pocket watches, watch chains and fobs, key ring chains, charms, and shirt studs were among the varieties of jewelry for the Victorian man. (Figure 2-52.) The tie stickpin especially received a great deal of attention in the press. The famous New York financier, Diamond Jim Brady, was nicknamed for the ostentatious, jewel-studded stickpins he wore. Style guides and magazine editorials of the time warned against wearing stickpins with the wrong form of tie, and cartoonists lampooned the dangerous fashion of wearing the pin point sticking out as seen in the photo shown here. Also sold in jewelry stores and catalogs that men carried or wore were suspender mounts, pocket knives, match boxes, cigarette cases,

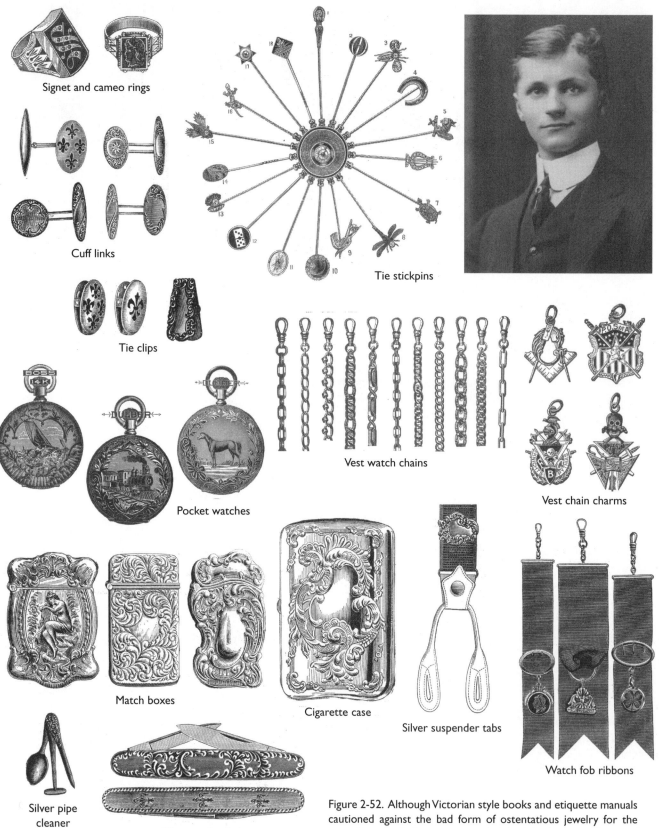

Signet and cameo rings

Cuff links

Tie stickpins

Tie clips

Pocket watches

Vest watch chains

Vest chain charms

Match boxes

Cigarette case

Silver suspender tabs

Watch fob ribbons

Silver pipe cleaner

Silver pocket knives

Figure 2-52. Although Victorian style books and etiquette manuals cautioned against the bad form of ostentatious jewelry for the masculine wardrobe, many men indulged in the many forms of precious metals and jewels available for accenting their somber dress. Jewelry and accessories from ads and catalogs, 1883–95.

cigar cutters, pipes and pipe cleaning tools, and spectacles cases. As with fine linens and fine leathers, fine jewelry was also replicated in simulated version by mass production. White metals made from alloys of base metals were electroplated with silver and gold, and semi-precious and faux stones made of glass or painted enamels substituted for genuine precious gems.

Men's hosiery of the nineteenth century was not much different from that made today except synthetic yarns were not available. Victorian men's hosiery came in two lengths: half hose (socks) and knee-high (stockings), both of which were made from varying weights of wool, cashmere, silk, and cotton yarns. Colors were subdued and dark although socks with horizontal stripes were often multicolored. For evening dress, fine silk stockings were knitted with decorative clocking along the ankles. In the 1880s, *Harper's Bazar* recommended English "digitated socks, with toes separated like the fingers of a glove" for men with "tender feet."[75] Although socks were made with ribbed tops, the best dressed men always wore garters to prevent socks from sagging or bunching about the ankles. (Figure 2-53.)

The walking stick or cane was the final touch to a gentleman's correct dress. Although most canes were plain, polished, or ebonized wood with simple caps, some were lavishly ornamented with handles of carved ivory or horn, silver or gold mounts, and inlaid mother-of-pearl or other semi-precious stones. (Figure 2-54.) In 1894, *Vogue* reported on the curious novelty of canes with watches set into the handle.[76] The shepherd's crook handle became popular in the late 1890s when the Prince of Wales adopted the style. These same handles used for adorning canes were also attached to umbrellas and riding crops.

Grooming 1860–1900

The Victorian male underwent a daily regimen of personal hygiene and grooming. Many style guides and physical culture magazines offered suggestions on the masculine "toilette" that were necessary for good health and for participating in polite society. Foremost, short hair prevailed throughout the nineteenth century. Only eccentrics such as General George Custer or theatrical performers like Wild Bill Hickock grew their hair long. *Vogue* even objected to bangs over the forehead, a trend among collegiates in the 1890s, as juvenile and effeminate.[77] The abundant display of facial hair was another form of masculine identity that was a significant shift from the eighteenth-century ideal. By the mid-1800s, men more often than not flourished a beard or mustache. Every U.S. president from the Civil War until the end of the century, except one, was fully bearded or mustached. Many of the cuts of facial hair were even named for famous men with whom the style became identified. For example, the combination of a short, pointed beard and long, thin mustache was called an "imperial" after Emperor Napoleon III of France. Likewise, the term "sideburns" was derived from the bushy jowl whiskers favored by Union General Ambrose Burnside during the Civil War. For some Victorian men, the restoration of masculine facial hair even became a religious cause, a return to the natural state of original man. In 1847, William Henslowe wrote *Beard-Shaving and the Common Use of the Razor: An Unnatural, Irrational, Unmanly, Ungodly, and Fatal Fashion among Christians* in which the Devil presents the razor to Woman who

Figure 2-53. To avoid sagging stockings or the worst case shown in this 1894 ad, the best-dressed men strapped on pinching, binding garters over the calves to ensure a smooth, secured fit of their hosiery.

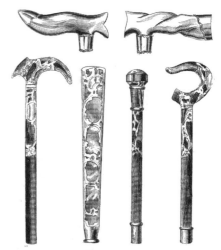

Figure 2-54. Throughout the nineteenth century, a walking stick was an indispensable accessory for the well-dressed gentleman. Although most walking sticks were simple and plain to complement the austerity of the Victorian masculine dress, some were capped with elaborate handles made of precious materials. Cane handles from Stern Brothers, 1897.

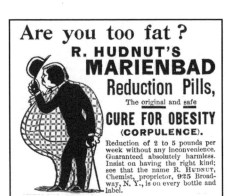

Are you too fat?
R. HUDNUT'S
MARIENBAD
Reduction Pills,
The original and safe
CURE FOR OBESITY
(CORPULENCE).

Reduction of 2 to 5 pounds per week without any inconvenience. Guaranteed absolutely harmless. Insist on having the right kind; see that the name R. HUDNUT, Chemist, proprietor, 925 Broadway, N. Y., is on every bottle and label.

R. HUDNUT, Chemist,
925 Broadway (only), New York City,
And Leading Druggists Everywhere.

MANLY PURITY AND BEAUTY

To cleanse the Blood, Skin, and Scalp of every eruption, impurity, and disease, no agency in the world of medicine is so speedy, agreeable, economical, and unfailing as the world-renowned CUTICURA REMEDIES, consisting of CUTICURA, the great skin cure, CUTICURA SOAP, the most effective skin purifier and beautifier, and CUTICURA RESOLVENT, the new blood purifier and greatest of humor remedies. Everything about the

Cuticura Remedies

inspires confidence. They are absolutely pure and agreeable to the most sensitive. They afford immediate relief in the most distressing of itching and burning eczemas, and other itching, scaly, and crusted skin and scalp diseases. They speedily cure humors of the blood and skin, with loss of hair, whether simple, scrofulous, hereditary, or ulcerative, when the best physicians and all other remedies fail. In a word, they are the greatest skin cures, blood purifiers, and humor remedies of modern times, and may be used in the treatment of every humor and disease, from eczema to scrofula, from infancy to age.

☞ "How to Cure Blood and Skin Humors," 64 pages, 300 Diseases, 50 Illustrations, and 100 Testimonials, Mailed free to any address. A book of priceless value.

CUTICURA REMEDIES are sold throughout the world. Price, CUTICURA, 50c.; CUTICURA SOAP, 25c.; CUTICURA RESOLVENT, $1. Prepared by POTTER DRUG AND CHEMICAL CORPORATION, Boston, U. S. A.

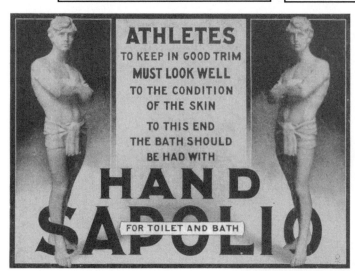

ATHLETES
TO KEEP IN GOOD TRIM
MUST LOOK WELL
TO THE CONDITION
OF THE SKIN
TO THIS END
THE BATH SHOULD
BE HAD WITH
HAND
SAPOLIO
FOR TOILET AND BATH

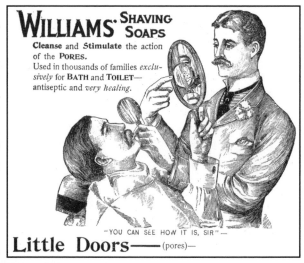

WILLIAMS' SHAVING SOAPS

Cleanse and **Stimulate** the action of the PORES.
Used in thousands of families *exclusively* for **BATH** and **TOILET**— antiseptic and *very healing.*

"YOU CAN SEE HOW IT IS, SIR"—
Little Doors——— (pores)—

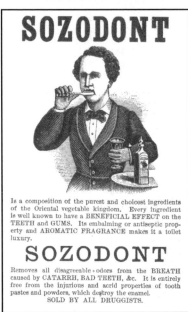

SOZODONT

Is a composition of the purest and choicest ingredients of the Oriental vegetable kingdom. Every ingredient is well known to have a BENEFICIAL EFFECT on the TEETH and GUMS. Its embalming or antiseptic property and AROMATIC FRAGRANCE makes it a toilet luxury.

SOZODONT

Removes all disagreeable odors from the BREATH caused by CATARRH, BAD TEETH, &c. It is entirely free from the injurious and acrid properties of tooth pastes and powders, which destroy the enamel.
SOLD BY ALL DRUGGISTS.

BUCKINGHAM'S DYE FOR THE WHISKERS

BISMARCK   HARRISON
FRANZ JOSEF   SHERMAN

REJUVENATES
GRAY BEARDS

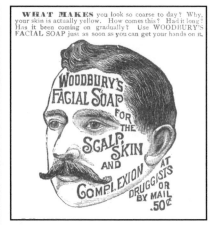

WHAT MAKES you look so coarse to-day? Why, your skin is actually yellow. How comes this? Had it long? Has it been coming on gradually? Use WOODBURY'S FACIAL SOAP just as soon as you can get your hands on it.

WOODBURY'S FACIAL SOAP FOR THE SCALP SKIN AND COMPLEXION AT DRUGGISTS OR BY MAIL .50¢

"DANDRUFF should never be neglected, because its natural end is in
BALDNESS."
"The chief requirement of the hair is cleanliness — thorough shampooing for women once a fortnight, and for men once a week." The best agent for the purpose is

PACKER'S TAR SOAP.

Figure 2-55. During the last quarter of the nineteenth century, makers of personal hygiene and grooming products tailored their mass marketing efforts to specifically target men. By using these products, advertising messages asserted, the Victorian male was promised "manly purity and beauty." Ads, 1880s and 1890s.

introduced the mutilating instrument to her husband.

By the last quarter of the nineteenth century, makers of personal hygiene and grooming products expanded their marketing efforts beyond targeting primarily the housewife and directly aimed their advertising at men. Manufacturers of bath and shaving soaps, shampoos, tooth brushes and dental powders, razors, brushes and combs, hair oils, and even hair dyes produced a barrage of ad campaigns urging men toward "manly purity and beauty" through better personal hygiene. (Figure 2-55.) The patent medicine industry especially capitalized on masculine vanity with promised cures for every condition from obesity to baldness. Women's magazines were filled with assorted home recipes for the masculine toilette. Some recommendations might even surprise us about the Victorians such as the "air bath"—remaining nude for some time after a bath or sunbathing in the nude.[78]

As an emphasis on hygiene and health expanded throughout the American medical establishment, an advocacy for circumcision began to emerge in the 1850s. Physicians increasingly recommended the procedure for infant boys as a prevention for various penile diseases and disorders, and even as a measure to curb masturbation. One of the best known advocates was Dr. John Harvey Kellogg of the cornflake fame who explained the many hygienic and health benefits of circumcision in his 1877 book, *Plain Facts for Old and Young: Embracing the Natural History and Hygiene of Organic Life.* Although the science supporting circumcision was incomplete and often misguided in the nineteenth century, the result was the foundation of a secular American culturalism that prevails still today.

Conclusion

By the time of the Civil War, the basic components of men's dress had become largely standardized. The sober, plain suit that evolved over the decades of the first half of the nineteenth century culminated in the ditto sack coat suit, which became ubiquitous throughout America by the time of the Civil War. The comfortable, boxy sack coat relegated the constricting, fitted tail coat to limited evening wear. The cut of the sack coat also influenced the silhouette and fit of the frock coat and morning coat, both of which kept the horizontal waist seams but with looser-fitting proportions. Trousers also became standardized with the button fly front that replaced the centuries-old fall front construction. The instep stirrups that had developed in the 1810s also had been abandoned by 1860.

Although the ditto sack coat suit had been standardized by the 1860s, many innovative details and new cuts occurred in subsequent decades. Versions of the sack coat were adapted to outdoor activities and formal wear, and trousers were cuffed, creased, and cropped.

The unlined blazer, or tennis jacket as it was also called with its bold awning stripes and patch pockets, was an adaptation of the sack coat. A similar version was the norfolk jacket with its self-belt and box-pleated front and back that became the golf suit jacket. Negligé forms of the sack coat, like the cowes or smoking jacket, were richly embellished with elaborate trim, quilted lapels, and vivid colors. For evening wear, a variation of the sack coat with satin lapels—the tuxedo—became a comfortable substitute for the dress tail coat.

Trousers were variously modified into new forms. Hemlines that had been rolled up on rainy days became tacked and pressed as cuffs. Baggy trouser knees were mitigated by steam-pressed creases. Knee britches were revived as knickerbockers and worn for golfing, hiking, bicycling, and similar outdoor activities. Another trouser revival inspired by the surge in sports activities was the belt-loop waistband. Jodhpurs were introduced as a new type of riding trouser.

Outerwear also lost the tightly fitted contours of the Regency redingote. Ulsters and overcoats were cut as capacious cylinders without waist seams. Pea jackets and the raglan sleeve were appropriated from military dress and adapted to civilian wear.

Some innovations of the era were fun and superfluous such as the cummerbund while others like the coat front shirt were significant enough to alter the way men dressed to the present day.

The subtleties of when and how menswear trends developed are often difficult to trace. Jeans had been around for decades from an unknown origin, but the launch of Levi's riveted jeans can be pinpointed to a patent date. Ready-to-wear advertising, mail-order catalogs, etiquette and style guides, and magazine editors provide an abundance of information in general, but, by the time a garment was in mass production, the first instance of use was lost to time. Trade periodicals like *Tailor and Cutter* and *Men's Wear* or consumer magazines like *Harper's Bazar* and *Vogue* provide enormous primary source material. Indeed, one of the most detailed chronicles of the subtle changes of menswear and accessories from season to season can be found in the "As Seen by Him" columns featured weekly in *Vogue* from 1893 into the 1910s.[79] The contributing editors were highly observant—and often critical—of the slightest changes in men's styles as represented to them by tailors, trade periodicals, haberdasheries, and their own social encounters.

At the close of the nineteenth century, menswear was permeated with striking dichotomies. The austerity of the business ditto suit contrasted with the peacock options in neckwear and vests. The conformist ubiquity of the penguin dress suit was balanced by the casual individuality expressed with blazers, sweaters, golfing suits, negligé jackets, sleepwear, and accessories. A gentleman was never to be without a jacket in the presence of ladies, and yet he dashed about public beaches in wet, formfitting knit swimwear unabashedly baring his legs and arms in the presence of ladies. All of these contrasts in silhouettes and fabrics, in detailing and trim and in use and purpose reflected the complexities of American society itself—one that rushed headlong toward a modern new century, trying to keep pace with the ever-quickening advances in science, technology, communications, transportation, manufacturing, and business.

Edwardianism
Fashions of la Belle Époque, 1900–1914

America on the World Stage

In January 1901, Queen Victoria died. Her eldest son, the Prince of Wales, ascended the throne as King Edward VII (1901–10). The era from the beginning of the twentieth century until the start of World War I is named for the jovial monarch whose amiable nature and vivacity were a sharp contrast to the mythical lugubriousness of his mother who mourned the death of her husband for forty years. Edward revived the royal court with a renewed effervescence and glamour not seen since the Regency era a century earlier. (The French called the period *la Belle Époque*.) With his elegant consort, the tall and slender Queen Alexandra, at his side, fashion and elite style once again reigned supreme. To his people, Edward was popularly known as "Good old Teddy"; among his friends, he was nicknamed "Tum-Tum" for his prodigious appetite and his insatiable pursuit of fun.

These early years of the century may be universally labeled Edwardian, but, in America, it was the era of a different Teddy—President Theodore Roosevelt. Everything about T.R. seemed bigger than life. As a child, he had built up his spindly, asthmatic body by a rigorous regimen of exercise. As a young man, he went out West and worked as a cowboy on a cattle ranch. When the war with Spain began in 1898, he led a group of volunteers called the Rough Riders whose daring exploits in Cuba made him a national hero. In 1901, he was elected vice president, and barely six months later, he came to the presidency when William McKinley was assassinated.

At age forty-two, Roosevelt was the youngest president thus far in American history. He plunged into being president with a high-voltage energy that electrified friend and foe alike. Incorrigibly boyish and pugnacious, he loved a good fight. His motto was the ancient proverb, "Speak softly and carry a big stick." (Figure 3-1.) In global politics, the Big Stick was "the power of the Executive in the government of the United States,"[1] and Roosevelt wielded it often during his eight years as president. He

Figure 3-1. The first decade of the twentieth century was named for Britain's King Edward VII, but, in America, it was the era of Teddy Roosevelt. Cartoon of Roosevelt and his famous "big stick" from the *New York World,* 1904.

intervened in the Panama revolution and secured the rights to build the Panama Canal. He engineered peace between warring Japan and Russia for which he won the Nobel Peace Prize. Most especially, he invoked the Monroe Doctrine a number of times to prohibit European powers from meddling in the affairs of Latin America.

On the home front, Roosevelt used the Big Stick to tackle social problems. It was an age of progressivism in America, and T.R. was a zealous reformer. His policy of a "square deal" for the American people sent his Big Stick crashing down on big business monopolies that exploited their workers and engaged in predatory practices like price fixing. He adopted the eight-hour workday for government employees when the national average was ten hours. He ushered into law a series of consumer protection reforms. But his most enduring tangible achievement was conservation. As an avid naturalist and outdoorsman, he crusaded for land preservation and reclamation, setting aside 125 million acres of American wilderness from timber and mineral exploitation.

When Roosevelt left office in 1908, his handpicked successor was his loyal disciple, the Secretary of War, William Taft. Although Taft promised to continue the progressive policies of Roosevelt, and he actually brought more proceedings against trusts, he soon came under the influence of the Republican Old Guard. The laissez-faire policies of the Taft administration once again eased the reins on big business, allowing those whom Roosevelt called the "malefactors of great wealth" a freer hand at their greedy, self-obsessed pursuits.

Outraged by the corrupt machinery of the reactionary party bosses and the undue influence of corporate special interests, Roosevelt formed a third party in the presidential election of 1912. "I'm feeling like a bull moose," T.R. barked to a reporter, and, from there, the antlered symbol of the Bull Moose Party charged onto the political landscape to challenge the entrenched Republican elephant and Democratic donkey. The ensuing campaign battle between Taft and Roosevelt—vicious and bitter—divided the Republican party, opening the way for the Democratic opponent Woodrow Wilson to be elected.

A Progressive American Society

The Edwardian era was the last age of innocence—a golden interlude—for the United States. Most Americans welcomed the new century with the promise of continued peace, prosperity, and progress. Theirs was not merely a hope for the best; theirs was the confidence of inevitability. The farmers were doing well with farmlands never more bountiful. Businessmen enjoyed minimal taxes and burgeoning trade. For the average citizen, jobs were abundant, and opportunities for earning a living ever more diverse.

Technology and mass production immensely eased the burdens of the Edwardian housewife. Food was plentiful and cheap. Fresh milk, eggs, and produce from the farms and meats from packing houses were quickly shipped around the country in caravans of refrigerated railcars. Grocers' shelves were stacked with numerous varieties of canned, bottled, and packaged processed foods from baked goods and meats to seasonal fruits and vegetables. (Figure 3-2.) Labor-saving home appliances continually improved. Oil and gas kitchen ranges with on/off switches were introduced, replacing the wood- or coal-burning cast iron stove. As more

Figure 3-2. For the Edwardian housewife, food preparation chores were greatly eased by the availability and convenience of a huge assortment of mass-marketed processed foods. Swift's ad, 1902; Van Camp's ad, 1903.

Plate 1. Front cover of a mail-order catalog from The Boston, St. Paul, Minnesota, 1887.

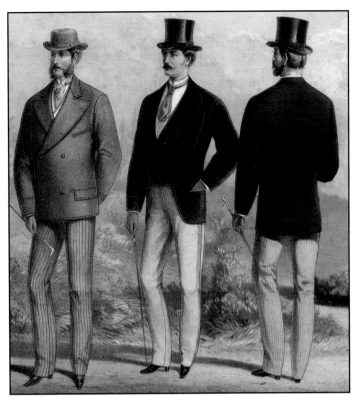

Plate 2. Sack coat designs by Butterick, 1870.

Plate 3. Sack coat suits by Babson Brothers Clothiers, 1914.

Plate 4. Pilgrim brand soft shirts from Sears, Roebuck, and Company 1929.

Plate 5. Young men's athletic style suits by Krafft and Phillips, 1935.

Plate 6. Ad promoting zipper fly trousers, 1935.

Plate 7. Corduroy walkshorts with crewneck "squash" shirt, 1938.

Plate 8. The Bold Look in neckties from Wembley, 1951.

Plate 9. Vividly colored and patterned sports jackets from McGregor, 1959.

Plate 10. Wash-and-wear sports shirts by Truval Shirts, 1959.

Plate 11. Sportswear with Velcro closures, 1959.

Plate 12. Flower power paisley print sport jacket from Clubman, 1967.

Plate 13. Embroidered Nehru jacket from JHC Suits, 1968.

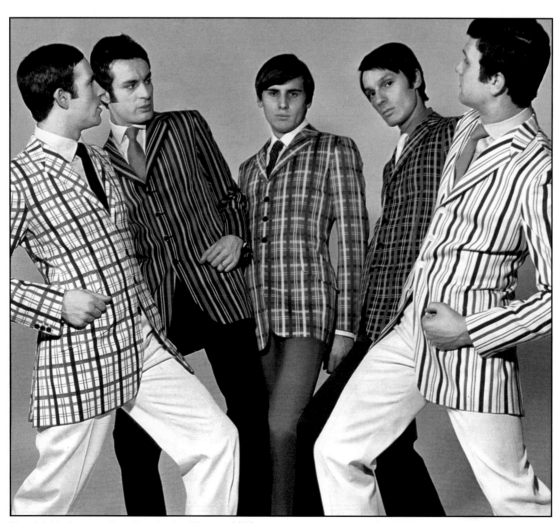

Plate 14. Mod sport jackets from Scotland Baratta, 1968.

Plate 15. "The uncommon shirt" from Carriage Club, 1968.

Plate 16. Peacock loungewear from Munsingwear, 1969.

Plate 19. Street designed "psychedelic" jeans drawn with permanent felt pens and colored with Rit Dyes, 1968.

Plate 17. Surfer trunks from Catalina and Brentwood, 1966.

Plate 18. The Apache scarf with a Nehru collar, 1968.

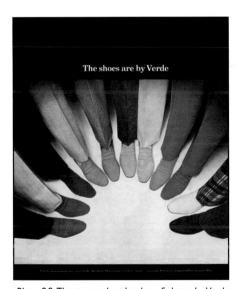

Plate 20. The peacock splendor of shoes by Verde Footwear, 1968.

Plate 21. Ruffled, embroidered, and pin-tucked tuxedo shirts from After Six Formalwear, 1973.

Plate 22. Revival butterfly bow tie by Rooster, 1973.

Shirts that speak out. If you're fat and forty, forget it.

This is the Age of Aquarius. And Arrow sews them as it sees them. Here, in a line of tapered, talkative prints that tell it like it is. Bright, colorful shirts that are as outspoken as the men who'll wear them.

Long, high-band collars, double-button cuffs, in a blend of Dacron® polyester and cotton. Shirts that speak out. But only if you have something really important to say.

-Arrow-

Mach II by Arrow

Plate 23. Tapered sports shirts with high collars in "talkative prints" by Arrow, 1971.

Plate 24. "Honeycomb" print shirt of 100% polyester interlock by D'Avila, 1978.

Plate 25. Wide-legged, high-rise baggies from Lee, 1973.

Plate 26. Polyester leisure suit by Lee, 1974.

DOUBLE KNIT SUITS

Green   Green plaid

Plate 27. Suits of polyester double knits from Montgomery Ward, 1975.

Plate 28. Stars 'n' Stripes design from Moss Shirts, 1971.

Plate 29. Branded designer label jeans as a "declaration of sensuality" from Studio 54, 1979.

Plate 30. Eighties big look jacket by Claude Montana, 1984.

Plate 31. Urban cowboy fringed jacket by Jeff Sayre, 1986.

Plate 32. Nylon Pop art ski jacket from Carrera, 1988.

Plate 33. Multiple Swatch watches, 1985.

Plate 35. Sixties' mod revival by Stacy Adams, 2003.

Plate 36. Avant-garde coat and trousers by Issey Miyake, 2000.

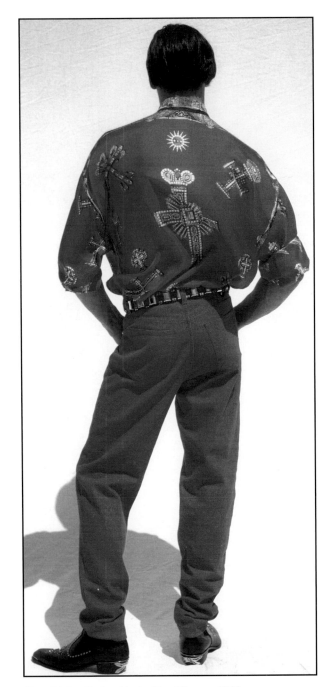

Plate 34. Scarf print shirt by Gianni Versace, 1992.

Plate 37. The short, trim fit of suits and sport jackets of the new millennium by Hickey, 2006.

Figure 3-3. At the beginning of the twentieth century, the United States was at peace, and the economy was booming. With their increasing affluence and leisure time, millions of working folks pursued the American dream, enjoying the materialism and consumerism of the industrialized age.

Women's fashions 1900–14: left, Edwardian S-bend silhouette, 1902; center, columnar hobble skirt, 1910; right, ankle-baring wartime dress, 1914

Edwardian suburban bungalow from *Ladies' Home Journal*, 1909

Mass-produced oak dining room suite from Sears, 1907

Golden Crown washing machine, 1908

Ansco box camera, 1905

Stereopticon movie projector, 1903

Locomobile "Type I" with 40 horsepower made in Bridgeport, Connecticut, 1908

The Teddy bear was a popular culture phenomenon named after Teddy Roosevelt who reportedly had spared a bear cub during one of his hunting expeditions. Teddy bear from Sears, 1912

Peerless Features of Excellence

The new drop frame and its advantages

The drop frame is an original adoption of the Peerless, in America. With this frame, and without reduction of road-clearance, the bulk of weight is brought down nearer center of gravity. The result is a better balanced car, handled more easily and safely at high speed with greatly lessened possibility of skidding; a saving of wear and tear on machinery and tires, and giving added ease and comfort to passengers

Our new illustrated book "N" showing new features in 1909 models, sent upon request

Peerless Motor Car Co. 2443 Oakdale Street. Cleveland, Ohio

1907

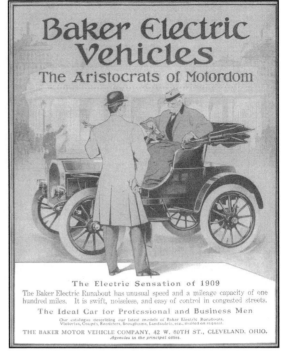

1909

Figure 3-4. Mass marketing by auto makers encouraged Americans to experience new horizons and adventures at the wheel of a modern motorized vehicle. From two-seat open roadsters to covered luxury limousines, there was a car that suited almost everyone's "personal requirements in speed, comfort, price and appearance," assured a 1908 Oldsmobile ad.

1908

homes were wired for electrical power, specialized electric appliances were developed to lessen the labor of housework: the electric vacuum cleaner replaced the roller carpet sweeper; the electric iron replaced the cast iron flatiron; the electric washing machine replaced the washboard and hand-cranked washers; the electric sewing machine replaced the foot treadle models. (Figure 3-3.)

Americans also became increasingly mobile. At the close of the nineteenth century, about 8,000 automobiles were registered in the United States.[2] Initially, the auto was largely a toy for the urban wealthy with some models of covered touring cars costing as much as $15,000 (equal to about $120,000 today). But in 1908, Henry Ford began mass production of the Model T. Priced at around $500, the basic "Tin Lizzie" opened a broader market of consumers, and, by 1914, 1.7 million autos trundled over American roads.[3] Automobiling to the country or seaside on weekends and holidays was no longer a pastime solely of the affluent classes. (Figure 3-4.)

Despite the continued rapid expansion of a consumer society, which fueled the nation's prosperity, not every citizen shared in the American dream. The new century dawned with many Americans living and working in horrific conditions. The social ills of America were thrust before its people by a group of young, reform-minded journalists and novelists who came to be known as the muckrakers. Their crusading zeal exposed the muck of iniquities in city slums, factory sweatshops, and prisons and reform schools. They exposed corporate and political corruption with withering, fact-based indictments that shocked the public. (Figure 3-5.) The most successful of the muckrakers was Upton Sinclair whose best-selling novel, *The Jungle,* described in lurid, nauseating detail the filth and putrefaction of the meatpacking industry.

The result of all the journalistic agitation was a groundswell of popular pressure on Congress and state legislatures. The era became one of the most progressive in American history. New safety and sanitation codes were enacted. Passed into law in 1906, the Meat Inspection Act subjected meatpacking operations to federal inspection, and the Pure Food and Drug Act protected consumers against the adulteration and mislabeling of products. For certain categories of workers, the workday was reduced to ten hours, and, in 1916, limited to eight hours. Child labor laws prohibited hiring minors for dangerous jobs. Public utilities commissions wrested control from crooked corporations. Insurance companies came under the governance of state regulations.

The women's suffrage movement also made new headway, especially during the early 1910s. The crusading women of the pre-World War I years who advocated emancipation and equal rights now began to call themselves "feminists."[4] Their goal was a constitutional amendment to guarantee the vote nationally. The suffragettes became increasingly militant and more organized. Instead of meeting in private homes and rented halls to hear circuit speakers like Jane Addams and Carrie Chapman Catt, they took to the streets, marching in ever larger numbers. In 1910, the first suffragette march in New York drew only a few hundred participants, but

Figure 3-5. The crusades of progressive journalists, pejoratively labeled "muckraking," exposed the corrupt and dangerous practices of manufacturers, insurance companies, absentee landlords, and political bosses. Exposés such as this one about the patent medicine industry influenced the passage of strict regulations and government oversight of food and drug manufacturers. Part V of "The Great American Fraud" published by *Collier's* in 1906.

"I HAVE HERE A RABID FEMINIST"
"GOOD! PUT HER IN THE HAREM OF THAT TURKISH WIFE-BEATER"

Figure 3-6. In the years before World War I, male-dominated publishers expressed their contempt for feminists and their fears of an independent, enfranchised American womanhood. Cartoons from the "Feminist Number" issue published by *Life* in 1914.

THE MODERN MAID AND HER FOREFATHERS

COUPLING KIPLING
"A FOOL THERE WAS"—AND—"THE FEMALE OF THE SPECIES IS MORE DEADLY THAN THE MALE"

five years later the event numbered over 40,000. They also handcuffed themselves to the White House fence and picketed state houses around the country. They suffered abuse, including beatings and arrest from both men and women who opposed their ideas and methods, but they did not relent. Finally, at the end of the decade, Congress passed the Nineteenth Amendment granting women the vote.

By the eve of the First World War, progressive leaders had won many battles to make government more responsive to the needs and welfare of the American people. In reviewing the progressive era from the perspective of the 1920s, social historian Mark Sullivan concluded that America had been "altered fundamentally" by the innovations of the reformers; the changes inaugurated during those early years "worked a political revolution...[that] changed measurably the basis of organized society in America, reflected the passing of some of the oldest of America's ideas, and either gave or reflected a new direction to social evolution in America."[5]

Dress and Identity: Ideas and Ideals of Edwardian Masculinity

Under pressures from industrialization, urbanization, immigration, science, feminism, and social progressivism, the Victorian constructs of separate spheres that had begun to erode at the end of the nineteenth century further disintegrated during the early years of the new century. The anxieties of manhood exacerbated by suffragettes, temperance unions, and rapidly advancing science and technology were at times utterly overwhelming for many American men.

In a backlash, men often turned their bewilderment and anger at their powerlessness into stalwart resistance, as in the sometimes violent opposition to feminist demands for women's rights. In 1914, *Life* issued a "Feminist Number" in which editorials from men (and women) expressed the tenor of the day. (Figure 3-6.) The masculine views invariably demonstrated the frustration of men in their helplessness to stem the tide of change. "Modern feminism is driving woman directly against nature," railed W. R. Hotchkin, "making her the rival and opponent of man—dragging her into the slavery of labor at the wheels of daily toil—

opposing her right to home and motherhood." He concluded by invoking the doctrine of separate spheres: "Man is designed to do the labor of the world. Woman is designed to be man's helpmate and comrade. She was never created to be his rival."[6]

Few social changes at the time were more threatening to men's view of self than having women compete in the job market. And women's rights—particularly enfranchisement—were widely thought to be an open door through which hordes of women would rush, capriciously abandoning their roles of homemaker, helpmate, and mother, and, worse, displacing men from their principal masculine role as breadwinner.

Yet even as an increasing number of women entered the workforce on all levels, including degreed professions, one of the few comforting certitudes for men to cling to was that some categories of jobs and places of employment remained exclusively male. It was inconceivable that women would ever be locomotive engineers, police officers, fire fighters, aircraft pilots, ship captains, or surgeons despite the continued inroads women were making in education, politics, and labor.

On the other hand, certain types of jobs became regarded as predominantly women's work such as fashion designer, interior decorator, hair stylist, nurse, secretary, and store clerk, to name a few. Men who worked in these jobs were likely to be perceived as effeminate and presumed to be homosexual on face value. (Figure 3-7.) Straight men who pursued careers with these jobs were usually subjected to the ignominy of guilt by association and all too often had to defend their choice of livelihood. In the ambiguity of such workplace roles, the stigma of effeminacy expanded during the Edwardian years, adding further to the anxieties of many men. "The twentieth century fears to be called effeminate," wrote social historian Gerald Heard in 1924.[7] From the earliest phases of boyhood, the American male learned that where there were many aspects of manliness, there were also many behaviors and conditions that were unacceptable. At the top of that list of intolerable qualities—in man or boy—was effeminacy. And one way for the American male to avoid being branded effeminate was to avoid the jobs that were viewed as women's work.

The Edwardian man then needed a new visual representation that expressed the modern image of the strong, dominant breadwinner and family protector. The new masculinity included a powerful manliness that could withstand the assault of feminism and the undermining threats of effeminacy. In the early 1900s, that role model of power and dominance was exemplified by the energetic, commanding president, Teddy Roosevelt whose athletic, broad-shouldered image was constantly depicted in the mass media. By emulating the look and presence of T.R., the average man could identify with the self-assured, decisive commander-in-chief who had succeeded in beating back the assaults of big business and other establishment powers on the home front and repeated threats from foreign powers on the world stage.

Thus, in the early twentieth century, the new masculine identity of strength and power required a revitalized visual representation that was a departure from the trim, reed-slender silhouette of the Victorian ideal. Masculine dress needed to symbolize and reinforce the strength and power that the modern American male had to possess to withstand the barrage of challenges to his manhood. Consequently, for a brief episode in the history of American menswear, the influences of London's Savile

Figure 3-7. By the beginning of the twentieth century, men who took jobs that were generally regarded as women's work were subjected to the stigma of effeminacy. Postcard, 1908.

Figure 3-8. The Edwardian sack suit featured coats constructed with broad, padded shoulders, short lapels, and loose, boxy bodies. In addition, sack coats were often closed only by the bottom button, which added to the loose, bulky fit. Trousers were peg-cut with a fullness through the hips and thighs tapering to the ankles. Above, sack suits from Hart Schaffner and Marx catalogs, 1907–1909; bottom, from Kohn Brothers, 1905.

Row were ignored as men's suits, sportswear, and outerwear were reshaped and padded with greater volume and bulk to represent a Herculean physique with a barrel chest, strong arms, and powerful thighs. It was an identity embraced by all socioeconomic classes of American men—an anchor of confidence and surety in the turbulence of social upheaval.

Suits and Formal Dress 1900–1914

With the beginning of a new century, women's fashions were completely transformed virtually overnight by the introduction of the S-bend corset in 1900. The fresh and exciting new look changed the upright, hourglass silhouette of the feminine form into that of a kangaroo stance with hips pushed back and the shoulders and bosom thrust forward. (Figure 3-3.)

In men's wear, though, no sudden drama occurred that was comparable to the feminine S-bend look. Instead, the change in dress for the Edwardian man was evolutionary and subtle over several years. However, by 1905, the look of men's suits was significantly different from the slim shapes and narrow contours at the end of previous decade. As the S-bend corset had altered the feminine form, a new, fuller, and broader cut of the sack suit redefined the American masculine ideal. The sack coat was constructed with pronounced, padded shoulders and a bulky, loose body.

Figure 3-9. Edwardian pegged trousers were cut with a fullness through the hips and thighs that tapered to sixteen-inch bottoms. Sporty styles for younger men were cuffed with an ankle-high crop, but dress trousers extended over the shoe heel with a break of the front crease over the shoe vamp. Left, pegged dress trousers; right, pegged trousers with cuffs, both from Reliable Tailoring, 1909.

(Figure 3-8.) Notched lapels were cut short with a high closure making the shoulders appear even more massive. Fronts hung straight and long from the built-up shoulders, and sleeves were wide, loose cylinders. Large pocket flaps added more bulk. Most coats were made with a center back vent although ventless skirts were common. Other skirts included short side pleats in addition to the vent, adding further volume about the hips. Skirt hems were rounded on single-breasted styles and square cut on the double-breasted versions. The most popular closure was the three-button single-breasted. Two-button styles were for younger men, and were sometimes listed in catalogs as "varsity models." Double-breasted coats were made with four- and six-button closures.

Another change that seems to be distinctively characteristic of Edwardian men's suits was the method of buttoning jackets. Catalogs and ads of 1905-1915 often show only the bottom button closed, even on six-button double-breasted styles. This was a notable reversal from the way the Victorian suit was worn, which for decades was fastened only at the topmost button. The Edwardian bottom button closure added even more of a loose bulkiness to the look of the sack coat.

Sack suit trousers were made with a plain-front, peg-top cut that draped with an exaggerated fullness at the hips and thighs and tapered to a narrow, straight line from the knees down. (Figure 3-9.) Pant leg hems were sixteen inches in circumference. Although cuffed trousers had been introduced a generation earlier for men's casual suiting and sports attire, for the Edwardian man, deep cuffs were a popular business suit alternative to plain hems. Cuffed trousers were slightly shorter than regular hemmed bottoms, so the cuff did not rest on the shoe vamp, causing it to gape and collect street debris. The regular hemmed trousers, though, extended over the heel of the shoe to the sole seam, and the front crease

Figure 3-10. Around 1910, men's suits were reshaped from the bulky, upholstered Edwardian look to a more narrow, trim cut. Coats were constructed without padding for a natural shoulderline, skirts were shortened, and sleeves narrowed. Side seams were tapered, and the waistline was raised. Persisting, though, were the single-bottom button closure and the high, stiff shirt collar. "Correcto" suits from Sears, 1914.

Figure 3-11. In the early 1900s, the frock coat was worn less as business attire and more as ceremonial dress for formal daytime events. As other suit styles evolved fuller dimensions, frock coats, too, were padded and constructed with greater bulk. Left, trim double- and single-breasted frock coats by Born Brothers, 1903; right, fuller sleeves and broad shoulders of frock and walking coats by Hart Schaffner and Marx, 1908.

Figure 3-12. For the Edwardian business executive, the walking coat, sometimes called a walking frock, became the preferred replacement for the old square-cut frock styles. Walking coat of striped worsted from *Vogue*, 1907.

broke over the vamp, the correct drape of trousers still today.

In 1908, the Parisian couturier Paul Poiret revolutionized women's fashions by creating the hobble skirt. The look was trim, narrow, and columnar. Corsets were reengineered for an erect posture that emphasized youthful, slim hips. Layers of frilly Edwardian petticoats were suddenly discarded. By 1910, the S-bend silhouette and the look of the ample, curvaceous, mature woman had been completely replaced by a more youthful, slender feminine ideal.

In the early 1910s, menswear likewise quickly abandoned the bulky, heavily padded looks of the preceding decade. As with women's fashions, men's styles emphasized a slim youthfulness. In 1910, Hart Schaffner and Marx Clothiers ran a campaign of full page ads to announce their new shape-maker suits. "The trousers are made to wear without suspenders, even without a belt; with comfort; they will not slip down," promised the ad copy. "They are shaped to fit snugly around the body; the wearer is constantly reminded to stand and walk erect; throw out the chest a little; the coat is made to fit such a figure."[8] To achieve the new slender, youthful look, suit coats had to be stripped of their upholstered padding. (Figure 3-10.) The natural shoulder now defined the masculine profile. Sleeves were narrowed and skirts shortened. As early as 1911, fashion journalists reported on the tapered, raised waistline that emphasized a leaner, leggier look.[9] Trousers also were reduced in volume and cut with slim legs and plain fronts.

One of the major changes in American men's dress during the pre-World War I years was the diminishment of the frock coat as the prevalent form of business attire. In England, the frock lingered longer because King Edward and his successor, George V (1910–1936), continued to wear the style regularly. But American fashion journalists repeatedly reported on the "passing of the frock coat" throughout the early years of the new century.[10] They did not mean that the frock coat was no longer worn, but rather that it was increasingly relegated to dress for ceremonial daytime events. The frock continued to be worn on Sundays, but it also became an acceptable suit for morning weddings and afternoon garden teas when once the cutaway morning coat was the standard.

Initially, the Edwardian frock coat varied little from its Victorian predecessor in cut or details. (Figure 3-11.) As the sack coat evolved into bulky, boxy proportions, the frock became somewhat fuller with padded shoulders and fuller sleeves, but retained the marked waistline. Skirts flared a bit more than previously but remained cropped just below the knee. Americans much preferred the single-breasted version since it could be comfortably worn open without the sagging caused by the asymmetrical weight of the double-breasted cut. Black or charcoal gray worsteds or vicunas were the most ubiquitous fabrics for the frock coat, vest, and trousers. Lapels were silk faced with an edge of worsted, and the collar was either velvet or worsted. Some style editorials noted that "peculiarities" such as lapel edging of braid or full silk facings were sometimes seen in shop windows, but "they are not much fancied by the best class of men."[11]

As the frock coat increasingly became viewed as semiformal dress reserved for ceremonial functions, the American businessman looked to a variation to fill the gap for daytime dress at the office. The English walking coat, also sometimes called a walking frock coat, was a popular option for junior executives in the 1890s. As with the squared-front frock, the walking coat was constructed with a marked waist seam to which the skirt was sewn. The walking coat, though, featured a skirt that was cut away beginning just below the waist button and angled out to the sides with rounded corners. (Figure 3-12.) The skirt of the Edwardian walking coat was also more flared than the fin de siècle versions. Flap pockets at the hips were designed to be tucked in if preferred, and an angled breast pocket accented the coat body—treatments absent on the traditional frock. Too, unlike the dressier frock coat made largely of somber black or dark gray fabric, the walking coat was acceptably respectable in many of the patterned and slubbed mixture textiles more often applied to the sack coat. Wide pin stripes were the most prevalent patterns although window pane checks were a favorite as well, especially in shades of brown. In case of a jaunty fabric color or pattern, though, style guides recommended the derby rather than a silk topper.

During the transition of the frock coat to an accepted garment for daytime formal affairs, etiquette guides and fashion editorials were at a loss with advice on when to wear the frock or the morning coat. "It is somewhat difficult to define the exact position of the two," conceded *Vogue* in 1908.[12] Nevertheless, the morning coat continued as the most popular daytime formal suit. The primary changes in the Edwardian styles were shoulder padding and fuller sleeves for a more robust silhouette than the trim, fitted Victorian versions. As with the earlier forms of morning coats, the cutaway skirt angled more sharply than the walking

Figure 3-13. The padded bulkiness of the Edwardian sack suit was also applied to formal dress and tuxedo suits. Tail coat and tuxedo by David Adler, 1908.

coat although, as some fashion editors noted, when a gentleman wore a morning coat with trousers of the same gray material, it "somewhat resembles the walking coat suit in appearance, that is therefore less formal in character."[13] The correct trousers for traditional formality were contrasting striped gray worsted or cassimere.

Evening dress was largely unchanged from a generation earlier. The notable alterations were the addition of shoulder padding and widened sleeves in keeping with the new broad-shouldered silhouette of the Edwardian male. (Figure 3-13.) Both shawl and peaked lapels were correct. In 1903, the *Sartorial Art Journal* reported a trend for the "imitation cuff" on sleeves, which was "not new" but more popular than previously.[14] The cuff was attached at the end of the sleeve with cording and closed with three or four buttons. Trousers were only slightly pegged and looked slim compared to those of the sack or walking coat suits. A rigidly starched white bosom front shirt, white silk bow tie, and white pique vest remained the required accouterment of the evening dress suit. During this time, the V-front vest became more prevalent than the U-front cut, which was regarded as old-fashioned in the new century. Patent pumps, silk top hat, white gloves, and ebony walking stick were the finishing accessories. Mother-of-pearl or possibly jeweled buttons were the only acceptable jewelry.

The tuxedo was originally a sack-style dinner jacket worn in casual settings where women were not present, particularly in the dining rooms of men's clubs. By the beginning of the twentieth century, the comfortable tuxedo was increasingly worn for a broader variety of evening functions. Edwardian versions such as that shown in Figure 3-13 followed the new shapes and dimensions of suit sack coats. Shoulders were upholstered with padding; the straight-front was boxy with a minimally tapered waist; skirts were extended longer; and sleeves were cut fuller. Unlike the tail coat, the tuxedo offered a wider assortment of detail options. Pockets were constructed as either corded besoms or flap covered. The notches of collars were shifted high or low as the gentleman preferred (or the tailor recommended), and lapels were cut with a straight edge or slightly convex. Options for the silk facing of the lapels included plain weave or a variety of textures such as diagonal ribbed, or self-striped, or basket weave. Buttons might be "hard" or fabric covered. Also, unlike the tail coat, the tuxedo could be worn with a white, black, or even slate gray vest in double- or single-breasted styles.

Although the white tuxedo had been introduced in the late 1890s, it was largely a novelty look for summer only. Even among the Edwardian dandies, few men braved the glaring notoriety of a white tuxedo. As one fashion journalist reminded gentlemen, "It rarely fails to attract attention, which good dress should not do."[15]

Shirts 1900–1914

One of the lingering debates from the Victorian dress reform movement was the "propriety of going about in a negligée shirt without a coat" as *Vogue* reported in 1902. Many men's ready-to-wear makers and retailers offered "shirt waists, so called, especially designed for the purpose." Although the shirts were of "pretty materials and neatness," the question was the "departure from long established custom" in men's dress. "A man without a coat has an unfinished appearance suggestive of

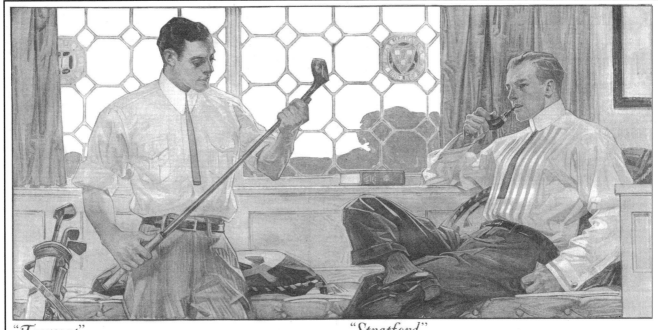

exercise or play, and while we expect it on a tennis court, on the golf links, or on a sailboat, and are not surprised to see it at a country place, in the public conveyance or upon the streets of the city, not to mention public restaurants and cafes, it produces rather an unpleasant shock. In short, it looks common and vulgar," admonished the editor.[16] Most men, however, were conformists and followed the conventional dress tenets exhibited in catalogs, ads, haberdashers' display windows, and, more importantly, by their peers on the street.

The coat-cut dress shirt with its open front design continued to eclipse the bosom front styles. Many men, though, steadfastly wore the old style overshirts, and makers produced them in an abundance of fabrics and cuts well into the 1920s. Menswear reports of the era often made note of the most popular colors of the seasons or the newest prints featured in men's shops, but rarely did news mention new shirt constructions except in sportswear. As with today's dress shirts, there were innumerable varieties of pocket treatments, cuffs, yokes, body seams, and similar details; however, the basic styling of the suit shirt remained fairly standardized. Through the prewar years, the correct dress shirt for any town suit remained the banded-collar style to which was fastened a two-inch high, detachable collar made of rigid celluloid covered with linen. (Figure 3-14.) As the soft shirt with its attached collar gained in popularity, shirt makers offered new designs to bridge both market niches. In 1912, Cluett Peabody introduced a new form of soft shirt with an attached collar that could be turned in to expose a band on which any white linen collar could be attached. This new design "gives you a soft collar for hot days in town or outing, or a soft shirt with a laundered collar for more formal wear," declared copy in an Arrow ad.[17]

Figure 3-14. Despite the increasing popularity and wide assortment of soft shirts with attached, turned-down collars, the correct daytime dress shirt still featured a high, stiff, detachable collar. The open-front coat cut styles increasingly replaced the pullover bosom-front shirt. Ad for Arrow collars and Cluett shirts, 1909.

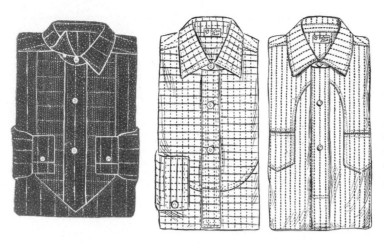

Figure 3-15. Work shirts came in a broader variety of textile patterns and constructions than dress shirts. In addition to attached, turned-down collars, work shirts were often made with layered front and back yokes for durability. Work shirts from Hart Brothers, 1908.

Work Clothes 1900–1914

Through the Edwardian era, *Vogue's* "As Seen by Him" and *Vanity Fair's* "The Well-Dressed Man" made no mention of what the working man wore. For those types of clothes, we have the catalogs of the mass merchandisers like Sears and Montgomery Ward that sold "working clothes" to "farmers, stockmen, ranchmen, carpenters, mechanics, and anyone who is obliged to work out of doors."[18] The drawings and photographs of the models were appropriately accoutered with the working man's tools—an ax over the shoulder or an oilcan in hand. The copy headers emphasized the important words: "strong," "heavy," "reinforced," "warm," "waterproof."

There were many specialized uniforms of various cuts, fabrics, and distinctive detailing for railroad workers, firemen, policemen, mail carriers, and barbers, to name a few. A number of specialty accessories such as bib aprons of "government standard" khaki for carpenters and of white cotton duck for butchers were common. For most average working men, though, whether for a job in a factory or chores on a farm, a comfortable work shirt and plain work pants were the basics.

Work shirts differed from business dress shirts in construction, color palettes, and textile prints. Work shirts not only included an attached, turned-down collar, but also featured a variety of yoke, pocket, and sleeve treatments. What appear to be bosom-front cuts illustrated in catalogs of the time are actually double-deck styles where fabric is layered double thick in both the front and back for durability. (Figure 3-15.) In addition, bold patterns and vivid colors such as peacock blue, bright cardinal red, or black cat were acceptable for work flannels, but never suit shirts. Work shirts of heavy chambray or cotton twill sold for about 45¢ compared to banded collar dress shirts of pongee or percale that cost three times as much.

Work pants remained a separate category from dress trousers in menswear catalogs. Sears assured catalog customers that their "working pants are cut large and roomy, and warranted not to rip or break."[19] Good work pants came with two front pockets and one back pocket. Until the 1910s, most work pants were still made with suspender buttons at the waistband instead of belt loops. Fabrics included heavy wool worsteds, cotton duck, corduroy, and denim in gray, blue, black, brown, or tan. Probably the most ubiquitous work pants of the time, though,

Figure 3-16. The norfolk coat with its squared front, box pleats, and belted waist remained the most popular style of outing jacket for weekend activities such as golf or fishing. Edwardian styles were more widely varied than Victorian versions and included innumerable arrangements of pleats, pockets, and sleeve cuffs. Left, drop-yoke norfolk jacket from *Vogue*, 1906; right, norfolk ditto suit from Chicago Tailor-Made Clothiers, 1908.

were the bib overalls made of heavy, 9-ounce blue denim that sold for 50¢. For the construction foreman or factory floor supervisor who was required to wear a tie, three-piece suits made of flannel-lined corduroy were a practical solution to working on chilly job sites.

Sportswear 1900–1914

For the average weekend sports enthusiast, clothing for outdoor athletics and recreation was largely freeform with few tenets for correct or incorrect dress. Comfort and common sense were the principal guides. "It must be remembered that nearly all costumes of sport are not within any rules of fashion," reiterated *Vogue* in 1903. "The dress of sport is that which is most suitable, most comfortable, and best adapted to the occasions on which it is to be worn."[20] Those types of sportswear that had become commonplace even among working and middle classes at the end of the nineteenth century—knickers, belted trousers, norfolk jackets, blazers, colorful negligée shirts—remained the prevalent styles of the Edwardian era. Jackets followed the changes of the sack coats and became bulky and boxy until the 1910s when they, too, narrowed and lost their padded structures. Pegged sports trousers with wide hips and thighs were also recut in the 1910s to fit trim and narrow.

The most prevalent form of sportswear coat was still the norfolk jacket.(Figure 3-16.) Although the basic style featured a square-front shape, box pleats, and belted waistline, innumerable variations on those components were available. "The name norfolk covers a multitude of sins nowadays," observed a fashion editor in 1902.[21] Among the variants were jackets with a pair of single-plait tucks in the front instead of box pleats. Back treatments included a single, wide box pleat instead of a pair or even loose gathers in place of pleats. Some norfolks were cut with dropped shoulder yokes from which the box pleats extended. Still others sported besom pockets at the side seams instead of the typically oversized patch pockets. In addition, norfolk jackets were no longer routinely worn with knickerbockers. Edwardian norfolk suits were as likely to come with ditto trousers.

Knickerbockers seem to have declined in popularity in the Edwardian era compared to previous decades. In 1907, *Vogue* reported that

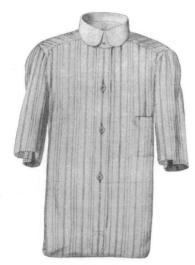

Figure 3-17. One of the dramatic innovations of Edwardian menswear was the introduction of short-sleeved sport shirts, specifically designed to be worn without a jacket even in mixed company. "Tennis" shirt from *Vogue*, 1903.

Figure 3-18. Sportswear makers experimented with innovative concepts such as a tennis shirt sewn to undershorts as a remedy for shirt tails pulling loose during the exertion of a match. One-piece tennis shirt and drawers from *Vogue*, 1904.

knickerbockers were more "restricted" in where they were worn, even to the point that it was difficult to find them from ready-to-wear makers. "For tennis, golf and general outing purposes at the country clubs and in many country places," continued *Vogue's* editor, "they are not only rarely worn, but less good style than long flannel trousers, but for the mountains, for camping, tramping, fishing, shooting, etc., nothing can be compared to them in point of comfort or good form."[22] Unlike sports flannels, though, the proportions of knickerbockers were not impacted by the reshaping of the Edwardian male silhouette since they were already voluminous and bulky. Instead, the cut had less "exaggerated fullness over the hips" than Victorian styles.[23] The one notable innovation was shifting the button closure of the kneeband extensions from the front to the outer sides.

Most outdoor sportswear continued to be made of heavy-duty worsted or durable cotton duck and corduroy. However, at the turn of the century, new textiles were introduced for outdoor clothing to be worn where the sportsman might encounter a lot of damp such as fishing and camping. Sports clothing made of waterproofed Duxbak brand materials was widely sold in sporting goods shops at the time. Ads noted that the soft, pliable cotton fabric, usually available in tan or olive green, was waterproofed by the Cravenette process. New technologies made waterproofing possible without smelly solvents that usually left many textiles used in outdoor clothing with a strong chemical odor. The patented Cravenette process rolled fabric under pressure over a slab of rubber compound, evenly coating the material by friction. The fabric then passed into a heater that melted the compound coating, which was absorbed into the fibers, rendering the material water-repellent.[24] The registered name of Cravenette was derived from the name of the street in London where the manufacturer was located.

Among the sportswear style innovations of the time was the short-sleeved sport shirt usually labeled a "tennis" shirt. (Figure 3-17.) Previously, the bared male forearms exposed by rolled-up sleeves were tolerated in mixed company only when the man was on the tennis court or golf links, and possibly with female family members on an outing; otherwise, the arms were to be decorously covered by the long shirt sleeves (and a jacket). However, in the early 1900s, reports in fashion journals began to make note of new forms of sports shirts with half sleeves, some with attached, turned down collars, and others with bands for detachable linen collars.[25] During the transition, before short sleeves were more widely accepted, some shirt makers even experimented with detachable sleeves, "the lower part of which buttoned to the upper part a few inches above the elbow and which could be taken off as one would take off a detachable cuff."[26] The idea of detachable sleeves failed to catch on with consumers, though, because the short-sleeved shirt became so popular so quickly.

Another sport shirt innovation that was introduced in the early 1900s was the combination one-piece tennis shirt and undershorts. (Figure 3-18.) The short-sleeved shirt of madras, linen, or batiste was sewn to the waistband of linen undershorts. The intent was to remedy the "shirt's wrinkling uncomfortably around the waist or pulling out over the belt" during the exertion of a tennis match.[27] The idea was not particularly popular and was not adopted by any of the mass merchandisers or

Figure 3-19. As high-speed knitting machines were improved, ready-to-wear makers could mass produce an endless variety of knit garments with complex constructions, yarn color combinations, and textures. The comfortable coat sweater quickly became a favorite alternative to the negligée sack coat and smoking jacket for leisure time at home. Left, V-front coat sweaters from Hart Brothers, 1908; right, shawl-collar coat sweaters from Clement Company, 1914.

ready-to-wear makers.

In addition to bare arms, another changing social more was the abandonment of the jacket in some sports activities. When once the striped flannel blazer had been the correct coat style for the tennis court in the 1880s and 1890s, by the Edwardian years, jackets were entirely discarded unless the sports event was also a lawn party.[28] Even then, men who might play extended matches to the point of becoming sweaty were expected to change into fresh clothes before joining the spectators.

Already at the end of the nineteenth century, various types of knit shirts and vests (in long- and short-sleeved styles), sweaters, shorts, and leggings had been common attire in assorted combinations for the athlete. Sweaters, especially, were a favorite cool weather garment for layering over athletic dress. As exertion increased the body temperature, sweaters were easily removed to keep cool. Pullover V-necks and particularly turtlenecks (called roll necks) were the best sellers. In 1905, Sears sold a dozen styles of roll neck sweaters priced 85¢ each for simple knits to $3.69 for heavy gauge "hunting sweaters."

The ease and comfort of knitwear was quickly adapted to everyday dress as well. During the Edwardian era, "coat sweaters" (sometimes listed as sweater coats or cardigan jackets) became a popular substitute for the sack coat in many casual settings. (Figure 3-19.) As one wholesaler catalog asserted in 1908, "Each year every man spends a certain percentage of his income on what you might call artificial or stimulated desires. It was particularly so with sweater coats when they first were shown. Today they are an absolute necessity."[29] Most coat sweaters were made with a collarless, V-front neckline, but others featured wide shawl collars and even double-breasted styling. Many coat sweaters featured complex knit

Figure 3-20. Swimsuits were a commodity clothing item like underwear and socks rather than a fashion item. The matching knit tunic and drawers set remained the most common style and changed little from the Victorian models. Left, wool jersey swimsuit from B. Altman, 1904; right, photo of father and son, 1910.

patterns to which large patch pockets were attached or into which were knitted concealed pockets. Oversized white mother-of-pearl buttons added a dressy accent. The coat sweater was a versatile casual garment for both indoors and outdoors. Catalogs and photos of the era frequently show models wearing high, detachable collars and neckties with their coat sweaters and holding a pipe or a newspaper indicating the garment was acceptable negligée dress for indoors at home; some models were also shown holding a golf club or walking stick.

With the improvements of high-speed knitting technologies and advances in mass production, an enormous variety of novelty knit patterns, textures, and color combinations were available in men's sweaters and knitwear. In 1914, *Vanity Fair* marveled at the great variety of knitwear in shop windows: "coats of soft lamb's wool, waistcoats, hoods, gloves, and great scarves all of this same luxurious stuff, and in the most brilliant of colors; also much else that calls forth such comments as 'Are those things for men, and when do they wear them?' "[30]

These three examples—short-sleeved shirts, jacketless dress in public, and coat sweaters—demonstrate a trend for increasing casualness in menswear as a result of the influence of sports clothing. Comfortable sportswear would continually be adapted to the everyday wardrobes of American men. As a result, the practical innovations, comfort, and casualness appropriated from sportswear would irrevocably alter the conventions of masculine dress, and, in turn, impact social protocols.

Styles of knit swimwear remained basically the same as those of the late nineteenth century. (Figure 3-20.) Men's swim suits were commodity items like underwear and socks, not fashion. Most mass merchandisers like Sears and Montgomery Ward offered only one or two variations of the short-sleeved tunic top with matching knee-length shorts in dark

Figure 3-21. Specialty sports clothes such as the shooting cutaway coat or the riding suit were largely the prerogative of the upper classes. For the middle classes, the norfolk jacket functioned sufficiently for hunting, riding, or other country activities. From Pope and Bradley, 1914: left, shooting cutaway coat; right, riding suit.

woolen knits or, for the flashy younger man, in horizontal stripes of navy, black, or red.

Despite the wide variety of men's ready-to-wear sports clothing, the upper classes still continued to opt for specialty clothing that reflected their sense of class propriety and decorum. The correct sports wardrobe of the Edwardian gentlemen contained a number of coat styles specially tailored for a specific activity. (Figure 3-21.) The shooting cutaway coat was constructed with sleeves "cut upon a pivot principle to allow unrestricted action to the arms," meaning deeper, ovoid armscyes.[31] Hunting kits featured a cutaway "pink" (actually scarlet) jacket, white buckskin jodhpurs, and a black silk topper as the proper dress for membership in American hunt clubs. For a morning ride in the park or countryside, the correct riding suit was made with a fingertip-length jacket designed to hang clear of the cantle of the saddle and jodhpurs reinforced with double layers of fabric in the thighs and seat.

Outerwear 1900–1914

In the early 1900s, *The Sartorial Art Journal* noted that more different styles of overcoats were available than ever in menswear history. "Their number is bewildering and their distinct differences seem infinite."[32] Indeed, the types of men's outerwear of the Edwardian era were widely varied; however, the differences between each were not always so distinct. The details of outerwear in tailoring trade publications like *The Sartorial Art Journal* were often quite precise and yet frequently overlapping. For instance, the proper length of an Edwardian chesterfield was

Figure 3-22. The Edwardian coat is notably defined by its massive bulk and capacious, tent-like shape irrespective of length. Ankle-sweeping hemlines typified most outerwear of the era although businessmen preferred the knee-length chesterfield, and commuters often opted for fingertip-length topcoats. Left to right: chesterfield, greatcoat, overcoat with military collar, and short topcoat from Hart Shaffner and Marx catalogs 1907–1909.

from "nine to ten inches more than one-half the wearer's height."[33] For a man of six-foot height, the coat length was about forty-four to forty-eight inches long. However, the details that differentiated a chesterfield from a Newbury, Newmarket, Berkeley, Blantyre, Gatwick, or any of the other dozens of styles of coats featured in tailor's guidebooks or menswear catalogs are far less precise. All of these forms of outerwear could be made with or without velvet collars, flap pockets, fly fronts, sleeve buttons, skirt vents, or any number of similar details. Hence, the descriptions and illustrations herein are based on those varieties where editorials or catalog copy is exact.

In general, Edwardian men's outerwear came in three lengths—fingertip, knee-length, and ankle-sweeping. Most styles were massive and shapeless. The capacious, tent-like cuts were necessary to adequately cover the padded bulkiness of suit jackets. (Figure 3-22.)

The chesterfield was regarded as the most versatile overcoat of the era—"the only overcoat that can appropriately be worn on every occasion...suitable for morning, afternoon or evening wear."[34] It was cut to hang loosely from the shoulders and extend to either just below the knees or, for younger men, almost to the ankles. The velvet collar that distinguishes most chesterfields was attached to silk-faced lapels.

Coats that were labeled ulsters usually featured a half-belt in the back or sometimes even a wide belt all around. Even with the belt treatments,

Figure 3-23. During the early 1900s, most American cars were made open without a roof or side windshields. To protect the driver from wind, dust, and inclement weather, outerwear makers produced assorted types of automobile dusters made of various impervious materials. Motor duster of waterproofed silk and rubber pongee with matching visor cap with neck guard from *Vogue,* 1906.

ulsters were as voluminous and bulky as other forms of overcoats. Lengths were cut to just below the knees or to the ankles as with the chesterfields.

The short box topcoat was about thirty-two to thirty-four inches in length and fitted as generously as its name implies. A fly-front and assorted pocket treatments made it a popular daytime coat, especially during transitional seasons like late autumn and early spring. This style was a commuter's favorite and usually included a ticket pocket on the breast or sometimes a pocket within a pocket at the hip. Side vents prevented the bulkiness from bunching up around the neck when the wearer was seated on a train or tram.

Caped coats such as the Inverness fell out of favor during the Edwardian era although varieties were still acceptable as outerwear for formal evening dress.

Despite the massive, loose-hanging shapes of most Edwardian outerwear, some types of coats were still cut with a tapered waist. The contours were less formfitting than the late Victorian styles, but the complex construction of darts and gores was retained. The trim coachman's coat with

Figure 3-24. By the 1910s, the bulky, voluminous shapes of earlier Edwardian outerwear were replaced by trimmer, more fitted styles. Lengths were shortened, and the emphasis was on detailing, especially military elements when World War I began. From Pope and Bradley: left, the Georgian overcoat, 1914; center, ulster with half belt, 1913; right, d'Orsay slips, 1914.

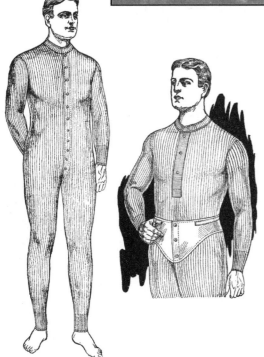

Figure 3-25. The wool knit union suit continued to be the preferred form of underwear year round for most men of the time. Coat cut undershirts increasingly replaced pullover styles. Top, coat cut undershirt, knee-length drawers, and sleeveless union suit, 1914; bottom, from Hart Brothers, 1908, wool union suit and ribbed cotton undershirt and drawers.

its darted waist seam and pleated skirt was called a paddock in the new century. Variations included single-breasted closures with fly fronts and half-waist seams that extended only across the front between the side seams.

During the early years of the twentieth century, the growth of auto ownership exploded. As one editorial noted in 1907, "The horseless carriage, as we were wont to call it in years gone by, has developed from a curiosity to a commodity, from a luxury to a necessity, from a thing of sport to an article of substantial business value."[35] Since most American cars were built open, that is, without a roof and side windshields, a significant assortment of motoring attire was produced to protect the intrepid wayfarers who ventured out over dusty cow path roads in their roadsters. Motoring dusters were made of assorted impervious materials ranging from waterproofed fabrics like rubberized silk or mohair to heavy-gauge cotton duck. (Figure 3-23.) The car was also credited with a revival in the popularity of fur coats for men.[36] Although masculine varieties of fur-lined and fur-covered coats had been common in the Victorian era, they were less favored by the late 1890s. Long coats of thick fur with high collars were almost a necessity for the man who trundled along at twenty miles an hour against a piercing winter wind. The variety of pelts used in making men's fur coats might surprise us today. Among those listed in a 1906 Vogue article included nutria, Manchurian dog, wombat, opossum, Russian pony, squirrel, muskrat, seal, raccoon, bear, civet cat, goat, mink, karakul, "and ironically as it may sound, horsehair." Costs might be equally surprising. Although some serviceable fur coats were available for as little as $12.50, some styles could cost more than $1000[37]—or about $12,000 in today's currency.

After 1910, though, slim, fitted coats returned in many varieties. On the eve of World War I, the attention of governments and their citizens in both the New World and the Old World focused on their young men who were about to march off to a deadly global conflict. The husky, barrel-chested masculine ideal of a mature Teddy Roosevelt now had been replaced by the slender, youthful silhouette of the young warrior. As men's suits narrowed and discarded upholstered padding for natural shoulderlines, overcoats, too, were reduced in mass, bulk, and length. The trim efficiency of military coats soon influenced the design of almost all styles of men's outerwear. (Figure 3-24.) The waistlines were raised; hemlines were shortened; armscyes were cut deeper and roomier; pockets were more capacious and numerous; and detailing such as epaulets, turned-back gauntlet cuffs, and vented or deep-pleated backs were applied to civilian coats.

Underwear 1900–1914

Underwear styles of the Edwardian era differed little from those of the late nineteenth century. The category of underclothing for most merchants and consumers was a commodity. "There is, of course, no such thing as actual fashion in underclothing," maintained one editor. "Every man wears what to him seems best as far as his pocket will permit without a thought of style and usually with little regard to looks."[38] Mass merchandisers emphasized fabric quality and price more than style or color even though ready-to-wear makers produced innumerable variations and hues of men's underwear.

For year-round wear, the union suit in any of its dozens of variations was the most common. When styled as a separate undershirt and drawers, the bottoms were reinforced with a deep waistband of woven sateen facing cut with a button front fly and reinforced with tabs at the sides to prevent stretching out of shape. (Figure 3-25.) Lamb's wool or worsted rib knits were preferred for cool months and "sanitary" cotton fleece or ribbed cotton for warm months. In the midteens, new knitting technologies made possible the "double body" union suits made with a double thickness around the torso and a single thickness over the arms and legs. Colors were mostly neutral grays, tans, or basic white although some catalogs offered fancy stripes and colors such as salmon, flesh pink, canary yellow, and pale blue. The coat front undershirt with a closure of mother-of-pearl buttons became a popular alternative to pullover versions that mussed the hair and waxed mustache. Clean-shaven young men, though, opted for the sleeveless or tank style pullover. Knee-length drawers in woven madras, linen, or silk were the upscale varieties of men's underwear. Although the abbreviated forms of underwear in light fabrics were usually for summer months, many affluent Edwardian men wore these styles year round since they spent most of their winters in overheated interiors. The primary objection to the shorts style was that "they expose the lower legs to the touch of the garters and trousers" although this was still preferable for many men to the "long, clinging drawers."[39]

In the early years of the 1900s, the sanitary clothing reform began to wane, and new varieties of light, cool mesh textiles were applied to men's underclothing. The Victorian notion of Dr. Jaeger's sanitary clothing program for keeping the entire body swaddled and protected from drafts faded quickly as men discovered the cool comfort and ease of the open-weave fabrics. The new idea was to let the body breathe. Contrary to the assertions of the old sanitary clothing advocates, *Vogue* insisted in 1903 that the open mesh underwear styles "have the reputation of being

Figure 3-26. Introduced in 1905, Porosknit brand fabrics were light, sheer, mesh knits used in the manufacture of men's underwear. The emphasis on undergarments that let the body breathe was antithetical to the late Victorian "sanitary clothing" movement, which advocated keeping the body fully covered and protected against drafts. Chalmers Porosknit underwear ad, 1914.

among the most healthful and sanitary of all kinds."[40] Among the most widely advertised types of knit mesh fabric was the Porosknit brand introduced in 1905. The porous sheerness of the Porosknit fabric was made as evident as decently possible in most of the posters and print ads from the Chalmer's Knitting Company. (Figure 3-26.)

Sleepwear 1900–1914

The nightshirt remained the most prevalent form of sleepwear for most Edwardian men. (Figure 3-27.) The basic bosom-front shirt construction did not change from the Victorian styles. Nightshirts were still cut to hang tent-like from the shoulders, and gathers in the back ensured a loose, sack-like comfort. Sleeves were wide and tubular, and armholes were cut in a curved line to drape off the shoulder for a non-binding fit. Skirts extended to the ankles and were vented at the side seams to prevent hemlines from riding up in the night. Despite the standardized silhouette, though, nightshirts were made with an infinite variety of details. Necklines were made with both collarless placket fronts or with attached turned-down collars. Front closures might be a simple three-button placket or an inserted shield-front bosom embellished with pleats, tucks, or even embroidery. Round-neck, collarless versions, sometimes listed in catalogs as the French neck style, were edged with all sorts of decorative stitching, trim, and contrasting fabrics.

Figure 3-27. Edwardian versions of the bosom-front pullover sleepshirt in wool for winter and cotton or linen for summer varied little from the ready-to-wear styles of the nineteenth century. Sleepshirts from Sears, 1905.

Despite the introduction of pajamas a generation earlier, the style was still viewed as a trendy option for young men. *Vogue* viewed pajama suits, especially in silk blends and fine flannels, as the "smartest things" in men's sleepwear found at the "best shops."[41] Unlike nightshirts, though, pajamas were available in a much wider assortment of designs. In addition to typical pullover bosom-front shirt styles, pajama tops were also made in a plethora of costume forms ranging from exotic, Asian-inspired looks with mandarin collars and imported silk prints to military uniforms replete with braid-trimmed jackets and frog closures. In 1907, the short-sleeved pajama jacket created fashion news, much the same as the short-sleeved sports shirt had a few years earlier.[42] (Figure 3-28.)

Cost, too, likely contributed to the continued preference of nightshirts over pajamas. In the 1907 Sears catalog, pajama suits cost 98¢ up to $1.48, but nightshirts were 42¢ for a good flannelette style and up to 98¢ for one made of the finest muslin.

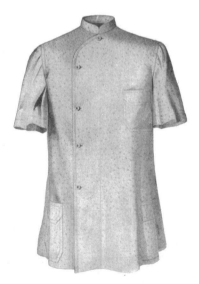

Figure 3-28. In addition to the basic striped pajamas offered in the catalogs of mass merchandisers, exotic costume styles included simulations of military uniforms and Asian-inspired looks. Silk pajama top from *Vogue*, 1907.

The two forms of robes also remained much as they had been in the late nineteenth century. Bathrobes were still made of knit terrycloth or thick, woven fabrics like pongee or cotton blanket. Colors and textile prints of men's robes were flamboyant to the extreme, many accented with lavish borders on cuffs and hemlines and tied with tasseled cords. While bathrobes were intimate apparel worn over pajamas or nightshirts for the morning bath or the evening toilet regimen before bed, lounging robes were dressy coverups worn over regular clothing in the evening for writing letters or reading before getting ready for bed. In some magazine editorial illustrations, a gentleman might be shown entertaining his closest friends with a nightcap while wearing a lounging robe, but he would still be wearing his dress shirt, necktie, suit trousers, and street shoes. The lounging robe was probably the most extravagant garment worn by an Edwardian gentleman. Some custom-tailored robes were made with such expensive, opulent fabrics like embroidered Chinese silk or brocaded

Figure 3-29. Smoking jackets of the era were as opulent as those of the nineteenth century. No longer a style primarily for the leisure classes, smoking jackets were mass produced by ready-to-wear makers and made available in most haberdasheries and menswear catalogs. Left, petite-floral satin smoking jacket with braid frog closures from *Vogue,* 1907; center and bottom, wool smoking jackets with silk cord piping from Hart Brothers, 1908.

satin that prices could exceed an astounding $500.[43]

Related to the lounging robe in purpose was the smoking jacket, also called a house coat. Similarly to lounging robes, smoking jackets were made with sumptuous fabrics and trim and cut with such extraordinary collar, cuff, or pocket treatments that most men would allow only the most intimate friends or family to see them wearing one. (Figure 3-29.) Nevertheless, by the Edwardian period, smoking jackets had become such a common negligée item for men in the middle classes that mass merchandisers included styles in their wishbooks priced around $4 up to about $7.50. "Year after year these things are shown in great profusion," observed a fashion editor, "and I suppose they must be bought for gifts by many hundreds of fond mothers, wives, and sisters, but if they are worn at all let us hope at least that it is within the privacy of their recipients' bedrooms and not around the house promiscuously."[44]

Accessories 1900–1914

The most important accessory for the Edwardian male, as with his Victorian father and grandfather, was the hat. (Figure 3-30.) Despite the dramatic progressivism of American society in the early twentieth century, masculine dress largely remained formal and conventional. Hence, the complexities of the protocols of headgear discussed in the previous chapter remained rigid and class bound. Style guides and fashion editorials frequently offered advice on the correct types of hats for the season and the man. Quite beyond the latest hat shape or color trend was the necessity of understanding the hat style that was most suitable to the individual. As the menswear editor of *Vogue* insisted in 1904:

> ...for the reason that in buying hats, rather more than any other one thing in the whole long list of men's attire, it is unwise to follow any particular shape simply because it is, or one may think it is, the smartest fashion. I do not mean to imply that one may defy prevailing modes to such an extent as to go about in some hat noticeably out of the season's vogue, no matter how becoming it may be, for it is never well to be conspicuous, but one must pay attention to one's own physical requirements in the matter of hats or one will certainly not look as well as one might. In other words, one must have a shape that is suitable, whether or not it is the exact shape put forth by the fashionable makers as the latest style.[45]

Even the mass merchandisers recommended that their customers choose their hat styles carefully before placing a catalog order. Sears catalogs included "illustrations of hats of different dimensions shown on different types and ages of men" so that the customer could be "assured of getting a hat to suit you."[46]

Derby, 1907

Pinched crown and peaked crown fedoras, 1908

Collegiate slouch hats, 1908

Summer straw hats, 1908

Panama hat, 1903

Left, collapsible opera hat of merino; right, silk top hat, 1908

Golf caps, 1907

Banded or engineers' cap, 1907

Yachting cap, 1907

Cowboy sombreros from Sears, 1903

Figure 3-30. As with his Victorian predecessor, the Edwardian man rarely went out of doors hatless. The derby remained the correct business suit hat, and the top hat was the only appropriate form for evening dress. In the summer, straw hats prevailed for every occasion except when a frock coat or tail coat was worn. Innumerable varieties of specialty hats were produced for sports, leisure, and work, often filling several pages of mass merchandisers' wishbooks.

The most important hat style of the era was the derby. Virtually all men who donned a ditto business suit and a high, stiff collar wore a derby in one shape or another. The Edwardian derby ranged from 5-1/2 inches to a tall 5-3/4 inches high. Young men preferred a derby called a "nobby" with a two-inch "dash" brim that dipped in the front and back. More conservative, older men opted for a derby with a rolled brim that was 2-1/2 inches wide and lacked the dash dip. Black was the most prevalent color year round although some men wore brown versions during cool transitional seasons. Materials were "selected Belgian [hare] fur stock, dyed by the best process known, assuring a jet black color that will not turn brown or green under the rays of the hot sun."[47] Wide hat bands were of grosgrain silk.

The top hat gradually vanished from daytime dress except, like the frock coat, for ceremonial purposes. The shiny silk topper worn with evening dress varied year to year in the contours of its bell shape, sometimes curving in at the sides and flaring slightly wider at the flat top than the crown opening. The cousin of the silk topper, the collapsible opera hat, persisted as the correct style for the theater. The tall, bell shape resembled the silk topper except opera hats were made with ribbed silk or merino and thinly banded with a fine fabric like vicuna rather than grosgrain ribbon.

For year-round weekend wear and outings, any of the numerous varieties of fedoras were immensely popular. Sometimes called "soft" hats or "tourist" hats, they were usually blocked of felt in assorted weights. Fedoras allowed men a bit of personal expression in how they arranged the pinched crowns and soft, wide brims. Hat bands varied from thin half-inch strips to wide, two-and-one-half-inch ribbons.

The "telescope" hat or "slouch" hat was a favorite of the collegiate young man. The wide "pan" brims were usually pushed upward in the front, and the shallow, creased crown could be flattened like a porkpie or pinched into a peak.

For warm weather, the panama and boater continued from the previous century as the preferred summer hat styles. Style guides suggested that straw hats of any type not be worn until June 1, but editorials noted that, in northern regions when springs were particularly warm, it was acceptable to see straw hats as early as mid-May.[48] Straw hats were regarded as correct for day or night, even with a tuxedo. The exceptions were a frock coat, if worn in warm weather for a ceremonial event, and formal evening dress, both of which required a silk top hat instead. The panama was not as popular during the Edwardian era as it had been in the nineteenth century. The boater, though, was common in smooth or coarse weaves and even in black-tinted straw. Wide hat bands were vividly colored and accented with prominent bows on the left side. (Figure 3-31.)

Utilitarian hats and caps ranged from tweed golf caps to toque-shaped fur hats with ear flaps that could be turned under or over the band. Outing or tourist caps included high-domed jockey caps, broadcloth visored yachting caps, or engineers' caps. Automobile caps of leather or fur were variously shaped ranging from low golf cap styles to tall engineers' caps, usually with ear flaps and sometimes a detachable neck guard.

Similarly, "cowboys' sombreros" with their shallow crowns and broad, five-inch brims were available from mass merchandisers in assorted styles for the western rancher and farmer. Sears offered versions made of "wool buckskin" accented with leather bands affixed with buckles or embossed with stars and other cattle-branding iron motifs.

Initially, neckwear for the Edwardian man was as varied and perplexing as that of his Victorian father. (Figure 3-32.) In the early years of the new century, the varieties of tie shapes, widths, and knots were too prolific even for fashion editors to agree on any one dominant look:

Here one sees a width of three inches or more, there one of an inch and a half or two, and there again a tie quite as narrow as were any of those when the derby was at the top of its vogue. The folded

Figure 3-31. For the Edwardian man, the wide, vividly colored and patterned hat bands popular for straw hats were, like neckwear and socks, one of the few elements of masculine dress broadly acceptable for personal expression. (Before World War II, the swastika was a common motif for men's accessories since it represented good luck.) Ad, 1908.

Patterned silk teck ties, 1908

Boxed gift set of print silk
four-in-hand ties, 1908

Imperial tie, 1908

Silk scarves, 1903

Round-end bow tie, 1908

Black peau de soie but-
terfly bow tie and floral
silk shield bow tie, 1908

Figure 3-32. The wide and confusing varieties of neckwear that had been available to the Victorian man gradually narrowed in the early twentieth century. Flamboyant puff scarves and ascots endured for a few years and then disappeared. Instead, the conformist Edwardian man was more comfortable with an assortment of silk teck ties or bow ties that took the guesswork out of tying the latest fashionable knots.

shapes for so long in evidence remain as fashionable as ever (yet by no means to the exclusion of the other styles), the varieties and weaves of silks are forever increasing, and there is practically no limit to the pattern designs and shades of color—some of them quite new in effect, but none so much in the lead from the fashion standpoint as to deserve more than others to be called preeminently smart.[49]

Style guides, catalogs, and promotional flyers from haberdasheries offered advice on which tie to wear with which suit and how to correctly tie the knot, but, even then, the ordeal was too much for many men. The solution to the stylistic dilemma for most men was the infinite assortment of preknotted teck ties and band bows that easily clipped around the collar. Not only were the mass-produced ready-made ties a great convenience but they also looked just as good as any of the troublesome, hand-tied varieties.

The most prevalent long tie for the business sack coat was the narrow four-in-hand tie. Most flared only slightly to about 2-1/4 inches at the

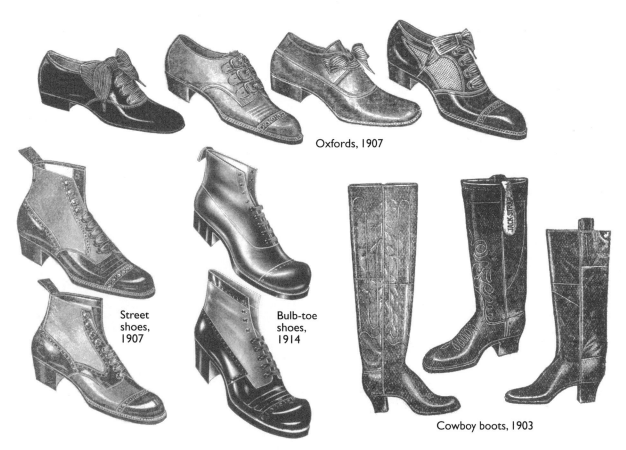

Oxfords, 1907

Street
shoes,
1907

Bulb-toe
shoes,
1914

Cowboy boots, 1903

Figure 3-33. The most common street shoe for the Edwardian man remained the ankle boot. The most prevalent form was constructed with a leather vamp and fabric upper. Younger men preferred the oxford, especially styles that sported the wide ribbon laces that formed huge bows when tied. Bulb-toe shoes were introduced as a hygienic alternative to the narrow fashion styles. Shoes from Sears and Montgomery Ward catalogs.

end. The more popular four-in-hand ended with a pointed tip although squared ends were a favorite of younger men. Boxed gift sets of four-in-hand neckties became a typical gift for American dads beginning with the first Father's Day in 1910. Imperials were broad versions of four-in-hand ties, some up to 4-1/4 inches wide.

The formal puff ties, Windsors, ascots, and other flamboyant scarf-type neckwear were still enough in demand for mass merchandisers to offer them in their annual wishbook catalogs during the early Edwardian years. However, as with the frock coat and tail coat, such exacting formal clothing gradually diminished in popularity until, by the beginning of the 1910s, such attire was viewed as quaint and eccentric.

The bow tie was almost as common for the business sack suit as the four-in-hand. The pointed-end batwing and butterfly bows continued to be the most typical shapes. A brief trend noted in some fashion editorials was the bow tie with rounded ends, evidence of "the entire absence of set standards."[50] Ready-made band bows were pretied and easily fastened at the back of the shirt collar with an adjustable elastic clasp.

Footwear for the Edwardian man was even more widely varied than headgear. (Figure 3-33.) The most standard form of street shoe remained the ankle boot style with a leather vamp and fabric upper although

Figure 3-34. Spats, or overgaiters, were viewed less as a semiformal accessory than in the previous century. Fashion editorials and catalog illustrations showed spats worn with sack coats as well as the traditional frock or morning coat. Illustration from *Vogue*, 1906.

all-leather versions were common. Button top boots disappeared around the turn of the century. Most lace-up styles were made with a looped pull tab at the heel, and pull on versions had a tab at both the front and back opening to prevent crushing the leather when putting them on. Pull ons also featured side panels of elasticized fabric. Sears' best men's shoes were made of colt, calf, or kangaroo skin with uppers made of heavy wool broadcloth or sateen. All black was most preferred although some young dandies opted for two-tones of gray and black or brown and cream in summertime. Tan shoes were a favorite topic of fashion editorials since they, more than any of the basic black forms, had a specific season and place for correctness; a tan boot in the city was incorrect; a tan oxford in the country was incorrect; a tan shoe of any variety worn other than during the summer was incorrect.[51]

The low shoe, or oxford, continued to gain in popularity after the turn of the century. When once oxfords had been viewed as casual footwear, mostly to be worn with outing sack suits and in cleated varieties on the tennis court or golf course, they were increasingly favored with street and business suits. The oxford was the correct style to be worn with the ankle-cropped, cuffed trouser. Most oxfords were made with lace-up lasts although slip-ons and even buckle styles were available.

Although the assortment of layered vamps, broguing (decorative punched holes), and toe shapes were seemingly infinite, most men's footwear varied little from the styles of the late nineteenth century. However, three fresh innovations were introduced during the Edwardian era. In the years following the Spanish-American War (1898), the Cuban heel, also called a military heel, became an exciting new look for almost all types of American men's street footwear. The shape was derived from the Spanish military boot heel, which was about 1-1/4 to 1-1/2 inches high and fashioned with a beveled slant all around the outside and sharp, straight edges at the inside arch. A second innovation was the introduction of the bulb-toe shoe made with a broad last and an upturned, bulbous-shaped toe. The bulb-toe shoe was intended as a hygienic alternative to the sharply pointed shoes and boots of the era that caused numerous foot ailments from blisters to bunions. The bulb-toe became immensely popular, lasting through the war years, and was applied to both utilitarian shoes and street shoes for men, women, and even children. A third innovation was the bow-lace oxford made with large eyelets through which were threaded broad, flat laces that tied into large bows. The bow-lace oxford, called a swagger style, was worn with the new, ankle-cropped cuffed trousers (and colorful socks with decorative clocking).

Spats had been a common shoe embellishment even in the Victorian years. During the first quarter of the new century, spotless spats, sometimes called overgaiters, symbolized the gentlemen who obviously never walked anywhere except along well-cleaned city boulevards. (Figure 3-34.) Nevertheless, unlike silk top hats and ebonized walking sticks, spats were not necessarily the accoutrement solely of frock and morning coat suits. As *Vogue* noted in 1906, boxcloth spats with inward pearl buttons and a buckle strap under the arch were "each year becoming a more general fashion, and are sometimes worn with sack suits as well as with more formal attire."[52]

Varieties of utilitarian boots, shoes, and slippers abounded in the wishbooks of the mass merchandisers. Cowboy boots made with high heels and lavishly embroidered lasts and tops were shipped to the remotest western outpost by the thousands. Thick-soled work boots were constructed with reinforced heels and toes for tough labors on the farm or city streets. Rubber footwear included assorted styles of wool fleece-lined Alaskas and Arctics made with molded soles of pure gum rubber and uppers of rubberized duck. Similarly, tennis shoes were made with cleated rubber soles and low canvas uppers.

Men's small leather goods such as belts, wallets, billfolds, change purses, and spectacles cases had been so standardized in the preceding century that little mention is made of them in style guides and fashion reports. Decade after decade, mass merchandisers offered the same types of each made mostly of calfskin leather in various finishes, debossed textures, and topstitching.

Dress gloves were still an important class differentiator during the Edwardian period. Gentlemen never went into the street without gloves, irrespective of the season. The proper dress glove featured three raised ridges stitched to fan across the back of the hand pointing to the separations of the fingers. A single button of bone or gilt at the wrist kept the opening from gaping. Various suedes, especially undressed reindeer, were popular in the early 1900s, but then convention prevailed, and most men limited their choices of gloves to dressed kid in shades of tan, brown, or gray. Increasingly, black became more common although mostly workman's or driver's gloves were made in black. Colored gloves, even in dark, subtle hues like plum, navy, or olive, were never as acceptable for self-expression as neckwear, pocket kerchiefs, and socks. As *Vogue* asserted in 1902, "In spite of the statements occasionally made as to the smartness of canary yellow or some other such impossible color, fashion is governed by what is worn by well-dressed men, and this class does not wear such things."[53] White gloves were never to be seen on the street, even if a gentleman were dressed in formal attire. Instead, he would wear dark dress gloves until arriving at his destination whereupon he would change into

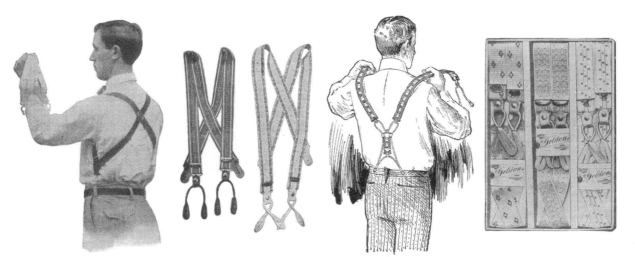

Figure 3-35. Even though the market for trousers with belt loops grew rapidly during the early 1900s, many men still preferred suspenders. From Hart Brothers catalog, 1908: left to right, model holding white coatless suspenders, two types of tab button loops, man putting on suspenders back to front, boxed set of fancy webbing suspenders.

Figure 3-36. Garters were a necessary discomfort endured by the well-dressed man to ensure a head-to-toe polished look. Young men who preferred the cropped cuffed trousers and oxfords that exposed their brightly-colored hosiery especially had to guard against the slovenly look of sagging socks. Goldenwear garters, 1908.

his white gloves. Some Edwardian dandies had experimented briefly with white evening gloves topstitched in lavender or black, but the fad was roundly criticized in the fashion press.

In the new century, trousers with belt loops continued to edge out styles with suspender buttons. In the early 1900s, a number of ready-to-wear makers produced trousers with both belt loops and suspender buttons to cover both market segments. The aging Victorian male who only knew suspenders in his era and many younger men who conformed to the conventions of their father and grandfather still chose suspenders despite the modern look and comfort of belted trousers. Since the market demand for suspenders remained steady, catalogs though World War I were filled with numerous varieties. Most suspenders were made of colorfully patterned elastic webbing with various forms of leather or metal button loops. (Figure 3-35.) Cantab suspenders featured a pair of elasticized tabs at the end of each strap to which the leather button loops were stitched, providing more give than ordinary suspenders. White coatless suspenders were widely advertised as an alternative to the eye-catching patterned styles for men who preferred to remove their suit coats in the office (if no women were present). But as one menswear editor chided, "If one must wear them, one must also wear a vest."[54]

Another support accessory were garters for holding up socks—an important finishing touch for the well-dressed man. (Figure 3-36.) Garters were made from the same types of rubber elasticized webbing as suspenders and came in an equally diverse assortment of colors and patterns. Garters were even more important for the Edwardian man than for his Victorian father because cuffed trousers were cropped at the ankles and worn with oxfords that exposed more of the colorful socks.

As noted earlier, high-speed knitting technologies had improved considerably by the beginning of the twentieth century. Complex combinations of knit patterns and techniques made possible a huge variety of mass-produced sweaters, vests, mufflers, gloves, caps, and neckwear. Similarly, men's socks, sometimes called half hose, were manufactured in a wide assortment of knitted constructs, multicolored yarn patterns, and

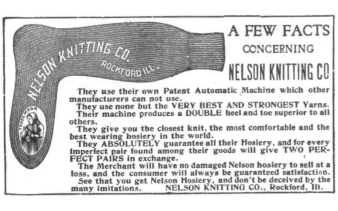

Figure 3-37. Advances in high-speed knitting technologies made possible the mass production of well-made socks in a huge variety of multicolored patterns. The Nelson Knitting Company of Rockford, Illinois, assured consumers in ads that their socks were of such superior quality—tight, strong knits with reinforced heels and toes—that they would give customers two free pairs if ever they found an imperfect pair. Left, Nelson Knitting Company ad, 1906; right, patterned half hose in multicolored combinations from Goldenwear, 1908.

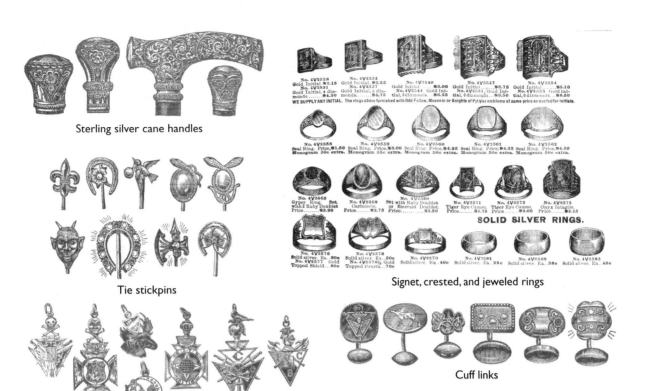

Sterling silver cane handles

Tie stickpins

Signet, crested, and jeweled rings

Cuff links

Watch chain charms (men's social organization emblems)

Vest chains

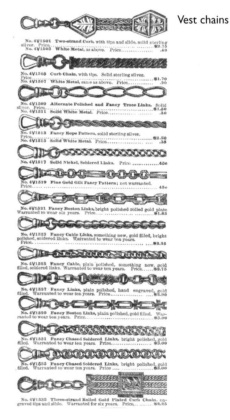

Figure 3-38. The types of jewelry acceptable for the conformist Edwardian man changed little from those of the late nineteenth century. Their use, symbolism, and decorative motifs extended the Victorian traditions into the new century. Men's jewelry from Sears catalogs, 1903–1907.

brilliant dye finishes. (Figure 3-37.) Six pairs of cotton socks were priced in Sears 1907 catalog at 68¢; in wool, six pairs for $1.47. For the youthful Edwardian dandy who rebelled against the ubiquitous plainness of most men's clothing, socks in colors such as red or purple with contrasting machine-embroidered clocking were the perfect finishing touch for cropped, cuffed trousers and oxfords.

The varieties and protocols of jewelry for men in the early 1900s remained largely the same as those of the Victorians. The December 1905 "Gifts Number" of *Vogue* recommended watches and watch chains, tie stickpins and clips, cuff links, dress shirt studs, monogrammed or crested rings, and "many styles of gold and silver, or other metal, pencils, key rings, key chains, pocket knives, etc., that make very acceptable presents."[55] The wishbooks of the mass merchandisers offered many pages of such ornamental accoutrement that replicated in plated metals the fine jewelry examples found in the better shops and upscale department stores. (Figure 3-38.) As one style editor complained in 1907, "smart fashion" for the well-dressed man must "suffer" because of the mass-produced replication of jewelry at "popular prices" in catalogs and haberdasheries. "I am often amazed to see how good are the styles and how perfect the imitations."[56] Consequently, every office boy and junior executive could afford a tie stickpin with simulated jewels and matching cufflinks, a fancy engraved pocket watch with vest chain and charm, and a monogrammed signet ring, all of inexpensive gold plate.

Grooming 1900–1914

A dramatic shift in men's grooming occurred in the years between the end of the nineteenth century and World War I. A number of social, scientific, and commercial forces coincided to bring the end to the Victorian masculine cult of facial hair.

In 1901, entrepreneurial salesman King C. Gillette approached a professor from the Massachusetts Institute of Technology with a concept for a new type of safety razor designed to hold disposable blades made by an innovative stamped sheet-steel process. Two years later, the Gillette Safety Razor was introduced to the American consumer. (Figure 3-39.) The idea was an instant hit, and, according to the 1908 ad shown here, more than two million razors and blades had been sold across America within the first five years of production. Throughout the prewar years, Gillette evangelized his idea nationwide with saturation advertising in mass media. In many instances, Gillette appeared in his ads revealing his persistent preference for a bushy mustache, but in all the other Gillette ads depictions of youthful men were thoroughly clean shaven.

At the same time Gillette introduced his improved safety razor, Americans were increasingly aware of germs, personal hygiene, and good health. As discussed in the introduction of this chapter, the relentless exposés of the muckrakers of the American press were instrumental in getting the Pure Food and Drug Act passed in 1906. Similarly, women's magazines expanded their roster of feature articles to include regular segments on family health issues. For example, in 1907, *Harper's Bazar* added "Reflections Concerning Women," which often focused on health concerns. That same year, "Reflections" tackled the issue of the insanitary conditions of men's facial hair in the "light of science." The clean-shaven masculine face, avowed the editor, "is, in our judgment, particularly grat-

Figure 3-39. The introduction of the safety razor by King C. Gillette in 1905 coincided with a hygienic movement in America that resulted in the Edwardian male abandoning the masculine traditions of facial hair in any form. Gillette ads, left, 1910; right, 1908.

ifying and should be encouraged in all proper ways." To substantiate their advocacy for clean-shaven men, *Harper's Bazar* enlisted the help of scientists to conduct an experiment: a clean-shaven man and a bearded man were sent about a city in the normal course of their daily activities. Afterwards, each was invited to kiss a young woman, whose lips had been sterilized. A swab was made of the woman's lips after each kiss and the swab was sealed in a petri dish. Four days later, the results were examined:

> The first, taken from the shaven man, was speckled with dots, each of which was a colony of yeast germs, such as cause mold, but are practically harmless. The second, from the mustached man, literally swarmed with malignant microbes. The long, thin tubercle bacillus was the first found, followed by diphtheria and putrefactive germs, minute bits of food, a hair from a spider's leg, and goodness knows what all—so great a variety, in any case that nobody had the hardihood to reveal the results of the experiment to the young lady.

The editors concluded that the best way to minimize such pervasive health risks was by "insisting upon the removal of mustaches."[57]

The theme of insanitary masculine facial hair became a national discussion and was happily taken up by the makers of shaving soaps, lather brushes, after-shave lotions, and, of course, razors. In 1910, Gillette's full-page ads emphasized the woman's point of view. "Woman is the great civilizer," stated the ad copy. "If it were not for her, man would revert to whiskers and carry a club." Other key words in the Gillette ad drove home the point: "clean, healthy skin," "massaged appearance," "wholesome," and "healthy look."[58]

Along with editorial campaigns to rid men of facial hair and the proliferation of clean-shaven faces of young men in ads, the commercialization

A **Cluett** SHIRT

deserves the approval of the man who wishes to avoid the commonplace in dress. *$1.50, $2.00, $2.50 and up*

Cluett, Peabody & Company, Makers, Troy, N. Y.

Figure 3-40. The ideal masculine aesthetic for the new century was youthful, trim, and handsome with a clean-shaven, square jaw and well-groomed hair. Two prolific illustrators of the time, J. C. Leyendecker and Charles Dana Gibson, perpetuated the new manly ideal through hundreds of commercial drawings and paintings in the mass media and advertising. Left, Gibson Girl and beau, 1902; right, Arrow shirt man by Leyendecker, 1910.

of a new idea of masculine beauty developed. The two best known proponents of this modern male aesthetic were the famous illustrators Charles Dana Gibson and J. C. Leyendecker. The idealized image of the American man of the new century as depicted by these two artists—and the many others who followed their lead—was handsome, square-jawed, clean-shaven, well-groomed, and youthful. (Figure 3-40.) And the American woman responded enthusiastically to this new ideal. The look of the Leyendecker man was featured for more than twenty years in ads for Arrow shirts, during which time the manufacturer received thousands of fan letters from women including marriage proposals and even threats of suicide.[59]

Conclusion

Although the pre-World War I years of the twentieth century are generally called the Edwardian era, named for Britain's King Edward VII, in America, it was the time of President Teddy Roosevelt. The burly, bigger-than-life Roosevelt was the masculine idea for the time. Consequently, men's fashions replicated the broad-shouldered, barrel-chested physique of the athletic president by reconstructing clothing with bulky padding, capacious shapes, and loose cuts. The new silhouette of the ideal American male was a Herculean build with massive shoulders and chest, strong arms, and powerful thighs.

The shoulders of most suit coat styles were built up with padding that extended to the chest, and sleeves were cut as wide, loose cylinders.

The body of sack coats hung shapelessly straight and long; when worn closed, only the bottom button was fastened, adding even more bulk to the coat shape. Frock and morning coats likewise lost their trim fit while retaining their distinctive darted waist seams. The plain-front pegged trousers flared from the hips over the thighs and down to narrow cuffs in such an exaggerated line that many illustrations of the time look almost like depictions of ankle-length jodhpurs.

To accommodate the bulk and mass of men's suits, outerwear overcompensated with an expansion in volume and length. The most typical shapes were tent-like, hanging loosely from the shoulders and sweeping about the ankles. Sleeves were cut huge to comfortably fit over the oversized suit sleeves without causing them to bunch up at the armscye and collar. Details such as patch pockets and lapels increased in dimension as well to balance the overall voluminous look.

By the beginning of the 1910s, women's fashions had abandoned the voluptuous S-bend silhouette and, instead, adopted the slim, columnar look of the hobble skirt. Menswear makers and tailors quickly adapted the youthful trimness of feminine styles to the shape of most forms of masculine clothing. Suits and outerwear were cut with natural shoulderlines devoid of bulky padding and mass. Volume was greatly reduced as waistlines were tapered and raised, sleeves were narrowed, and skirts were shortened. Trouser legs lost the exaggerated pegged draping and narrowed to a slender legginess emphasized by the short jacket skirts.

In addition to the shifting of bulk and mass of menswear during the Edwardian era, changing social mores inspired some innovative new looks. On the tennis courts across America, men began to wear short-sleeved sport shirts when competing. However, the players were expected to change into long-sleeved negligée shirts before joining the spectators.

Increasingly, American menswear reflected the market demand for casual comfort in clothing styles. At home and for weekend wear, men opted for the ease of coat sweaters and pullovers instead of the sack coat. The myriad of comfortable work and negligée shirts available at every haberdashery and in mail-order catalogs gradually eroded the social barriers of when and where a man might go jacketless. The sanitary clothing reform movement of the previous century that totally encased men in heavy woolen underwear and outerwear faded as men adopted briefer forms of underwear made of new, lightweight fabrics that let the body breathe. By the eve of World War I, the days of the upholstered Edwardian look had come to an end.

The Jazz Age

Fashions from World War I through the Great Euphoria, 1915–1929

The World at War

In the summer of 1914, the heir to the vast Austro-Hungarian Empire was assassinated in the Balkan kingdom of Serbia. To clean out the perceived nest of terrorists, the Vienna government declared war on tiny Serbia, setting off an explosive chain reaction across Europe. When Russia began to mobilize its army to aid its Slavic ally in the Balkans, Germany became alarmed and demanded that the Czar stand down. When Russia refused, Germany declared war and entered the conflict as an ally of Austria. Two days later, anticipating a military threat from the French on its western borders, Germany also declared war on France and marched on Paris through neutral Belgium whose treaty with England then drew the British into the continental conflagration on the side of France. By the fall of 1914, the German race to the sea had been halted just inside the northern French border, and the opposing armies settled into a deadly stalemate of trench warfare for the following four years, during which a narrow few miles of devastated farm fields changed hands repeatedly.

The United States viewed the war in Europe as a localized fight. Overwhelmingly, Americans wanted to remain neutral despite their sympathies for the British, French, and Belgians. (Figure 4-1.) Nevertheless, the U.S. government shipped enormous quantities of munitions to the Allies and extended credit for those purchases while, at the same time, diverting supplies once designated for countries like Denmark that had been passing them on to Germany. Thus, inexorably, the United States was gradually pulled toward entering the conflict. As a reprisal for the British blockade that was slowly starving the Fatherland, German U-boats increasingly targeted any merchant ships that entered the war zone, including those of the United States. In 1915, without warning, a German submarine sank a British passenger ship, the *Lusitania*, killing 1198 of whom 128 were Americans. By the spring of 1917, the United States had

"Strictly Neutral"

Figure 4-1. For the first three years of World War I, the United States maintained a policy of neutrality despite the sympathies of the American people for Britain, France, and Belgium. Cartoon from *Life*, 1915.

Figure 4-2. For those Americans who might complain of the shortages and other privations of wartime, Bauer and Black, makers of surgical dressings, published a full color ad in 1918 reminding them of the ultimate sacrifice of their young men "over there." "In behalf of the brave men who have enlisted in the fight of right against might," the ad reprinted the poem, "We Shall Not Sleep," by John McCrae whose "body now lies buried in Flanders fields."

had enough. On April 2, President Wilson went to Congress and asked legislators to recognize that a state of war had been "thrust" upon the Republic, and America went to war.

From all across the country, more than 600,000 young men volunteered to "make the world safe for democracy" in 1917; and the following year, the newly instituted draft called another 2,700,000 to the colors.[1] The battalions of American doughboys soon found themselves fighting the same bloody, muddy trench warfare that had plagued the British and French for the previous three years. The destruction wrought by the modern war technologies of machine guns, armored tanks, gigantic howitzers, stealthy aeroplanes, and lethal gas killed over 10 million men and wounded another 20 million by the end of the war.

On the home front, rationing had been immediate from food and fuels to many of the basic raw materials for clothing, housing, and other consumer products. "Wheatless, meatless, and heatless," the nation hunkered down for the duration. Women by the tens of thousands stepped into the jobs vacated by the men who went to war. Home-bound citizens knitted socks, scratched out victory gardens, rolled bandages, and collected mountains of peach pits used in making gas mask filters. Everyone bought war stamps and bonds. Advertisers and the media joined the government's propaganda machine to mobilize Americans toward greater conservation and increased productivity. (Figure 4-2.)

Finally, in November 1918, battered and exhausted, depleted of supplies, and deserted by their allies, the German army retreated. Kaiser Wilhelm was forced to abdicate, and, after four agonizing years, the First World War ended.

America after the war was radically different from what it had been at the close of the Edwardian era just a few years earlier. Worn out by the anxieties of the war, Americans simply wanted a return to normalcy—but, in those few short wartime years, too much had changed. Normalcy now had to be redefined.

The returning doughboys were not the wide-eyed rural lads who patriotically lined up at recruiting centers in 1917. Not only had they eagerly explored the many new horizons offered by the sophisticated cultures of Europe, but they had also witnessed more horrors and suffering

Figure 4-3. Many Americans viewed the push for Prohibition by puritanical temperance groups as an assault on their personal liberty. Cartoon from *Life,* 1918.

of humanity than ever they would have known in a lifetime in their heartland hamlets and farms. In addition, the soldiers came home to find that the sweethearts, wives, sisters, and mothers they left behind to keep the hearth fires burning had, instead, become the New Woman. Following the passage of the Nineteenth Amendment in 1919, women could vote. The vicissitudes of war had made them self-assured and independent, having run households in the absence of their menfolk or having earned paychecks working in hundreds of jobs previously viewed as men's work only.

Moreover, the very core of American society had been shattered. The soldier heroes were welcomed home to a "dry" nation. The Prohibition against alcohol that had been instituted in 1917 as a temporary measure to conserve grain for the war effort had become permanent in 1919, largely at the vociferous urging of antisaloon leagues. (Figure 4-3.) Nor could the soldier assimilate back into the civilian workforce as easily as he might have hoped. A postwar depression caused widespread unemployment as industries shifted from war production back to consumer goods. The economic downturn also led to an increase in racial tensions. The wartime labor shortage had triggered a mass migration of African Americans from southern plantations to northern factories and services—jobs that returning vets demanded as rightfully theirs. As the recession deepened, race riots erupted in several northern cities.

As the turbulent decade drew to a close, America was ravaged by a virulent flu pandemic during the winter of 1918–19. Although originating in Asia, the disease was called the Spanish flu because Spain had been especially hard hit. By the time the epidemic had run its course, more than half a million Americans had died.

The Golden Twenties

For so many Americans, the beginning of the 1920s was a chance, at last, to put the tumultuous 1910s behind them. Perhaps with a new decade, they hoped, a fresh start toward that elusive postwar normalcy was possible. Instead, the Great War, as the First World War was commonly known through the 1920s and 1930s, lingered still at the forefront of American foreign policy. A wave of isolationism engulfed the country, and the U.S. Congress responded by refusing to allow America to join the League of Nations. It took until 1921 for the United States to finalize the peace pacts with Germany and Austria.

In addition, a new xenophobic hysteria swept the land—a fear of the Red Menace. Seemingly around every corner, someone spotted anarchist communists from Russia bent on overthrowing the U.S. government and violently destroying the American way of life. In response, the reactionary U.S. Attorney General energetically rounded up thousands of perceived Reds and radicals who were jailed or deported to Russia.

Figure 4-4. In the post-World War I years, the U.S. economy roared, fueled by the mass production and mass consumption of the Machine Age. After years of wartime shortages, rationing, and privations, Americans gorged themselves on the abundance of consumer goods instigated by mass advertising and enabled by liberal payment installment plans.

Women's fashions 1915–1929: left, military inspired dress, 1918; center, dropped-waist dresses, 1923; right, knee-length flapper dresses, 1929

Tudor Revival suburban home, 1927

Mass-produced parlor suite from Ward's, 1928

Electric refrigeration from Frigidaire, 1927

Ford coupe, 1926

Thermiodyne Radio, 1924

Kewpies by illustrator Rose O'Neill were a popular culture favorite throughout the 1920s. "Kewpieville" from *Ladies' Home Journal,* 1925

By 1922, though, the postwar depression ended, and the economy began a quick recovery. Jobs became plentiful again. Within a year, the Big Bull Market had surged upward, and a broad spectrum of Americans got in on the action. Just about everyone, it seemed, from office girls and delivery boys to blueblood socialites and business moguls, was playing the stock market by buying on margin—making a minimal down payment—and then cashing in quick. The twenties now roared with prosperity.

One of the key drivers of the economic boom was an explosion in consumerism. The years of wartime shortages followed by deprivations of the postwar depression had left most Americans with pent-up needs and wants that erupted into a buying frenzy. Materialism was the new American dream in the 1920s. Manufacturers fueled the consumer spending binge with an endless array of new products. (Figure 4-4.) Marketers encouraged the aspirations of the American consumer with saturation advertising: Magazines were ponderously filled with pages of alluring color ads; mail order catalogs flooded into every home; and radio began to bombard the airwaves with lively sell messages from sponsors. For high-end merchandise like cars and major household appliances, makers and retailers introduced the payment installment plan that allowed consumers to own today and pay tomorrow. (Figure 4-5.)

Although the Great War had turned American society inside out, that trauma was but a prelude to what the new cultural materialism fomented. With the revved-up production of new cars, an abundance of used cars, and easy payment installment plans, almost everyone could own a car. New experiences were suddenly opened to restless America. From the countryside, rural folks ventured into the nearby babylons to discover the progress of the Machine Age. For the urbanite, the automobile made possible a commuter lifestyle for which the tendrils of sprawling suburbias increasingly extended far beyond city limits.

Traditional values were further eroded by the introduction of commercial radio broadcasting in 1920 when a Pittsburgh station went on the air to announce the returns of the presidential election. At the beginning of the decade, fewer than 5000 hobbyists toyed with radio sets that might, on a good day, pick up ship-to-shore signals or voice transmissions from naval stations. But within a few short years, more than three million home radios tuned in daily to 600 commercial stations across the country broadcasting a variety of programming.[2] "The wonder of it!" exclaimed a radio ad in 1927. "Just one turn of that single dial will filter from the air any kind of music you want—jazz, a symphony, a voice of beauty; music to put toes to dancing or tired brain to sleep."[3] Into homes grand and small across America wafted new sounds of music, entertaining dramas and comedies, instantaneous news and sports reports, educational information, thought provoking commentary, and enticements from advertising. Through these widely diverse radio programs were disseminated new ideas of modern culture and social change to the masses.

Even more influential than the automobile and the radio in reshaping America's postwar social mores were the movies. Each week, millions of Americans flocked to their local movie palaces to escape into the fantasy worlds that flickered on silent screens before them. Besides escapist entertainment, the movies also provided guidance on the Jazz Age way to look, dress, and behave. Stars like Clara Bow and Joan Crawford were emulated by flappers from Maine to Montana who bobbed their hair,

Figure 4-5. During the 1920s, jobs were plentiful and credit was easy for most Americans. For big ticket items like cars and appliances, manufacturers and retailers developed easy payment installment plans. With a paycheck stub to prove employment and a small down payment, consumers could buy now and pay later. Ford ad, 1925.

Figure 4-6. During the 1920s, millions of Americans thronged to their local movie houses every week to thrill at the flickering images on silent silver screens. In addition to escapist entertainment, movies also presented a new mass culture of modern behavior and fashion. Spreads from *Motion Picture Magazine*, 1925.

kohled their eyes, and rouged their lips in imitation of their screen idols. Rudolph Valentino made hearts race with his seductive tangos and desert romances. Movies such as *Flaming Youth* (1923), *Flesh and the Devil* (1926), and *Don't Deceive Your Children* (1925) depicted the postwar "new morality" of sexual permissiveness, social sophistication, and other such escapades of the modern youth. The sexual revolution of the 1920s was especially advanced by movies. One billboard for *Tarnish* (1924) proclaimed "Moments of love—hours of sorrow—nights of rapture."[4] The formula for such sex films, asserted *Motion Picture Magazine*, "for the most part consisted of an old grandmother who quavered around with a cane and shook with horror at the conduct of the younger generation.

And the younger generation flapped defiance, bobbed hair, cocktail shakers, hip flasks, and cigarettes at her, and told her that 'times have changed since your day, old dear'....Indiscreet young ladies were carried off to bed. Automobile joyride parties forgot to come home until daylight."[5] And the masses devoured it all. Fan magazines proliferated, bringing moviegoers photos from their favorite films and pin-ups of their favorite stars, accompanied by inventive behind-the-scenes stories of Hollywood and the players. (Figure 4-6.)

Indeed, the sexual revolution of the 1920s was a social phenomenon in itself. The young men who went to fight the Great War "over there" had encountered societies where sex in its many varieties was much more open than in America. While the doughboys experimented with sex abroad, the New Woman on the home front learned about birth control from heroic advocates like Margaret Sanger, who was jailed on the charge of distributing obscene materials from her clinic. And both sexes discovered the writings of Sigmund Freud and Havelock Ellis, whose pronouncements assured readers that sex was healthy and necessary for a happy, fulfilled life. Hence, by the second half of the twenties, the sexual revolution was in full swing. As *Vanity Fair* noted in 1928:

> The young no longer regard [sex] with that feeling of rather guilty excitement and thrilling shame which was for an earlier generation the normal reaction to the subject. Moreover the practice of birth control has robbed amorous indulgence of most of the sinfulness traditionally supposed to be inherent in it by robbing it of its socially disastrous effects....[Sex] has ceased to be the rather fearful, mysterious thing it was and become a perfectly normal, almost commonplace activity—an activity, for many young people, especially in America, of the same nature as dancing or tennis, a sport, a recreation, a pastime.[6]

All across America, the young embraced the sexual revolution in various degrees, from teenage petting parties to premarital sex with multiple partners, as their most potent form of generational rebellion—the one topic most alarming to their Edwardian parents and Victorian grandparents.

Inadvertently and ironically, Prohibition further undermined prewar traditions and values. The puritans who had so stridently driven the nation to Prohibition had envisioned a Constitutional Amendment to fend off what they perceived as one of the chief evils—drinking liquor—of moral decay in America. But the law simply did not prohibit. Instead, Prohibition led to an age of urban gangsterism and violent turf wars between rivals of smuggling bootleg hooch. The neighborhood saloons were replaced by speakeasies that, with the right password, admitted women, including many teenagers, who imbibed bathtub gin in teacups. And, since the law was against the sale and distribution of alcohol, not against its possession, many average citizens carried a hip flask filled with liquor of some form. (Figure 4-7.) Between 1925 and 1927, *Ladies' Home Journal* visited the campuses of several major universities coast to coast to interview students and faculty about "college morals" and "the drinking question." "We do not find national prohibition a help," concluded one college administrator. "Drinking...is a serious problem"—a problem "carried to such excess and the sex irregularities were so numerous that it became a matter of college scandal."[7]

The 1920s was a heady era in America. The economy boomed and

Figure 4-7. Instead of Prohibition curbing the "moral decay" perceived by dry advocates, liquor was more available than ever—and to a younger market. Flaming Youth readily added hard drinking to their other indulgences of jazz music, wild dancing, fast cars, and easy sex. Cartoons from F. Scott Fitzgerald's *Tales of the Jazz Age,* 1922.

Figure 4-8. In 1925, the great Exposition Internationales des Arts Dècoratifs et Industriels Modernes held in Paris was a showcase of international modern style known to us today as art deco. The event helped France recapture its preeminence as the world's style leader following the disruptive war years. Expo pavilions designed in the art deco style.

the stock market soared fueled by materialism and consumerism. A youth-obsessed society drank hard and played hard to forget the pain of the Great War. The young and the young at heart danced the Charleston to the blare of jazz bands, smoked ceaselessly, and experimented with unconventional sex. The exhilarating Great Euphoria swept all America along its dizzying course right through to the end of the decade.

The Fashion Industry in America 1915–1929

American ready-to-wear makers, tailors, and apparel retailers had always looked to Paris for the latest in women's fashions and to London for direction in menswear. During the early 1900s, though, some fashion editors and journalists, most notably Edward Bok at *Ladies' Home Journal,* crusaded vigorously for the establishment of an American fashion leadership that could equal—or better—that of Europe. "Are *all* the clever women who can add a new touch to women's clothes in Paris?" asked an editorial in 1910.[8] Not at all, insisted the *Journal:*

> It is not that we can originate, but we actually have originated our own fashions. The growth of our own ideas in dress, as in all other ideas, has been so natural that we ourselves hardly know what has happened. And so positive has become both the need and design

in the evolution of an American style of dress that we shall instinctively go on and develop a distinctively American art of dressing until we shall not only be co-equal with Paris, but perhaps, excel it in cleverness and originality, just as we have excelled and are excelling today along other lines.[9]

Indeed, when the war erupted in 1914, *Vogue* was so fearful of the loss of fashion guidance and news from Paris and London that publisher Condé Nast organized a three-day fashion fete to publicize the best in New York fashion design. The event was ostensibly a charity benefit, but in reality, the magazine hoped to promote and validate American designers nationally to ensure a steady supply of fashion news and editorials in the event Europe became completely cut off. Unfortunately for American designers, the war did not cause the Chambre Syndicale de la Couture in Paris nor Savile Row in London to cease business. Consequently, American clothing makers and retailers continued to follow the established leaders, and the opportunity for the emergence of an American preeminence in fashion design faded. It would take another world war a generation later before American designers would be challenged to stand on their own fashion creativity and originality.

One of the most significant events in postwar Europe that ultimately influenced American fashion design for more than a decade was the Exposition Internationales des Arts Dècoratifs et Industriels Modernes held in Paris in 1925. (Figure 4-8.) The great Expo was a showcase of international modern style known to us today as art deco. (At the time, though, the look of the era until World War II was called "moderne" by designers and style editors.) The elements of art deco were, in essence, hard-edged geometric shapes, flat patterns, and stylized motifs often emphasized by a juxtaposition of bold, contrasting colors. The antecedents of art deco were the myriad of European avant-garde art movements that experimented with new approaches to pictorial space and use of color, particularly the Cubists and Fauves in Paris, Futurists in Italy, Constructivists in Russia, Secessionists in Vienna, and De Jugenstil in Germany. Into the mix was blended the exoticism of the ancient world—influences from the Near East following the dismantling of the Ottoman Empire after World War I and especially from ancient Egypt when the treasures of Tutankhamen were discovered in 1922. These many inspirations developed into the fresh, modern look in the visual and applied arts that was on exhibit at the Paris Expo. The world's foremost architects, sculptors, furniture makers, jewelers, and fashion names were represented. The result of the expo's success, according to economist Paul Nystrom writing a few years later, was that "A deep impression was created favoring the modernistic art movement, and most of the people who attended it, including producers and distributors, have since been inclined to give Paris the credit for the whole modernistic art movement."[10]

Notably absent from the Expo, though, was the United States. The Secretary of Commerce, Herbert Hoover, had determined that American designers could not meet the modernist requirements outlined in the expo charter, so the Coolidge administration declined participation. But the influence of the art deco style in America was profound, impacting the look of everything from fashion and accessories to advertising and kitchen appliances. (Figure 4-9.) Among the icons of art deco in America are New York's Empire State Building and the spired Chrysler Building.

Figure 4-9. Although the United States did not participate in the Paris Expo of 1925, the resulting influence of the art deco style was immediate in all arenas of American culture. From advertising and fashion to automobiles and appliances, the sleek geometry of art deco design proclaimed the modernity of the Machine Age. Lord and Taylor ad, 1928.

Although American fashion design did not achieve international leadership in the postwar years, American style greatly influenced both Paris couture and London tailoring. During the prewar nationalist push for American fashion designers to break free of the influences of Europe, the *Ladies' Home Journal* reminded readers that America "has given even Paris more distinct fashions that have a sense of permanency about them than Paris has ever given her."[11] Among the examples cited were forms of sportswear including the shirtwaist, rainy-daisy skirt, pleated skirt, and jumper.

Likewise, by the 1920s, the fashion press began to acknowledge that the influence of American men's style of ease and comfort also extended across the Atlantic. In 1925, *Men's Wear* reported from Paris that "Countless numbers of American tourists and college boys journeying through France this year are certain to lend much additional emphasis to the manner in which the average Frenchman is taking to American clothes....The aim of the Frenchman [is] to look as much like an American as is possible."[12] The following year, the British style guide *Clothes and the Man* noted that English men particularly liked the "American semi-soft collar" made of comfortable, unstarched cotton and, in summer, the "American idea" of cool tuxedos without vests for evening dress instead of a formal tail coat.[13] Most significant of all, however, was the influence of the Prince of Wales (later Edward VIII) who was much taken with the comfortable casualness of American men's clothing. Following his first trip to the United States in 1919, the young prince almost single-handedly overturned many of Britain's masculine sartorial conventions during the next two decades. Because Edward was one of the world's most high-profile arbiters of men's fashion throughout the 1920s and 1930s, his style choices were avidly watched by the press and every detail reported. In 1929, for instance, *Vanity Fair* noted several examples of American casualness demonstrated by the Prince. "The Prince of Wales on occasion wears no waistcoat with his formal day dress. He frequently wears a [turned-down] collar with this turn-out during the summer. And last winter, on one informal occasion, he wore a sweater and a polo shirt with his dinner jacket."[14] Throughout the 1920s, the Old World centers of fashion and their style setters increasingly looked to America for inspiration and innovation in menswear design. More and more, men's apparel makers and tailors around the world responded to the market demand for the easy-fit, easy-care styling of American men's clothing.

In addition to the sportiness of American men's style, American technology also significantly influenced world fashion. In 1910, the American Viscose Company introduced a synthetic "art silk" they called rayon. However, the early cellulose-based fibers produced textiles with too much sheen and brittleness to be an acceptable alternative to natural silk. Throughout the 1920s, a number of American manufacturers such as DuPont, Glanzstoff, and Enka refined the optical properties of rayon with delustering techniques and improved its tensile strength. The resulting forms of art silk were widely used in the mass production of a wide variety of ready-to-wear, especially hosiery, underwear, and sleepwear. (Figure 4-10.)

Another important technological innovation from America was the zipper. The earliest slide closure mechanisms were hook-and-eye fasteners introduced in the 1890s. But these early devices easily broke open and often rusted shut after laundering. In 1913, the first slide closure made

Figure 4-10. The quality of rayon fibers was greatly improved by American chemical manufacturers during the postwar years, resulting in yarns that more closely replicated the look and feel of natural silk. Textile makers applied the "art silk" yarns to numerous types of mass-produced apparel and home textiles. As this 1928 ad by the Rayon Institute avows, "rayon is serviceable, long wearing. Its smooth, fine textured surfaces resist soiling and launder easily. No special care is necessary—merely launder rayon as you would launder any other fine fabric. Rayon will not lose shape with repeated washings. Perspiration will nor injure it and, properly laundered, it will neither stretch nor shrink."

with interlocking metal teeth was developed, though with the same problems as the earlier fasteners. By the 1920s, the rubber manufacturer B. F. Goodrich had reengineered the slide closure, making it stronger and more rust-resistant as an innovative fastener for golashes. (Figure 4-11.) An executive of the firm gave the zipper its name. Throughout the late 1920s, the zipper was used for a wide assortment of accessories, luggage, and durable, utilitarian purposes such as removable coat linings and detachable children's leggings. A broader application to fashion, such as men's trousers and women's dresses did not occur until the mid-1930s.

In the postwar years, as American fashion businesses assimilated art deco from Europe and reciprocated with innovative technologies and influences of comfortable sportswear, the home-based industry began to get organized. In 1918, a group of investors collaborated with about fifty ready-to-wear manufacturers to develop a centralized location of showrooms and workshops in New York. Retail buying staffs from all over the country would have a one-stop market for virtually every category of apparel. The co-op selected two building sites on the west side of Seventh Avenue and, in 1921, opened with full occupancy. Over the following several years, more buildings were added along the avenue to provide merchants with ever more fashion options from American designers and makers. Seventh Avenue soon became America's "Garment Center Capital." In her book on the U.S. ready-to-wear industry, former *Vogue* editor-in-chief, Jessica Daves wrote:

> Seventh Avenue, as practically anyone not of the New Math generation knows, is a generic term. It includes a small section of New York, both on and off an avenue called Seventh, from 36th to 42nd Streets; a body of gamblers who are engaged in something called the dress business or the coat business or the suit business; each man gambles every season on his new collection–a collection that can run into hundreds of thousands of dollars at cost.[15]

Today, retail buyers and manufacturers from coast to coast know Seventh Avenue simply as "the market." The initials "S.A." used by trade publications for Seventh Avenue are instantly understood.

Dress and Identity: Ideas and Ideals of Masculinity During World War I and the 1920s

The 1910s was a decade of the world at war. American masculinity was defined by manly duty whether a man was serving as a doughboy in the trenches of France or supporting the war on the home front. The American soldier "glorified the male camaraderie of the trenches," wrote historian George Mosse.[16] Traditions of male honor and chivalry were played out amidst some of the most lethal forms of combat the world had ever known. Ultimately, by defeating the Kaiser and making the world safe for democracy, a generation of American men rescued the threatened sense of manhood that had persisted for decades.

The era was an age of warrior tribalism whether military or civilian. The homosocial bonding of men into exclusionary organizations reached its peak at this time: The military had not been larger since the Civil War, the varieties of college fraternal orders expanded, the Boy Scouts was founded, a resurgence of the Ku Klux Klan flourished, men's associations like the Rotary, Lions, and Kiwanis proliferated. (Figure 4-12.) Men who participated in these groups found comradeship and support for their

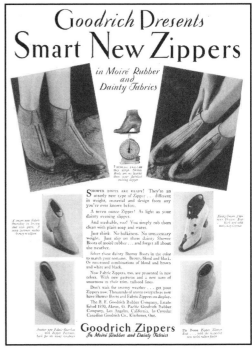

Figure 4-11. B. F. Goodrich reengineered the slide-closure fastener made with interlocking teeth as a convenient, water-tight closure for rubber golashes. Their version was christened the "zipper," named by a company executive for the sound it made when pulled close. The apparel industry of the 1920s quickly recognized the practical and modern style of zipper closures and adapted the device to numerous other clothing, accessory, and utilitarian items. B. F. Goodrich ad, 1928.

Figure 4-12. The turbulence of the war years in the 1910s kindled a new intensity of homosocial bonding for American men through the military, social organizations, and civic associations. Words in this Bull Durham tobacco ad like "clean-cut manhood," "comrade," and "brotherhood" not only suggested an enticing exclusivity for white middle-class men, but also emphatically asserted exclusion. The copy suggests that no matter where men meet, even through a brand of tobacco, "each recognizes in the other a man to his own liking." Ad 1914.

respective ideas of masculine purpose and behavior. Their unity was a significant factor in achieving goals for the common civic and social good, as they saw it. They also found solidarity in what they opposed. The "Red Scare" that Bolshevism might spread from Russia to America caused riots by demobilized soldiers in the late teens. Books like *The Rising Tide of Color* by Lathrop Stoddard (1920) inflamed racism and anti-immigration fears. D. W. Griffith's film *Birth of a Nation* (1915) institutionalized black stereotypes for millions of Americans. Sensationalized newspaper reports of the Navy's witch hunts for homosexuals between 1917 and 1919 further marginalized gay American men into a subculture class.

In the home, though, women's views of wartime masculinity were more pragmatic. They recognized the sacrifice and peril their men faced as warriors, but they knew that that masculine adventure would eventually conclude. Men would soon return to their homes and family and to normalcy. The counter to the chaos of world war was to be found in the stable, traditional roles of the "average" man, "who counts his life as empty unless he has a helpmate and children," asserted *Ladies' Home Journal* in 1916. In addition to, or in spite of, his warrior duty, and before he can in good conscience "write the great world poems, or paint the great world pictures, or uncover the vast and secret ways of nature," he must "be able to support himself and his family." Anything else, even the lure of war or any other compelling means for proving or reaffirming manliness, was a "selfishness of pure individualism." Within this "curse" of masculine selfishness as the *Journal* called it, might dwell the obsessive quest for power whether through the pursuit of money "as an end in itself" or through social status. "After enough money for comfort has been earned, then what?" asked the editors. To be "secure of meat, clothes, and fire" was a satisfactory validation of manhood while, on the other hand, the superfluity and "the desire to be fashionable" was an unsuitable ambition for men. "The restless and insatiable passion to pass for creatures more distinguished than they are" causes "more positive misery...than all the desolations of war or the accidents of mortality." To women of the turbulent 1910s, "The really successful man is he who has lived a happy and useful life with wife and children."[17]

Hence, during the crisis years of the 1910s, both sexes seemed to agree that conformity, not individualism was the preeminent attribute of manliness. Masculine power was achieved and sustained by belonging—whether as members in the military or in civic and social groups, or through a familial patriarchy.

After the war, though, the American soldier hero came home to discover enormous change. The world war had transformed and reshaped more than European regimes and global geography. American society was suddenly so different that a return to normalcy for the soldier was not possible. In just a few years during the teens, the languid world of Edwardian simplicity had been abruptly and irrevocably supplanted by a frenetic era of fast machines, mass marketing, and consumerism. The Ford Motor Company epitomized the blend of all three phenomena by its rapid, assembly-line production of the Model T, which was mass marketed to the American consumer at a cost of less than $500. Everyone was suddenly mobile and in a hurry. "A first-class revolt against accepted American order was certainly taking place," wrote Frederick Lewis Allen in *Only Yesterday*. "A whole generation had been infected by the eat-drink-and-be-merry-for-tomorrow-we-die spirit."[18]

Likewise, the traditional roles of women had significantly shifted. In 1920, women were at last enfranchised, but the long-anticipated threat to the American male from this diminishment of masculine power did not materialize. Contrary to the alarm raised for decades by many men, the New Woman with her power of the vote did not take over statehouses, governorships, Congress, or boardrooms. The New Woman did, however, cast off the remnants of the Victorian corseted "gentler sex" and emerged as the flapper—a woman of age nineteen to forty-nine who wore dresses cropped to the knees, bobbed her hair, dabbed on makeup in public, smoked, drank, danced the shimmy, and experimented with pre- and extramarital sex. This further erosion of traditional gender identities and roles was far more threatening for some men than sharing power at the polls.

Popular culture of the 1920s often represented young men as collegiate sheiks with scantily-dressed shebas on their arms. Older men were represented as business tycoons in three-piece tailored suits who were preoccupied with the stock market tickertape and indulgence in a lavish lifestyle. F. Scott Fitzgerald's Gatsby epitomized both types of men. The Victorian natural gentleman had become a faded memory. If the former doughboys could not return to prewar normalcy, then they could forget the trauma of that masculine experience in the ballyhoo of the Jazz Age high life. "The man's man," according to *Vanity Fair* in 1928, "is a jolly old Dick, who leads his friends to his den where his choicest drinks, smokes and stories are dispensed." For the New Woman, continued *Vanity Fair,* the "perfect husband" of the time had few prerequisites: "checks in the checkbook, money in the bank, and ink in the good old fountain pen."[19] (Figure 4-13.) Men of the 1920s had thus surrendered their masculine conventions to a modern, youth-oriented pop culture and gone "soft" according to journalist Edward Ruttenber in 1924: "soft fabrics, soft hats, and soft heads."[20]

From the mid-1910s until the second half of the 1920s, men's dress and masculine identity reflected a national obsession with the youthful warrior. The power look of the bulky, over-padded clothing of the Edwardian era was abandoned in favor of the slim silhouette of the lithe young man. Jackets and trousers narrowed significantly for a tight, contouring fit. Natural shoulderlines emphasized a feline agility rather than brawn, and shorter jackets made legs look longer and slimmer.

In addition, dress and identity became more generational than ever before in American history. In the Victorian and Edwardian eras, the

Figure 4-13. The legacy of a transformed masculinity in the Jazz Age boomtimes of the 1920s is of hedonistic young men and money-focused older men. The reality, though, was that, for most working- and middle-class American men, the manhood orthodoxies of their Victorian fathers largely remained the norm. Silhouettes by Erma Paul Allen, 1928.

It's all right to be stylish if—

the style is not wasteful of material and labor; if it is refined and in keeping
with these war days; if it is applied to lasting all-wool fabrics that represent
the highest clothes economy

The quality in our clothes saves for you; the styles are made without wasting material

Hart Schaffner & Marx

Figure 4-14. Men's suits of the war years into
the early 1920s retained the trim fit of the early
1910s. Sack coats were cut with natural shoulders, tapered sleeves, and short hemlines;
trousers were slender and snug. Hart Schaffner
and Marx suits, 1918.

young men of eighteen dressed in the same suit styles as their
fathers and grandfathers, differentiated only minimally by accessories such as slouch hats or, within reason, a bold necktie.
Instead, the Jazz Age youth adapted sportswear more broadly,
dispensing with suits and altering social conventions in the
process. Fads in dress such as elephantine Oxford bags combined
with boldly patterned sportscoats expressed a new freedom in the
interpretation of masculinity. The collegiate embraced his youth
rather than trying to rush through it by growing whiskers and
replicating the conventions and dress identity of older generations.

Suits and Formal Dress 1915–1929

The First World War brought an end to the Belle Epoche—
the beautiful era. In America, the prewar years had been a time of
the Bull Moose Teddy Roosevelt and his successor, the ponderous
Big Bill Taft. American men's clothes had reflected the physical
power of its leaders and, by extension, the nation's power on the
world stage. The massive, bulky suit coats were over-padded and
cut with a full, loose body and big sleeves as if encasing the
physique of a Hercules; trousers were pegged with an exaggerated
fullness through the thighs as if to accommodate powerful, energetic legs. The look asserted that all American men were mature,
beefy, and commanding.

All that changed when the world went to war, and nations
around the globe focused on the new hero: the youthful, lean
warrior. Men's suits lost their padded bulk and mass, becoming instead
slim and narrow. Sack suit coats were cut with natural, unpadded shoulders; narrow, tapered sleeves; raised, articulated waists; and shortened
skirts. Trousers, too, narrowed so much that, as one editor observed, "No
gentleman would accept a pair of trousers from his tailor if he could get
into them with his shoes on. Every time he bent over he must have mur-
mured a prayer that his seams would have strength."[21] (Figure 4-14.) In
addition, the slender look of menswear was bolstered by the wartime
conservation restrictions on the use of wool and many other materials of
the fashion industry. Among the sartorial reductions in "superfluities" to
help the war effort—what *Vanity Fair* called a "skeletonization" of men's
clothing—were the back belts on jackets that had become so popular in
the mid-1910s, patch pockets and pocket flaps, double-breasted closures,
gauntlet sleeves on outerwear, trouser cuffs, and even the linings of summer sack coats.[22] Moreover, for warm weather attire, silk became an
acceptable alternative to rationed wool. "The time was, not so very long
ago, when a man was conspicuous—and to that degree in bad taste—
when he wore a silk suit," noted a fashion editor. "But fortunately...we are
becoming more sensible in matters of dress as time goes on and silk is
taking its rightful place as a material for summer clothes for men."[23]
Ready-to-wear retailers were more than happy to stock suits of Shantung
silk rather than have empty racks and shelves from wool shortages.

Another wartime shortage that impacted the look of menswear was
the depletion of textile dyes. Germany had been the world's foremost
exporter of aniline dyes and related chemicals. When the war began in
1914, the production of dyes was limited as the German and Austrian

Figure 4-15. The postwar jazz suit was notorious for its tight, "sausage casing" fit. The jacket was cut with a cinched, raised waist accentuated by a seam all around or a three-quarter back belt and a flared skirt with a deep center vent at the back. Jazz suits from Reliable Tailoring catalog, 1920.

chemical industries converted to wartime production needs. Ironically, this abrupt cut off of dyes coincided with an effort by menswear makers to push for a greater variety of colors in men's suits. In a style guide from 1914, a contributing editor praised the Bond Street tailors Pope and Bradley for producing suits "in the most beautiful shades of subdued purples, blues, greens, browns, and even reds."[24] And why not, insisted another writer. "Why should men's noble form be imprisoned in blacks and browns and non-committal blues? Why should his evening wear insist upon the funereal note of the mute and the habit of the waiter?"[25] The answer became only too apparent as the battles in France and Belgium began in earnest. Simply put, the zeitgeist of the war years precluded the application of vivid color and ornamentation in dress. The "war spirit," a journalist reminded Americans in 1918, was "both sober and steadfast," and men's clothing should be "no less so."[26] Consequently, late Edwardian era suits of vivid colors like mulberry, heather green, and sienna brown, were no longer appropriate.

When the doughboys at last came home, they immediately discarded their khakis and climbed back into their civvies (civilian clothes). They were delighted to discover that the slim cut suits they had mothballed almost three years earlier were still the correct style. One of the slim suit variations popular with young men during 1918–23 came to be known as the jazz suit. In addition to the perpetuation of what one editor referred to as the tight, "sausage casing" fit,[27] the jazz suit jacket was variously cinched by a raised, military-style waist seam all around or a three-quarter back belt, and the skirt was given a flare by a deep center vent at the back. (Figure 4-15.) Other details sometimes included open-vent sleeve cuffs, a close set of the button closures, and a deep roll shawl collar.

As has been the standard for menswear over the centuries, when a shift in style occurs, it begins slowly, almost imperceptibly, until it is done and can be recognized in hindsight as a significant change. Thus was the transition from snug, narrow suits of the war years that actually lasted into the early 1920s to a more muscular silhouette with broad shoulders, subtly tapered waist, and slim hips. (Figure 4-16.) The transition began around 1922–23, and was distinctive enough by 1925 to be the subject of fashion reports and ads. "We are making them now," proclaimed a Hart Schaffner and Marx suit ad in 1925. "The shoulders are considerably wider; chest effects are fuller; buttons and pockets are higher; the coats are snug at the hips and suggest greater height."[28] This new broad-shoul-dered look was not a revival of the Edwardian upholstered look, though. The athletic "V" silhouette of jackets was achieved instead with a new cut that retained the popular natural shoulderline of the war years. "In order to have broad shoulders," reported *Vanity Fair* in 1925, "which give not

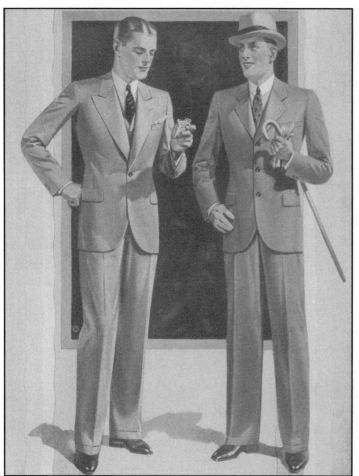

Figure 4-16. During the early 1920s, men's suits evolved from a slim, tight silhouette into the athletic look with wide shoulders, broad chest, trim hips, and full trousers. Single- and double-breasted suits by National Tailoring, 1928.

only style, but freedom of movement and comfort, the tailor is forced to cut a coat which has wrinkles, both in front and back, in the vicinity of the armholes; for without this extra material, the coat would have to be unnaturally padded, and then *comfort* of the broad shouldered coat would be nonexistent."[29] In addition, the waist was more subtly defined by the cut in the back rather than the contoured side seams of the 1910s. The new shoulder dimensions were a particular challenge for ready-to-wear makers because the unpadded width affected the fit of the collar, which could gap and look "disarranged."[30] With the correct cut, the result of the new sack coat was a fuller, looser fit with a straight hang in the front from broad shoulders and a slight definition of the waist in the back.

The origins of this athletic aesthetic of suit coats is credited to the famous London tailor Frederick Scholte. During the 1910s, the Dutch immigrant had been apprenticed to the tailors who furnished the Royal Household Guards. When he set up his own shop after the war, his goal was to endow the average man with the ideal masculine silhouette of the young guardsman but without the Edwardian artifice of restrictive padding and heavy linings. To achieve the V-shape Scholte admired, he developed his famous drape cut, sometimes called the blade cut, whereby

Figure 4-17. Color options and ensemble product marketing helped feed the materialism and insatiable mass consumption of the 1920s. Advertising and catalogs printed in full color coaxed and cajoled the American consumer into wanting more and buying more. Ads 1927-1929.

discreet horizontal drapes narrowed across the shoulder blades from the roomy armholes down to the raised waistline. Also, by aligning the shoulder roll of the sleeve with the triceps, the unpadded shoulder line looked natural and broad. Other details included rolling the lapels rather than making them lie flat and tapering the sleeves to the wrists thereby providing the illusion of athletic pectorals and a trim waist.

The trousers, too, became fuller with pleated fronts and wide legs that tapered slightly from the knee to the ankle. Cuffed styles were still shorter, extending to just at the instep so as not to break the front crease; plain hems were longer with a break in the front crease. With the return of a greater fullness, pleats became an important detail again. The inverted pleat (facing in) was a popular variation in the 1920s. No longer were men's hands "trapped" in pockets as before, and the fuller cut was "more graceful looking while walking," producing a "better stride" than the slim snugness of the wartime fit.[31]

With the advent of a new look in men's suits in the second half of the 1920s, menswear makers reopened the debate about color, clothing, and masculinity. The exigencies of wartime conservation and conservatism had ended the flurry of color advocacy by some tailors and ready-to-wear makers more than a decade earlier. But in the Jazz Age, color exploded across American mass culture like never before. (Figure 4-17.) Auto makers such as Dodge and Chevrolet introduced car models in vibrant hues with matching interiors, eroding the dominant market share of Ford, whose Model T famously was available only in black. The ubiquitous black telephone yielded to vivid color options. Even furnaces, locked away in dark, dank basements, were now produced in rich jeweltone enamels. Ensemble merchandising became a tour de force marketing strategy of the era, encouraging consumption with color-coordinated bedrooms, kitchens, and bathrooms. Tiles, countertops, cabinets, flooring, wallpaper, fixtures, appliances, textiles, and decorative accessories were designed and marketed with an emphasis on color. As a trade publication advised in 1927, "No better idea of getting goods quickly into the hands of the consumer has shown itself than this idea of putting color in the product....If you believe your customers are not spending enough, then give them color. They will spend more and will be happy while they do it."[32] In his study of advertising and the American dream in the 1920s, Roland Marchand explained the economic phenomenon: "The popularization of the idea of the ensemble not only expanded the definitions of consumer 'necessities' and schooled the eye in the recognition of obsolescence; it also represented a notable success in the transfer of elite tastes and ideas to the consumer masses and provided a new vehicle for the 'personalization' of mass-produced goods."[33] And to showcase this burgeoning of color in mass production and mass merchandising, color advertising likewise surged. Color ads abounded in magazines, and entire mail-order catalogs were printed in full color to the delight of the American consumer.

For the apparel industry, the idea of the color-coordinated ensemble was applied with the same fervor as that of the makers of cars, appliances, and bed linens. Sportswear, discussed later in this chapter, was especially receptive to influences of moderne design and the use of color. But the traditionalists in the suit-making business were more wary and resistant. Modernity was not a hallmark of men's suits despite the distinctive new shapes and dimensions of the athletic silhouette. Thus, the application of color to men's suits faced two obstacles: the traditions of more than a century of simple, sober masculine dress—the postrevolutionary renunciation of eighteenth-century aristocratic splendor—and, according to fashion stylists of the time, the inability of men to understand color. In 1928, *Vanity Fair* addressed the issue:

> The question of whether it is good taste for men to use color freely in their dress has long been the subject or discussion. Most of the prejudice against the introduction of color in men's clothes is really based on the fact that certain colors are not and never will be appropriate for men. But that does not mean that all colors should be barred. Another factor which has mitigated against the use of color is that very often, either through carelessness or ignorance of color harmonies, effects are achieved which, in themselves are not smart or becoming and which immediately attract undue attention.[34]

When in doubt about color, style guides suggested a relatively safe rule for men who were "not color conscious." "Instead of combining contrasting colors with uncertain results...stick to the one basic color for clothes and accessories."[35] In other words, for a blue suit, coordinate the shirt, tie, pocket handkerchief, and socks with matching shades of blue.

Although suit makers and consumers were reluctant to experiment too creatively with colors, they were receptive to a wide assortment of fabrics. Wool flannel increasingly became a favorite for summer suits even though the material is not at all cool. Flannel had been common for casual suits worn in the country, but, in the postwar years, it was a popular alternative to the traditional worsteds even for town wear. As resort wear, a dark blue flannel jacket was worn with white flannel trousers. (Figure 4-18.) White flannel was the epitome of affluence since its pristine appearance attested to a large wardrobe and sufficient income to

Figure 4-18. The combination of a dark blue flannel jacket and white flannel trousers was the most popular suiting attire for resorts and country visits. Because white flannel seldom could be worn more than a couple of times before needing to be dry cleaned, the look was the epitome of affluence and class distinction. Bruner flannel jacket and trousers, 1928.

Figure 4-19. Unlike the sack suit of the 1920s that evolved into the new athletic proportions, the formal dress suit retained the trim snugness of its Victorian predecessor. In addition, changes in details such as the width or length of coat lapels were so subtle and minimal that fashion journalists seldom took notice. Tail coat by National Tailoring, 1929.

afford frequent dry cleaning. "White flannel trousers are not good for more than two wearings without being sent to the cleaners," complained a fashion journalist in 1921, "and unfortunately few cleaners return them the same shade of white they originally had from the tailor."[36] For the middle class male who sometimes spent weekends in the country rather than joining seasonal migrations to resorts and who may have only one pair of flannel trousers, a popular alternative to white was one of several off-white shades variously called names like oatmeal or putty. These shades did not require cleaning so often. When summertime heat and humidity made wearing flannel suits especially disagreeable, the comfort-seeking man gladly donned one of the new tub cotton suits, so named because they could be washed in a tub instead of requiring dry cleaning. White was the most popular, but tub cotton suits also came in light shades of gray, taupe, and tan, or dark mixtures of blue, green, and brown. White or natural linen also remained a favorite warm weather material for suits. In the 1920s, summer suits made of linen came to be called the Palm Beach suit, named after the famous Florida resort.

The frock coat suit largely vanished in America during the 1920s. Mass-merchandiser catalogs no longer offered the frock coat after the mid-teens. However, since it persisted in England because George V insisted that his sons and courtiers wear one, the Edwardian-styled frock coat occasionally surfaced in America as a ceremonial garment for diplomatic or academic events.

Like the sack suit, formal suits underwent a myriad of style changes. The general look of the tuxedo or tail coat may have remained largely consistent, but, to the trained eyes of the tailor and the gentleman, the alterations in details that developed during the postwar years were significant. In his 1926 style guide, George Curtis asserted that the evening dress suit had "changed drastically in the last few years":

Figure 4-20. As with the formal tail coat, the semiformal morning coat also remained trim with a narrow-fitting cutaway coat and slim trousers. Morning suit with one-button cutaway coat, matching vest, and striped chervot trousers by Bruner, 1928.

> The prewar evening coat with its long lapel and mid-Victorian appearance, and the white waistcoat rounded in front and lacking its present day character, would, cut with care, fit almost any chest and waist, however protuberant either may have been. Now, the evening coat with its short lapel and the V-shaped white waistcoat are both the most difficult garments to make for any man which is not absolutely normal in build, and almost impossible to fit correctly upon a man who does not put them on properly and wear the right kind of well-fitting dress shirt beneath.[37]

Despite these drastic changes, though, the tail coat was an exception to the major reconstruction of men's suit coats that evolved during the early

He Opens It Up

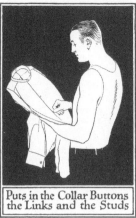

Puts in the Collar Buttons the Links and the Studs

Buttons the Back Button

Figure 4-21. Open back dress shirts for evening wear allowed men cooler comfort during summertime balls and dances. Open back shirt by Arrow, 1926.

1920s. Unlike adopting the new, looser fit and athletic shape of the sack coat, the tail coat remained snug and trim with a natural shoulder line, narrow sleeves, and a tight, contoured waist. The white stiff-front shirt with wing collar, plain white pique or silk vest, and white bow tie remained the standards. (Figure 4-19.) Any variations on the formula were regarded as "atrocities in clothes," especially the "cabaret" trend that briefly emerged at the end of the war, which included a "freakish" soft shirt with turned down collar, white bow tie edged in black, and white silk brocade vest with long end points extending below the coat front.[38]

For daytime formal dress, the cutaway morning coat was still de rigueur. As with the tail coat, the look remained the same as a generation earlier and was also impervious to the new athletic cut of the sack coat. (Figure 4-20.) Its one-button closure cinched the waist and hugged the hips. Traditionalists preferred coats of black cheviot while younger men, influenced particularly by the Prince of Wales, opted for slate gray. Vests could contrast with the coat in white pique, pearl gray, or faun, or the vest could be of the same cloth as the coat. The proper trousers for a morning coat were gray worsted with black pin stripes or black with white pin stripes. For men who wished to follow the style variation of the Prince, check trousers were acceptable as well so long as the checks were so tiny that, from a distance, the appearance was of a solid gray. Even the Victorian puffed ascot tie lingered into the 1920s as the correct neckwear for the cutaway suit.

In America, the comfortable tuxedo continued to eclipse the tail coat for evening wear. The favored dinner jacket style alternated year to year between the shawl collar and the peaked lapel. Widths of lapels and V-front depths also varied, but always in miniscule measurements. Collegiate men opted for one-button closures; young businessmen preferred the double-breasted style; and mature men more often chose the two-button single-breasted coat. In any case, the key was for the jacket "to be cut in a manner to set well, when not buttoned; that is, close into the figure and not dependent on the one usual button to hold it to the body."[39] Tuxedo trousers followed the trends of the sack suits and became full with pleated fronts. A black tie and black vest remained correct—for the most part. One of the numerous dress controversies of the era initiated, of course, by the younger generation was the combination of a white vest with a dinner jacket.[40] Traditionalists viewed the look as bad form despite its popularity.

By the end of the 1920s, young men even abandoned the dinner suit vest. Its form-fitting snugness was hot in summertime and impeded the freeform exuberance needed for a good turn on the jazz dance floor, particularly the Charleston. To distinguish the dinner jacket sans vest from a sack coat, lapels were made with "glossy" silk.[41] For the mature traditionalist who refused to depart from the vest, a backless version became immensely popular. So the garment would sit correctly and not shift about as the wearer moved, it was designed with a hidden linen tab in the front that fastened to the trouser waistband button, and in the back a strip of linen buttoned across the shoulders, and a second adjustable strip buckled in the back at the waist.

Adding to the comfort of the loose tuxedo jacket and full, pleated trousers were the open back dress shirts that became popular in the 1920s. (Figure 4-21.) The bosom front and cuffs were made of a stiffly starched pique to preserve the formal look. The cotton sleeves and body coupled with the vented back made the open back shirt cool and comfortable.

The rigorous debate in the fashion industry about color in men's suits extended to evening dress as well. "Black cloth takes the character and personality out of a man's face," complained a style guide of the time.[42] In 1928, The *American Mercury* insisted it was "ridiculous" that the tuxedo was only made in black. "One of the great strides in man's emancipation should come in the guise of colorful dinner suits," continued the editor.[43] Because men are "slaves to tradition and 'correctitude'," said stylist George Curtis, it would take a revolution for the "extreme smartness" of dress like a "maroon evening coat and trousers."[44] But the dangers of breaking certain rules of evening dress propriety could be dire. A man dare not "alleviate the funereal aspect of his evening mode in the smallest degree," concluded the *Mercury*. "He must wear white shirts, black ties, and black socks, or get black looks."[45] In 1925, *Vanity Fair* reported on a gentleman who wore a dark blue dress suit to a fashionable ball, for which he was "regarded with suspicion ever since."[46] Even though in many aspects, menswear had begun to edge away, by degree, from the century-old sober simplicity of men's dress, evening attire remained a last bastion of finite conservatism.

Shirts 1915–1929

The ongoing controversies about the use of color in men's suiting did not apply to shirts. Even at the despairing depths of the Great War in 1918, when all Americans were expected to behave and look serious, men's shirts were vividly colored and boldly patterned. One objecting journalist reminded readers that shirtings in "rainbow stripings...are neither in keeping with the spirit of the times nor are they at any time in keeping with the dictates of good taste."[47] Nevertheless, throughout the wartime and postwar years, the American male could not get enough of colored and patterned dress shirts, sports shirts, or work shirts. (Figure 4-22 and Color Plate 4.) Ready-to-wear manufacturers responded to the market demand with an infinite variety of palettes and prints applied to a wide assortment of textiles. Even men who wore custom-made shirts opted for the modern look of vivacious hues and patterns.

The American male also demanded comfort in his shirts. Following

Figure 4-22. For the younger generation, the unstarched soft collar shirt increasingly became a preferred alternative to the stiff, detachable collar shirt for business dress. In addition, the market demand for vivid colors and bold prints was eagerly met by ready-to-wear makers that mass produced an endless variety of richly hued, affordable styles. Patterned dress shirts from Montgomery Ward, 1928.

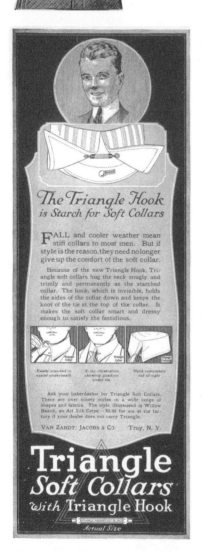

Figure 4-23. Soft shirt and collar manufacturers introduced numerous constructs and devices for holding the points in place and preventing curling or unevenness. Triangle hook ad, 1919.

the war, the stiff detachable collar declined rapidly in popularity in favor of the soft collar. It was the era of the "cult of the soft collar," as George Curtis referred to the new preference:

> Quite a few years ago no self-respecting man would be seen wearing a limp, unstarched soft collar, unless engaged in taking some form of exercise or sport in the country. Today the soft collar has become almost universal on almost all occasions, except those ceremonial. You will see the best-dressed and most conservative of men wearing silk, thin woolen taffeta, poplin or unstarched zephyr...and very nice they look.[48]

Despite the great comfort and convenience of the soft collar, though, some styling problems emerged that many men found objectionable. To hold the collar ends in place, collar bars and pins were employed behind the tie knot, but pins often pulled the collar out of shape causing the tips to curl up. Innumerable stays and other devices were invented to hold the ends of the soft collar in place, but most were not successful, especially when compared to the starched detachable collar. (Figure 4-23.) But the problems with the soft collar holding its shape was less important to the American male than being free of the immovable chokehold of the rigid, starched collar. Still, enough men continued to wear the stiff detachable collar for haberdasheries and mail order retailers to keep them inventoried through the end of the twenties.

As the soft collar shirt edged out the detachable collar, the economic impact on the menswear business was significant. By the midtwenties, *Men's Wear* warned the shirt and collar businesses, "Today there are hoards of young men who have never bought a starched collar and the gloomy analysis of some collar producers is that these fellows will span the distance from the cradle to the grave and never know the dignity of the 'great white wall of China,' the starched collar."[49] In addition to the reduction in the manufacturing of detachable collars, related businesses such as collar button makers and even advertising firms were also negatively impacted.

Work Clothes 1915–1929

Following a brief postwar recession, jobs were again plentiful in the America of the 1920s. Great masses of men went to work at jobs that did

Figure 4-24. Work shirts were mass produced in heavy, durable chambray, denim, and wool in almost as many colors and prints as soft collar dress shirts. Work shirts from Charles Williams catalog, 1925.

not require a business suit. They did not think about the proper cut of a sack coat shoulderline or the correctness of a tuxedo lapel. The clothes they wore to work daily needed to be comfortable, functional, and durable. Ready-to-wear makers and mass merchandisers provided broad assortments of work clothes suited to every hard-working Joe.

Work shirts were mass produced in heavyweight chambray or denim for summer and thick cotton or wool flannel for winter. (Figure 4-24.) In keeping with the market demand of the time, work shirts were produced in colors and prints as striking as those of dress shirts. The 1929 Sears wishbook offered an assortment of Hercules brand work shirts that were "good to the eye—good for the body." Each style featured twelve points of quality including:

Extra wide cuffs; a fist will go through without unbuttoning

Extra long side seams; no unsightly opening above the trousers

Triple stitched seams

Double thick shoulder yokes

Interlined collar and cuffs[50]

Sears work trousers were "stubborn brutes for wear" made with "indestructible pockets" and a waistband with outside belt loops and inside suspender buttons.[51] Curiously enough, though, many styles of work pants were made with cuffs, which not only would easily collect dirt or factory debris, but also could catch on equipment and tools causing an accident.

Figure 4-25. Work breeches were worn by men whose specialized jobs required significant time out of doors. The distinctive flare at the outer thighs and tight closure below the knee had been a traditional look for military uniforms and riding jodhpurs since the late nineteenth century. Moleskin work breeches from Dutchess Trousers, 1926.

Figure 4-26. Denim bib overalls and jackets were the preferred work clothes of the laboring man. Mass merchandisers offered numerous varieties cut with plenty of fullness for ease of movement and nonbinding comfort. Seams were reinforced with copper rivets for greater durability and wear. Blue denim overalls, jeans, and matching jackets from Montgomery Ward, 1928.

Another variety of work pants that was more specialized were jodhpurs, more commonly called breeches. Their distinctive shape featured a balloon-like fullness from the hip to the knee at the outside thigh that tapered to a tight fit over the knee and calf. They fastened variously with laces, buckles, or buttons at the outside knee seam. The inside thigh fitted closely to the leg and was reinforced with various stitches. Styles were made of corduroy, moleskin, cotton whipcord, and leather. (Figure 4-25.) Breeches had been a popular sports and riding garment as well as a distinctive part of U.S. military uniforms since the late nineteenth century. After the Great War, volumes of surplus khaki army breeches were sold by Sears and other mail order retailers for less than one dollar per pair. Breeches were popular with aviators, chauffeurs, surveyors, and field construction foremen.

Blue denim bib overalls, coveralls, and buckle back jeans—worn with a matching blue denim jacket—were the work uniforms of farmers, ranchers, railroad crews, miners, carpenters, and bricklayers, to name a

Figure 4-27. As more and more Americans took up various sports, they scrutinized and copied the casual, comfortable clothing styles of their favorite athletes both on and off the field. Where once sports clothes had been specialized apparel usually found in sporting goods sections of stores and catalogs, sportswear now became a category of casual fashions for weekends and other leisure time. Sportswear Inc. ad, 1929.

few. (Figure 4-26.) The garments were cut fuller than other work clothes for the maximum ease of movement and nonbinding comfort. Quality denim work clothes were reinforced with copper rivets at every strain point.

Sportswear 1915–1929

Much has been written about the sports-obsessed American male of the postwar years. The 1920s especially was an era of tremendous sports achievements and fan enthusiasm. Everywhere the athleticism of America's Flaming Youth triumphed and was heralded with great fanfare and mass publicity. Names of sports heroes of the time still resonate today: the awesome baseball slugger Babe Ruth; boxing brawler Jack Dempsey; gridiron legend Knute Rockne; tennis champion "Big Bill" Tilden; golfing great Bobby Jones; and Olympic swimming gold medalist Johnny Weismuller. Radio broadcasts, mass media, and endorsement advertising made these and other athletes household names.

As the middle and working classes pursued their consumer aspirations, they emulated their sports idols and ventured outdoors to play hard on weekends and holidays. Golf and tennis were no longer largely the provenance of the affluent. With the conveniences of the modern machine age, working Joes and Janes enjoyed ever greater leisure time and carted their golf and tennis equipment to the local community or college fields to play.

They also scrutinized the images of star athletes in movie newsreels, magazines, and ads for how to dress the part of the seasoned golfer and tennis player. As a result, the expansion and variety of sportswear in the 1920s was explosive. Where once sports clothing had been specialty

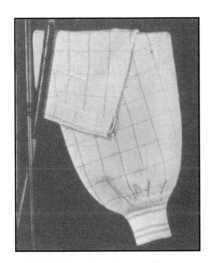

Figure 4-28. The old style of golf knickers became looser and fuller in the 1920s. The new styles came to be called "plus fours" because the baggy excess of fabric formed a blouson at the knees that drooped about four inches over the tops of the stockings. Left, plus fours from B. Altman, 1929; right, plus fours with knit kneebands from Knitgrip, 1928.

apparel that mass merchandisers usually scattered about in their mail-order catalogs adjacent to the corresponding athletic equipment, sportswear now became a category of fashion apparel. (Figure 4-27.) "This question of style in sportswear is a ticklish thing!" declared a 1929 apparel ad. "From Atlantic to Pacific and from the Canadian line to the Rio Grande authentic sports style is now available to the man who wants to be properly turned out."[52] The comfort and style appeal of American sportswear quickly and broadly extended beyond the golf links and tennis courts to become acceptable dress for the spectators as well. As the Prince of Wales noted in his autobiography (writing as the Duke of Windsor), "[Sports clothes] above all mark the democratic century with its swing towards freedom and ease. The change in this direction has been strikingly rapid."[53]

The most versatile and common sports clothes were baggy knickers. Following the end of wartime rationing and textile conservation, knickers ballooned into voluminous "plus fours," so named at the time because the cut was so full that they formed a blouson that drooped about four inches over the tops of the knee stockings. By the late 1920s, knickers were so baggy that some fitted more as plus sixes or even plus eights. One of the innovations of the plus fours was the introduction in 1924 of an elasticized rib knit band at the knees, which tucked more neatly into golf stockings than the usual buckle straps. (Figure 4-28.) Although the plus fours were still largely associated with golf and country leisure wear, the style was more broadly adapted to other activities as well, particularly winter sports. Style guides mostly insisted that fitted breeches, modeled after riding breeches, were the proper dress for winter sports, but overwhelmingly men preferred the comfort of plus fours.

The baggy plus fours initiated one of the most famous fashion fads of the 1920s—the Oxford bags. Credit for the enormously wide trousers, some with legs at twenty-five-inches in circumference at the cuff, is given to the college boys at Oxford and Cambridge in England.[54] There, students were prohibited from wearing the sporty, comfortable plus fours to class, so rather than rush back to their rooms to change clothes after classes, they had trousers made with legs wide enough to wear over their plus fours. In the midtwenties, American college boys returning from England brought the fad back to the United States where the look was an instant hit on campuses coast to coast. (Figure 4-29.) British style guides of the time objected not so much to the cut and fit of Oxford bags as to the pretentious usurpation of a university trait. "Thousands of young men about the country who had never been up at Oxford, and would never be likely to get there, flaunted themselves before the eyes of an amused populace in the snobbish desire, one can only suppose, to be taken for a varsity undergraduate," sneered a British menswear stylist.[55] But in America, such class distinctions were irrelevant. Instead, the look itself was objectionable. One journalist complained of the Oxford bags:

> The way they bag around the ankles, all but smothering the crude but generous square-toed shoes, is a subject about which much might be written, There is very little shoe visible at all because the back cuff of the trousers rests so loosely upon the ground that the sagging super-structure seems in imminent danger of falling down completely. These strange trousers are usually made of a grey material which, when they are viewed from the rear, completes the illusion of a departing elephant.[56]

Figure 4-29. Oxford bags were trousers cut with exaggerated, wide legs—some expanding to a circumference of twenty-five inches at the cuff. The look was especially popular with collegiate young men in the second half of the 1920s. Illustration from *Grim Youth,* 1929.

Flaming Youth, however, embraced the new style that was uniquely theirs—a distinct departure from the commonplace navy or charcoal sack suit and a clear rebellion against convention. "There is a demand for absurd things," wrote a *Men's Wear* editor in 1927. "Absurdity wins. One has only to gaze reflectively on the apparel of young men and women to grasp the fact that both sexes are hell-bent for extremes."[57]

Another collegiate fashion fad of the postwar years was the beer suit. "These suits are nothing more nor less than overalls and jackets made of white denim," reported *Vanity Fair* in 1926. "They are the same as the outfits worn by plasterers and masons."[58] According to "Tigernet," Princeton's alumni Web site, beer suits were first adopted by their class of 1917. The costume was exclusively the prerogative of the seniors of the graduating class worn in the early spring. Princeton lore holds that students wore the utilitarian costumes to protect their clothing while quaffing beer at a local tavern. Black arm bands were added to the sleeves in 1920 to mourn the enactment of Prohibition.[59] The backs of the white denim jackets were soon covered with various graffiti, hand drawn cartoons, and stenciled college emblems. "These 'beer' suits are never laundered," *Vanity Fair* noted, "and by commencement time this is evident."[60]

Although the short-sleeved sport shirt was introduced at the beginning of the century, it was to be worn only while playing tennis. Once off the court, men were expected to change into long-sleeved shirts, ties, and jackets to join the spectators. By the 1920s, though, the comfortable short-sleeved sport shirt was increasingly seen among the spectators, especially at resorts like Palm Beach where style trendsetters explored new ideas of fashion and dress protocol. Similarly, the short-sleeved knit polo shirt with its keyhole neckline and short, ribbed collar also became a favorite at vacation spots in the late 1920s. (Figure 4-30.) One of the notable innovations of sport shirt designs of the period was the introduction of the banded bottom shirt in 1925. (Figure 4-31.) The hip-hugging style, as the ad copy shown here cites, was promoted by its makers as ideal for action on the tennis court or golf greens, but versatile enough to be tucked into trousers for a comfortable, dressier look.

Increasingly throughout the 1920s, comfort was a chief consideration of the American male's wardrobe choices even at the expense of discarding some masculine dress conventions. "Men in America will disregard anything for the sake of their comfort," observed an editor in 1921.[61] The soft collar shirt edged out the starched, detachable collar for business dress; short-sleeved sport shirts were adopted for leisure time at home and weekend play; and knitwear became a favorite alternative to suit coats. Although for decades sweaters had been popular commodity clothing items offered by mass merchandisers, styles and colors were usually limited despite the efficiency and variety of mass-production knitting technologies. But in the early 1920s, icons of men's fashion and style

Figure 4-30. Among the new types of casual sportswear appropriated from athletic apparel by the comfort-seeking spectator was the knit polo shirt. Polo shirt and riding jodhpurs from B. Altman, 1929.

Figure 4-31. The banded bottom sport shirt was introduced in 1925 as a solution to the discomfort and disheveled look of shirt tails pulled loose during exertion on the tennis court or golf links. Wachusett Shirt ad, 1925.

Figure 4-32. In 1922, the Prince of Wales began playing golf dressed in colorful, boldly patterned Fair Isle sweaters instead of the traditional tailored golf jacket. Almost immediately, men around the globe followed his example, adapting multicolored cardigans, pullovers, and sweater vests as favored casual dress. U.S. knitwear makers could hardly keep up with the demand for Americanized versions of the famous British woolens. Tom Wye Sweater ad, 1925.

began to advocate a wider application of the comfortable and striking sweaters in the masculine wardrobe. In 1922, the Prince of Wales appeared at the St. Andrews Golf Club in Scotland wearing a "multicolored Fair Isle sweater with its jigsaw of patterns" rather than his usual belted golf jacket.[62] The Prince so enjoyed the comfort and eye-catching style of Fair Isle sweaters and boldly patterned knee stockings with his plus fours that he was often photographed wearing them on the golf course and in other casual settings. The style leadership of the Prince was a boon for the British woolens export business. In America, ready-to-wear makers quickly responded to the popularity of the brightly colored and patterned knits by mass producing an endless variety of knitwear. Haberdasheries stocked up, and mass merchandisers filled their catalogs with affordable Fair Isle-inspired sweaters, stockings, mufflers, neckwear, and gloves. (Figure 4-32.) By the end of the decade, the colors of men's sweaters and other sportswear were produced in such extreme hues as to "appear garish or effeminate," worried one journalist.[63]

For the American male who was reluctant to indulge in peacock splendor, the V-neck tennis sweater was a popular alternative. The V-neck tennis sweater, made of solid colors and usually with a contrasting narrow stripe or two outlining the V-neck and ribbed cuffs or waistband, had actually been a staple warmup garment of tennis players for decades. But in the 1920s, tennis champions such as Bill Tilden were often featured in mass media smartly outfitted in a cable knit V-neck and flannel trousers on and off the court. (Figure 4-33.)

Another sweater style that came into its own during the 1920s was the turtleneck. The design was not new, just the name. (Figure 4-34.) Called a roll neck in menswear catalogs prior to World War I, the style was a utilitarian garment for winter wear and sports. But in 1924, the turtleneck became a fashion item when Noel Coward wore one with a blazer in his highly successful play, *Vortex*. The new fashion look was especially popular in England from which it spread to France and America along with the Fair Isle sweater and Oxford bags.

Among the most radically changing garments of the postwar years were swimsuits. Like so many other forms of sports clothing of the Victorian and Edwardian eras, for decades, swimwear was a commodity item akin to other knitwear like sweaters, socks, and underwear. In 1915, though, Danish emigrant Carl Jantzen invented a specialized knitting machine that produced lightweight, elasticized knits that held their shape even when wet. Initially applied to the usual standardized knitwear items, Jantzen's knitting technology was adapted to the production of swim-

Figure 4-33. Men who were less adventuresome in their knitwear choices than those who donned the colorful, boldly patterned Fair Isle varieties were content with the comfort and subdued looks of club sweater styles. V-neck cable knit tennis sweater from Minerva, 1925.

Figure 4-34. For decades, the roll neck sweater primarily had been a worker's and athlete's cold weather garment. In the 1920s, though, the style was rechristened the "turtleneck" and became a fashion fad when Noel Coward wore one with a blazer in a popular play of the time. Ad for "Turtle Necks" by Puritan Knitting Mills, 1925.

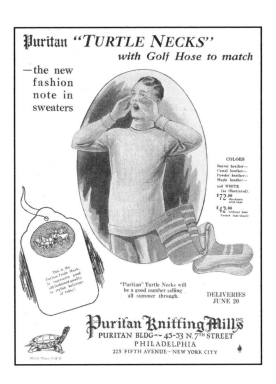

suits in 1920 and revolutionized both men's and women's swimwear designs. During the early 1920s, the length of the trunks gradually shortened, armholes and tank scoopnecks became deeper, and the backs and sides were pierced with wide openings that created thin straps of material. (Figure 4-35.) For two-piece models, trunks were secured with belts of white canvas or sometimes of multicolored horizontal stripes. The pierced swimsuits were popularly called "crab backs" because the cutouts and straps resembled the silhouette of a crab.

However, for the mature man, or the less athletically built man, or the more modest young man, swimsuits of longer, loose-fitting woven flannel trunks and jersey knit tops of assorted color combinations were also common.

The sleek fit of the new knit swimwear was especially appreciated by

Figure 4-35. Between the end of World War I and the end of the 1920s, men's swimwear dramatically changed from a styleless commodity garment to an ever briefer fashion item. Knit and woven versions were produced in riotous colors and patterns never seen on beaches or poolside before. New methods of knitting technologies made swimwear more formfitting and revealing. More and more skin was exposed. At the resorts, some men began to appear in trunks only without the usual tank or crab back tops. Left, photo, c. 1920; right, Jantzen ad, 1929.

competitive swimmers, and Jantzen one-piece racer suits were the preferred choice of collegiate and Olympic teams. By the mid-1920s, Jantzen ads included a tagline beneath their logo proclaiming the company's contribution to the sport: "The suit that changed bathing to swimming." Moreover, the formfitting stretch swimsuits were an immediate hit with Flaming Youth whose heightened sense of sexuality was complemented by the exhibitionism of the new styles of swimwear. Jantzen, and their copyist competitors, emphasized the second-skin fit of the new styles of swimsuits in their advertising. "Tightly knitted from long-fibred wool by the Jantzen-stitched process," stated a 1928 ad, "a Jantzen graces your body lightly, snugly, smoothly...without a wrinkle. Being extremely elastic, it retains its shape permanently."[64]

The revealing swimsuit styles also had the added bonuses of shocking the older generations and of challenging staid conventions. By the end of the decade, fashion reports noted how the skimpier swimsuits and masculine exhibitionism had altered social protocols. As one editor noted in 1929, young men vacationing at the resorts in Europe or the Caribbean spent their entire day dressed only in their swimsuits, sometimes topped by a sweater: "Every man starts out early in the morning from his hotel, or the villa at which he is staying, hops into a taxi, or drives a car to his favorite bathing place, and so attired, passes the whole day,—lunching, playing tennis, bathing again in the afternoon, and going about the countryside until long after sunset, when he dresses for a late dinner."[65]

By the second half of the 1920s, swimwear was undeniably a fashion item. Colors and prints were as uninhibited as the fit. Bold, Fair Isle knit patterns were adapted to the tank tops of swimwear. In 1928, Jantzen introduced the "twosome"—a short trunk with a tank that buttoned to the waistband. Most twosomes were made with solid-colored trunks and a horizontal-striped tank although some versions included matching solid-colored tops. The twosome was a marketing response to the new trend of topless swimwear for men that had begun at the European Riviera resorts and even in Hawaii in the late teens. The wintertime suntan became the fashionable testimonial of the affluent who could afford a vacation at a warm climate resort in January. To maximize their exposure of flesh for basking in the sun, the leisure class men stripped to only their trunks on the beaches and poolside at Nice and Honolulu while, on American beaches, they were required by puritanical community ordinances to keep their tops on. In 1921, a fashion journalist reminded readers that "a man should be most careful about his bathing attire....It is only in America that prudish regulations are enforced. Even a one-piece bathing suit is not allowed as a rule, and trunks are considered indecent."[66]

Another form of casual resort dress that fashion reports often mentioned because of its startling modernity and sophistication was beach pyjamas (spelled with a "y" to distinguish from the sleepwear). For the young exhibitionist who may not have the athletic build to carry off spending much of his day wearing solely a swimsuit, the eye-catching pyjama suit was a coverup worn over the swimsuit between dips. Most styles were made of boldly patterned and vibrantly-colored silk foulard. Long-sleeved wrap tunic tops were worn untucked over flowing trousers. When worn without the jacket, the bottoms were called cabana trousers.

Although the dress of the masses was not always directly influenced by what the affluent wore in Palm Beach or abroad, the continued

Figure 4-36. Men's wartime overcoats were trim and snugly fitted. Military influences included a raised waistline and flared, knee-length skirt. World War I overcoats by Majestic Tailors 1917.

inroads of casual style upon the conventions of menswear had a pronounced cumulative effect during the 1920s. American ready-to-wear makers were a couple of years behind the trend of skimpier swimsuits seen on the Riviera, and Sears and Montgomery Ward never offered cabana trousers in their mass-merchandise catalogs. However, the growing popularity of sportswear such as sweaters, short-sleeved tennis shirts, and knit polos had mass appeal, and American mass production supplied the market demand. Whenever the masses embraced the rapid changes in fashion during the postwar years, changes in social conventions followed as quickly. The barricades of many entrenched taboos and protocols of dress were brought down by Flaming Youth, and the foundations were laid for the next generation to explore ever more casual comfort—not only in sportswear, but also in most categories of menswear.

Outerwear 1915–1929

By the beginning of World War I, men's coats had lost the capacious dimensions and ankle-sweeping lengths of the Edwardian styles, becoming, instead, trim and fitted. (Figure 4-36.) Among the military influences applied to overcoats during the war years were a practical, flared skirt with a knee-length hemline, a raised waistline, deep armholes, and wide sleeves for maximum freedom of movement. Even the long ulster was shortened to about mid-shin. Although press reports often mentioned the "elimination of all superfluities" to conserve fabric for war needs, catalogs and fashion editorials still featured coats with belts, pocket flaps, gauntlet cuffs, wrist straps, epaulets, and double-breasted closures.[67]

As fuel shortages limited public transportation and even the use of private cars, men did more walking even in the depths of winter. As a result, fur coats of all kinds became especially popular. For men who could not afford full-length furs, coats with large fur collars, irrespective of the quality or scarcity of the pelt, were a favorite alternative. "During the war, every man attached a cat skin, of one variety or another, to his rain coat or his [overcoat]," recalled a journalist.[68]

Another military influence on civilian outerwear was the widely adopted trench coat for all cool weather seasons. Aptly named for its "acid test of service on the British front" in the trenches of France, the trench coat was a way for civilians not only to express their support of the doughboys but also to share in some degree a bond with the soldiers.[69] The trench coat was basically a wartime name for the traditional Burberry raincoat made of waterproof gabardine and interlined with waterproofed silk to which a detachable wool lining buttoned.

In the postwar years, outerwear construction was altered to fit over

Figure 4-37. By the mid-1920s, men's overcoats and ulsters were cut with wide, tubular shapes to fit over the new, broad-shouldered suit styles. With the end of wartime rationing, skirt lengths dropped once again, and details such as capacious patch pockets and turned-back cuffs returned. Overcoats and ulsters from Sears, 1926.

Figure 4-38. Oversized raccoon coats were a fad of collegiate men in the 1920s. Ad, 1923.

the new athletic cut of men's suit coats. The shapes of overcoats and ulsters were tubular with broad shoulders and wide lapels. (Figure 4-37.) "In the wide shoulders, long full skirt, half belted back, large pockets, and general careless appearance of a coat of this sort, lies its sportsman-like smartness," asserted a fashion columnist.[70] Even belted styles had a thicker, heavier look. For the young man who preferred a more slender silhouette, collegiate cuts were slightly fitted with contoured back seams rather than the tight, delineated side seams of the 1910s versions. With the end of rationing, hemlines of overcoats dropped a few inches from the wartime knee-length crops, and fabric-indulgent details such as inverted back pleats, pleated patch pockets with large flaps, breast welt pockets, and deep, turned-back cuffs were revived.

Fur coats were less favored in the 1920s although fur-lined topcoats and ulsters were common. Long, fluffy raccoon coats were a fad of the Ivy Leaguer who could afford the pricey style to wear to football games and cruising in open flivvers with a stylish flapper. (Figure 4-38.) Cartoonists such as John Held often featured his sheiks and shebas enveloped in massive "coonskins."

Figure 4-39. The belted double-breasted Mackinaw had been a favorite winter coat for the working man for decades. During the postwar years, the middle classes increasingly adopted the colorful short coat for weekend winter outings and sports. Mackinaws from Sears, 1926.

Utilitarian jackets remained largely uniform with prewar styles. The repeated headlines of "warmth and comfort" in the copy of Sears catalogs expressed the chief selling points of the numerous styles of fleece- and wool-lined jackets made of cowhide, calfskin, horsehide, twill moleskin, and thick army wool. The thigh-length mackinaw had been a working man's winter wear for decades, but in the postwar years the colorfully plaid style became a casual, comfortable alternative to long overcoats for the middle classes to wear during weekend pursuits of winter sports and activities. (Figure 4-39.)

Underwear 1915–1929

Prior to World War I, most American men largely viewed underwear as a prosaic item of clothing that they bought when needed. In winter, long woolen union suits remained the most favored, and, in summer, combed cotton union suits, perhaps with half sleeves and knee-length legs, were sufficiently functional.

But in the postwar years, Flaming Youth demanded greater comfort and freedom from the body armor forms of underwear that were all-enveloping and binding. Doughboys had become accustomed to the easy fit of the athletic tank undershirt and boxer type shorts year round. Ready-to-wear makers and mass merchandisers quickly responded to the demands of youth-oriented America, and, by the early 1920s, offered

Figure 4-40. Returning doughboys and the Flaming Youth generation of the postwar years preferred the comfort, freedom, and convenience of the briefer forms of "athletic" underwear. Left, BVD Athletic Underwear, 1926; right Commander tank-style union suit, 1928.

wider assortments of ever briefer underwear. Catalogs and haberdasheries were well stocked with sleeveless step-ins and separate tanks and shorts called "athletic undershirts" and "running pants." (Figure 4-40.)

By the midtwenties, underwear makers were swept up in the color frenzy of the era and mass produced the duos of athletic shirts and shorts in a rainbow of colors and prints. *Men's Wear* noted in 1925:

> Colored underwear is no novelty abroad but here color effects are displayed that are bound to startle the man whose former impression was that underwear was neither to be seen nor heard. Made of printed shirting materials, athletic drawers are to be had in ideas that support the belief that underwear men, cognizant of what color has done for garters, suspenders, belts, hose, items that generally are not conspicuously on public view, have decided to get some attention for their product.[71]

And despite the alarm for many men that "athletic underwear in pink, pale blue, peach, blazer stripes, etc...has a feminine look about it," such designs became widely available from mass merchandisers like Sears and Montgomery Ward "for the proletariat."[72]

In addition to choosing from among the broad assortment of vibrant colors and prints in underwear, new fabrics were also worthy of consideration when a man shopped the furnishings counters of his local department store. Silk had been a popular fabric for men's underthings for centuries, but they were primarily upscale items available only at the exclusive smart shops. In the 1920s, though, imported Asian and Indian silks were in abundance, and silk underwear was more affordable to a wider market. When rayon was mass produced in the second half of the decade, underwear makers offered numerous styles made of the cool, comfortable synthetic fabric marketed as "art silk" or "artificial silk." Underwear made of open-weave mesh also remained popular for summertime wear. More than half a century before Calvin Klein promoted the eroticism of men's underwear, Jeanne Lanvin exported to America trim athletic shirts and brief shorts made of the sheerest mesh netting in vibrant colors.[73]

Sleepwear 1915–1929

For the upper income echelon, men's sleepwear became even more luxurious and high styled. The Cossack pajama suit was often featured by fashion writers as the epitome of high style although the look had been popular since the end of the nineteenth century.[74] Former military men were especially fond of the imperial uniform look of the circular standing collar, asymmetrical button closure down the right side, and braid trim or contrast piping. By the 1920s, even mass merchandisers like Sears offered fancy pajamas and robes designed with art deco prints or jacquard-textured graphics ornamented with corded piping, passementerie trim, and mother-of-pearl buttons. (Figure 4-41.)

Technological advances that were applied to men's sleepwear included pajamas and robes made of silky rayon or accented with trim made of the artificial silk. In addition, comfortable, elasticized waistbands were introduced as an alternative to the constructed button or drawstring waistband. (Figure 4-42.)

Basic white muslin sleep shirts were still offered in the catalogs of mass merchandisers although in ever fewer varieties as the 1920s pro-

Figure 4-41. In addition to the standard plain and vertical-striped cotton pajamas, mass merchandisers offered men of the 1920s new varieties of high style sleepwear. Pajamas for the mass market were made of fine broadcloth and rayon in vibrant colors and prints accented with braid, piping, and frog closures. Pajamas from Montgomery Ward, 1929.

Figure 4-42. Advances in rubberized yarn production and elasticized fabric weaving made the elasticized waistband a much more comfortable alternative to drawstring and button belt constructions of pajamas. Detail of Faultless Pajama ad, 1926.

Figure 4-43. Lounging pajama suits were the modern casual dress for the private time of the sophisticated gentleman of means. Etiquette even allowed these costumes to be worn to dinner on occasion. Lounge PJ suit from a *Vanity Fair* editorial, 1926.

gressed. The sleep shirt, like the starched detachable shirt collar, was viewed by Flaming Youth as a clothing anachronism associated with old fogies who were unable or unwilling to adapt to modern times. As *Men's Wear* observed in 1928:

> It is reported on fair authority that in a few remote spots, probably where wild Indians still range, the nightshirt can be worn without occasioning a guffaw from a sophisticated, modern person who expects to see the nightshirt topped with a tasseled night cap...There are obese persons and independent individuals who wear nightshirts to bed. These have vents on either side of the shirt to permit a liberal stride when putting out the cat and blowing out various lamps and candles, but the modern gentleman who reads in bed by the aid of a soft boudoir light while reclining on tinted sheets, is horrified at the mere thought of a nightshirt....[75]

The sleep shirt was further denigrated by Hollywood where it was a favorite archaism used in silent movies as a prop to convey to audiences characters who were unsophisticated and behind the times.

Smoking or cowes jackets had faded from fashion at the end of the Edwardian era. Instead, the luxurious dress for the private time at home of a man of means included even more comfortable options such as lounging or pajama suits. These lounge suits (not to be confused with the British term for sack suits) were more tailored than sleepwear pajamas, but colors and textile prints were equally vibrant. (Figure 4-43.) Jackets

Figure 4-44. The traditional house robe made of opulent fabrics and tailored with fine details remained a popular form of negligée dress at home in evenings. The cotton blanket bathrobe was worn during the morning and nighttime toilet. From Sears: top, cotton blanket cloth bathrobe; bottom, brocaded rayon lounging robe, 1929.

were usually made with wide shawl collars with deep V-front openings and sometimes with contrasting satin facings. The loose-fitting trousers were made of the same fabric and were cuffed. As a fashion editor advised in 1921:

> A suit of this kind can be worn at dinner in one's own house when alone with one's family and also when there are only intimate friends as guests. They take the place of dinner jackets and are looser and more comfortable and need not be worn with stiff shirts....These suits are more becoming than the regular dinner jacket, because they are more interesting in color and material and also because they can be made in a much more individual cut without treading on any of the conventionalities of formal evening clothes. They are admirable to lounge about in, do not come out of shape and need no repressing, as evening clothes do.[76]

The pajama suit, though, was a dress eccentricity of the affluent. Mass merchandisers did not offer versions of pajama lounge suits in their wishbooks.

House robes were still an option for negligée dress at home. (Figure 4-44.) The tradition of the businessman arriving home and exchanging his street boots for pumps or slippers, necktie for a muffler, and suit or frock coat for a silk robe continued from the Victorian era. By the same token, the house robe was never to be worn as a substitute for the terrycloth or waffle-woven bathrobe since the fine fabrics and trim used to make lounging robes could get ruined by splashes of soapy water or daubs of shaving cream.

Accessories 1915–1929

As with many fashions in menswear of the postwar years, headwear preferences shifted significantly during the second half of the 1910s. The prewar businessman had been comfortable in his round-domed derby in black (winter), brown (autumn), or gray (spring and summer), which all his peers likewise wore to town year round. By the end of World War I, though, the homburg became more preferred to the derby for town—but never to be worn in the country. As noted in chapter 3, the homburg was introduced to Britain by the Prince of Wales (Edward VII) in the 1880s. The Prince often went to the German Alpine resorts in summer and had visited the hat factory in Homburg where he purchased the conical-shaped hat that came to be named for its town of origin. In the 1920s, the Americanized homburg was shortened, and the conical angle of the crown became more subtle. (Figure 4-45.) The brim remained narrow and turned up all around with a finished rolled edge although the curl became less pronounced. The reputation of the homburg, though, was that it was not flattering to every man, especially those with irregular features or large heads. Hat makers assiduously fought this perception with extensive advertising. "To homely men," exclaimed the header of a 1925 Berg Hats ad: "An irregular face, according to phrenologists, is a sign that its owner has character. That's a comforting thought to most of us. But it's still more comforting to know that this is a hat with a positive talent for grouping miscellaneous features into an ensemble that approaches good looks."[77] Despite the marketing efforts of American hat makers, the homburg was regarded by most men as a stiff, uncomfortable style of the equally stiff, mature businessman.

Snap brim fedora, 1927

Pinched front fedora, 1929

Homburg, 1929

Panama, 1927

Golf caps, 1928

Western sombrero, 1926

Figure 4-45. The homburg replaced the derby as the favored headwear of the American businessman, and, for young men, the snap brim fedora was the most popular. In summer months, the straw boater was still the most common hat style although assorted new variants of the panama were a trend at resorts and country retreats. Hats from Sears and Montgomery Ward.

Even though the derby remained the more prevalent choice of the British businessman, American men resisted the influence from London, and U.S. hat makers responded by producing fewer derbies. In the 1918 Sears catalog, only one derby was offered against more than two dozen soft hat varieties. By the 1920s, the derby was completely absent from mass merchandise wishbooks.

Instead of the homburg or the derby, young American men opted for a variety of soft hats, especially the snap brim fedora. The wide brim of the fedora could be snapped into a number of shapes to reflect its wearer's personality. One of the most prominent male fashion plates in America at the time was New York City's handsome young mayor, Jimmy Walker, who was often photographed wearing his fedora snapped up at the left side and down on the right. The more common way to snap the brim was down in front and up in the back. Another variety of the fedora was the pinched front, which featured indentations on the front sides of the center-creased crown.

For summertime, the straw boater was still the most ubiquitous style. Panamas once again gained in popularity—now with versions made of brown leghorn and coarse coconut fiber. Traditional fedora-style panamas endured with high, pinched crowns and curled brims. But the newest panamas of the midtwenties were blocked with flat-top crowns and wide,

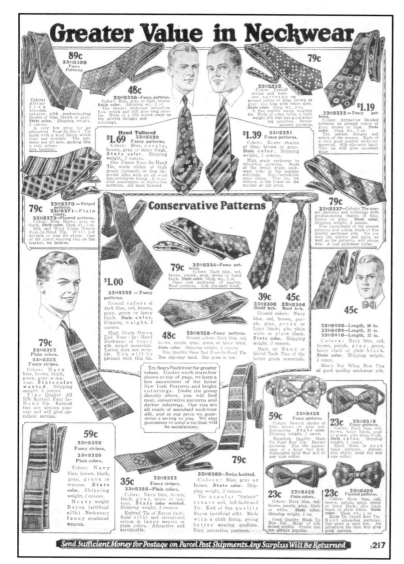

Figure 4-46. By the 1920s, most men wore the four-in-hand long tie, which had become largely standardized in blade shape and width. Bow ties were much less common than a generation earlier except for evening wear. Vibrant Jazz Age colors and art deco prints provided men with neckwear style options to express their personalities and modernity. Ties from Sears, 1927.

flat brims. Both boaters and panamas were banded with wide, colorfully striped and patterned ribbons with a large flat bow on the left side.

Golf caps, as they were called in catalogs, were the most common casual headwear for outdoor activities and weekends in the country. Most golf caps were still made the same as those of the Victorian era with a soft, deflated fabric sack that sagged over a rigid visor covered in the same fabric. At the end of the 1920s, a visorless version became popular with collegiates worn with the soft fullness pulled forward over the brow. Tweeds, checks, herringbones, and similar traditional fabrics were cut in pie-wedge pieces and stitched together with a covered button in the center. Some single-piece constructions featured striking art deco patterns in vivid colors.

The cowboy's sombrero remained a popular catalog item for western ranchers and cowhands. In the 1920s, western styles towered with seven-inch crowns variously named for their dents. A deep, single depression at the front was commonly known as a Carlsbad style; others with side dents or depressions all around were given colorful names like Stampede and Dakota.

Among the collegiate crowd of the late 1920s, many young men began to abandon headwear of any kind. Similarly, fashion reports noted that men at resorts like Palm Beach were conspicuously going about unhatted even in the sun-drenched daytime.[78] The hatless trend, though, remained limited to youthful rebellion and resort sun-worshippers.

Neckwear of the postwar years was also subjected to the two tenets of style of the times: comfort and vivacious color. By the late 1910s, men had two principal forms of ties from which to choose: the long, four-in-hand tie and the bow tie. The assortment of broad scarves, puff ascots, imperials, and similar neckwear variants that had been common for the Victorian and Edwardian man had been relegated to ceremonial dress along with the frock coat and day top hat. (Figure 4-46.)

The four-in-hand tie became the preference for most men of the 1920s. Unlike the versions of a generation earlier, which came in all sorts of widths, long ties were now fairly standardized at about 2 1/2 inches at the flared tip. It was still tied to extend only about three-quarters down the shirt front, unlike today where the correct length ends just at the belt buckle. Flaming Youth especially demanded ties that would "proclaim its wearer loudly afar off," as *Vanity Fair* noted. "Why such material should ever be made into neckwear is difficult to understand," lamented the editor who examined the vivid bouquets of ties on display in store windows and color inserts in catalogs. "The men who wear neckties of this gay and peculiar type have evidently forgotten the truth that civilization reverses nature when evolution reaches the stage of man."[79] Among the fads of necktie patterns of the 1920s were repeat designs "inspired by radiator caps and insignia of foreign cars,"[80] emblems of the fast-paced, mobile era. Another popular necktie novelty of the time was made of imported Javanese handprinted silk batik.

In addition to the bold colors and patterns of men's neckwear of the era, squared knit ties were resurrected as a particular trend with collegiate men. New versions of knit ties featured dynamic art deco patterns in multicolored yarns that held their knitting structure better than those of prewar styles, which easily stretched out of shape from the repeated knotting. Similarly, the quality of printed rayon was such that realistic screen prints of snake and reptile skins were a fad of young men of the late twenties.

The bow tie was mostly limited to evening wear. In the late 1920s, the Prince of Wales was credited with reviving the bow tie with a sack coat suit. As one journalist asserted in 1928, because the bow tie "belonged to the fashions of our grandfathers," when the Prince adopted the look, it seemed "as quite an innovation to this generation."[81] The new bow ties of the time, like the four-in-hand ties, were also available in brightly hued patterns, art deco prints, and multicolored stripes.

Footwear styles complemented the trends of shape and fit of men's suits. Until about 1923, postwar suit styles remained slim and narrow; shoes likewise were slim and narrow. By the midtwenties, the new cut of the athletic suit featured broad shoulders and full trousers, including variations of the exaggerated Oxford bags. Correspondingly, after 1923, shoes became wider with squared toes and thick soles to balance the visual effects of the larger suit silhouette. (Figure 4-47.) At the same time, the high ankle-boot style of street shoes declined, replaced increasingly by oxfords. The variety of mass-produced oxfords was enormous. Mass merchandisers featured almost as many pages of men's shoes as women's. Wing tips and straight tips were especially favored for city wear with business suits. Fanciful perforations and decorative pinking all around the edges of the overlays added even more variety. Snakeskin, lizard, and alligator—genuine or simulated—offered still more high style options. Two-tone jazz shoes showed the influence of art deco design in the second half of the decade. In a shoe ad featuring jazz shoes, the copy, with dropped vowels and phonetic spellings, was clearly written for the young man seeking modern, high-style looks: "A shoe to uze—a shoe to abuze. One that is supremely comfortable and outstandingly correct. Designd and bilt for servis but not, on that account, neglectful of good looks. Plantation crepe rubbr soles, upprs of soft, pliabl calfskin and smokt horse."[82]

As recreational sports became more broadly pursued by the masses, particularly the middle classes, sports shoes became an important category for shoe manufacturers and retailers. Previously, athletic footwear was often available in the sporting goods sections of stores and catalogs.

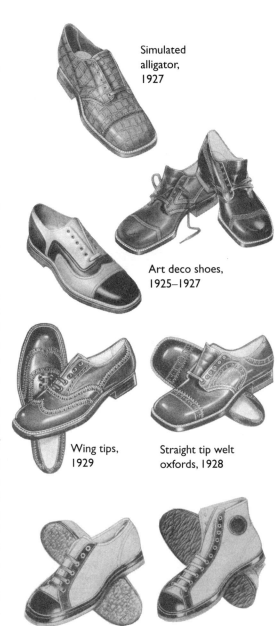

Simulated alligator, 1927

Art deco shoes, 1925–1927

Wing tips, 1929

Straight tip welt oxfords, 1928

Tennis and basketball shoes, 1928

Figure 4-47. The ankle boot, which had been the most prevalent street shoe for decades, gradually faded from style in the 1920s. Instead, the versatile oxford became the favorite of all ages of men. Shoes from Sears and Montgomery Ward catalogs.

The smart and sensible gift for THIS Christmas is

Suspenders!

Smart—because they are in fashion. Well-dressed men wear them to make the new cuffless trousers hang properly.

Sensible— because they are healthful—comfortable—a practical gift that "he" will use and appreciate.

The Suspender Manufacturers' Advertising Committee, Inc. 395 Broadway. New York

Figure 4-48. In their quest for greater comfort in dress, the younger generation discarded binding suspenders in favor of the basic, waist-flattering belt. The makers of suspenders pooled their resources for an aggressive but futile marketing effort to bring back suspenders as the correct form of trouser support. Ad by the Suspender Manufacturers' Advertising Committee, 1921.

By the 1920s, sports shoes were made in such a wide assortment of styles, including specialty versions for basketball, baseball, and golf, that they were made an integral part of the retailer's shoe division. Most active sports shoes were made with "mail bag" canvas uppers and flat, rubber crepe or molded soles. Some outing sports shoes featured "air cushioned" heels molded to the sole. Cleated golf shoes were styled after the newest looks in street styles, including two-tone art deco overlays and punched decorations.

The first significant change in men's wallets and billfolds in decades occurred at the end of the 1920s when the U.S. Treasury Department redesigned all currency. Because paper money was reduced to about two-thirds the size it had been previously, wallets and billfolds were likewise reduced.

In their continual pursuit of comfort and convenience with dress, the young men of the postwar era discarded a number of accessories that their fathers and grandfathers had regarded as correct masculine accoutrement. Walking sticks were viewed as superfluous anachronisms although many mature gentlemen still carried them. Except for the shepherd's crook cane—more associated with the lame than the fashion-conscious—mass merchandisers discontinued offering the silver-capped walking stick in their wishbooks.

Similarly, men ceased wearing gloves except the thick, lined winter

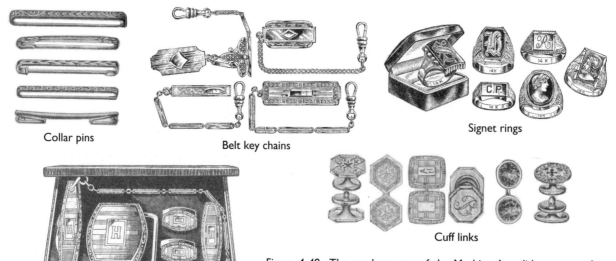

Collar pins

Belt key chains

Signet rings

Cuff links

Monogrammed gift set with cuff links, belt buckle, key chain, and pocket knife

Figure 4-49. The modern man of the Machine Age did not encumber himself with much jewelry. He did not need cuff links with his soft collar shirt nor stick pins with his slim four-in-hand tie. The pocket watch with its lengthy swag of chain and cluster of charms was made obsolete by the wristwatch, and the bejeweled walking stick was abandoned as one less item to carry. Jewelry from various catalogs, 1926–1929.

varieties necessary for protection against cold weather. The buff or gray kid gloves that had been a key daytime accessory of the properly dressed Edwardian gentleman had been abandoned by their sons in the 1920s. Even white gloves for formal dress were no longer endured by the comfort-oriented young men. "White kid gloves for evening wear are more and more disregarded," wrote a journalist in 1921, "despite the fact that women complain that their dresses get dreadfully soiled when they are with men who do not wear them."[83]

Suspenders and sock garters were also consigned to the trash heap of irrelevant clothing by young men. These binding straps of elasticized webbing were not only uncomfortable, but were impractical for the fuller cut trousers, particularly Oxford bags. Like the detachable collar industry of the time, suspenders makers suffered the impact of the changing fashions. As one trade journal noted in 1925: "It became the fashion several years ago for men to wear belts and to leave off suspenders. The suspender industry went from bad to worse until finally in self-defense the various manufacturers got together and decided that they would forget their competition for the time being and unite in a campaign to make suspenders the fashion again." The problem was, continued the editor, "the public paid no attention to it, since to read in an advertisement labeled 'Suspender Manufacturers' that suspenders were coming back again would hardly be convincing."[84] (Figure 4-48.) More fuel was added to the debate between advocates of belts vs. suspenders when, in 1925, President Coolidge met with a group of college men and later remarked that "the use of suspenders rather than belts would improve the sartorial appearance of his callers."[85] The generation gap in dress and identity was further reinforced from the publicity of the President's comment.

Jewelry for men was, as ever, a tricky style endeavor. Since the days of Queen Victoria, style guides and fashion editors had chided men who opted for any jewelry that was conspicuous. The protocol had largely been conservatism, a preserving of that renunciation that separated postrevolutionary era men from the effeminate luxuriousness of the Old World aristocracy. Those potent, nineteenth-century conventions endured into the post-World War I years. "There is nothing more destructive of successful dressing than the theory that men can wear, on any occasion, many or conspicuous jewels," reminded an editor in 1918.[86] But postwar young men, now at the helm of masculine style instead of their traditionalist elders, had already demonstrated in so many ways that dress conventions were too often meaningless to them. Their push en masse for comfort in their clothing impacted jewelry as well as most other categories of menswear.

With the replacement of the soft collar shirt, the gold or pearl collar buttons necessary for the old-styled detachable collar disappeared from men's jewelry boxes. In place of the collar buttons were collar pins that held the unstarched soft collars in place and prevented tips from standing out or curling under. (Figure 4-49.) Tie pins likewise fell out of favor with young men although mature men, perpetuating the looks of their Edwardian era youth, continued to insert jewel-encrusted pins into their four-in-hand blades. Cuff links were also a casualty of the soft collar shirt since few ready-to-wear styles were made with turned back French cuffs. For men who still donned formal dress, though, a panoply of jewelry was available for the evening ensemble including cuff links, pocket watch,

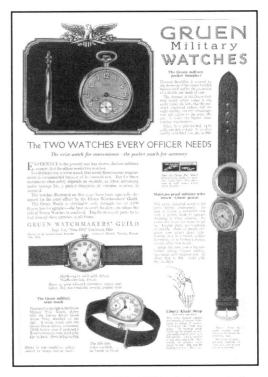

Figure 4-50. During World War I, the practical and convenient wristwatch was mass produced for the U.S. military and immediately became a civilian style trend. Gruen Watches ad, 1918.

Figure 4-51. The automatic cigarette lighter was the newest jewelry accessory for the sophisticated man of the late 1920s. Especially popular was the high styling of monogrammed and art deco casings. Cigarette lighters from Sears, 1927–1929.

watch chain and charms, key chain, shirt studs, signet ring, cigarette case, lighter, and pocket knife.

One of the most convenient pieces of jewelry for men of the era was the wristwatch. Although wristwatches were introduced at the turn of the century, it was during the First World War when the practicality of the wristwatch was recognized and advanced into mass production by the U.S. military. (Figure 4-50.) A sliding clasp was developed that allowed soldiers to quickly loosen the wristband and push it up the arm to wash their hands rather than unbuckling the strap and having to fumble with reclasping it. The returning doughboys continued to wear their wristwatches, and the pocket watch, along with detachable collars, suspenders, daytime gloves, and walking sticks became a quaint eccentricity of the older generations. In 1928, metal-linked wristwatch bands were the fashion news of the day, including smart art deco designs imported from France.

Another new jewelry item of sorts was the cigarette lighter. First introduced in 1925, the automatic lighter was fueled by gasoline or benzene. The thin, flat lighters were less bulky in the pocket than the match case, and flicking an automatic lighter was a testament of a man's modern sophistication. (Figure 4-51.) By the late twenties, even the mass merchandisers offered art deco designed lighters with matching cigarette cases.

Grooming 1915–1929

Hairstyles continued to be cut in one of two variations: short all over or short at the sides and full on top. During the war years, many young men opted for the military cut, which was short all over and trimmed or sometimes even shaved all around the back of the head even with eyebrows. Like bulb-toed shoes and longjohns, the extreme military cut lingered in western and rural regions long after being abandoned by eastern urbanites and became a cartoonist's caricature of the country cousin.

Normal, healthy hair looks well because it is well

Does your hair need help to make it vigorous?

MOST men suffer from one, or both, of two common hair ailments — *dandruff* and *thinning hair*.

Neglected, they can result only in complete loss of hair.

Yet all that is needed to overcome them and keep the hair clean and strong is a moment's special care each day. Even long established cases yield to this simple treatment:

EVERY MORNING moisten hair and scalp generously with Ed. Pinaud's Eau de Quinine. Just shake the bottle, with its convenient shaker top, over your head. Then with the fingers pressed down firmly, move the scalp vigorously in every direction, working the tonic thoroughly into every inch of the scalp. Comb and brush your hair while still moist. It will lie smoothly just the way you want it.

You will feel the difference in your hair the very first time

you use this treatment. After only a few days the change in its appearance will astonish you!

For Ed. Pinaud's Eau de Quinine does the two things needed to promote hair health—destroys dandruff infection and stimulates active circulation, which nourishes the hair at its very roots.

Keep Ed. Pinaud's Eau de Quinine near your toothbrush and make its use as regular a part of your morning toilet as brushing your teeth.

Get Ed. Pinaud's Eau de Quinine today at any drug store or department store. Look for the large signature of Ed. Pinaud in red on each bottle. Pinaud Incorporated, 90 Fifth Avenue, New York—sole distributors for Parfumerie Ed. Pinaud, Paris.

ED. PINAUD'S *Eau de Quinine*

Figure 4-52. The two variations of men's hair cuts were short all over or full on top and short at the sides. Most men preferred the fuller style, which was oiled with pomades and combed into a fixed shiny helmet. Left, Pinaud's ad, 1926; right, Hollywood leading men Ben Lyon and Lloyd Hughes, 1925.

Hollywood influenced the look of men with fuller hairstyles whose lengthy locks atop the head were greased with pomades and combed back into a fixed shiny helmet. (Figure 4-52.) Rudolph Valentino epitomized the helmet hair of the 1920s both on and off screen.

Shaving cream and razor manufacturers maintained a relentless advertising barrage to ensure no return of the Victorian bewhiskered face. (Figure 4-53.) But since Flaming Youth dominated the era, most men preferred the youthful modern look of the clean shaved face. The exception were the pencil-line mustaches that edged the upper lip, which became popular in some urbane social circles during the late 1920s.

Besides the expansion of varieties of shaving and haircare products for men, other grooming and hygiene products tailored to the masculine market proliferated during the 1920s. Marketers effectively employed scare tactics in their advertising to warn men of dire social consequences if they were careless with their personal hygiene. (Figure 4-54.) All socioeconomic classes of American men were now made painfully aware of body odor, bad breath, bad teeth, and dandruff—topics their Edwardian predecessors would have found shocking so openly and graphically discussed in ads.

Beyond personal hygiene products, beauty products were extended to the male consumer as well. Sun tanning emerged as a style trend for both women and men in the postwar years. Previously, the bronzed skin was a telltale identity of the man who had to work outside to a large extent. But in the early 1920s, young men began returning home from summer holidays and resort vacations sporting the coppery evidence of their leisure time in the sun—to the envy of their pale peers. Swimwear was even redesigned with detachable tops for the maximum exposure to the sun (where allowed in public). But to prevent the vacation suntan from looking like the rough, burnt-red hide of a field worker, skincare product makers advertised "how to be smartly sun-tanned yet keep your skin smooth and evenly browned." Pond's solution in 1929 was a regimen of four different "exquisite preparations...to help achieve a smooth clear skin toned to an even brown."[87]

Skincare products like Williams Aqua Velva also emphasized preservation of the skin for the era's prized youthful look. "Because it helps conserve the natural moisture of the skin, Aqua Velva keeps your face like velvet all day," promised a 1925 ad. "It keeps the skin pliable and flexible...It prevents face shine. It delights with its man-style fragrance."[88] Such copy in an ad targeting the American male would have seemed feminine or, at best, unmanly, to the prewar Edwardian man, but not to the Flaming Youth of the Jazz Age. "Today few men object to scent, even if they have not the habit of using it," concluded a men's style editor in 1928, "because every toilet preparation is now more or less scented and so the prejudice against it has disappeared along with that against wrist watches."[89]

Figure 4-53. Manufacturers of shaving products emphasized in their advertising the youthful look of the clean shaved face and the archaism of whiskers. Colgate Shaving Cream ad, 1925.

Figure 4-54. Makers of personal hygiene products expanded their market share by targeting men with the same scare tactics in their advertising that had worked so effectively on women consumers. Ads forewarned men of the dire social consequences of bad breath, body odor, dandruff, and a host of other hygienic dangers. Listerine ad, 1929.

Figure 4-55. The masculine aesthetic changed in the postwar years to emphasize a muscular, athletic ideal. To get in shape for the formfitting knit sport shirts, sweaters, and ever briefer swimwear, many men joined gyms and subscribed to mail order fitness regimens. *Physical Culture*, October 1920.

In addition to a focus on the youthful face and hair, a new aesthetic of the ideal masculine physique emerged during this time. (Figure 4-55.) Movie news reels and heavily illustrated mass media presented a constant stream of images of vigorous champion athletes to the sports-obsessed American public. Too, hordes of fit young doughboys returned home after the war and donned formfitting knit sport shirts and sweaters for leisure time or displayed their honed bodies on the beach clad in the new briefer, revealing forms of swimwear. Moreover, the V-silhouette of the athletic suit coat reinforced this new masculine aesthetic. In response, men joined gyms to get in shape or bought home exercise equipment and programs such as the Charles Atlas mail order regimen. "Men, how do you look in a bathing suit?" asked the header in a 1925 physical training farm ad. "Do bathing suit manufacturers annoy you when you go swimming by trying to get you to sign a contract agreeing to pose exclusively in their bathing suits?...We thought not," cajoled the copy, concluding with a promise to help the hapless American male get in shape so he might "appear in a bathing suit without being laughed at."[90]

Conclusion

The mid-1910s through the end of the 1920s was an era of exhilarating social and economic change in America. The United States entered the First World War reluctantly in 1917. In the eighteen months of the war, thousands of wide-eyed young doughboys were forever changed by their experiences "over there"—not only from exposure to the sophisticated cultures of Europe but also from witnessing the worst horrors of modern warfare. Back home, the New Woman found independence and self-confidence from the right to vote and from unprecedented opportunities in employment due to the wartime labor shortage. In the postwar years, an economic boom was fueled by an explosion in consumerism. Jobs were plentiful, and materialism became the American dream. Society was reshaped by Flaming Youth who rejected the traditional values of their Edwardian parents and Victorian grandparents. The youth of America played hard, drank hard, drove fast, wildly danced to jazz, and experimented with sex.

Fashion, too, was youthful and vivacious. Suits, coats, and sportswear of the war years were cut with the slim silhouette of the youthful, lean warrior. Clothing fitted with a trim snugness devoid of the exaggerated padding and bulk of a generation earlier.

During the early 1920s, men's suits evolved into a totally new look. Suit coats were reshaped into an athletic profile with an unpadded, broad-shouldered cut, trim waist, and narrow hips. Trousers became fuller with pleated fronts and wide legs that were more comfortable than the tight, "sausage casing" fit of wartime styles. As a result of the new contours of the athletic suit, other clothing styles were redesigned with greater fullness and comfort, most notably outerwear that had to be reconstructed to fit over the suit coats.

Comfort was the demand of the modern American male in almost every garment he wore. The soft collar dress shirt was preferred to the starched detachable collars of yesteryear. Sweaters and knit vests increasingly replaced tailored sports coats for leisure time and outdoor activities. Sports attire of all types from baggy plus-fours to fitted knit polo shirts was adopted for spectator and weekend wear. Innovative pajama suits were worn to dinner with close friends. Swimwear, ever briefer year by year, was worn day long at resorts in place of conventional casual dress. Daytime gloves and walking sticks were abandoned. Belts were favored over suspenders. The wristwatch replaced the pocket watch and vest chain.

The other big fashion story of the era was color. A resurgence of peacock splendor marked virtually all categories of menswear. Soft shirts were especially popular in vibrant colors and textile prints, and were complemented with neckwear of bold art deco patterns. British Fair Isle sweaters with matching knee stockings and the many Americanized replications were knitted with multicolored yarns into bold jigsaw designs. Some men even dared to extend color experiments to evening wear, donning tail coats and tuxedos of deep blue despite the risk of opprobrium.

From Bust to Berlin
Fashions from the Great Depression
through World War II, 1930–1945

Crash and Crisis

The Great Euphoria of the prosperous twenties came to an abrupt end in 1929 with the crash of the U.S. stock market. From the beginning of the bull market in 1922, the American stock exchange had continued to spiral ever higher despite a number of significant corrections periodically. Everyone wanted in on the action. Office workers, store clerks, errand boys, and many thousands of other average Joes and Janes bought stocks on margin with a small down payment and watched their paper treasure grow in value. But in 1929, interest rates in Europe had begun to edge up in an effort to bring capital investments back from the American market. The resulting credit crunch forced many speculators to dump their securities, and, on the panicky "Black Tuesday" of October 29, 1929, more than 16 million shares were sold at fire-sale prices. Over the subsequent two months, stockholders lost $40 billion in paper value. The consequences were catastrophic, plunging the United States into the Great Depression.

What had caused the calamity was discussed at length by economists and journalists at the time. At the lowest point of the economic disaster in 1932, *Vanity Fair* encapsulated what had happened:

> It began with a contraction of credit. This was followed by a fall in the prices of stocks. Commodity prices fell. Production declined. Sales were reduced. Unsold goods piled up. Profits shrank. Workers were laid off. Wages were reduced. Purchasing power diminished. Confidence was impaired. Banks failed. Loans were called. Money was hoarded. Credit had to contract further....And so on and on and on.[1]

Despite the simplicity of this editorial recap, though, for the millions of Americans who lost their jobs, the Depression was baffling and severe. They wanted to work, but jobs were scarce. In the first three years of the Depression, 86,000 U.S. businesses failed, and unemployment leapt from

Figure 5-1. The dustbowl droughts of the Depression era destroyed farmlands all across America's heartland from the Mississippi River basin to the Great Plains. Thousands of families lost their farms and were forced into migratory lifeways as itinerant field workers. Dustbowl farm and displaced family, 1936.

less than 2 million in 1929 to more than 12 million in 1933.[2] Many thousands of Americans lost their homes and farms to foreclosure. Over 10 million savings accounts were wiped out when more than 9000 banks collapsed.[3] For the first time in their lives, many millions of Americans experienced the misery of poverty and real hunger.

As if the prolonged economic crisis were not enough, nature compounded the traumas of the era with spectacular natural disasters. In 1930, a scorching drought destroyed farmlands throughout the Mississippi Basin. Between 1934 and 1938, the topsoil from millions of acres of poorly managed farms in the Great Plains was lifted into massive dust storms that swept as far east as Boston. Floods continually inundated the Ohio, Tennessee, and Mississippi River valleys. Displaced farming families collected what few belongings they could and migrated elsewhere to seek work. (Figure 5-1.) The plight of the "Okies" and "Arkies" from hard-hit Oklahoma and Arkansas was poignantly captured in John Steinbeck's novel, *Grapes of Wrath* (1939).

Although President Herbert Hoover was profoundly distressed by the widespread suffering of the American people, he was a staunch individualist whose views of pioneer industry and self-reliance were rooted in the nineteenth-century notions of free enterprise. He genuinely felt that a government "dole" would undermine the national fiber and impede recovery. Instead, his administration assisted the banks, railroads, and businesses at the top of the economic pyramid with the intention that a "trickle down" effect would resolve unemployment. When that policy failed and the Depression deepened, the American people increasingly blamed Hoover for the continuing crisis. With the election of 1932, Hoover was voted out of office in a landslide.

In 1933, Franklin Delano Roosevelt took office as President. The Democratic campaign theme song had been "Happy Days Are Here Again," which aptly befitted the indomitable optimism of Roosevelt. His cheerful smile and high-spirited speeches inspired a renewed hope with the American people. During his famous First Hundred Days, the President inaugurated his "New Deal" program of relief, recovery, and reform. An alphabet soup of new federal agencies like the WPA (Works Progress

Administration) and PWA (Public Works Administration) provided thousands of new jobs through works projects. Dozens of emergency reform and relief acts from the New Deal Congress addressed fair labor standards, minimum wage regulations, unemployment insurance, banking reform, social security, and agriculture soil conservation, among others. In addition, Prohibition was repealed that same year. (Figure 5-2.)

Recovery was slow but tangible. When the federal government tried to rein in the skyrocketing national debt in 1938, a sharp recession set in forestalling economic improvements. The New Deal had relieved the worst of the crisis, but it had not cured the economic ailments of the era. Unemployment declined but in 1939 was still six times what it had been a decade earlier. The Great Depression persisted until the beginning of World War II when wartime labor needs put America back to work.

The Pendulum Swings

One of Hoover's miscalculations was just how severe the Depression was. In March 1930, he had assured Americans that the setback would not last more than sixty days before the pendulum of prosperity would swing back. But as the crisis worsened, the President turned his energies toward mitigating the fear that gripped the nation with a campaign of optimism to bolster confidence, but to no avail. When FDR became president in 1933, he, too, recognized that the psychological state of the American people was critical to a recovery. "The only thing we have to fear, is fear itself," he asserted in his inauguration speech. Still, even though most Americans felt hopeful and renewed, the dark clouds of fear were not dissipated.

The social pendulum likewise began to swing away from the youth cult and ballyhoo of the Jazz Age. The guidance of sober, serious grownups was needed now. Frederick Lewis Allen wrote in 1931:

The young people of the early nineteen-thirties presumably knew just as much about life as those of the early and middle twenties,

Figure 5-2. When Prohibition was repealed in 1933, distillers, vintners, and breweries scrambled to recapture as much of the U.S. market as possible through aggressive advertising. Dixie Belle Gin and Pabst Blue Ribbon Beer ads, 1934.

Figure 5-3. Despite the economic hard times of the Great Depression and the privations from rationing during the Second World War, American consumerism was sustained with an endless array of new products, advanced technologies, and changing fashions.

Women's fashions 1930–1945: left, curves and ankle-sweeping dress, 1932; center, shoulder-interest dress, 1937; right, short, narrow dress, 1943.

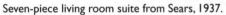

Seven-piece living room suite from Sears, 1937.

American colonial style home, 1938.

Walt Disney's Mickey Mouse was a pop culture phenomenon in the Depression era. *The Band Concert,* 1935.

Pontiac, 1935.

Heterodyne console and table radios, 1934.

but they were less conspicuously and self-consciously intent upon showing the world what advanced young devils they were....What had departed was the excited sense that taboos were going to smash, that morals were being made over or annihilated, and that the whole code of behavior was in flux. The wages of sin had become stabilized at a lower level.[4]

Those early stark, dark days of the Depression were not the time for any flux and social nihilism, but rather a recentering of the bread-and-butter matters of daily life. The postwar Flaming Youth vanished with the crash, and Americans circled the wagons to retreat into a regressive social conservatism.

In 1933, *Good Housekeeping* sent journalists to college campuses across the country to find "the real story" of the new modern youth. "The rah-rah days are over," declared one co-ed. "Few students are concerned with athletics, and the campus activities that dominated former student generations are laughed at now."[5] Depression era youth were more serious and cynical than the collegiate sheiks and shebas of the previous decade:

Gone, too, is youth's romantic, rose-colored glasses. It is beginning to see through much of the sham and hypocrisy that has characterized its parent's generation....Youth has seen its fathers and mothers swung from their sane and decent grooves by unexpected profits, by speed and gin and divorce and an insatiable craving for bigger and more showy things....They have seen the dethroning of many of our national heroes—bankers, financiers, statesmen, industrialists.[6]

But for most of modern youth, there was little to fill the vacuum. "Underneath there is a feeling of uncertainty and insecurity," avowed a Columbia senior. Instead of promise, many young people felt the burden of an uncertain social reconstruction. "Naturally we're upset and worried," continued the senior. "We don't know how to do it, but we realize that it will be up to us to do it."[7]

More important than the influence of teachers and schools, though, noted *Good Housekeeping,* was the "responsibility" of the "average American home...to instill fine ideals, correct standards, wise viewpoints, proper niches for money, and a breadth of tolerance and understanding that is all important in dealing with youth."[8] Those fine ideals, standards, and viewpoints, though, were based on a broadly pervasive social regression—one that was surveyed, measured, and documented by marketers, social scientists, and educators. For example, in their 1935 study of "Middletown in transition," social researchers Helen and Robert Lynd revisited the American heartland ten years after their first landmark study and discovered a greater intensity of fear and intolerance than in 1925. "Middletown is meeting such present issues and present situations as it cannot escape by attempting to revert to the old formulas [which] leads to the stating of such social problems as may arise defensively and negatively."[9] In their assessment of the new "Middletown spirit," the researchers noted that middle America "is *against* the reverse of the things it is for"—a collective and endemic attitude that resulted in an acute xenophobia ("most foreigners are 'inferior'"); a rampant racism ("Negroes are inferior"; "Jews may be alright but that as a race one doesn't care to mix with them"); a pronounced religious bias ("Protestantism is superior to Catholicism"; "having a Pope is un-American"); and a renewed homophobia ("culture and things like that are more the business of women than men"; "deviant members...have been thrown off to the Chicagos, the Clevelands, the New Yorks").[10]

The Depression-era backlash against the social permissiveness and progressivism of the 1920s was often manifested in stark contrasts between the two eras. One example of the new conservatism cited at the time was the drop of women's hemlines from the knees almost to the ankles.[11] (Figure 5-3.) In actuality, though, most of the Paris couturiers had lowered the hemlines and redefined the waist at its natural position with their spring collections in 1929. Still, many people in the early 1930s perceived the style change as a moral counteraction to the short skirts of the flapper or even a corresponding response to the drop in the stock market.

Similarly, sex and sin were largely banned from movies as Hollywood imposed a self-censoring Production Code in 1934. Instead, moviegoers escaped the harsh realities of the era in the lively musical fantasies of Fred Astaire or Shirley Temple, the slapstick riots of the Marx Brothers, the visual delights of Disney color cartoons, or the swashbuckling historical dramas of Errol Flynn and Tyrone Power.

War Ends the Depression

The Great Depression was a global economic calamity. Throughout the 1920s, the industrialized nations of Europe had continued to struggle with postwar reconstruction and rehabilitation only to be set back anew with the world financial crisis. Into the chaos marched fascist military regimes with the promise of stability and order. (Figure 5-4.) In Italy, Benito Mussolini initiated a restoration of the imperial glory of the Roman Empire by attacking and occupying Ethiopia in 1935. In Spain, Francisco Franco set up a brutal dictatorship touching off a civil war in 1936–1939. In Asia, Japan invaded China in 1937 in a quest for the natural resources demanded by its burgeoning military-industrial complex. In Germany, Adolf Hitler led the Nazis to power in 1933 and defiantly rearmed the German military in 1935. In 1938, Germany seized Austria and Czechoslovakia and, in the following year, invaded Poland. As allies to Poland, Britain and France promptly declared war and the long-feared Second World War commenced.

As the tumult raged around the world, the U.S. Congress passed a series of shortsighted Neutrality Acts between 1935 and 1937 to prevent being drawn into another war as it had in 1917. Key to the American isolationism was the ban against the sale or transport of munitions and supplies or providing

Figure 5-4. In Europe, public fears from the lingering Depression, the spread of social unrest, and nationalist movements opened the door for fascist governments and totalitarian regimes. Throughout the 1930s, the self-serving, expansionist policies of Japan, Germany, and Italy continually threatened a new world war. Editorial cartoon from *Saturday Evening Post*, 1936.

loans to any belligerents engaged in a war.

Desperate to replace sources for oil, fuel, and steel that the United States had embargoed, Japan chose to expand its war of conquest across southeast Asia. On December 7, 1941, the Imperial Japanese navy attacked Pearl Harbor in Hawaii, and America was thrust into war. Four days later, Italy and Germany, both allies of Japan, also declared war on the United States.

America immediately geared up for war production. Industries retooled and expanded operations for war needs; shipyards reorganized into mass production assembly lines. Almost overnight unemployment dropped to about one percent. Women by the hundreds of thousands went to work outside the home to fill critical vacancies left by enlisted men. As had their mothers and grandmothers in 1917–1918, women stepped into trousers, cut their hair, and worked in armaments factories, drove trucks, operated heavy equipment, repaired cars, and delivered the mail, among many other jobs.

The U.S. War Production Board quickly implemented priorities for most industries and imposed rationing consumer goods. Books of ration tickets with allocations of points for gasoline, clothing, and food were issued to all American families. To offset food shortages, "Victory Gardens" were cultivated in suburban backyards and city parks. Community organizations sponsored recycling drives to collect metal, rubber, paper, and even nylon stockings for the war effort.

Despite the rapid response of America and its economic might, the tide of the war turned slowly. Rather than a direct assault on Hitler's Fortress Europe, the Allies opted for an invasion from North Africa through Italy. In June 1944, the Allies launched a second front in northern France. From the east, the Russians pushed into Germany, linking up with the Americans just south of Berlin the following spring. Within his bunker in Berlin, Hitler committed suicide in April 1945, and Germany surrendered in May.

In the Pacific, the United States and Allies continued to suffer setbacks throughout 1942 until the Battle of Midway in June where the Japanese lost four aircraft carriers before withdrawing. After halting the Japanese military advance, the Allies began their strategic leapfrogging across the Pacific from island to island until they were within bombing range of Japan in 1944. The fanatical resistance of the Japanese on these outer islands convinced President Truman to drop the atomic bomb on Hiroshima in August 1945. Only after a second bomb annihilated Nagasaki three days later did Japan surrender.

Dress and Identity: Ideas and Ideals of Masculinity During the Great Depression and World War II

With the crash of the American stock market at the end of 1929, unemployment leaped from less than 4% that year to nearly 25% in 1933.[12] The ideology of work as the cornerstone of male identity for the American working- and middle-classes was substantially undermined by the massive loss of jobs. Even for men who retained their jobs, many were subjected to wage cuts and reduced hours, and the threat of unemployment was ever present. The masculine ethos of self-reliance and the manly role of breadwinner were preordained for American men as it had been for their fathers and grandfathers. In their research of American

Figure 5-5. Consumer ads of the Great Depression often represented the American working-class male in photographic apotheoses of man, machine, and honest labor. These depictions of men as breadwinners helped restore the nation's confidence and instill hope that recovery was "just around the corner." Ads 1936.

Figure 5-6. During the Depression of the 1930s, ideas of American manhood reverted to Victorian notions of separate spheres where men were the family breadwinners and women were homemakers. New anxieties about gender identities and behavior norms induced a renewed focus on fears of effeminacy and homosexuality. According to this 1937 toothpaste ad, if fresh breath could dispel the gossip about an unattached male, then the twenty-cent purchase price would be an exceptional value.

society and culture of the mid-1930s, Robert and Helen Lynd noted in their *Middletown in Transition* study, "One's job is the watershed down which the rest of one's life tends to flow in Middletown. Who one is, whom one knows, how one lives, what one aspires to be—these and many other urgent realities of living are patterned for one by what one does to get a living and the amount of living this allows one to buy."[13] Unemployment and the loss of economic power left men feeling emasculated. They lost status among their peers, in their community, and most especially with their wives and children. They saw themselves as impotent patriarchs unable to ensure stability in the home and properly provide for their families.

In 1933, the emphasis of New Deal initiatives was to put American men back to work. In fact, during the 1930s, many companies and government institutions enacted policies and regulations that prohibited married women of childbearing age to work. The New Deal work programs reinforced gender norms of men as family breadwinners and women as mothers and homemakers. Participants felt a sense of worker solidarity that grounded the values of manhood. This new sense of collectivity and cooperation inspired a resurgence of unionism and labor organization actions. Advertisers featured the working-class man rather than the typical middle-class office worker. (Figure 5-5.) The "be yourself" attitude of the Jazz Age was abandoned and would not resurface until the first stirrings of the counterculture groups of the 1950s.

Popular culture of the Depression era reflected a twentieth-century adaptation of the Victorian concept of separate spheres for men and women. Through rigid conformity, both sexes found their footing again after the disorienting social revolutions of the 1920s and the trauma of the Depression. The masculine values for the average Middletown man, for example, were centered on conformity—"being like other people," explained one citizen. "Practically all of us realize that we are common men, and we are prone to distrust and hate those whom we regard as uncommon."[14]

Among the "uncommon" types of men at the time who were "hated" in Middletown—and throughout America—were homosexuals. During the 1930s, the specter of feminization and the resulting fear of effeminacy reemerged. (Figure 5-6.) Pop-psychologists distilled Freudian assumptions about sexuality and sexual development in childhood into the notion of the strong mother/weak father = gay son. To counter such possibilities, gender-role socialization of children evolved into a social science during this time. IQ and personality tests, first introduced into school systems in the 1920s, were expanded to measure and chart gendered behaviors in greater depth. Manhood could now be scientifically tested. Although in the end the test results actually were counterintuitive, revealing, for instance, that boys brought up primarily by their mothers tested more masculine than boys brought up by their fathers or both parents equally, the fear of their sons growing up to become a "pansy" as defined by these personality tests caused parents much anxiety. Childcare authorities emphasized discouraging boys from interests in art, reading, or cooking while encouraging participation in sports and rugged outdoor activities to assure manliness in the adult.

Men likewise overcompensated to guard against effeminacy in themselves. In 1932, *Vanity Fair* offered "tortured wives" advice on the Depression-era husband. "His fear of being caught in the act of being

Figure 5-7. To fill the labor shortage caused by the massive troop deployment, government and industry reversed policies of discrimination against working women and encouraged them to leave the home and join the labor force. Mass media depictions of women working in factories and service sectors confidently operating complex machinery aided recruitment of women. Ads 1943.

sentimental," suggested the editor, was "part of a national male fear that he will be thought a sissy." This explanation, and many similar pronouncements in the mass media of the time, did little to comfort women who complained about the lack of affection from their men. "The American husband is positively the worst lover in the world," continued *Vanity Fair.* "His occupation with himself and his definite lack of romanticism...is an appalling immaturity."[15] Sentiment and romance were, after all, qualities of woman's sphere.

At the end of the decade, masculine conventions—exercised through a pervasive conformity—had once again become firmly entrenched. Those in society who were not among the trusted common men of the Middletown social order—nonwhites, gays, and especially women—were relegated to subculture and subclass stereotypes. Men fiercely guarded their renewed sense of power and dominance within the revived separate spheres of the sexes. Especially telling was a promotional ad for *Ladies' Home Journal* in 1939, in which American men were criticized for their "barriers of silence and conventional prejudice" when it came to editorial material that women needed "for solving problems of living." Despite objections from male heads of household, the *Journal* affirmed that it would continue to provide information about "birth control, morality, double standards, drinking, and divorce" for their more than three million women readers to help them make decisions that could "lead to better living."[16] Ironically, without knowing it, the fathers and husbands who wrote angry letters to the *Ladies' Home Journal* in 1939 were on the threshold of change unlike anything a women's magazine could hope to instigate. The societal norms of separate spheres that men had found comforting and necessary during the Depression were once again about to be overturned entirely as the Second World War began.

The U.S. mobilization for the Second World War occurred on a scale not seen since the Civil War. Millions of men were quickly deployed around the globe to serve in the military and provide support. In combat, American men could prove their masculinity in ways they had found difficult in the workplace and in their homes during the Depression. The battlefield validated their roles as dedicated providers and protectors of family, hearth, and country. Furthermore, the moral crusade to save the world from Nazi genocide and Japanese tyranny enhanced the American male's manhood with newfound masculine virtue and noble purpose. Images of the strong, manly warrior and his very real heroism and sacrifice saturated the mass media, movies, newsreels, and advertising during the war years.

Despite this reinforcement of masculine power, though, wartime needs forced substantial changes on the home front that challenged traditional male and female roles. As the labor shortage increased due to the expanding military mobilization, women were called upon by the

Figure 5-8. Although Americans understood the need for temporary women's branches of the military, many men resented the female in uniform. She was viewed as a usurper of masculine identity and a negator of feminine respectability. Ads 1943–44.

government to leave the home and take jobs in industries and service sectors that were traditionally male occupations. Union, corporate, and government policies against hiring married women had to be rescinded. During the war years, more than three million women donned overalls and workpants, cropped their hair or tied on bandannas, and joined "Rosie the Riveter" in munitions plants, shipyards, airplane and tank factories, and hundreds of similar workplaces that were previously for men only. (Figure 5-7.) Women, especially married women from the middle classes, suddenly enjoyed personal and economic freedoms that had been denied them by the Depression era revival of the cult of separate spheres. Even more alarming to traditionalists than women in the workplace was women in the military. In 1942, the War Department initiated women's branches of the military. (Figure 5-8.) Although these auxiliary women's corps were strictly segregated and women served primarily in support roles to free more men for combat functions, female recruits in uniform were viewed by many men as usurpers of their warrior-protector role.

The surge in numbers of women in the workplace was not the only contributor to the erosion of conventional gender identities in the 1940s. Almost overnight, wartime pressures erased gender norms and undermined established social order. Now women were not only breadwinners, but, in the absence of soldier husbands, they were often the head of the household with the power of decision-making for the entire family. Women owned their own cars and traveled when and where they chose. They went to bars and dance halls unaccompanied by men. They jitterbugged, drank cocktails, and experimented with sex. "Traditional barriers against women are gone," avowed *Ladies' Home Journal* in 1944. Women of wartime America "may drink and smoke in public, be as free as they like in extremes of dress and adornment, and may even be sexually promiscuous."[17]

The wartime "letdown of the barriers respecting women," continued the *Ladies' Home Journal*, had resulted in the "hurt ego" of the "frustrated male" who "felt it necessary to assert superiority much as a frustrated Hitler attempted to prove he belonged to a 'master race'." Modern American men were frustrated, maintained the *Journal's* editors, because of their "fear of women" who had successfully challenged the "mythical male superiority" by overturning the "double standards" of the Victorian separate spheres. The "sexual revolution,"—a prescient term used by the *Journal*— coupled with women's economic independence, self-reliance, and self-determination, had allowed women to prove themselves against challenges that, for decades, had been a masculine prerogative. "A large part of maleness consists in the ability to endure disabilities and defeats." By the end of the war, women had demonstrated their resilience and capacity to confront and overcome the "vicissitudes to which men have long since been subjected."[18]

When the war ended, millions of American soldiers returned stateside hoping for a return to normalcy. But as with their fathers following the First World, American men discovered that home was not the same as they had left it. Wives, girlfriends, and even mothers and grandmothers had become entirely different beings. One of the consequences of the wartime socioeconomic shifts was a substantial leap in the divorce rate, which for 1946 was more than double that of 1940.[19] Nevertheless, the American government and especially mass market interests with their power of advertising and pop culture went to work with full force to tip the scales back to a masculine order of social authority and economic control—a wholesale endeavor that became manifest in the 1950s.

With the reassertion of a dominant, patriarchal male orthodoxy in American society of the Depression years, followed by the ideal of the tough, rough warrior GI in the war years, masculine dress evolved to reflect and reinforce these prevalent masculine identities. The broad-shouldered, athletic silhouette in men's dress that had begun to emerge in the late 1920s expanded to the American mass market. The strongly delineated athletic look complemented the seriousness of the dutiful, take-charge working man of the 1930s and the combat soldier of the 1940s. Indeed, by the early war years before rationing and War Production Board restrictions on clothing manufacturing, the shoulder and back dimensions and arm and leg proportions of some styles of men's suits became exaggerated almost to the point of caricature. Even after the war, the pronounced contours of the athletic suit persisted, transitioning only reluctantly to a new look for the postwar ideas and ideals of masculinity.

Men's Style During the Depression

American men's suits of the early years of the Great Depression continued under the influence of Anglomania that prevailed for decades. The reticent English look was particularly suited to the revived conservatism that had firmly gripped American society in the 1930s.

Where American men departed, initially, from the dress guidance of London was in color and pattern choice. The Brits continued to relish and expand color options and especially pattern mixing in men's suiting. To the American male, experimentation with colorful suiting was as much a part of the previous Jazz Age as Oxford bags and raccoon coats. Then, too, most American men possessed an inherent inferiority complex

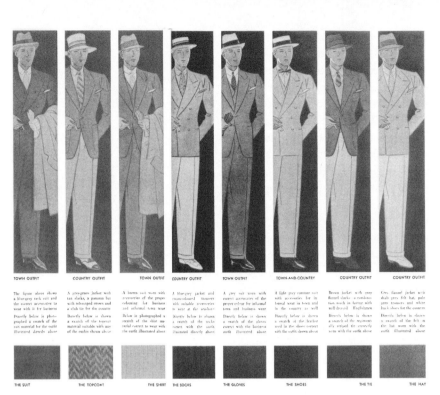

Figure 5-9. To help American men with selecting combinations of colors and textile patterns in their wardrobes, fashion editorials provided illustrations of fabric swatches matched to guidelines for dressing correctly. Style guide in color with fabric swatches from *Vanity Fair*, 1931.

when it came to fashion. It was common knowledge that London dictated the correctness of men's dress, and Americans were all too prone to dress incorrectly as journalists constantly reminded their male readers: "For while colors in men's things are rarely new, the fashion for different combinations moves in a faster cycle, and one of the great differences between the man who dresses smartly and the one who fails to present a smart appearance, lies not so much in fashionable colors, but rather in fashion combinations of color and the general effect achieved."[20] Ever mindful of such potential failures, most American men steered clear of such fashion minefields as color coordination. "Plain grey for the well-dressed man," a columnist suggested to the wary businessman in 1932. The "leaders of fashion" in New York "are all wearing grey flannel suits just as they were wearing them five years ago and will probably be wearing them five years hence."[21]

Moreover, the fear of effeminacy was as strong as ever. The renunciation of aristocratic ideas of masculinity from a century earlier prevailed still, so the less interest a man exhibited in "feminine" pursuits—such as fashion—the less suspect he would be among his peers. In her 1937 autobiography, American designer Elizabeth Hawes expressed her frustration with men's attitudes about color and fashion. When she was invited to design a collection of menswear for a color spread in *American Magazine*, she asked the male editorial board about their personal preferences in clothing colors. " 'Color!' They snorted. 'Only pansies wear colored clothes.'" Dejected by this feedback, Hawes lamented, "God help the American male with his background of having to be Masculine."[22] The following year, *Esquire* similarly asserted contemptuously that because "the world of fashion is riddled with fairies," the dangerous "influence of the lily lads...is gradually emasculating the country." Warned the editor, "Be on your guard for the taint of swish....It is up to the hundred-percent normal males of the land—if there be any such still extant—to combat and subdue this tendency."[23]

To shake the American male out of his dress complacency and fear of fashion, though, many men's dress guides and magazine articles began to produce color layouts and wardrobe charts showing photos of color-coordinated fabric swatches for jackets, trousers, overcoats, and even matching socks and ties. (Figure 5-9.) "Certainly men's clothes are not so gay as women's, nor are they so obvious, but they are much easier to live with and in, and it requires a discriminating eye to select the proper combinations," coaxed a fashion writer in 1932.[24] *Vanity Fair* continued to feature the monthly column "Our London Letter" with reports of the Englishman's dress and personal style. An especially favorite topic was the activities and wardrobe of the Prince of Wales who was as much as ever an ambassador of the English apparel and textile trade. *Esquire* so frequently reported on the Prince that editorials identified him simply as "P. of W." Ever on the vanguard of men's style, the Prince was a perpetual source of masculine fashion and taste, sometimes going too far according to his tailors and critics. During a visit to France in 1930, the Prince shocked the reception attendees when he wore a pink shirt with a matching attached collar. In 1934, he and his brother, the Duke of Kent, began having their trousers made with a zipper fly front rather than the typical button fly, for which the Prince had to supply his own zippers.[25] (Because Scholte and other London tailors regarded this sartorial shift as too extreme, the Prince had to have his trousers made in New York although Scholte continued to make the Prince's suit coats.[26])

In 1931, additional help arrived for the fashion-befuddled American male when *Apparel Arts* began publication. These oversized, colorful style guides were put on countertop displays in department stores and men's shops to not only aid salesmen but also to reassure style-shy customers. Two years later, the editorial staff of *Apparel Arts* launched a new men's magazine, *Esquire*, to further democratize fashion and contemporary style for the average American man.

Hollywood became an even more important influence in American masculine stylishness during the 1930s than it had been during the silent film decades. Rather than relying on studio costume departments for their clothing, leading men often had allowances for tailor-made wardrobes specified in their contracts. Hence, on the movie screen before them, American men could watch and learn about modern masculine style. At one end of the spectrum were European imports—the English gentleman such as Leslie Howard and Ronald Colman and the sophisticated Frenchman like Charles Boyer. Simpler, homegrown elegance was exemplified by Fred Astaire, Gary Cooper, and Jimmy Stewart. The epitome of masculine style of the era was Anglo-American Cary Grant who wore everything from three-piece suits to sportswear with an understated ease and confidence.

Gradually, as economic conditions began to improve in the midthirties, men once again began to dress with a renewed interest in color and style. The popularity of bold patterns especially represented the lighter, more hopeful zeitgeist. Putting the right face on one's dress was as important to one's well-being, suggested some editorials, as it was to the improvement of one's business prospects. "The lack of ready cash may be betrayed, upon occasion, by your features, but shouldn't, under any circumstance, be indicated by your dress," *Esquire* opined in 1934. "This is not spoken by way of preamble to a revival of that trite and tiresome and

Figure 5-10. The drape cut dominated men's suiting throughout the 1930s. The athletic silhouette featured broad shoulders, full chest, trim waist, and narrow hips. Drape cut suits from Detmer Woolens, 1937.

obviously untrue maxim that clothes make the man, but merely by way of gentle reminder that they have been known to hinder, in the attainment of business objectives."[27]

Suits and Formal Dress 1930–1945

The athletic silhouette in suits, introduced in the late 1920s and gradually and subtly refined into the drape cut (also called London cut or blade cut) by Frederick Scholte and his Savile Row followers, remained the preferred look. (Figure 5-10 and Color Plate 5.) The suit style was unchanged, familiar, and safe in such uncertain times. The lines were flattering and easy to wear for most men. A man's shoulders looked broad with the fluid draping of blade cut flannels; his chest appeared full with the deeply rolled lapels; and his waist and hips were made trim with the raised coat waistline and ventless skirt. One key design difference between British and American drape suits was the treatment of the sleevehead at the shoulderline. American men insisted on a smooth roll of the sleeve fabric where it was stitched into the armscye whereas Eng-

Figure 5-11. Trousers of the 1930s were full and baggy with wide legs at twenty-two inches at the cuff. Young men's styles called "high waisters" were made with a raised, wide waistband often worn beltless and with attached metal monograms. Left, novelty trousers from Ferris Woolens, 1938; right, high waisters from Bellas Hess, 1937.

SWING OUT IN NIFTY SLACKS   . . . WITH YOUR INITIALS

lishmen accepted the tiny puckers from stitched tucks. For the American male who was especially picky about his shoulderline, some tailors offered a "rope shoulder" construction whereby the sleevehead was sewn with a slightly raised roll as if encasing a coil of rope.

By the midthirties, two subtle changes added a touch of modernity to the athletic style suit. First was a modification of the peaked lapel that had become so popular in the late 1920s. The lapel width was expanded slightly, and the peak was angled upward more. When combined with a deep roll, the new peaked lapels added even more breadth to the athletic look of the masculine chest. Second was a narrowing and raising of the sleeve armholes, which emphasized the broad, natural shoulderlines and made the waist appear more trim.

Certainly not all men could wear the athletic suit silhouette. For men who were heavyset, box back cuts, with or without center seams, allowed ample room for a non-binding fit.

For the sake of comfort, many American men had abandoned the suit vest by the 1930s although ready-to-wear and tailored suits still came with a vest and a second pair of trousers. Suit vests were greatly varied, depending upon the jacket style. The most common version was the collarless, five-button, single-breasted cut. Tailor-made variants included double-breasted closures, notched lapels, and even cropped, straightline hems for high-waisted (British style) trousers. Athletic style vests featured deep armholes, narrow shoulders, and tucks or even inverted pleats at the waist seam for a snug fit.

Trousers were enormous all through the 1930s. Some catalog illustrations looked more like the depictions of capacious Oxford bags from a decade earlier. (Figure 5-11.) Both pleated and plain front trousers were made with wide legs at twenty-two inches at the cuff, diminishing only an inch at the end of the decade. Waistbands were constructed with novelty dimensions and detailing. In the late thirties, a young men's fad was the high style (also called high waister) with a raised, wide waistband.

Stand...Sit...Slouch...
TROUSERS TAILORED WITH TALON
always keep their good appearance

Today . . . well-tailored trousers are closed with the **TALON** *slide fastener*

Ward's Newest Fashion
in All Wool Slacks
with Slide Fastener
$3.98

New Tunnel Belt Loops
and Fancy Diamond Pleats!
Snappy 1-button Waistband!
Wide 22-inch Cuff Bottoms!

Figure 5-12. One of the most significant changes in men's trousers was the introduction of zipper fly fronts in the early 1930s. Tailors resisted the innovation, but American ready-to-wear makers were quick to mass produce the new trouser styles. Left, Talon ad, 1936; right, detail of Montgomery Ward catalog page, 1935.

WHAT?
air-conditioned
clothes?

And why not? You live in your suit. It's the very thing that ought to bring you comfort on a warm day...

That's why we have equipped the

NEW PALM BEACH

with a "cooling system." The patented fabric is porous, and every little pore (by the new method of weaving and finishing) is set to stay open and admit the air. (See test below).

That's just one of the surprises that makes the New Palm Beach a greater value this summer. Another is its happy faculty of shedding dirt and dust. A third...its "cleverness" in resisting muss and wrinkle.

But the greatest surprise of all is the way the New Palm Beach jacks up your good appearance. Smart's the word...

At your clothier's, today...new weaves...new patterns...light colors, dark colors, and dashing whites. In suits, ensembles and comfortable SLACKS.

GOODALL CO · CINCINNATI

$18.50
COAT AND TROUSERS

Look for this Label...your assurance of the Genuine

SHOWING HOW PALM BEACH LETS IN THE AIR AND EVAPORATES BODY PERSPIRATION... Your body is apt to give off a pint of perspiration on a warm day. Hence, these five jars, each containing a pint of liquid, were exposed to the air.

JAR NO. 1   JAR NO. 2   JAR NO. 3   JAR NO. 4   JAR NO. 5

In 4½ hours Jar No. 1, without any covering, evaporated all the "perspiration." In the same length of time, 95% was evaporated in Jar No. 2, covered by porous Palm Beach Cloth. It is highly interesting to note that jars Nos. 3, 4, 5, which were covered with other summer fabrics, retained from 25% to 41% of "perspiration." **The air walks right through a Palm Beach Suit to cool your skin.**

Many high style trousers were made without belt loops to be worn beltless, and others were made with deep belt loops that were worn with skinny belts. Some high waisters also included machine-stitched or affixed metal monogram initials on the wide waistband. Metal ring tabs at each side could be pulled taut for a snug fit at the hips.

The most significant change to men's trousers in the early 1930s was the introduction of the zipper fly. Despite the publicity from the Prince of Wales adopting the zipper fly trouser in 1934, most men were reluctant to try the new closure. The location of the metal locking teeth of the zipper was unnerving. In addition, traditionalist tailors were resistant to the notion and refused to employ the device. Nevertheless, makers of zippers, particularly the Hookless Fastener Company, maker of the Talon slide fastener, campaigned extensively to change men's attitudes toward the fashion innovation. (Figure 5-12 and Color Plate 6.) The artwork of some ads showed a before-and-after comparison that emphasized the "shabbiness" of gaping, button fly closures versus the smooth, seam-like lay of the zippered fly. In 1935, mass merchandisers introduced the new style nationwide.

Further evidence of comfort as a critical market force in men's suiting is evident from the emergence of the summer or tropical weight suit. For decades, the summer suit had been a collateral style preferred regionally by gentlemen living in hot, southern states or acquired as resort wear by the affluent for trips to Florida and the Caribbean in winter. In the 1930s, though, men increasingly chose summer suits of lighter materials for town dress, and the struggling menswear industry responded by offering fresh assortments of styles in even more lightweight fabrics. The classic Palm Beach suit was made of a cotton and mohair blend woven into a "porous" fabric "set to stay open to admit the air." "The air walks

Figure 5-13. Summer suits of lightweight fabrics became generically known as Palm Beach suits, named for the cool dress styles preferred at the Florida resorts in the 1930s. In addition to traditional cotton and mohair blends, new synthetic rayon blends and seersucker became widely popular for summer suits. Palm Beach suit ad, 1934.

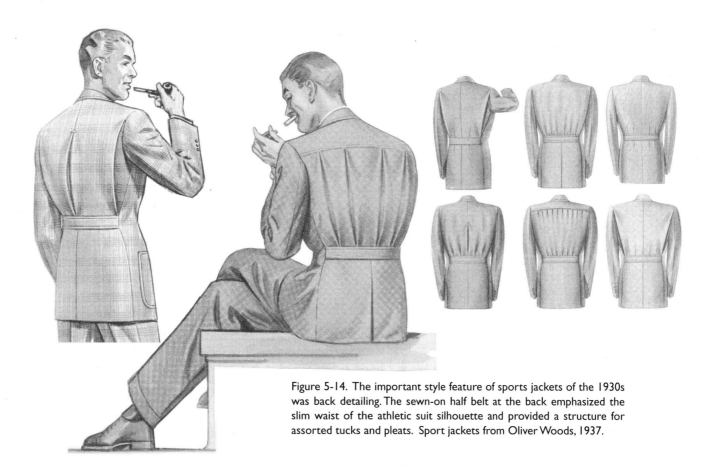

Figure 5-14. The important style feature of sports jackets of the 1930s was back detailing. The sewn-on half belt at the back emphasized the slim waist of the athletic suit silhouette and provided a structure for assorted tucks and pleats. Sport jackets from Oliver Woods, 1937.

right though a Palm Beach suit to cool your skin," promised ads of the time.[28] (Figure 5-13.) Much to the chagrin of the Goodall Manufacturing Company, makers of the Palm Beach suit label, the term became a catchall for summer suits in general and was sometimes written in lower case, not unlike oxfords, ulsters, and norfolks. As *Fortune* reported in 1937: "You may be wearing a summer suit, and you may call it a Palm Beach suit, but unless it has a Palm Beach label and was made by Goodall Co., Inc., it isn't Palm Beach and Goodall would like you to stop calling it that."[29]

Among the newest tropical blend fabrics of the decade were rayon and worsted, rayon and wool, rayon and cotton, and rayon and acetate. Seersucker also reached a wider popularity at the time. Although for decades, men's summer jackets had been made from seersucker—an Anglicized word from the Persian *shiruschakar* for puckered textiles— variations of the fabric broadened its appeal. "Did you think that seersucker always came in those crinkly stripes that looked like ribbons of toothpaste on a ground of corrugated board?" asked *Esquire* in 1935. "Well, you're partly right. It always did, until fairly recently. But now you can get it in such brave new patterns as small brown and white checks, and it's a case of handsome is as handsome does."[30] The preferred tropical weight fabric for daytime suits, though, was gabardine. It was heavier than the other summer fabrics, which made it tailor well and yet feel much cooler than typical worsteds. Not only were gabardine suits favored for street wear in warm weather, but, at the resorts, the gabardine suit was combined with colorful polo shirts for a look of casualness. "The French have a word for it, dègagè," noted a fashion editorial.[31]

Figure 5-15. Among the most prevalent menswear influences from London in the 1930s were the rich color options and bold textile patterns such as herringbones, window pane checks, and plaids. Especially popular were any of the assorted "glenurquhart" tartans, or glen plaid for short. Cover of National Bellas Hess catalog, Spring 1937.

The tremendous popularity of the summer suit and its flexible casualness led to an expansion of sports coat styles. All varieties of belted-back jackets were designed as both suit coats and sports coats. (Figure 5-14.) The sewn-on half belt added to the trim waistline of the athletic silhouette while the many arrangements of tucks, pleats, and vents between the shoulder yoke and belt provided an easy fit. The sports jacket suit also blurred the "correctness" line between town wear and country wear. Depending upon the nature of their work and location of their offices, many men opted for the sports style suit as business attire.

Summer suits and sports jackets also provided men with the opportunity to revive an interest in color, especially after the Depression began to ease in the second half of the decade. Catalogs featured gabardines in rich palettes of blues, browns, and golden tans in addition to pale neutrals ranging from pearl gray to oatmeal. Some hues called "red-back gabardine" were warmed with a warp weave of red cotton threads that were believed to help filter the intensity of the sun's rays. The Prince of Wales observed that the popularity of Palm Beach suits made "in sky blues and other vivid colors" could be attributed to the "cosmopolitan nature of the American people" since "Latins and other southern Europeans tend to dress more gaily than Anglo-Saxons."[32]

In addition to more color options, American men eagerly embraced the patterned suit. The two most popular forms were the "Belbourne" plaid with its evenly spaced checks of contrasting double lines, and the "Glen" plaid variously woven of intersecting bands of four to eight lines. (Figure 5-15.) Derived from the Scottish *glenurquhart* tartan of the nineteenth century, the glen plaid was popularized by the Prince of Wales who admired the precise tailoring required to align the horizontal bands of lines at coat closures and seams.

With the beginning of the Second World War, the exigencies of shortages and rationing significantly altered men's suit designs. Although the athletic silhouette of the suit coat, with its broad, unpadded shoulders, trim waist, and slim hips carried over into the 1940s, the cut and details were altered by the requirements imposed upon the menswear industry by the U.S. War Production Board (WPB). During the spring of 1942, the WPB instituted a series of sweeping regulations affecting the design of clothing and the use of materials. The restrictions were an emergency stopgap to conserve wool for uniforms and blankets, silk for parachutes, leather for boots, and metals for munitions and materiel among others.

On the other hand, though, cotton, rayon, acetate, plastics, silver, and many other nonessential raw or manufactured materials were still plentiful and accessible to the apparel industry. As the American people girded themselves for privation and sacrifice, journalists emphasized the importance of buying American- and Allied-made goods to sustain the newly recovered U.S. economy. "That the male consuming public will of necessity be compelled to tighten the belt a little and forego some of the apparel pleasures which have been his for many years, seems to be in the cards," warned *Men's Wear* in early 1942. "This does not mean, however, that there will not be sufficient apparel of far from an inferior class to go around."[33] *Vogue* similarly weighed in with a reminder that "the makers of fashion...are operating with full government approval. Whatever is on sale in a shop is there to be bought, with the government's full permission. Refusal to buy only helps to dislocate the public economy."[34] But within the year, ration coupons, acute shortages, and products made with substitutions that consumers did not like impeded apparel sales and profits, depressing clothing businesses even as other industries were booming.

The Victory Suits of World War II were more a variation on the athletic cut theme than a radical departure. Suit coats made of 100% wool were still tailored with the drape cut shoulder breadth, but WPB restrictions altered many details. As *Esquire* reported in 1942, the new "streamlined suits" were courtesy of Uncle Sam: Jacket lapels were narrowed, and skirt hemlines were shortened slightly to 29 3/4 inches (regular size 37); patch pockets, back belts, tucks, pleats, and vents were eliminated.[35] Double-breasted suits did not include vests. Trousers were made without pleats, cuffs, and tucks; leg widths narrowed to 22 inches at the knee, tapering to 18 1/2 inches at the bottom. High waisters with their excessively wide, overlapping waistbands disappeared. Vests could not have collars, lapels, or patch pockets. *Esquire* further noted that contrasting vests of cotton or rayon blends took on "new significance with men who still like the idea of wearing a [vest]."[36] Design proposals for a variety of Economy Suits presented at the 1942 Merchant Tailors and Designers Association even went so far as to recommend suit coats without collars and lapels.[37]

In addition, most of the bolder textile patterns and hues were abandoned in the face of wartime seriousness and conservation. Military colors were favorites for civilians to express their patriotism and support of the troops. Air blue, inspired by the uniform color of the U.S. Army Air Force, was especially popular. Shades of khaki, sand, and even olive drab were adapted to wartime suits during the North Africa campaigns (1942–43).

Figure 5-16. In the early years of the Second World War, double-breasted suits were cut with an elongated lapel roll that dropped to the bottom button. Double-breasted suit from Pioneer Tailoring, 1942.

Figure 5-17. Between the late 1930s and the early 1940s, young urban blacks and Latinos found self-expression and ethnic identity with the zoot suit. Styles of zoot suits varied widely but featured common design elements such as exaggerated padding in the shoulderlines of coats and high-waisted trousers with full, multipleated legs. Under pressures from War Production Board regulations, local law enforcement, and social opprobrium, zootsuiters were forced to abandon their distinctive dress. Photos c. 1941–42.

Figure 5-18. For rebellious white teens and young men, adaptations of the exaggerated styling of the zoot suit were applied to the athletic cut silhouette and labeled "swing" or "swank" suits in the early 1940s. The jackets were reconstructed with extremely wide, padded shoulders, long skirts, and huge lapels. Trousers were deeply pleated with wide legs and high waistbands. War Production Board regulations prohibited such excesses, and, by 1943, tailors and retailers discontinued the styles. Swank suit from Pioneer Tailoring, 1942.

One of the style innovations noted in the fashion press of the early war years was the lapel roll that dropped to the bottom button of double-breasted jackets. (Figure 5-16.) The look was especially popular with slender young men who liked the elongated sweep of the jacket and the deeper V-front opening.

Unlike with the World War I generation, a youth culture did not dominate much of society during the Second World War. These were serious times, and grownups were in charge now. Nevertheless, rebellious youth found a means of expression in clothing that riled parents and authority figures, ultimately with tragic results. During the first couple of years of the war, teenage boys and young men not in the military donned exaggerated zoot suits that came in a wide assortment of styles. (Figure 5-17.) Within the urban jazz culture of the late thirties, the term "zoot" referred to "something worn or performed in an extravagant style."[38] In 1942, *Life* described the details of the "jive-garb" of the "long-haired hepcats":

> A really 'solid set of threads' has a garish-colored coat with from three to six inches of padding in each right-angled shoulder, a tapering waist, a length which comes to within a few inches of the knees, slash pockets and pegged sleeves. The different-colored trousers, snatched up high to the diaphragm by flashy suspenders, have a 'frantic' full 32-in. knee, then drape to a narrow peg (from 12 to 15 in.) which makes the cuffs snug around the ankles.[39]

Sometimes long watch chains hung from the waistband in a low swag nearly to the floor. The look became associated with urban blacks in the East and Latino gangs on the West Coast. "Rather than disguise their alienation or efface their hostility to the dominant society, the [zoot-suiters] adopted an arrogant posture," notes social historian Stuart Cosgrove. "They flaunt their difference, and the zoot suit became the means by which that difference was announced."[40] However, when the look was worn by rebellious suburbanite whites, the styles were called "swing" or "swank" suits and were benign enough to be available in most tailoring catalogs of the early forties. (Figure 5-18.) The problem for zoot-suiters arose when the WPB instituted its conservation restrictions in early 1942. The production of zoot suits, said one WPB official, "was interfering with the U.S. war effort and must stop."[41] Latino gangs in California, particularly, continued to wear the exaggerated suits even though the excessive use of fabric clearly violated the law. Consequently, in the summer of 1943, groups of servicemen stationed in Los Angeles instigated fights with zoot-suiters, some confrontations of which escalated into full-scale bloody riots. With the negative publicity in the press, the constant scrutiny of the police, and the relentless persecution by servicemen, zoot-suiters were compelled to abandon their distinctive expressions of culture and personal style.

Evening formal dress returned to the forefront of men's style in the 1930s. The youthful casualness of the previous decade was replaced by a resurgence of Edwardian formality. Old money resurrected its position of prominence as the nouveau riche vanished from the social scene after the crash.

The morning coat was updated with the draped cut shoulders, peaked lapels, and tapered sleeves. The exceedingly wide trousers looked even more voluminous when patterned with strong vertical stripes or herringbone and topped with snug-fitting morning coat. Solid gray trousers, though, were still the preferred option.

The tail coat of the 1930s was renovated with a new look. Instead of the smooth, tight fit of previous designs, the tail coat was constructed with the drape cut that allowed the vertical wrinkles over the chest and shoulder blades to be evident. (Figure 5-19.) Broad, sharply angled peaked lapels with a deep roll looked fresh for the era. The shiny gros-grain silk facings of the lapels, favored by Americans but not the British, emphasized the deep rolls and wide expanse of the lapels. In addition, tails were notably shorter and wider. Black remained the preferred color for evening dress although, in the second half of the decade, midnight blue became all the rage since it actually appeared blacker than black in the dim lights of evening soirees.

The accoutrement of evening dress did not vary. The correct accessories included a white piqué V-front vest, wing collar bosom shirt (with or without an open back) fastened by white or black pearl studs and matching cuff links, white butterfly bow tie, and patent pumps.

Whereas the single-breasted tuxedo had been the most prevalent with Flaming Youth of the twenties, the double-breasted version was the favorite of young men in the 1930s. The tuxedo, too, was reshaped with the soft, fluid drape cut. Also, as with tail coats, the sharply angled peaked lapels gave the dinner jacket a look of modernity. In addition to traditional black worsted and, later, midnight blue, textured black-on-black vertical stripes were a popular fabric variety for tuxedos. White tropical weight gabardine, linen, and even cotton duck were correct for warm weather and resort wear.

During World War II, the single-breasted tuxedo returned to dominance because the wool double-breasted style was restricted by the WPB in 1942. Likewise, production of the tail coat and cutaway morning coat were prohibited.

Figure 5-19. The drape cut suit construction of the early 1930s was also applied to evening dress. Both the tail coat and the tuxedo were reshaped with broad shoulders, deeply rolled lapels, and fuller trousers. The comfortable, roomy fit at the armscyes and across the back resulted in fluid, vertical wrinkles that previously had been unacceptable. Tuxedo and tail coat from Mitchell Fashion Company, 1932.

Figure 5-20. Although the spencer-style mess jacket was not new in the 1930s, the look became popular with trim young men as an alternative to the tuxedo and tail coat. Mess suit ad from Cohen Brothers, 1935.

For a few seasons in the midthirties, the mess jacket was a trendy alternative to the tuxedo. In essence, the mess jacket was a tail-less tail coat as the ad shown here explains. (Figure 5-20.) The short, spencer-style cut with its high waist crop and skeleton back construction was particularly flattering to the slender build of young men. As with the tuxedo, either a vest or a cummerbund was correct. Similarly, a white or black bow tie could dress up or dress down the look. Mess jackets were most common in white gabardine or duck although black and midnight blue were acceptable in cooler climates. By the end of the 1930s, the mess jacket was seen less because it had been widely adopted by jazz bands and waiters as a uniform.

Shirts 1930–1945

By the 1930s, the banded collar dress shirt with its detachable starched collar was almost as archaic as the Victorian pullover bosom shirt. In 1937, *Fortune* commented on the decline, "The explanation was simple enough: During the War some 1,000,000 U.S. soldiers and marines had grown accustomed to a soft collar attached shirt and most of them refused to go back into the starched neck harness."[42] The wishbooks of mass merchandisers like Sears and Montgomery Ward still offered one or two versions of the detachable collar, but they were relegated to the notions or men's furnishings sections rather than with men's dress shirts.

Despite the return of subdued conservative colors for suits and outerwear in the early years of the Depression, men's soft collar shirts in vibrant colors and patterns remained popular. Vertical stripes of varying widths and color combinations were the most common pattern followed by small checks in equally as many colors.

The continued fashion news in shirts was collar treatments. The unstarched soft collar remained a problem for makers and consumers alike. "For almost two generations the industry has been striving to produce a collar which would hold its shape," acknowledged an ad in 1935, "which would be comfortable and yet not wilt under perspiration, which would maintain its neat appearance without starch, and which could be washed and ironed simply and easily without requiring restarching with each laundering."[43] The result was a wide assortment of permanently fused collars that were constructed of plies of fabric with cellulose acetate heat sealed and topstitched to hold the shape of the collar and the point flat. The most widely licensed process was Trubenizing, which was a patented, branded method invented in 1934 by America's largest shirt maker Liebovitz Company. (Figure 5-21.) The process improved on earlier fused collar methods in which the collar was made more durable and the resulting fabric was porous and breathable. Even then, though, fused collars could crack, blister, or separate after repeated washings and ironings. By the beginning of the 1940s, makers such as Van Heusen had perfected methods of weaving collars on circular looms that fitted the neck without added linings or thick topstitching.

Collar pins remained a favorite solution since they not only held the collar points flat, but they also prevented the tie knot from shifting out of place. Collar pins, though, broke the yarns of tightly woven broadcloth eventually causing frays. In the mid-1930s, the button down collar was introduced to a mass market as an alternative to collar pins. The button

Figure 5-21. The banded collar dress shirt with its detached stiff collars was largely abandoned in the 1930s in favor of the soft collar shirt. To address the problem of unstarched collars curling out of shape, shirtmakers experimented with varieties of fused methods in which plies of fabric and synthetic materials were heat sealed to hold the shape of the collar. Royal Ascot dress shirts with Trubenized collars from Sears, 1938.

down broadcloth collar achieved the same fixed-point effect as the pinned collar. "Button-down collars is the one style note that 'clicked' and kept on clicking," asserted the copy in a 1937 Sears catalog. "Collars stay neater when points are held in place by buttons."[44]

Other shirt fashion news of the 1930s was with fabrics. Open weaves were among the smartest summertime looks for both dress and sport shirts. Advances in high-speed textile weaving made possible drop-stitch broadcloths with screen-like textures that were light and cool yet strong and durable. Another popular porous weave fabric that became a favorite trend in the late thirties was a spongy crepe in rich deep tones. Satin stripes with their alternating raised-weave texture were a year-round look influenced by the shirtings of London's custom shops. Silk was in such demand for dress shirts that even mass merchandisers offered assortments in their catalogs. For men who liked the rich-hued look and feel of silk shirts but not the upscale price, color-fast rayon shirts were a popular option.

During the Second World War, the design of dress shirts was little impacted by shortages or WPB restrictions. Cotton was plentiful, and textile mills ran around the clock producing yards of cotton and cotton-blend fabrics to fill in the gaps of other textile shortages. Some dyes were scarce, but, on the whole, men still had a wide range of hues and colorful prints from which to choose.

Work Clothes 1930–1945

The average working man of the Depression era who was fortunate enough to have a steady indoor job with a factory or warehouse likely wore the standardized, long-sleeved work shirt made with two chest pockets and various reinforcing details. Elbows and shoulder yokes were double-layered; pocket corners were bar tacked to prevent tears; sleeves were triple stitched at the roomy armholes; and shirttails were longer to

Figure 5-22. Work shirts of the 1930s were newly constructed with additional reinforcements and detailing such as bar tacking to ensure durability and longer wear. Cast Iron brand work shirts from Sears, 1938.

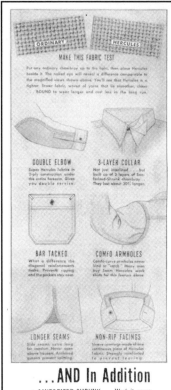

stay tucked. Mass-merchandise catalogs emphasized the durability and comfort of their private label work shirts with hard-sell copy and illustrations. (Figure 5-22.) Montgomery Ward touted the "non-skimping features" of their work shirts that included triple-stitched strain points, large pockets, and preshrunk, closely woven fabrics.[45] Key words in the catalog text such as "longwearing," "reliable," "sturdy," and "heavy duty" were reassuring to the working man who was reluctant to spend much of his hard-earned wages on clothes.

The most common fabrics for work shirts were heavy chambray and twilled covert, usually in blue, gray, or tan. A crossover wintertime shirt for some working men was the wool flannel sportsman shirts commonly advertised for hunters and winter activities. These vividly-hued flannels in bright solids and multicolored plaids were pricey, though, at $3.49–$4.98 compared to covert twill work shirts at 45¢–98¢.

By the start of World War II, the variety of work shirts had broadened to include adaptations from sportswear such as knit crewneck "industrial" shirts and short-sleeved cuts for warm weather. Zipper front versions of work shirts were adapted from flannel jacket-shirts that were popular transitional sportswear between the cool seasons.

After wool became a restricted resource, work clothes makers increasingly relied on assorted blends of fabric, especially mixtures of spun rayon. By 1943, part wool work shirts made of 15% reused wool and 85% cotton were common.

Work shirts were paired with rugged and tough work pants made of heavy wool kersey, cotton whipcord, khaki twill, or cotton moleskin. Leg widths were huge ranging from twenty to twenty-two inches at the cuffs. Strain points were reinforced with tapes and double or triple stitching. As with dress trousers, zipper fly closures gradually replaced button fronts in the second half of the thirties although button flies remained common through World War II. During the war years, work trousers narrowed and were made without pleats and cuffs in keeping with WPB regulations.

Jodhpurs, or breeches as they were commonly known, were still a favorite uniform look of working men who were specialists or field man-

SHORT
For men up to 5 feet 7 inches tall. Order 30 or 32 inches inseam.

MEDIUM
For men between 5 ft. 7 in. and 5 ft. 11 in. Order 32 or 34 in. inseam.

TALL
For men 5 feet 11 in. and over. Order 34 or 36 inches inseam.

LOW BACK   HIGH BACK   FULL BACK

Figure 5-23. Work clothing of the Depression era such as denim overalls and jeans was made in greater varieties, including proportional sizing and varying textile weights. Left, proportional overalls from Sears, 1937; right, low, high, and full back overalls from Montgomery Ward, 1938.

agers such as surveyors, aviators, site foremen, explorers, and archaeologists among others. The same reinforced, knee-length styles were also worn for horseback riding, hunting, hiking, and similar outdoor activities. Not only was the zipper applied to the fly front, but it was also used at the knee on some styles in place of cumbersome laces or tiny buttons.

Denim work clothes were made in ever more varieties in the 1930s. (Figure 5-23.) Bib-front overalls were available in low back styles with denim suspenders that crossed over the back; high back styles with wide straps forming an "X" over the shoulder blades; and full back styles with a shallow scoop neck at the back. Work jeans with copper-riveted pockets were the top quality styles. In 1937, Sears introduced "graduated patterns...scientifically and practically designed to fit every man."[46] Placement of the waistband, dimensions of the bib, and lengths of the inseams were proportioned to short men under 5' 7", medium men 5'7" to 5' 11", and tall men over 6'. Indigo blue denim was the most prevalent fabric for most overalls although dairymen styles were made of blue and white stripes, and white boat sail drill was preferred by plasterers and painters. "In their weight lies their strength!" advised Sears catalog copy. On the "value" end for price-conscious customers was the "government standard" 2.20 weight, which meant every yard of cloth weighed 7 1/2 ounces or 2 and 20/100 yard to the pound. "It exceeds the government standard for breaking strength, which is 150 pounds warpwise and 65 pounds fillingwise."[47] Better grades of denim, though, were eight-, ten-, or twelve-ounce weights.

During the Second World War, denim was more widely worn in factories and other work sites. Since cotton textiles were not restricted during the war, denim work clothes were cheaper and more easily available than those in wool, rayon, or blends.

Although denim apparel was commonly viewed as work clothing and mass merchandisers always grouped them together in their catalogs under that category, during the 1930s, jeans also began to take on the cachet of Western costume. Hollywood's "horse operas" that starred singing cowboys like Gene Autry and Roy Rogers featured idealized Western wear with yoke cut shirts—sometimes with contrasting color panels,

Figure 5-24. The influence of Hollywood's many Western-themed movies coupled with the popularity of dude ranches for vacationers inspired city slickers back east to begin wearing jeans as weekend play wear. Western sportswear featured in *Esquire* in 1938 as "being the McCoy" included a black leather vest with contrast fringe, jeans turned up at the cuff, and ponyskin high-heel boots. The cowboy on the right is in his "Sunday-go-to-meetin' clothes" including a red sateen shirt, silk scarf, and riding trousers reinforced at the thighs and seat.

piping, or fringe—and trim jeans with turned up cuffs. (Figure 5-24.) In addition, dude ranches became a favorite vacation destination in the 1930s, for which brochures provided wardrobe checklists that included jeans for both men and women. City slickers returning from their holidays in the West brought back slim jeans to wear in their suburban backyards on weekends. During the Second World War, denim was plentiful, but jeans were not always available since civilian clothing production had been reduced as war production needs increased. When a retailer advertised a shipment of Levi's, for instance, customers would line up before opening time with ration books in hand to get their allotted pair.

Sportswear 1930–1945

During the 1930s, businesses increasingly implemented the 40-hour work week, eliminating 10-hour days and half Saturdays. More than ever, American workers enjoyed full, 2-day weekends and many more hours of leisure time than their parents had been allowed. "Where there was once talk of a 'growing leisure class', today there is more leisure for the masses," noted *Men's Wear* in 1935. "Even the man who knows the utility of denim overalls and shirt five days a week, who is used to dressing for work specialties, is an easy mark for a specialized play costume."[48]

As a guide for the latest trends in leisure time sportswear, fashion journalists and ready-to-wear makers continually looked to the affluent style leaders who still flocked to the resorts in season. The old money had been little impacted by the economic woes of the Depression, and, in mid-winter, many of them shipped off to Palm Beach, Jamaica, Bermuda, or Cuba to socialize and to bronze in the tropical sun. Those who preferred skiing and other snow-bound activities boarded trains for the Adirondacks or Rockies.

In addition to gaining greater leisure time, the masses were also inspired to use that leisure time in the pursuit of sports. The New Deal program funded new public parks, swimming pools, tennis courts, and golf courses. In addition, the extensive news and publicity of the 1932 Summer Olympics hosted by Los Angeles and the Winter Olympics held at Lake Placid, New York, encouraged many more Americans to experiment with new sports such as decathlon combinations and cross-country skiing. Mass merchandisers offered affordable sporting goods such as golf club sets with bag for $4.95, tennis rackets for $1.95, and skis for $3.49. The variety of sports attire also expanded to include new garment constructions such as zipper closures and even licensed screen prints of pop culture icons like Mickey Mouse.

As in previous decades, styles of active sports attire of the Depression era influenced casual sportswear, either from direct adoption such as with sweaters and blazers in the nineteenth century or through adaptations such as with the knit polo shirt and walking shorts in the 1930s. Despite the American male's penchant for casual comfort, though, since the end of the First World War, fresh looks and style innovations in men's sportswear originated at the resorts in Europe. In the specialty shops of the Riviera and St. Moritz, European fashion designers and makers test-marketed their ideas which, if successful, then appeared in the international press worn by the Prince of Wales and other prominent style leaders. In 1935, *Men's Wear* reported from the French Riviera: "The Americans were easily in the majority amongst the visitors. I have not seen so many on the Riviera since the boom days. I emphasize this because what they take home and what they wear there will have its influence in America during the summer of 1936."[49] For those Americans who did not go to the Riviera, the fashion press obligingly reported on the newest looks from abroad. "From this year's Riviera notes," observed *Esquire* in January 1935, "the coming season's southern resort fashions may be predicted with a minimum of guesswork."[50] In turn, the shops of Palm Beach and Palm Springs stocked up on Americanized knock-offs of European styles, from which trends were picked up by ready-to-wear makers and mass merchandisers.

Throughout the 1930s, the knit polo shirt was continually reconfigured into endless variations with assorted collars, neckline closures, sleeve treatments, colors, and knit patterns. (Figure 5-25.) Short-sleeved pullover variants of the polo were also produced in a variety of woven

"Dishrag" polo shirt and tennis shorts by Chemisier, 1935

Knit sports shirts from Wilson Brothers, 1935

Cotton ribbed polos from National Bellas Hess, 1936

Figure 5-25. Short-sleeved active sports shirts such as polos were broadly adapted as leisure wear in the 1930s. By mid decade, innumerable versions of sports shirts were made with assorted collars and closures and in innumerable fabrics, particularly the trendy mesh weaves.

Figure 5-26. Among the fashion influences from the American resorts during the 1930s were the numerous varieties of sports shirts and jacket shirts with matching trousers and shorts. Among the new concepts of comfort wear were shirts designed with tailored hemlines to be worn untucked. John David ad, 1938.

fabrics, particularly rayon. Among the biggest trends in men's sports shirts were the many forms of cotton mesh, sometimes referred to in the press as "dishrag materials."[51] The favorite mesh styles were boldly colored plaids often sewn on the bias forming a diamond pattern. Zippered keyhole necklines were new for spring 1936. Among the favorite short-sleeved sports shirts was the boldly colored Hawaiian print. By the second half of the decade, men all over America wore eyecatching cotton or silk sports shirts covered with graphics of stylized pineapples, coconut palms, and tropical flowers. An influence from South America was the gaucho sports shirt made of linen or slubbed cotton, which featured loops rather than button holes.

Jacket shirts in long- and short-sleeved versions were a popular addition to the masculine sportswear wardrobe. Jacket shirts were tailored with squared skirts, dropped patch pockets, and side vents to be worn untucked. (Figure 5-26.) The most prevalent style was the Cuban jacket, an adaptation of a sugar planter's work shirt with four oversized pleated patch pockets and a capacious, tubular hang from the shoulders. The bush jacket, sometimes called a hunter jacket (known today as a safari jacket), was made with large patch pockets, buttoned pocket flaps, and a self-belt that either tied or buckled.

One of the most debated sportswear trends of the 1930s was shorts—both on the tennis court and in the spectator crowds. Tennis shorts, like those shown in Figure 5-25, had appeared on college and community courts even in the 1920s. But in 1932, they became mainstream fashion when British tennis champion Bunny Austin wore a pair of white flannel shorts cropped well above the knees in competition at the Men's National Tennis Championship in Forest Hills, Long Island. Photos of Austin wearing the "ventilated pants" were in all the major newspapers. The following year, a number of ready-to-wear makers offered the "new mode for shorts." "Active men are getting down to elementals," advised one maker's ad, "and wearing them high and brief."[52] By the midthirties, white shorts were ubiquitous on tennis and squash courts nationwide.

The rapid popularity of walk shorts likewise caused a stir within certain conservative circles. For some years, knee-length walk shorts had been common town wear in tropical British colonies like the Bahamas, Jamaica, and Bermuda (for which the shorts would later be named). The practicality of such cool comfort was happily adopted by American tourists who then introduced even shorter versions to stateside resorts. (Figure 5-27 and Color Plate 7.) By 1935, the fashion news was the "shortness of shorts," reported *Men's Wear* with photos from the Riviera of young men in thigh-high shorts and formfitting tank tops. "Shorts grow shorter and wider, but great attention is being paid to the fit so that the leg does not droop in at the back or front, but hangs straight. The popularity of shorts is increasing and will be even greater in the summer of 1936."[53]

The primary controversies about shorts arose when the garment began to appear in places less casual than resorts like on Middle America's city streets and in public buildings. Moreover, shorts were increasingly seen on golf courses in bright hues and patterns and paired with equally colorful knee socks and polos. In addition to vivid colors, many of the textured mesh, rough linen, and slubbed cotton fabrics were also applied to walk shorts to match sports shirts of like materials. The khaki

Figure 5-27. Shorts on and off the sports fields were among the most controversial fashion changes of the 1930s. Debates centered on the "shortness of shorts" and where shorts might be worn in public. Khaki shorts and sports shirt, 1936.

Figure 5-28. By the end of the 1930s, skiwear had evolved into much more specialized and sophisticated sports clothing. Lightweight, water-repellent synthetics such as "satin ski twill" made of rayon allowed skiers greater freedom and comfort than layers of knitwear. Poplin pullover wind jacket with a zipper across one shoulder paired with matching peg-top trousers, 1939.

shorts and sports shirt "turnout" shown in Figure 5-27 "owes its original inspiration to the British Army officers of India," noted *Esquire*, and was "typical of what was worn at Nassau this past season."[54]

In addition to shorts being worn increasingly on America's fairways, trousers made of bold patterns and bright colors were likewise a favorite in the 1930s. If the trousers were not cuffed, golfers would roll up the hems as their Victorian forefathers had done—which had led to the development of cuffed trousers in the first place. Only a few diehards in America continued to traipse about the links in golf knickers. The look continued to thrive in Britain during the thirties because the royals still donned the ensemble of tweed knickers, Fair Isle sweater, and matching knee stockings The plus fours, sixes, and eights of the preceding decade were now tapered to a more narrow fit somewhat like the cut of the Edwardian styles.

Although knickers were less favored on the golf course, they remained a staple for the ski slopes. They were practical since they easily tucked into heavy woolen stockings, and their roomy, nonbinding fit was necessary for maneuvering down the snowy mountainside. Combined with knickers were the many varieties of ski jackets, parkas, and sweaters, each of which was subject less to the practicality of the garment than to the style preference of the winter sportsman. One of the most fashionable but illogical ski coats of the midthirties was the double-breasted short jacket. The double-breasted closure gaped open to mid-chest and caught the wind when a skier leaned forward, and the short crop at the waistline gaped at the back, allowing freezing draughts and snow underneath. In 1935, *Men's Wear* advised retailers that "there's a reason behind winter sportswear...The customer has to be hypnotized into buying what he should, which is very different from what he may like or what he thinks he needs."[55]

By the end of the decade, skiwear had become more sophisticated in design. "The ultimate evolution of the ski outfit," noted *Esquire,* featured a poplin pullover wind jacket with a zipper across one shoulder seam and a snug, knit waistband and wristbands. (Figure 5-28.) Instead of knickers, various long, peg-top trousers were preferred. New synthetic fabrics allowed skiers to discard layers of heavy sweaters in favor of lightweight jackets. For example, in 1939, Puritan sportswear introduced winter active wear made of "satin ski twill," a water-repellent rayon "in the colors of famous racing stables."[56]

At the beginning of World War II, the military looked to the practicality of winter sportswear as a guide for mountain infantry. "What play-loving Americans learned about skiing for the sheer hell of it during the past decade now has a vital military application," wrote an editor in 1943. "Knowledge thus gained about the most practical types of fabrics, comfortable designs for parkas and other details furnished a pattern for uniforms for the armed forces."[57] Worn by both soldiers and civilians were hooded parkas with zipper front closures and matching, baggy trousers made of reversible processed cotton. One ply was white, to be worn turned outside as camouflage during day patrols. Civilian versions were still in brilliant colors that made it easier for rescue teams to find lost or injured skiers.

As during the 1920s, swimwear of the 1930s underwent some of the most radical changes of any masculine clothing of the era. At the beginning of the decade, American tastes lingered a couple of years behind the sophistication of Europeans. Until the end of the of decade, many U.S. communities retained—and enforced—community ordinances prohibiting men from appearing on public beaches or at public pools bare-chested. Consequently, the crab back top and squared-leg trunks remained the prevalent swimsuit until the end of the decade. One difference was the ever greater exposure of torso skin as tops became little more than bibs over the chest held in place by thin, knit tendrils. Still, even as topless swimming was increasingly accepted, up until World War II, mass merchandisers offered both the trunks alone and also swimsuits with tops attached to the waistband with a zipper for easy removal. (Figure 5-29.) But along the Riviera and at the Caribbean resorts, men not only discarded their crab back tanks, but they also opted for ever briefer cuts of swimwear made of the thinnest, skintight knits. In 1931, *Men's Wear* noted that swimsuits once designed "to conceal nakedness" had become "more revealing than concealing."[58] In that year, the brief style trunk, with its lower waistband and leg openings cut in a high arc over the hips, made its debut in Europe. Over the following few years, ever briefer versions were introduced. A photo from the midthirties featured in a *Men's Wear* retrospect editorial showed a male model wearing a

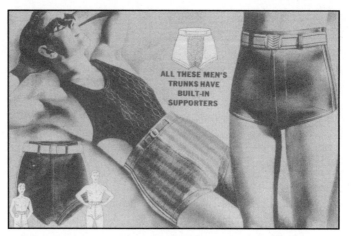

Figure 5-29. Swimwear of the 1930s became ever skimpier as men abandoned crab back tops and long, skirted one-piece styles in favor of the European-inspired brief cuts. Left, B.V.D. Swim Suits ad, 1938; right, swimsuits from Montgomery Ward, 1937; bottom, detail of Sun Dogs swimwear ad, 1935.

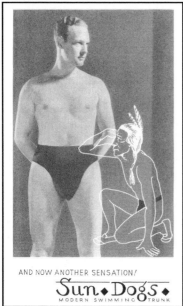

white brief that was cut with barely two inches of fabric at the sides high on the hip and a narrow triangle at the back that exposed the buttocks.[59] Today, the style is called a French bikini. However, even as the leg cuts rose higher and the knits became thinner and more revealing, ironically, waistbands remained high to conceal the navel. For men whose modesty or non-athletic physique precluded them from slipping on a knit brief, the baggy boxer made of woven fabrics and lined with a mesh supporter was available in all varieties of prints and colors.

By the same token, beach robes were more important as swimsuits became topless and skimpy. It was one thing to swim and sunbathe on the beach or poolside in a topless brief, but to stroll about a hotel lobby or seaside cabana bar so nearly nude was carrying exhibitionism too far. Flannel and terrycloth robes in solid colors were the most favored although multicolored vertical stripes were fairly common as well. Prints with tropical or nautical themes prevented the beach robes from looking too much like bathrobes.

Outerwear 1930–1945

One of the newest styles of overcoats in the 1930s was the double-breasted guard's coat modeled on the uniform greatcoat of the British Grenadiers. (Figure 5-30.) The Americanized guard's coat featured the trim fit, broad shoulders, and deeply rolled lapels of the grenadier's greatcoat that had been the inspiration for Frederick Scholte's drape cut construction. The double-breasted closure was made with three pairs of widely-spaced buttons although the top pair were never fastened. Side slash pockets aligned with front darts that defined the waist and emphasized the athletic silhouette. Peaked lapels modernized the style. Instead of a single inverted pleat from collar to hem, as with British versions, the Americanized guard's coat had two inverted pleats: one between the shoulder blades and belt and the second from the belt to the skirt hem.

Although not new, the raglan sleeve coat in both single- and double-breasted styles became hugely popular in the midthirties. The style was a

Split Raglan
Sleeve Coats

Guard's Coat

Figure 5-30. The two newest looks in men's outerwear of the era were the guard's coat, modeled on the British grenadier's greatcoat, and fingertip coats. The Victorian raglan sleeve was given fresh appeal with variations such as the split raglan that featured a center seam down the outer sleeve. Left, raglan sleeve topcoats and fitted guard's coat from Krafft and Phillips, 1935; right, fingertip coats from Sears, 1943.

favorite of the Prince of Wales at the time. A new take on the design included the split raglan with a topstitched seam from collar to cuff down the outer sleeve. Glen plaids, plaid-over-plaid, window pane checks, and herringbones were among the bold textile patterns applied to topcoats in the second half of the thirties. For the affluent, fur linings with matching collars and lapels were an assertion that their fortunes were intact after the crash.

On the college campuses, fingertip coats became a new trend in the late 1930s. During the war, these short coats were a fabric-saving alternative to traditional knee-length topcoats. They were especially popular in reversible variations of reused wool blends on one side for warmth and water-repellent poplin on the other side.

After the United States entered World War II, men's coats were also subjected to WPB regulations. Details such as oversized patch pockets, pocket flaps, sleeve cuffs, sleeve straps, and "railroad stitching" (four rows) were restricted. Skirts narrowed and were shortened to the knees. Wartime textiles included make-do blends and substitute synthetics, especially rayon. Sears' "famous Bengora topcoats" were made of a "surface fleece of 61% virgin wool and 39% sturdy reused wool anchored to a strong, close knitted cotton back that is 49% of the total fabric."[60] Rain-

Figure 5-31. During the Second World War, civilian outerwear was influenced by military service jackets and coat styles. Top, army field jacket from Sears, 1943; bottom, bomber's (bombardier's) leather jacket from Spiegel, 1945.

wear was made of reclaimed rubber. Leather jackets were available in capeskin (sheep) and goatskin.

Military influences were particularly evident in the designs of jackets. (Figure 5-31.) The bomber's (also bombardier's) jacket was made with a knit waistband and sleeve cuffs. The army field jacket had adjustable shoulder, wrist, and waist tabs. The battle jacket featured big pockets, a fly front, and buttoned waistband similar to the original. The hooded duffel coat had rope frogging that fastened with wooden pegs. Army blue, khaki, and olive drab were typical colors for outerwear of the war years.

Underwear 1930–1945

Underwear styles of the 1930s followed closely behind the ever briefer innovations of swimwear. In 1934, Coopers, a knitwear manufacturer in Kenosha, Wisconsin, introduced the Jockey Y-front brief. "'Jockeys' are snug and brief," declared a 1936 ad, "molded to your muscles...Built-in masculine support made of lightweight, porous, absorbent knitted fabric with the famous Y-front, no-gap front opening."[61] (Figure 5-32.) The super flexible Lastex waistband was nonbinding and much more comfortable than the typical sewn band with a button closure. The brief style was a huge success and other knitwear makers quickly produced their branded versions with assorted open fly fronts. Among the variations were forms with elasticized supporter bands and belts designed to give men with a waistline bulge a trimmer look— the better to fit the ideal masculine profile of the athletic drape cut suits.

Boxers also became briefer with legs cropped to the upper thighs. Through the midthirties, most boxers were constructed with yoke-front waist bands that fastened with three buttons above an open fly. The metal snap closure called "Grippers" was introduced in the mid-1930s as a solution to buttons, which often got broken in the laundry or, worse, popped off when dressing. Influenced by the popularity of the elastic waistband of briefs, manufacturers began making buttonless shorts with the same elasticized waistband used for the new brief styles. Other experiments to make the boxer less binding included knit gussets at the crotch and adjustable button tabs at the sides in place of yoke button fronts.

The tank-style athletic shirt was the most prevalent undershirt of the 1930s. The short-sleeved, button front styles of a decade earlier were too cumbersome compared to the easy pullover athletic shirts. According to fashion lore, though, for a few years in the mid-1930s, undershirt sales declined after the release of the movie *It Happened One Night* (1934), in which Clarke Gable undressed to reveal a bare torso. Men all across America abandoned undershirts entirely in warm weather, and some preferred no undershirt year round. In answer to this new trend, some shirt makers attempted to produce dress shirts with built-in liners that "makes the undershirt superfluous," but the added bulk was uncomfortable and made the shirt look thick.[62]

During the Second World War, boxers and briefs varied little from the previous decade. Since cotton was not a restricted wartime material, a plentiful supply of the ubiquitous ribbed cotton briefs, undershirts, and broadcloth boxers was available. Rayon, too, was readily available as a substitute for silk and as a durable fiber blend with wool or cotton. Wintertime union suits, though, were often made of part wool blends, usually

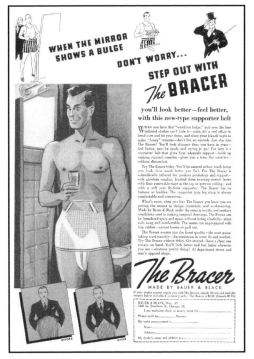
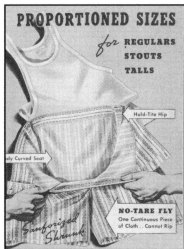

Figure 5-32. Influenced by the ever skimpier forms of swimwear, underwear styles also became more snug and abbreviated. In 1934, Jockeys were introduced. By mid-decade, most underwear makers and retailers mass produced their own versions of the new brief cut. Left, Jockeys, 1935; center, The Bracer, 1936; right broadcloth boxers from Montgomery Ward, 1938.

with 75% cotton. As fuel shortages forced reduced thermostat settings of home furnaces, men appreciated the warm army style undershirts with long sleeves and ribbed cuffs paired with long drawers with elastic waistbands and ribbed cuffs. In warm weather, the white cotton T-shirt was increasingly favored over the tank style during the early forties.

Sleepwear 1930–1945

With so many news headlines about Russia and the Stalinist regime in the 1930s, the influence of imperial Cossack uniforms on sleepwear was as strong as ever. Some were even emblazoned with an embroidered escutcheon of the Romanov double-headed eagle. Although the pajama top with a stand-up circular collar, off-center button closure at the right side, and wide satin sash had been around since the late nineteenth century, the look was refreshed with new trimmings and fabrics, especially the latest forms of rayon. As a Sears catalog explained: "Science has improved rayon, until many of the new ones are not only 'like' silk or wool, but have added properties that make them even better—they're not substitutes for, or imitations of anything, but have important new qualities of their own....more crush-resistant, easier to keep clean, and the lustrous brocaded rayons, fine, long wearing fabrics in their own right."[63] Similar in design to the Cossack styles were Asian looks with mandarin collars or collarless scoop necklines, asymmetrical closures, and Chinese-inspired motifs embroidered or screen-printed on the back and chest. (Figure 5-33.) For the less adventurous American male, the prevalent

Figure 5-33. Exotic foreign costumes inspired sleepwear trends of the 1930s. Pajama jackets with stand-up collars and off-center closures replicated Cossack uniforms and Mandarin tunics. Adding to the vivacity of the styles, many were embroidered or screenprinted with Imperial Russian emblems or Asian motifs. Left, paisley print pajamas; right, Chinese dragon pajamas from Montgomery Ward, 1938.

Figure 5-34. A fresh take on the lounge robe in the 1930s was the double-breasted closure. New fabrications included luxurious, brocaded rayons and lustrous broadcloths with a glossy finish. Double-breasted lounge robes from Sears, 1937.

type of pajama was the standard candy-striped flannelette shirt and trousers. New styling included improved elastic waists, inset panels at the back called "balloon seats," and bellows pleats under the arms to prevent bunching and binding while in bed.

The blanket cloth bathrobe changed little from its Victorian predecessors. Art deco motifs—called "moderne" in the 1930s—were more updated looking than the typical Indian blanket patterns. Lounge robes, though, were newly constructed with double-breasted closures and even peaked lapels. (Figure 5-34.) Luxurious fabrics for lounge robes included silk, brocaded rayon, and new types of lustrous broadcloth with a glossy finish. The old-fashioned smoking jacket had somewhat survived through the 1920s primarily as a Father's Day and Christmas gift, but, with the repeal of Prohibition in 1933, the short cocktail coat "arrived as an integral part of the American scene."[64] (Figure 5-35.) As with the smoking jacket before it, the cocktail coat was worn in place of the dinner jacket while entertaining intimate friends. Instead of the upholstered

THE BACARDI—All wool flannel with black and white checked trim. Ground Colors: Black, Brown, Navy and Wine. $3.50

Figure 5-35. With the repeal of Prohibition in 1933, the cocktail coat became a trendy loungewear replacement for the old-fashioned smoking jacket. Cocktail coat from Van Baalen and Heilbrun, 1935.

look of smoking jackets with their quilted cuffs and lapels, fringe trim, and sumptuous fabrics, cocktail coats were simpler and sleeker with contrasting opulence limited primarily to lapels, cuffs, and pocket trim.

The double-breasted lounging robe disappeared during World War II as WPB restrictions were applied to all menswear. Winter robes and pajamas were made with the new Teca rayons, which were spun into yarns that had the texture and warmth of wool and the softness typical of rayon. As T-shirts became the more popular undershirt in the 1940s, the crewneck style was applied to knit pajama tops in horizontal stripes of varying widths and solid colors that contrasted with the hues of the bottoms.

Accessories 1930–1945

During the Depression, many millions of men had to economize when faced with lost jobs, reduced hours, and salary cuts. That meant buying only a single hat or one pair of shoes and making due with last year's ties and handkerchiefs rather than acquiring a fresh, seasonal wardrobe of accessories. However, for those men whose fortunes and jobs were little impacted by the era's economic woes, accessories were as much a critical component of being well-dressed as ever. As *Vanity Fair* noted in 1932, a three-piece suit was made with thirteen pockets, which men daily populated with more than half a dozen accessories:

> Consider all the things for a man's pockets. What with handkerchiefs, pens, pencils, cigarette case and lighter, watch, pocket knife, key ring and keys, bill clip, wallet for papers and bill fold, notebook and watch and key chain... man's burden is at the same time augmented and alleviated. Augmented by that much more weight and alleviated insofar as these accessories are necessary conveniences on which we have learned to depend.[65]

In addition to this list of pocket accoutrement were the other accessories of hats, shoes, ties, and belts that were the critical finishing touches of modern masculine dress.

Headwear styles in the 1930s were influenced primarily by two sources—affluent vacationers in Palm Beach and the Prince of Wales. For these men, a hat wardrobe of multiple styles was a necessity. In 1936, *Esquire* presented "a complete hat wardrobe" that included two types of snap brim fedoras, homburg, derby, porkpie, Tyrolean, sports cap, and silk opera topper. "Only one snap brim is necessary," advised the editors, "and one type of country hat. However, every other hat on this page should be included in the wardrobe of those men who wish to be dressed correctly for every occasion."[66]

During the Florida resort season, the panama remained as ubiquitous as it had been in previous decades. (Figure 5-36.) A new shape for the panama was the porkpie with its low, flat top and the brim snapped down all around. In the second half of the decade, the larger shapes returned, and wider brims were snapped up at the back. Also later in the decade, the plain bands gave way to a fad for horizontal striped ribbons that represented the colors of private clubs, either those back home in the North or the Palm Beach clubs. Some men still preferred the classic boater, which was adorned with colorful, vertically striped bands.

The fur felt version of the porkpie became popular at race tracks and ball games after 1934. College men modified the porkpie by denting the

Homburg, 1938

Panama, 1937

PERFECT FITTING — BECAUSE IT SHAPES ITSELF EXACTLY TO YOUR HEAD

ROUND HEADS   REGULAR HEADS   LONG HEADS   This Is The Lastex Insert That "Does The Trick"

HAND CRAFTED OF LUXURY FUR FELT!

$4.85

Snap brim fedora 1936

Tyrolean, 1935

Porkpie, 1936

Figure 5-36. For business attire, the homburg remained the preferred hat of the urban executive during the 1930s. Variations of the snap brim fedora were favored by younger men for both town and country dress. The greater variety of hats during the Depression and Second World War was with casual headgear, including the conical Tyrolean, flattop porkpie, and close-stitched fedora among others.

Wartime close-stitched fedora of rayon, 1944

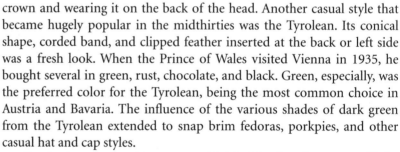

Sports caps of reprocessed wool, 1943

crown and wearing it on the back of the head. Another casual style that became hugely popular in the midthirties was the Tyrolean. Its conical shape, corded band, and clipped feather inserted at the back or left side was a fresh look. When the Prince of Wales visited Vienna in 1935, he bought several in green, rust, chocolate, and black. Green, especially, was the preferred color for the Tyrolean, being the most common choice in Austria and Bavaria. The influence of the various shades of dark green from the Tyrolean extended to snap brim fedoras, porkpies, and other casual hat and cap styles.

For business attire, the gray or midnight blue homburg was still the standard. Its distinctive brim roll, grosgrain edging, and wide ribbon with bow was distinguished and traditional. The derby was still around in the 1930s where English influences prevailed, but most American men had abandoned the style a decade earlier. Younger men opted for any of the snap brim fedoras with their high, 5 3/4-inch crown and broad, 2 1/4-inch brim. The basic, lightweight fedora offered men any number of ways for personal expression. "What is your favorite hat shape?" asked the copy in a 1937 Sears catalog. "Snapped down in front or up all the way around? Long side pinches or short pinches? Diamond shape crown or narrow dent crown? Any shape you choose is yours...and can be blocked with your own fingers into any shape that strikes your fancy."[67]

The best quality hats were made of fur felt. Hats blocked of beaver fur felt cost twice that of wool styles. Next in quality and price were the hare fur felts from the long-haired European hare, and rabbit fur felts from Australian rabbits. The least expensive hats were of varying wool felts, which were heavier and sturdier than fur felt.

Figure 5-37. Neckwear of the Depression and World War II years was as boldly colored and patterned as ever. The influence of art deco design—called "moderne" in the 1930s—dominated. Improvements in neckwear construction made washable ties of wool or cotton more practical. In addition, synthetic materials such as rayon and nylon were adapted to neckwear. From Montgomery Ward catalogs: left, reversible silk ties, 1937; right, wartime rayon and rayon blend ties, 1943.

Despite the emphasis on a hat wardrobe, ironically, throughout much of the decade, the fashion press reported that the men in Palm Beach and the Prince of Wales were frequently seen hatless when out-doors—the former for the purpose of ensuring a deeper tan and the later for the sake of comfort. A broader influence did not spread, though, and most men automatically reached for a hat whenever going out.

During the war years, hats were made of wool and synthetic blends as wool rationing went into effect. By 1943, many dress hats were blocked with 40% reused and reprocessed wool. New casual styles made of cotton or rayon were closely row-stitched to help brims and crowns hold their shape. Military influences included pale shades of khaki like "sandune," made popular during the North Africa campaigns.

Neckwear of the Depression era was as colorful and vivaciously pat-terned as in any previous decade. (Figure 5-37.) With an eye to the styles of London, American makers appropriated many English regimental and school stripes, much to the chagrin of the British. The Duke of Windsor wrote that Americans wore such ties "blissfully regardless of any right to do so, [and] ignorant of their origin."[68] New in the 1930s were reengi-neered washable ties in wool or cotton. The new twin-ply constructions were reinforced with spiral stitching and bar tacking for greater resilience and longer life—a key selling point to the economy-minded man of the Depression. By the same token, to give more value for the tie cost, some makers developed reversible ties made of the same material and stitched with hidden side seams in case one side got soiled. As with sportswear of the decade, textured fabrics like slubbed silk and dishrag linen were also applied to neckwear. At the end of the decade, the newest synthetic, nylon, was woven into DuPont Nylard brand twills for ties that were

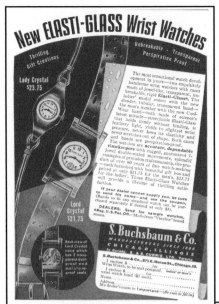

Figure 5-38. Accessory fads just before World War II included clear vinyl wristwatches, belts, suspenders, and garters. Ads, 1940.

advertised as wrinkle proof and easy to launder.

The long tie was still most commonly tied with a four-in-hand knot and short blades that still ended a few inches short of touching the belt. In the midthirties, the additional loopings of the Windsor knot produced a large, triangular-shaped knot that better filled the spread collar. Although the elaborate knot was attributed to the Prince of Wales (who was of the House of Windsor), he denied originating the look.[69]

The new spread collar dress shirts also inspired a resurgence of the bow tie, which had been largely abandoned by Flaming Youth in the preceding decade. The bow ties of the 1930s, though, were slim and ribbon-shaped compared to the earlier wide butterfly bows.

Colorfully patterned scarves and oversized handkerchiefs were used to add color and style at the open neckline of sports shirts. At resorts and country clubs, these richly hued squares and oblongs also were twisted into waist handkerchiefs and inserted through the trouser belt loops in place of a belt to add a splash of color to the stark, all-white tennis ensemble. In 1934, *Esquire* declared the waist handkerchief "smart as all get out...in recognition of the fact that many tournament officials still stick to the letter of the traditional rule against any deviations from plain white in the attire of contestants."[70]

When the WPB restricted silk, nylon, and wool primarily for war use in 1942, neckwear makers substituted abundantly available fabrics of rayon, rayon blends, and, for summer, cotton. One of the fads of the war years was the hand-painted tie, many of which were almost garish in their color combinations and oversized graphics of flowers, landscapes, and animals. To allow the maximum "canvas" for hand painting, many of these ties were a broad 4 1/2 inches at the end, for which they were called "belly warmers."

Among the novelties in men's accessories just before the war were belts, suspenders, garters, and wristwatches made of flexible clear plastic vinyl. (Figure 5-38.) Polyvinyl chloride, known commonly today as PVC, had been known to chemists since the nineteenth century but was only plasticized for commercial use in the 1920s. The vinyl accessories were guaranteed in ads as unbreakable, water- and perspiration-proof, and, because of the decorative perforations, cool and "healthful." The fad for vinyl accessories was brief since PVC was among the critical synthetic materials restricted by the War Production Board for war use.

Men's dress footwear of the Depression era changed little through the early 1930s. The toes remained wide and squared until about 1935 when they once again were tapered to a more round, pointed tip. (Figure 5-39.) Wingtips became sharply pointed. Although most men preferred any of the sleek oxfords, catalogs still offered assortments of the Edwardian high-top street boot. New forms of oxfords included the trouser crease with a center seam down the toe, and the "bel-style" with a V-shape formed by side wings. The monk-front moccasin with a wide buckle strap became especially popular in the late 1930s. The universal fad for mesh sportswear throughout the second half of decade likewise extended to casual shoe lasts, which were ventilated all around with punching. Red rubber soled buckskins were a fad at the end of the decade.

New to the era were the slip-on moccasin styles. The Norwegian peasant moccasin featured a strap of leather across the instep with a diamond cutout in the center. The style, called "loungers," was first imported to England, from which it made it way to the United States with

Monk straps and trouser crease oxfords, 1938

Bel-style oxford, 1937

Moccasin-styled loungers, 1943

Punched buckskins, 1938

Figure 5-39. The sleek oxford in its countless variety of styles was the preferred choice for the modern man of the 1930s and 1940s. Among the innovative new looks were buckle monk straps, bel styles, and trouser crease lasts. The slip-on moccasin was imported from England and quickly became the favorite of American teenagers.

Sandals, 1937–1938

returning American tourists. The famous Weejuns were introduced in 1936. Later, American teenagers would insert pennies into the cutouts, and the style would become popularly known as penny loafers.

Two forms of summer footwear that crossed over from the high styles of the resorts to mass merchandising were sandals and espadrilles. The variety of strappy and pierced sandals with leather or crepe rubber soles was endless. Colorful canvas espadrilles with wide rope soles were favorite beachwear at the end of the decade and especially during World War II since they were not rationed.

During the war, molded tire cord and other "compo" (composition) materials were used for soles to conserve leather for soldiers' boots and belts. Horsehide was a common substitute for leather for work shoes. A new look for the war years was the military oxford constructed with a smooth last across the rounded toe and specially treated to hold a shine.

As noted in the previous chapter, during the 1920s, walking sticks and daywear gloves had largely been abandoned by the comfort- and convenience-conscious American male. Although both accessories were still provided by upscale menswear shops in the 1930s, such superfluous accoutrement was largely relegated to Hollywood's image of financiers and the leisure class and to cartoon characters such as the Monopoly board game icon of a tycoon.

Jewelry for men was as popular as ever during the Depression years.

Military oxford, 1944

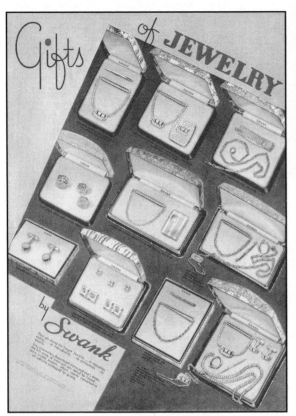

Swank jewelry gift sets, 1936

Sterling silver I.D. bracelet with dual photo locket and embossed branch of service, 1943

Figure 5-40. Despite the economic constraints for most men in the Depression years, masculine jewelry remained an important accessory item. Matching sets of monogrammed tie bars, collar grips, key chains, and belt buckles were especially favored. Surfaces of jewelry and other men's accessories were decorated with contrasting moderne patterns and motifs.

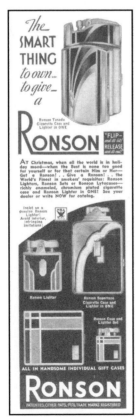

Moderne design cigarette cases and lighters, 1934

Favorite sets included matching collar grips, tie bars, and cuff links. (Figure 5-40.) Although button down collars became trendy in the 1930s, many of the spread collar shirts still required collar grips to hold their shape and keep the tie knot centered. Tie bars were made even more eye-catching with the addition of chains with attached monogrammed ingots that hung in a swag over the tie. The moderne style dominated the surface ornamentation of masculine jewelry and accessories such as cigarette lighters and cases. The stylized, geometric designs were enhanced by contrasting segments of etched metal and inlays of enamels or semiprecious stones. Colored stones were preferred for white dinner jackets, especially if they coordinated with vividly hued cummerbunds. Traditionalists opted for more representational motifs like animals and sports equipment. Equestrian motifs and enwreathed horse heads became a fad in 1938 when two descendants of the famed Man o' War ran against each other in the Match of the Century—a horse race that had been broadcast on radio to 40 million listeners nationwide. Similarly, men who knew little of golf, tennis, or hunting, happily selected jewelry adorned with crossed rackets, nine irons, and game rifles. Other sports motifs were inspired by the 1932 Summer and Winter Olympics, both of which were hosted by the United States.

Even though wartime restrictions on the use of white metals (alloys of tin) limited the availability of some forms of men's jewelry, two trends reemerged in the early 1940s. The identification bracelet with either a full first name or set of initials had been a favorite of young men in the years after the First World War and was revived by their sons as the Second World War began. In addition, the chunky chain of the I.D. bracelet influenced the looks of keychains and watch chains for men who still carried a pocket watch.

Grooming 1930–1945

The shiny helmet hair of the Jazz Age disappeared with the Crash of '29. In the 1930s, men's hair remained short on the sides but became fuller and softer on the top. Most men combed their hair back from the forehead with a slight pompadour contour at the front and a part on the left side. Faces were still mostly clean shaven. Some men opted for the pencil moustache thinly lining the upper lip that had begun to appear in the late 1920s. Hollywood movie stars notable for the look in the 1930s included Clark Gable and Errol Flynn.

In 1931, Canadian inventor Jacob Schick revolutionized shaving with his introduction of the electric shaver. Competitors such as Remington and Gillette among others quickly jumped into the dry shaver market with their own versions. (Figure 5-41.) Ads promoted the benefits of the electric shaver: "No soap! No blades! No cuts! Saves as it shaves!"[71] The related market of after-shave products grew exponentially. "There are two halves to every shave," declared the copy in a 1937 Mennen ad. "The first is to get rid of your whiskers. The second is to take care of your skin."[72] Alcohol-based after shave colognes, skin balms, lotions, and talcum powders promised to "banish razor rawness," eliminate face shine, make the skin look younger, and add a masculine scent.

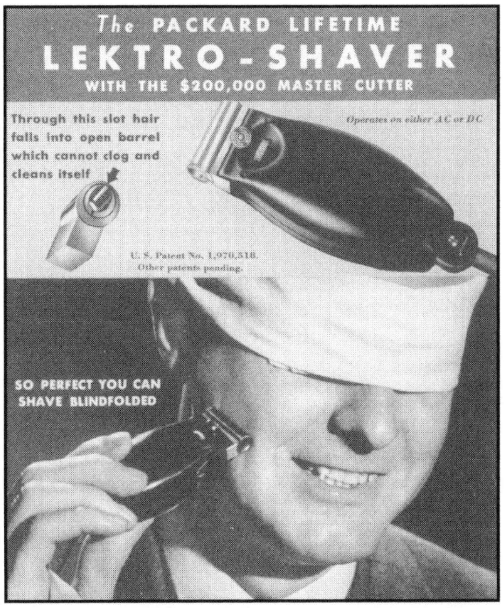

Across all socioeconomic levels in the 1930s, men increasingly became aware of their personal hygiene as makers of personal hygiene products directly targeted men with their marketing efforts. (Figure 5-42.) An endless array of ads warned men to guard against bad breath, dandruff, body odors, and other health and hygiene concerns. The term "halitosis" was invented by an advertising executive in the 1920s and became a permanent fixture in advertising during the 1930s. Copywriters used words like "handicap," "afflicted," and "ailments" to goad men into buying their products or risk failing with their careers, families, and friends.

Figure 5-41. The electric shaver made its commercial debut in the early 1930s, and became as popular as the safety razor had been a generation earlier. Lektro-Shaver ad, 1936.

Conclusion

Beginning with the crash of the U.S. stock market at the end of the 1920s, the Great Depression was an economic disaster that lasted more than ten years. At the beginning of the 1930s, millions of Americans lost their jobs, homes, and life savings as thousands of businesses went bankrupt and banks collapsed. Further misery was heaped upon the people of the heartland when floods, drought, and dust storms destroyed farmlands, driving desperate families to leave their farms in search of work. The economic hard times only came to an end with the outbreak of the Second World War in 1941 when the nation mobilized manpower and industry for wartime needs.

The Depression had a profound effect on the American clothing industry. Where the working and middle

Figure 5-42. Makers of personal hygiene products were relentless in their mass marketing efforts. Ads frequently focused on promises of protection from the dire social and career consequences of bad breath, dandruff, body odors, and all manners of other personal care concerns. Listerine ad, 1932.

classes of the Roaring Twenties had indulged in the consumption frenzy of the era, including fashion and style trends, in the 1930s, most men were forced to economize either because of lost jobs, cut wages, reduced hours, or the fear of these hardships as imminent. In response, ready-to-wear makers and retailers focused on clothing that men were still willing to buy. And foremost in the minds of most men when shopping for clothing was comfort and ease.

The drape cut suit, introduced from England in the late 1920s, was further refined in the 1930s. The cut of the coat fit comfortably and projected an athletic silhouette with broad shoulders, full chest, and trim waist and hips. By mid-decade, American men began to accept new color palettes and especially textile patterns like glen plaids that were influenced by London's Savile Row. Among the advances in easy dressing was the adaptation of the zipper to trousers. In addition, warm weather suitings, generically called Palm Beach suits made of cool, summer weight fabrics, became hugely popular in the griddle-hot cities all across the nation.

Despite the economic conditions for millions of working and middle-class Americans, many of the affluent families retained their wealth and enjoyed their lives of leisure as before. Their social pursuits included winter trips to tropical resorts like Palm Beach and ski vacations to Sun Valley. At these fashionable gathering spots for the wealthy, men found shops filled with the latest sportswear imported from the Riviera and other European centers of high society. American fashion makers and journalists looked to the men who attended the social scenes at these resorts for guidance on what was current in menswear and what would translate for the masses the following season.

One of the fastest-growing clothing categories for men in the Depression era was sportswear. Variations of the polo shirt were among the most popular weekend wear of the 1930s. The biggest trends in sports shirts were in fabrics, ranging from improved rayons to many types of mesh dishrag materials and rough weaves like slubbed cotton. Shorts increasingly became mainstream throughout the decade, ranging from thigh-high tennis and beach shorts to the longer walk shorts. On the golf links, trousers in bright colors and bold patterns replaced knickers. Swimwear evolved ever scantier cuts that, by the mid-1930s, included topless briefs made of formfitting knits. The new shapes of swimsuits inspired the development of similar underwear briefs first introduced in 1934 as Jockeys.

Among the new trends in accessories for the well-dressed man of the thirties were the conical, befeathered Tyrolean hat; the low-crowned porkpie hat; the slip-on Norwegian moccasin and assorted sandals; nylon and wide, hand-painted neckties; and monogrammed jewelry sets, including matching chain tie bars, cuff links, and belt buckles.

As World War II commenced, the design of men's clothing was subjected to restrictions imposed by the U.S. War Production Board. Suit jacket lapels narrowed, and hemlines shortened. Trousers were made without pleats and cuffs. Overcoats lost patch pockets, sleeve cuffs, and wide, flared skirts. Alternative and substitute materials replaced rationed wool, silk, rubber, and nylon. Suits and outerwear were made of reprocessed wool blends, and shoes were soled with molded tire cord. Patriotic colors dominated menswear—Air Force blue suits, khaki trousers and walk shorts, olive drab hats and jackets, and red-white-blue sports shirts.

On the one hand, from the beginning of the Depression through World War II, men's clothing was comfortingly predictable and staid as exemplified by the long run of the drape cut suit. On the other hand, sartorial rules were challenged by the continually innovative and fresh designs of sportswear—sports shirts in every color and fabric, active shorts and leisure walk shorts everywhere, topless and skimpy swimsuits, sporty accessories like Tyroleans and nylon ties. This dichotomy of convention and innovation in menswear was a challenge and, at the same time, a delight for most American men despite the economic conditions of the Depression and the privations of the war years.

Postwar Boom Times

Fashions in the Atomic Age, 1946–1959

Consumerism, Conformity, and Communism

With the surrender of Japan in August 1945, the demobilization of America's mighty military forces from all around the world began almost immediately. More than fifteen million men and women in the armed services were rapidly deployed back to civilian life while American industries shifted gears to retool and restructure for peacetime business.

During the war, most citizens who wanted to work enjoyed well-paying jobs with plenty of overtime. Unemployment dropped to 1.2 percent.[1] Yet there was little on which they could spend their money. The manufacturing of cars, appliances, clothing, and most other categories of consumer goods was greatly reduced or even prohibited so that factories could mass produce planes, tanks, and other war materiel; new home construction virtually halted as supplies of building materials were diverted to war needs. After four years of rationing and the privations from wartime conservation, Americans went on a spending spree. The U.S. economy boomed as pent-up demand for consumer goods was unleashed—much of it centered on the home and family.

The economic boom was further boosted by postwar marriage and baby booms. During the war, many couples had postponed weddings, and married couples had deferred having children. Moreover, women who had joined the wartime workforce were now encouraged by business and government to quit their jobs and return to homemaking.

Millions of postwar families moved into rapidly expanding suburbs that sprawled over the landscape surrounding cities. With the help of mass marketing and saturation advertising, the American dream became ownership of a contemporary subdivision house filled with all the mass-produced marvels of modern comfort and convenience. (Figure 6-1.) Backyards were furnished with barbeque grills and matching patio sets. Kitchens were accoutered with specialized, color-coordinated appliances. Danish-modern living room suites were arranged around television sets and stereo hi-fi consoles. Children's rooms brimmed with toys and games

Figure 6-1. In the post-World War II years, Americans enjoyed a sustained economic boom fueled by a renewed consumerism. The American dream was middle-class membership validated by a suburban home filled with all the modern conveniences of the era.

Women's fashions 1946-1959: Left, Dior's New Look of long, full skirts, rounded shoulders, and cinched waists, 1948; center, the ultrafeminine pencil skirt, 1954; right, the knee-length sack dress, 1958.

Drexel furniture, 1959

Suburban ranch style house, 1956

Specialized electric appliances for the modern kitchen, 1956

Jet Age fins on a Ford Fairlane, 1957

'Coonskin caps and mohawk haircuts in the mid-1950s were inspired by the popularity of a Disney movie and TV programs about frontiersman Davy Crockett.

branded with licensed icons from movies and TV shows. Many families became a two-car household as breadwinner men commuted into the city from their quiet suburban neighborhoods, leaving housewives to drive the kids to neighborhood schools and shop at the new suburban supermarkets and shopping centers.

One burgeoning new segment of the consumer market in the post-war years was the teenager. With previous generations, the precollegiate teen was a "junior miss," or "juvenile," or "youth"—miniature versions of adults dependent upon their parents for choosing everything from their clothes to their social life. But teens of the 1950s asserted their independence and self-awareness with a collective purchasing power. They bought millions of rock-and-roll records, flocked to see movies like *Rebel Without a Cause* (1955), ate with friends at drive-in restaurants and soda shops, consumed vast quantities of snack foods, and chose trendy fashions and fads that differentiated them from their younger siblings and especially from the older generations. Marketers quickly recognized the uniqueness of the teen consumer niche and targeted them with mass-media advertising tailored to their age group. (Figure 6-2.)

In addition to the economic significance of the new suburban lifestyles, suburbia itself—with its orderly subdivision streets lined with neat, uniform houses of predictable designs inhabited by neat, predictable families—became symbolic of a societal shift toward a regressive and pervasive conformity. To many Americans, the relentless progressivism and modernism of the postwar world moved too fast even to comprehend let alone adjust to. Rapid advances in science and technology were at once marvelous and frightening. World politics on the stage of the newly formed United Nations were too complex and often too subtle to grasp.

In the wake of the vanquished Nazis and Japanese militarists, new and even more terrible evils confronted America and threatened peace and prosperity. The postwar Soviet Union renewed its zealous machinations for world domination by bringing down an "iron curtain" over East Germany, Poland, Czechoslovakia, Romania, Bulgaria, and Hungary. In 1949, China fell to the Communists while Greece, Italy, and France, among others, teetered on the brink. The struggle of democratic nations against Communism came to be known as the "Cold War." Also in 1949, the Soviet Union exploded an atomic bomb, and the Cold War took on a new dimension with a terrifying nuclear arms race. A year later, Communist North Korea invaded the U.S.-sponsored South Korea, and Americans were drawn into another war (1950–1953) that ended only with a tenuous truce. In 1957, the launch of Russia's first orbital satellite, Sputnik, fueled more unease. It was not so much that the Soviets had beat America into space as it was that the Russians possessed proven rocket technology that could deliver nuclear warheads anywhere around the world.

At home, McCarthyism terrorized the nation for almost five years as Senator Joseph McCarthy headed a Congressional witch hunt for Communists in the government. As fruitless as it was ruthless, the investigation employed slander and smear tactics that heaped irrevocable injury on the lives and livelihoods of law-abiding citizens from nonconformist writers and entertainers to political adversaries.

In the face of such uncertainties—and ever mindful of the social upheavals caused by the still-too-recent Depression and World War II—

Figure 6-2. During the 1950s, the American teenager became a significant consumer demographic. Marketers specifically targeted teens with ads tailored with messages and images to appeal to young interests and buying habits. Coca-Cola ad, 1955; Canada Dry ad, 1956.

Figure 6-3. Advertising and TV programming of the 1950s perpetuated an idealized, mythical concept of the middle-class American family with a bread-winner father, homemaker mother, and well-behaved children. Left, Dumont TV ad, 1950; right, ABC Network ad (featuring Ozzie and Harriet Nelson with real-life sons David and Ricky in the family sitcom *Adventures of Ozzie and Harriet*), 1951.

Americans sought comfort in the familiar, including age-old social constructs of separate spheres for men and women. The American male of the 1950s embraced and advocated conformity to a masculine ideal defined by patriarchal dominance, order, and control. The ubiquitous man in the gray flannel suit was the breadwinner, and masculine identity was defined by marriage, family, and a suburban house filled with consumer goods. For women, wrote Betty Friedan, remembering her role as a 1950s housewife, "their only dream was to be the perfect wives and mothers; their highest ambition to have five children and a beautiful house, their only fight to get and keep their husbands."[2] Antiseptic TV programs of the era with their scripted formulas about the mythical, white middle-class family reinforced the illusion of a harmonious America. (Figure 6-3.) To critics of the time, these middle-class men and women were the "Silent Generation," whose preoccupation with preserving socioeconomic status and conventions of respectability was viewed as hypocritical and phony. At the end of the decade, *Esquire* worried that "the pall of conservatism and hypocrisy that has been hanging over America for the past decade can only get blacker and fouler in the next few years."[3]

The American people also found comfort in their president, Dwight D. Eisenhower (1953–1960), whose avuncular demeanor and preference for golfing over governing were ideally suited to the national temperament, if not to the seriousness of the times. The simplistic campaign slogan, "I like Ike," reflected, perhaps more than anything else, the narrow comfort zone of 1950s Americans. In 1958, John Galbraith wrote in *The Affluent Society,* "These are the days when men of all social disciplines and all political faiths seek the comfortable and the accepted; when the man of controversy is looked upon as a disturbing influence; when originality is taken to be a mark of instability; and when...the bland lead the bland."[4]

Despite the self-satisfaction of so many Americans in the postwar years, volatile social and cultural changes began to challenge the nation's complacency and staid comfort. In 1954, the Supreme Court's decision in *Brown v. Topeka Board of Education* ordered desegregation in public schools. Two years later, another high court ruling declared bus segregation laws unconstitutional. Through non-violent protests and boycotts, the civil rights movement was galvanized under the leadership of Martin Luther King, Jr. In 1957, the first civil rights legislation since Reconstruction was passed by Congress.

At the same time that African Americans were making their collective voices heard, the "Beat Generation" of young people, feeling stifled by traditionalism and convention, expressed rebellion in popular literature and music. Writers such as Jack Kerouac and Allen Ginsberg rejected "square" middle-class values and explored ways to expand the consciousness through sex, drugs, and exotic Eastern philosophies. For mainstream teenage rebellion, there was rock-and-roll music. The songs and orgiastic performances of Elvis "The Pelvis" Presley drove adolescent fans wild. A host of Elvis imitators quickly followed, spreading the gospel of rock-and-roll on TV programs such as *American Bandstand*. That teen music shocked parents and offended the establishment was all the more reason to turn up the volume.

As teens rocked their way to the threshold of a new decade, America faced numerous challenges. More and more, the younger generation questioned the sociopolitical values of their parents and what *Esquire* called their "wholesome suburban boredom,"[5] setting the stage for the youth activism of the 1960s. Growing impatient with slow desegregation in the South and continued discrimination in the North, civil rights advocates increased their efforts to effect change through sit-ins at lunch counters, large-scale marches, and boycotts of retail chains. Around the globe, friction between Cold War adversaries intensified. In America's backyard, Cuba fell to the Communists, and the stability of other Latin American countries lay in doubt. On the eve of the 1960 presidential election, the space race with the Soviets was opening new frontiers of competition and raising the stakes of national security.

Dress and Identity: Ideas and Ideals of Masculinity in the Postwar Boom Times

In the first few years after World War II, the American economy struggled to adjust to peacetime market conditions. Despite the immediate difficulties of high unemployment, debilitating labor strikes, and soaring inflation, the economy rebounded quickly. Pent-up consumer demand from the privations of rationing and War Production Board restrictions set off an economic boom that continued for years.

More than eight million returning soldiers took advantage of the GI Bill, which provided for college or vocational training and low-cost loans for business start-ups. This government action prevented veterans from swamping the transitioning job market while, at the same time, reasserting the role of men as primary breadwinners and providers.

Almost immediately upon the end of the war, women were asked to give up their jobs and resume their roles as homemakers and wives. Many women were fired as companies went through the process of retooling and restructuring for postwar manufacturing and services with the new jobs largely reserved for men. Layoffs of women were 75 percent higher than those of men.[6] The Selective Service Act ensured that veterans received priority for their old jobs, displacing still more women workers. Major corporations such as IBM, Detroit Edison, and Thompson Aircraft among others reintroduced so-called "marriage bars"—policies against hiring married women or allowing continued employment of single women if they married.[7] "Too many women should not stay in the labor force," declared the head of the National Association of Manufacturers in 1946. "The home is the basic American institution."[8] At every turn, single working women were encouraged to marry, leave the workforce, and have children; married women were expected to be content with home-making.

Popular culture reinforced the nation's sudden social reversals. In the 1946 movie *Every Girl Should Be Married*, working woman Betsy Drake sets out to snare bachelor Cary Grant any way she can. She is not expected to advance her career, strive toward any personal development goals, or seek higher education; instead, she is to persevere single-mindedly in her goals of stalking and, if necessary, deceiving Grant into a marriage vow. The following year, *Life with Father* represented the ideal nuclear family albeit in the guise of a Victorian middle-class family replete with a stereotypical patriarch, doting wife, and assorted children with benign developmental challenges. (Figure 6-4.) This nuclear family theme would serve as a model for many of the family-situation TV programs of the 1950s such as *The Adventures of Ozzie and Harriet*, *The Donna Reed Show*, *Father Knows Best*, and *Leave It to Beaver*. With this relentless barrage from popular culture and mass media, Americans were led to believe that a return to the family constructs and traditions of yore would secure America against outside threats such as communism and socialism, as well as internal threats from inner-city youth crime and delinquency and intellectualism and effeminacy.

In the postwar years, fatherhood provided one of the most solid anchors for masculine identity and success. From 1946 to 1964, America sustained a baby boom. Social sciences of the era urged and cajoled men into taking on more active parenting roles than had previous generations. It was up to men to assure proper gender-role socialization of their sons to offset the feminizing influences of stay-at-home mothers. In the 1950s, pop psychology blamed negligent parents for delinquent sons in inner cities, and overprotective, domineering mothers for effeminate—meaning homosexual—boys in the suburbs.

Another arena where American manhood was redefined was the home. Low-interest mortgage rates for veterans fueled a housing boom. In the postwar years, suburban sprawl extended out into the countryside surrounding every U.S. city. The design

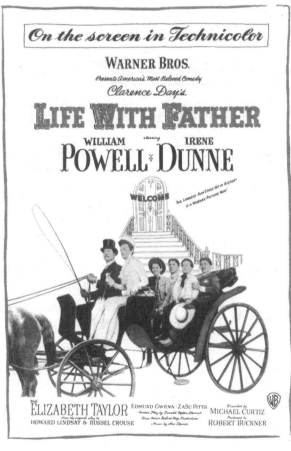

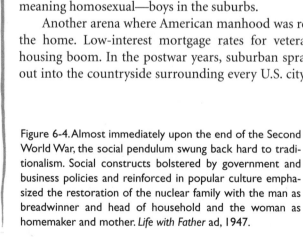

Figure 6-4. Almost immediately upon the end of the Second World War, the social pendulum swung back hard to traditionalism. Social constructs bolstered by government and business policies and reinforced in popular culture emphasized the restoration of the nuclear family with the man as breadwinner and head of household and the woman as homemaker and mother. *Life with Father* ad, 1947.

Figure 6-5. From the end of the 1940s into the mid-1960s, the white suburban middle-class family was the ideal representation of America. In ads, TV programs, and thousands of other mass media images, the nuclear family was sanitized and idealized. Men tended lawns and backyard grills in their role as family provider, and women wore skirts, earrings, and high heels to do housework and to run family errands. Ad 1956.

of suburbia from the layout of the streets and parks to the style of the houses, emphasized the orderly nuclear family unit. (Figure 6-5.) The white suburban middle-class family became the ideal representation of America from the late forties into the midsixties. For men, success or failure in their masculine role was measured in terms of consumption—the quantity and quality of consumer goods a man could provide for his family. It was an era of what some scholars call "masculine domesticity."[9] Men took an avid interest in their houses and property. Lawncare and landscaping represented the traditional masculine attachment to the outdoors while the backyard barbeque grill symbolized man's role as family provider.

The cost of the American dream for men, as many saw it, though, was

Figure 6-6. A true man's man of the 1950s was decisive and in control of his work, his emotions, his home, and his woman. He is appealing, suggested *Woman's Day*, because he is hard to handle and maybe even a little bit dangerous. Top, Cigar Institute ad, 1959; bottom, Chase and Sanborn ad, 1952.

the loss of their souls. Men became passionate conformists in the 1950s from their banal gray flannel suits worn in their cookie-cutter offices to the uniformity of their suburban ranch-style houses. In Arthur Miller's *Death of a Salesman* (1949), the Willy Loman character symbolized "those stolid, middle-class American men, frightened into conformity and saddled with familial responsibilities."[10] Men of the postwar years had become dependents of the corporate enterprise whether as blue-collar factory workers or white-collar middle management. Without even recognizing it, the American male had assumed one of the chief characteristics of the nineteenth-century feminine sphere—dependency.

To millions of American women, the cost was "the forfeited self," a complete surrender to what Betty Friedan would describe in 1963 as the "feminine mystique":

> The American housewife—freed by science and labor-saving appliances from the drudgery, the dangers of childbirth and the illnesses of her grandmother. She was healthy, beautiful, educated, concerned only about her husband, her children, her home. She had found true feminine fulfillment....She was free to choose automobiles, clothes, appliances, supermarkets; she had everything that women ever dreamed of.[11]

All the challenges and compromises for women of the fifties led to one goal: a successful marriage. That success was predicated on her responses and adaptation to the masculine qualities of her husband. In the early 1950s, *Ladies' Home Journal* ran a series of articles on "Making Marriage Work." Quizzes provided directions to women on "what you can do to increase his happiness—and your own." (His clearly came first.) The editors even recommended correspondence courses for women who were "interested in making good marriages." Among the themes in the *Journal's* series were how to handle dependent males who were spoiled by a "doting mother" and little influence from his father; how to structure a "hospitable home...which is man's best preparation for withstanding the pressures of modern life"; how to fend off his threat of a divorce; how to deal with in-laws; how former working women should adjust to a "change of jobs" from a career tract to "her principal occupation of running a house."[12]

In 1953, *Woman's Day* provided a similar view of dealing with the traditionalist American male. "Is ours a beat-up or a built-up man?" the editors asked. "On the answer will depend his happiness—and our own." The man that women dream about, the editors conceded, is "decisive, secure in himself, hard to handle, perhaps even a little dangerous." (Figure 6-6.) But once "caught," women must "set about to tame him," that is, to ensure he conforms to proper social standards of husband and father; that he is safe and predictable for the security of the marriage, family, and home. "So the men light their pipes and lapse into a silence that eventually becomes habitual." And when his "dreams of great success die out and disillusionment sets in,...a sympathetic, understanding, intelligent woman can reinforce a man's sense of well-being by recognizing the things he *has* done and admiring him for them."[13] The *Woman's Day* woman of the 1950s could then count herself successful in life if, after building up her man year after year regardless of his failures and mediocrity, she feels secure in her marriage and home. And by default, men expected to be tamed, to conform complacently to what was expected of them as workers, husbands, and fathers, and possibly to endure the stroking manipulation of wives at times of disillusionment.

These and countless similar articles in women's magazines of the 1950s provide a glimpse of how "women lived their lives—and were counseled, studied, treated, taught—according to that feminine mystique which defines women only as a husband's wife, children's mother, server of physical needs of husband, children, home, and never as a person defining herself by her own actions in society."[14] Moreover, the women's mass market press also deciphered the masculine cachet of the American male in the complacent 1950s—how his archetypical role-playing as husband, father, and family provider was defined for him by women, government, corporations, mass marketing, and pop culture.

By the end of the 1940s, the new tenets of postwar American masculinity were broadly entrenched. To be a successful breadwinner, tens of millions of American men were reconciled to a status of dependency whether on government-financed education, mortgages, and business loans, or corporate-based employment. Marriage, 2.5 children, and suburban living further defined the masculine ideal. To sustain manly success, the American male had to conform to a narrow scope of sociopolitical precepts: anticommunism, antisocialism, antifeminism, and antieffeminacy. To reflect the conformist identity of postwar American men, masculine dress was transformed in the second half of the 1940s. As discussed in detail in the next section, the powerful, broadshouldered athletic silhouette of the Depression-era working man and the wartime combat soldier was deflated. Instead, suits and outerwear adopted what came to be known as the American Ivy League look with its shapeless, straight-hanging lines and timid, diminutive details such as thin lapels and narrow natural shoulderlines. The blandness of the Ivy League gray-flannel suit hallmarked the masculine identity of the era.

At the end of the 1950s, though, the influence of an emerging youth market and a social counterinsurgency inspired not only new, nonconformist ideas of masculinity but also a radically new dress identity. The European-inspired Continental look was youthfully trim, shaped, and sexy. For young men who wanted to break free of the gray-flannel herd, the Continental suit asserted their independent thinking. It was also the prelude to the style drama of the Peacock Revolution of the 1960s.

Suits and Formal Dress 1946–1959

In the early postwar years, the shaped, athletic silhouette of the draped cut suit came to be viewed as dated—a relic of the previous generation, which, like the Depression and the war, was best left to history. During the late 1940s, the transition away from the delineated athletic contours was subtle but distinctive. Shoulders were still broad, hips snug, and rolled lapels deep, but the draped back and marked waist were cut to a straight hanging line. (Figure 6-7.) A men's suit ad in 1948 described the changing look as "architecturally tailored...with graduated straight line back and blade fullness."[15]

By 1950, the evolution was complete. The new look in men's suiting was broadly introduced by a fictional menswear stylist in *Esquire* named "Mr. 'T' Esquire." Mr. T (as in "dressed to a T") "has everything the American male has been wanting in his wardrobe," advised the editors, "a

Figure 6-7. During the late 1940s, men's suits transitioned away from the shaped, athletic fit of the draped cut designs toward a less articulated silhouette with loose-fitting, straight-hanging lines. Northampton suit, 1948.

Figure 6-8. The conservative Ivy League suit featured natural shoulders, straight-hanging lines, and narrow lapels. The look became the uniform of the corporate masses and symbolized the conformist identity of the American man in the 1950s. Suits from Surrétwill, 1953.

strictly new and masculine closetful of clothes." Chief among the new postwar changes in menswear was "a trim new look" in suits.[16] The old Superman effect in the suit silhouette with its broad shoulders, defined waist, and narrow hips had been completely replaced. But unlike the revolutionary New Look in women's fashions that virtually reinvented feminine style, men's suits instead reflected the conservative tilt of American society, and the masculine new look was a shapeless, tubular sack with natural shoulders, narrow lapels, and the straight-hanging lines of fifty years earlier, though without the exaggerated Edwardian padding. "No tug at the shoulders; no taper at the waist; no tightness at the hip," proclaimed a 1950 suit ad in differentiating the "new shape" from the old drape cut styles.[17] (Figure 6-8.) Because the new forms of subdued, single-breasted suits were adopted by the collegiate crowd (and young college-graduate businessmen), the style was soon labeled the "Ivy League look." It was the archetypal uniform and ideal dress identity for the army of traditionalist American men of the early postwar era.

The ubiquity of the plain, sober Ivy League suit and all that it symbolized even inspired a best-selling novel, *The Man in the Gray Flannel Suit,* by Sloan Wilson (1955). The title became an instant catchphrase in the American cultural lexicon with a widely understood meaning. To social critics, "The man in the gray flannel suit came to represent all that was perceived to be wrong with American business—the conformity, the stodginess, the lack of true creativity, the unquestioning obedience to executive authority."[18] But to the millions of men who suited up most workdays in a gray suit, it symbolized something different. As *Esquire* noted in 1951, "If you own a grey suit, we'll wager it ranks among your favorites; if you haven't one, you don't know what you're missing. Grey has a knack of giving you assurance, a manner that can best be described as satisfying—and if you are pleased with yourself, the rest comes naturally."[19] A gray Ivy League suit bespoke the success of conformity, of surviving in the great corporate herd, and, with that, the comfortable reward of fulfillment and self-satisfaction.

In the second half of the 1950s, though, change in America was palpable. The oppression of McCarthyites had been rejected, the unpopular Korean War had ended, the civil rights movement gained momentum, and the cult of conformity was beginning to erode. Many of the Silent Generation, particularly under-thirty males, began to seek a look other than the shapeless Ivy League suit in shades of gray for their workday wardrobes. Suit makers found fresh inspiration and opportunity from three sources: Italian style, a resurgence in color and textile patterns, and a profusion of new synthetic yarns and materials.

In the 1956–57 season, American men's suit makers introduced the "Continental look"—influenced by postwar Italian models. The new "shaped" styles, said *GQ*, were "the most provocative new suit silhouette in many years." Compared to the Ivy League styles, the Continental look was distinctly "evident in the shorter length jacket with natural shoulders, cutaway front, high-cut armholes, peaked lapels, angled pockets and cuffed sleeves. Trousers are pleatless, tapered."[20] (Figure 6-9.) The Continental look was shapely slim and trim, almost reminiscent of the youthful, narrow cuts of the First World War. The "slim-line suit," *Esquire* predicted in January 1958, "is going to reshape the look of suits this year from Fifth Avenue to Sunset Boulevard."[21] An accompanying graphic illustrated the decided distinction between the shaped Continental look and the straight-hanging Ivy League styles. (Figure 6-10.)

The inspiration for the Continental look had come from Italy, which for the first time challenged the menswear leadership of London. "Probably the most striking postwar phenomenon in men's fashions has been the emergence of Italy as the world's chief center of sartorial influence," observed *GQ*.[22] In the years following the fall of fascism, Italy opened its doors to the world, and tourists flooded in. Visitors were impressed with the elegant vitality of the people and especially the smartly attired men who lounged along the sidewalk cafes and strolled through the ancient piazzas. This masculine preoccupation with the *fare figura*, notes fashion historian Farid Chenoune, stemmed from the triple heritage of Italian society: "Latin (life is lived on the streets, which all lead straight to the forum), baroque Catholic (there is always a trace of pomp in the most secular appearance), and humanist (the body, as seat of the soul, merits care and respect)."[23] In addition, Italian luxury goods were in abundance for Americans to take back home, in contrast to the shortages still suffered by London and Paris. Moreover, the costs of finely crafted leather goods and hand-tailored suits from Rome's Via Condotti were a fraction of comparable products in, or imported from, London and Paris.

Unlike the Italian suit makers, though, American designers eagerly explored variations on the Continental look. "Now that the Continental style is established, designers can experiment within its basic design," reported *GQ*.[24] One of the first variations was the addition of trouser cuffs, which Italian tailors thought ruined the suit line (besides collecting dirt). One- and three-button closures soon joined the preferred two-button style. By 1959, the first double-breasted variants were marketed, retaining the shaped contours, tapered sleeves, and natural shoulderline but losing the telltale cutaway front of the original model. That same year, Pauline Trigere even went so far as to offer coat versions with raglan and split raglan sleeves.[25] One of the novelty experiments with the Continental look was a jumpsuit comprising a one-piece vest and beltless trouser combination featured in *GQ* in December 1958.[26]

Some of the most important fashion news of the 1950s was the explosion of synthetic fibers and materials. The era's new synthetics had numerous advantages over natural fibers and solved many age-old problems confronted by clothing makers. Synthetic filament yarns in combination or blended with natural fibers produced fabrics that were durable, stain and moisture resistant, wrinkle-proof, and, most lauded of all at the

Figure 6-9. In the second half of the 1950s, the Continental look became an alternative to the Ivy League suit. Inspired by Italian styling, the Continental suit was designed with a shaped, shorter jacket that featured a cutaway front, peaked lapels, and angled pockets. Trousers were tapered and pleatless. Continental suit from Promenade, 1959.

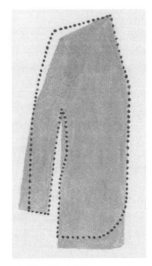

Figure 6-10. The differences between the shaped Continental suit and the straight hanging Ivy League styles were subtle but distinctive. Graphic from *Esquire*, 1958.

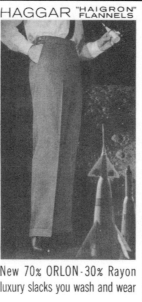

Figure 6-11. The 1950s was an era of "miracle fabrics" woven or knit from many new synthetic fibers. Left, "wash 'n' wear" suits of Dacron/cotton by Palm Beach, 1958; right, "wash and wear" slacks of Orlon/rayon from Haggar, 1959.

time, machine washable ("wash 'n' wear"). (Figure 6-11.) The new "miracle" yarns also made it easier for textile and clothing makers to control dyeing, shrinkage, and crease and pleat retention.

In addition to the development of new chemical-based fibers, advanced processes for extruding filament yarns were refined that could produce varied thicknesses and even shapes. The synthetic yarns were made by forcing liquefied polymers through tiny holes in spinnerets resembling bath shower heads where, upon contact with air, the chemicals solidified into filament yarns. The holes in the spinnerets could be cut to the shapes of triangles, hearts, Ys, or 8s among others for the production of yarns with optical and textural properties such as luster, sparkle, opacity, coil, and crimp.

Among the most highly promoted synthetics was nylon. Although introduced in 1939, its production had been restricted largely to war needs until the late 1940s. In the postwar years, nylon was continually refined for use in tricot and woven textiles; in 1954, a more versatile "Nylon 6" was engineered for specialized uses such as shaped carpet yarns. Cellulose-based acetates had been around for decades, but in 1954 a triacetate trademarked Arnel was produced that had a high heat resistance for better crease and pleat retention. In 1951, DuPont announced its polyester fiber Dacron, which was a superb blending fiber for wrinkle resistant fabrics used in making suits. Light and springy acrylic fibers, variously branded as Orlon, Acrilan, Creslan, and Zefran, were used in blends for sweaters, knit sportswear, and, in 1953, the first manmade "furs."

In addition to the myriad of new synthetics for men's suits and sports jackets, silk became more broadly popular in the 1950s. (Figure 6-12.) As American tourists returned from Italy with lightweight jackets made of handloomed silk shantung, U.S. ready-to-wear makers began to import the colorful, slubbed material for mass production of suits and sports coats. American textile mills quickly responded to the market demand with imitations of silk made of the new synthetics and blends woven into nubby fabrics that had the look and feel of the real thing, but were more durable and easier to clean.

Although the man in the gray flannel suit was comfortable with his conformity and herd mentality in the office, at home, he allowed himself some degree of individual expression by opting for leisurewear that contrasted sharply with his workweek restraint. In the early fifties, he ventured to don a silk blazer in a daring color such as teal, ochre, or even dusty rose or perhaps a tweed jacket with an oversized windowpane check or shadow plaid. In the second half of the decade, patterns and colors became riotous for sports coats. (Color Plate 9.) "Men have been conservative too long," complained designer Pauline Trigere. "Enough of that self-imposed sobriety which alternates between shadow-grey and semi-black; why not dark green and deep red? And don't men realize there are blues other than navy?"[27] Madras plaids in the most vivid combinations of colors were applied to lightweight summer jackets. Fashion editorials featured print jackets in fussy paisleys and even an all-over reproduction of the medieval Bayeaux tapestry. Yet, as dramatic as such stylistic versions seemed at the time, critics claimed these were but variations on a bad theme. In 1958, Pearl Binder wrote in *Peacock's Tail*, "To add color (sadly lacking though it is in man's dress today) would only make the dress worse than it is already. It would not bring man's dress back to life, but merely be painting the corpse."[28]

One of the more unusual anomalies of business dress occurred in the early 1950s when some younger men donned tailored knee-length shorts and knee-high stockings with their business coats, white dress shirts, and foulard ties. At a time when most offices were not air-conditioned, the steamy summer months could be unbearable in wool trousers. The

Figure 6-12. Throughout the 1950s, suits and sports jackets made of nubby-textured shantung silk were favorite warm weather options for business dress. American textile manufacturers capitalized on the popularity of silk and replicated the look and feel in many new synthetic weaves. International Silk Association ad, 1958.

Figure 6-13. As a solution to wearing wool suits to work in oppressively hot office buildings in summer, some suit makers offered a three-piece suit or suit separates that included tailored, bermuda-length shorts. The addition of air conditioning to most office buildings by the late 1950s soon made the idea obsolete. Left, city shorts by Corbin, 1955; right, city shorts by Everfast, 1954.

Figure 6-14. The design of evening attire followed the trends of business suits. In the early 1950s, the tuxedo was cut with the straight-hanging lines of the Ivy League suit; in the second half of the decade, the shaped Continental look was an option. Left, Ivy League tuxedos from After Six, 1950; right, Continental tuxedo from Lord West, 1959.

concept was certainly not innovative in menswear since suit shorts and knee stockings had been common for decades in tropical British colonies like Bermuda, Jamaica, and the Bahamas where vacationing American businessmen would have seen the look. In 1953, *Life* photographed men on the streets of Manhattan and in offices attired in business shorts. "In saloons and restaurants, in offices and along scorching streets, wearers of knee-length bermuda shorts were cropping up, not frequently but boldly and regularly," noted the editor. "Properly worn with knee-length wool socks, which somewhat cancel the cooling effect, bermuda shorts take on formality as a jacket or tie is added."[29] When Manhattan bank clerks were permitted to wear suit shorts, and Sardi's and the 21 Club admitted men in jackets and shorts, some menswear retailers began to offer a two-and-a-half piece suit that included a matching pair of knee-length shorts with the jacket and trousers.[30] (Figure 6-13.) Suit shorts never became a broadly accepted trend and lasted just a few summer seasons before most office buildings were fitted with air conditioning. In addition, most men of the era were too conformist to risk the opprobrium of peers and the disapproving stares on city streets.

Evening attire followed the trends of business suits. In the early postwar years, tuxedos were cut in the same tubular, straight-hanging lines as the Ivy League suit coat; and in the second half of the 1950s, they adopted the shaped Continental look. (Figure 6-14.) For the most part, the tail coat was seldom worn anymore, having been a casualty of War Production Board restrictions. For men who were obligated to dress formally for an embassy ball or haute cultural event, traditional tail coats of the era were "nearly all blue," reported *Men's Wear*.[31] The morning suit, with its cutaway black or charcoal coat, striped gray trousers, and puffed ascot, likewise, was rarely seen except for weddings of the affluent. "This is the favored outfit for a formal day wedding," noted *Esquire*, "but it is not the only one."[32] Otherwise, the simplicity and comfort of the tuxedo dominated after-six formal dress.

The key news for tuxedos, though, was color and texture. The black and midnight blue for winter and white for summer remained the standards for evenings in the city. When at resorts or a country club dance evening dress became peacock expressive. The vividly colored prints and bold plaids that were so popular in sports jackets were adapted to tuxedo coats as well—always worn with black or dark blue trousers. In 1956, dazzling tuxedo jackets of textured, iridescent silk and woven metallic threads in turquoise, russet, silver, and patterned white, each accented with a ruffled or embroidered bosom shirt, were introduced as "the lustrous look" in *Esquire's* "Fashion Forum."[33]

For the man who was reluctant about wardrobe splendor, new forms and fabrications of tuxedo accessories offered him opportunities for tentative experimentation. Cummerbunds and matching ties were made with a wide variety of sumptuous, vibrantly colored textiles. An alternative to the bow tie introduced in 1957 was the Continental tie, also called a "cross-over," designed as two flared tabs that overlapped and fastened with a covered button beneath the collar. Cummerbunds were embellished with insets of richly patterned fabrics or reconstructed as cummervests with various single- and double-breasted button front closures and even vest points.

The caution for the well-dressed man, though, was when and where to wear the splendor of a colorful or patterned tuxedo jacket or accessories. In their look at "designs under the moon" at a resort, *Esquire* noted in 1958 that "when you dress for dinner, patterns still prevail."[34] However, warned *GQ*, keep "the red and brocade jackets for cruises and country clubs"; for dinner parties and casinos, "evening elegance" required "formal black."[35]

Shirts 1946–1959

In 1948, *Esquire* announced the emergence of the Bold Look in men's fashions. With men's suit designs in transition and millions of ex-servicemen trying to catch up on the current, correct dress for the modern, atomic-age male, the focus of the Bold Look was on accessories, including the new ideas in dress shirts and collars. "The newest styles that are appearing wherever the leaders of fashion gather exemplify the Bold Look," declared *Esquire*. "Ties, shirts, socks—they're designed with the accent on authority. They're unrestrained; they use wide borders, big patterns, bold colors—more colors. They have a look of definite good taste. Wearing them, you'll have that look too."[36] The Bold Look also symbolized what *Esquire* assessed as the new masculine identity in America:

It's a look that's worn by successful, distinguished men—men who are the leaders in their fields and who want the clothes they wear and the appearance they make to reflect their positions in life. It's a look that's worn with head held high and shoulders pulled back. It's a keen, direct, look-you-in-the-eye and take measure look... It's a look that only begins with what you're wearing and runs all

Figure 6-15. The "command collar" shirt of the late 1940s was constructed with a wide-spread, stayed collar and stitching that was a half-inch in from the edge instead of the usual eighth of an inch. Bold Look shirt by Wachusett Shirt Company, 1948.

Figure 6-16. Dress shirt collar styles were widely varied in the 1950s, including the new round points, short points, and modified spreads. Van Heusen introduced a fresh look in dress shirts made without visible stitching on collars, cuffs, or button pleats. Fourteen styles of dress shirt collars by Van Heusen, 1953.

the way to how you feel in it...In the Bold Look you'll feel like the self-confident, dominant, successful man that you do look![37]

And typical of the socially regressive postwar period, the editorial featured an illustration of a smartly suited, "dominant" man striding confidently forward while dragging a leopardskin-clad "cave woman" by the hair.

The new Bold Look in dress shirts of the late 1940s was the command collar style. (Figure 6-15.) It featured a spread, stayed collar with stitching a half-inch from the edge instead of the usual eighth of an inch. The same stitching was also applied to the longer French cuffs and to the center button pleat, which was wider than usual with larger buttons.

The command collar was short-lived, though, since the subdued, minimal details of the Ivy League suit coat required a complementary dress shirt with equally simplified detailing. In contrast to the bold stitching of the command collar shirt, the fresh look of dress shirts in the early 1950s was without visible stitching on the collar, cuffs, or button pleat. In addition, shirt makers like Van Heusen offered an increasingly broader assortment of collar styles that were much reduced in band depth and point length. (Figure 6-16.) The new and modified shapes of collars included wide spreads, modified spreads, round points, short points, and button down variations.

Figure 6-17. In the postwar years, jeans were elevated to fashion status although they were largely promoted as "Western wear." Teenagers adopted jeans as a form of rebellion, emulating pop idols such as James Dean in *Rebel Without a Cause*. Above, Marlboro ad, 1959; below, Western jeans from Sears, 1952.

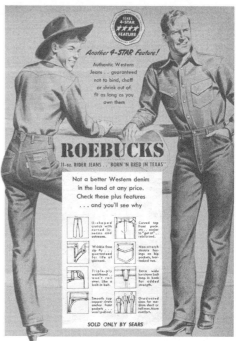

Shirt makers also joined the synthetic revolution of the 1950s and applied various fabric blends throughout the decade. Easy-care wash-and-wear fabrics were emphasized in dress shirt ads.

One of the key developments in style shifts of the era was the introduction in the early 1950s of the short-sleeved business shirt for summer dress. So that men did not confuse the colorful and patterned varieties with sports shirts, stores were advised by trade journals to display the styles with correctly coordinated neckties.

Work Clothes 1946–1959

In the postwar years, work clothes followed the trends of sportswear and were made with an increasingly varied assortment of synthetic fabrics. In addition to the continued use of rayon in wool and cotton blends, nylon was once again available after war restrictions were lifted in 1946. Work clothes made with nylon "fortified" fabrics were promoted as "50% more abrasive resistance."[38] Blends of durable Dacron and rayon were promised to "resist acids, wrinkles, and abrasion." Utility pants made of 90% Orlon and 10% wool "look like wool but wash like cotton." Acrilan acrylic fiber whipcord had a "wool-like texture" and resisted "shrinking, wrinkling and creasing."[39] Wash-and-wear was a welcomed advance in synthetic fabric manufacturing for the housewife whose laundry chores included ironing heavy-duty work clothes. Marketing names like "Wash-fast" suggested both wash-and-wear convenience as well as non-fading, colorfast dyeing. For the ex-serviceman, "army chinos"—shirts and pants made of preshrunk 2-ply cotton—assured familiar comfort.

Denim overalls and jackets were largely unchanged from prewar styles. Even as sportswear became more trim and fitted, work clothes of heavy denim remained baggy and loose for the requisite nonbinding fit.

Jeans became elevated to fashion status in the 1950s. TV westerns like *Gunsmoke* and *Bonanza* further popularized the dude-ranch look that had begun to emerge in the 1930s. The cachet of the rugged cowboy in his iconic tight-fitting jeans became even more commercialized when the Marlboro Man was introduced in 1955. (Figure 6-17.) For suburban teenagers, jeans were a benign expression of rebellion. Counterculture

Figure 6-18. The vivid colors and flamboyant prints of sports shirts allowed men to break out of the gray flannel conformity of workday dress and express themselves with flair and personality. Wash-and-wear sports shirts from Sears, 1952.

groups such as the Beats, bikers, and inner city hoodlums wore jeans almost exclusively. School dress codes prohibited jeans to be worn to class, but, at home and with peer cliques on weekends, teens emulated the jeans-clad look of Elvis Presley in *Jailhouse Rock* (1957), James Dean in *Rebel Without a Cause* (1955), and Marlon Brando in *The Wild One* (1953). As a menswear ad asserted in 1958, the new look and slim fit of jeans were "calculated to flip the socially oriented BMOC [big man on campus], the Angry Young Man, and sophisticated delinquents in all age groups."[40]

Sportswear 1946–1959

In 1946, *Men's Wear* looked ahead at "things to come" in postwar men's fashion. The editors took the sartorial pulse of the American male and determined that "men are in the mood for change. Never has the urge toward masculine fantasy in the field of raiment been more marked."[41] But when serious, sober dress became the workday identity, that masculine fantasy found an outlet through sportswear. "Often designers try out new ideas in sportswear before they are adopted for general use," noted a 1957 style guide. "Perhaps the feeling is that sport clothes can be way out or extreme without much danger. And if an innovation catches on, you've got a trend."[42] The conservative "man in the gray flannel suit" responded enthusiastically to the designers' colorful and innovative sportswear experiments as a relief from the stuffy conformity of his workday dress.

On weekends and at play, a considerable number of American men donned sports shirts in startlingly vivid colors and prints. In 1957, *GQ* advised readers that "the avant-garde dresser of fine taste will be the man with the boldly patterned [sports shirt]."[43] Year after year, the mass merchandisers provided fresh prints and new palettes of colors. (Figure 6-18.) In addition, the myriad of wash-and-wear synthetic fabrics ensured that colors were more brilliant and retained their brilliant hues better than natural fiber styles. (Color Plate 10.) The oversized plaids and vibrant colors of madras prints were especially popular on sports shirts in the 1950s. African-inspired batik prints flourished as a result of so much news about former colonies achieving independence from Europe. Hawaiian prints had remained a favorite since the 1930s and found a new market with the postwar generation. Stylized graphics of Mexican, American Indian, and folk art motifs were also recurring fabric designs.

Figure 6-19. For the Ivy Leaguer who was more comfortable with conservative, understated sportswear, mass merchandisers always stocked assorted sports shirts in safely traditional colors and patterns. "Ivy Look" button down sports shirts from Montgomery Ward, 1957.

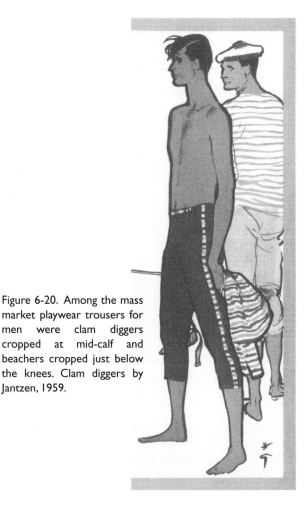

Figure 6-20. Among the mass market playwear trousers for men were clam diggers cropped at mid-calf and beachers cropped just below the knees. Clam diggers by Jantzen, 1959.

Figure 6-21. A new preppy look for the Ivy Leaguer was the slim, buckle tab back trouser. Reston Slacks ad, 1956.

In the late 1950s, American sports-shirt makers introduced another technological innovation called Velcro. (Color Plate 11.) The Swiss inventor had experimented for ten years perfecting the idea of a new closure formed by opposing strips of nylon, one with thousands of tiny hooks and the other with tiny eyes. When pressed together, the hooks locked into the eyes securely but could be pulled apart easily. Success came when a French textile lab developed the complex process of weaving nylon under infrared lights that hardened the fibers into the durable, interlocking hooks and eyes.

Not all men were comfortable with the attention-getting prints and colors or fancy new constructions of sports shirts. The ultraconservative Ivy Leaguer preferred sports shirts in small, traditional plaids, stripes, and the occasional tiny print in a basic button front, button down collar variety. (Figure 6-19.)

To complement the vast array of sports shirts, sportswear trousers also became more varied than ever. "News is the length," proclaimed an editorial in 1956, which featured five lengths, including regular cuffed casual trousers, bermuda shorts, the ankle-length beach trouser, "peon pants" cropped at mid-calf [more commonly known as clam diggers], and "beachers" that extended to just below the knees.[44] (Figure 6-20.) Fabrics, though, were even more important news in men's sportswear trousers. In 1958, *Esquire* featured a double-page color photo of six "fancy pants," including a multicolored madras plaid, foulard pattern,

Figure 6-22. The bulky, baggy ski suits and thick, coarse knit sweaters of the war years evolved into sleek, formfitting ski pants and high style knitwear at the end of the fifties. Jantzen lambswool sweater with knit ski pants, 1957.

and paisley print. "Let your wildest impulse be your guide," the editor recommended "the brighter the trousers, the better to relax in a holiday mood."[45] For the conservative Ivy League man, a new look in sportswear trousers appeared as well. The cut was narrow with cuffs at 17 inches, unpleated, and affixed at the back with a buckle tab just above the welt pockets. (Figure 6-21.)

Skiwear of the 1950s continued the trend toward less bulky and more comfortable clothes for easy maneuvering down the slopes. Fabrics made of the new synthetics and blends, especially nylon and Dacron, were lighter and yet more windproof and moisture repellent than the heavy knits and the rayon wovens of the war years. In the mid-1950s, ski pants were made from elasticized fabrics with a silicone finish that fit snugly to reduce wind resistance. The stirrup ski pants featured in the 1954 Winter edition of *Gentry* were made of "a revolutionary new fabric called Elastisse," which was 40% nylon blended with 60% wool. The innovative fabric, reported *Gentry*, "actually stretches vertically, thus allowing a freedom and comfort impossible in conventional fabrics."[46] By the end of the decade, sleek ski pants of stretch nylon and one-piece skisuits lined with nylon fleece were the favorites of serious skiers. (Figure 6-22.)

Swimwear varied little for the first several postwar years. The short, baggy boxer with an internal brief-cut liner and the knit brief of nylon, rayon, or wool Lastex were the two options. As in the 1930s, both styles still featured a high waistline to cover the navel. By the early-1950s,

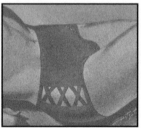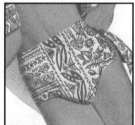

Jantzen swim briefs from left to right: Seaflame 1951, Daredevil 1952, Kontiki 1954

"Skimmer" boxer trunks from Jantzen, 1955

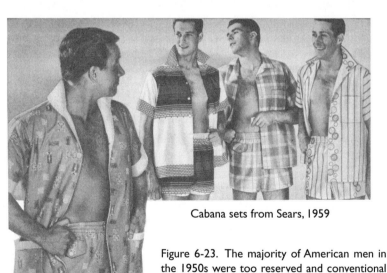

Cabana sets from Sears, 1959

Figure 6-23. The majority of American men in the 1950s were too reserved and conventional for most of the skimpy swimsuits influenced by European designs. The preferred style of the American male was the loose-fitting poplin or nylon boxer that still concealed the navel.

Figure 6-24. Two popular outerwear revivals of the 1950s were the raglan sleeve topcoat and the buttonless wrap coat. Left, wrap coat of Bactrian camel's hair from Savile Row, 1951; right, raglan sleeve topcoat of wool tweed from Montgomery Ward, 1956.

though, swimwear makers began to experiment with skimpier looks influenced by the Italians. In 1952, Jantzen introduced the Daredevil which had a waistline cut below the navel and open sides held together by three crisscrossed straps. Two years later, Gantner produced its version of the lower cut, open-sided brief with four thin straps over the hips. In 1955, *Gentry* reported seeing the first "abbreviated Italian Bikini knit trunks" at the resorts.[47] As noted in chapter 6, European men had worn a form of high-waisted bikini-style swimwear as early as the mid-1930s, but, in the 1950s, the Italians lowered the waistline to the hips and cut the oval leg openings higher. At the other extreme, swimwear makers produced a variety of retro looks from bygone eras. Three of those were shown in a color spread of *Esquire* in 1958: a knit square-cut trunk reminiscent of the 1930s; a horizontal striped, knee-length knit trunk of the Edwardian era, sometimes called a "swim-walker"; and the calf-length knit Bongo Pants modeled on long Victorian styles.[48] For men who did not like the baggy boxer shorts nor the formfitting knit briefs, Jantzen developed the Skimmer in 1956—a snug-fitting boxer constructed with a darted front of woven cotton and the back half of elasticized knit.

Despite a willingness to don all varieties of flamboyant sportswear in the most attention-getting colors and patterns, most American men were reluctant exhibitionists on the beach and poolside. The long styles of swimwear were rejected because they were too unorthodox and too uncomfortable when wet, and the bikinis became associated with homosexuals. Overwhelmingly, the loose-fitting, high-waisted boxer trunks, often with matching sports shirts in cabana sets, were the most preferred swimwear for the average American male. (Figure 6-23.)

Outerwear 1946–1959

Overcoats followed the trends of suit jackets. In the early 1950s, outerwear adopted the natural shoulders and straight-hanging lines of the Ivy League suit. Two revivals that were popular with Ivy Leaguers were the raglan sleeve (and its variant the split raglan) and the buttonless wrap. (Figure 6-24.) In keeping with the conservative mood of the time, fabrics for overcoats were drab with medium gray, medium brown, or medium tan being typical in menswear catalogs. Even tweeds were less colorful than in the 1930s. The Bold Look textile patterns of the late forties diminished to small checks or herringbones in the early fifties. As with suits and sports jackets, silk became fashion news for topcoats in the 1950s. "The silk topcoat...another way in which silk is finding it way into the wardrobes of well-groomed men....Soft to the hand, rich to the eye, giving the warmth desired," lauded *Gentry* in 1952.[49] Slubbed silks set the

trend for other textured fabrics especially the nubby Donegal tweeds.

As the Continental suit became more prevalent in the late fifties, top-coats began to adopt elements from the look. "The Continental influence [is apparent] in topcoats: shorter length...horizontal peak lapels, slanted flap pockets, cuffed sleeves," reported *GQ*.[50] Variations included shawl collars and half raglan sleeves that were set-in at the front but cut with diagonal raglan seams at the back. Color and patterns also returned with the Continental-styled coats. "Flecked" tweeds were textured with nubs of bright yellows, reds, royal blue, and teal green to warm or cool the charcoal gray, navy, or chocolate ground. Another revived favorite was the overplaid woven as a single- or double-line window pane check in red, sienna, or hunter green over the flecked tweed.

Short coats became especially popular during the 1950s as suburbanites spent ever more time in their cars. (Figure 6-25.) The short crops were more comfortable and allowed greater maneuverability for operating floorboard pedals. The two most common short coats were car coats, some-times called "surcoats," which were cropped short at about the wrist, and the slightly longer suburbans with fingertip-length hemlines. For high school boys and collegiates, the duffel coat, also called a "duffer," was the favorite. The style had become a civilian adoption of a military coat during World War II, but grew even more popular in the 1950s. The duffel was a "most desirable *extra* coat," noted *Gentry* in 1951, "for country walking, for exercising the dog, for driving in an open car, for sitting in a stadium. The duffel coat fits all these uses superbly."[51] Because the duffel—and other

Figure 6-26. Although numerous men's style guides and fashion editorials promoted the cape as a new outerwear trend, American men regarded the look as too eccentric and too British. Burberry Inverness coat, 1958.

short coat styles—often had removable, zippered linings, they were easily adapted to the transitional weather in fall and spring when topcoats were too heavy. In addition, duffel coats, parkas, windbreakers, and trench-coats were often made of the more durable, easy-to-clean synthetics, especially blends of nylon, Orlon, and Dacron.

In the second half of the 1950s, two outerwear ideas were popularized in the fashion press but largely ignored by consumers. Capes were repeatedly mentioned. In 1958, *Esquire* tried to put an American spin on the look of capes: "New directions in outerwear reflect the flair and colorful imagination of American industrial design. Capes are coming back in force this year...textured for country life but precision-seamed to fall in stylized folds from raglan shoulders to a generous sweep."[52] The look of capes was simply too eccentric and too British for the average American man. (Figure 6-26.) Likewise, the fake furs of the late fifties never achieved mass popularity despite their frequent coverage in the fashion press. Various blends of Orlon, Dynel, Verel, and Arnel were extruded into shaped filaments that could be woven into deep pile textiles with a furry feel. "Looks like fur," proclaimed a *GQ* editorial. "Deep pile fabric—warm but surprisingly lightweight—lends a rich furry look to sporty new winter coats in suburban and jacket lengths."[53] (Figure 6-27.) However, not only did fake furs have an artificial sheen, they tended to flatten and matt easily.

Underwear 1946–1959

In 1946, *Men's Wear* offered merchants an extensive "inside story" on men's underwear. "In selling men's underwear, comfort is the activating principle, with durability a runner up." The five essential points a man considered in choosing underwear, advised the editor, included: "(1) no binding, but not too loose; (2) non-irritating to the skin; (3) free from bulginess; (4) staying put—climbing and rolling may be good exercises but are most annoying in underwear; (5) free from irritating fasteners."[54] Fashion style, colors, or prints did not make the list.

Until the end of the 1950s, men's underwear changed little from a generation earlier: knit or woven union suits in long or short varieties; yoke front "gripper" (metal snap) boxers and elastic waist boxers in woven solids and prints; and white knit briefs. (Figure 6-28.) In the second half of the 1950s, colorful, novelty print boxers were promoted by makers as Father's Day gifts, and mass merchandisers like Sears and Montgomery Ward offered briefs with tiny scatter prints on white. Knit T-shirts with crewneck or the new V-neck designs were preferred over the tank-style athletic undershirt largely because millions of servicemen had become accustomed to the fit and feel of the T-shirt as part of their military uniforms during World War II and the Korean War.

As with most other categories of menswear in the age of miracle fabrics, men's underwear was produced in a variety of synthetics and blends as well. Since the underwear styles remained the same regardless of fiber, makers and retailers marketed the higher-priced synthetics as good-better-best options. Cotton briefs were prepackaged three for about $1, but the same style of brief in spun nylon was $1.65 each, and in spun Orlon $1.89 each.[55]

In 1959, though, a hint of big changes to come in masculine self-

Figure 6-27. Among the new forms of textiles made possible by various blends and extrusion processes of synthetic fibers were deep pile fabrics used in making fake furs. "Wolf's coat" of Dynel and Verel fake fur by Fredwin, 1959.

Figure 6-28. "Since men are creatures of habit, many go on buying the same type of underwear indefinitely," noted *Men's Wear.*[56] For most men of the 1950s, either the traditional woven boxer or knit brief was the underwear style of choice. Yoke front "gripper" (metal snap) boxers, elastic waist boxers, and knit briefs from Montgomery Ward, 1956.

Figure 6-29. Men's underwear became an erotic fashion accessory in 1959 when Jockey introduced its nylon bikini-styled Skants. Jockey Skants ad, 1959.

awareness and identity manifested with the introduction of the Jockey Skants bikini. (Figure 6-29.) For a major underwear maker like Coopers to take this product marketing initiative at this time is significant. Although bikini-style swimsuits for men had been around since the 1930s, the look had been limited to certain Mediterranean resorts in France and Italy, and, unlike the brief cut swimsuit of the 1930s (model for the original Jockey knit brief), the bikini-style swimsuits had not influenced the design of underwear. Even though men's bikinis had been spotted on the beaches of North American resorts and reported in the fashion press, by the 1950s, American men largely rejected the skimpier swimsuits. After all, to the traditionalist American male, such sexual exhibitionism was regarded as a feminine trait, or, worse, a subculture trait of homosexuals and competition-circuit body builders. Thus, at a time when catalog photos such as those from Montgomery Ward shown in Figure 6-28 were still scrupulously airbrushed to eradicate any hint of the genitals or nipples, the idea of masculine sexuality expressed in underwear was radical. The copy in Jockey ads specifically emphasized male erotic exhibitionism: "Bikini-styled Skants are tailored of 100% stretch nylon that molds to your body...with minimum coverage."[57] The horizontal "candy stripes" further delineated the contours of the genitals and buttocks. At the close of the 1950s, the colorful peacock splendor of men's sportswear was joined by the sexual exhibitionism of swimwear and underwear, setting the stage for a revolutionary era of masculine dress and identity.

Sleepwear 1946–1959

A recurring fashion trend in men's sleepwear of the postwar years was Asian-inspired motifs, influenced by the constant headline news from Pacific Rim nations. In 1949, China fell to the communists; the Korean War was fought 1950–53; the U.S. military occupation of Japan ended in 1952. The "Yokojama" featured a coat with half sleeves, Mandarin collar, and a calligraphy print body; the short "coolie" trousers were cropped just below the knees. (Figure 6-30.) Even the old Cossack styles, with their stand-up, circular collars and off-center closures were redesigned with Asian motif trim and renamed "mandarin" pajamas. Similarly, in 1957, *GQ* reported on the new silk kimono robes for men that included varieties designed with oversized, square-cut samurai sleeves and a collarless neckline.

For the most part, though, men's sleepwear and robes varied little from styles of a generation earlier. Fresh detailing included the new "Italian collar," which was a roll form without the lapel extension. Skijamas were knit crewneck pullover tops and matching or contrasting trousers with ribknit banded cuffs somewhat resembling Victorian underwear. For the diehard Ivy Leaguer, some robes were made with button down collars. The most contemporary look of the era was the contrasting coat and trouser set often marketed as mix-and-match to encourage multiple purchases. Coats were usually of prints and patterns that coordinated with the solid color trousers.

The screen-printed fabrics for pajamas and robes were updated with modern art interpretations of traditional animal, nautical, or sports motifs; others resembled high-tech schematics of Jet Age industries. In addition, many of the new synthetic fabrics were ideal for sleepwear. Nylon or Dacron blends were more durable and longer lasting than natural fiber fabrics, and the wash-and-wear synthetics were conveniently drip-dry, requiring no ironing.

Accessories 1946–1959

As noted previously, men's fashions of the postwar years were declared as the Bold Look by the style editors of *Esquire*. As a general guide, the editors advised that Bold Look accessories:

use big patterns, bold colors, more colors—but none of them go overboard in the matter of color or design. And each accessory is related to the outfit as a whole: notice how the color of a suit stripe is picked up in the color of a tie figure, how the color of the stones in the big cuff links repeats the color of the suit. There's a definite relationship between these accessories—they're selected not just for their own sakes but because of the way they complement each other. That's important, because the Bold Look isn't just in a shirt or a necktie or a hat—it's in the complete, overall appearance you'll have when you're wearing the Bold Look clothes and accessories and when they are related to each other.[58]

For millions of returning ex-servicemen, the Bold Look was a welcome relief from years of standard government-issue uniforms; for civilians, the abundance and variety of accessories enabled men to indulge in fashion and self-expression after the conservation and restrained looks of the war years.

When it came to hats, the Bold Look was all about proportion and size. The recommendation from *Esquire* was a "snap brim in a rich cinnamon brown with a black band." The contrasting gun-metal grey binding along the edge of the broad brim was a wide 5/8 of an inch on the underside. "From the rear it's a wide band of color."[59]

By the beginning of the 1950s, the Ivy League suit with its narrow sil-

Figure 6-30. Asian-inspired motifs and garment constructions were popular for sleepwear and loungewear of the 1950s. His and Her Yokojamas by Pleetway, 1957.

Pinch front, snap brim fedoras; flat top porkpie, and business-man's homburg, 1950

Summer straw and boater with tele-scope crown, 1959

Figure 6-31. The oversized Bold Look in hats of the late 1940s diminished in scale and propor-tion during the 1950s. Crowns were tapered to look as slim as the Ivy League and Continental suits, and brims were trimmed to as narrow as two inches. At the end of the decade, the tele-scope crown was a fresh variation of the tapered styles.

houette and reduced collar, lapels, and other detailing influenced a new look in hats. (Figure 6-31) Crowns were more tapered, giving hats a lighter, trimmed shaped. The brims also narrowed from 3 inches at the start of the decade down to about 2-1/8 inches and even 2 inches on some styles. In the late 1950s, the new telescope crown featured a promi-nent taper and appeared to tilt backward from its high front angled to a lower back. Even summer straws and boaters were reshaped with the new telescope shapes. In keeping with the resurgence of color in men's wardrobes in the second half of the decade, summertime hat bands pro-vided another opportunity for personal expression. "Even conservative dressers these days have taken to bright and colorful bands (and they can be changed for a variety and fashion coordination) and novel weaves in their summer straws," noted *GQ* in 1958.[60]

Toward the end of the 1950s, American men were increasingly going hatless despite the insistence of style guides and fashion editorials. "Not every man wears a hat, of course," conceded *GQ* in 1958, "but no well-dressed man opens his front door without one....Not that we advocate wearing a hat because it's 'correct,' because one 'has to.' A hat is a smart accessory....The right hat should make you look better than nature intended—slimmer, or taller, or younger, or less dissipated than you are."[61] Young men, especially, discounted such sartorial advice, however, and the most notable hatless example at the time was the presidential candidate for the 1960 election, John F. Kennedy.

The Bold Look of the late 1940s was particularly notable with neck-wear. Wild-figured prints and strong patterns were eye-popping in their size and color combinations. A continued favorite novelty gift for dad

Bold Look rayon ties from Haband, 1950

Figure 6-32. The Bold Look in neckwear persisted until the mid-1950s when figures and patterns were scaled down to work better with the narrower cut of ties. In the second half of the decade, tie makers experimented with new shapes to complement the sculpted Continental suits. By the end of the decade, ties had narrowed to two inches.

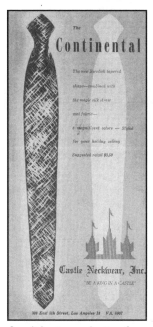
Swedish tapered tie from Castle Neckwear, 1956

was a handpainted tie embellished with multicolored tropical landscapes and hunting scenes. The four-in-hand remained a broad 4-1/2 inches wide at the pointed end of the blade, and bow ties were 1-3/4 inches wide at the ends.

Even in the face of the regressive conservatism in men's suits in the 1950s, ties continued to be visually aggressive. (Figure 6-32 and Color Plate 8.) "If you've an overwhelming urge to toss caution to the winds, express it in your tie," *Esquire's* Mr. T recommended in 1951.[62] The vividly hued madras plaids that were so prevalent in everything from sportswear to formal accessories were particularly popular. In 1953, *Esquire* featured coordinated sets of ties and socks in which the "graduated-stripe patterns [of the ties] are repeated on the front of French lisle socks" in the same design and colors.[63] For the ultraconservative, an abundance of understated ties in traditional stripes, checks, and tiny repeats were options. Throughout the decade, widths of the four-in-hand gradually narrowed to 3-1/2 inches in the early 1950s, about 3 inches by mid-decade, and a slim 2 inches at the close. Thin knit (crocheted) ties in school colors remained as much a favorite of collegiate men as a generation earlier. For the new, shaped Continental suit of the second half of the decade, some tie makers experimented with new shapes of ties although none displaced the narrowed four-in-hand. Makers also produced neckwear made of the new synthetics, particularly Dacron and acetate.

Shoe shapes in the early postwar years were wide, thick, and round-toed. As the 1950s progressed, the Italian influence inspired sleek, dagger sharp proportions with thinner soles and lower heels. (Figure 6-33.) One of the newest complements for the Continental suit was the chiseled square toe. For the conformist Ivy Leaguer, innumerable varieties of the perforated wing tips, medallion tips, and the new tassel loafer were available. Engineers finagled with shoe designs and developed the "Shu-Lok," which was a mechanical fastener hidden under a high tongue. Preppy teens opted for black and white saddle oxfords with thick crepe soles or the new concept in loafers with changeable instep trim. Another teen favorite was the ripple-sole oxford or low boot made with thick soles of

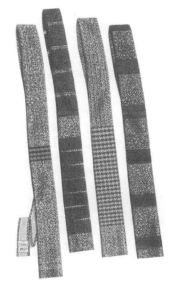
Skinny knit ties from Wembley, 1958

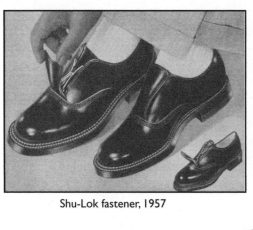

Shu-Lok fastener, 1957

"Snap-Happy Preps" with changeable trim, 1957

Ripple-sole oxfords, 1957

Saddle oxford, 1954

Suede chukka boot, 1956

Australian bush boot, 1956

Open-front buckle, 1958

Continental look slip-ons, 1958

Figure 6-33. The heavy, rounded shoes of the postwar Bold Look gradually evolved into the trim, sleek Continental styles of the late 1950s. Among the nontraditional shoes of the era were styles engineered with lock-fastener tongues, changeable trim, and springy ripple soles. The Australian bush boot, chukkas, and other low boot styles were hugely popular with young men in the second half of the decade, setting a boot trend that would extend through the next decade.

deeply angled rubber ridges that bent backward as the wearer stepped forward. In 1956, the Melbourne Olympics inspired a fad for the Australian bush boot made with elastic insets at the sides. With the popularity of the bush boot came a resurgence in the suede chukka boots as well as monk-front jodhpurs and other forms of low jeans boots. The bush boot is often credited with initiating the boot frenzy of the next decade.

The variety of jewelry for men greatly diminished in the conservative postwar years. Wristwatches, wedding bands, and sets of matching tie clips and cuff links were the most acceptable jewelry for the traditionalist American man. Mass-merchandise catalogs of the 1950s still offered a few signet rings, but gone were the pages of pocket watches, key and watch chains, charms, shirt studs, tie stick pins, and collar pins.

For both the Ivy Leaguer and the Continental dresser, the newest jewelry flash was any of the new expansion bands for wristwatches. A Montgomery Ward catalog suggested that men could "dress up that old watch with a smart new expansion band...All are designed to fit snugly, yet comfortably on any man's wrist, look flatteringly trim and tailored. Moreover, they are so convenient to wear—easy to put on and remove, no unfasten-

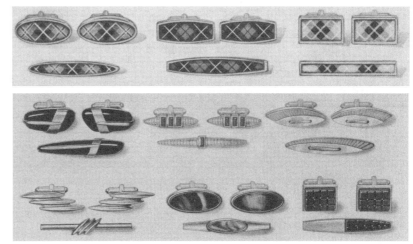

Figure 6-34. The conservative man in the gray flannel suit of the 1950s wore little jewelry other than a wristwatch, wedding band, tie clip, and cuff links. Matched sets of bejeweled or vividly enameled tie clips and cuff links provided corporate men with an opportunity for adding a subtle but distinctive touch of color without risk of opprobrium. Tie clip and cuff link sets from Anson, 1956.

ing buckles of unhooking catches."[64] If the corporate man wanted to add a subtle touch of color to his gray flannel uniform, he could choose from sets of tie clips and cuff links embedded with gemstones—real or simulated—or enameled with multicolored plaids. (Figure 6-34.)

Grooming 1946–1959

The well-groomed man of the postwar years was clean shaven and kept his hair short at the sides and back but full at the top. Ads for hair tonics not only offered advice on hair care but also depicted the masculine hair styles that would catch the attention of the ladies. (Figure 6-35.) To break the visual monotony in advertising, some agencies began to depict male models with mustaches, and a well-publicized campaign for Hathaway shirts included a model with an eye patch. As part of their anti-establishment rebellion, some subculture groups of young men like the Beats grew beards of varying lengths. The beatnik character on the TV sitcom *Dobie Gillis* sported a scruffy variation of the vandyke. One of the more popular haircuts for teenagers was the military style crewcut, which featured extremely short sides and back but was variously shaped on top from a spiky round volume to a sculpted flat plane. Preps preferred soft bangs angled from the part over the brow. Bikers and inner city "toughs" like those represented in *West Side Story* opted for longer hair that was combed in a sweep around the ears and into a point at the nape of the neck called a "D.A." ("duck's ass" or more politely, "ducktail"). In the mid-fifties, rock-and-roll stars such as Elvis Presley, Jerry Lee Lewis, Tommy Sands, and others grew their hair into huge pompadours amassed atop the head with fuller sides covering ear tips and sideburns extending down to the earlobes. (Figure 6-36.) Their fans loved the look, and a number of teenagers imitated their rock idols, but most of American society objected. "That long hair stuff has got to go!" insisted an editorial at the time. "It's really too, too much—those ducktails, those sideburns. And now they're even getting permanents....In vying among themselves to see who can get the deepest wave in his pompadour or grow the longest head of hair, our new rock and roll heroes are in danger of losing some of their masculine appeal."[65]

Personal care products proliferated in new—and sometimes curious—forms in the 1950s. For a few years, deodorants, tooth paste, chew-

Figure 6-35. Most men of the 1950s were clean shaven and kept their hair short. Ads for men's hair care products emphasized the unacceptable "over-slick, plastered-down look." Vitalis ad, 1954.

Figure 6-36. The well-oiled and carefully coiffed pompadour was a favorite hair style of young men in the 1950s. Actor Ed Byrnes from the TV series 77 *Sunset Strip*, 1958.

Figure 6-37. In the 1950s, personal care product makers promoted the use of chlorophyll, a green plant derivative, for protection against various body odors. Ennds ad, 1952.

ing gum, vitamin supplements, and dozens of other products were formulated with chlorophyll, a compound derived from plants. The Ennds ad shown here promised to "protect you from all three forms of odor offense (breath, body and other personal odors)...and keep you fresh as a daisy from head to toe." (Figure 6-37.) With or without chlorophyll, the variety of specialized personal care products for men continued to expand throughout the 1950s. Advertising convinced men that they needed to wear cologne for greater sex appeal; they even needed to "dim that face shine" with a tinted talcum powder after every shave.[66]

Conclusion

The postwar era was an economic boom time. Americans were preoccupied with consumerism and materialism in ways not seen since the 1920s. The American dream was a nuclear family living predictable, middle-class lives in their well-accoutered suburban home.

It was also an era of social conservatism and mass conformity. In his study of American "character and politics" of the postwar years, David Riesman submitted that it was "exceedingly unlikely" that the privileged, middle-class suburbanites would "some day wake up to the fact that they over conform. Wake up to the discovery that a host of behavioral rituals are the result, not of an inescapable social imperative but of an image of society that, though false, provides certain secondary gains for the people who believe in it." Those secondary gains, Riesman concluded, were "the economic richness of our middle-class life...and the banalities of our leisure," both of which were defended and preserved by a herd mentality.[67]

The conservatism of the times manifested in the new forms of suits. The contoured, athletic drape cut styles of the 1930s and early 1940s transitioned after the war into a shapeless, tubular silhouette with natural shoulders, straight-hanging lines, and narrow lapels. Because the new, subdued suit style was readily embraced by the collegiate and young college-graduate businessman, the style became known as the Ivy League look.

In the second half of the 1950s, American suit makers introduced the Continental look inspired by the fitted, slim suit styles from Italy. The Continental suit featured a trim, shaped jacket with a shorter length, cutaway front, peaked lapels, and angled pockets. Trousers were slim, pleatless, and tapered.

Despite the weekday conservative dress and identity of the corporate man, at home in his leisure hours, he explored personal expression through the many styles of vividly colored and boldly patterned sportswear. Madras plaids, African-inspired batiks, Hawaiian prints, and stylized graphics of all types were applied to sport shirts, trousers, jackets, shorts, and beachwear. "Miracle fabrics" created from the many new synthetic fibers and blends of the era made clothing of all types more durable and comfortable.

Accessories likewise were options for adding flair and personal style to the dress of the man who was weary of a gray flannel wardrobe and gray existence. In the late 1940s, *Esquire* proclaimed the Bold Look in men's style—an emphasis on rich colors and pattern mixing for ties, shirts, and socks. This Bold Look in accessories continued through the 1950s even as shapes and proportions changed. Ties gradually narrowed from the 4-1/2-inch-wide belly-warmers of the late 1940s to the trim 2-inch-wide blades of the Continental look at the end of the 1950s. Shoes were reduced from heavy, wide shapes to the sleek, dagger-sharp lines of Italian models. Hats, too, were reshaped with narrow brims and telescope crowns that tilted back on the head.

By the end of the 1950s, conservatism still dominated men's dress and identity. Hints of things to come in the next decade, though, surfaced in many forms. Peacock flamboyance became acceptable to some degree in masculine sportswear and accessories. Increasingly, young men abandoned wearing hats. Masculine eroticism was mass-promoted with the introduction of bikini underwear by Jockey. Most significant of all, teenagers were recognized as a dominant marketing demographic, and they asserted their style preferences with jeans, boots, and longer hair.

Revolution

Fashions from the Age of Aquarius to Disco, 1960–1979

Youthquake and Aftershock Transitions

In 1960, America elected its youngest president, John F. Kennedy, at age forty-three. "Let the word go forth from this time and place...that the torch has been passed to a new generation of Americans," the handsome and youthful new president proclaimed in his inaugural speech. In that same year, the first baby boomers entered high school, and, by mid-decade, half the U.S. population was under twenty-five years old.

Unlike the conformist and complacent Silent Generation of the 1950s, the youth of America in the 1960s expressed themselves loudly, en mass, in their efforts to effect change. Young people in America were acutely aware of the social injustices and inequalities perpetuated by their parents and grandparents, and they wanted to make a difference. Just as the man in the gray flannel suit was the representative icon of the previous decade, the university student was the image of the new era. Student unrest and demonstrations rocked campuses and communities all across America, challenging the status quo of the "establishment" whether it be established government, law, society, economics, politics, or religion.

When U.S. troops were first sent into Vietnam in 1965, antiwar protests erupted almost immediately nationwide. In October 1967, more than 50,000 antiwar dissenters gathered in Washington, D.C., for the March on the Pentagon. The following summer, American families watched in horror as TV news reports showed teenage protesters being brutalized and arrested in Chicago during a police riot at the Democratic Convention. Two years later, when the Nixon administration escalated the war into other Southeast Asia countries, campuses exploded in revolt. Unarmed student demonstrators were shot and killed by National Guardsmen and police at colleges in Ohio and Mississippi. The protest marches and student actions helped turn public opinion against the war, and, in 1973, the United States finally negotiated a cease-fire with North Vietnam.

What's wrong with this picture?

Somebody forgot to include the women. Each day decisions are being made in all-male boardrooms, in city councils, on the boards of education, and elsewhere, that affect all of our lives. Intelligent, educated women—and they are legion these days—belong in this picture. They can help to build the kind of society we all want. What's wrong with this picture is that half the talent and brainpower of our country is missing...an important half—women.

Womanpower. It's much too good to waste.

For information: NOW Legal Defense and Education Fund Inc., 127 East 59th Street, Dept. K, New York, N.Y. 10022

Figure 7-1. The second wave feminism that emerged in the 1960s demanded equity and fairness for women in society and in the workplace. Postmodernist women successfully challenged all levels of masculine power bases ranging from the home patriarchy to the corporate boy's club. NOW ad, 1973.

Other forms of protest and activism were generated by the civil rights movement. Activists staged local pickets and sit-ins and organized massive marches throughout the South to demand enforcement of court-ordered desegregation. A provocative new phase of militant activism emerged in the 1960s that inspired groups like the Black Panthers and the SNCC (Student Nonviolent Coordinating Committee.) Young African American leaders like Malcolm X and Stokely Carmichael represented a new perspective of black identity and pride. In addition, the tacit racism of the North and West that deprived blacks of jobs and housing became a target of black activists as well. Repressed frustration and rage sparked riots in a number of cities including Los Angeles, Boston, Philadelphia, Newark, Detroit, and Washington, D.C. In 1964, a new Civil Rights Act provided the legal basis for the desegregation of public facilities such as restaurants and extended federal authority for the enforcement of public school desegregation. The following year, the Voting Rights Act prohibited discriminatory election practices.

The Second Feminist Movement was also rooted in the social consciousness of the 1960s and, ultimately, achieved significant progress for women in the 1970s. In 1963, Betty Friedan published her groundbreaking book, *The Feminine Mystique,* in which she examined the "problem that has no name"— "a sense of dissatisfaction"—that women experienced, "of yearning" for more than motherhood and housekeeping.[1] Three years later Friedan founded NOW (National Organization for Women) with two principal goals: equal opportunities for women, particularly equal pay for equal work, and the right of reproductive self-determination. Through rallies and mass demonstrations, "women's liberation" became a powerful movement. In 1972, Congress responded by passing the Equal Rights Amendment (later defeated by antifeminist and religious groups), and, in 1973, the Supreme Court ruled in favor of abortion rights. Larger numbers of women went to college and entered the professional workforce than ever before. Feminists raised the public awareness of violence against women, sexual harassment, discrimination in hiring policies, and inequality in pay scales for comparable work. (Figure 7-1.) "As long as feminism diverts women from their fate as servants—forever, we hope—men are going to have to figure out how to relate to them as equals," avowed *Ms.* in 1974.[2]

Inspired by the advances of civil rights for women and blacks and emerging from the brutal McCarthyite witchhunts of the 1950s, the gays of America began to demand equal protection under the law. Advocates of gay rights began to organize in the mid-1960s against a hostile society, legal system, and press. "The gay world takes to the city streets," reported *Life* in 1964. "Today, especially in the big cities, homosexuals are discard-

Figure 7-2. The youthquake of the 1960s shook American culture and society to its foundations. Many young men found self-expression in the peacock splendor of mod clothes, love beads, and long hair. Poster for the rock opera *Hair,* 1968.

ing their furtive ways and openly admitting, even flaunting their deviation."[3] But in 1969, the Stonewall riots against police harassment—named for a gay bar in Greenwich Village, New York—ignited the gay rights movement. The GLF (Gay Liberation Front) and GAA (Gay Activists Alliance) were organized on a national scale as revolutionary in purpose and confrontational in method. This was "a true liberation movement aimed to remake, not reform, society," noted John Loughery in his history of American gays.[4] Public institutions such as the civil service and universities abandoned policies against hiring gays; community ordinances were enacted to prohibit housing discrimination; and progressive states repealed Victorian sodomy laws. In 1973, the National Gay Task Force succeeded in convincing the American Psychiatric Association to drop homosexuality from its list of mental disorders. In 1977, though, an antigay group led by citrus industry spokesperson Anita Bryant formed the "Save Our Children" campaign to roll back antidiscrimination ordinances across the country. In reaction to right-wing attacks, gays mobilized nationally and succeeded in electing openly gay government officials, organizing the first Gay Pride parades, and instigating an effective boycott against the citrus industry that got Bryant fired.

"Times they are a-changin'," sang Bob Dylan in 1964. It was the Age of Aquarius named from a song in the rock opera *Hair*. (Figure 7-2.) The era was fired and fueled by a youth revolution—a "youthquake" as a *Vogue* editor proclaimed in 1965. The youthquake in America was "what's happening," declared a 1967 study from the editors of *Look*. "Turned-on and tuned-in...Teeny-boppers, hippies, long-hairs, short-hairs...Sunset Strip to Washington Square...Conversations parents never hear—sex, drugs, God, morality, success...The OUT and the IN...Beatles, Monkees...mod and mini...psychedelic lights."[5] Unlike their older siblings—the teens of the 1950s who viewed themselves as a consumer demographic—the youth of the 1960s regarded themselves as a counterculture apart from mainstream society. A favorite refrain of the young was "Trust no one over thirty." The symbol of disaffected youth in America became the hippie—a term derived from the beatnik word "hip," meaning "with it." The young rejected the materialism and sociopolitical conformity of their parents. They expressed their antiwar feelings with "flower power" by wearing flowers in their hair and painting symbols of flowers on themselves and their clothing. They freely experimented with drugs, especially the new hallucinogen LSD, and with sex, freed from pregnancy by the availability of the birth control pill in 1960. Rock-and-roll was a universal driving force of the young to which they danced exuberantly. Tens of thousands of the young gathered at outdoor rock concerts beginning with Monterey in 1967 and culminating in the massive Woodstock event in 1969, for which the generation became named. (Figure 7-3.)

As the 1960s convulsed into the 1970s, many Americans felt disoriented and uncertain. The optimism of the post-World War II years had vanished with the race riots, the youth revolt, and the assassinations of President Kennedy, Robert Kennedy, and Martin Luther King, Jr. The Vietnam War ended in defeat, and the last U.S. troops were withdrawn in 1976. The United States had reached the moon in 1969, but space exploration of the seventies seemed less spectacular. President Nixon resigned in 1974 after the Watergate hearings revealed criminal conspiracy at the

Figure 7-3. The Woodstock music festival held in upstate New York attracted more than 400,000 young people in the summer of 1969 for a counterculture celebration of sex, drugs, and rock-and-roll. For years afterwards, young people in America were often collectively called the "Woodstock generation." Woodstock movie ad, 1970.

Figure 7-4. Streamlined Space Age styling in the 1960s and 1970s was applied to everything from fashion to automobiles to interior design. Personal convenience and instant gratification were satisfied by suburban apartment living, color television, and 8-track cassette players.

Women's fashions 1960–1979: left, miniskirt by Ronnie, 1968; center, polyester pantsuit from Sears, 1973; right, layered look by Geoffrey Beene, 1978.

Color is better in Philco 20/20 Color Vision.

Color television, 1965

Minimalist furniture by Founders, 1972

Suburban apartment living, 1968

Microwave Oven, 1975

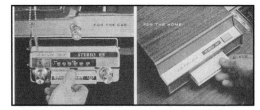

8-track cassette players for home and car, 1966

Ford Mustang, 1967

The blockbuster movie *Star Wars* (1977) initiated a three-decade franchise of sequels and multimillion dollar merchandising.

highest levels of government. An oil embargo in 1973 by Middle East nations severely impacted the U.S. economy, prompting a deep recession.

Americans had lost faith in traditional institutions and, instead, turned inward in the 1970s, becoming preoccupied with self-interests. The 1976 cover of *New York Magazine* proclaimed "The ME Decade." People saw themselves more as constituents: "women," "grays" (the elderly), "greens" (environmentalists), "gays"; ethnic identities were asserted as "Afro-American," "Latino," "Asian," and "Native American"; religious cults flourished; a New Right gained momentum in the backlash against a progressive society and the failings of government.

With a jaded cynicism, the second wave of baby boomers came of age, accepting the benefits but not the idealistic legacy of the sixties youthquake. College men cut their hair and pursued business degrees; young women donned pantsuits and climbed the corporate ladder. (Figure 7-4.) Hedonistic indulgence with sex, drugs, and rock-and-roll became a rite of passage. With abandon, the young danced the night away in discos and prowled for recreational sex. The cult of youth had become a cult of narcissism.

Dress and Identity: Postmodernist Ideas and Ideals of Masculinity

To many historians, the modern era and cultural modernism begins in the late nineteenth century with the Second Industrial Revolution and its mass production, mass communication, mass marketing, and mass consumption and lasted through the 1950s. The term "postmodernism" has come to mean a rejection of the traditions of modernism. According to art historian Anthony Janson, postmodernism first emerged in the humanities during the 1960s when an "eclecticism in the arts" began to reflect the "new sensibility" of a "generation not in search of its identity." Where once the arts inevitably developed a mainstream ideal, now postmodernist ideas in literature, painting, sculpture, architecture, and the performing arts, instead, became a "loose collection of tendencies" rather than "a unified movement." "Postmodernism makes no attempt to pose new answers to replace the old certitudes it destroys. Instead, it substitutes pluralism in the name of multicultural diversity."[6]

Just as the specific characteristics of Cubism, Surrealism, Abstract Expressionism, and other modernist art movements are easily discernible in their representative artworks, the standardized norms of modernist masculinity had developed orthodoxies of character and behavior, which respectable men were expected to possess and demonstrate. Many of these accepted forms of masculinity are evident in the artifacts of pop culture presented in this and preceding chapters from the visual representations in movies and advertising to the editorials about manliness and manhood published in mass-market magazines.

These late nineteenth-century and early twentieth-century orthodoxies of masculinity were subsequently passed on to sons through gender-role socialization. Unlike art movements, though, which continually replaced old ideologies with radically new ones, the succeeding generations of modernist sons were loath to overturn the social precedents of their fathers even as the younger generation acknowledged flaws with their elders such as misogyny, racism, homophobia, and other biases. "Boys are ultra-conventional," complained a *Vogue* editor in 1931. "Ritualists. Standpatters. Dyed-in-the-wool conservatives. Like father, like son."[7] Thus, the linearity of white middle-class male dominance was sustained throughout the modern era.

However, by the 1950s, those groups of people who had been subordinated and marginalized by the generational constructs of privileged white male authority—women, nonwhites, gays, social nonconformists—began to make their voices heard in the public arena. During the 1960s and 1970s, the social revolutions of the civil rights movement, the rise of second wave feminism, gay liberation, and the increase of nonnuclear family structures reflected the broad diversity of the American people in ways the cultural standards of previous decades had not. For the American male, this pluralism of society further eroded the institutionalized conventions of masculinity and power on which men anchored their identities. In his 1960 speech to the Democratic National Convention, John F. Kennedy had predicted this generational shift when he spoke of young men "who are not bound by the traditions of the past—men who are not blinded by the old fears and hates and rivalries —young men who can cast off the old slogans and delusions and suspicions."

For a great many white middle-class American men, the consequence of postmodern pluralism was a sense of displacement. No longer was an uncontested definition of manhood evident. Nor was a monolithic dress identity. "The day when some self-proclaimed pundit handed down incontrovertible edicts from fashion's own Mount Olympus is long gone," confirmed an *Esquire* editor in 1969. "Now it's a matter of personal taste and common sense—which probably comes harder to a lot of men than a flat-out rule would."[8] Just as pluralism in society reflected the dramatic social changes that rocked America in the 1960s, men's dress began to express the pluralism of gender identities that emerged during that turbulent decade. The Peacock Revolution was imported from England and exploded across America in the mid-sixties. (Figure 7-5.) In 1966, *Life* reported on the "revolt in men's wear" with a cover story about the "mod" look. "Things are moving mighty fast in a field where change has always been measured in quarter inches per decade," marveled the editor. Almost as important as the photos of the "way-out" styles was the story title: "The Guys Go All-out to Get Gawked At."[9] Not only did the youthquake men embrace their narcissism and exhibitionism as personal expression, they also rejected their fathers' notions of effeminacy. They were unafraid of being different, and the moral symbolism of menswear traditions was meaningless to them in the social revolution of the time.

The dress options of the peacock generation ranged from commercial fashion looks like the vest suit or space-age variations from Pierre Cardin and Paul Wattenberg to the distinctive self-expressions typical of the hippies. "The biggest of all the plusses that have emerged from this Peacock Revolution," noted *Esquire* in 1969, "[is] the enormous variety of choice that today's man has when it comes to clothes."[10] Bravery—that hallmark of manliness—was now measured by the degree of individualism that a man was bold enough to exhibit in his attitude, life choices, and clothing identity compared to the easy and safe traditions of the conformist.

Color as much as new styles also became important news in postmodernist men's fashions. For many men, the opportunity to unleash the

Figure 7-5. The Peacock Revolution was imported to America from "Swinging England" in the mid-1960s. Specialty boutiques for young men provided new forms of masculine dress that were regarded by traditionalists as subversive or effeminate. Top, Capability Brown Boutique, Carnaby Street, London, 1967; below, interior of Different Drummer Boutique, East Village, New York, 1969.

peacock from within was long overdue. Menswear stylist Dennis Bradley had foretold in 1922 that "when the revolt comes, as it will come some time during this century...we shall see a different world of life and color."[11] Certainly the American male never fully abandoned color in his wardrobe, even as the sobriety of dress became prevalent in the postrevolutionary years of the early nineteenth century. Men continued to indulge in little splashes of color in their wardrobes so long as the hues were largely or entirely concealed: brightly colored and patterned vests were sequestered beneath suit coats; vibrant neckwear barely peeked above a vest neckline; and silk underwear in hues such as lavender or rose were to be seen by no one but the wearer and his launderer. With the increasing popularity of sportswear all through the first half of the twentieth century, though, bold colors gradually moved outward. But even then, vivid colors were worn sparingly in one or possibly two garments—a sports shirt and maybe socks or a cardigan with coordinating tie. The Peacock Revolution changed all that and, with it, the comfortable conventions of clothing that were representative of masculine identity.

One other important aspect of the new narcissism of the Peacock Revolution was a sexualized body consciousness. In addition to choosing clothing in striking colors and bold prints to attract attention, young men also opted for fitted shirts and snug trousers to exhibit youthful masculine attributes. Formfitting bikini underwear for men was introduced by Jockey to the mainstream market in 1959, and similar styles of swimwear became common on American beaches in the 1960s and 1970s. Shirts were worn open several buttons down to display manly chests. The basic styles of dungarees favored by the teenager in the 1950s were reconstructed in the disco era with raised rear pockets, higher inseams, and narrower thighs for a body-enhancing, painted-on fit.

Postmodern Fashion Pluralism

In 1895, *Vogue* acknowledged that Victorian men's dress had become "too utilitarian...to indulge in the foibles and follies of the [eighteenth] century....We may modify," concluded the editor, "but I doubt much if we will ever become again extremely picturesque, unless a revolution occurs."[12] Almost seven decades later, that revolution at long last erupted—an incandescent rebellion in men's dress and identity widely recognized at the time as the Peacock Revolution.

Unlike the overhaul of women's fashions with Christian Dior's 1947 collection that launched the New Look, no single event or individual ignited the Peacock Revolution in American men's dress. Rather, it was the result of a confluence of mass marketing, popular culture, foreign influences, and dramatic societal shifts that, taken as a whole, only became clear at the end of the decade when those who were swept along in the forceful currents of the era looked back to see what had hit them.

One of the most potent influences on the metamorphosis of American men's dress was the British Invasion. Two fronts from across the "pond" helped shatter the stylistic conventions of the Ivy Leaguer. First was a retail and marketing phenomenon; second was a tidal wave of pop music.

By the beginning of the 1960s, a number of menswear shops were established along a few short blocks of a narrow thoroughfare in London's Soho called Carnaby Street. During workday lunch hours and on

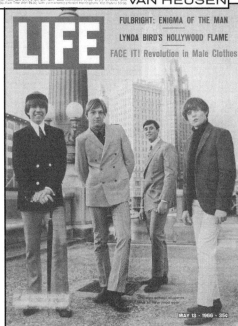

Figure 7-6. The pop culture British Invasion of the mid-1960s brought to America the music of the Beatles and the Rolling Stones among others and the swinging mod fashions of Carnaby Street. Top, mod fashions from Van Heusen, 1966; bottom, mod looks on the cover of *Life*, May 13, 1966.

weekends, throngs of young men would converge on the boutiques to shop, compare, and compete for the latest "mod" looks named for the modernist teenagers who donned vividly-hued, boldly patterned, and unconventionally-styled fashions. "Visits to the street are so much a part of the routine of England's youth that they have a special word for it—"Carnabying," reported *Life*.[13] "The pervading motif" of the men's mod look, suggested a guidebook of Carnaby Street at the time, "is simply sexuality, which is why the place attracts so many women....You can see these girls stroked out, draped on chairs or up against shirt racks watching their boyfriends squeeze into pants that are tight in the calf, in the thigh, in the buttocks, in the crotch and put on shirts that are billowy and satiny and ties that explode with flowers."[14] In the American fashion press, and especially retail advertising, "Carnaby Street" and "mod" were used interchangeably to describe the British Invasion styles of men's fashions. (Figure 7-6.) The British mod look featured mixes of skinny-rib body shirts in brilliant colors; dress shirts in bold stripes or striking, graphical prints; skin-tight hiphuggers in denim, suede, or synthetic knits; and fitted jackets in velvet, silk, and other opulent fabrics. Accessories included skinny ties in vibrant hues and prints, silk neckerchiefs and scarves, hip chains and three-inch-wide belts, beaded necklaces and oversized pendants, and razor-toed Chelsea boots.

Mod clothes were seldom well made since they were not expected to last more than a season. Planned obsolescence kept merchandise turnover quick as young men continually returned to their favorite boutiques in the newest fashion trends. Typical of the boom and bust of styles was the Nehru jacket discussed later in this chapter—a fashion phenomenon that came and went in 1968.

The mod look was introduced to American youth on a nationwide scale through the dress of the British pop bands that first hit U.S. shores in 1964. The Beatles appeared on *The Ed Sullivan Show* in February of that year, and more than 72 million Americans tuned in to see the Fab Four dressed in mod jackets, slim pants, and Cuban-heeled boots. Their long hair covered their ears and brushed their back collars. Also in 1964, the Rolling Stones toured the United States, sporting even longer hair and wilder mod fashions than the Beatles. In a sudden avalanche of Brit bands, U.S. radio stations and teen TV programs like *American Bandstand* and *Hullabaloo* featured the music and appearances of The Who, The Birds, The Kinks, The Animals, Herman's Hermits, and dozens of similar groups, each distinctively costumed in peacock mod styles. (Figure 7-7.) In 1966, a *Life* cover story stated the case for American men: "Face it! Revolution in Male Clothes....Mod fashions from Britain are making a smash in the U.S."[15]

Ironically, many fashion reports used the confusing term "New Dandy" to characterize the flamboyant dress of the mods. But where the dandy of yore actually dressed to achieve the ultimate in simplicity and conformist correctness in dress and manner, the new interpretation of dandy was the young, rebellious peacock whose showy mod attire was worn to attract attention—especially that of girls. *Esquire* explained the 1960s distinction: "The New Dandyism is a revolt against sedateness—against the Establishment and the staidness of successful men, against the traditional Brooks Brothers suit."[16] For some men, even slight variations in masculine dress that were sudden and unpredictable constituted a

At last, there's a place for you.

A groovy kind of scene. TV's HULLABALLOO SCENE. Dance clubs that are strictly for teenagers. A place where you have to prove how *young* you are to get in. Not how old.

The Hullabaloo Scene clubs really move. To the beat of our time — live rock groups and folk groups. Real entertainment. Your kind of fun. Your kind of socializing. Without undue restrictions. Soft drinks and comfortable tables and chairs. And swinging decor. With Hullabaloutiques — where you can buy buttons and stuff.

FREE ROCK 'N ROLL RECORD AND HULLABALOO BUTTON

Yours for the asking. For your free record and button, and if you want to know where the nearest HULLABALLO is at — just print your name and address on a card and mail to HULLABALOO, Dept. 68, 810 Hobson St., Union, N.J. 07083.

TV's HULLABALOO scene™

Figure 7-7. Television programs such as *American Bandstand* and *Hullabaloo* not only presented the most popular rock-and-roll music each week, but also served as style guides to teens for how the cool kids dressed and danced. Ad, 1967.

Figure 7-8. The peace-and-love young men of the 1960's expressed their anti-establishment views with eclectic clothes, long hair, and body paint. Haight-Ashbury hippies and flower children, 1967.

revolt—the L-shaped suit collar or the eight-button jacket, for instance. But for others, subtle change was still sedateness, and the revolt had to be much more emphatic and visually dramatic.

Another tectonic challenge to the comfortable and predictable Ivy League style was the influence of street looks. In 1967, the national press focused on counterculture events taking place around the Haight-Ashbury intersection of San Francisco. Tens of thousands of young people migrated there from all over the country to join in the Human Be-In. It was a "Gathering of Tribes" for the Summer of Love. (Figure 7-8.) On the streets and in the parks, young men dressed in a dual expression of the individual—an embracing and celebration of global multiculturalism and, at the same time, an antifashion, nonconformist protest of the Vietnam War, of middle-class values, of social injustices, of government oppression. The peace-and-love young men of the late 1960s rejected the soulless gray flannel suits of their fathers' generation; they disdained the wash-and-wear, permanent press, synthetic fabrics of the mass market; and they dismantled the rigid barriers of gender dress identity. Instead, they combined layers of East Indian batik tunics, fringed cowboy leather vests, and Afghan carpet coats. They tie-dyed T-shirts, cotton vests, and flea market granddad dress shirts. They embellished thrift store castoffs and army surplus garments with handpainted protest symbols, embroidery, beading, fringe, feathers, and other decorative trimmings. They sometimes discarded underwear and even trousers, opting for long, flowing Arabian kaftans. They grew their hair long and adorned themselves with strands of love beads, handcrafted bracelets and rings, Native American headbands, and silk scarves in exotic Eastern prints.

The ultimate challenge to centuries of masculine dress and identity occurred in 1966, when French designer Jacques Esterel presented a "skirt suit" for men. The short skirt cropped just above the knee, was actually a pair of shorts cut so that the left leg was open and wrapped across the front. The plaid fabric of the jacket and skirt and knee-high stockings gave the suit the somewhat safe look of a Scottish kilt. The following year, though, *Life* reported on a global "happening" of miniskirts for men:

> In a 'spontaneous' fashion happening miniskirts for men have begun showing up in Paris, Munich, London and Tokyo. In Scotland the minikilt raised the [hem]line to nine inches above the knee. In Japan the outfits include tops and can be worn by men and women. 'You can tell the men by their hairy legs,' one lady said. '...or at least I think so.'[17]

The accompanying photos depicted young men around the world (except

Figure 7-9. Although a few designers experimented with skirts for men as the ultimate iconoclastic challenge to traditional masculine dress, the look was largely confined to the runway and publicity photos. Even a practical application such as a bath wrap was rejected by American men. Skilt by Weldon, 1967.

America) in thigh-high tailored skirts, some full and pleated, others trimly fitted. On the U.S. home front, the man's skirt was reported by *GQ* in 1966 as the costume of a New York eccentric rather than a sweeping iconoclastic trend. "I wear a dress—a man's dress," exclaimed the World War I veteran. "I want to be free from conformity, but I still act like a man."[18] In their fall 1967 *Campus and Career Annual* for collegiates, *GQ* found that "kilts are exhibiting more than a wee bit of on-campus acceptability and could go on to become the latest fashion fad in dormitory gear or suburban at-home wearables. Actually quite comfortable and equally adaptable to sweater or sport coats, the kilts are woven of rousingly tartan-plaided wool closured by a brace of buckled leather straps."[19] From a broader commercial perspective, ready-to-wear makers experimented with forms of skirts for men that were less threatening. In 1967, sleepwear maker Weldon produced "skilts" promoted as "kilts for sleeping." (Figure 7-9.) "They should appeal to non-top or bottom pajama-ists. The bare brigade might like them getting to and from the shower with decorum."[20] Similarly, a version of skirts for men as sarong-like wraparounds for poolside was offered by American designer John Wietz in 1970, but, since big beach towels and robes served the same purpose, the skirt seemed superfluous.

In the end, the street looks of the hippies blended with the avant-garde styles of the mods in commercial forms that American ready-to-wear makers tamed, distilled, and offered to a mass market of young men who, not willing to completely abandon the safety of their middle-class identities, nevertheless wanted to be in the groove to some degree. Young men could selectively introduce a few mod items into their wardrobe without appearing radical. Among the commercially successful adaptations of street-pop-mod looks were the Nehru jacket, Apache scarf, flower power print shirts, bell bottom pants, and tie-dyed and psychedelic screenprinted T-shirts. Gender-bending unisex fashions even became mainstream enough to be offered in the wishbooks of mass merchandisers. (Figure 7-10.)

This is not to say that the Peacock Revolution was welcomed by everyone any more than any of the other social upheavals of the era. There was an abundance of objections and complaints from pulpits, classrooms, and government halls, and, most especially, in the press. "What of traditional manly elegance?" complained an *Esquire* contribu-

Figure 7-10. As women donned pantsuits and joined the second wave feminist movement and men experimented with Peacock Revolution fashions, the lines between gender dress identity were often blurred. American ready-to-wear makers capitalized on the moment and produced a wide variety of unisex styles. "Mr. and Ms." shirt jac and high-rise jeans from Aldens, 1974.

tor who squarely blamed the Beatles "for the excesses and effeminacy of so much of the male look in the sixties....What is sartorially wrong with the Beatles and those who ape them is not that their clothes are radical, but they place far more emphasis on flamboyance than fit, that they display a lot more trickery than taste. Their appearance startles rather than seduces." "The Beatles syndrome," continued the editor, "is an abnegation of the dominion of the male...but even more self-defeating, it gives women a choice in picking out men's clothes, thus depriving the male of initiative."[21] In other words, the neo-Victorian revival of the separate spheres of men and women that dominated American culture in the 1950s had been irrevocably overthrown in large part because of the Peacock Revolution.

But in case the denunciation of effeminacy was not enough, archconservatives often peppered their rantings with that most vituperative of all accusations—second only to "communist"—homosexuality. "Fashion consciousness that has been the exclusive domain of the female and the fag is seeping into the male population," grumbled *Men's Wear* in 1969. "At some fronts the peacock revolution is condemned with the cry that it shows an alarming increase in homosexuality."[22] Such cause-and-effect thinking was fueled in part by the emerging gay rights movement at the end of the decade and the more open acknowledgement of gay fashion designers in the realm of men's apparel.

Resist as traditionalists may, though, there was no denying the impact of the revolution. It not only had effected significant and abrupt changes in men's fashions, but, even more important, it had altered the way the American male thought about masculine dress and identity.

Moreover, the Peacock Revolution with its many contributing factors was popular fashion from the bottom up—youthful, iconoclastic looks inspired from the street rather than imported from the upper-class tailors of Savile Row or the couturiers of Paris and Milan. The new men's fashion, even inaugurated a fresh approach to retailing. The sedate haberdasheries of old with their polished wainscotting and boxed merchandise behind glass counters were replaced with colorful, creative boutiques where merchandise was displayed for customer browsing and self-service beneath colored spotlights and piped-in rock music. Store names now reflected the new approach to retailing; instead of marquees bearing the names of the owners, men's boutiques were branded with generic names like Merry-Go-Round, Chess King, and His Shops or lifestyle-expressive names like Vivienne Westwood's Too Fast to Live, Too Young to Die.

In the Me Decade of the 1970s, youth culture devolved from the idealism of the sixties into a self-absorbed hedonism. The glittery, shimmering look of glam rock that influenced American menswear throughout the decade originated with a second wave of Brits. In 1970, Elton John made his legendary American debut in Los Angeles where his bespangled wardrobe was as much of a draw as his stage antics and music. But two

Figure 7-11. Following the hit movie *Saturday Night Fever* in 1977, young people all across America dressed in body-accentuating fashions and packed into their local discos to do the Hustle and to hook up for casual sex. Monticello Shirt Company ad, 1978.

Figure 7-12. Beginning in the 1960s, many urban African American men expressed black pride by adopting African-inspired clothing such as the dashiki. Old Village Shop ad, 1969.

years later, glitter and glam rock achieved its apotheosis with David Bowie's *Ziggy Stardust* show. Bowie presented a new look of androgyny with his long, spiky magenta hair, heavily applied makeup, oversized jewelry, and glittery, second-skin clothes. The influence of glam rock was an application of rhinestones, sequins, and other sparkly trim to denim and leather jackets, dressy T-shirts, bell bottom cuffs, shirt collars, belts, and caps—all worn as much in daytime as night.

The glam rock looks of the early 1970s transitioned easily into the sexually provocative styles of the disco era in the second half of the decade. Slender young men dressed in skintight satin, leather, or polyblend pants topped with clingy nylon print shirts opened several buttons down to reveal hairy chests and astrology pendant necklaces. In 1977, John Travolta epitomized the era's exhibitionistic young men as he gyrated across a strobe-lit dance floor wearing a fitted white suit in *Saturday Night Fever*. Almost in an instant, the new hedonism spread nationwide, and virtually every town suddenly had its own version of New York's infamous Studio 54 disco packed with young people dressed for the night life. (Figure 7-11.)

Ethnic consciousness was also a key segment of the new pluralism in the 1960s and 1970s. Native Americans adapted historical tribal dress to modern attire. African Americans expressed black pride with adaptations of traditional African garments such as the wide, collarless tunics called dashikis.(Figure 7-12.) Black men and women grew their hair into full and fluffy afros ('fros) and, in the 1970s, trimmed the natural look into shaped cuts like the "Full Round" and the "Watusi." Many urban blacks preferred the high styles of "flash" or "funk" looks that included fitted silk or nylon shirts, tight pants, vividly hued sports coats, black leather jackets or maxi-length dusters, and high platform shoes. The funk looks were popularized by entertainers like James Brown and the so-called "blaxploitation" movies such as *Shaft* (1971) and *Superfly* (1972).

The most notable new protest look of the 1970s was the emergence of punk. This was a curious social phenomenon, noted Tom Wolfe in *Esquire* in 1979, because "punk had no American roots at all. It was a concept that had vitality only as a gob of spit in the face of the British class system. American children had to read about it in *People* or *Vogue* in order to know what to wear or how to act."[23] Still, the shock value appealed to some urban young people who felt disaffected by family life, a negligent school system, and the faltering U.S. economy. "Their sound is awful. They're awful," an editor wrote of punk bands in 1977. "Won't you make them happy by getting upset?"[24] The punks dressed in slashed or ripped clothes sometimes held together with rows of safety pins or duct tape and adorned with chains. (Figure 7-13.) They imprinted T-shirts and jackets with obscenities, swastikas, and cultist symbols. Some copied their British counterparts and lacquered their hair into spikes and

Figure 7-13. As a new way of expressing youthful rebellion, some American urban teens of the 1970s appropriated the punk look from disaffected British youth. Their antifashion looks included slashed and torn clothing, spiked leather jewelry, and chains. The punk band The Viletones, 1977.

Figure 7-14. The two-button single-breasted suit (worn hatless) became known as the "JFK look" after President John Kennedy who popularized the classic style. Also in the early sixties, the three-button Britisher was widely promoted by suit makers as a fresh alternative to the lingering Ivy League suit. Left, three-button Britisher from Fashionbilt Suits, 1961; right, JFK look from Palm Beach Suits, 1961.

crests of all dimensions and colors.

By the close of the 1970s, the eclectic pluralism of American men's dress was expansive. Some men opted for a specific tribal identity, but most men preferred to cobble together a look that suited their personal lifestyle and the many roles they might play daytime, night time, and weekend. For his workday, the American male might be a corporate traditionalist while Saturday night he might become a disco exhibitionist. Self-expression in dress was never more broadly accepted in American society.

Suits and Formal Dress 1960–1979

At the beginning of the 1960s, Ivy League and Continental suitings continued to dominate. "To some, clothes are in 'good taste' only if they are acceptable to the strong, conservative prejudices of an Eastern coterie of Ivy League orientation," observed *GQ* in 1961. "Still others consider good taste to apply with equal correctness to new designs or Continental innovations that justify themselves on the grounds of aesthetics."[25] In either case, as the fashion drama of the 1960s unfolded, the gray flannel corporate uniform represented a man with a lack of imagination and modernity. In 1965, *GQ* featured a full-page photo of a man in typical business attire with a large "X" crayoned over it. "There is nothing *wrong* with the way the man at the right is dressed," the editor asserted:

> His dark suit fits well and is neatly pressed. The white of his shirt collar and cuffs makes their proper appearance at the neck and sleeves, and his trousers just touch his shoes. His tie does not clash, his shoes are proper, The outfit is not dated or rumpled or poorly coordinated. It just happens to be dull. To believe that all there is to dressing is to be neat and clean is stultifying to a man with any creative urge about his visual personality.

It was a new age, the *GQ* editor was trying to say. "What we would like to see is men dressing more to the limits of their own personality and inven-

Cloverleaf

Double-stitched
Cloverleaf

L-shaped

Inverted L-shaped

Figure 7-15. For traditionalist men who were not ready to go afield with mod suit styles, American makers offered updated variations of lapel treatments including the innovative L-shaped and inverted L cuts. Details of suit lapels, 1965–1966.

tiveness instead of following the patterns of dress set by other men in their professional or social milieu....There is much exploring that can be done to find an expressive, satisfying, personal mode of dress."[26] And the variegated opportunities for that personal journey of the American male was never greater than in the 1960s.

Within the unyielding conservatism of men's suit designs in the early 1960s, two subtle but distinct departures from the norm were notable. The two-button closure became a preference for young men who emulated the style of the newly elected, youthful President Kennedy. The deeper V-shape of the jacket front emphasized a leaner appearance, and the wider expanse of shirt made the chest seem broad and masculine. (Figure 7-14.) The other variation on the conservative suit was widely promoted in 1961 as the Britisher. The jacket was more structured than the natural-shoulder Ivy style with slightly padded shoulders, wider lapels, and a raised three-button front. In that same year, *GQ* reported on the "invisible construction" of suit coats that was "engineered into the shoulder and armhole" as a solution to complaints from men that they felt "constricted" by the "more natural-shoulder, trimmer-chested suit."[27] This was the beginning of the end of the natural shoulderline in suits, a shift in style that would evolve through the 1960s and settle into the armor-plated look of the next decade.

As the new constructions of suit coats were evolving, news of startling color palettes for suits began to filter to American makers from England, France, and Italy. In the spring of 1964, *GQ* ran a feature story about the new suit colorings. "The long-promised brighter, lighter suit colors have become a reality, and the suit-searching gentleman can now find outspoken colors—many of them iridescent mohair or silk mixtures—mingled with the expected charcoals and navies."[28] The key was the mingling with, and predominance of, expected traditional colors. The American male was not quite ready for the peacock vividness he allowed in his sport jackets to translate into suits.

Similarly, the new approach to constructed suits had to be eased into. While the inside of suit coats was undergoing a reengineering, on the outside, some fresh ideas in the details were gaining ground. "First, about four years ago, the two-button suit arrived...then the one-button suit. Next came the cloverleaf and fishmouth and L-shaped lapels, and some of the many other variations," *GQ* recapped in 1965. (Figure 7-15.) "Now designers are looking thoughtfully at other areas of the jacket...to create an individual, customized look in the detailing of a ready-made coat."[29] Among those newsworthy details were leather piping, double stitching, and outer side-seamed sleeves.

Yet these details were benign stylistic advances compared to what designers presented in the second half of the decade. Between 1967 and 1969, suit coats and sport jackets were reshaped, restructured, and transformed into many new forms. (Figure 7-16.) In addition to the British

One-button suit from Ratner California Clothes, 1969

Eight-button, double-breasted "Tiger Suit" by Schwartzman, 1969

"The Taj" with Nehru collar shirt by Cardinal Clothes, 1968

Bal collar suit by Ermenegildo Zegna, 1968

Collarless fencing jacket by Bertotto, 1968

Polyester/wool "sculpted" suits from Europe Craft, 1968

Figure 7-16. In the second half of the 1960s, the shaped suit replaced the dated looks of the tubular Ivy League styles. Influences from Italy and France included a wide assortment of collar treatments and closures ranging from one- to sixteen-button styling.

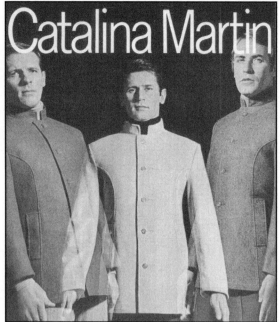

Figure 7-17. The Nehru jacket was the most universal of the shaped suit looks in the late 1960s. The style was named for the famous prime minister of India who dressed principally in the native sherwani, a long tunic coat with a stand-up collar. Pin wale Nehru jackets by Catalina Martin, 1968.

invasion with its importation of mod looks, other influences on the new sculpted looks included the sleek linearity of Andre Courrèges' 1964 Space Collection for women, and more important, the many innovative suit styles from Pierre Cardin. Front closures ran the gamut from one button to sixteen buttons. Collars disappeared or were refreshed with revivals such as the high Napoleonic collar. Lapels spread widely across the chest and were cut at all angles. Mod-influenced colors and exotic prints were adapted to American menswear. (Color Plates 12 and 14.) Suit trousers adapted trends from sportswear by lowering waistbands and flaring cuffs.

Between 1967 and 1968, the Nehru jacket was the most popular of the shaped suit variants. The design featured a long, fitted tunic jacket with a round, stand-up collar. It was introduced in 1965 by French designer Gilbert Féruch, which the pro-Chinese French called a "Mao collar" after the Communist dictator Mao Tse-tung. Disavowing any influences from Communist cultures, no matter how remote, American designers adopted the look as the Nehru collar, named for the former prime minister of India, who usually wore a similar tunic style called a sherwani that was native to his country. *Esquire* noted in 1968 that "in a world of progressively bitchier international relations," the Nehru-collared jackets, coats, and shirts "testify to the influence being exerted on male fashions by the remembrance of the thirties and the nostalgia for Nehru."[30] But the look quickly spun off in directions quite beyond the simplicity of Nehru's nationalist dress. The Americanized Nehru jackets were made of richly patterned and vibrantly colored fabrics. Collars, closure edges, cuffs, and breasts were lavishly embroidered or embellished with other sumptuous trim, and the look was accented with oversized chains and jeweled pendants. (Figure 7-17 and Color Plate 13.) "IS THIS YOU?" asked a two-page banner in *GQ* in 1968.

Are you ready for the Nehru, the sideburns, the chain and pendant—the break with conformity?...Suddenly the rules are changing....Not just kids, not just a few show-offs, but men of all ages in all parts of the country buying new-direction clothing and jewelry. Not just a lapel an inch wider but no lapels. Not just a tie an inch wider, but no tie.[31]

But although *GQ* proclaimed the Nehru an instant classic, it was short-lived and had completely vanished by 1969.

The meteoric rise and fall of the Nehru style was symptomatic of the idea of planned obsolescence in men's fashions—another radical departure from traditional concepts and economics of the menswear industry. This notion of an abbreviated lifespan of men's fashions had been the success of the mod craze earlier when young men bought trendy, cheaply made styles that were likely worn only for a season before the next fad surfaced and last year's styles discarded. Thus, at the height of the Nehru style popularity in the fall of 1968, *Esquire* predicted that:

> ...it is but a matter of time before the Nehru jacket, which is now the rage, also becomes part of the dead past. But this will be for different reasons [other than instantaneous obsolescence] not the least of which is that it can be bought so inexpensively that its ubiquitousness abolishes the sartorial distinction, the individuality, that well-dressed men cherish. Furthermore, the Nehru is now being worn in their professional capacities by musicians, bellhops, room clerks, waiters, and elevator operators. And if there is one factor in male fashion that cannot be called fickle it is what has been referred to as 'strangulation by servitors'.[32]

A third point not mentioned by the editor was that the Nehru had not occurred in an evolutionary style sequence where its conversion to the next level was possible. Hence, its uniqueness was its rapid undoing. (And it was a curious oversight by the *Esquire* editor that the tail coat had been worn as formalwear by both gentlemen and servants for more than a century.)

In 1969, *Men's Wear* looked ahead to the new decade and attempted a prediction about men's suiting. "The costume look is dead. The excesses of Edwardian[ism] are being discarded," the editors foretold. Instead, a "cool conservatism" had taken hold, and men would want clothing "with the designer or custom tailored look."[33] Mod fashion and its derivatives like the Nehru jacket were passé. The signposts for suits in the 1970s were already clear: "Wide lapels up to five inches, notched or peaked, with 'hard' construction for the crisp, custom look. The Tube Look which is tall and slim, narrowed chest, higher roped shoulder, lower 'natural' waistline, less flare in the coat skirt, straight leg trousers....Bodyline shaping is automatic. Now tracing moves up to the chest. Jackets continue to 'open up' to show more shirt, more tie."[34] The engineered interfacings, linings, and substructure of the suit jacket that had been predicted by the fashion press in 1961 finally developed at the end of the decade.

In the 1970s, a resurgent conservatism was epitomized by the landslide reelection of Richard Nixon in 1972. The new conservatism was a backlash against the riotous permissiveness and perceived anarchy of the sixties. Unlike during the 1950s, the reasserted conservatism was not a monolithic white, middle-class conformity to regressive Neo-Victorianism. Pluralism was too firmly established for that to happen despite the best efforts of rightists to roll back the clock. Women's organizations, civil rights activists, and gay rights advocates had successfully mobilized and achieved significant milestones toward their varied objectives.

With the renewal of conservatism in the early 1970s came a new dress identity—a business uniform more evocative of the postmodern Ivy Leaguer—the college graduate who eschewed the protest marches, pot parties, and dorm orgies to focus, instead, on his graduate degree in business administration. But unlike the natural shoulder, gray flannel corporate dress of his dad in the 1950s, the Me Decade businessman suited up in rigid, shaped armor fashioned of indestructible double knit polyesters. It was a stiff, assertive big look. Suit coat lapels with thick, stiff interlinings lay immovably flat as if blind stitched into place. The broad expanse of hard lapels spread across the chest with points that almost touched the armscye seams. Deep pocket flaps complemented the other oversized details. Trousers were cut with a high-rise waistband. Flared

Figure 7-18. Suits of the first half of the 1970s were re-engineered with stiff padding, wide lapels, and deep pocket flaps. Wrinkle-free, double knit fabrics added to the armor-plated look. Two-button suit from Witty Brothers, 1973.

Figure 7-19. The shaped look of the English drape cut from the 1930s was revisited in a number of Hollywood movies in the late 1960s and early 1970s. The Gatsby look on the cover of *GQ*, 1974.

hemlines disappeared and legs widened, often finished with deep cuffs. The 100% machine washable polyester fabrics seemed barely to bend, disguising the body beneath. Permanent creases were knife-edge sharp. (Figure 7-18.)

In 1976, *GQ* examined the evolution of suitings thus far in the decade. "The past few years have seen somewhat 'good taste' cautiously offset by literally hand-me-down ideas about recycled clothes. The first few years had been " a 'resting period'—a time when innovation was conspicuously discreet and new design talents who came to the fore did so on the overly secure foundation of period revivalism."[35] These revivalisms were especially influenced by Hollywood. The engineered, hard-lapel suits that dominated much of the 1970s received their first inspiration from the costumes worn by Warren Beatty in *Bonnie and Clyde* (1967). As *Men's Wear* recognized in 1969, the "traditionalists revisit the '30s" for their suit design inspiration.[36] Other hit movies of the time, such as *Cabaret* (1972), *The Sting* (1973), and especially *The Great Gatsby* (1974), revisited the vintage suits of the 1920s and 1930s, adapting the English drape cut silhouette to modern synthetic fabrics and engineered constructions. (Figure 7-19.) The peacock influence endured in the color palettes of men's suiting. With the new rage of polyester double knits, suit fabrics were made in a wealth of rich colors and patterns.

Figure 7-20. One of the most popular forms of the casual, unconstructed suit styles of the early 1970s was the vest suit. Early versions were worn belted, but, by 1972, vest tops were more commonly worn open. Vest suit from Celanese, 1971.

Figure 7-21. The knicker suit was among the historical costume revivals that appeared at the end of the 1960s and early 1970s. New interpretations were narrower than the original plus fours and were matched with a padded, shaped jacket. Knicker suit from Clubman, 1970.

Figure 7-22. One of the definitive iconographic looks of the 1970s was the unconstructed leisure suit made of polyester double knits. With its endless variety of collars, pocket treatments, and other detailing, the style remained popular throughout the decade. Leisure suits from Montgomery Ward, 1976.

Teal, steel blue, hunter green, wine red, and sienna brown were among the fabric colors typical in the mass-merchandise catalogs of the mid-1970s. "Sport suits" were often topstitched with contrasting colors, and plastic buttons were replaced with flat metal varieties that resembled brass or pewter washers. Plaids were bold, and gangster pin stripes regained credibility.

For those men who preferred a less formal alternative to the padded, engineered sport jacket and suit coat, American ready-to-wear makers produced a variety of casual, unconstructed suitings. Jackets were unlined and unpadded; collars and detailing were more inventive; and the fit was looser and more comfortable. Young men of the early seventies opted for the vest suit. The sleeveless tops were cut with long skirts and deep V-front openings, over which long, pointed collars were layered. Early versions were usually belted, but, by 1972, loose, open-front varieties were more favored. (Figure 7-20.)

Other forms of casual suits included the revival of the knicker suit in the early 1970s. (Figure 7-21.) Instead of a replication of the voluminous plus fours of the 1920s, the modern interpretations were pared down and matched with a padded, shaped jacket. But other than wearing them as novelty attire at the country club or golf resorts, the nostalgic costume effect of knickers was lost on most men, even jaded former mods. Jumpsuits likewise had been offered by makers in a variety of designs and fabrics in the late sixties, but, despite the fashion ads and editorials, the look too much resembled the work clothes of repairmen and cleaning crews.

The most popular casual, unconstructed suiting was the polyester double knit leisure suit. Mass-merchandise catalogs abounded with numerous varieties in striking plaids and vivid colors such as mint green, aqua, peach, and maize yellow. (Figure 7-22 and Color Plate 26.) The initial forms were derived from the many types of bush or safari suits popular throughout the 1960s and were made to be worn belted. By 1973, the open-front shirt jacket variety became the dominant look. The leisure suit remained a comfortable favorite of all ages of men and boys nationwide into the early 1980s.

Just as the stiff, engineered suit became the standardized look in the mid-1970s, fresh and innovative news arrived in America from Milan. Between 1975 and 1977, Giorgio Armani experimented with a different fit of the men's sport jacket and suit coat. "Armani goes soft, with a hint of biceps beneath fluid, draped lines," announced *GQ* in the spring of 1977.[37] The following year the editors featured a full report on Armani's suits:

> All construction was removed, leaving a supple and easy-to-wear shell. The shoulders were subtly emphasized, indirectly leading to this season's squarer, more exaggerated shoulder; and the jacket's cut was carefully worked to showcase a man's body. Armani calls it 'a study in making men look sexier.'[38]

GIORGIO ARMANI

Figure 7-23. In the second half of the 1970s, Milan designer Giorgio Armani deconstructed the stiffly padded suit jacket and created a new look in men's suiting that fluidly accentuated the masculine anatomy. Armani ad, 1979.

Figure 7-24. The lavish embellishments and sumptuous fabrics of the tuxedo preceded the peacock mod influences of other suitings. Black mohair dinner jacket with corded scroll collar and cuffs, 1965.

Figure 7-25. As a complement to the opulence of tuxedos in the 1960s, formalwear makers added a profusion of ruffles, embroidery, or complex pin tucks to the bosom fronts and cuffs of after-six shirts. Lion of Troy ad, 1965.

Figure 7-26. In the late 1960s, richly embellished eveningwear versions of the Nehru jacket became an avant-garde alternative to the tuxedo. Brocade Nehru jacket from After Six Formalwear, 1968.

Figure 7-27. The tuxedo styles of the 1970s followed the shaped, stiffly padded silhouettes of business suits. Tuxedos from After Six Formalwear, 1973.

The emphasis became less on the man as a business warrior properly armor-plated to compete in the glass and steel offices of corporate America. Instead, the suit of the late seventies was all about the male anatomy sensuously accentuated and draped in fine fabrics woven of natural fibers. (Figure 7-23.)

Formalwear for most American men in the 1960s and 1970s was the tuxedo, even though style guides still referred to the style as informal. The most formal version was the traditional black suit with white or black vest and black tie; less formal was the color jacket with black or color tie and cummerbund. The white dinner jacket remained a popular summertime variant even for town. Peacock splendor in formalwear actually preceded the influences of the sixties' revolution with vibrant hues, sumptuously patterned fabrics, and boldly colored accessories becoming a trend in the late 1950s. As with the business suit coat, tux jackets of the 1960s were recut with a variety of lapel treatments and reengineered with padding and interfacings for an updated look. (Figure 7-24.) The iconoclastic ideas of the mod look, though, began to permeate even the formalwear industry in the late 1960s. *Men's Wear* reported in 1967 that "our leading formalwear manufacturers have performed a more-than-commendable service for the American man by showing him that 'Black Tie' need not mean that every man at the party must look like a headwaiter."[39] Contemporary dinner jackets were made of the new synthetic blends such as triacetates and Fortrel polyesters woven into shimmering paisleys

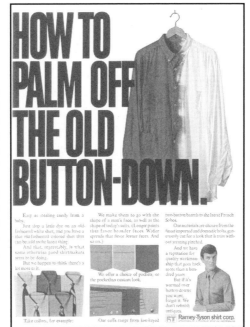

Figure 7-28. In the early 1960s, the news in men's dress shirts was permanent press fabrics. By mid-decade, dress shirt makers began responding to the influence of the Peacock Revolution and produced styles with more varied detailing and a broader color palette. In the 1970s, dress shirts followed the trends of the shaped suits and became fitted. As suit lapels and ties expanded in width, shirt collars were made longer with a wider spread to accommodate the big knots. Left, Ramey-Tyson ad, 1968; right, Manhattan dress shirt, 1973.

and other brocades or cotton batiks that replicated the psychedelic prints of youthquake wear. Added to the richness of the peacock splendor in eveningwear were the self-described "frou-frou" shirts with their Edwardian "riot of ruffles on bosom and cuffs."[40] (Figure 7-25 and Color Plate 21.) In 1968, the Nehru jacket became a fleetingly popular alternative to the jacket and tie ensemble. After Six Formals advertised their brocaded Nehru jacket as the "no black tie black tie" dress. "Besides allowing you to leave your black tie at home," the ad copy suggested, "our new Nehru Formal also allows you to dispense with some thing else you may find confining these days: your inhibitions."[41] (Figure 7-26.) By the 1970s, the tuxedo had all the stiffness and big detailing of business suits, including broad lapels, deep pocket flaps, and rigidly padded shoulders. (Figure 7-27.)

Despite the imaginative variations in tuxedos, the tail coat and morning coat lingered still as unchanging anachronisms. Style and etiquette guides continued to recommend the tail coat as the correct "full dress" formalwear for diplomatic balls or similar society events, and the cutaway morning with striped trousers was still preferred for society weddings. As stylist Charles Hix wrote in 1978, "Formalwear customs vary according to geographic regions and—let's be honest—social strata."[42] The "old money" of the Northeast and, to a lesser degree, the Old South, still found occasion to bring the full dress out of mothballs.

Shirts 1960–1979

The major news in dress shirts of the early 1960s was permanent press fabrics—sometimes referred to in the press at the time as "durable press." "Permanent press is considered the most important fabric development since synthetics were introduced," declared GQ. "Everything we wear will probably one day be treated in some manner that assures us the creases we want in our clothes will stay there and the wrinkles we don't want will never appear."[43] The first attempts at achieving a permanent press finish was patented in 1961 by Koret. But the problems with the

Figure 7-29. In the mid sixties, the locker loop stitched to the back yoke pleat of young men's shirts became a target to be ripped off by teen girls and added to their "trophy" collections. Ad 1965.

Figure 7-30. In the mid-1960s, makers of work clothes began applying permanent press processes to their clothing lines. Lee-Prest ad, 1967.

early processes came from "precuring" a flat fabric, which caused seams to pucker as garments were constructed and prevented sharp creases and pleats when pressed. In the following few years, advances in "post-cured" methods made it possible to treat garments after they were made and pressed, thereby ensuring the "memory" of the shape of the garment. By the mid-1960s, all U.S. shirtmakers were manufacturing permanent press styles.

Also in the mid-1960s, American dress shirt manufacturers began to respond to the demand for greater color variety and styling. "Are you ready for the revolution—not just a lukewarm evolution—that transforms everything from white to blue, melon, gold, raspberry...and more?" *Men's Wear* asked in 1967.[44] In addition to color, style distinctions became more worthy of note. Ads for Ramey-Tyson shirts in 1968 not only promoted their color palettes and the quality of their dyes, but also emphasized the science of choosing the right collar. "We make them to go with the shape of a man's face, as well as the shape of today's suits. (Longer points that favor broader faces. Wider spreads that favor leaner faces. And so on.)"[45] (Figure 7-28.) One of the most significant shirt design developments in the late sixties was the tapered silhouette inspired in part by the youth culture of the era and partly from the popularity of snug-fitting Italian imports.

A somewhat destructive fad of the mid-sixties caused many a teenage boy to return home from high school or college classes with a torn shirt. As the ad in figure 7-29 explains, "Have you heard about the latest girl grabs boy tactic now in vogue in our best colleges? It's called 'Loop de locker loop.' When a girl spots a guy she likes, she grabs him by his locker loop. Tug. And a new trophy is added to her bulletin board collection."[46] The point of the Moss ad was that the locker loop had been redesigned to be too wide and flat for girls to latch on to.

By the 1970s, dress shirts mirrored the look of the stiff, engineered suit coat. Collars were architectonic with high bands and long points that spread wide to accommodate huge tie knots. The fit was made smooth to the contours of the body with tapered side seams and darted backs. Any hint of a blouson of the shirt tail over the belt was considered slovenly. Formfitting knit dress shirts were introduced as a solution to the billowing woven shirts. The assortment of colors, prints, and patterns became so diverse that, by 1977, *GQ* wondered, "Who can say what's a *dress* shirt, as opposed to a *sport* shirt, or if there even is a difference?"[47]

Work Clothes 1960–1979

Denim overalls and work jeans continued to be staple commodities in the mass-merchandise catalogs. In the second half of the 1960s, permanent press processes were applied to work clothes. (Figure 7-30.) New stretch synthetic fabrics and tri-blends of polyester, nylon, and cotton made work clothes more comfortable, longer lasting, and easier to launder. Since the jumpsuit was widely promoted as fashion leisurewear beginning in the late sixties, the work jumpsuit also gained more style appeal. In the 1970s, Sears created a department of "Work 'n' Leisure Clothes" that included mix-and-match separates of twill or minicord work shirts, pants, and jackets that could look good on the job weekdays or at play weekends. Some ready-to-wear makers took advantage of the national publicity about flame-resistant clothing for children and produced a line of work clothes treated to meet tests of the U.S. Flammability Standard No. FF5-74. Disclaimers in catalogs warned consumers that "flame-resistant fabrics are not fireproof, and they do not protect their wearer from intense heat," but rather the flame would spread more slowly and could be more easily smothered.[48]

Sportswear 1960–1979

As with just about every category of American menswear in the early 1960s, the fashion news for sports shirts was permanent press. (Figure 7-31.) "Never needs ironing. No—not even touch-up," promised a Montgomery Ward catalog in 1965. "The smooth, allover press of these shirts is automatically reset every time they're washed and dried."[49] Such reassurances were typical of ads, hangtags, packaging, in-store signs, and other marketing materials for permanent press clothing.

When the British Invasion of mod looks hit America in the midsixties, sportswear was especially receptive to the influences, beginning with new interpretations of prints. "The adventuresome among you, take heart!" declared GQ in 1965. "After a considerable interim of conservative striped and check quietude, sportswear this coming spring promises to return to the celebration of big, bold patterns."[50] One of the primary sources for the fresh approach with prints was the art movements of the decade: Op art with its optical illusions of flat patterns and Pop art with its appropriation of images from popular culture. (Figure 7-32.) Shirt designers also looked to the streets for ideas in shirt prints and silhouettes. The flower children of the counterculture wore blossoms in their hair and painted stylized flowers on clothes, accessories, and themselves as symbols of peace and love. Ready-to-wear makers depoliticized the flower power message and applied innumerable variations of floral prints to men's sports shirts, pants, and accessories, laying the groundwork for the popularization of unisex fashions. (Figure 7-33.) Other design influences from popular culture included historical styles with massive Renais-

Figure 7-31. Women, even more than men, were the target of advertising for permanent press men's clothes. "Your wife, girl friend or what have you will never iron this shirt," promised a Truval ad in 1966.

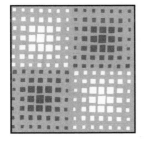

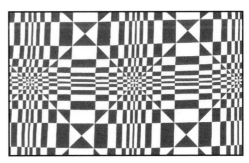

Figure 7-32. The Op art paintings of the 1960s with their flat, graphical patterns provided fresh design ideas for textile manufacturers and shirtmakers. Op art shirt prints in GQ, 1965.

Figure 7-33. The Peacock Revolution opened the possibilities of new fabric designs for men's sports shirts. Mod-inspired floral prints, viewed by traditionalists as effeminate or worse as a flower power antiwar protest, were nonetheless hugely popular with young men. Sports shirts with "pow patterns that frug it up on King's Row" from Lion of Troy, 1966.

Go Mod in Lord John's Shirt His Swingin' Highness, Lord John of Carnaby Street, gave Lion of Troy the shirt off his back, told them to make rockin' copies for all you stateside byrds. The result? A way-out whirl of dots, paisleys, stripes, patterns. The same high-roll, long-point collars that hullabaloo down High Street. The same pow patterns that frug it up on King's Row. The London look, by a top American maker: M. Nirenberg Sons, Inc. Write, phone or make the in-shirt scene at the Tiger Shop, Second Floor, Macy's Herald Square, or the Macy's near you.*

Lion of Troy at Macy's

Dress and sport shirts in cotton denims, paisleys, grannies, stripes, dots, solids. Also, white collar and cuffs on contrasting stripes or solids. $5 and $6. Shirts available at Macy stores listed on page to left. Come, write or phone LA 4-6000 or your nearest Macy number. On C.O.D.'s in our delivery area, 50¢ will be added for handling. Outside delivery area, add 60¢ for handling. In N.Y.C. add 5% sales tax. Elsewhere in N.Y. State add 2% plus local tax. 3½% in Conn. Dept. 181.

sance sleeves or neo-Edwardian ruffles, military raglan styling, and Western yoke fronts. (Color Plate 15.)

If floral prints, peacock color palettes, big puffy sleeves, and ruffles were not enough to alarm archconservatives of the era, the "naked look" sent most of them over the edge. (Figure 7-34.) For a few seasons at the end of the decade, shirts of the sheerest materials were a trend. "The voile see-through shirt is defying all the rules," reported *Men's Wear*. "The sales are overwhelming."[51] For those parents and community leaders who were convinced that the new styles in menswear were a conspiracy of homosexuals, the near nude display of see-through shirts—always worn without an undershirt—was too extreme. Social scientists saw it differently. *Men's Wear* noted in 1969 that "man's tendency to peacock it has led to what these scientists call an increase in exhibitionism. This is evidenced by styles and garments that unabashedly emphasize the male form—or as [analyst Dr. Philip Eisenberg] puts it: 'Much of what people wear today is meant to expose the body while covering it.'"[52] "If you have it, flaunt it," was how trim young men felt about the "non-stop see-throughs" in masculine dress of the time, concluded another Fairchild contributor.[53]

Even more controversial than sheer shirting was the use of motifs of the American flag. Beginning in the mid-1960s, hippies and antiwar protesters stitched pieces of the flag to the backside of jeans and shorts or affixed flag decals upside down on shirts and jackets as an expression of dissent. On the other side of the fence, conservatives wore neckties with flag images and flag pins on lapels to express their view of patriotism. Ready-to-wear makers seized the marketing opportunity to produce clothing and accessories with stars and red stripes that could appeal to both sides of the explosive issue. (Color Plate 28.) In 1971, *GQ* editorialized on the subject:

The current 'fad fashion' is the American flag. Many seem to have suddenly discovered that Old Glory is eminently wearable, whether merely as fashionable panache or as an expression of deeply felt—either pro or con—patriotic emotionalism. Flag shirts, flag pants, flag shoes and belts and pins and decals and patches and hats and jewelry: you can't walk the streets of an American city without seeing the Stars 'n' Stripes displayed in varying degrees of boldness on hardhats, hippies, police cars, taxi-

Figure 7-34. The naked look of see-through shirts at the end of the 1960s was the epitome of the new masculine sexuality. Social scientists viewed these clothes as expressive of an aggressive exhibitionism among young men. Left, stretch lace shirt and trousers from PJ Boutiques, 1969; right, black voile shirt by unknown maker, 1969.

cabs, Volkswagens, chests, buttocks and heads.[54]

In 1976, the United States celebrated its bicentennial, and flag motifs became even more pervasive on menswear. Ironically, more than thirty years later, the controversy of if, how, and when to "wear" the flag persists still with some citizens calling for a Constitutional ban against desecrating the flag—although even advocates are unable to determine what constitutes desecration any more than they could in the 1960s.

More direct protest messages on apparel were offered in specialty boutiques where T-shirts imprinted with peace signs, antiwar statements ("Make Love, Not War"), and trendy one-liners from TV's *Laugh-In* ("Sock it to me"). When a student stenciled "State Prison" with a number on an old shirt and got arrested as an escaped convict in 1966, commercial versions of the "prison shirt" became a hit.[55]

In 1965, Paris commemorated the fortieth anniversary of the Exposition Internationales des Arts Dècoratifs et Industriels Modernes, which had given birth to the art deco style of the 1920s and 1930s. From the late 1960s into the 1980s, art deco motifs recurred on all varieties of men's clothing and accessories, but especially on the slinky, nylon acetate sports shirts of the 1970s. (Figure 7-35.)

In addition to formfitting nylon fabrics, sports shirts of the 1970s were tailored to fit the body snugly. Side seams were tapered, and backs were darted for a smooth, contoured fit. (Figure 7-36 and Color Plate 23.) As with dress shirts, collars became high with long points that could spread wide over expansive leisure suit lapels. At the end of the seventies, the nearly forgotten banded collar was revived although, unlike its Gatsby era predecessor, it had no back button for affixing a detachable collar. For the disco nightlife, shirts that shimmered and shined in the strobe lights were preferred—usually worn with several buttons undone to display chest hair. (Color Plate 24.) For a smooth fit during a workout on the dance floor, skinny rib knit pullovers fit the body like a second skin. Some knit shirt makers even revived the 1920s tennis shirt that was stitched to

Figure 7-35. From the late 1960s into the 1980s, art deco-inspired patterns and stylized images were trendy motifs for men's sports shirts. Art deco nylon acetate shirt from D'Avila, 1979.

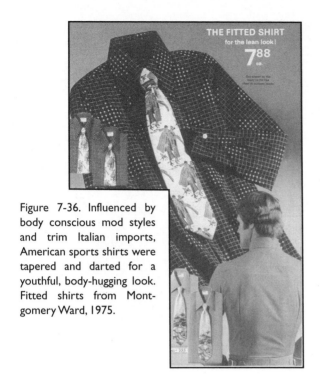

THE FITTED SHIRT
for the lean look!
7⁸⁸

Figure 7-36. Influenced by body conscious mod styles and trim Italian imports, American sports shirts were tapered and darted for a youthful, body-hugging look. Fitted shirts from Montgomery Ward, 1975.

Fortrel: for the good life.

CELANESE FORTREL
A CONTEMPORARY FASHION FIBER

Figure 7-37. In the mid-1960s, young men's pants were cut so narrowly that they fit almost as snugly as tights, especially when made of synthetic blend fabrics. Celanese ad, 1966.

Figure 7-38. Swept in with the British invasion of mod looks, the tight-fitting, low-slung hiphugger was an instant hit with American young men. Hiphuggers from Metro, 1966.

matching drawers, only the seventies' one-piece versions called "turtle suits" featured high cut briefs with a snap front closure.

Trousers, too, were recut and redesigned with new contours and new textiles. By the midsixties, young men's pants were so narrow that they fit almost as snugly as tights, especially when made of synthetic blend fabrics. (Figure 7-37.) One ready-to-wear maker aptly branded their line "Broomsticks" to emphasize the slim profile. Levi's 13's were twill and midwale corduroy pants that tapered to an ankle-hugging thirteen inches at the leg hem.

One of the key influences from Britain's mod looks in the 1960s was the hiphugger. (Figure 7-38.) Carnaby Street designer John Stephen is credited with lowering the waistband of pants when he observed young men pushing down the belt when trying on pants in his shop. As the waistband was lowered on the hips, it was also widened, some deep enough for a three-inch belt.

The reconstruction of pants also focused on the cuff, which flared into the quintessential style of the sixties youthquake: the bell bottom. The look was not new, first having been appropriated from the navy by resortwear makers in the 1920s and periodically revived as beachwear during the following forty years. *Men's Wear* reported from St. Tropez in 1963 that "the bell flare is new again" and now "fits current slacks trend in slimness through hip and thigh." The editors suggested that the style "may have appeal for the young fellow by way of its novelty and the amusing way it can be accessorized. But if it goes, it will be an 'extra'—a just-for-the-heck-of-it item."[56] By 1966, bell bottoms were more widespread, but were still viewed as summertime "pants for beach or boat-

Figure 7-40. Among the street looks commercialized and mass produced by U.S. ready-to-wear makers were flower power prints. Flower power jeans from Spiegel, 1969.

Figure 7-39. In the early 1970s, bell bottoms expanded into huge dimensions called "elephant bells" that completely covered the shoe except for the toe. Canvas elephant bells from Spiegel, 1973.

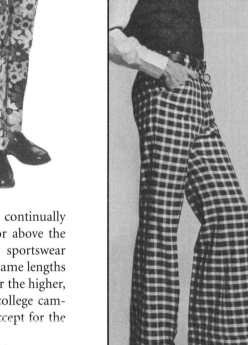

Figure 7-41. In the mid-1970s, high-rise baggies were a fresh look after years of bell-bottomed hiphuggers. Although baggies still fitted snugly about the hips, the legs were wide and columnar. Baggies from Rappers, 1973.

ing."[57] Photos and illustrations of the beachwear versions continually showed the bell bottom pant cuffs cropped short, just at or above the ankles. As ready-to-wear makers adapted bell bottoms to sportswear pants and jeans in the late sixties, the inseam was cut to the same lengths as other trousers. In 1972, elephant bells were the solution for the higher, broader platform shoes. (Figure 7-39.) The right look on college campuses was for the huge bells to completely cover the shoe except for the toe, dragging the ground, even at the cost of frayed edges.

Another fashion innovation for men's trousers (and other sportswear) was the introduction of the nylon zipper in 1968. "Unlike its metal counterpart, its nylon coils won't jam or snag," promised the launch ad campaign. "It's light as today's fabrics. And it can be permanently dyed to match any of the wild colors slacks now come in."[58]

For sixties' flower children, a favorite, well-worn pair of faded or white jeans could be personalized with felt-tip pens and packages of home dyes. (Color Plate 19.) By the end of the decade, ready-to-wear makers produced street-inspired pants in flower power and psychedelic prints for the mass market. (Figure 7-40.) In the early seventies, multicolored blanket plaids and awning stripes were new looks. Polyester double knit pants were manufactured in a myriad of textures and intricate patterns. In 1973, high-rise baggies became an alternative to the skintight

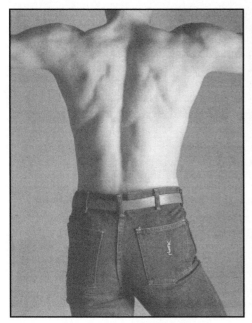

Figure 7-42. At the end of the 1970s, designer jeans with their painted-on fit and logo-branded patch pockets were a favorite for the disco nightlife. Ads from 1979: left, Yves St. Laurent jeans; right, Calvin Klein jeans.

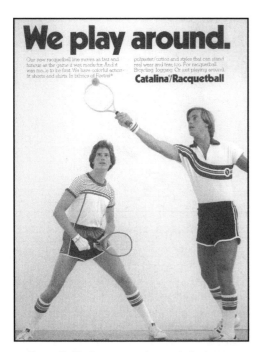

Figure 7-43. As more and more baby boomers turned thirty in the 1970s, a fitness craze swept America. Sportswear makers developed active wear ensembles in mix-and-match colors that men could add to in future seasons. Catalina ad, 1978.

low-rise bell bottoms. (Figure 7-41 and Color Plate 25.) In the second half of the 1970s, men's casual trousers became more standardized with a looser fit over the hips and thighs, but with narrower legs than the baggies. Flared legs and hiphuggers disappeared by mid-decade. Natural fibers regained popularity as a backlash against the look and feel of the many synthetics.

In the 1960s and 1970s, jeans became the single most important fashion item in America. Blue jeans had evolved from cheap, durable work clothes early in the century into dude ranch Western sportswear and then into the rebellion look for 1950s teenagers. By the time of the sixties youthquake, jeans were an American institution that transcended all socioeconomic classes. In 1968, *Men's Wear* acknowledged that "jeans produce a close-to-the-body fit which began to influence thinking about bodyline suits, shirts and more."[59] For the first time in its century-old history, blue jeans were subjected to the fashion trends of the day. Makers recut them with low-rise waistbands and flared legs in the 1960s and high-rise waistlines in the early seventies. Blue, black, and white jeans were joined by red, yellow, green, brown, and a dozen other new dyes. New jeans fabrics included stretch denim made with 50% nylon and 50% cotton and faded or indigo denim simulations made of polyester double knits. For the Me Generation, jeans became a "declaration of sensuality," said *GQ* in 1974. "The way jeans fit, the velvety feel of worn denim, the way they hug the body—curving when it curves, bulging when it bulges—makes them one of the most sensual garments that can be worn."[60] At the end of the decade, the designer label phenomenon consumed America. In 1978, Calvin Klein reconstructed the basic blue jeans with higher inseams, slimmer legs, and smaller patch pockets placed higher to contour the buttocks. He and other designers branded their rebuilt jeans with distinctive topstitching and logo labels on back patch pockets. (Figure 7-42 and Color Plate 29.) "The new designer jeans," wrote a style editor in 1979, "which are only pricier, sleeked-up improvi-

Figure 7-44. Traditional tennis whites continued to be the most prevalent dress for most U.S. tournaments and tennis clubs. By the 1970s, some tennis wear makers introduced styles accented with bold colors and even complete ensembles in pastel hues. Tennis separates by Gant, 1977.

sations on standard western jeans, fit perfectly into today's terminally trendy, supra-casual, hey-look-me-over disco syndrome of dance and romance, sex and status."[61] In fact, many disco doorkeepers refused admission to anyone wearing jeans without the imprimatur of a designer label; pedestrian Levi's or Wrangler jeans were turned away.

Active sportswear was largely utilitarian through the 1960s. Basic sweatshirts and sweatpants made of cotton or polyester blends were the most common. During the seventies, though, a fitness craze swept the country. The first baby boomers turned thirty in 1976, and they were not willing to go quietly into middle age. They took up outdoor running and jazzercise aerobics; they rode their neon-colored ten-speed bikes long distances into the countryside; and they joined gyms in droves. Racquetball and handball were the trendiest workouts for the fittest and most competitive jocks. Roller skating to disco music beneath mosaic-mirrored globes was recommended for firming and shaping thighs to better fit into designer label jeans. For the successful male who had the means and leisure time to pursue fitness activities, active sportswear was designed on the same principles as women's fashion coordinates. Makers produced workout ensembles in mix-and-match colors that consumers could add to in future seasons. (Figure 7-43.) Shorts, T-shirts, sweatshirts, sweatpants, and zip-front jackets were designed in dozens of coordinating colors often styled with contrasting trim and color blocking that the manufacturer would carry over into the new lines of the following year. Traditional cotton knits were replaced with more durable triple knit acrylics.

On the tennis courts, traditional white continued to dominate into the 1970s. The Peacock Revolution eventually began to make some headway with color accents on shorts, knit shirts, and jackets. (Figure 7-44.) At some resorts and tennis clubs, tennis ensembles entirely of soft pastels were beginning to be more acceptable.

For skiers, fashion looks were far more varied. The sleek nylon knit skipants that originated in the late 1950s remained the favorite of serious ski buffs. A sharp crease was permanently pressed into the legs to prevent the formfitting pants from looking like dancer's tights. Black was the preferred color although, in the second half of the 1960s, versions with wide, brightly colored stripes down the outside legs matched the new styles of quilted nylon jackets. (Figure 7-45.) In the midsixties, nylon jumpsuits with a zip front from neck to inseam gave skiwear a Space Age look "meant not for Martian mountains but slopes of earthly snow," reported GQ.[62] In the 1970s, nylon knit skipants were made in brilliant primary colors. Polyester-filled quilting on jackets and pants became finer and more aerodynamically constructed over the legs and arms for greater speed and control.

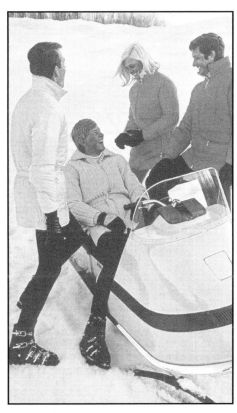

Figure 7-45. Nylon quilted jackets in bright, primary colors worn over formfitting nylon knit skipants were the favorite look at winter resorts. Unisex skiwear from White Stag, 1968.

Figure 7-46. Colorful, complex intarsias and other sophisticated knit techniques were the hallmark of Italian knitwear. Intarsia sweater by Gino Paoli, 1966.

For college kids wanting to spend spring break in the snow rather than on Florida's beaches, jeans were paired up with any of the new Italian-styled sweaters. Beginning in the 1960s, Italian knitwear makers like Missoni and Gino Paoli attracted the attention of the American press with innovative knit fashions. High style Italian sweaters with colorful, complex intarsia designs won awards, headlines, and the approval of winter resort-bound Americans. (Figure 7-46.) Sweater and jean duos on the slopes became especially popular at the end of the 1970s when designer label jeans were the fashion-must look.

Swimwear was the one category of menswear that, surprisingly, lacked innovation in the exhibitionistic, Peacock Revolution decade. Many of the newsworthy designs of the 1960s actually had been introduced a decade or more earlier. Designer Rudi Gernreich made headlines in 1962 with his Porthole spandex boxer that opened each side with a circular cutout, but Jantzen and other makers had produced open-sided styles ten years earlier. Surfer jams—named for the pajama-styled baggy fit with drawstring waistband—were a continuation of the 1950s swimwalker, only updated with different fabrics and prints. In 1966, *Esquire* invested two full pages on the new basketball trunks cut with tulip-edged side seams and white piping, a style men had worn swimming for decades. The two most notable influences of mod styling on swimwear were the lowered waistband that replicated the hiphugger look and the many psychedelic and flower power prints, often in bright, clashing neon colors. The bikini was ignored by the annual *GQ* summer issues until a one-line mention in 1968. As noted in the previous chapter, the men's

Jantzen "Surftrunks" and Cabana Set, 1966

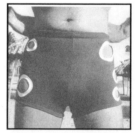

Jantzen cutout boxer, 1966

Nylon spandex bikini, 1966

Belted hiphuggers, 1967

Figure 7-47. For most American men in the 1960s, boxer-style swim trunks in various lengths and fabrics remained the most common. Mod influences included the belted hiphugger and Op art patterns. Bikinis and briefs became more revealing when made of the new nylon-Lycra tricots.

Figure 7-48. Outerwear in the early 1960s changed little from the styles of the preceding decade. Short suburbans, car coats, and knee breaker topcoats were favorites of urban commuters. Fresh variations included the hooded "chimney sweep" coat with a double-front closure to keep out cold winds. Left, glen plaid knee breaker topcoat from I.C. Coats, 1961; right, chimney sweep coat from Hudson's, 1962.

bikini had first appeared at resorts in the midfifties. Even so, few American men tried the bikini in the 1960s, primarily because it was more associated with gay men. Bikinis and briefs made of the new Lycra-nylon tricot fabrics, introduced by DuPont in 1960, contoured rather than constrained the genitals and buttocks. Some seaside communities even enacted anti-gay ordinances prohibiting men's bikinis on public beaches. For the most part, though, in the 1960s and even into the 1970s, American men continued to prefer the cabana sets of matching shirt jackets and high-waist swim shorts that looked much the same as those of twenty years earlier. (Figure 7-47 Color Plate 17.)

The options for men's swimwear in the 1970s continued to expand in all directions. Tank and unitard swimwear were featured in editorials, but the styles covered too much skin for the suntan enthusiast. In 1972, the bikini gained mainstream popularity when Olympic champion Mark Spitz posed for a best-selling poster wearing only his seven gold medals and a Stars 'n' Stripes bikini. In 1974, Rudi Gernreich was once again in the fashion news with his launch of the thong. The following year, *GQ* featured the style with its one-inch side straps, noting that the "thong pares down to a new minimum."[63] Despite the variety of extremes in men's swimwear of the seventies, though, most Americans remained traditionalists when it came to baring all on the beach or poolside. "You'll not only be splashing around mostly in solid colors that span the spectrum," advised *GQ* in 1977, "but in more traditional designs, too, as briefs and boxer models prevail."[64]

Outerwear 1960–1979

Through the first half of the 1960s, men's outwear retained the conventional looks of the preceding decade. Short suburbans and car coats

Figure 7-49. By the end of the 1960s, the calf-length midi and the ankle-length maxi greatcoats were two fresh alternatives to the prevailing short, knee breaker styles of topcoats. From 1970: left, midi by Datti; right, maxi from Palazzi.

were best sellers. Fresh variations on favorite themes included the hooded chimney sweep coat with its double-front closure to keep out cold winds. Overcoats called "knee breakers" were relatively short as well with hemlines breaking a few inches above the knees. (Figure 7-48.) In the second half of the decade, though, outerwear began to show the influences of youthquake fashions and street styles. The maxi made its debut in 1968, heralded in *Esquire* as a "return to the past," a revival of the long great-coat that first appeared in the eighteenth century. "It has such authority that it fairly swirls on a man, transforming him into some swashbuckling figure out of the Napoleonic wars."[65] Compared to the short, compact knee breaker coats, the maxi with its longer skirts and larger, military-style collars was a dramatic look. What became confusing, though, was the term "maxi." The men's style of the late 1960s was only a few inches below the knee, but, in women's versions, that was a midi, and maxi styles were ankle-length. A few years later, some men's outerwear makers offered ankle-sweeping maxis (especially as Western-styled dusters) for men, and the mid-calf varieties came to be called midis. (Figure 7-49.)

Another influence from youthquake styles was the shaped coat. (Figure 7-50.) *Men's Wear* reported: "The signals for fall '67 and the tip-offs for next year are these: Shaped outerwear, man-sized pockets and short jackets, big collars and no collars, more button fronts and bigger zippers, fresh, vibrant colors for suedes, wools, nylons, super blends."[66] Parallel with the padded and fitted constructions of suit jackets, many outwear makers adapted the same snug, shaped contours to town coats.

Leather coats and jackets also made a significant comeback in the late sixties. In the 1950s, leather jackets came to be associated with urban hoodlums and roughneck bikers as portrayed by Marlon Brando in *The Wild One*. After such a long absence, the leather coat, like the maxi great-coat, was a revival that seemed new and vital. (Figure 7-51.) Leather "is often referred to as the most masculine of all materials," avowed *Esquire*. "And leather is a smell—one of the richest and most meaningful smells in the world, suggesting not only cowboys and World War I aviators, but also club chairs and the volumes in a university library."[67] One of the key reasons for the renewed popularity of leather, continued *Esquire*, was "that leather now happens to be a far better clothing material than it was....Now it is supple where once it was stiff, for, until recently, the dyes used in the tanning process starched rather than softened. And then, too, animal fats are now removed and emollient agents added, and, after that,

Figure 7-50. Padded, shaped topcoats with tapered waists and architectonic detailing reflected the trend in suit coats at the end of the 1960s. Shaped topcoat from Botany 500, 1969.

Figure 7-51. New methods for tanning leather achieved greater suppleness and range of colors in the 1960s. The new buttery-soft varieties of leather contributed to a resurgence in popularity of leather outerwear. Knee breaker topcoat, suburban, and sport jacket in cabretta leather from Spiegel, 1968.

such aniline dyes as were not even envisioned at the time of World War I are used to bring out the natural qualities."[68]

Whereas the natural qualities of leather were a significant selling point for men's outerwear, fur became problematic for coat makers. Environmentalism became one of the many social conscience issues of the revolutionary sixties in America. In response, Congress passed the first Endangered Species Preservation Act in 1966 and a second one in 1969, banning the importation or sale of 247 animals in the United States. In 1970, twenty million Americans celebrated the first Earth Day. The following year the U.S. Post Office issued endangered wildlife stamps to increase public awareness. These actions were a serious blow to the fur industry, which had enjoyed an expansion into the menswear market throughout most of the sixties. In 1970, *GQ* had to acknowledge a lack of "conscience" in its previous, enthusiastic fashion editorials on men's furs. "Short of outlawing the fur trade," wrote the editor, "the best way of conserving fur-bearing animals may be to persuade the public that wearing furs is arrogant, ecologically unsound and, in general, pretty rotten."[69] But alternatives were recommended by *GQ*, such as farm-bred animals: "Mink, besides being a good-for-nothing weasel, is bred solely for its fur and is in no danger of extinction." Even at this pronouncement, advocates for the humane treatment of animals began to publicize how farm-bred pelt animals were kept and killed, which further discouraged men from wearing natural fur. Better still for the environment, animals, and the wallet were fake furs. "Financially and ecologically, fake furs are clearly ahead of the genuine article."[70] Shaggy acrylic pile textiles had been introduced in the 1950s and were mass produced in weaves that could easily be dyed and textured to replicate furs of every kind. (Figure 7-52.)

Similarly, in one of those curious dichotomies of fashion and social change, just as laws protecting endangered species were enacted and public awareness was broadened, the look of snakeskin and alligator became

Figure 7-52. An alternative to natural furs was outerwear made of deep pile synthetic fabrics. Men's and women's Yaks of Dynel and Verel Modacrylic pile from Robert Lewis, 1962.

Figure 7-53. Despite a broad public awareness of the Endangered Species Acts, the look of reptile skins was hugely popular in the early 1970s. Textured cotton print jacket and trousers, 1970.

Figure 7-54. Despite the new social sensitivity to endangered species, many of which were the result of over hunting, the bush or safari jacket became a favorite casual coat style during the 1960s and 1970s. Bush coat from Peters Sportswear, 1968.

hugely popular. (Figure 7-53.) "Suddenly, and for no better reason than that the fickleness of fashion is its own raison d'etre, the seventies are becoming an age when the simulation of snakeskin is everywhere," reported *Esquire* in 1970. "The look of the decade is the look of the reptile as much as the look of anything else."[71] Coats, jackets, shirts, ties, scarves, jeans, and sportswear were printed with replications of rare and exotic reptile skins; and all varieties of accessories were made of alligator and snakeskin-textured leather, vinyl, and plastic.

Despite the new awareness of endangered species, the bush or safari jacket, an adaptation of the norfolk, became a favorite casual outerwear style for seasonal transitions in early autumn and spring. (Figure 7-54.) Called a bush jacket in the 1960s and safari jacket in

Figure 7-55. At the end of the 1970s, outerwear became softer and more capacious. Topcoats were cut fuller and longer to fit over the layered look of bulky sweaters, vests, sports coats, and multiple shirts. Valentino ad, 1977.

the 1970s, the style was produced in vibrant fashion colors, textile patterns, and synthetic blend fabrics never seen on the Serengeti.

In the early 1970s, outerwear was manufactured with polyester double knits. When treated with Scotchgard fabric protectant, polyester coats were advertised as more water resistant than natural fibers coated with plastic or rubber.[72] By the midseventies, natural fiber fabrics became preferred to the artificial look and feel of polyester. The midi and maxi had disappeared, and coat lengths stabilized at just below the knees. At the end of the decade, some longer greatcoat styles were reintroduced. The fashion now was for a soft, loose layered look with capacious topcoats that could comfortably fit or drape over several garments underneath. (Figure 7-55.)

Underwear 1960–1979

As noted in the previous chapter, the first styles of men's bikini underwear were launched by mainstream makers at the end of the 1950s. Just as the introduction of underwear briefs in the 1930s had been inspired by brief-cut swimwear, so, too, the radical, sexualized forms of sheer bikini underwear of the peacock era may have been influenced by the appearance of men's bikini swimsuits on American beaches in the second half of the 1950s. Whatever inspired the leaders in underwear design to make this innovative leap into such sexualized styles, sales were good, prompting even mass merchandisers like Sears, Penney's, and Ward's to add bikini styles to their inventories as early as 1961.[73]

Esquire viewed the briefer forms of underwear more parochially. "The evolution of the new trim look has progressed from the outside in. It began with the shaped suit (suppressed waist and narrow, cuffless trouser legs), then the tapered shirt and now a new line of close-fitting underwear."[74] Others, recognized that the new, sexy forms of men's underwear were more than a mere fashion trend. Like the "naked look" shirts of the late sixties, see-through mesh and form-molding nylon styles of underwear were a sign of the times: the sexual revolution. (Figure 7-56.) The famous psychologist and author Dr. Joyce Brothers wrote in 1969:

Women today react to men as sexual objects. Up to a few years ago

Figure 7-56. The eroticization of men's underwear that began with the nylon knit bikini at the end of the 1950s reached an apogee of extreme forms in the early 1970s. A myriad of form-fitting boxers, briefs, bikinis, microbikinis, thongs, and G-strings were available in every color and print, and for the ultimate exhibitionism, see-through tricot and mesh. Underwear from Adam Briefs and Ah Men, 1972–1977.

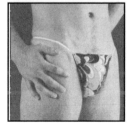

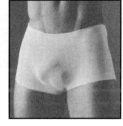

men were seen as security objects. Men were supposed to convey an impression of financial stability. A woman wanted to know whether a man could take care of her and the children. Now she is interested in the man as a sexual being, because in most cases she can provide her own financial security if she has to.[75]

This idea of the objectification of the American male launched a thousand essays and analyses in the 1960s and especially in the 1970s. Perhaps nothing was more telling of the times than the debut of *Playgirl* in 1973, which *Newsweek* reported "promptly sold out 600,000 copies," and immediately afterwards, mailbags stuffed with subscriptions flooded in to the entrepreneurial publisher.[76]

It is also during this time that boxers versus briefs became a debatable personal style issue. In a look at the sexy new underwear styles of the seventies, *GQ* featured a multipaged editorial in 1971 depicting male models wearing the briefest and sheerest of underwear in intimate scenarios with seminude female companions. "Judge a man by the company he keeps," added the editor, "but what is his company to judge him by?"[77] Two years later, Germaine Greer wrote about "what turns women on" for *Esquire*. "It is your duty to know," she insisted, "but first take off those silly boxer shorts....No more repellent garment than boxer shorts has ever been devised."[78] Even traditionally conservative men's style guides entered the fray: "Boxers are safe," observed stylist Bill Gale, "but let's be truthful, *dull*."[79] Nonetheless, for those millions of American men who were not interested in, or not possessing the trim physique for, sexual exhibitionism, the practical boxer and the functional white cotton brief remained the two most prevalent choices.

Sleepwear 1960–1979

The standardized pajama set was modernized to some degree with permanent press fabrics in the 1960s and acrylics or polyester blends in the 1970s. The most common pajama style was still the button front shirt (usually called a coat) with pants or shorts. Ski knits were still made with pullover tops with rib knit cuffs and collar and elastic waist bottoms with rib knit ankles. In keeping with the many revivals that occurred in the late sixties, the nightshirt became popular with young men. Most commodity nightshirts extended to just below the knees with deep side vents, but some were cropped at mid-thigh and came with matching bikinis. Mass merchandisers offered sleep shorts and pants separately to be worn topless or with a favorite sports jersey or T-shirt. Some specialty retailers offered sleepwear in colorful prints that copied the psychedelic and Op or Pop art designs of sports shirts. The psychedelic art of Peter Max and the Beatles' *Yellow Submarine* (1967) was a huge trend at the end of the sixties, and in the 1970s, Bernard Kliban's pen-and-ink cats were on everything for bed from sleepshirts and soft-sculpture kitty slippers to coordinating linens and curtains. Despite the variety of comfortable and trendy sleepwear, though, most men preferred to sleep in their underwear or in the nude. "Whatever happened to pajamas?" *GQ* wondered in 1970. "Suddenly the country is filled with men who sleep stripped to the shorts and don't even feel deprived. Or ashamed. Or unsexy."[80]

Robes in the 1960s were mostly knee-length kimono styles in cotton terry, flannel, or broadcloth. At the end of the sixties, robes and

Figure 7-57. Loungewear reflected the multicultural pluralism of the era. Groovy jumpsuits, exotic kaftans, hooded maxi robes, and embellished lounging suits were designed to be worn in private hours. Left, belted robe, lounge suit, and jumpsuit by Pleetway, 1969; center, "Tangiers" kaftan by Lew Magram, 1972; right, "Chinese Horse" lounging jumpsuit from Ah Men, 1976.

loungewear became much more varied, designed to be seen in intimate company rather than simply as utilitarian transition attire just before bed or out of the shower in the morning. "Live a little. Relax a lot. Today's sleep/loungewear has come a long, long way from old fashioned standard p.j.'s. Now you can feel at home in something that grooves a bit," suggested a Pleetway "Sleeperinos" ad in 1969.[81] Kaftans were made of silk or Antron nylon in exotic prints and vivid colors. Lounging pajamas and jumpsuits were detailed with mandarin collars, wide sashes, and braid trim. (Figure 7-57 and Color Plate 16.) Ankle-length maxi robes, some hooded, were made of thick triacetate velours trimmed with insets of contrasting colors and corded edging.

Accessories 1960–1979

"What John Fitzgerald Kennedy did for the two-button suit, he did *not* do for the hat," noted a men's style guide in 1969. "Even in the most severe weather, JFK would appear hatless, snowflakes flecking the famous Kennedy thatch—a many-splendored thing all too rarely seen atop a man of forty-plus, and for that reason alone a point of pride as well as a distinguishing feature for a media-conscious politico. It is hardly surprising that hatlessness was thus encouraged among many of the young who were almost excessively hair-conscious."[82] Despite President Kennedy's

The Britisher, 1963

The slip stream, 1963

Nureyev cap, 1966

Panamas, 1961

Figure 7-58. At the beginning of the 1960s, hats were still an important component of smart dressing. The British look in hats featured a tapered, V-creased crown and a narrow brim with a deep roll at the back. For men under thirty, the new "slip stream" hat was blocked with an edge to the crown that tapered off to a round dome at the back. In the second half of the decade, youthquake teens opted for nontraditional headgear such as the Nureyev cap.

example, most American men in the early 1960s still considered the hat a critical accessory. Just ahead of the Carnaby Street British Invasion, a new look in hat styles was imported from London's Savile Row to complement the new three-button Britisher suit styles. The crowns were low and tapered with a deep V-crease, and the narrow brims, at about 1-1/2 inches, were snapped up at the back in a deep roll. (Figure 7-58.) One of the most innovative hat shapes in decades was called the "slip stream," a short-lived style preferred by collegiate teens in the early sixties. The slip stream was blocked with a crown edge along the front and sides that tapered to a rounded dome in the back.

In the summertime, the panama, made of fine sennit straw or a broad weave of rough coconut, was shaped like town hats with narrow brims and tapered crowns. "Everybody's got a black or dark straw," wrote a *Men's Wear* editor in 1963. "Barring accident, the same hat can be worn for two or more seasons. Unless you press your nose against it, it looks just like the dark winter felt....Joe Blow is not as style-conscious as Joe Hatter, and tiny changes in the brim and crown don't mean much. But the switch from black to light or medium is a change, and he knows and enjoys it."[83] Most men looked forward to the late spring switch over from the monotony of dark-colored felts to light-colored straws with their colorful hatbands.

The youthquake generation discarded the conventional blocked hats of their dads, opting instead for headgear that was anti-traditional. The Nureyev cap—named for the famed Russian ballet dancer who popularized the style when he defected to the West—became a favorite of mod youths in the late 1960s. The cap's Soviet proletariat origins achieved the desired effect for the young peacock male by infuriating authority figures of "the establishment." Likewise, hippies donned assorted broad-brimmed hats made of suede and other soft materials as a statement of

Skinny ties, 1961

Button down tie from Prince Consort, 1963

Contoured tie from Damon 1963

Apache scarves, 1969

Butterfly bow tie, 1973

Figure 7-59. The two-inch-wide skinny ties of 1960 gradually widened through the decade until they spread across the shirt front more than four inches at the tip. By the end of the 1970s, skinny ties had returned as a young men's trend. Neckwear revivals included the bow tie, expanding into enormous butterfly widths in the early 1970s.

Broad tie, 1973

Return of skinny ties, 1979

gender-bending dress.

From the late 1960s through the mid-1970s, town hats disappeared from mass-merchandise catalogs. Caps and hats were worn primarily for utility in inclement weather. Vividly colored knit caps, often called "toboggans," were popular on ski slopes. For chilly nights in open stadiums, football fans of both sexes showed their team spirit—and kept warm—with knit caps in school colors or with the school logo knitted into the edge roll. At the end of the 1970s, the wide-brimmed fedora was revived as an ideal accessory for the layered look. *GQ* observed in 1977: "Once a gentleman wasn't dressed without a hat. Then hair grew longer. Now that it's getting short again, it's time to look headward. Not that GQ believes a hat should be obligatory. But do consider wearing one as a dra-

Mod Chelsea boot, 1965

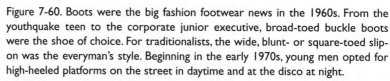

Figure 7-60. Boots were the big fashion footwear news in the 1960s. From the youthquake teen to the corporate junior executive, broad-toed buckle boots were the shoe of choice. For traditionalists, the wide, blunt- or square-toed slip-on was the everyman's style. Beginning in the early 1970s, young men opted for high-heeled platforms on the street in daytime and at the disco at night.

Buckled boots, 1969

Wide, square-toed slip-ons, 1969

Stacked-heel platforms from Italia, 1972

Earth Shoes, 1974

matic—albeit optional—extra."[84] Other revivals at the end of the seventies included the befeathered Tyrol, the tweed golf (or newsboy cap), and even the Edwardian deerstalker sometimes advertised as a "Sherlock."

Between 1960 and 1980, men's neckwear went full circle. Styles at the start of the 1960s retained the thin 1-1/2- to 2-inch blades of the Ivy League look. (Figure 7-59.) New textures and more durable constructions were achieved with application of the new polyesters. As the decade progressed, ties began to widen to about 3-1/2 inches around 1965. The following year, *Esquire* predicted ties at widths of 4, perhaps eventually, even 5 inches. "Last seen in the late forties, the broad-model tie made a hasty exit with the advent of narrow shoulders and overall slim styling....But lately the trend has been to break up the straight lines with angles: the new shaped suit has wider shoulders, suppression at the waist, flair at the skirt....It is clear that with the shape of men's clothes what it is today, only the wide tie is fit to be tied."[85] By the beginning of the 1970s, *Esquire's* predictions had become fashion fact. Ties of the first half of the decade expanded to a broad 4-3/4 inches. By the late seventies, the circle was completed, almost abruptly, when the skinny tie reappeared. "The most radical reduction in tie widths since the mod era over a decade ago is now upon us," declared *GQ* in 1978.[86] This time, however, the ties that once again shrunk to a mere 2 inches at the end point were not a universal look, but rather became a trend for young men. Business suit ties stabilized at 3-1/2 inches.

Bow ties largely vanished in the 1960s except for eveningwear. If a TV or movie character was supposed to be geeky, he was dressed in a checked or polkadot bow tie. In the early 1970s, the bow tie was revived thanks mostly to the influences of period costume movies like *The Great Gatsby* and *The Sting*. In keeping with the huge jacket lapels, long shirt collars, and broad four-in-hand ties, the butterfly bow tie became enormous. (Color Plate 22.) Within a few years, however, when the skinny long tie resurfaced, bow ties were reduced to a thin 1 1/2-inches wide.

In addition to the traditional four-in-hand and bow ties, the peacock male of the 1960s adapted other, more resplendent neckwear to his expressive dress. Silken ascots tied into large puffs were perfect for the

Figure 7-61. Mod styling was also applied to men's pocket accessories. Wallets, billfolds, checkbook covers, and keycases were covered with silk and synthetics in bright colors and prints. Also, thinner billfolds were designed for the tight-fitting trousers of the 1960s. Left, silk pocket accessories by Shields, 1966; right, the "Super Skinny" by Enger Kress, 1969.

new Edwardian velvet and brocade jackets. The Apache scarf in vivid paisleys and floral prints could be worn Western style to the side of an open collar or knotted at the front of a Nehru or spread collar. (Color Plate 18.)

Footwear of the early 1960s was not much varied from the styles of the preceding decade. The razor sharp Continental look vanished as shoe toes widened and became more blunted. At the end of the sixties, shoes and boots followed the trend of lapels and ties, becoming wide and shaped with square or blunted toes. (Figure 7-60.) The most important footwear news was boots. The bush boot of the late 1950s initiated a mod fad for the high Cuban-heeled Chelsea boot popularized by the Beatles. In the second half of the 1960s, junior executives wore ankle boots and half boots with business suits much to the chagrin of corporate traditionalists. The new honey browns were even worn with blue and gray suits, an anathema of men's dress just a few years earlier. Buckles and other hardware abounded on both boots and slip-on dress shoes. Some shoe styles were available in a rainbow of colors never seen in men's footwear. (Color Plate 20.)

In the early 1970s, toes remained broad and heels began to rise. In the spring of 1971, *GQ* reported on the first three-inch-stacked heels, though with regular flat soles. Within a year, high chunky heels and thick platform soles were ubiquitous. In 1977, John Travolta strutted down a Manhattan street in platforms in the opening scene of *Saturday Night Fever*. The platforms gradually diminished at the end of the decade, but the wide, squared toes and some high heels remained common into the early 1980s. For a few years in the early 1970s, white shoes with matching white belts were a popular combination for mature men of the country club set. As part of the new body and health consciousness of the 1970s, the Earth Shoe, or "negative heel" footwear, was imported from Denmark. According to ads, the concept of the wide molded sole with a heel lower than the toe allowed the wearer to walk more naturally, "like when you walk barefoot in sand and your heel sinks down lower than your toes."[87]

Among other leather goods impacted by the Peacock Revolution were wallets. The last time wallets had been significantly altered was in the 1920s when the U.S. Treasury Department reduced the size of paper currency by one-third, and billfolds were likewise resized. In the 1960s, trousers became so slim and snug that the thick back pocket wallet not only ruined the look and fit but also felt uncomfortable to sit upon. Leather goods makers responded to the market with slimmer, lighter wallets. "We've stripped away the excess linings, fillers, folds and flaps that make a billfold bulge," one ad noted.[88] Another peacock influence was the addition of colorful fabrics to wallets, billfolds, key cases, and other pocket accessories. Prints and patterns were adapted from popular textiles used for sportswear. (Figure 7-61.)

The reduced wallet was not as practical a solution as leather goods makers had hoped. The modern man of the 1960s had far more things to carry around than his father did. In the 1960s, credit cards became common. But because its acceptance was not as universal as today, a man might need separate pieces of plastic for one or more gas station brands, specialty stores, and department stores. In addition to an expanding wallet, the American male might also carry a key ring or case, a business card case, pen, notepad, cigarette pack or case, lighter, checkbook, and possibly one of the new pocket calculators. Then there was the annoying accumulation of coins weighing down trouser pockets, spilling out into car seats, and jangling like sleigh bells with each stride. The answer was a handbag or, more accurately, a man bag. The idea was not new to the 1970s, though. In 1947, Bernard Rudolfsky complained about the "pocket system" of EuroAmerican dress:

> The need for always carrying innumerable objects with us is a penalty of our civilization only. Still, the solution appears to be rather simple—a single container may hold the scattered contents of all our pockets. Women's handbags are a half-hearted attempt in this direction; they are however organized on the principle of the ashcan. Toolbags and businessmen's briefcases are better examples. The disadvantage of a loose bag to be carried by hand, could easily be remedied if an attached strap would enable us to hang it on to the shoulder. Southern European and Latin American countries, where the carrying of considerable loads is a daily necessity, have developed ingenious contraptions worth studying. The thoughtless but widely held opinion that the shoulder-hung bag is only for females seems hardly worth discussing The virility of postmen remained unimpaired by years of letterbag carrying, and the soldier, equipped with a shoulder bag, does not protest against this sort of effeminacy.[89]

Despite the practicality of a shoulderbag, the fearful stigma of effeminacy in any form, especially during the repressive conformist postwar era, remained considerable for American men. But with the iconoclasm of the Peacock Revolution, shoulderbags joined the list of articles of clothing stripped of their rigid gender identity, first with the mobile youth and then gradually becoming mainstream. "Future shock rages around us, and our poor dizzy heads demand that we get organized," *GQ* declared in 1971. "A bag probably won't take the place of therapy, but it can help tie up some loose ends....A bag is a cornucopian accessory. And today's form-fitting clothes make the bag virtually essential."[90] The key was to make the man bags not resemble ladies' handbags in any way. Makers copied luggage totes, the postman's mail pouch, or the photographer's utility case to achieve a masculine look. (Figure 7-62.) Still, until the late 1970s, American men were largely uncomfortable with man bags except those carried for travel.

The array of jewelry worn by the traditionalist American male in the 1960s changed little from that of his Victorian grandfather. Collections of monogrammed pieces were as much a favorite as they had been for

Figure 7-62. Another men's dress convention shattered by the Peacock Revolution was the introduction of man bags in the early 1970s. Styles were modeled after luggage totes and cases to avoid any resemblance to women's handbags. Napa cowhide shoulder bag from International Male, 1978.

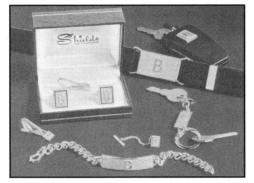

Monogrammed jewelry set, 1965

Youthquake protest pins, 1968

Nehru jacket pendant, 1968

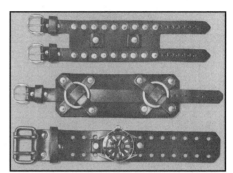

Figure 7-63. In addition to the traditional forms of masculine jewelry—tie clips, cuff links, signet rings—men began adorning themselves with pendant necklaces, strands of love beads, and matching chokers and bracelets.

Leather cuff watchbands, 1969

decades. (Figure 7-63.) To complement the mod look, jewelry makers designed oversized cuff links with huge faux gemstones or stylized Pop art graphics such as spiders' webs and bear-hatted British Redcoats. Egyptian motifs like the ankh and the scarab, astrology sun signs, and protest symbols such as peace emblems were applied to all forms of jewelry for the youthquake market. Necklaces for men became more prevalent in the second half of the decade despite the protests of some critics. "Now really!" complained an *Esquire* editor in 1968 at the trend of pendant chains for Nehru jackets. "Such affronts to fashion are sometimes born of contemporary man's mania to be in the swim...as is so egregiously the case [with] medallions on grown men."[91] (Figure 7-64.) Reportedly, Tiffany's even refused to sell medallions to any man "who looks as if he might wear it himself."[92] Once the fad caught on, retailers were unsure where and how to display the new styles of chains and pendants. Since they served as a unisex look, many stores put them in the women's jewelry department; other merchants displayed them in the men's sportswear sections next to the Nehru jackets and turtlenecks. A few years later, *GQ* looked at "jewelry fit for a man" and concluded, "Whether in the shape of a relic- (or garlic-) filled amulet that warded off the devil and his ways, or a World War II dog-tag chain or the most recent pastel-colored beads, necklaces for men are OK, and only the seriously uptight can condemn them as being unmasculine."[93] By the disco era, chains and chokers were standard accoutrement for the man who wanted

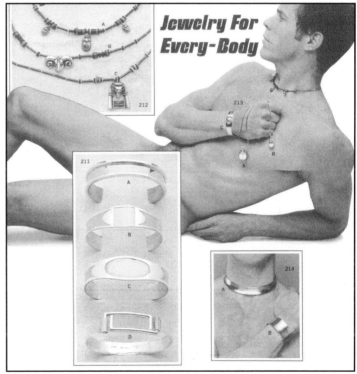

Necklaces, bracelets, collar, and cuff, 1977

Figure 7-64. Heavy chains with jeweled pendants were a popular complement to Nehru jackets and turtleneck sweaters in the late 1960s. Such flashy adornments were added to the lengthy list of changes in men's dress inspired by the Peacock Revolution to which traditionalists objected. Nehru jacket with jeweled pendant, 1968.

to draw attention to the open-shirt display of his hairy chest. Silver, gold, and stainless steel cuff bracelets and oversized rings also added attention-getting shimmer under the strobe lights.

Grooming 1960–1979

Of all the changes in American social norms wrought by the Peacock Revolution—skintight pants, see-through shirts, love beads, man bags, bikini underwear, high-heeled platform shoes—the new ideas of masculine beauty, especially long hair, upset people the most. (Figure 7-65.) At the peak of the mod British invasion in the mid-1960s when images of the Beatles' "mop tops" were influencing young men all across the country, *GQ* insisted, "Off with their hair!" In a double-page spread, the editors depicted the Fab Four in a "before" photo with their long hair covering their ears and brushing their shirt collars beside a touched-up "after" version in which the hairstyle of each was recut and slicked down into an Ivy League look from a decade earlier.[94] In 1967, *Vogue* asserted that, historically, the term "longhairs" had been applied to a breed of men "always suspected of sexual inauthenticity." Continued *Vogue*: "Psychiatrists and sociologists complain that boys and girls today look alike and are often mistaken for each other."[95] In 1968, psychologist Charles Winick went so far as to suggest in *The New People: The Desexualization of America* that, because of such confusions of sexual identity, we might cease to reproduce, and the human race could come to an end.[96] Nonconformist young men with long hair were considered such a threat to an orderly society in the movie *Fahrenheit 451* (1966) that police "mop-up squads" ambushed the subversive "messy know-it-alls" and forced them to submit to a barber's sheers.

As discussed in chapter 2, with few exceptions (such as General George Custer and frontier trappers), American men had traditionally cropped their hair short since the start of the nineteenth century. Short hair was one of the most important components of masculine dress. In the nineteenth-century social order of separate spheres—a precept periodically revived in phases of neo-Victorianism of the twentieth century—long hair was a woman's "glory." But for many young men of the

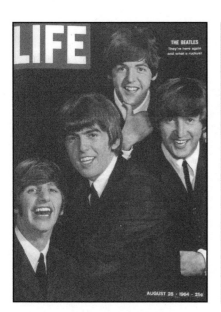

Figure 7-65. Short hair for men had been a principal component of masculine identity since the beginning of the nineteenth century. In the 1960s, though, many youthquake men opted for long hair as an expression of modernity and individuality. Left, the Beatles on the cover of *Life*, August 28, 1964; right, the Strawberry Alarm Clock, 1969.

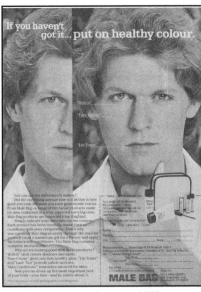

Styling hair dryer for men, 1970 · Specialty haircare products tailored to African American men's market, 1972 · Cosmetics for men, 1978

Figure 7-66. As men began to grow their hair long, makers of haircare products developed regimens of shampoos and conditioners formulated for the American male. By the 1970s, cosmetics were increasingly marketed to men, including makeup for camouflaging flaws and enhancing facial features.

youthquake generation, there was no rolling back the clock on their clothes, their hair, or their self-determinant notions of masculine identity. In examining the "new man" of 1966, the *GQ* editors concluded:

> He cares how he looks. The clothes came first—that we all know. Then cologne—the great decision. Now it's hair styling—and hair coloring—and, failing those possibilities, a hairpiece. Next: cosmetics for the man....Sybaritic? Why not? Puritanism—'self-enhancement and gratification are sinful'—has lost its stranglehold. Vanity? Perhaps...men, too, are vain....Effeminate? Only because our age is not used to all this—as other ages were. And it may be that men just don't have to worry about proving their virility as much as they used to.[97]

But the new iconoclastic approaches a man took for his grooming and for preserving a youthful appearance were more than sybaritic pursuits, or rejection of puritanism and ideas of effeminacy, or indulgence in vanity. It was being a part of a new vitality in an era of palpable change. In a four-page editorial, *Esquire* outlined how to "look like new in '65," which included trying a "new way of styling your hair," or letting the barber "tone down the grey," or even getting a hairpiece.[98] Makers of women's commercial hair and skincare products quickly expanded their lines to include specially formulated and packaged products for men. (Figure 7-66.)

Long hair did not mean an unkempt tangle atop the head, growing wildly and unmanaged. Even longhairs whose tresses extended to the shoulders or down the back learned the importance of the right haircare regimen that often included specialized shampoos and conditioners chemically balanced for different types of hair. Specialty haircare products were developed for African Americans who wanted to style their hair with a natural look and add sheen. The sale of hairdryers exploded as men grew their hair longer, and short hair became more carefully styled without the aid of old-fashioned greasy creams and tonics. "The wet head is dead," rang the jingle of a TV commercial for men's haircare products in the early seventies. Hair coloring kits such as Clairol's Great Day were also introduced in the 1960s for men who wanted to hide the gray or add highlighting in the comfort and privacy of home. For balding men, affordable ready-to-wear wigs became more common. The improved acrylic strands duplicated the look of real hair and could easily be attached to stretch-fit netting. "These wigs are ideal for a wide range of downtrodden minorities," suggested GQ in 1971, "bald or balding men; military reservists; long-haired freaks who want to cross the Spanish border; hirsute types who work in banks; anybody who gets bored with his own hair and wants a change."[99]

Cosmetics for men were also coming into their own. In 1969, GQ detailed the new "cosmetic camouflage" for men: "As practically everybody knows, men's cosmetics are solidly established as an entity unto themselves, worthy of occupying counters of their own in department stores, rather than being an adjunct to the women's sections."[100] Although initially few makers produced "actual camouflaging makeup preparations comparable to pancake makeup for women," an abundance of skin conditioners, moisturizers, face-firmers, skin-toned blemish coverups, and bronzers appeared on the market. By the end of the 1970s, complexion kits even included a semiglossy "lip toner" and "lash tint." "Now you can dress up the most important part of your body—your face—and be subtle about it," offered a men's cosmetic ad in 1978.[101]

Longer hair, styling blow dryers, hair coloring, wigs, fragrances, and even cosmetics were common men's grooming accoutrement by the end of the 1970s, but the debate on how all this impacted American society's ideas of masculinity raged on. In his 1978 book *Looking Good,* stylist Charles Hix cautioned men: "Although it's expected that women will try even the weirdest concoctions to improve their looks,...that a man should do anything at all in the same interest has often been suspect....From infancy a male is trained not to look in a mirror except as a hasty once-over before rushing out the front door."[102] And what seemed especially confusing to many American men was the reversal of conventional differentiators in manly looks. At the end of 1979, Tom Wolfe assessed some of the more notable reversals of the concluding decade:

> So it's the shit kickers with their Camaros up on cinder blocks beefing up the suspension on Saturday afternoon in the Teen Burger hamlets of Oklahoma who now wear the hair of the much hated hippies of the 1960s down to the shoulder blades, complete with head bands, while the college boys go in for the short, fluffy, thatchy look of Oxford undergraduates from the Evelyn Waugh period. Meantime, the shortest hair of all, the crew cut, or butch cut—formerly associated with military macho—is now affected by the more trendy male homosexual of the gay life. They also go in for big Nautilus Center high-definition mondo-gorgo biceps, deltoids, trapeziuses, and latissimi dorsi, while heterosexual males now favor the more feminine forms of exercise conceivable, namely, jogging and tennis, both of which were scorned as "nancy" activities in the original 1950s era of crew cuts.[103]

The most fundamental explanation was the ever-shifting cultural pluralism of the era. The peacock iconoclast of the mid-1960s with his brilliant-colored and sexually expressive raiment instigated a dismantling of predictable, glacially evolutionary men's dress. The new man cared about how he looked much more than was traditionally acceptable. And he was comfortable exploring fresh ideas about his looks and dress. The new masculine identity was whatever a man wanted it to be. The dress and style hallmarks of the long-haired student protester of 1960s became the look of many rural midwesterners in the 1970s. The sheared, buff look of the Vietnam War marine became the look of the disco era gays. American men's dress and identity would never again be static.

Conclusion

The 1960s and 1970s were decades of social turbulence and rapid change in America unlike in any era since the Civil War. By the mid-1960s, half the U.S. population was under twenty-five years old, and a youthquake rocked the nation with a social revolution. Young people all across America rejected the middle-class conventions and materialism of their parents, and pursued new ideas of self-expression with sex, drugs, and rock-and-roll. Protest marches and student unrest on campuses helped turn public opinion against the Vietnam War. The actions of civil rights advocates effected new federal legislation guaranteeing voting rights and the dismantling of segregation laws. The second feminist movement inspired the founding of the National Organization for Women, which focused attention on equal opportunities in the workplace and reproductive self-determination. The Gay National Task Force pursued equal protection under the law and succeeded in getting the American Psychiatric Association to drop homosexuality from its list of mental disorders. By the 1970s, American society was defined by a pluralism of constituencies. It was the Me Decade—a time of greater introspection and self-absorbed pursuits.

The postmodern social pluralism in America that emerged during the 1960s was initiated in part by the Peacock Revolution in men's fashions. A British invasion of pop culture, music, and mod fashions rolled over America in the mid-1960s. The Carnaby Street look, named for a London fashion district, introduced radical new concepts of masculine dress and identity to American men that included attention-getting styles and colors, sexual exhibitionism, and long hair. It was a "new masculinity," observed *Men's Wear* in 1969, in which men "feel freer to express their individuality in their dress and experiment with styles."[104]

The slow, methodical evolution of style that had been typical of American menswear for decades was transformed almost overnight. Men's fashions were designed with the same planned obsolescence as cars and appliances. In many instances, yesterday's styles looked too yesterday to linger in a man's wardrobe for more than a couple of seasons. The Nehru jacket, for example, was the hot look in 1968, but completely gone a year later.

Almost abruptly, the nearly twenty-year-old styling of the Ivy League suit was displaced in the second half of the 1960s by shaped suits that had padded shoulders, stiff interlinings, hard lapels, and fitted waists. Traditional two- and three-button fronts were recut for one- to sixteen-button closures. Lapels expanded across the chest almost to the armscye seams. Some jacket collars rose into Napoleonic military styles or were removed entirely. By the beginning of the 1970s, polyester double knits gave suits a smooth, indestructible look with permanent, knife-edge creases and stiff, oversized details. Within a few years, though, the shaped, armor-plated suit was deconstructed. At the end of the decade, stiff padding and interlinings were stripped out, and suits became softer—draping and accentuating the male anatomy with fluid fabrics.

Outerwear followed the trends of suits, becoming more fitted and shaped with padding and architectonic lines. The midi and maxi lengths were high-style alternatives to the usual short suburbans and knee breaker topcoats. In the 1970s, polyester double knits made coats more durable and varied in texture. At the end of the decade, natural fiber fabrics returned, and coats were cut fuller for the prevailing layered look.

American men's sportswear was the most expressive of the Peacock Revolution and the era's evolving multicultural pluralism. A convergence of influences on sportswear included British invasion mod styles; flower power and antifashion street looks; historical revivals spanning from the Renaissance through the Edwardian era; replicas of East Indian, Arab, Asian, and Native American clothing; art deco, Stars 'n' Stripes, and psychedelic motifs; and Hollywood's costume films like *Bonnie and Clyde* and *The Great Gatsby*. The sexual revolution inspired fitted body shirts and skintight trousers. The designer jean phenomenon consumed the fashion-obsessed. And the pursuit of comfortable, easy-care clothing launched the leisure suit.

The sexual revolution also influenced sports shirts, swimwear, underwear, and loungewear styling. Styles of swimwear and underwear were cut to be more exhibitionistic. Diaphanous voile shirts were worn open to the waist for the naked look. The bikinis of the early 1960s were pared down to microbikinis and thongs in the 1970s. Nylon spandex fabrics provocatively molded and displayed the male anatomy.

New types of men's accessories also challenged traditions of masculine dress and identity. Love beads and pendant necklaces adorned hippies and cosmopolitan urbanites alike. Gold chains at the open-throat shirts of disco partyers brought attention to hairy chests and muscular pecs. Boots and high-heeled platform shoes, many with vividly colored finishes, provided exciting alternatives to the usual black or brown wingtips. Man bags were a practical solution to organizing and managing the dozens of personal and workday pocket items needed by the postmodern American male.

Changes in grooming practices likewise altered ideals of masculinity. Men grew their hair long—covering the ears and extending over the shirt collar—for the first time in 150 years. They went to hair salons instead of barbers, and they indulged in grooming regimens at home that required multiple haircare products and blow dryer styling. They even applied makeup to camouflage flaws or enhance facial features.

In the final analysis, the postmodern American male was freed from decades of prescribed, standardized norms of dress and identity. Through the evolving multicultural pluralism in American society, he could express himself and his independence through a broad variety of tribal looks and fashions. The peacock could be splendidly radiant or not. It was his choice.

Pluralistic Tribalisms

Fashions since 1980

The Reagan Counterrevolution

The current era that began in 1980 was the culmination of a political and societal shift in America initiated during the post-Watergate years. The "imperial presidency" of Richard Nixon had collapsed in ruin when he was forced to resign in disgrace in 1974. His successor, Gerald Ford, had been tainted by his pardon of Nixon, and consequently lost the election of 1976. The presidency was further tarnished under Jimmy Carter with the Iran hostage crisis, in which the American embassy in Teheran had been attacked and U.S. diplomats were held in captivity for 444 days. Moreover, America had lost its first war ever when U.S. troops were pulled out of Vietnam in 1975 and the Communists took over. Years of campus unrest, violent street protests, assassinations, and persistent demands of women's organizations, civil rights activists, gay rights advocates, and other constituency groups had exhausted most Americans.

It was then a simple answer for most citizens when presidential candidate Ronald Reagan asked during a campaign debate in 1980 if they were better off than four years ago. In response, Americans elected Reagan as president and, with him, the hope of a clean break with the troubling and troublesome previous era. Peter Jennings, senior editor of ABC News, wrote, "Feelings of nostalgia for less complicated times ran so high it felt occasionally as if the society had been transplanted to the grounds of an elaborate theme park where a tidied-up, even cinematic, version of the past could be lived out in comfort."[1] Reagan suited both criteria—a representative of the idealized, simpler past and a personable, cinematic image: As the oldest man ever elected to the office of president, and as a staunch conservative, Reagan was often accused of being "frozen in the fifties."[2] And as a former B-movie actor, he and his handlers masterfully marketed the cinematic personality that appealed so comfortingly to many Americans. (Figure 8-1.) Reagan's vision of a return to a premodern, Norman Rockwell-Disneyesque America represented a society not so much as it had been but rather a fantasy of what many wished it might

THE REMAKING OF THE PRESIDENT, 1981

This is not a political story. You'll get no comment from us on Ronald Reagan and his right-wing-tip shoes. Consider this a follow-up of sorts. In an earlier article in this magazine (*The Dressing of the President*), we spoke of the importance of good looks to a prime political candidate. And we told you how Ronald Reagan won that important battle with Jimmy Carter. But that doesn't mean we think Reagan is a fashion plate. Or even that we like what he wears. Quite the contrary. To us, he still looks like he's wearing that Notre Dame football uniform under his suits. And that hair. It resembles an explosion in a Wildroot factory.

So, to do our bit for America, we decided to make the President look more Presidential, and certainly more up to date. For advice on clothes, we went to master tailor Peter Dezirel. For input on hair, we spoke with Ron Mancuso at the Jamilton salon in New York City. We had them work with our recent photo of Reagan. Here's what they said:

GET THE GREASE OUT!
REMOVE BULK FROM TOP OF HEAD
BALANCE, SHAPE AND PROPORTION HAIR LAYER TO GIVE A SLIGHT ELEVATION
PUT DOWN THE SHOULDER PADDING
THE COLLAR'S ALL WRONG, TOO SPREAD
KISS THAT DOUBLE-WINDSOR KNOT GOODBYE
COLLAR SHOULD BE HIGHER TO HIDE WATTLE
BLAZER NOT "PRESIDENTIAL" ENOUGH
WAIST SHOULDN'T BE THIS TUCKED. IT CREATES TOO SEVERE A V-LOOK
DUMP THE POCKET SQUARE—IT'S TOO SQUARE ALREADY
TOO HIGH A RISE

We took that advice and had an artist put it all together. Are you reading this, Ronnie? We've gone to a lot of trouble here for you. Now all you've got to do is turn the page. . . .

Figure 8-1. As a former movie actor, Ronald Reagan was the most image-conscious president of the century. Among his nicknames in the press, he was sometimes referred to as the "Celluloid President." Soon after taking office in 1981, *Playboy's Fashion for Men* offered some tips for updating Reagan's look.

have been.

Reagan's approach to the job of president was simple. Like his idol, Calvin Coolidge, he started work late, knocked off early, and took frequent and extended vacations. He set an agenda of broad themes and left the details to staffers. Chief on his list of domestic goals were tax cuts for the wealthy, deregulation of business, reduction of government, and a buildup of the military. The theory of the so-called supply side "Reaganomics" was that a rising tide would lift all boats; that is, the tax cuts and deregulations would encourage investment by big business, thus generating new jobs and stimulating economic growth. The result was the biggest bull market in U.S. history. But instead of expanded growth in productive enterprises and entrepreneurship, it was a financial frenzy of takeovers and mergers that dismantled companies for quick profits, resulting in mass lay-offs and high unemployment, peaking near 11 percent. The "trickle-down" effect of Reaganomics failed, and the middle class actually shrank by the end of the 1980s.[3] A sharp increase in the social security tax and higher state and local taxes increased the tax burden of average Americans. Of the 18 million new jobs claimed by the Reagan administration, most were low-paying service sector positions, called "McJobs" after the fast-food chain McDonald's.[4] His attack on the "welfare state" slashed government spending on social programs, and the number of Americans living in poverty rose twenty-five percent during his years in office.[5] In addition, Reagan's enormous military buildup helped increase the national debt from $600 billion to $3 trillion,[6] breaking one of his most sacred campaign promises to balance the budget.

Another pledge that Reagan was unable to meet was a restoration of integrity to the office of president. In 1987, the Iran-Contra scandal broke. In violation of several laws, White House operatives had illegally sold arms to Iran and used those funds to aid contra rebels in the Nicaraguan civil war. Although in subsequent trials and Congressional hearings, the central question of "what did the president know and when did he know it" remained unclear, Reagan was portrayed as either a forgetful and disengaged leader or, worst, the remote figurehead of a corrupt government.

Despite the regressive harshness of the Reaganites' right wing vision for American society, the predatory business climate that crashed the stock market in 1987, and the criminality of the Iran-Contra scandal, most Americans somehow still felt their lives had improved over the not-too-distant, tumultuous seventies. Consequently, the 1988 presidential election was a referendum on the Reagan years—or at least on the economy of the time—and most Americans wanted to continue on the course they were traveling. They elected Reagan's vice president, George H. Bush, as the heir apparent to the Reagan mantle. But as the 1990s dawned, Bush was increasingly perceived as an anachronism. The Cold War had ended, and Reaganomics (once called "voodoo economics" by Bush) spiraled into another deep recession under the weight of its $3 trillion national debt, numerous financial scandals, and substantial middle-class job losses. Bush's strength as a veteran Cold War warrior was foreign policy. When Iraq invaded Kuwait in 1991 and threatened the Middle East oil supplies, Bush put together an international coalition to intervene. The brief Persian Gulf War was a success, but Bush was widely criticized for not continuing with an invasion of Iraq to depose the dictator Saddam Hussein. Despite his triumph with the war, the lingering sour economy plagued Bush's administration and cost him reelection in 1992, losing to Democrat Bill Clinton.

The Fin de Siècle and a New Millennium

In 1992, William Jefferson Clinton became the first baby boomer elected president. Although he won on a progressive platform, his advisors steered him toward a more balanced, centrist approach to governing. On the liberal side of his agenda, he achieved stricter gun control regulations and placed thousands of acres of environmentally sensitive lands under federal protection. On the conservative side, he signed NAFTA (North American Free Trade Agreement) in spite of pressures from labor supporters within his own party and the Defense of Marriage Act, which allows states to ignore gay marriages from other jurisdictions. Most important of all, Clinton's economic policies disproved the tenets of supply-side Reaganomics. Not only were taxes increased on the wealthy and government was expanded considerably, but the federal budget was balanced, wiping out the enormous national debt of the Reagan-Bush years and actually resulting in a surplus for the first time since 1969.[7] The economic good times earned Clinton reelection in 1996.

Clinton's second term was marred by a sex scandal that led to an impeachment effort spearheaded by hostile Congressional Republicans. Although the Senate voted not to remove Clinton from office, the issue of the integrity of the presidency, once again, became a political campaign topic in the 2000 presidential election.

For weeks following the contentious election of 2000, the outcome was inconclusive. Although Vice President Al Gore had received 500,000 more popular votes than former Texas governor George W. Bush, neither candidate achieved the requisite electoral college number. During the hand recount of ballots in Florida, the U.S. Supreme Court intervened with a controversial decision in favor of Bush.

On September 11, 2001, Muslim terrorists highjacked U.S. planes, crashing them into the New York World Trade Center and the Pentagon, killing thousands. The Bush administration responded quickly and effectively by invading Afghanistan to destroy the bases of terrorist organizations and overthrow the regime that supported them. Two years later, military objectives were expanded to include an invasion of Iraq on the pretext of eliminating nonexistent "WMDs" (weapons of mass destruction) that White House officials falsely claimed included biological and even nuclear bombs.[8] Despite the unpopularity of the Iraqi War, issues of national security during the 2004 election earned Bush the narrowest reelection in U.S. history.

On the domestic front, Bush's claim of being a "compassionate conservative" was negated by many of his partisan actions and inactions. He vetoed a healthcare plan that would benefit 10 million low-income children. He vetoed federal funding for medical research on embryonic stem cells that could aid in cures for debilitating diseases. He instituted a Reaganesque tax cut for the wealthy, but the economy fell into a deep, lingering recession. When Hurricane Katrina devastated the Gulf Coast and flooded New Orleans in 2005, he was widely criticized for his slow response and for the inept leaders he appointed to manage the disaster. In addition, the deregulation policies of the Bush administration led to a financial crisis in 2008 and a stock market crash with the worst losses

Figure 8-2. In the presidential election of 2008, Americans went to polls in record numbers, choosing Barack Obama as the 44th President of the United States. "Change has come to America," Obama declared in his election night speech. Cover of *Time*, January 26, 2009.

since the Great Depression.[9] Bush's approval ratings remained consistently the lowest since Nixon's during the Watergate investigations.

In the presidential election of 2008, a record number of voters—more than 132 million—went to the polls and chose Barack Obama as the 44th president of the United States. (Figure 8-2.) As the first African American president, Obama was the embodiment of his simple campaign slogan: change. Among the first hurdles faced by his administration was significant unfinished business left by the Bush administration including a deep recession, a trillion-dollar debt, a financial crisis on Wall Street, the highest unemployment in thirty years, and costly wars in Iraq and Afghanistan. In addition to dealing with the demands of these national concerns, Obama's signature achievement was the 2010 Health Care Reform Act; until then, "an unmet promise," noted the president in his signing speech, since Teddy Roosevelt first acknowledged the need more than a century earlier. Healthcare was now recognized as an American right, not merely a privilege.

The End of the Cold War

The post-World War II competition between communist states and the democracies of the world had come to be known as the Cold War in the 1950s. By the 1970s, the Soviet Union struggled with massive housing shortages and food scarcity, crumbling industries, obsolete technologies, and rampant political corruption and government mismanagement. The Afghanistan War (1979–1988) had been devastatingly costly. The aggressive buildup of the U.S. military under Reagan was simply beyond the capacity of the Soviet economy to match. Even the fossilized Politburo leadership recognized the desperate need for change. In 1985, Mikhail Gorbachev became the new leader of the USSR, and with him a fresh breeze of reform swept the country. Not even Gorbachev could have anticipated that his reforms would so transform global politics and the lives of hundreds of millions of people. He instituted a program of *glasnost* (openness) and *perestroika* (restructuring) that he hoped would reinvigorate the communist state. Industries began to offer worker productivity incentives. The press became more open. Citizens tested their new freedom with open expressions of dissent such as signing petitions of protest. Real elections were held for the first time in decades. In 1989, Gorbachev announced that the Soviet Union would no longer prop up the regimes in the Eastern Bloc nations of central Europe. One by one, the communist power structures fell in Poland, East Germany, Romania, Czechoslovakia, Bulgaria, Hungary, and Yugoslavia. The height of the drama in that "year of miracles" came when the citizens of communist East Berlin joined West Berliners with pickaxes and hammers to dismantle the wall that had separated them since 1961. East and West Germany reunited the following year. China and Vietnam began to encourage a capitalist market approach to business and industry. In 1992, the Soviet Union separated into fifteen independent republics. The Cold War had ended.

American Business and Technology 1980–Present

The 1980s was the Greed Decade. The Reagan administration's fiscal policies, tax cuts for the wealthy, and laissez-faire deregulation of busi-

Figure 8-3. During the 1980s, the yuppie (young urban professional) became the icon of the Greed Decade. The yuppie worked hard to achieve success and spent lavishly on the trappings of affluence. "You can have it all," declared a Michelob ad campaign in 1985. Top, *The Yuppie Handbook*, 1984.

nesses ushered in a New Gilded Age comparable to its counterpart of a century earlier in which robber barons, financiers, and industrial magnates conspicuously flaunted their vast wealth. Unlike the nineteenth century, though, where railroads, steel mills, oil refineries, and similar Industrial Revolution tangibles were built, the 1980s was an era of lawyers, brokers, and investment bankers who made fortunes by paper manipulation—orchestrating company takeovers and restructuring, dismantling, or liquidating businesses. "Greed is good," asserted the corporate raider portrayed by Michael Douglas in *Wall Street* (1987). More than fifty billionaires and scores of new multimillionaires emerged in the 1980s. The "yuppie" (young urban professional) became the new breed of corporate worker. Yuppies worked long hours in cutthroat competition to climb the corporate ladder to power and financial success, and they spent their substantial salaries and bonuses lavishly on upscale cars, big houses, fine furnishings, the latest in technological gadgets, and designer label clothes. "You can have it all," proclaimed a beer ad campaign in the mid-1980s. (Figure 8-3.) For evening events, women overdressed in extravagant couture gowns and jewels, and men once again donned traditional white ties.

Meanwhile, a technological revolution began to take root in the 1980s that blossomed into the Information Age of the 1990s. Megafortunes were made by computer and software innovators and, in the 1990s, by dot-com entrepreneurs. In 1981, IBM introduced the personal computer and, three years later, the Macintosh debuted with its easy-to-use graphical interface. (Figure 8-4.) Software developers such as Microsoft and Adobe produced specialized programs for business as well as home use. Video games became an obsession for a generation of new-agers. (Figure 8-5.) In 1994, the "Information Superhighway"—the World Wide Web—became accessible to the masses. By the start of the new millennium, hundreds of millions of people around the world communicated instantly through e-mails, viewed billions of Web site pages, and shopped online for every imaginable commodity. Wireless connectivity and portable laptops, Blackberries, and iPhones made possible global communications virtually anywhere, anytime. PDAs (personal digital assistants) vibrated, chimed, or chirped from belt attachments, pockets, business cases, and handbags. Cell phones were indispensable and seemingly everyone from grade schoolers to great-grandmas had one. A new etiquette developed of when and where phones could be answered: Movie theaters and concert halls displayed reminders to turn off phones; in some communities, laws were enacted prohibiting driving while talking on cell phones. Safety concerns aboard planes and in hospitals restricted use of many personal electronic gadgets.

In the first decade of the twenty-first century, a greed revival reminiscent of the 1980s emerged during the presidency of George W. Bush. Once again, broad tax cuts for the wealthy were instituted and big business was granted special regulatory exemptions. At a Republican fund raiser, Bush addressed the affluent-looking audience as his "base"—"the haves and have-mores."[10] The Bush White House was widely criticized for convening secret meetings with oil and other business groups on strategic economic decisions. The war itself was a huge opportunity for enormous profits for many service and supplier companies such as Haliburton where Vice President Cheney had been CEO. The lax accountability of the Bush administration cost taxpayers billions in missing funds and waste.[11]

Figure 8-4. The personal computer was introduced in 1981, revolutionizing the American workplace and lifestyle. With the emergence of the Internet in the mid-1990s, communications and commerce became truly global. Above, Macintosh, 1984; below, Dell laptop, 2008.

Figure 8-5. The continual advances in electronic and digital technologies since 1980 improved and quickened the pace of American life. Personal computers and the "Information Superhighway" changed the workplace and home with new forms of communication and entertainment and methods of consumption.

Women's fashions 1980-present: left, big look power dressing by Versace, 1987; center, minimalist suiting from Spiegel, 1996; right, fitted, skinny looks by Shape FX, 2005

Computers changed home entertainment with video games (above, Atari 1983) and shopping by global e-commerce (Web site 2010)

Yuppie opulence, antiques, and collectibles, 1984

Yuppie gentrification: restoration and preservation of vintage houses, 1986

Sony flat screen TV, 2008

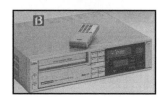

Sears Beta VCR, 1984

Toyota SUV (suburban utility vehicle), 1991

Helio cell phone with slider texting keyboard, 2007

In addition, scandalous excesses such as the looting of pension plans by corporate executives rocked financial markets. The most egregious was the collapse of the multibillion-dollar energy commodities giant Enron when it became public in 2001 that executives lied about corporate earnings, leaving thousands of stockholders and employees with nothing. "Outsourcing" became the bane of the working and middle classes as all levels of jobs were contracted abroad by American companies seeking to lower labor costs and eliminate worker benefits. Unlike the 1980s, though, there was not an exuberant exhibitionism of wealth amongst the haves during the Bush years. The unpopularity of the president and his circle, the uneasiness most people felt about their jobs, and the scandals of misconduct by corporate CEOs and executives cast a pall over the economic good times of the affluent.

American Culture and Society 1980–Present

In the 1980s, the "Reagan counterrevolution" was achieved by a cobbling together of strange bedfellows: Northern fiscal conservatives, Southern right wing populists, militant evangelical Christian organizations, anticommunist militarists, and small government libertarians, each of which demanded a place at the table of power to institute their agendas. Their views of antifeminism, antiabortion, antigay, antigun control, antiaffirmative action, and antiwelfare were sanctioned by the Reagan-Bush administrations. The harsh rhetoric and extremist policies from the partisans who were given roles in the White House further polarized the nation into deeply divided constituency groups.

The rise of the religious right in the 1980s was in part a result of their support for Reagan and in part a backlash against the liberalism of the sixties and seventies. The Moral Majority (which opponents insisted was neither) was a coalition of religious groups ranging from Protestant fundamentalists who objected to banning prayer and Bible reading in schools to Catholic organizations against birth control and abortion rights. These paleoconservatives, as they were later labeled,[12] put their weight and dollars behind defeating the Equal Rights Amendment in 1983 and in organizing stealth campaigns on the local level to pack city councils and school boards. Their political influence peaked in the early 1980s but waned precipitously after a series of widely publicized sex-and-money scandals of some televangelists. The religious right remained a core constituency of the Republican party without which George W. Bush could not have eked out his narrow reelection win in 2004.

Despite the advances wrought by the civil rights movement in the 1960s and 1970s, the racial divide remained prevalent in American society. Throughout the 1980s, Reagan officials undermined affirmative action policies in government. When Supreme Court nominee Clarence Thomas came under scrutiny by the Senate in 1991, he accused the committee members of conducting a "high tech lynching of an uppity black man."[13] The following year, Los Angeles erupted into the most violent rioting in decades when four white police officers were acquitted of beating a black motorist, Rodney King—an incident that had been captured on videotape and repeatedly shown on television news reports. In 1995, the racial division was again evident in the reaction of whites and blacks to the acquittal of double-murder suspect O. J. Simpson. To blacks, Simpson had been framed by racist police officers; to whites he was

Figure 8-6. By the second half of the 1980s, AIDS was recognized as a growing worldwide pandemic. Mass media campaigns by AIDS organizations and condom makers emphasized that anyone could contract the disease. Ads, 1987.

unarguably a murderer. Even into the twenty-first century, the issue of racial division persisted. When Hurricane Katrina destroyed New Orleans in 2005, the Bush administration was accused of racism because of the slow response to the victims, the overwhelming majority of whom were poor blacks.[14]

Among the events and occurrences that have substantially impacted American society since 1980, the discovery and spread of the HIV virus and the resulting disease, AIDS (Acquired Immune Deficiency Syndrome) is one of the most significant. Although medical professionals assured the public that the disease could only be transmitted through unprotected sex, sharing needles by infected drug addicts, transfusions of contaminated blood, or from mother to unborn child, most people were initially unconvinced and reactionary. The gay rights movement was set back because the disease was first classified and widely reported in the press as a condition specific only to gay men. (Originally AIDS was called GRID: Gay-Related Immune Deficiency.) Until 1987, religious partisans in the Reagan administration kept any reference to the epidemic out of presidential speeches until public pressure finally forced Reagan to acknowledge the crisis and the need for public education on the disease.[15] AIDS organizations and condom makers used mass media to get the message out that anyone could contract the disease. (Figure 8-6.) In the 1990s, new advances in regimens of medicine "cocktails" helped deter the onset of AIDS, but the treatments were expensive. Although Americans gradually became more educated on the subject and altered their lifestyles, elsewhere in the world, AIDS spread unchecked. Unlike Reagan, George W. Bush could not ignore the devastating global pandemic. In 2003, he outlined a five-year plan and pledged $5 billion dollars for emergency worldwide AIDS relief.

Concerns for the environment also impacted American society. The green movement that began in 1970 with the first Earth Day and the establishment of the Environmental Protection Agency (EPA) continued to increase public awareness and to effect legislation for clean air and water, nuclear waste disposal, and endangered species. The American people began to think about the use of spray cans containing fluorocarbons and about recycling. During the 1990s, studies of global warming began to warn of the consequences of melting polar icecaps and the effects on ocean currents. Terms such as "the greenhouse effect" where gases in the earth's atmosphere trap solar radiation, causing global warming came into the lexicon of average Americans. In 2007, former Vice President Al Gore won an Academy Award, an Emmy, and the Nobel Peace Prize for his campaign of awareness on climate change.

Fashion Merchandising 1980–Present

Ready-to-wear retailing continued to expand the new merchandising strategies that had emerged in the 1960s and 1970s. Department stores increasingly adopted the self-serve boutique concept with floor space dedicated to famous maker labels. Downtown shopping districts suffered a rapid decline as suburban strip centers and malls proliferated. Long-established haberdasheries lost market share to youth-oriented, mass market chains like Chess King, Merry-Go-Round, and Casual Male. During the merger-acquisition fervor of the 1980s and 1990s, numerous hometown department stores vanished gobbled up by megachains like Macy's and Dillard's whose apparel merchandising spread a homogeneity of looks and brands nationwide. Acres of off-price outlet shopping centers made upscale designer labels more widely available to the masses. In 1985, the first home shopping network was launched on cable television, making fashions and accessories accessible to consumers in small towns and rural areas far from malls. In the second half of the 1990s, the Internet brought the world of fashion news and shopping into millions of American households. (Figure 8-7.)

Dress and Identity: Postmodernist Ideas and Ideals of Masculinity

By the beginning of the 1980s, the emergence of pluralism in postmodern American society left a significant segment of the white male population feeling displaced and confused. For most of them, the certitudes of masculinity and identity that had been sustained by their fathers and grandfathers were now obsolete. The peacock generation had overturned many decades of conventions of masculine behavior and dress, discarding in the process the age-old mandate of conformity in favor of individualism and self-expression. The legacy of the iconoclasm of the postmodern peacock male inspired new models of masculinity for the end of the millennium. Beginning in the 1980s, growing numbers of men explored their "feminine" side by participating more in homemaking arenas such as cooking and childcare. Movies like *Mr. Mom* (1982), *Three Men and a Baby* (1987), and *Mrs. Doubtfire* (1993) reflected the postmodern sensitive male and the dismantling of historic gender distinctions. (Figure 8-8.)

Likewise, despite relentless opposition from religious groups, by the end of the twentieth century, gay male identities were increasingly featured in popular mass media as alternative masculinities. As *Details*

Figure 8-7. In the late 1990s, the Internet became a significant distribution channel for menswear makers and retailers. From the comfort of their homes, American consumers could access the most current news on fashion trends, comparison shop for best prices and style selections, and order for home delivery with the click of a mouse. Zappos.com ad, 2007.

observed of homophobia in America of the new millennium, "Ideals of what's 'heteronormative'—the term social scientists use for the sets of behavior that define 'heterosexuality'—have become one big blur."[16] Stereotypes of the mincing, limp-wristed male as the archetypical gay man were broken in popular movies such as *Philadelphia* (1993) and *In and Out* (1997) and in TV series like *Will and Grace* (1998-2006) and *Queer As Folk* (2000-2005). (Figure 8-9.) Advertisers increasingly targeted the gay market with images of same sex couples and gay-friendly messages in ads placed in mainstream magazines and newspapers. In academia, queer studies programs were added to gender studies curriculums.

As a consequence of the social progressivism and expanding pluralism in America, numerous men's seminars, research reports, books, and academic programs were developed to help the postmodern American male deal with the perceived crisis in masculinity. In 1990, for example, Robert Bly's best-selling *Iron John: A Book About Men* inspired the mythopoetic movement. Urban middle-class men were urged to revitalize their masculinity through therapeutic "wild man" weekends in the woods where they could remedy their softness through fellowship, rugged outdoor activities, and Native American rituals. Religious groups also provided a haven for white working- and middle-class men who felt adrift in the social progressivism of the postmodern era. Evangelical organizations like the Moral Majority of the 1980s and the Promise Keepers of the 1990s emphasized doctrines of Christian fundamentalism and dogmatic morality for defining manhood. For evangelicals, manliness was based on the early modernist conventions of masculine authority through exclusion from power: Women were subordinated; nonwhites were scarcely represented; and gays were habitually vilified. Though short lived, these diverse groups reflected the continued anxiety and distress that conservative white men experienced with America's new social pluralism.

Today, almost fifty years after the first postmodernist shifts in social constructs, many American men still struggle with their understanding

Figure 8-8. The second wave feminist movement is often credited with influencing new models of manhood including the role of nurturing father. Left, Lauder ad, 1998; right, Calvin Klein ad, 2000.

of masculinity and gender identity in a pluralistic society. The continuing debate over whether or not there even can be a universal idea of masculinity in our postmodern world has transformed American culture. "Yes, times are confusing," acknowledged *GQ* in 2006. The rules of manly behavior and masculine etiquette had "remained hard-and-fast" for generations, "but that was before your Treo [Smartphone] became an appendage, a woman became your boss, and your good buddy married a man."[17] The impact of new perspectives in academia, the relentless advances in technology, and the confident assertiveness of women, non-whites, and gays has generated a reassessment of what it means to be a man in America of the twenty-first century.

Although the peacock male had overturned traditions of masculine dress and identity in his quest for individualism, a dichotomy persisted whereby men with more conventional inclinations could maintain a conformist comfort zone. Parallel with the peacock's self-expression in dress, a relatively consistent form of masculine dress has continued for more than 150 years: the three-piece suit. Even as peacock influence deconstructed the standardized sack suit, and an endless assortment of variations has been offered by avant-garde designers since the 1960s, the menswear market never abandoned the basic look. The three-piece sack suit has continued to make a fundamental statement about the wearer just as it had when introduced in the 1850s. The utilitarian business suit, typically in black, navy, or gray, continued to serve as an optional form of masculine identity, a signal to any observer that the wearer was likely a member of that vast masculine pool of the corporate world. Over the past fifty years of the postmodernist era, business suit styling has remained much the same with minimal adjustments to lapel widths, shoulder contours, trouser constructs, and similar small design elements. "While the context and connotations of men's suits have changed, their basic form hasn't," affirmed *GQ* in 2002. "The tailored jacket with matching trousers remains the uniform of official power, suggesting civility, diplomacy and physical self-control."[18] Like any uniform, the business suit has continued to convey an identity message of presumed masculine conservatism, respectability, and class distinction.

By the 1980s, though, men increasingly became more comfortable in experimenting with a variety of new looks that might express identities beyond the typical conventions of the herd. Most American men now often went shopping for themselves, making a conscious effort to understand fashion and how clothing reflected or transformed their masculine identity. The decade was a New Gilded Age, and, like its counterpart of the 1880s, the display of status, wealth, and accomplishment was unabashed. With the image-obsessed Reagans in the White House and a proliferation of style magazines for men, masculine exhibitionism was not only enabled by the social climate, it was encouraged. Fashion writer Charles Hix noted in 1984:

> Society is finally allowing men a new visibility, the opportunity to emerge from the anonymous crowd. This sanction reflects the fact that society's view of acceptable male behavior is broader, less limiting, than it has ever been in this century. New concepts—and images—of maleness are emerging. To take full advantage of this enriched social climate, many men must learn new techniques in outfitting themselves. The desired end is not to look 'fashionable.' The goal for men is to use clothing as a tool

Figure 8-9. By the end of the twentieth century, gay male identities were pervasively represented in mainstream movies, TV programs, and advertising. Stereotypes were broken as portrayals of gay men were presented in what social scientists call "heteronormative" behavior.

Figure 8-10. In 1980, Richard Gere portrayed a male prostitute in *American Gigolo*. In one scene his character spends considerable time coordinating and accessorizing outfits—an activity that left movie audiences of the time questioning the character's masculinity.

for self-expression, even self-discovery.[19]

These new concepts and images of maleness swept across American popular culture in the 1980s, most especially in movies and advertising.

In *American Gigolo* (1980), Richard Gere spends considerable time carefully laying out ensembles of shirts, trousers, and neckties, thoughtfully assessing the complementary colors and textures of each. (Figure 8-10.) He is the next generation of the peacock, confident in his wardrobe choices and secure enough in his masculinity to find pleasure and satisfaction in the activity of coordinating and accessorizing outfits. Moreover, Gere also presents a new attitude about the male physique. As a male prostitute, he must look good for his upper-class female clients who are accustomed to paying well for the best, but his motives for attaining an athlete's body go beyond the trim masculine contours that he knows appeal to women. He straps on Gravity Guiding Inversion Boots and hangs inverted from a doorway bar to make his torso exercises even more intense. His build must be as superlative as the other expressions of his masculinity: his wardrobe, sports car, and apartment.

This notion of the male body as an object of social contemplation and as an expression of masculinity akin to the ditto suit is largely a postmodern phenomenon. As social historian J. C. Flugel observed in 1930, Western culture had developed "a very considerable intolerance of the male body."[20] In the nineteenth century, the idealized manly body was defined in terms of health and moral purity rather than physiological aesthetics. During the first decades of the twentieth century, societal concerns about the emasculation of the American male by sedentary office work and confining factory jobs prompted a shift from an emphasis on inner ideals to more outward markers of masculinity. In the 1920s and 1930s, Hollywood presented the natural, athletic male body virtually nude on screen in the form of the fictional hero Tarzan, choosing athletes such as gymnastics champion Frank Merrill and Olympic swimming gold medalist Johnny Weissmuller to represent the hero. At the same time, bodybuilder Charles Atlas widely promoted his home program for developing "the build of a HE-MAN...smooth muscled, perfectly balanced," not the "knotted-up bulges of a circus weight lifter."[21] (Figure 8-11.) By mid-century, though, conventions of masculinity resembled more the inward concepts of the nineteenth century than the extroverted exhibitionism of Tarzan and Charles Atlas. With the all-consuming fears of Soviet communism, juvenile delinquency, and homosexual deviancy, the focus regressed to the Victorian ideas of masculine health and moral fitness. The aesthetic or erotic aspects of the male body were downplayed in popular culture, and bodybuilding was viewed

Figure 8-11. In the years between the two World Wars, a new aesthetic of masculinity was represented by the muscular exhibitionism of the bodybuilder. As two-time title holder of "The World's Most Perfectly Developed Man," Charles Atlas promoted an exercise regimen that promised "the build of a HE-MAN." Ad 1936.

with suspicion as subversively narcissistic, meaning gay. Rugged facial good looks epitomized by Rock Hudson and a trim but thoroughly *clothed* body were the ideal in this era of repression and conformity.

Following the Peacock Revolution of the 1960s and 1970s, an increasing number of men joined gyms and took up jogging, roller skating, or riding ten-speed bicycles. Movie stars like Arnold Schwarzenegger and Sylvester Stallone inspired average, middle-class men to pursue workouts with aesthetic goals of a sculpted, muscular body. Men's magazines, menswear catalogs, and advertising began to show male models in this new masculine aesthetic. Store mannequins were sculpted with delineated pecs and abs to reflect the change in ideals of masculine beauty. The postmodern man now confronted the new image of the slim, muscular male body at every turn in mass media and mass marketing. "The male torso is the new, pansexual symbol of health—a crossover image that appeals to men and women, young and old," observed *Adweek* in 1999.[22] Ironically, though, according to researchers such as Martin Levine and Erick Alvarez, this new aesthetic of a trim, muscular body emerged from the gay rights movement in the 1970s when a "clone culture adopted a more hypermasculine affect"—including the cult of muscles—to negate the "swish" stereotype of the effeminate homosexual.[23] Nevertheless, more than ever, American manhood was measured and defined by the new body ideal. (Figure 8-12.)

In tandem with the emergence of the muscular aesthetic was the development of complementary phallic fashions. Flugel had noted in 1930 that phallic exhibitionism was not new to men's dress—most particularly the exaggerated padding of the codpiece or "phallic substitutes" such as the pointed toes of poulaines or the pointed sugarloaf hats and liripipe hoods of the Renaissance. Such "phallic symbolism," which was "to draw attention to the genital organs," had become more subtle in the masculine dress code of Flugel's era but was nonetheless discernible.[24] The tailored suit with its erect peaked lapels and deep V-front cut of the jacket like an arrow directing the eye toward the crotch combined with the verticality of a necktie, a sturdy walking stick, an upright breast pocket kerchief, and emphatically pointed wingtips conveyed a phallic power. More blatant was the creased crown hat, which in shadow profile resembled the glans penis. And even in the twenty-first century, subtleties of men's phallocentric dress still harken back to the Renaissance with the revived razor-toe shoe, a contemporary interpretation of the poulaine, and pointed skicaps that replicate the liripipe. These "penis substitutes," as sociologist Tim Edwards proposed, serve as "the fetishization of men's fashion...through the hyper-masculinization of other parts of the male body....The penis was, necessarily, never seen though constantly invoked and empowered through the implication of the phallus."[25] Thus, phallocentrism as a representation of masculine power and potency has remained a cultural construct reinforced and expressed by dress.

With the widely variable masculine identities of postmodernist pluralism and the sexualization of men's bodies and men's clothing, phallic symbolism also took on a literal meaning. As men increasingly spent many hours in fitness regimens to develop an ideal muscular physique, they sought ways to exhibit the results—a display of their manly achievement. Straight men of the 1980s adopted the hypermasculine looks of the 1970s gay clones and donned skintight jeans or short shorts, ripped muscle shirts and tank tops, and clingy knits of all styles. Coinciding with this

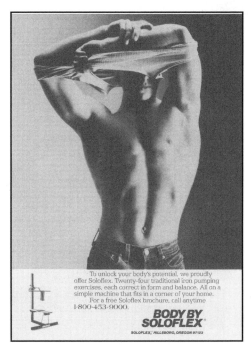

Figure 8-12. The postmodern male revived an interest in the muscular aesthetic. Millions of men joined gyms and purchased home exercise equipment to achieve the ideal slim, sculpted body. Ad 1983.

Figure 8-13. Beginning in the 1960s, the eroticism of the sexualized young male body became a focus of men's underwear marketing. Previously, photos of male underwear models were heavily airbrushed to disguise any nipple show-through or genital articulation. By the twenty-first century, images of men's underwear in ads and editorials became explicit, virtually to the point of nudity. Left, airbrushed photo from a Montgomery Ward catalog, 1957; right and below, ads 2007–2009.

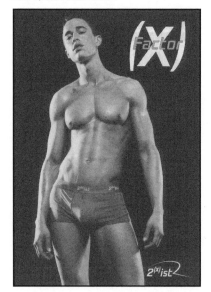

phallocentric exhibitionism was the entry into the menswear market of more gay and women designers such as Gianni Versace, Giorgio Armani, Donna Karan, and Jhane Barnes. Armani, especially, is credited with deconstructing the men's suit and transforming men's fashions in the late 1970s. Fashion historian Harold Koda noted: "Armani emphasized the sexuality of his clothes in a way that had never been done before....Trousers were loose but revealing. Suits were tailored to flatter and flaunt. Fabrics had a sheerness that was barely acceptable even in women's fashion."[26] Clothes like those from Armani and Versace that fluidly revealed the male form were now added to the narcissistic male's wardrobe of form-fitting designer jeans, knitwear, underwear, and swimwear. "Even an ordinary pair of blue jeans or white underpants can be a sexual fetish if it seems to hold a big penis," concluded Valerie Steele.[27] In 2003, a TV commercial for Old Spice Body Spray featured a woman executive remarking to a young man in tight pants delivering a parcel: "nice package." Phallocentrism had seemingly come full circle—from the subtle symbolism of the ditto suit constructs back again to the literal exhibitionism of the male genitals as in the Renaissance.

Perhaps nowhere is the literal exhibitionism of the penis more pronounced than in underwear marketing—from five-story-high billboards to TV commercials to page after page of color images in magazines and catalogs. Whereas photos of men in their underwear prior to the 1960s were heavily airbrushed to conceal any genital definition, men's underwear ads of the postmodern decades were explicitly erotic, emphasizing the sexualized body consciousness of a significant segment of American men. (Figure 8-13.) Even brand names of underwear evoked the unabashed emphasis on the genital package: Cocksox, Baskit, Priape. Models posed provocatively, expressing the self-awareness and self-confidence of their exceptional bodies, good looks, and sexual desirability. Women's studies professor Susan Bordo wrote that these images of the sexualized muscular male seemed to deliberately invite her to linger over them and provoked her into "erotic consciousness."[28] These specimens of male physical perfection were aware of the effect of the phallic power of their genital exhibitionism. The effect on women, whether through viewing a photo or seeing such men in person, was unadulterated sexual attraction; on other (straight) men, the effect was one of dominance, leaving the competition who could not measure up feeling inadequate.

By the end of the twentieth century, the heightened visibility of masculine self-expression through a buff body, fashion bravado, and haute living set the stage for a new American male. Enter the metrosexual into the landscape of masculine pluralism. *GQ* editor Mark Simpson defines the metrosexual as "a young man with money to spend, living in or within easy reach of a metropolis, because that's where all the best shops, clubs, gyms, and hairdressers are."[29] Twenty years earlier, the American Gigolo's impeccably tailored Armani wardrobe had been an extroverted expression of his business self while his tastefully designed apartment, superbly accoutered with designer furniture and coordinating accessories, was an introverted expression of his private self. At the beginning of the new millennium, taste and style was worthy of a public display for the narcissistic heterosexual male: body, clothes, job, car, home. Even trophy wives and orthodontically perfected children were accessories. By their nature, qualities of refinement and sophistication capture attention, and they set men apart from those whom they view as inferior specimens. The two brothers in the TV sitcom *Frasier* (1993-2004) were the epitome of the natural metrosexual—urban, erudite, stylish, cultured, and supercilious. They were undeniably heterosexual, a point the story lines often overemphasized, yet they loved opera, literature, art, antiques, fine dining, travel, and smart clothing—"sissified" interests previously associated primarily with "swish" gay men. They eschewed rough contact sports, strenuous outdoor activities, and manual labor, none of which

Figure 8-14. Pluralistic manhood in the twenty-first century included a broad spectrum of definitions for masculinity ranging from cliché mainstream stereotypes to all varieties of nonconformist individualists. In 2006, J. C. Penney's ad for BVD underwear is a tongue-in-check representation of a faux men's magazine cover depicting a "regular dude" with headlines of interest to him. He wears baggy boxers and a rumpled tank undershirt proving he is no metrosexual, and his shaggy, unkempt hair and choice of snack foods indicates he is not a body conscious narcissist.

impeded their appeal to women. As typical metrosexuals, they were comfortable in expressing their manhood through a superior intellect and sophisticated lifestyle. The big brain of the metrosexual was an alternative phallocentric ideal for the new millennium. Although the term "metrosexual" quickly became passé—evolving into more benign forms such as "metro male"—refined narcissism was an established masculine identity that many men wore comfortably.

Despite the emergence of the body-conscious sexualized male with his underwear model muscles and the sexually ambiguous metrosexual, "Neanderthal macho" continued to thrive as a masculine identity in pluralistic millennial America, noted *Fitness RX* editor, Steve Blechman. "Think a bit more of an unshaven, unkempt look." On Madison Avenue, the look and attitude of "the manly man...the anti-metrosexual" that was captured in advertising became known as "menergy," a direct appeal to a marketing segment of "bona fide fellas."[30]

After more than fifty years of postmodernist pluralism, to attempt an academic definition of masculinity in the 2010s would yield an impossibly broad array of different and often contradictory ideas and ideals. Within certain social silos, some certitudes of manliness have remained constant, becoming safe and easy identities, even clichés, for some men. (Figure 8-14.) For most men, though, the cultural debate about what constitutes a man in the new millennium has blurred what were once absolutes. Within the realm of pluralistic masculinities are overlapping tenets of behavior and transitory dress identities. At one end of the identity meter is the constancy and continuum of the business suit, reassuring to many men in its representative principle and utility. In the vast middle of dress options is a host of personal styles that fluidly bleed into each other, providing men with a freedom of self-expression that our postrevolution era forefathers could not have imagined. And at the extreme opposite of the standardized suit tradition is iconoclasm. The Peacock Revolution launched a deconstruction of masculine identities that balkanized into diversities of personal expression ranging from frilly Edwardian revivalism to punk, goth, and grunge. Even that most taboo of all forms of attire for men, the skirt, was wrenched from women's exclusivity and offered in menswear design collections as early as the 1960s. (See Figures 7-9 and 8-34.)

As postmodern concepts of masculinity continue to metamorphose in an ever increasingly global culture, men's notions of self and identity are destined to face relentless new challenges, opportunities, and for some men, threats. The metaphysical cleaving of postmodern pluralism will ensure an unending variety of qualifying options for manhood as the coming generations seek their own distinctive identity and expression in dress.

Pluralistic Tribalism 1980–Present

The stylistic pluralism of American men's dress and identity since 1980 has been the subject of numerous books, magazine articles, research studies, and museum exhibits in recent years. Even as early as 1981, *GQ* observed: "Today, fashion isn't merely in a state of disarray in terms of chronology and evolution—actually, there's little of it—but it also lacks the totality of any single agreed-upon ideal....The sheer open-endedness of contemporary ideals means that personal style has become the yardstick of fashionability, rather than up-to-datedness."[31] But the editors were uncertain how to label the divergent repertories of style that were the result of the revolutionary changes in men's dress of the 1960s and 1970s. Among the general categories they identified for the 1980s were "terribly predictable prep dressing" typified by classics such as Lacoste shirts and Burberry coats; "survival clothes" like L.L. Bean duck boots paired with Icelandic sweaters that "appear somewhat ludicrous in the wilds of shopping malls"; military surplus looks that "smack somewhat of the faded sixties"; Western themes inspired by John Travolta in *Urban Cowboy*; "clone dressing" of leather bomber's jackets, sweatshirts, jeans, and construction boots; "American Boy," a tousled look of Fair Isle sweaters and loafers; and, lastly, the "International Star" who "dresses around the globe" including looks ranging from Gianni Versace and Fiorucci to Calvin Klein.[32]

The following year, though, *GQ* recognized a chronology of postmodern "youth cults" (largely British) in which "enormous numbers of kids are bonded stylistically, musically, sociologically, and sometimes ideologically."[33] Tribal pluralism in America since 1980 has run two parallel courses: music groupies and trend followers. The music groupie emulated the fragmented, thematic looks of pop music idols but usually with minimal adherence to the social ideas and behavior of the stars; the trend follower adopted whatever traditionalist masculine identity was current such as the power chauvinism of the hard-edged corporate yuppie of the 1980s or the softer, style-conscious metrosexual of the early 2000s. The music groupie is youth-oriented; the trend follower is more broadly demographic. Whereas with earlier counterculture groups such as the beatniks of the 1950s and the hippies of the 1960s and 1970s, clothing was often a freeform self-expression of personal rebellion, especially through rejection of dress and identity conventions, post-1980 music groupies and trend followers are just the opposite. They are, instead, conformists who dress to reinforce a specific social role and identity. They and their exclusive looks are the heirs, in a straight line, to similar herds from previous eras: the manifest-destiny Victorians in their blue serge sack suits; the beefy imperialist Edwardians in their oversized, overpadded suits; the Depression-era breadwinners in their athletic drape suits; or the post–World War II Ivy League conformists in their gray flannel suits.

As a possible subcategory of the trend follower are consumers with a social agenda. Their dress objectives are less about visual style identity than the substance of clothing. For example, PETA members (People for the Ethical Treatment of Animals) "believe that animals are the moral equals of human beings and should not be exploited by humans for any purpose."[34] On the extreme side, this credo includes a ban on wearing clothing made of fur (including fake furs since they perpetuate the fashion), any animal skin, wool (shearing is painful to animals), feathers, silk (worms are boiled alive), pearls, bone, or ivory. Similarly, the Ecos or Greens prefer eco-friendly clothing made of natural fibers and dyes. They also avoid certain brands and types of personal hygiene and grooming products produced by makers whose manufacturing processes may be ecologically questionable. Unlike the music groupies and trend followers, though, neither PETA members nor Ecos conform to a tribal look.

In 1994, London's Victoria and Albert Museum presented an exhibit of fifty years of subcultural clothing. In the post-1980 era, the curators identified ten tribal categories that also occurred simultaneously in America including hip-hop or B-Boy, punk, gay (clones), goth, grunge, preppy, rockabilly, skater, skinhead, and techno or cyberstyle.[35] Add to this pluralistic tribal list a recurring popularity of Western looks, the various cachets of designer brands, and an endless resurgence of retro or revival styles to round out the dress and identity tribalism of fin de siècle and new millennium dressing:

• **Hip-hop or B-Boy**: Hip-hop is a rhyming rap recitation blended with sung choruses. The name B-Boy may have derived from the rap band the Beastie Boys. "Hip-hop fashion is one of appropriation," noted a style editor in 1992. "Typically, a prominent B-Boy will take a shine to a perfectly ordinary article of clothing—a Los Angeles Raiders jacket, an anorak, a pair of boxy, oversized glasses–and, by repeatedly wearing it in public, transform the item into a staple of every homey's wardrobe."[36] (Figure 8-15.) Among the ordinary clothing identified with B-Boys dress are Kangol logo hats, Adidas shoes worn unlaced, oversized quilted parkas, baggy Ben Davis work jeans, and big gold chains and pendants known as bling-bling (later shortened to just "bling"). In the 1990s, the B-Boys began to wear their loose, baggy jeans pushed low on the hips, revealing the tops of colorfully patterned underwear. Just as the look was becoming passé at the beginning of the new century, school and community dress policies prohibiting the look prompted a rebellious resurgence among ethnic teens.

• **Punk**: As noted in the previous chapter, American punks of the 1970s derived their look from the original punks in Britain. Over there, "groups of disaffected, brutalistic and carefully styled kids...perfected their alienation and announced loudly and obnoxiously what they presumed to be Britain's terminal decline."[37] Their music idols were the Ramones and the Sex Pistols, led by Johnny Rotten and Sid Vicious. The "neopunks," reported *Rolling Stone* in 1985, "slam-dance" to the "two-chord rock" of Black Flag, Minutemen, and the Meat Puppets.[38] Urban American teens who opted for the attention-getting punk look eschewed the Brits' protest attire made of black trash bags and soiled, ankle-high tartan plaid trousers, preferring instead all-black clothing accented with metal chains and hardware; metal-studded leather jackets, dog collars, belts, and cuff bracelets; and thick-soled workboots or dirty sneakers. They continued to gel their hair into vividly hued spikes and even some crests or mohawks. By the 1990s, the multiple ear piercings expanded to other parts of the body including eyebrows, lips, tongues, noses, navels, nipples, and even genitals. Tattoos were increasingly popular with punks, especially images and messages with shock value.

• **Goth**: Short for Gothic, the dress and attitude of the Goths of the 1980s were a reaction to the colorful and vivacious disco culture. Their dress was a funereal derivative of the punk look. Trim, fitted clothing was all black except for accents of deep purple. Heavy leather belts, chokers, pendant necklaces, earrings, and rings were embellished with religious or occult motifs. Dyed black hair was usually spiky or closely cropped. Deathly pale complexions were accentuated with white powder. Some men wore black lipstick, nail polish, and thick eyeliner. They read somber poetry and occult novels while listening to the music of Bauhaus, Dead Can Dance, and Sisters of Mercy.

• **Grunge**: The grunge phenomenon of the early 1990s originated in

Figure 8-15. *Hip-hop or B-Boy dressing featured an appropriation of everyday articles of clothing popularized by repeated wearing in public. A B-Boy's identity was sustained by choosing ill-fitting, oversized versions of ordinary clothing or by modifying standards such as removing laces from branded athletic shoes. B-Boy in oversized FOG parka, cargo jeans, and knit cap, 1996.*

the Pacific Northwest where "frustrated students and minimum-wage slaves banded together and created a lifestyle, ever cynical and utilitarian that more accurately reflected their conditions."[39] Like the hippies of a generation earlier, these "lost Gen X'ers" rejected the comfortable, middle-class materialism of their parents. The grunge look was a nonchalant "hobo" casualness assembled with layers of ratty sweaters, torn or patched flannel shirts, faded rock tour T-shirts, baggy corduroy pants or jeans, baseball caps, and clunky Doc Martens. Seattle-based rock bands like Pearl Jam and Nirvana popularized the grunge look with their videos and national tours.

• **Preppy**: The preppies of the past few decades have been the heirs of the 1950s Ivy League look. Named for the plain, conservative clothing allowed by prep (preparatory) school dress codes, the preppy look includes basic navy blazers, striped ties in school colors, button down collar shirts, gray flannel trousers, and Weejums. The quintessential casual uniform of the preppy has been the polo shirt (double-layered in contrasting colors in the 1980s and with the collar flipped up in the 1990s) worn over a white crewneck T-shirt and with chinos and deck shoes. (Figure 8-16.)

• **Rockabilly**: The cult of the rockabillies stemmed from a music revivalist blend of 1950s and 1960s rock-and-roll mixed with country-western sounds. In the 1980s, these bands included Kid Creole and Blue Rondo. Rockabillies had a dual look either of selected retro-fifties and Carnaby Street styles or rural Americana. The preferred jeans were relaxed-fit Levis 501s with denim jackets to match over white crewneck undershirts or well-worn plaid flannel workshirts. For the retro fan, authentic bowling shirts imprinted with names of business sponsors topped the baggy, high-waisted trousers of Ricky Ricardo. Quiffed hair à la Elvis 1955, Carnaby Street granny glasses with blue or yellow lenses, and two-tone saddle oxfords completed the retro rockabilly look. Sometimes the looks, like the music, were cross-over blended.

• **Skater**: The skateboarder look that had emerged in the 1950s and 1960s along the coasts simulated the styles of surfers including Hawaiian print shirts and baggy jams. By the 1990s, though, televised national skateboard competitions reached a broad audience of teen boys who wanted to emulate the looks of top performing alpha skaters. Baggy jeans and oversized rugbies were favored. In the early 2000s, to better differentiate themselves from the baggy, hip-hop looks of urban ethnic groups, white teen skaters opted for the new low-rise, slim-fit jeans topped with button-front shirts worn open to flap dramatically in the breezy wake of a fast-rolling skateboard.

• **Skinhead**: The cult of skinheads, like punk, originated from the lower working classes of Britain. The groups of ultra-right wing young men resented hippies (whom they regarded as lazy), immigrants (whom they felt took their jobs), and yuppies (of whom they were jealous). They often expressed their anger through "agro" (aggression) by bashing minorities "on their turf" and starting fights at soccer matches. The most distinctive element of their dress was their sheared hair cropped so closely that the shine of the pate gleamed. Shirts were basic discount store styles, tucked into tight, high-rolled jeans or pants with high-water cuffs either cut short or rehemmed to reveal their heavy boots. Rather than belts, skinheads preferred narrow suspenders made with an X- or Y-shape in

Figure 8-16. The epitome of the preppy look was the polo shirt—whether emblazoned with an alligator or polo pony logo—worn over a white crewneck T-shirt. Double polo shirts in contrasting colors by Ralph Lauren, 1986.

Figure 8-17. The techno tribalist of the 1980s compiled his high-tech look from mainstream styles such as nylon parachute pants, screenprinted T-shirts, and military-inspired accessories available at young men's boutique chains. T-shirt, parachute pants, and metal mesh belt from Oak Tree, 1984.

the back. Thick-soled workboots called bovver boots (after their pronunciation of "bother") completed the uniform.

In America, the look of the skinheads was appropriated by neo-Nazi and neo-fascist militia groups who promoted a racist "white power" agenda. Although American skinheads had favorite bands—notably Skrewdiver, Iron Cross, and Forced Reality—these young men were ideologue trend followers in their choice of dress rather than music groupies.

• **Techno- or Cyberstyle:** The techno- or cyberstyle of the 1980s and 1990s was a sci-fi-meets-B-Boy look worn by rave scene teens who danced to the frenzied rhythm of industrial-sounding, synthesizer music by Circus Bedlam or Spiral Tribe. Their favorite movie was the 1926 silent film *Metropolis* by Fritz Lang. The preferred clothing was made of high-tech materials and accessorized with army surplus or industrial worker gear. In the 1980s, they adopted parachute cargo pants and jackets made of silky, shiny nylon blend textiles that were quilted and multistitched into hard-edged spacesuit looks. (Figure 8-17.) In the 1990s, the costumes for movies such as *Kika* (1993) designed by Jean Paul Gaultier, inspired cyberpunks to embellish their clothes with body-molded plastic pieces, electrical wires, silvery CDs, computer chip circuitry, and similar tech hardware. Neoprene boots with thick rubber cleats, fingerless weightlifting gloves, and skater's knee and elbow guards were sometimes added for a futuristic military combat look.

• **Urban Cowboy:** In 1980, John Travolta two-stepped across the dance floor of Gilley's megabar in the movie *Urban Cowboy*. He wore snug, boot cut jeans, yoke front shirts, cowboy boots, and Stetson hat. The standardized Western look had never diminished in the True West, nor in country-Western entertainment centers like Nashville and Branson, Missouri. But since 1980, the popularity of various designer versions of the Western look resurged every few years even in East Coast urbania, often inspired by TV series like *Dallas* (1978–92) and movies like *Silverado* (1985) and *The Quick and the Dead* (2003). (Figure 8-18.) Even President Reagan, who was never a cowboy, notes Pulitzer Prize writer Alison Lurie, often wore "Western gear of the Good-Guy type, reminding us—and possibly himself—of his mythological role of the noble cowboy."[40] In 1988, Ralph Lauren launched his Chaps cologne with a multimedia ad campaign promoting "the spirit of the West that's inside every man." In addition to the typical Western fare of yoke front shirts, boot cut jeans, and cowboy boots, updated versions of dusters and fringed jackets were periodically reintroduced with silhouettes and detailing of the time. In the 1980s, that meant broad, heavily padded shoulders and jeweltone hues; in the 1990s, trim fits and natural shoulders; in the 2000s, microfiber and polymide fabrics. (Color Plate 31.)

• **Gay Clones:** The dress of the gay clone as identified by *GQ* in 1981 and presented a decade later in the Victoria and Albert Museum exhibit was viewed as a "play on and parody of 'accepted' notions of dress, gender and sexuality."[41] But the clone was much more than that. In his study of gay men's dress in the twentieth century, Shaun Cole examines the "macho man clones and the development of a masculine stereotype." As the gay rights movement gained momentum in the 1970s, asserts Cole, many gay men strived to counter the public perception that "to be homosexual means not to be masculine....As a positive move away from effeminate stereotypes, and in search of an 'out' masculine image, gay men

Figure 8-18. The urban cowboy look consistently recurs every few years, usually inspired by stylish Western-themed movies or popular TV programs. Western fare is often updated with contemporary silhouettes such as the big shoulders of the 1980s, the trim fits of the 1990s, or new technotextiles of the 2000s. Left, urban cowboy look by Calvin Klein, 1986; right, Chaps ad, 1988; below, Western duster from J. Peterman, 1988.

The J. Peterman coat.
Unintentionally very flattering.

looked towards traditional images of rugged masculinity, such as the cowboy or lumberjack, for their dress inspiration....As this new masculinity became more popular and more gay men adopted the look, these men became known as clones."[42] For humorist Clark Henley, this appropriation of hypermasculine dress and behavior was simply "a whole new drag," the tenets of which he codified in his 1982 *Butch Manual*.[43] One of the key distinctions, though, was that gay clones rejected the nonchalance of most straight men's approach to dress—the lack of attention to fit or color and pattern coordination or grooming. Instead, gay clones "kept their hair short, beards and mustaches clipped, and clothing fitted and matched." Their machismo attitude and the carefully tailored dress of their cowboys, lumberjacks, construction workers, bikers, and preppy jocks were an eroticization of the male ideal, a self-conscious effort "to make one appear sexy and attractive to other men."[44] By the end of the decade, though, to be called a clone was a put-down, an accusation of being phony and lacking imagination. Ironically, thirty years later, the Oscar-winning film (for original screenplay) *Milk* (2008) featured actors such as James Franco portraying mustachioed macho gay men of the 1970s, which inspired a revival of the look with some Gen Yers.

• **Metrosexual:** The archetypically male gay clones of the 1970s and 1980s blurred the line between that great divide in American masculine identity. As a result, straight men unwittingly began to adopt elements and attitudes of gay dress. "Many men don't realize it, but [Manhattan's] Christopher Street is our sartorial Ellis Island" advised *Esquire* in 1993.

Mall meatheads today dress like the gay clones of fifteen or twenty years ago. In the '70s, gay men chose to wear single earrings. A

Figure 8-19. Beginning in the mid-1990s, straight men who were fashion and style conscious came to be identified as metrosexuals. In the early 2000s, a proliferation of style guides were produced to advise this new breed of American male in his self-indulgent pursuits. Metrosexual style guides and studies by Michael Flocker, 2003; Peter Hyman, 2004; David Coad, 2008.

decade or so later, decorated earrings and simple studs had passed so completely into mass culture that a lot of gay men were avoiding earrings as infra dig [undignified] and too much identified with beefy suburban boys. Even the most testosterone-laden high-school-quarterback type from the 'burbs can be seen wearing his earring, gold chain, butch haircut, oversize athletic gear, generic jeans, and work boots or high-tops, with Calvins hoisted into view.[45]

Ironically, these and other similar forms of masculine dress spearheaded by gay men had originated as identity codes and communications to each other that became diluted and lost in translation by straights. Nevertheless, as *GQ* noted in its review of the confusingly pluralistic menswear from the runway showings in Milan and New York in 1993, the designers rely on "a few fashion sophisticates—homosexual men, often—who act as filters by wearing the pieces that fall outside mainstream tastes but which over time will percolate to the mass culture."[46]

By the mid-1990s, that percolation of style consciousness so long associated with gay men began to be unabashedly experienced by a new breed of straight men who became identified as metrosexuals. (Figure 8-19.) As noted previously in this chapter, the satirical term "metrosexual" originated in 1994 by cultural journalist Mark Simpson to identify the emerging self-indulgent, consumer-oriented male. The new millennium's metrosexual was, in essence, "a narcissist, persuaded by consumer culture to desire to be what he sees in glossy magazines...a sensitive guy who went to malls, bought magazines and spent freely to improve his personal appearance."[47] In the early 2000s, dozens of style guides were published to ease the anxieties of straight men who enjoyed the indulgent luxuriousness of the metrosexual "while simultaneously keeping homos safely on the other side of the divide," observed *Details* in 2005. "That's certainly the impetus behind...*The Metrosexual Guide to Style*—a handbook that's basically all about how to be gayer without turning into a fag."[48] In fact, editors began to use alternative terms like "metro male" to preserve the meaning for their straight readers, but excise the original play on and derivation of homosexual.

Logo PLUs: Some men who were seeking an identity through dress but were not affiliated with a youth cult or lacked the originality and style bravado to be a metrosexual, designer logos were an easy option.

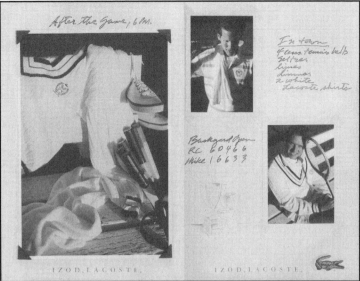

Figure 8-20. In the age of multicultural and counter-cultural pluralism in menswear in the closing decades of the century, many identity-challenged men found comfort in the marketed cachet of the branded designer label. Logo wear conveyed the image and attitude of certain lifestyles and provided a sense of identity as well as a tribal kinship with like-minded consumers. Left, collegiate "relaxed elegance" from Sisley, 1987; right, the legacy of Lacoste, 1988; below, the exclusivity of the Polo University Club label, 1992.

Although logo wear had a long history, most notably the Lacoste alligator originating in the 1920s, the promotion and marketing of designer names in American menswear only began to emerge in the late 1960s. By the 1980s, many designers had established certain cachets that conveyed the image of specific lifestyles that appealed to niche market segments. The reliable consistency of such logo wear was comforting for men who bought into the image marketing of the designer label and thus joined the tribe of logo PLUs (People Like Us). The unmistakable country club look of Ralph Lauren was reinforced with the embroidered polo pony; the upscale active sports enthusiast was marked by Fila logos on his clothing and sports accoutrement; and the sophisticated urbanite was evident by his display of Donna Karan's DKNY acronym. (Figure 8-20.) Ralph Lauren even marketed a line of sportswear labeled the Polo University Club, giving its wearers a special sense of exclusive club membership. These external logos were tribal markings emblematic of the social attitude and status of the wearer and a visual communication to other like-minded PLUs.

Suits and Formal Dress 1980–Present

By the beginning of the Greed Decade of the 1980s, the business suit took on a new meaning. Dress and identity in the office suites of corporate America were a statement of power and aggression. Editorials in men's magazines—and fashion advertising copy—throughout the era were couched in battle terms. "When duty calls," declared a 1982 report, "captains of industry slip into the universally recognized emblem of

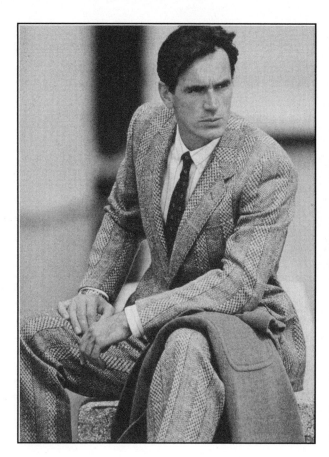

Figure 8-21. The broad, shaped shoulders of the 1980s power suit asserted the corporate warrior's confidence and seriousness. Left, Italian-styled pattern mixing by Canali, 1984; right, four-button double-breasted suit by Hugo Boss, 1983; right,

authority: the business suit. The nucleus of corporate style, a finely fashioned, suitably fitted suit projects the confidence and cool that's essential in the heat of boardroom battle."[49] TV programs such as *Dynasty* and movies like *Wall Street* presented to the American masses the look of the new power brokers. Even without dialog, the dress of John Forsythe's Blake Carrington and Michael Douglas' Gordon Gekko were an unequivocal identity of their alpha male status.

Looking back from a decade later, *GQ* defined the quintessential power suit of the eighties as a "shoulder-padded uniform that fairly proclaimed, 'Look at me,' I've expensively riveted myself together for today's business battles....The bigger the suit, the bigger the man."[50] But unlike the tight armor plating of the rigidly constructed and padded suits of the 1970s, the silhouettes of the 1980s were a blending of Italian style and English drape suit tailoring. The naturalness of the Italian cut and craftsmanship coupled with the use of soft fabrics allowed the body to inhabit the suit rather than be constricted and shaped by it. Where previously padding, interfacings, and hard lapels virtually adhered to the male torso, the softly fluid fit of the power suit allowed the man a comfortable freedom of movement despite the broad, shaped shoulders. Suit trousers became more generously cut with a fit snug at the waist rather than the hips.

Although the silhouette of the eighties power suit was distinctive, the details were much more variable. Most rolled notch lapels extended to just short of half way to the armscye seams, but some styles favored by junior execs were slightly narrower. For the veteran Wall Street warrior, an assertive choice was the four- or six-button double-breasted jacket with peaked lapels that spread broadly across the manly chest.

For the most part, caution and subtlety in fabric choices were more critical than silhouette. Gray or navy wool was always the safest, but the pin stripe was omnipresent throughout the eighties. In the creative executive suites of ad agencies or publishing houses, the successful young entrepreneur might dare to choose one of the Italian suits made with an edgy, boldly patterned fabric—but not too often. (Figure 8-21.)

Following the 1987 stock market crash and the subsequent deep recession, the exaggerated shape of the power suit began to diminish. By 1990, the suit had deflated into a more natural fit:

> Gone are the huge padded shoulders and the roomy jackets with their severe, angular lines. In their place: a narrower, less constructed silhouette with natural shoulders and a slightly suppressed waist. The higher armholes make the jacket's shape trimmer; the easy drape keeps it from being tight. Jackets are long, and the overall feeling is more relaxed than that of the typically beefy eighties power suit.[51]

Although jackets had been pared down even before the end of the eighties, trousers remained high-waisted and billowy until the early nineties when the waistband was lowered, legs narrowed, and hips became more fitted.

The three most influential forces on suit styles of the nineties were Milan, London, and revivalisms.

The two titans of menswear design from Italy were undeniably Armani and Versace. From these two designers came styles of masculine dress and identity as polarized as national politics. "If Armani is the inscrutable shaman for whom even eating represents excess, Gianni Versace, his great equal and adversary, is the fashion world's gourmand, wearing his heart on each of his wildly printed sleeves." Where Armani recognized that "men use their wardrobes to repress as much as to express themselves," Versace designed clothes for men who "like the rest of the world to gawk at them."[52] The classic Armani suit of the 1990s was trim, subtly shaped, and masterfully tailored in neutral tones. In contrast, Versace offered unconstructed suits in bright vermilion or jackets and vests in sapphire blue with slim striped trousers.

From London came an influence of style reminiscent of the 1920s and 1930s: pattern mixing. Although style guides and fashion editorials frequently offered advice on how to wear mixed patterns, American men were reluctant. Even when provided examples in store displays and color photos in catalogs or ads like that in Figure 8-22, most American men were not convinced.

Retro styles and revivalisms dominated fashion in the 1990s. Headers and editorials from *GQ* showed the constantly shifting retro influences:

Figure 8-22. Among the influences on American men's suit styles from abroad was the British penchant for striking pattern mixing. Most American men, though, were uneasy with how to successfully achieve mixed patterns without appearing clownish and, consequently, avoided the effort. Pattern mixing by Ralph Lauren, 1991.

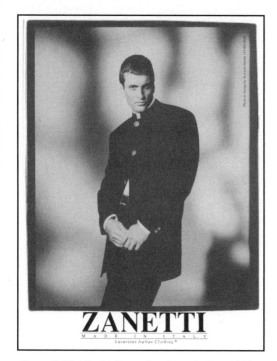

Figure 8-23. The Nehru jacket from the late 1960s was among the many retro looks that have constantly recurred from the 1980s through today. Nehru jacket revival by Zanetti, 1996.

"Back to the future...Menswear designers have looked to the forties for inspiration." (1992)

"A thirties staple, the three-button suit, makes a comeback." (1993)

"The '70s are back." (1996)

"Ultramod suits in the spirit of Dr. No." (1996)

"In the past two years, we've seen clothes from every decade since the 1930s."[53]

In some instances the retro look might be as simple as the brief revival of the ticket pocket or the hip-hugging ventless skirt in the early nineties to the revisiting of an iconic look such as the Nehru jacket of the 1960s. (Figure 8-23.)

By the end of the 1990s, the dominance of the ultraslim, fitted looks of the 1960s began to dominate men's suit styling. "New shapes" and "new rules" for dressing correctly were now in effect, advised *GQ* in 1997. Like the youthquake styles of thirty years earlier, the new shapes had "less sack and more classical statue." One of the key revivals once so popular with the young peacock male was the one-button closure—"a sharp, formal-looking silhouette guaranteed to give you that chiseled, wasp-waisted look."[54] And despite the many revivals of the time, sartorial rules remained for the proper suit:

1. The jacket hem should be about mid-palm with the arms at rest.
2. The tie should never extend past the belt buckle.
3. About 1/2 inch to 3/4 inch of the collar should be visible at the jacket collar.
4. Precisely 1/2 inch of the shirt cuff should show at the wrist.[55]

But as most designers will assert, the rules were made to be broken, and by the beginning of the twenty-first century, the transition of the suit silhouette had already evolved dramatically.

The first decade of the new millennium was an era of the short, slim suit. "Not since the early '60s have suits been cut so short and trim," noted *GQ* in 2004.[56] (Figure 8-24 and Color Plate 35.) As in the 1960s, the new suit silhouettes were a look for the young and thin. "Here's what you should know these days about the fit of your suit," suggested a "style anatomy" editorial in 2006. "It should be slim and trim—and shorter too. Not tight or ill-fitting, but precise. When a suit is worn this way it makes a statement without relying on loud colors or patterns. It's a confident look that speaks volumes." Although the editors advised against a fit that is too tight, still, to achieve the trim look, they suggested "going down a suit size."[57] The danger with the new slim silhouette, though, warned *Project Runway* style guru Tim Gunn was the "Pee-wee Herman" look of "shrunken jacket and shrunken pants."[58]

In addition to the slim cut of the new suits, details were thinner, narrower, and smaller as well. Lapels were sixties' narrow, and pocket flaps were shortened. Trousers hugged the hips and thighs, and waistbands were lowered and narrowed. Belts and ties were thinner, and shirt collars were reduced to complement the abbreviated cut of the suit. Curiously,

Figure 8-24. The new short, trim look for the new millennium suiting was actually a revival of the ultraslim, fitted styles of the 1960s. Single-breasted suit from Dior, 2007.

for one- and two-button jackets, a gap beneath the closed button and the belt buckle often resulted in a display of the tip of the tie and sometimes a flash of the shirt, which took the eye straight to a man's trouser front. (Color Plate 37.)

Other sixties suit revivals in the new millennium revisited the innovative experiments of Pierre Cardin, Paco Rabanne, and André Courréges. Design variations such as bal collars—or no collars—were a tribute to the peacock individualist in the distant age of revolution as well as a twentieth-century iconoclasm against the prevailing trend of slim and short suits. (Color Plate 35.)

One of the key developments in men's suiting that made possible the new trim, fitted silhouettes was the advancement in synthetic blended fabrics. At the end of the 1990s, high quality suits were commonly made of wool blended with about ten percent elastane, acetate, polyamide, or even Lycra and spandex. "Elastane and fibers like it are added to fabrics today for two reasons," advised a 1997 editorial. "First, they give wool a bit of resilience, which means no matter how long you wear your suit, its two pieces aren't going to bag like the borrowed clothes on a Bowery bum. Second, they give the garment stretch, which means it will move when you do."[59] (Figure 8-25.) By 2008, American textile manufacturers had perfected the production of fabrics woven from lightweight, high twist wool yarns. "To make the fabrics," reported *GQ*, "mills choose the finest, softest fibers, then coil two strands tightly together. This not only strengthens the material, it also makes it elastic, allowing the finished suits to bounce back and stay relatively wrinkle-free."[60]

Full dress eveningwear had virtually disappeared from the American social scene by World War II. The exception was a highly formal event such as a state visit or an embassy ball (or as the dress for a symphony orchestra conductor). During the New Gilded Age of the 1980s, formal attire enjoyed a brief resurgence. "The rich are no longer so self-conscious about looking rich," declared *Esquire* in 1985.[61] When the nouveau riche and old money rich reemerged during the exhibitionistic Reagan years, many new-agers scurried to tailors and referenced style guides for the rules of formal evening dress. The proper style of the tail coat and accessories "is engraved in stone," warned *Esquire*. "A red bow tie is neither clever nor attractive, just demented."[62] The correct assemblage of a tail coat suit had not changed in a century. The cutaway coat was always worn open over a white pique vest and a well-starched bosom shirt with winged collar. A white pique bow tie matched the vest. White kid gloves, black patent pumps, and silk top hat completed the archaic look. (Figure 8-26.)

For most American men, though, the tuxedo or dinner coat was considered formalwear. With the neoconservatism of the 1980s, the basic black tuxedo returned, and the peacock extravagance of sumptuous print fabrics, jeweltone colors, lavish embroidery, and ruffled shirts was happily forgotten. As with the tail coat, the rules for the tuxedo remained largely unchanged. With a single-breasted coat, a white, black, or colorfully brocaded vest was required. The cummerbund and coordinating tie were an acceptable alternative to the vest. The preferred bow tie was black, charcoal gray, or midnight blue—but never white. Most American men, though, preferred to personalize the somber look of the tuxedo with a print or richly colored tie to coordinate with a fancy vest or

Figure 8-25. As suits became more trim and fitted in the new century, makers increasingly used fabrics blended with the new synthetics for greater comfort and ease of movement. Haggar's "Has It" ad campaign of 2003 promoted their wool and Lycra suits with the message that "they move with you for added comfort."

Figure 8-26. During the New Gilded Age of the 1980s, the tail coat was briefly revived. Hand-tailored full dress from Saks Fifth Avenue, 1987.

The most extraordinary formalwear bears the mark of Lord West.

Figure 8-27. To the casual-minded American male, the tuxedo was widely regarded as formalwear. Although style guides provided specific rules for the correct tuxedo, many men often preferred to personalize the basic penguin look with colorful ties, cummerbunds, or vests. Left, shawl collar tuxedo with cummerbund from Redaelli, 1983; right, notch collar tuxedo with brocade vest from Lord West, 1990; below, slim cut tuxedo from Burberry, 2006.

cummerbund. (Figure 8-27.) As with men's business suits, the tuxedo followed the business suit silhouette trends of the day. In the 1980s, the dinner jacket shoulders were broad and padded though not as wide as most power suits. The tuxedo jacket and trousers narrowed in the 1990s and, by the 2000s, were made in short, trim versions with low-rise trousers.

Shirts 1980–Present

Dress shirts continued to be fitted into the early 1980s. As the first baby boomers turned forty in 1986, though, the fuller cut shirt regained dominance in American markets. Comfort, as always, was the guide for most men's clothing choices, particularly clothes that they spent a majority of their day wearing. Even as suit styles became more fitted and narrow in the 2000s, full cut dress shirts were still preferred. After all, most corporate men worked in shirt sleeves all day and only put on a jacket for special meetings or luncheons downtown. "American traditionalists have long sported a baggy aesthetic," noted *GQ's* "Style Guy" in 2003. Besides, since "a majority of Americans are overweight...guys think this bagginess disguises incipient corpulence."[63]

Fashion editorials and retailers continually promoted the idea of a wardrobe of Gatsby color-rich dress shirts. To prevent the typical American male from reverting back to a closet full of whites only, shirt makers continually refreshed color palettes every few years, fluctuating from earthtones to neutrals to brights and assorted combinations. Through the mid-1990s, stripes were the pattern of choice, ranging from fine pencil stripes to bold awning stripes, even some multicolored candy stripes. Petite prints, checks, plaids, tone-on-tones, and textured fabrics were occasional options but were not as popular as they had been in the 1960s and 1970s.

The basic spread collar was the most common followed closely by the traditional button down. In the early 1990s, variations like the wide cutaway spread collar (for the double Windsor knot), the round-edged club collar (in white against a contrasting body color or pattern), and the English eyelet (requiring a collar bar) were trendy. For a couple of years in the mid-1990s, some men rebelled—ever so slightly—against the standardized corporate uniform by wearing their button down collars unbuttoned. Other men opted for some unorthodox dress shirt variations such as Perry Ellis' shoulder pin-tucked sleeve. (Figure 8-28.)

Sportswear 1980–Present

Sportswear became more broadly pluralistic than any other category of menswear. When once the latest trends of sportswear appeared at the resorts first, and then became selectively assimilated into the wardrobes of the average American male, now casual dress could be assembled into an endless variety of personalized looks. For the everyday Joe who did not belong to one of the uniformed tribes previously discussed in this chapter, sportswear could be used as an expression of personal style, lifeways, or even day-to-day mood. And just to spice up their average looks, many ordinary guys might occasionally try a touch of unexpected whimsy—anything from choosing a sports shirt in an out-of-character color or print to piercing an ear to slipping a baseball cap on backward hip-hop style.

Inspiration for a man's personal style came from all directions—peers and social cliques, television and movies, the workplace, and particularly the street. Since the 1960s, "street smarts," as *Esquire* observed in 1984:

> set the pace for both the avant-garde and, eventually, those in the mainstream. While not expensive, [commercialized] streetwise fashion...should be worn with an unstudied sense of style. This approach often combines such diverse elements as topcoats with

Figure 8-28. To break the monotony of the standardized business uniform, some men opted for dress shirts in bold prints or colors, or perhaps even styles with unorthodox construction features such as Perry Ellis' shoulder pin-tuck sleeves. Ad, 1990.

Figure 8-29. As sportswear became increasingly pluralistic, many menswear retailers shifted their merchandising strategies to niche marketing, especially targeting the 18–24 age demographic. Abercrombie and Fitch catalogs, 1990s.

jeans, rolled trouser cuffs, shirts buttoned up without neckties, and even berets. What emerges is a relaxed and spontaneous way of dressing.[64]

And that unstudied sense of style and spontaneity that *Esquire* noted was the hallmark of the American male's casual dress made all the easier by the vast array of mass marketed sportswear styles from which to choose.

Because of the broad pluralism of sportswear, many ready-to-wear makers and retailers increasingly focused their merchandising strategies on niche marketing, particularly by age groups. The Gap, Benetton, Abercrombie and Fitch, Banana Republic, and other similar chains provided a safer, more generalized look for young men in the 18–24 age demographic. (Figure 8-29.) Street looks were distilled and tamed: baggy jeans were given fake street looks with acid- and stone-washed finishes; "worn" T-shirts bore non-controversial captions and images; khaki cargo shorts and pants were standard commodities; board shorts changed prints year-to-year but kept the oversized fit. For thirty-something (and up) men, the heirs to the old haberdasheries of yore were Bachrach's, L.L. Bean, Eddie Bauer, and the sedate men's shops within department stores. There a standardized and predictable inventory of relaxed-fit jeans and chinos, bermuda shorts, knit polos and rugbies, and tartan shirts were available in mix-and-match separates collections that did not require much style-consciousness to coordinate.

Despite the balkanized niche marketing and generic merchandising of sportswear, many trend currents were universally adopted by designers and ready-to-wear makers. In the 1980s, the big look of power suits translated into big shoulders, big textile patterns, and big details in sportswear. The shoulders of shirts and sweaters were padded; logo sweatshirts were cut fuller and with bigger sleeves; pockets were oversized and given larger dimensions with pleats and bellows; pegged trousers were made fuller through the hips with multiple pleats and wider through legs.

Another trend for a few years in the mid-1980s was the *Miami Vice* look inspired by the TV crime drama. Unconstructed sports jackets in sherbet colors were worn with the sleeves pushed up to the elbows. Underneath, equally colorful crewneck T-shirts without screenprints or collarless button front shirts in textured linen and cotton blends complemented or contrasted with the jackets. Poplin or cotton duck pants were in a complementary third color or neutral. Deck shoes without socks and big, dark sunglasses completed the look.

Among the most important foreign influences on American sportswear were the Italians. By the 1980s, the labels of Armani, Versace, Zegna, Ferré, Valentino, and Missoni among others were recognized in America as high style and superior quality. To appeal to the American market, Italian designers

Figure 8-30. Gianni Versace's bold and dramatic use of vividly colored prints and pattern mixing influenced even his archrival, classicist Giorgio Armani. Top, paisley print shirt and checked trousers by Armani, 1993; bottom, scarf print shirt by Versace, 1992.

borrowed "the free-flowing vocabulary of Anglo-American dressing" to blend with "Italy's traditionally crisp and careful designing" for a "dolce eclecticism."[65] Where Giorgio Armani presented "American classics seen through the eyes of Italy's fashion craftsman,"[66] his archrival, Gianni Versace, produced collection after collection of wildly colorful sportswear. "The idea was to be like a painter," said Versace in 1991, "to paint people like a tattoo."[67] By the 1990s, the print drama of Versace's sportswear had altered the perspectives of most men's sportswear designers, including Armani. (Figure 8-30 and Color Plate 34.)

From the Far East (via Paris sometimes) came a "revolutionary approach to fit and silhouette" in the 1980s from Japanese designers. "Contemporary Japanese fashion is sportswear at its most relaxed, and yet, sometimes, at its most elegant," assessed *GQ* in 1984:

> The loose, oversized shirts and unconstructed jackets are correct for most casual occasions. The fit is meant to be big; the clothes should drape over the body rather than restrict it. And because many of these garments are cut from prewashed linen and cotton, wrinkling is the desired effect.[68]

The resulting loose and layered look was everywhere in American sportswear throughout the 1980s and 1990s, influencing masculine identities from power dressing to hip-hop to grunge. (Figure 8-31.) In addition, the emphasis on textile surface and texture in Japanese clothing especially influenced knitwear where combinations of knitting techniques created new forms of sweaters that were stunning art to wear.

By far, though, American sportswear since 1980 has continually recycled its past. "Can fashion be saved from retro quicksand?" wondered an editor in 1982. "Virtually every youthquake of the past two decades" had already resurfaced.[69] In the subsequent years since that observation, designers and ready-to-wear makers have continually ransacked the attics, trunks, and closets of bygone eras for inspiration. (Figure 8-32.) The iconoclastic 1960s especially was a favorite era to revisit. In the mid-1990s, the hiphugger, now called low-riders, was reintroduced after disappearing more than twenty years earlier. For the new millennium, the fly length was further shortened to such a brevity that "the alarming creep of male pubes" was evident—a look curiously credited to that most conservative of societies, Japan.[70] In addition, as a counter look to the baggy, oversized fit of jeans preferred by the hip-hop crowd, young millennials began to opt for skin-tight cuts of jeans. In 2008, Levi's expanded its line to include the 511 Skinny Jean and the 510 Super Skinny Jean; similarly, the following year, Calvin Klein launched CK Jeans Body "with a body-defining fit...designed for a more contoured shape and engineered for an enhanced profile."[71] That enhanced, contoured profile, which emphasized the buttocks, thighs, and crotch, was a revival of the exhibitionistic looks of the early 1980s (which itself had been a revival of the peacock sexuality of the 1960s.)

Also from the sexual exhibitionism of the 1960s was a return of the "naked" look of shirts made of sheer materials, particularly favored for displaying tattoos and body piercings. Traditional renewals included the banded collar from the late seventies that recurred every few years, often alternating with a reiteration of the Nehru collar. Among the renewed textile prints were art deco, Op art, flower power, and psychedelic designs that were repeatedly applied to shirts and pants of the 1990s and 2000s.

Figure 8-31. The loose, layered looks of men's sportswear owes an allegiance to the relaxed, "big look" of Japanese fashions in the 1980s. Knit sportswear from Max Studio, 1988.

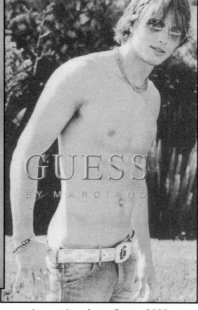

Reintroduced hiphuggers
by Mossimo, 1996

Low-riders from Guess, 2005

Retro-sixties "naked" look shirt by Mossimo,
1996

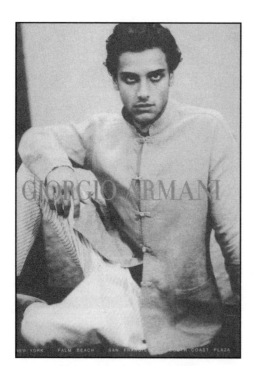

Nehru collar by Armani, 2003

Op art print jeans, 1991, and shirts, 1992, by Versace

Figure 8-32. Fashion designers and ready-to-wear makers constantly revisited the styles of past eras—particularly the iconoclastic 1960s—for inspiration and fresh perspectives.

Figure 8-33. For many avant-garde designers, the semiannual runway shows were opportunities to present innovative and unexpected concepts of masculine dress mixed with their more commercially viable prêt-a-porter fashions. Left, peplum trouser suit by Jean-Charles de Castlebajac, 1991; center, shorts suiting by L'Homme Bis, 1990; right, corset by Jean Paul Gaultier, 1997.

Retro styling was but one form of creative ammunition in the arsenal of the men's sportswear designer. The prêt-a-porter collections of the major European houses were broadly marketable fashions that financially sustained the label. But semiannual runway shows were also opportunities for the designer to experiment and present fresh, innovative ideas to a wide public audience and the fashion press. Designers assailed social conventions and barriers by exploring culture collisions, gender bending, theatrical art school looks, and techno sci-fi fantasies. (Figure 8-33 and Color Plate 36.) But despite the Peacock Revolution more than forty years ago and the advent of the metrosexual in the 1990s, hard lines remained in American masculine dress and identity, far more so than with feminine dress. In looking at the menswear runway shows of 1997 that included velvet evening suits, sheer polos, halter tops, and asymmetrically cut spandex tanks, *GQ* scoffed, "We're not saying that they're not finely made or that such clothes shouldn't be worn. We're just saying that while [*X-Men* actress] Rebecca Romijn can wear them, we can't."[72]

One of the recurring gender bending looks that always caught the attention of the press was the reinvention of the man-skirt. (Figure 8-34.) As noted in the last chapter, designers first attempted pulling down that masculine/feminine barrier in the 1960s. (To give her proper credit though, American designer Elizabeth Hawes created a men's eveningwear kaftan type robe for her 1937 fashion show, for which she concluded, "It made me quite certain, once and for all, that for being alluring, the skirt is the thing and there is no difference between the sexes."[73]) Throughout

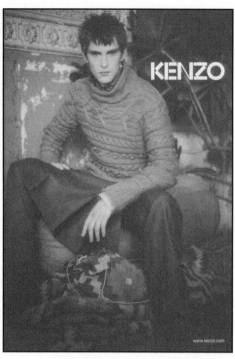

Figure 8-34. Since the 1960s, designers have continually chiseled away at the masculine/feminine distinctions of dress. Gender bending concepts of the man-skirt have been revisited by many of the most prominent names in men's fashion. Left, three-piece skirted suit by Copperwheat Blundell, 1999; right, trouser-skirt by Kenzo, 2005.

the subsequent decades designers such as Vivienne Westwood, Jean Paul Gaultier, John Galliano, and Alexander McQueen featured man-skirts in their collections. On occasion, some men found the shock value of the man-skirt useful. In 1992, Guns and Roses lead singer Axl Rose performed in concerts wearing knee-length leather skirts (and bare legs), and *Vogue* featured grunge guys in tartan kilts wrapped over ragged jeans. "No doubt men will like it not," responded *GQ* to the fin de siècle man-skirt.[74] "In these liberated times a man in a skirt causes considerable anxiety and hostility," notes Elizabeth Wilson in *Adorned in Dreams*, "[because] in order to wear a skirt a man has to define himself as a transvestite, that is, a sexual deviant."[75] Despite the continual rejection of the look by men, though, designers have not relented and keep coming back with fresh concepts of the man-skirt.

Active sportswear continued its trend towards greater performance efficiency. In the early-1980s, formfitting spandex bicycle shorts, running tights, tanks, and jerseys were ubiquitous. The cyclist had "legitimate reasons" for the newly engineered sports clothes, suggested John Forester, author of *Effective Cycling*. "The shorts should be skintight and have a chamois (or polypropylene, which is easier to take care of) crotch lining to protect skin against saddle rub."[76] In addition, the new synthetic fabrics were perfect for strenuous activities. Nylon spandex provided comfortable support for the genitals and did not constrict muscles as they warmed and expanded. Pro athletes and weekend enthusiasts alike took to the backroads on their multi-speed bikes, jogged through community parks, or traipsed to the gym in their spandex sports clothes. By the late 1980s, though, men were seized by a renewed modesty. Although the practical aspects of the newly engineered sports clothes were broadly acknowledged, the contouring fabrics were too exhibitionistic for many men. In reviewing the primary-colored, nylon-and-Lycra-blend athletic wear of 1997, *GQ* concluded: "Can any man wear these clothes? Yeah, but for chrissake, let's pray they don't."[77] Consequently, men continued to

Figure 8-35. In the early 1980s, newly engineered fabrics and sports clothes that fitted like a second skin became ubiquitous for the pro and weekender alike. But by the end of the decade, American men were seized with a sudden modesty that banished the formfitting sports shorts beneath a top layer of baggy shorts. Nike sports clothes, 1991.

wear the spandex shorts but layered over them a pair of baggy gym shorts or fleece pants. (Figure 8-35.)

During the early 1990s, layered athletic shorts led to a totally new look in men's activewear—the long, baggy shorts. Michael Jordan is often credited with initiating the look. Fashion lore holds that when Jordan began playing for the Chicago Bulls, he had long, baggy uniform shorts custom made that he could wear over his lucky college team shorts. However, in a 1997 interview, he claimed, "It started in '85....I just felt like the shorts were too tight. And I was always thin, so I wanted to seem bigger than I actually was, and I wanted room to move around."[78] The look quickly became a national trend for all ages and was soon adopted by women's athletic teams as well. By the start of the 2000s, men's athletic shorts were so wide legged and baggy that they looked like the divided skirts of 1970s. Skinny teens often opted for shorts that were a couple of sizes too large to fit low on the hips and hang below the knees.

Newly engineered synthetic fibers were also applied to winter sports clothes. "Technology is advancing up the ski slopes," noted a 1986 editorial. "Those archenemies of skiing—cold, wet, and burn—are being buried in an avalanche of super-insulating fibers like Themolite and Gore-Tex."[79] For glacier hikers and snowmobilers who spent extended hours outdoors in frigid air, mylar thermal reflector oversuits retained vital body heat and helped prevent hypothermia. In 2004, Under Armour introduced sports clothes made of microfibers specifically designed for cold, hot, or in between extremes that drew sweat away from the skin while allowing the body to adjust its temperature regardless of the elements. Colors and prints of skiwear were produced in bright primary colors and neon palettes "loud enough to start an avalanche."[80] Vibrant-hued Pop art graphics and medieval particolor patterns added personality to skiwear both in the snow or at the resort lodge. "Skiwear has become more than just functional," asserted an ad in 1988, "it has become an attitude."[81] (Figure 8-36 and Color Plate 32.)

Swimwear became a significant differentiator between American male dress and identity and that of most of the rest of the world. At the beginning of the 1980s, swim briefs, collectively called "Speedos" after the famous-maker brand, were common on U.S. beaches. (Figure 8-37.) In the second half of the eighties, though, *GQ* reported that the "tide has turned on racing briefs and nylon swimsuits."[82] Instead, boxer and walk-short lengths (the sixties surfer jams that became "board shorts") in colorful cartoon graphics, tropical motifs, and abstract prints filled the editorial pages of swimwear editions for several years. Although U.S. Olympic swimmers, divers, and water polo teams continued to wear the brief cut swimsuits into the 2000s, American men eschewed the style. In 1997, *GQ* made an off-handed recommendation for the new Aquablade briefs "made from the same water-shearing fabric worn by Olympians": "While the pig-in-a-wet-blanket effect might make you feel self-

Figure 8-36. In addition to new fiber technologies, winter sportswear designs emphasized eye-catching style with graphical prints and vibrant colors. Graphic-printed nylon ski jacket, survival belt, and neon orange skipants from Luhta, 1988.

conscious at first, after a swim or two you'll appreciate the second-skin quality. So save the baggy trunks for the beach, unless you happen to be French."[83] In 2004, *GQ* examined why "men all over the world swear by Speedos; but baggy-minded Americans...refuse to surrender":

> Slip into a Speedo-style swimsuit...and what you notice most is everything *but* what's supposed to be filling out your trunks. You notice how pasty your upper thighs are, you notice how the hair down there doesn't neatly contain itself within the suit, and you notice how your love handles are more pronounced than you ever imaged. In short, it's not pretty.[84]

A few years later, Mark Simpson looked at the persistent speedophobia in America and to some degree, agreed with *GQ*: For the past twenty-five years, American men have been and remain shy about their bodies. But Simpson saw far more socially complex reasons for the abandonment of swim briefs than pale thighs and errant pubic hair. First, as the U.S. population has aged—the first baby boomers turned forty in 1986, fifty in 1996, and sixty in 2006—obesity increased significantly and steadily. "Baggy shorts hide baggy buttocks. They also wear higher, and their large profile makes a baggy stomach considerably less obvious than when hanging over the waistband of a Speedo." Second was the sexual objectification of the youthful, athletic male in popular culture and advertising since the late 1970s as discussed earlier in this chapter. "The bar for male beauty was being set higher and higher as the reality was getting heavier and heavier." Third was the "self consciousness, self-loathing and paranoia both of being 'checked out' and not measuring up." Fourth, the baggy layered shorts look popularized by Michael Jordan translated easily into swimwear, where baggy surfer's shorts had been common for decades. Finally, the Speedo brief irrevocably became associated with gays. "Gays are flamboyant Speedophiles," concluded Simpson. "They are less likely to be overweight. They are more likely to be worked out. Hence their wearing Speedos really rubs people's noses in it."[85]

Despite the demure, comforting coverage of baggy boxers and board shorts, they were very uncomfortable. "Too often, board shorts hang like a baggy pair of knee-grazing culottes and hold water like a fish tank," commented *GQ* in 2006.[86] Complained another fashion writer: "Apart from looking like clown's pajamas, they feel horrible when wet and gritty."[87] As a result, swimsuit designers in the 2000s retained the length but trimmed the wide legs and used softer, quick-drying fabrics. In addition, board shorts covered a lot of skin, leaving more than a third of the

Speedo suits

Swimmers

Speedo suits champions! World record holders! Gold Medalists! And you!

SPEEDO®

Speedo suits America!

ANTRON LYCRA
DuPont registered trademark   Speedo® is a registered trademark of Speedo Knitting Mills Pty. Ltd.

Figure 8-37. During the late 1980s, American men abandoned brief, formfitting styles of swimwear in favor of baggy, concealing boxers and board shorts. Left, Speedo ad, 1983; right, board shorts from International Male, 2007.

Figure 8-38. To accommodate the big look of power suits and sportswear, topcoats and jackets of the 1980s expanded to huge proportions. Details such as collars, lapels, and patch pockets were enlarged to complete the big look silhouette. Top, raglan sleeve overcoat by Basile, 1984; bottom, leather jacket from Tannery West, 1984.

body sunscreened and pale and causing a knee-socks-looking tan on the legs. For the sun-worshipper who wanted no tan lines and an even tan all over without stripping nude on the beach, the solution was the Solar Tan Thru swimwear introduced in 1999. The boxer style swimsuits were made with a patented fabric perforated with thousands of tiny holes through which the sun could penetrate.

Although the boxers and board shorts were the commonplace choices for the majority of average American men, for the competitive athlete, new forms of swimwear were developed in the 2000s. Technological advances in synthetic fibers for swimwear became ingenious performance enhancers. New weaves of microfiber fabrics simulated the smooth sleekness of shark skin, improving a swimmer's speed and maneuverability in water. Where once Olympians shaved their bodies and stripped to the barest of swimsuits, today's champions wear suits cut like long bike shorts or even full bodysuits to cover more of their skin surface. In February 2008, Speedo introduced the LZR Racer made of a specially engineered fabric, which is ultrasonically welded to appear seamless. The unique design of the swimsuit helped a swimmer hold the optimum body position in the water and provided additional buoyancy. Within the first two months of the LRZ Racer's release, twenty-two world records in swimming were broken.

Outerwear 1980–Present

In the late 1970s and early 1980s, Japanese designers experimented with big look fashions for both men and women—oversized proportions that featured "a hint of Samurai warrior styling in the martial swoop of the shoulders."[88] That influence was especially felt in the power suits and outerwear of the 1980s. As shoulders of business suits expanded, overcoats had to be made even wider and more capacious to fit over them without crushing and rumpling the suit. (Figure 8-38.) Even casual jackets, trench coats, suburbans, and other more utilitarian forms of outerwear were constructed with the decade's big look silhouette. (Color Plate 30.) Details, too, were decisively sized up to balance the new proportions: Collars were larger, lapels wider, patch pockets bigger, sleeves fuller, hemlines longer. Raglan sleeves and shoulder yoke constructions best accommodated the massive padding and interlinings. For set-in sleeves, the sleeve caps were either virtually at right angles to the padded, squared shoulderlines or designed to hang off the shoulder at an angle. A superfluity of details such as pleats, tucks, epaulets, and sleeve straps added still more dimension.

By the beginning of the 1990s, the big look had been deflated, and outerwear proportions began a decade-long reduction. Padding was eliminated, and the natural shoulder returned. Lapels on dress coats narrowed. Tapered waistlines reappeared. Even details were reduced to a minimum; extraneous hardware, straps, and belts were omitted. As suits

Figure 8-39. By the beginning of the 1990s, the oversized scale and capacious fit of overcoats began to diminish. Over the subsequent years, coats and jackets became narrow and trimmed with minimal details. Among the favorite revivals was the duffle coat, famous since World War II for its economy of line and simple, functional styling. Left, cowl overcoat by Burberry, 1999; right, duffel from Hermès, 2000.

became ever slimmer and narrower in the 2000s, the shape of overcoats followed. "Your overcoat should be as trim and well cut as the suit beneath it," advised an editorial in 2004. "So ditch that baggy, belted number.... No matter what a salesman tells you, your overcoat should be the same size as your suit."[89] In many instances, the new coats of the twenty-first century nostalgically resembled the youthful drape cut styles of the post-World War I years. Also, revivals such as a shorter, trimmer trenchcoat and a revitalized duffel were a new look for the young Gen X urbanite and the Gen Y undergrad. (Figure 8-39.)

Underwear 1980–Present

Styles of men's underwear changed only superficially. The snug fitting white cotton brief and the loose, baggy boxer remained the two most preferred styles. The innumerable varieties of fashion underwear—bikinis, G-strings, and thongs—were refreshed with new details, colors, and fabrics each year by niche marketers like Ah Men and International Male. "Men are more adventurous and discerning than ever before when it comes to their undies," observed an editorial in 2006, "and this season has something for all moods, whether it's retro porn star smalls, unique sling systems that enhance your schlong, organic briefs, newsprint boxers or wildly patterned Y-fronts."[90] A popular trend with young men that emerged in the 1990s was the square cut boxer brief, an abbreviated variation of the knit "athletic" drawers that had been around since Victorian times. In the 1980s, briefs and bikinis were reengineered with contoured pouches that more comfortably supported the genitals than the earlier

Calvin Klein Underwear

Calvin Klein

Figure 8-40. In the 1980s, Calvin Klein revolutionized the marketing of men's under-wear in two ways. First he branded the basic commodity garments with his logo on the outside of the waistband. Second, he promoted an erotic masculine mystique with provocative, exhibitionistic images of the ideal male dressed only in his branded prod-ucts. Left, pole vault champion Tom Hintnaus in Calvin Klein briefs, 1982; right, Mark Wahlberg in Calvin Klein boxer briefs, 1992.

constricting styles made with stretch knit flat fronts. The wild prints, screened graphics, and vibrant colors that had been so popular for briefs and bikinis in the 1970s largely disappeared except for novelty styles as gifts for Valentine's Day or Father's Day. Besides white, only heather gray, black, and the occasional navy were the usual limits of knit underwear in department stores. Boxers, were always available in bold tartans and brightly colored allover prints. In 2003, underwear maker 2$^{(X)}$ist resolved two problems with the undershirt that had plagued men for decades: they introduced a T-shirt with a raglan sleeve to prevent the underarm bind-ing and bunching of the regular set-in styles; and they attached the collar label on the outside to eliminate the annoying itch caused by tags that were heat-seared at the edges to prevent unraveling.

By far the more important news about men's underwear after 1980 was the marketing tactics. In 1982, master marketer Calvin Klein, flush with success from his sensational sex-sell advertising of designer label jeans, went the next step in marketing his label on underwear. Just as he had put his name prominently on the patch pockets of jeans, he moved the underwear label from an inside tag to a repeat motif all around the outside of the waistband. And just as he had so successfully marketed his jeans as masculine eroticwear, he redefined underwear marketing. His famous image of Olympic pole vaulter Tom Hintnaus in nothing but Calvin Klein briefs ran in full page, full-color ads between 1982 and 1985. (Figure 8-40.) When the photo was made into a three-story billboard towering over New York's Times Square, the marketing campaign made international news—worth millions of dollars in publicity and brand recognition. As sales of his underwear soared, Klein continually presented fresh variations on the sex-sell theme for his underwear (and fragrances and sportswear). In 1992, he achieved more free publicity with his ads and billboards displaying Marky Mark (Mark Wahlberg) wearing only CK boxer briefs. The year before, the controversial rapper had prefaced a book about himself with: "I wanna dedicate this book to my dick." And as a copywriter for the ad campaign recalled, "There was plenty of dick, both in the Calvins and in our model's personality....Ka-ching!"[91] The result was yet another dimension of the sexual-sensuality image associated with the Calvin Klein label—a harder-edged narcissism and a rougher male eroticism than a decade earlier.

Other underwear makers quickly followed Calvin Klein's lead, replacing the static presentations of models posing like store mannequins with erotic exhibitions of male strip-tease, narcissistic self-adoration, and soft-core porn imagery that invited the consumer to become a voyeur. The product itself sometimes became almost incidental to the narrative of the photo. (Figure 8-41.) And since the day that gigantic building-size image of Tom Hintnaus was unveiled, hunks bearing all have become a common sight in public, upon billboards, bus wraps, airport posters, and, of course endlessly, in mass-publication magazines.

Why then was the American male so willing to indulge in sexual exhibitionism with underwear, buying styles for the way they looked rather than solely for utility but became "speedophobic," as Mark Simpson asserted, when it came to swimwear? The answers lay with the audience. As Simpson observed, in the 1980s, the American male developed a paranoiac fear of "being checked out" in public and not measuring up. Certainly by the 1980s, marketers had set the bar high with their endless images of male gym-rat models who spent hours each day in workout routines perfecting an ideal body far beyond that of the average American male. But in private, intimate circumstances where undressing was intended as an erotic display or sexual foreplay for a partner, the audience was invited to see all, and the right type of underwear was as much an expression of a man's identity as his suit and tie.

Figure 8-41. Since 1980, marketing tactics for men's underwear have repeatedly used images that invited viewers to become voyeurs of erotic narratives such as the male strip-tease and soft-core porn. Jordache ad, 1985; 2(x)ist ad, 1995; C-IN2, 2004.

In the 1990s, the partial display of underwear became a nonerotic insurgency dress identity of some urban teens. As a result of their preference for "fifties" (large size jeans sometimes with a size fifty waist), the waist bands continually slid down over the hips exposing their underwear. Rather than display pedestrian "tighty whities," teen boys opted for colorful, eyecatching boxers to reinforce the antifashion fit and look of the baggy jeans. (Figure 8-42.) The cachet of the look, according to *The New York Times* in 1994, originated with the bad-boy look of prison inmates, "who aren't allowed to wear belts."[92] When parents, schools, and even some community ordinances increasingly attempted to prohibit the exposed underwear, even more boys adopted the look as a statement of defiance.

Sleepwear 1980–Present

The commodity styles of sleepwear were largely unchanged from those of a century earlier. Mass merchandisers still carried the standardized pajama sets, sleep pants, nightshirts, and bathrobes in cotton and synthetic blends. Most American men, though, slept in their underwear, or, in cold seasons, in fleece sweatshirts and bottoms.

In the New Gilded Age of the 1980s, some affluent yuppies revived the tradition of the lounge robe. "While some men have been wearing them in public (as amusing evening wear), robes are still best donned in the intimacy of one's own home," advised an editorial at the time.[93] As with the undress styles of past generations, the lounge robes were distinctive from bathrobes in their design and materials. Styles were cut with either short, coat-length skirts or mid-calf lengths. Sumptuous silk or velvet in deep, rich hues was preferred to multicolored brocades and satin stripes. Logo crests and heraldic monograms were a popular affectation of the yuppies, and lounging robes could be customized with lavishly embroidered escutcheon or oversized initials in nests of filigree. Even after the age of greed, some men opted for the tradition and social pretension of lounging robes.

Accessories 1980–Present

The resurgence in hat wearing that emerged as part of the layered look of the late 1970s continued to grow in the 1980s as yuppies discovered that a sharp fedora added a sophisticated accent to a power suit and camel hair overcoat. Fashion journalists revisited old style guides to provide advice on choosing the right hat. For the upscale Wall Streeter, only hats made of real fur felt, not wool, were acceptable. One maker of the era even produced hats made of mink fur felt priced at $350. "A felt hat may return in social recognition what it costs in cash," suggested *Esquire* in 1984.[94] Well-made hats were lined with silk for insulation and a finished look, and interior bands were made of leather, which molded to the shape of the head and stayed on better during blustery days. More casual styles of the crushable wool fedora with a wide brim, sometimes made with braided leather bands and even grommet vents, became popular after Harrison Ford wore one in *Raiders of the Lost Ark* (1981).

As the Greed Decade imploded into a stock market crash and lingering recession, the image of the Gordon Gekko power suit faded, including the accoutrement of hats. In the more casual 1990s, hats were once

Figure 8-42. During the 1990s, urban teen boys began to wear their oversized, baggy jeans pushed low on the hips exposing the upper portions of their colorfully patterned boxer shorts. Banana Republic ad, 1992.

Figure 8-43. The baseball cap was not only a practical head covering, but it functioned as a prominent form of tribal identity. Through the color, insignia, or logo of a baseball cap, a man could declare his sports team loyalty, home state origin, club membership, or work association. Izod logo baseball caps, 2004.

again largely utilitarian—for protection against northern winter snows and southern summer sun. Ideally suited to both needs was the baseball cap, which became a universal head covering all over America. They were not only practical but served as an added reference of identity for many men. Their color, logo patches, or embroidered insignia proclaimed a favorite sports team, college, or home state; some affirmed a work membership when trimmed with a company name; others were generic in style but could complement a tribal look or age when worn backward or with the brim cocked to one side. (Figure 8-43.) The other advantage of wearing baseball caps was the accepted disregard of hat etiquette. Because the baseball cap was regarded as a unisex item, there were few places a man would not wear a baseball cap. No man removed his baseball cap upon being introduced to a lady, nor did he take it off aboard airplanes or inside movie theaters, stores, hospitals, or even in the home. Only if a school dress code was enforced would a young man doff his cap.

Neckwear became almost as varied as the Victorian styles. Widths were no longer standardized although makers tended to keep business suit ties at about 3 to 3-1/2 inches. "Unless you're a hardcore fashion guy who favors a superskinny tie, stick with one that measures about three inches," advised a style editor in 2006.[95] The skinny tie that had been revived in the late 1970s became a widespread trend through much of the 1980s and endured into the new century. "A skinny tie gives a modern look," noted a 2004 editorial, but "it's not traditional business attire."[96] In addition to woven silk, rayon, and synthetic fabrics, skinny ties of the 1980s were made of textured knits and leather in bright solid colors. (Figure 8-44.) A skinny tie variation of sorts was the urban cowboy bolla—a string tie of knit cord braided leather affixed at the throat with a decorative fastener. In the 1990s, a brief fad for "street art" ties featured hand-painted designs that looked like graffiti. "[They] look an awful lot like just about any untended vertical surface in a broken-down part of town," complained an editor in 1996, "not exactly the thing to wear for a meeting with investment bankers."[97]

The bow tie had largely disappeared in the 1980s except for formal wear. Even then, many men began wearing long ties with notch-lapeled tuxedos. Preknotted skinny versions of bow ties made of red leather or

Figure 8-44. Skinny ties were among the retro-sixties looks that became a widespread trend in the 1980s. As fashions narrowed in the 1990s and the skinny look prevailed in the 2000s, the skinny tie endured. Left, skinny leather tie from Vincente Nesi, 1984; right, skinny knit tie from Henry Grethel, 1983.

Slip-ons and demi-boots by Foti, 1982

Figure 8-45. Designs of men's footwear were among the most varied since the eighteenth century. In addition to a wide assortment of conventional wingtip lace-ups and tassel slip-ons, innovative and retro styles ranged from clunky rubber-cleat platforms to razor-toed poulaines.

Square-toe lizard and crocodile oxfords and belt by Mauri, 1987

Deco inlays from Foti, 1984

silk foulards reappeared briefly in the mid-1980s and again in the early 1990s as an eccentric look for daytime.

With all the inconstancy of tie widths through the past three decades, the shirt collar became a more important sartorial differentiator of correct (and incorrect) dressing. If "chunkier, baby-fist-sized knots" were the preference, then a spread collar was advised; when wearing a skinny tie, the spread collar should be avoided since the knot would be too small.[98]

Shoes were as varied as neckwear. (Figure 8-45.) Throughout the past three decades, men's shoes have been made in more varieties of styles than any other era since the eighteenth century. The most innovative looks came from Italy. "Fans of footwear have come to expect pleasant styling surprises, as well as streamlined classics from Italy's designers," noted *GQ* in 1982.[99] The Italians constructed shoes into every conceivable toe shape, tongue treatment, and heel type. They were also fearless with colors that year, offering men's leather shoes in aqua, powder blue, jade green, dusty rose, cranberry red, and caramel. Among the revivals of the affluent eighties were art deco inlays and two-tones and thirties style crocodile and lizard skin oxfords. During the late eighties, the throats of loafers were cut low, omitting the tongue for an opening nearly down to the toe cleavage. Western films like *Urban Cowboy* and the TV soap opera *Dallas* made highly decorated cowboy boots a nationwide favorite in the mid-1980s. By the turn of the century, shoe shapes reached extremes ranging from broad, square toe widths with high heels and rubber cleat platforms to thin-soled poulaines with long, razor-sharp toes. For most men, the standardized wingtip or tassel loafer remained unchanged with moderately rounded toes and low heel. For some reason, the black vs. brown debate continued. Despite the constant reassurance from style guides (since the 1930s) that "dark brown shoes go with everything, even black," most men remained unconvinced.[100]

Among other leather goods that reflected postmodern changes in men's dress were the many new looks of the shoulder bag. (Figure 8-46.)

Rubber cleat platforms from Guess, 1997

Sharp-toed poulaines in crocodile and snakeskin by Dolce and Gabbana, 2004

Louis Vuitton signature shoulder bag, 1996

Pierre Cardin signature envelope, wallets, dop bag, belts, lighter, and cuff links, 1982

Contoured billfold by Amity, 1981

Figure 8-46. Advances in business gadgets and communications technology caused a proliferation of pocket tools that became necessities for the modern American male. The practical shoulder bag, so controversial in the 1970s, became commonplace by the 1980s. For the status-conscious yuppie, designer leather goods with prominent signature logos were a must have.

Revival mod look wallet by Jerry Garcia, 1996

Fanny pack from Luhta, 1986

Earlier versions resembled luggage or utility cases, but the metrosexual was not afraid to carry a high style designer label bag. Throughout the 1980s, small leathers and other accessories with designer logos were important status symbols for the yuppie. On the practical side of accessories was the contoured billfold designed to minimize the unsightly back pocket bulge that often caused men's trousers to pull asymmetrically. In 2007, TechnoBrands introduced the Rogue Wallet, which was shaped with rounded corners to fit in the front trouser pockets, thus "eliminating ergonomic problems [such as lower back pain] caused by sitting on a traditional wallet."[101] Also the nylon "fanny pack" carryall became popular in the mid-1980s for cyclists, street skaters, and runners although the item became a favorite with urbanites and mallites who wanted to keep their hands free for browsing flea markets and mall boutiques. For the most part, fanny packs were actually worn on the hip or at the front for easier access. As men's trousers became more trim and narrow in the 2000s, *GQ* advised men to "get rid of your wallet and, while you're at it, trash all the receipts, video cards, and other unnecessary crap that's stuffed in it. Buy an elegant slim leather credit card holder and stock it with your essential cards. Then, fold your cash in a money clip. All that other nonsense can go in your desk drawer. You don't need it."[102]

Belts became a much more significant accessory than previously. Designers discovered that logo-branded belts were as popular with men as they had been with women. The master of logo licensing, Pierre Cardin, had been putting his initials on men's belt buckles since the 1970s. By the 1990s, men paid premiums for belts with buckles made of

Figure 8-47. White accessories such as belts and sunglasses were eyecatching style options for millennial young men who wanted to break the monotony of the usual conformist niche dress of jeans or khakis topped with nondescript shirts. Top, Guess ad, 2009; bottom, Prada ad, 2010.

the oversized initials or logos of famous labels such as the DG for Dolce and Gabbana, Armani's stylized eagle, or Versace's Medusa head. In the early 2000s, white belts became a trend again—a 1970s revival, only this time favored by millennial young men rather than the over-thirty country club set and now worn without the matching white shoes. (Figure 8-47.)

Another bold white accessory adopted by young men in the new millennium were white frames for eyeglasses and sunglasses. The attention-getting white belts and white glasses were tentative expressions of individuality for the Gen Y male who more often preferred the low profile of conformity to the dress identities within their respective social niches.

Among the revivals of the 1980s was the reintroduction of suspenders such as those shown in Figure 8-28. For the corporate junior executive in the Greed Decade, the look of suspenders was suddenly fresh and new and, at the same time, traditionally masculine. It was also a class differentiator, an assertive distinction of dress for successful men who could afford suit trousers tailored with suspender buttons.

Jewelry for men took on new significance after 1980. During the New Gilded Age (a.k.a. Greed Decade), the exhibitionism of fine jewelry was as important as the proper fit of an Armani suit, the distinctive look of Gucci loafers, or the recognizable pattern of an Hermés necktie. (Figure 8-48.) "Live with a sense of pleasure," coaxed an ad for 18K gold jewelry in 1983.[103] The typical jewelry for men of the eighties remained the same as decades before: rings, wristwatches, cuff links, and perhaps a chain bracelet or discrete necklace.

By contrast with the abundance of fine jewelry was the popularity of disposable jewelry like Swatch watches, sometimes worn in multiples of different designs and colors. At only about $25 each, when the battery ran down, they would be discarded and a new one purchased. (Color Plate 33.) In the 2000s, rubber bracelets signified the support of various causes—pink for breast cancer research, yellow for cancer research in general, red for AIDS education and research, green for Muscular Dystrophy.

Also in the 1980s, a critical change in the American male's dress and identity developed when average men began wearing earrings. The look had been pioneered a decade earlier by iconoclastic punks and out-and-proud gay men for whom the earring was socially subversive. But when straight men began wearing one or more earrings, the growing trend prompted a number of editorials examining the phenomenon. Women, especially, resented and were perplexed by this latest shift in masculine style. The notion of earrings for men, wrote Susan Ferraro in 1988, was a "Rubicon, as it were, of male adornment...that was only a generation ago, utterly, exclusively feminine. On men of the recent past, jewelry meant glitter and gay. Real men—which Americans understood to be the hard-fisted, tight-lipped, ruthless, blunt instruments of efficiency and busi-

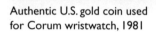

| Authentic U.S. gold coin used for Corum wristwatch, 1981 | 18K gold ring and cuff links by Henry Dunay, and watch by Daniel Mink, 1983 | High-tech titanium jewelry by The Titan Factory, 2006 |

Figure 8-48. For traditionalist men, well-designed rings, cuff links, and watches were always acceptable forms of masculine jewelry. During the Greed Decade of the 1980s, ostentation of wealth included big, bold, and flashy jewelry.

ness—didn't touch the stuff. The jewelry they had was functional, not decorative."[104]

A decade later, Lucy Kaylin gave her views of the homosocial world of pro sports, noting: "Then there's [NFL Superbowl champion] Deion Sanders, who insists on wearing two earrings instead of one—and big, gold Fortunoff-type hoops at that. Does anyone else think he's starting to look like a wigless drag queen?"[105] For Rebecca Johnson in 1997, "This earring business is not about vanity. It's about putting women off." To her, the masculine earring represented a man's "way of prolonging adolescence." Where Susan Ferraro had viewed the pierced earring as a "serious commitment" by a man, Johnson saw it as just the opposite: "It's utterly pliant. In for the blind date, out for the office. It's the perfect accessory for the ambivalent guy....His driver's license may say he's 35, but when there's a ruby in the lobe, he's really 15."[106] By the beginning of the new millennium, the prevalence of the style-conscious metrosexual made the earring controversy moot. He was a committed family man who could take or leave earrings as easily as choosing between a striped or print tie or wingtip or tassel loafer. Despite the furor about man-earrings in the 1980s and 1990s, Susan Ferraro had deduced correctly that men were wearing earrings "because they feel more comfortable with themselves, freer to be playful and stylish and sassy, confident enough to ignore societal norms and to make their own rules, and—perhaps bravest of all—more willing to take the blunt, macho coarseness of stereotypically tough manhood less seriously."[107] Moreover, as the first decade of the twenty-first century progressed, the ever changing style cycle began to shift toward a renewed minimalism in men's dress—trim, simplified suits; sportswear with clean lines, devoid of excesses—which included less jewelry. All a man needed, suggested *GQ* in 2006, was a stainless steel watch since it could be "both dressy and sporty."[108]

In addition to pierced ears, many Gen Y men opted for more varied piercing and jewelry. As pierced eyebrows and tongues became more common by the end of the nineties, some young men expanded their piercings to include the nostrils, septum, nose bridge, lips, navel, nipples, and penis. Jewelry included straight or horseshoe barbells, rings of varying thicknesses, and beaded or jeweled studs. Preferred metals included titanium, sterling silver, gold, and tungsten; retainers and expanders were of acrylic or surgical steel.

Grooming 1980–Present

Men's hairstyles since 1980 have been the most varied and creative since the powdered wig colonial era. (Figure 8-49.) The long hair of the youthquake generation that had so dismayed traditionalists in the 1960s became commonplace with Gen X and Gen Y men. In addition to flowing manes—sometimes tamed into a ponytail low at the back of the neck—trendy long-style cuts came and went with regularity. In the late eighties, the mullet was cut with a short, spiky top and sides but a shoulder-length back. In the 1990s, the mullet devolved into the rat tail, short all around the head except for some long strands at the nape of the neck that were tightly braided and affixed at the end with a few beads. And, as noted previously in this chapter, versions of punk mohawks and spiky crests or the Goth's blue-black shag cut still survived.

By and large, though, most men preferred the easy-care maintenance of short hair. Depending on the hair type, a man could express himself by varying the short cut into anything from a top-heavy, retro-fifties pompadour to the ultra-sheared caesar of the mid-1990s. For the corporate-bound yuppie, "the neat look" with its short sides and side part was as de rigueur as it had been in Victorian times. Following the Greed Decade's quintessential movie, *Wall Street,* in which the Gordon Gekko character always appeared with slicked-back helmet hair, the wet head became the smart look of the urbanite executive. "Gordon Gekko's hair has been turning up everywhere," reported *GQ* in 1988:

> In the most exclusive men's clubs, in boardrooms, in restaurants, at dinner parties and at country clubs, the same men who once used to blow-dry their hair to the flash point now appear to have had their heads dipped in Pennzoil. They're pomaded, moussed, gelled, Vaselined, Brylcreemed, and in some cases, their hair is literally wet.... It's a power statement, an obvious pronouncement of ego...so popular in the 'power' fields—investment banking, public relations, advertising.[109]

By the beginning of the new century, the helmet head subsided, replaced instead with the "slope," a variation of the caesar with the short bangs gelled and pushed flat up from the forehead. Noncorporate types sported the bed head—a moussed styling of the hair atop the head carefully finger arranged into a studied casualness.

African American men likewise enjoyed a broad range of expressive hairstyles unlike any before. The wet sheen of the "jheri curl" look of the mid-1980s was achieved by the repeated application of spray moisturizers. Urban blacks sometimes opted for geometric shapes and "waves" that required the use of relaxers. In the 1990s, young black men expressed their individuality with the "fade," a cut with extremely short sides, into

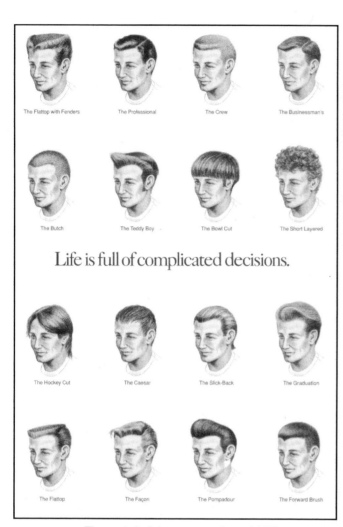

The myriad of short cuts in the mid-1990s

The corporate "neat look," 1984

"Jheri curls," 1983

Shaped and "wave" styles, 1985

The mane, 1985

Punk, mohawk, and dreadlocks, 1984

Bed head, 2005

Figure 8-49. By the 1980s, long hair for men was no longer the social concern it had once been. Most men, though, preferred the easy-care maintenance of short cuts, which could be styled into dozens of looks.

which was razored patterns, emblems, and initials. Dreadlocks (often shortened to "dreads") were a favorite look for proclaiming ethnic and cultural pride; the hair could either be twisted into long, matted ropelike strands or arranged into a profusion of braids.

For the aging baby boomer who was losing his hair, a topical treatment of minoxidil branded as Rogaine was introduced in 1988, and a pill form of finasteride branded as Propecia was available in 1999. These hair-loss aids were moderately successful for some younger men. For other men, the chrome dome or cue ball look was cultivated by completely shaving the head. In 2004, a new safety razor called the HeadBlade was developed with a finger ring attached for easier control than a regular razor.

Besides the pluralistic assortment of hairstyles, some men at the fin de siècle also explored a renewed interest in facial hair. Although the full, bushy beard of the Victorian was rarely seen, many young men experimented with vandykes, goatees, shin curtains, and soul patch. In the second half of the 1980s, the three-days-old stubble became a favorite look of men with strong facial features, especially chiseled jawlines. The stubble look came to be known as the *Miami Vice* look popularized by the TV program's star, Don Johnson. Still, as one bearded editor complained in 1988, the bewhiskered American suffered "denigration as an eccentric, a misanthrope or a poor credit risk."[110]

In addition to all the attention men gave to their hair atop the head and on the face, "manscaping" the body also became a trend in the late 1980s. Hairy chests (and bushy mustaches) became associated with the passé disco era. And with all the swimwear and underwear ads of the era depicting hairless models, many men began shaving or waxing away body hair, especially "bearskin" backs. Some pop culture researchers credit the Calvin Klein "Underwear Man" campaign of 1982–85 shown in Figure 8-40 as the beginning of the hairless torso masculine aesthetic.[111] The ultimate in manscaping for millennial men was the full Brazilian wax, which was a specialized salon treatment for removing all hair around the genitals, perineum, and buttocks except for a small, shaped pubic patch above the penis and sometimes a "treasure trail" extending from the navel downward. (The name was derived from Brazilian sisters who offered the service in their New York salon; it was not a common practice among Brazilian men.) "Who cares if he mows it like a lawn?" asked an editor in 2003. "It doesn't make him a go-go boy....Grooming is for the entire body, including the mind."[112] Even if a man opted to keep his hairy chest, he would unhesitatingly trim ear and nose hair, and maybe even pluck heavy eyebrows—particularly those that grew together forming a monobrow or unibrow. Makers of grooming products responded to the manscaping popularity with a number of specialized shavers designed for the face, nose and ears, and sensitive parts of the body. (Figure 8-50.)

Another significant shift in twentieth-century masculine dress and identity came with the popularization of body remolding treatments. "Forget the days of the 50-year-old face-lift," noted *GQ* in 2004. "Today is the age of cosmetic surgery as youthful maintenance routine....Cosmetic surgery has become an evolutionary extension of the modern health-and-fitness routine—another tool to complement Clinique Skin Supplies for Men, the pilates machine, and the $60-a-month Propecia habit."[113] Men combated perceived genetic deficiencies by getting pectoral, bicep,

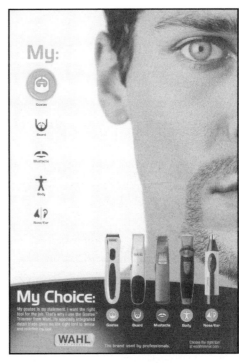

Figure 8-50. In response to the growing trend of manscaping, makers of grooming products developed specialized shavers designed for the face, nose and ears, or body. Wahl ad, 2007.

Figure 8-51. Cosmetics makers developed regimens of skincare products formulated specifically for men. Increasingly, marketing campaigns aggressively targeted men's concerns about aging. L'Oréal ad, 2006.

and calf implants when gym workouts failed to achieve the ideal shapes. Liposuction eliminated love handles and stubborn umbilical donuts (fat deposits encircling the navel) to ensure six-pack abs. Botox injections turned back the clock on crows' feet and brow creases. For the daily battle against telltale signs of aging, men had a wide array of skincare products formulated for masculine complexions. Makers stepped up their marketing scare tactics with a barrage of messages that played on the fear of aging. "What you think are great lines, she thinks are premature wrinkles. Fight back!" chided an ad for L'Oréal's "Wrinkle De-Crease" cream.[114] (Figure 8-51.)

For many young men, tattoos ("tats") were used to express themselves and their generation. Like body piercing, a tattoo was a sign of rebellion for many teens. Tough guys in prison, criminal gangs, and the military got tattoos. Rock stars and professional athletes made them seem cool. For the average man, a tattoo might commemorate a life event such as marriage, commitment to a lover, a newborn child, or a religious conviction. AskMen.com advised readers to be discrete in choosing a tattoo and, equally important, where to place it. Sexy parts included the upper back, hip, shoulder, calves, and chest, but exposed areas such as the neck, face, forearm, hands, and fingers might be problematic since "not everyone is open-minded" about body art and, at times, a tattoo would need to be concealed.[115] For men who wanted only a temporary tattoo, transfer decals that would last several days could be applied with isopropyl alcohol. Also, tattoo salons offered a wide assortment of temporary body art achieved with airbrushed stencils. But by the end of the new century's first decade, tattooing became so commonplace that it lost much of its cachet as an expression of youthful rebellion. "When every baller, rocker, celebutard, and regular Joe is covered in bad tattoos, new ink is not gonna make you look like a badass," advised GQ in 2009. "Want to rebel? Keep it all-natural."[116]

Another temporary skin enhancement was the tantoo, made with an adhesive-backed decal applied to the skin that formed a light silhouette of the design after sunbathing. Similarly, for many gay men, the swimsuit tan line was carefully cultivated by wearing the same cut of swimwear for the season, particularly the brief or bikini. For decades, such styles of swimwear themselves had been erotic—even fetishistic—garments, and the nude shadow of such garments cast by a contrasting tan line extended that eroticism indoors after sunset. "Nothing is as lust-inducing as an August tan line," observed Out in 2009. "To glimpse the porcelain buttock of an otherwise tanned body is to spy an intimate area untouched by the sun."[117]

One of the more astonishing body modifications a few men undertook in the new century was penile foreskin "restoration." In America, the circumcised penis has been a cultural preference since the late nineteenth century sustained by repeated science and medical research regarding hygiene and health. The question about the cut or uncut American male became a debate in the 1970s when some communal hippies began to choose the "natural" state for their children. Finally, in 1989, the American Academy of Pediatrics sponsored a task force to reexamine the procedure. Their conclusions reinforced the age-old arguments: circumcision is a successful preventive health measure; uncircumcised men are ten times more likely to get urinary infections and twenty times more likely to get penile cancer. Also, because foreskins commonly have tiny abrasions, uncircumcised men are more likely to contract HIV/AIDS when exposed. As for the favorite argument of foreskin restorers, no study has shown that uncut men "enjoy better sex."[118] To the contrary, asserted a 2007 study for the *Journal of Sexual Medicine*: "circumcision does not decrease sensitivity....Greater penile sensations in uncut men is an urban legend."[119] Nevertheless, some new age men opted for a contrivance of tape and suspended ball bearings that, over a couple of years, gradually stretched the skin from the penis shaft into a simulated partial foreskin. Despite the debate, thousands of adult men in America underwent circumcision each year largely for aesthetic and cultural purposes. As novelist John Sedgwick wrote for *GQ* about his uncircumcised penis, when a woman would see him naked, "They'd go like, *ew*." Citing a 2000 survey, he noted that American women "preferred a man's penis to be circumcised, largely because it's cleaner and more 'normal.'" For him, as well as many other American men, being uncircumcised "was an oddity...a subject of some mild shame."[120] In part, the mild shame was also socioeconomic since the procedure was an additional cost to those of delivery and hospital maternity care. The uncut penis suggested a lower socioeconomic status in America.

Conclusion

Following the socially divisive and turbulent 1960s and 1970s, the dress and identity of American men became increasingly pluralistic with an ever-widening array of dress options that could be adapted to man's personal lifestyle. In 1982, *GQ* foresaw far into the future an endless "kaleidoscope of tribes and revivals, eccentricity and ethnicity, cross-pollination and insularity" in American menswear.[121] Previously, style changes in men's fashions had been glacial with new looks becoming distinct only by a glance backward over several years. For decades, American ready-to-wear largely took its fashion guidance principally from London and, after the 1960s, from Paris and Milan selectively. Even from these capitals of style, traditional looks evolved gradually, redefining a universal correctness of style, sometimes by only millimeters. With the Peacock Revolution of the 1960s came a fragmentation of the universality of style. Savile Row was no longer the dictator of men's fashion. Designers from Paris, Milan, New York, and the West Coast began to challenge menswear conventions, laying the foundations of postmodern pluralism in masculine dress and identity.

Finally, by the 1980s, the pluralistic dress and identity of American men was divided into dual paths: one of distinctive and inexorable change, the other of tribalistic continuity. The silhouettes of men's suits have demonstrated the clearest evidence of a continuum of fashion change, a sustained correctness of style that has developed in a straight line since the first sack coat suits of the 1850s. Sportswear, however, has been fluidly adaptable; its components formed composite tribal costumes that remained constant for long periods of time and provided many men with a comfortable social and dress identity. The preppy uniform of polo shirt and chinos has not changed in seventy-five years; it serves as an identity for preppies of all ages from grade schooler to elder retiree. Similarly, the hip-hop look of baggy jeans worn sagging low on the hips with crotch inseams corrugated at midthigh—branded sneakers, oversized T-shirts, capacious nylon jackets, and baseball caps worn backward remained as standardized today as twenty years ago. The same can be said of the tribal dress preferred by punks, a look now more than thirty years old, and urban cowboys with their appropriation of the century-old Western style. Other tribal styles were brief and regionalized. Grunge was a widely publicized youth hobo look of the Seattle area that just lasted a couple of years in the early 1990s.

The 1980s was the era of a New Gilded Age—also often called the Greed Decade because of its frenzied stock market driven economy. It was an era of big business and power brokers. To reflect the power of the big man and his big ego, the power suit of the 1980s was engineered with broad, shaped shoulders and a generous, softly fluid fit that allowed the maximum freedom of movement for fighting corporate battles. Outerwear expanded to even greater dimensions to adequately cover the wide suit shoulders. Following the Reaganomics stock market crash of 1987 and the resulting lengthy recession, the business suit was deflated. In the 1990s, suits began a decade-long narrowing. By the new millennium, suit silhouettes were fitted, trim, and short with minimal details.

With the New Gilded Age also came a revival of affluent exhibitionism. Women donned opulent gowns and accompanied their men to galas and balls where they rubbed shoulders with other PLUs (people like us). The tuxedo lost its peacock flamboyance and reverted to the traditional sober penguin look. Some men even resurrected the full dress tail coat and white tie.

The design of sportswear in the 1980s was equally influenced by the big look of power suits and outerwear. Looks were broader, bigger, and baggier. Sweaters and shirts complemented power suits with padded shoulders, full sleeves, and generous body constructions. Pants were cut with multiple pleats and wide, billowing legs. As suit silhouettes diminished in the 1990s, sportswear followed with trimmer cuts and simpler shapes. By the early 2000s, the look was skinny.

Revivals were a hallmark of American sportswear in the fin de siècle decades. Retro looks recurred with regularity, especially styles of the 1960s. The most prominent and lasting revival was the hiphugger reinvented as low-rider jeans and trousers that reduced the fly front even more than the original designs.

As American society further fragmented into a pluralistic culture, ready-to-wear makers and retailers increasingly focused their business strategies on niche marketing, particularly age groups. Some branded labels and store chains such as the Gap and Abercrombie and Fitch exclusively targeted the coveted 18–24 age demographic. Another niche marketing strategy for sportswear makers was the logo cachet. Brand advertising promoted the images of certain casual lifestyles that ranged from the urbanite sophistication of Donna Karan and Versace to the country gentry style of Ralph Lauren and Armani. "Fashion is a magical system," concludes Elizabeth Wilson in *Adorned in Dreams,* and fashion marketing has "moved from the didactic to the hallucinatory....What we see today in both popular journalism and advertising is the mirage of a way of being, and what we engage in is no longer only the relatively simply process of direct imitation, but the less conscious one of identification."[122]

Preface

1. William Harlan Shaw, *American Men's Wear 1861–1982* (Baton Rouge, LA: Oracle, 1982), i.

2. Joanne B. Eicher and Ruth Barnes, eds., "Definition and Classification of Dress: Implications for Analysis of Gender Roles," *Dress and Gender: Making and Meaning* (Oxford: Berg, 1992), 15.

3. John Harvey, *Men in Black* (Chicago: University of Chicago Press, 1995), 19.

4. Earnest Calkins, "Fashion Versus Advertising," *Printers' Ink*, October 5, 1922, 3.

5. Percy Waxman, "Are We As Mean As All That?" *Printers' Ink*, June 23, 1927, 41.

Chapter 1

1. W. J. Machett, *The Tailor's Compass* (Baltimore, 1829).

2. Brown, King and Company catalog, Boston, 1893, 4.

3. Sears, Roebuck and Company catalog #117, 1907, 942.

4. Anon., "New York Fashions," *Harper's Bazar*, June 12, 1875, 379.

5. Josephine Redding, ed., "As Seen by Him," *Vogue*, May 24, 1894, 215.

6. Ibid., March 22, 1894 (supplement), 1.

7. Sara Hale, ed., "The Queen of Inventions: The Sewing Machine," *Godey's Lady's Book*, July 1860, 77.

8. Ibid., "The Sewing Machine," August 1860, 174.

9. Catherine Allen, "In A Garret," *Peterson's*, September 1883, 193.

10. Harry Corbin, *The Men's Clothing Industry: Colonial Through Modern Times* (New York: Fairchild, 1970), 45.

11. United States Hoffmann Company brochure, 1914.

12. Hale, "Fashions: Notice to Lady Subscribers," July 1857, 95.

13. Montgomery Ward ad: *Lady's World*, September 1904, 29.

14. The Boston catalog, 1887, 4.

15. Oscar Herzberg, ed., "We Are Seven," *Printer's Ink*, December 29, 1897, 39.

16. Anon., "New York Fashions: Men's Clothing," *Harper's Bazar*, December 1, 1883, 755.

17. Redding, "As Seen by Him," May 24, 1894, 215.

18. Ibid., "Answers to Correspondents," April 12, 1894, 5.

19. Gifford Hart, "Why Is Men's Style a Joke?" *Printer's Ink*, November 30, 1922, 36.

20. Jim Nelson, ed. "How to Be a Self-Made Man," *Gentlemen's Quarterly*, November 2007, 80.

21. F. S. Richards, "History of the Men's Wear Industry," *Men's Wear*, February 10, 1950, 260.

Chapter 2

1. Roger Butterfield, *The American Past* (New York: Simon and Schuster, 1947), 111.

2. U.S. Bureau of the Census, *Historical Statistics of the United States: Colonial Times to 1970*, Part 2 (Washington, D.C.: U.S. Department of Commerce, 1975), 958–9.

3. Ibid., 728.

4. Ibid., 140.

5. James McCabe, *The Illustrated History of the Centennial Exhibition* (Philadelphia: National Publishing, 1876), 848–50.

6. H. T. Coggin, "Manners Make the Man," *Gentlemen's Journal*, August 1871, 202.

7. Eliza Bisbee Duffey, *The Ladies' and Gentlemen's Etiquette: A Complete Manual of the Manners and Dress of American Society* (Philadelphia: Porter and Coates, 1877), 19.

8. Ibid., 13.

9. Ralph Waldo Emerson, *The Works of Ralph Waldo Emerson*, vol. 2 (New York: Hearst's International Library, 1914), 79.

10. George Fox, *Fashion: The Power that Influences the World*, 3rd ed. (New York: Sheldon, 1872), 17.

11. Duffey, 225.

12. Fox, 41.

13. Ibid, 23, 41.

14. William Cobbett, *Advice to Young Men* (1830; reprint, London: Oxford University Press, 1980), 14.

15. Fox, 143.

16. Duffey, 260.

17. Thomas Carlyle, *Sartor Resartus* (1833; reprint, New York: MacMillan, 1927), 221.

18. John Doran, *Habits and Men with Remnants of Record Touching the Makers of Both* (New York: Widdleton, 1865), 373.

19. Elizabeth Wilson, *Adorned in Dreams: Fashion and Modernity* (New Brunswick, N.J.: Rutgers University Press, 2003), 180.

20. Orson Fowler, *Creative and Sexual Science: Manhood, Womanhood and Their Mutual Inter-Relations* (New York: Physical Culture, 1870), 165.

21. Christine Frederick, *Selling Mrs. Consumer* (New York: Business Bourse, 1929), 344–52; Daniel Delis Hill, *Advertising to the American Woman 1900-1999* (Columbus: Ohio State University Press, 2002), vii.

22. Duffey, 225, 256, 260.

23. Fowler, 397.

24. Esther Singleton, "Beau Brummell," *Cosmopolitan,* June 1891, 228.

25. Olive Schreiner, "The Woman Question," *Cosmopolitan,* November 1899, 48.

26. Albertus Dudley, "That Hilton Game," *Youth's Companion,* October 20, 1892, 517–18.

27. Michel Foucault, *The History of Sexuality: An Introduction,* vol. 1, Robert Hurley, trans. (New York: Vintage, 1978), 43.

28. Brian Pronger, *The Arena of Masculinity: Sports, Homosexuality, and the Meaning of Sex* (New York: St. Martin's, 1990), 88.

29. Warren Steinberg, *Masculinity: Identity, Conflict, and Transformation* (Boston: Shambhala, 1993), 161.

30. Anon., "Gentlemen's Fashions," *Harper's Bazar,* June 13, 1868, 515.

31. Redding, "As Seen by Him," November 22, 1899, v.

32. Ibid., May 16, 1895, 311.

33. Anon., "New York Fashions: Men's Clothing," *Harper's Bazar,* June 20, 1885, 395.

34. Redding, "As Seen by Him," May 16, 1895, 311.

35. Anon., "New York Fashions: Spring Styles for Gentlemen," *Harper's Bazar,* April 17, 1869, 243.

36. Fox, 55.

37. Redding, "As Seen by Him," April 5, 1894, 3.

38. Ibid., May 16, 1895, 311.

39. Ibid., November 22, 1894, v.

40. Ibid., May 16, 1895, 311.

41. Anon., "New York Fashions: Men's Clothing," *Harper's Bazar,* December 1, 1883, 755.

42. Montgomery Ward catalog #57, Spring and Summer 1895, 267–69.

43. F. S. Richards, "History of the Men's Wear Industry," *Men's Wear,* February 10, 1950, 229.

44. Ibid., 230.

45. George Bradford Tripler Men's Outfitter ad, *Vogue,* April 26, 1894, 12.

46. Work Brothers and Company catalog, Fall and Winter 1892, 80.

47. Lynn Downey, et al, *This Is a Pair of Levi's Jeans* (San Francisco: Levi Strauss, 1995), 126.

48. Ibid., 79.

49. Montgomery Ward catalog #57, Spring and Summer 1895, 488.

50. Redding, "As Seen by Him," May 16, 1895, 312.

51. Phyllis Tortora and Keith Eubank, *Survey of Historic Costume,* 3rd edition (New York: Fairchild, 2000), 375.

52. Peter Brown, *The World of Late Antiquity* (New York: Harcourt, Brace, Jovanovich, 1971), 29; Millia Davenport, *Book of Costume* (New York: Crown, 1948), 89.

53. Fox, 48.

54. Vittoria de Buzzaccarini, *Elegance and Style: Two Hundred Years of Men's Fashions* (Milan: Lupetti, 1992), 73.

55. Montgomery Ward catalog #57, Spring and Summer 1895, 296.

56. Redding, "As Seen by Him," January 31, 1895, 70; February 21, 1895, 119.

57. Anon., "New York Fashions: Men's Clothing," *Harper's Bazar,* December 1, 1883, 755.

58. Redding, "As Seen by Him," April 19, 1894, 7; May 16, 1895.

59. Ibid.

60. Fox, 44.

61. Redding, "As Seen by Him," March 21, 1895, 183.

62. Duffey, 157.

63. Fox, 46.

64. Redding, "As Seen by Him," June 17, 1897, 384.

65. Ibid., "The Well-Dressed Man," November 2, 1899, v.

66. Redding, "As Seen by Him," June 21, 1894, 280.

67. Havelock Ellis, "Sexual Inversion," vol. 1, part 4, 3rd ed. of *Studies in the Psychology of Sex* (New York: Random House, 1942), 299–300.

68. Davide Mosconi and Riccardo Villarosa, *Getting Knotted,* trans. Clive Foster, (Milan: Ratti, 1985), 67.

69. Avril Hart, *Ties* (New York: Costume and Fashion, 1998), 80.

70. Anon., "New York Fashions: Men's Clothing," *Harper's Bazar,* December 1, 1883, 755.

71. Redding, "As Seen by Him," May 2, 1895, 282.

72. Ibid., "The Well-Dressed Man," November 2, 1899, v.

73. Fox, 47.

74. Ibid., 55.

75. Anon., "New York Fashions: Men's Clothing," *Harper's Bazar,* December 1, 1883, 755.

76. Redding, "As Seen by Him," April 19, 1894, 7.

77. Ibid.

78. Duffey, 231.

79. *Vogue* was a weekly publication from 1892–1909.

Chapter 3

1. Butterfield, 313.

2. U.S. Bureau of the Census, *Historical Statistics of the United States: Colonial Times to 1970,* Part 2 (Washington, D.C.: U.S. Department of Commerce, 1975), 716.

3. Ibid.

4. Mark Sullivan, *Our Times 1900–1925,* vol. 4 (New York: Charles Scribner's Sons, 1936), 128.

5. Ibid., vol.1 (1926), 67.

6. W. R. Hotchkin, "Feminism," *Life,* June 4, 1914, 1012.

7. Gerald Heard, *Narcissus: An Anatomy of Clothes* (New York: E. P. Dutton, 1924), 118.

8. Hart Schaffner and Marx ad: *Colliers,* September 24, 1910, 3.

9. Marie Harrison, ed., "The Well-dressed Man," *Vogue,* December 15, 1911, 94.

10. Ibid., October 18, 1906, 532.

11. Ibid., November 5, 1908, 760.

12. Ibid.

13. Ibid.

14. J. J. Mitchell, ed., *Sartorial Art Journal,* August 1903, 42.

15. Harrison, August 5, 1909, 159.

16. Ibid., May 8, 1902, 497.

17. Arrow ad: *Literary Digest,* August 17, 1912, 270.

18. Sears catalog #117, 1907, 986.

19. Ibid., 995.

20. Harrison, June 25, 1903, 888.

21. Ibid., October 9, 1902, 488.

22. Ibid., August 22, 1907, 212.

23. Ibid.

24. Henry Pearson, *Crude Rubber and Compounding*

Ingredients: A Textbook of Rubber Manufacture (New York: India Rubber, 1909), 243.

25. Harrison, June 28, 1900, 447.

26. Ibid., August 30, 1900, 142.

27. Ibid., June 9, 1904, 750.

28. Ibid.

29. Hart Brothers Men's Furnishing Goods catalog #45, Fall and Winter 1908–1909, 1.

30. Frank Crowninshield, ed., "The Well-dressed Man," *Vanity Fair,* January 1914, 57.

31. Dennis Bradley, *The Man of Today* (London: Pope and Bradley, 1914). 40.

32. Mitchell, August 1903, 39.

33. Ibid.

34. Ibid.

35. Harrison, January 24, 1907, 136.

36. Ibid.

37. Ibid., December 27, 1906, 958.

38. Ibid., June 4, 1903, 800.

39. Ibid., May 16, 1907, 800.

40. Ibid., June 4, 1903, 800.

41. Ibid., May 16, 1907, 800.

42. Ibid.

43. Ibid., December 26, 1907, 936.

44. Ibid.

45. Ibid., September 8, 1904, 232.

46. Sears catalog #117, 1907, 1045.

47. Ibid.

48. Harrison, May 28, 1903, 766.

49. Ibid., January 9, 1908, 44.

50. Ibid.

51. Ibid., June 22, 1905, 894.

52. Ibid., October 18, 1906, 532.

53. Ibid., October 9, 1902, 488.

54. Ibid., May 24, 1906, 822.

55. Ibid., December 7, 1905, 768.

56. Ibid., December 26, 1907, 936.

57. George Harvey, "Reflections Concerning Women: Mustaches in the Light of Science," *Harper's Bazar,* December 1907, 1252–53.

58. Gillette ad: *Colliers,* November 10, 1910, 32.

59. Michael Shau, *J. C. Leyendecker* (New York: Watson-Guptill, 1974), 30; John Chamberlain, ed., "Cluett, Peabody," *Fortune,* February 1937, 120.

Chapter 4

1. Sullivan, vol. 5, 303,313.

2. Ibid., vol. 1, 383.

3. Atwater Kent Radio ad: *Vanity Fair,* April 1927, 17.

4. Harry Carr, "Sex Pictures Are on the Wane," *Motion Picture,* July 1925, 28.

5. Ibid.

6. Aldous Huxley, "Fashions in Love," *Vanity Fair,* December 1928, 73.

7. Charles Seldon, "Fashions in College Morals," *Ladies' Home Journal,* December 1925, 40; March 1926, 222.

8. Edward Bok, ed., "Are the Only Clever Women in the World in Paris?" *Ladies' Home Journal,* January 1910, 1.

9. Anna Westermann, "Can America Originate Its Own Fashions?" *Ladies' Home Journal,* September 1909, 81.

10. Paul Nystrom, *Economics of Fashion* (New York: Ronald Press, 1928), 183.

11. Bok, "American Fashions for American Women," September 1909, 1.

12. Louis Fairchild, ed., "Around the Shops: Paris," *Men's Wear,* June 10, 1925, 85.

13. George Curtis, *Clothes and the Man* (London: Jonathan Cape, 1926), 34, 89.

14. Crowninshield, "For the Well Dressed Man," August 1929, 72.

15. Jessica Daves, *Ready-made Miracle* (New York: G. P. Putnam's Sons, 1967), 40.

16. George Mosse, *The Image of Man: The Creation of Modern Masculinity* (New York: Oxford, 1996), 112.

17. Bok, "Men: In Answer to the Oft-Asked Question: 'Why Do You Not Have Just One Page for Men in the Home Journal?'" October 1916, 32.

18. Frederick Lewis Allen, *Only Yesterday: An Informal History of the Nineteen-Twenties* (New York: Harper and Brothers, 1931), 88.

19. Erma Paul Allen, "Classified Husbands," *Vanity Fair,* June 1928, 65.

20. Edward Ruttenber, *The American Male: His Fashions and Foibles* (New York: Fairchild, 1948), 11.

21. Frances Allen, "The Vestments of the Male," *American Mercury,* June 1928, 213.

22. Robert Trevor, "For the Well Dressed Man," *Vanity Fair,* September 1918, 62; "Clothes for the Business of Life," October 1918, 82.

23. Ibid., "For the Well Dressed Man," September 1918, 62.

24. Herbert Norris, "Men's Modern Costume," in *The Man of Today,* ed. H. Dennis Bradley (London: Pope and Bradley, 1914), 103.

25. George Warrington, "The Craving for Colour," in *The Man of Today,* ed. H. Dennis Bradley (London: Pope and Bradley, 1914), 113.

26. Trevor, "For the Well Dressed Man," March 1918, 72.

27. Frances Allen, 213.

28. Hart Schaffner and Marx ad: *Men's Wear,* June 10, 1925, 98.

29. Crowninshield, February 1925, 63.

30. Ibid., February 1928, 82.

31. Ibid., 108.

32. Alex Walker, "Color in Merchandise—A Sales Stimulant," *Printers' Ink,* April 21, 1927, 209.

33. Roland Marchand, *Advertising the American Dream: Making Way for Modernity 1920–1940* (Berkeley: University of California Press, 1985), 132.

34. Crowninshield, February 1928, 82.

35. Ibid.

36. Heyworth Campbell, ed., "For the Well Dressed Man," *Vanity Fair,* May 1921, 69.

37. Curtis, 28.

38. Trevor, August 1918, 54.

39. Crowninshield, April 1921, 74.

40. Ibid., August 1921, 69.

41. Ibid., April 1927, 92.

42. Curtis, 78.

43. Frances Allen, 215.

44. Curtis, 79.

45. Frances Allen, 215.

46. Crowninshield, January 1925, 64.

47. Trevor, March 1918, 75.

48. Curtis, 87.

49. Fairchild, "Shirts and Collars in Family Row," June 10, 1925, 86.

50. Sears, Roebuck catalog #159, Fall and Winter 1929, 428.

51. Ibid., 478.

52. Sportswear Incorporated ad: *Vanity Fair,* March 1929, 10.

53. Edward, Duke of Windsor, *A Family Album* (London: Cassell, 1960), 125.

54. Crowninshield, "Our London Letter on Men's Fashions," July 1925, 66; "What the College Man Really Wears," September 1926, 92.

55. Curtis, 80.

56. Crowninshield, "What the College Man Really Wears," September 1926, 94.

57. Ruttenber, 52.

58. Crowninshield, "What the College Man Really Wears," September 1926, 94.

59. Martin Sawicki, ed., "Princeton Beer Jackets: History and Lore," tigernet.princeton.edu, 1999.

60. Crowninshield, "What the College Man Really Wears," September 1926, 94.

61. Campbell, "For the Well Dressed Man," March 1921, 68.

62. Edward, Duke of Windsor, 130.

63. Crowninshield, "For the Well Dressed Man," January 1929, 74.

64. Jantzen ad: *Vanity Fair,* May 1928, 122.

65. Crowninshield, "Our London Letter on Men's Fashions," August 1929, 70.

66. Campbell, "For the Well Dressed Man," May 1921, 71.

67. Trevor, October 1918, 82.

68. Campbell, "For the Well Dressed Man," January 1921, 80.

69. Trevor, October 1918, 90.

70. Crowninshield, "For the Well Dressed Man," October 1929, 96.

71. Fairchild, "Color the Novelty Note in Underwear," June 10, 1925, 89.

72. Ibid.

73. Crowninshield, "Our London Letter on Men's Fashions," August 1925, 70.

74. Ibid., "For the Well Dressed Man," March 1921, 68.

75. O. E. Schoeffler and William Gale, *Esquire's Encyclopedia of Twentieth-Century Men's Fashions* (New York, McGraw-Hill, 1973), 380.

76. Campbell, "For the Well Dressed Man," March 1921, 69.

77. Berg Hats ad: *Vanity Fair,* November 1925, 94.

78. Crowninshield, "For the Well Dressed Man," April 1925, 79.

79. Trevor, August 1918, 54, 68b.

80. Crowninshield, "Our London Letter on Men's Fashion," February 1929, 84.

81. Ibid., March 1928, 84.

82. John Ward Shoes ad: *Vanity Fair,* June 1925, 109.

83. Campbell, "For the Well Dressed Man," January 1921, 80.

84. John Romer, ed., "Hands Off the President," *Printers' Ink,* February 12, 1925, 208.

85. Ibid.

86. Trevor, "Informal Evening Clothes," October 1918, 79.

87. Pond's Extract Company ad: *Good Housekeeping,* July 1929, 112.

88. Williams Aqua Velva ad: *Collier's,* April 11, 1925, 32.

89. Crowninshield, "Our London Letter on Men's Fashions," September 1928, 84.

90. Bill Brown's Farm for Physical Training ad: *Vanity Fair,* April 1925, 119.

Chapter 5

1. Walter Lippmann, "Vicious Spirals," *Vanity Fair,* June 1932, 44.

2. Donald J. Mabry, "Great Depression and Herbert Hoover 1929-33," historicaltextarchive.com, January 2010.

3. George M. Constantinides, Milton Harris, and René M. Stulz, eds. *Handbook of the Economics of Finance,* vol. 1 (Amsterdam, The Netherlands: Elsevier, 2003), 511.

4. Frederick Lewis Allen, 348.

5. Frazier Hunt, "America Is Dreaming Again," *Good Housekeeping,* June 1933, 60.

6. Ibid., 159.

7. Ibid., 61.

8. Ibid., 158.

9. Robert and Helen Lynd, *Middletown in Transition: A Study in Cultural Conflicts* (New York: Harcourt, Brace and Company, 1937), 493.

10. Ibid., 402–17.

11. Frederick Lewis Allen, 347.

12. Nick Taylor, "A Short History of the Great Depression," topics.nytimes.com, January 2010.

13. Lynd, 7.

14. Ibid., 406–7.

15. Janice Taylor, "Footnotes on the American Husband," *Vanity Fair,* January 1932, 45.

16. *Ladies' Home Journal* ad: *Ladies' Home Journal,* February 1939, 87.

17. Marynia Farnham and Ferdinand Lundberg, "Men Have Lost Their Women," *Ladies' Home Journal,* November 1944, 23.

18. Ibid., 132–5.

19. U.S. Bureau of the Census, *Historical Statistics of the United States: Colonial Times to 1970,* Part 1 (Washington, D.C.: U.S. Department of Commerce, 1975), 49.

20. Crowninshield, "For the Well Dressed Man," April 1931, 82.

21. Ibid., "Smart Flannels in Plain Grey for the Well-dressed Man," August 1932, 46.

22. Elizabeth Hawes, *Fashion is Spinach* (New York: Random House, 1938) 297.

23. Helen Lawrenson, "Fashion Is a Fairy," *Esquire,* April 1938, 36,116.

24. Crowninshield, "For the Well Dressed Man," April 1931, 82.

25. John A. Murdocke, "The Riviera Presents Many New Ideas for the Men's Wear Trade," *Men's Wear,* October 9, 1935, 19.

26. Edward, Duke of Windsor, 59, 103.

27. Arnold Gingrich, "At Least Look As If You Had a Little Money," *Esquire,* January 1934, 116.

28. Palm Beach Suit ad: *Saturday Evening Post,* June 30, 1934, 51.

29. Chamberlain, "Palm Beach Cloth," August 1937, 18.

30. Gingrich, "Sail for a Seersucker for a Cool Change," June 1935, 154.

31. Ibid., "Southern Wear is Elaborately Casual," January 1935, 119.

32. Duke of Windsor, 122.

33. J. C. Atchinson, "War and Men's Wear," *Men's Wear,* February 25, 1942, 9.

34. Chase, "Fashion in America Now," February 1, 1942, 50.

35. O. E. Schoeffler, "Streamlined Suits by Uncle Sam," *Esquire,* June 1942, 76.

36. Ibid.

37. Fairchild, "Defense Fashions," February 25, 1942, 18.

38. Stuart Cosgrove, "The Zoot-Suit and Style Warfare," *History Workshop Journal,* vol. 18 (Autumn 1984), 77.

39. Henry R. Luce, ed., "Zoot Suits: WPB Order Ending Jive-Garb Production Outrages Nation's Teenage Jitterbugs," *Life,* September 21, 1942, 45.

40. Cosgrove, 79.

41. Luce, 44.

42. Chamberlain, "Cluett, Peabody," 120.

43. Trubenizing Process Corporation ad: *Men's Wear,* April 24, 1935, 62.

44. Sears, Roebuck catalog #175, Fall and Winter 1937, 357.

45. Montgomery Ward catalog #128, Spring and Summer 1938, 245.

46. Sears, Roebuck catalog #175, Fall and Winter 1937, 428.

47. Ibid., 430.

48. Fairchild, "Get in the Swim," May 8, 1935, 9.

49. Murdocke, 18.

50. Gingrich, "The Riviera's Tip On Florida Fashions," January 1935, 108.

51. Murdocke, 19.

52. Hockmeyer Brothers ad: *Vanity Fair,* March 1933, 10.

53. Murdocke, 18.

54. Gingrich, "The Golfer as Glorified Boy Scout," June 1936, 148.

55. Fairchild, "There's a Reason Behind Winter Sportswear," October 9, 1935, 32.

56. Puritan Sportswear ad: *Esquire,* January 1939, 27.

57. Schoeffler, "Skiing in the Military Manner," *Esquire,* February 1943, 79.

58. Schoeffler, *Esquire's Encyclopedia of Twentieth-Century Men's Fashions,* 424.

59. Walter Raymond, ed., "Seventy-five Years of Fashion: 1930–1940," *Men's Wear,* June 25, 1965, 124.

60. Sears, Roebuck catalog #187, Fall and Winter 1943, 453.

61. Cooper's ad: *Esquire,* September 1936, 188.

62. B.V.D. Combonair ad: *Vanity Fair,* June 1933, 54.

63. Sears, Roebuck catalog #187, Fall and Winter 1943, 531.

64. Van Baalen, Heilbrun ad: *Men's Wear,* October 9, 1935, 10.

65. Crowninshield, "For the Well Dressed Man," March 1932, 58.

66. Gingrich, "A Complete Hat Wardrobe for Fall and Winter," September 1936, 124.

67. Sears, Roebuck catalog #175, Fall and Winter 1937–1938, 374.

68. Duke of Windsor, 115.

69. Ibid., 116.

70. Gingrich, "Court Costume for the Season of 1934," August 1934, 115.

71. Remington ad: *Esquire,* September 1937, 28.

72. Mennen ad: *Esquire,* August 1937, 194.

Chapter 6

1. U.S. Bureau of the Census, *Historical Statistics of the United States: Colonial Times to 1970,* Part 1 (Washington, D.C.: U.S. Department of Commerce, 1975), 126.

2. Betty Friedan, *The Feminine Mystique* (New York: Laurel, 1983), 18.

3. Norman Podhoretz, "Where Is the Beat Generation Going?" *Esquire,* December 1958, 150.

4. John Galbraith, *The Affluent Society* (Boston: Mentor, 1958), 15–16.

5. Podhoretz, 150.

6. William Chafe, *The Paradox of Change: American Women in the Twentieth Century* (New York: Oxford University Press, 1991), 159.

7. Claudia Goldin, *Marriage Bars: Discrimination against Married Women Workers 1920s to 1950's* (Cambridge, MA: National Bureau of Economic Research, 1988), 1.

8. Chafe, 156.

9. Bret Carroll, ed., *American Masculinities: A Historical Encyclopedia* (Thousand Oaks, CA: Sage, 2003), 440.

10. Michael Kimmel, *Manhood in America* (New York: Free Press, 1996), 234.

11. Friedan, 18.

12. Clifford Adams, "Making Marriage Work," *Ladies' Home Journal,* January 1951, 26; February 1951, 26; March 1951, 26; April 1951, 28; May 1951, 26; June 1951, 28.

13. Henrietta Ripperger, "Is Ours a Beat-up or a Built-up Man?" *Woman's Day,* March 1953, 66.

14. Friedan, xi.

15. Goldman and Brothers ad: *Esquire,* June 1948, 114.

16. David Smart, ed., "Mr. 'T' Esquire's New Trim Look Takes Over," *Esquire,* November 1950, 88.

17. Belmont Clothes ad: *Esquire,* November 1950, 121.

18. Bob Greene, "Required Reading: The Man in the Gray Flannel Suit," *Esquire,* June 1986, 200.

19. Smart, "Grey to a T," March 1951, 65.

20. Everett Mattlin, ed., "The Shaped Suit," *Gentlemen's Quarterly,* October 1958, 101.

21. Schoeffler, "The Slim-line Suit," January 1958, 72.

22. Melton Davis, "The Tailors of Rome," *Gentlemen's Quarterly,* November 1959, 102.

23. Farid Chenoune, *A History of Men's Fashion,* trans. Deke Dusinberre (Paris: Flammarion, 1993), 242.

24. Mattlin, "The Three-Button and the Double-Breasted Continental," September 1959, 70.

25. Ibid., "Pauline Trigere Designs for Men," May 1959, 74–5.

26. Ibid., "Foreign Portfolio: A Bolder Britain," December 1958, 114–5.

27. Ibid., "Pauline Trigere Designs for Men," May 1959, 74.

28. Pearl Binder, *Peacock's Tail* (London: Harrap, 1958), 14.

29. Henry Luce, ed., "Men Try Shorts for Town," *Life,* August 3, 1953, 61.

30. Arlene Cooper, "Casual, But Not That Casual: Some Fashions of the 1950s," *Dress,* vol. 11, 1985, 49.

31. Tony Williams, "Things to Come," *Men's Wear,* January 15, 1946, 49.

32. Schoeffler, "The Esquire Guide for the Bridegroom," June 1948, 84.

33. Ibid., "First Run Smash Hit," December 1956, 144–5.

34. Ibid., "Patterns in the Sun...Designs under the Moon," February 1958, 70.

35. Mattlin, "The New Age of Evening Elegance," November 1959, 68.

36. Schoeffler, "The Bold Look," April 1948, 78.

37. Ibid., "It's the Bold, Dominant Male Look for You for Fall 1948," September 1948, 58.

38. Sears, Roebuck catalog #207, Fall and Winter 1953, 467.

39. Sears, Roebuck catalog #215, Fall and Winter 1957, 596.

40. The Domino ad: *Esquire,* September 1958, 161.

41. Tony Williams, "Things to Come," *Men's Wear,* January 25, 1946, 48.

42. John Berendt, *Esquire Fashion for Men,* (New York: Harper and Row, 1957), 14.

43. Mattlin, "The Bolder Approach: Sports Shirts," Winter 1957, 102.

44. Jacques Faure, "Pants Go to All Lengths," *California Men's and Boy's Stylist,* January 1956, 57.

45. Schoeffler, "Fancy Pants," February 1958, 69.

46. Christopher Fremantle, ed., "Red Offset with Black," *Gentry,* Winter 1954, 96.

47. Ibid., "Ocean Beach...Pool Side," Summer 1955, 74.

48. Schoeffler, " '90s in the Swim," February 1958, 73.

49. Fremantle, "Gentry Fashions for Fall," Fall 1952, 81.

50. Mattlin, "A Report on the New Continental," March 1959, 94.

51. Fremantle, "The Story of the One and Only Authentic Duffer," Winter 1951, 30.

52. Schoeffler, "Capes for Inner Space," August 1958, 74.

53. Mattlin, "Looks Like Fur," November 1958, 94.

54. Fairchild, "The Inside Story—Men's Underwear," January 25, 1946, 66.

55. Spiegel catalog, Spring and Summer, 1954, 261.

56. Fairchild, "The Inside Story—Men's Underwear," January 25, 1946, 66.

57. Jockey Skants ad: *Esquire,* December 1959, 64.

58. Schoeffler, "It's the Bold, Dominant Male Look for You for Fall 1948," September 1948, 58.

59. Ibid., "The Bold Look," April 1948, 81.

60. Mattlin, "Straws to Turn All Heads," Summer 1958, 75.

61. Ibid., "When Buying a Hat," November 1958, 99.

62. Schoeffler, "Coordinate to a T," March 1951, 63.

63. Ibid., "Cross-Channel Reports," April 1953, 95.

64. Montgomery Ward catalog, Fall and Winter, 1956, 623.

65. John Howard, ed., "The Long Hair Stuff Has Got to Go!" *TV Headliner,* January 1959, 75.

66. Mennen ad: *Esquire,* August 1951, 19.

67. David Riesman, *The Lonely Crowd: A Study of the Changing American Character* (New Haven: Yale University Press, 1950), 371–2.

Chapter 7

1. Friedan, 15.

2. Robert Christgau, "Are You Ready for Men's Liberation?" *Ms.,* February 1974, 16.

3. Paul Welch, "Homosexuality in America," Life, June 26, 1964, 66.

4. John Loughery, *The Other Side of Silence* (New York: Henry Holt, 1998), 323.

5. *Youthquake* book ad: *Look,* May 16, 1967, 11.

6. H. W. Janson and Anthony Janson, *History of Art,* 6th edition (Upper Saddle River, NJ: Prentice-Hall, 2001), 908.

7. Edna Woolman Chase, ed., "The Rising Son," *Vogue,* April 1, 1931, 84.

8. Bill Gale, *Esquire's Fashions for Today* (New York: Harper and Row, 1969), 8.

9. Edward Thompson, ed., "The Guys Go All-out to Get Gawked At," *Life,* May 13, 1966, 82A.

10. Gale, 8.

11. Bradley, 243.

12. Redding, "As Seen by Him," May 23, 1895, 331.

13. Thompson, "The Guys Go All-out to Get Gawked At," 84.

14. David Block, *Carnaby Street* (London: Lord Kitchener, 1967), 7–8.

15. Thompson "Revolution in Men's Clothes," May 13, 1966, 3.

16. Harold Hayes, ed., "College Clothes Circa Sixty-Nine—A New Sprightliness," *Esquire,* September 1969, 136.

17. George Hunt, ed., "Now the Mini Has a Man in It," *Life,* August 11, 1967, 29.

18. Mattlin, "Sidewalks of N.Y.," *Gentlemen's Quarterly,* November 1966, 125.

19. Ibid., "Kilts A'comin'?" *GQ Campus and Career Annual,* Fall-Winter, 1967, 94.

20. William Arthur, ed., "Bedtime Sleeper: Skilts," *Look,* July 25, 1967, 69.

21. George Frazier, "The Peacock Revolution," *Esquire,* October 1968, 207, 212.

22. Mort Gordon, ed., "The New Masculinity," *Men's Wear,* July 11, 1969, 63.

23. Tom Wolfe, "Tom Wolfe's Seventies," *Esquire,* December 1979, 37.

24. Matt Cohen, "Toronto Punk," *Quest,* December 1977, TE3.

25. Mattlin, "Off the Cuff...Random Observations on Fashion and the Fashionable," October 1961, 16.

26. Ibid., "Look Like New in '65," February 1965, 84.

27. Ibid., "Off the Cuff...Random Observations on Fashion and the Fashionable," October 1961, 164.

28. Ibid., "Color Comes to Suitings," March 1964, 107.

29. Ibid., "Detail Makes All the Difference," November 1965, 118.

30. Hayes, "One Touch of Nehru Makes the Whole World Kin," July 1968, 95.

31. Mattlin, "Is This You?" September 1968, 62.

32. Frazier, "The Peacock Revolution," 212.

33. Gordon, "The Individualist: He'll Wear the Hard, Wide Lapel," July 11, 1969, 41.

34. Ibid., 42, 46.

35. Jack Haber, ed., "The Sum of the Parts," *Gentlemen's Quarterly,* November 1976, 178.

36. Gordon, "The Individualist: He'll Wear the Hard, Wide Lapel," 49.

37. Haber, "Europe Takes It Easy," April 1977, 88.

38. Ibid., "Armani on the Loose," September 1978, 120.

39. Stanley Gellers, ed., "Black Tie," *Men's Wear,* August 11, 1967, 57.

40. Lion of Troy ad: *Gentlemen's Quarterly,* Summer 1965, 23.

41. After Six Formalwear ad: *Look,* December 10, 1968, T28.

42. Charles Hix, *Dressing Right: A Guide For Men* (New York: St. Martin's, 1978), 136.

43. Mattlin, "Permanent Press: A Progress Report," February 1966, 41.

44. Gellers, "The Urbane Shirt," November 17, 1967, 49.

45. Ramey-Tyson Shirt Corporation ad: *Gentlemen's Quarterly,* Winter 1968, 29.

46. Moss Shirts ad: *New York Times Magazine,* April 25, 1965, 80.

47. Haber, "Shirting the Issue," March 1977, 90.

48. J. C. Penney catalog, Spring and Summer, 1977, 645.

49. Montgomery Ward catalog, Fall and Winter, 1965, 595.

50. Mattlin, "Put It in Print," February 1965, 81.

51. Gordon, "The New Masculinity: What Retailers Say," July 11, 1969, 74.

52. Ibid., "The New Masculinity: What the Social Scientists Say," 64.

53. Gellers, "Advance '70 Sportswear: The Resort Look," September 5, 1969, 67.

54. Arthur Boehm, "Does Every Heart Beat True for the Red, White and Blue?" *Gentlemen's Quarterly,* February, 1971, 96.

55. Haber, "Now," *GQ Scene,* Fall-Winter, 1966, 129.

56. Walter Raymond, ed. "Some Things New for Summer," *Men's Wear,* May 10, 1963, 168.

57. Iris Bauer, "Summer Pants: Ringing in the Bell-Bottoms," *Look,* May 31, 1966, 86; Mattlin, "Bell-Bottoms," February 1966, 63.

58. Talon ad: *New York Times Magazine,* April 21, 1968, 24.

59. Gordon, "The Slack Rack," October 4, 1968, 64.

60. Kim Foltz, "The Wearing of the Jeans," *Gentlemen's Quarterly,* April 1974, 93.

61. Brant Mewborn, "Smart Ass Jeans," *After Dark,* November 1979, 53.

62. Mattlin, "Way Out on the Slopes," Winter 1965, 72.

63. Haber, "Keep on Trunking," Summer 1975, 64.

64. Ibid., "Water Colors," Summer 1977, 68.

65. Hayes, "The Maxi: A Great Coat in More Ways Than One," November 1968, 138.

66. Gellers, "New Outerwear Directions," November 3, 1967, 48.

67. Hayes, "A New Look of Leather," November 1968, 140.

68. Ibid., 138.

69. Haber, "The Fur Furor," November 1970, 69.

70. Ibid., "Consider the Alternatives," 77, 79.

71. Hayes, "The Reptile Syndrome: The Look of Snakeskin and Imitation Alligator," August 1970, 119.

72. Sears catalog, Fall and Winter 1973, 661.

73. "Action cut bikini brief" of stretch nylon: Montgomery Ward catalog, Fall and Winter, 1961, 710.

74. Hayes, "Inside Story: Fundamentals of the Slim Look," March 1966, 102.

75. Gordon, "The New Masculinity: What the Women Say," July 11, 1969, 71.

76. Osborn Elliot, ed., "The Beefcake Mags," *Newsweek,* May 28, 1973, 113.

77. Haber, "Brief Encounter," Summer 1971, 93.

78. Germaine Greer, "What Turns Women On?" *Esquire,* July 1973, 150.

79. Gale, 124.

80. Lillian Borgeson, "Whatever Happened to Pajamas?" *Gentlemen's Quarterly,* October 1970, 95.

81. Pleetway Sleeperinos ad: *Esquire,* December 1969, 66.

82. Gale, 85.

83. Ernest Hubbard, "Hat Life," *Men's Wear,* September 27, 1963, 116.

84. Haber, "Head Lines," November 1977, 96.

85. Hayes, "Esquire Predicts," February 1966, 105.

86. Haber, "What's Hot," March 1978, 154.

87. Earth Shoes ad: *Gentlemen's Quarterly,* November 1974, 23.

88. Enger Kress ad: *Esquire,* November 1969, 252.

89. Bernard Rudolfsky, *Are Clothes Modern?* Chicago: Paul Theobald, 1947, 219.

90. Haber, "Getting Your Junk Together," April 1971, 103.

91. Hayes, "Now Really!" August 1968, 106.

92. Ibid.

93. Haber, "Jewelry Fit for a Man," October 1970, 156.

94. Mattlin, "The New Man," February 1966, 50–51.

95. Harold Rosenberg, "Masculinity: Real and Put On," *Vogue,* November 15, 1967, 106.

96. Charles Winick, *The New People: Desexualization in American Life* (New York: Pegasus, 1968), 356–58.

97. Mattlin, "The New Man," February 1966, 46.

98. Mattlin, "Look Like New in '65," February 1965, 87.

99. Haber, "The Wigs: Ready-to-Wear," April 1971, 82.

100. Mattlin, "Grooming: Cosmetic Camouflage," October 1969, 46.

101. Male Bag ad: *Gentlemen's Quarterly,* November 1978, 91.

102. Charles Hix, *Looking Good: A Guide for Men* (New York: Hawthorne, 1978), xiv.

103. Tom Wolfe, "Tom Wolfe's Seventies," *Esquire*, December 1979, 48.

104. Gordon, "The New Masculinity: What the Social Scientists Say," July 11, 1969, 64.

Chapter 8

1. Peter Jennings and Todd Brewster, *The Century* (New York: Doubleday, 1998), 470.

2. John Karaagac, *Between Promise and Policy: Ronald Reagan and Conservative Reformism* (Lanham, MD: Lexington, 2001), 144; Paul Carter, *Another Part of the Fifties* (New York: Columbia University Press, 1983), 27.

3. Olaf Gersemann, *Cowboy Capitalism: European Myths, American Reality* (Washington, D.C., Cato Institute, 2004), 112.

4. Ibid., 111.

5. Dinesh D'Souza, *Ronald Reagan: How an Ordinary Man Became an Extraordinary Leader* (New York: Simon and Schuster, 1999), 105.

6. Will Bunch, *Tear Down This Myth: How the Reagan Legacy Has Distorted Our Politics and Haunts Our Future* (New York: Free Press, 2009), 59.

7. George Hager, "Decades-Old Era of Budget Deficits Ends," *Washington Post*, September 30, 1998, C10.

8. William Walton Keller, Gordon R. Mitchell, *Hitting First: Preventive Force in U.S. Security Strategy* (Pittsburgh: University of Pittsburgh Press, 2006), 220.

9. Henry Blodget, "Crash of 2008 Now Worse Than Crash of 1929," businessinsider.com, March 5, 2009; Dan Gainor, Julia A. Seymour and Genevieve Ebel, *The Great Media Depression: News Reports Depict Economy Far Worse Now Than During the 1929 Stock Market Crash* (Alexandria, VA: Business and Media Institute, 2008), 1.

10. Bob Herbert, "Bush's Not-So-Big Tent," *New York Times*, July 16, 2004, A21.

11. Robert Scheer, "Taxpayers Lose, Halliburton Gains," *The Nation*, June 27, 2007.

12. John Micklethwait and Adrian Woolridge, *The Right Nation: Conservative Power in America* (New York: Penguin, 2004), 102.

13. Sylvia Flanagan, ed. "National Report," *Jet*, November 4, 1991, 6.

14. Andy Barr, "Bush low point: 'Being Called a Racist'," politico.com, January 14, 2009.

15. Lou Cannon, *President Reagan: The Role of a Lifetime* (New York: Public Affairs, 2000), 733.

16. Simon Dumenco, "The New Homophobia," *Details*, September 2005, 138.

17. Glenn O'Brien, "Modern Manners," *Gentlemen's Quarterly*, September 2006, 318.

18. Allan Flusser, "The Suit," *Gentlemen's Quarterly*, September 2002, 368.

19. Charles Hix, *Man Alive! Dressing the Free Way* (New York: Simon and Schuster, 1984), 18.

20. Flugel, *The Psychology of Clothes*, 208.

21. Charles Atlas ad: *Physical Culture*, May 1938, 3.

22. Barbara Lippert, "Here's the Beef," *Adweek*, April 19, 1999, 36.

23. Martin Levine, *Gay Macho: The Life and Death of the Homosexual Clone*, ed. Michael Kimmel (New York: New York University Press, 1998, 56; Erik Alvarez, *Muscle Boys: Gay Gym Culture* (New York: Routledge, 2008), 99.

24. Flugel, 28.

25. Tim Edwards, *Men in the Mirror: Men's Fashion, Masculinity and Consumer Society* (London: Cassell, 1997), 45.

26. Germano Celant and Harold Koda, *Giorgio Armani* (New York: Guggenheim Museum, 2001), 85.

27. Valerie Steele, "Phallic Fashion," *Vogue Hommes International*, Fall/Winter 2002, 160.

28. Susan Bordo, *The Male Body: A New Look at Men in Public and in Private* (New York: Farrar, Straus, and Grioux, 1999), 169.

29. Mark Simpson, "Meet the Metrosexual," salon.com, July 22, 2002.

30. Steve Blechman, "Trend Alert: The New Look for Guys Is Butch," *Fitness RX for Men*, January 2008, 62.

31. Peter Carlsen, "Express Male: Keeping Up with Fashion's Fast Moves," *Gentlemen's Quarterly*, March 1981, 104.

32. Ibid., 108–9.

33. Jeffrey Miller, "English Youth Has Its Say," *Gentlemen's Quarterly*, April 1982, 170.

34. Gregory Cerio, "What Becomes a Zealot Most?" *Gentlemen's Quarterly*, November 1993, 235.

35. Amy de la Haye and Cathie Dingwall, *Surfers, Soulies, Skinheads, and Skaters: Subcultural Style from the Forties to the Nineties* (Woodstock, NY: Overlook, 1996), 10–15.

36. Bob Mack, "Off the Cuff: Everything Old Is Dope Again," *Gentlemen's Quarterly*, October 1992, 215.

37. Miller, "English Youth Has Its Say," 173.

38. Michael Goldberg, "Punk Lives," *Rolling Stone*, July 18, 1985, 28.

39. Grace Coddington, "Grunge and Glory," *Vogue*, December 1992, 260.

40. Alison Lurie, *The Language of Clothes* (New York: Henry Holt, 2000), 160.

41. Carlsen, "Express Male: Keeping Up with Fashion's Fast Moves," 108.

42. Shaun Cole, *Don We Now Our Gay Apparel* (Oxford: Berg, 2000), 94.

43. Clark Henley, *The Butch Manual: The Current Drag and How to Do It.* (New York: New American Library, 1982), 138.

44. Cole, 95.

45. Richard Martin, "The Gay Factor in Fashion," *Esquire Gentleman*, Spring 1993, 135–6.

46. Hilary Sterne, "Seventh Avenue: Report from Milan," *Gentlemen's Quarterly*, December 1993, 176.

47. Marc Van Bree, *The Metrosexual Defined: Narcissism and Masculinity in Popular Culture*, (n.p., 2004), 9.

48. Dumenco, 138.

49. Haber, "Company Style," August 1982, 106.

50. Scott Omelianuk, "Fall Preview 1993," *Gentlemen's Quarterly*, July 1993, 66.

51. Arthur Cooper, ed., "The Armani Revolution," *Gentlemen's Quarterly*, January 1990, 150.

52. Sterne, "Seventh Avenue: Report from Milan," 174.

53. Cooper, "Back to the Future," July 1992, 78; Cooper, "Button, Button, Button," November 1993, 251;

Omelianuk, "The Minimalists," February 1996, 114; Omelianuk, "Seventh Avenue," September 1996, 216.

54. Cooper, "All About Fall Suits," August 1997, 133.

55. Ibid., 138.

56. Jim Nelson, ed., "The Short Suit," *Gentlemen's Quarterly*, October 2004, 319.

57. Ibid., "How a Suit Should Fit: The New Rules," February 2006, 48.

58. Ro Costello, "Gunn Control: The Project Runway Style Master Dishes on Your Duds," *Genre*, December 2007, 25.

59. Cooper, "All About Fall Suits," August 1997, 140.

60. Nathaniel Goldberg, "The Man in the Gray (Indestructible) Suit," *Gentlemen's Quarterly*, January 2008, 113.

61. John Berendt, "Classics: White Tie and Tails," *Esquire*, October 1985, 40.

62. Ibid.

63. Glenn O'Brien, "The Style Guy," *Gentlemen's Quarterly*, October 2003, 68.

64. John Mather, "The Esquire Collection: Street Smarts," *Esquire*, September 1984, 62–3.

65. Haber, "Italian Overview," March 1982, 174.

66. Marshall Field's Store for Men ad, *Gentlemen's Quarterly*, March 1982, 6.

67. Cooper, "Viva Versace!" June 1991, 188.

68. Ibid., "Made in Japan," April 1984, 257.

69. Philip Smith, "Past Imperfect," *Gentlemen's Quarterly*, August 1982, 48.

70. William Berlind, "Bush Men," *Gentlemen's Quarterly*, October 2004, 190.

71. Nelson, "The Low Down," August 2009, 41.

72. Cooper, "Seventh Avenue," March 1997, 207.

73. Hawes, 305.

74. Cooper, "Off the Cuff: Skirting the Issue," November 1992, 212.

75. Elizabeth Wilson, 165.

76. Steve Tesich, "The Compleat Biker: Leader of the Pack," *Gentlemen's Quarterly*, May 1986, 176.

77. Cooper, "Men in Tights," June 1997, 225.

78. Mim Udovitch, "Fly Guy: Michael Jordan, the King of Ball Media, Holds Forth," *Details*, January 1997, 37.

79. Laurie Schechter, "Snow Motion," *Rolling Stone*, October 23, 1986, 85.

80. Cooper, "Rocky Mountain High Tech," December 1986, 209.

81. Head Skiwear ad: *Gentlemen's Quarterly*, November 1988, special section insert.

82. Cooper, "His Girl Friday," January 1986, 122.

83. Martin Dugard, "Finding Your Stroke," *Gentlemen's Quarterly*, March 1997, 180.

84. Adam Rapoport, "Battle of the Bulge," *Gentlemen's Quarterly*, May 2004, 72.

85. Mark Simpson, "Speedophobia," *Out*, February 2007, 57.

86. Jim Moore, "The Parke and Ronen Swimsuit," *Gentlemen's Quarterly*, July 2006, 25.

87. Andrew Creagh, ed., "Is the Boardshort Back?" *DNA*, February 2007, 18.

88. Peter Carlsen, "Made in Japan," *Gentlemen's Quarterly*, May 1982, 165.

89. Nelson, "The Coat that Suits You," October 2004, 325.

90. Frank Strachan, "Privates on Parade," *Fashion Inc.*, Spring 2006, 116.

91. Glenn O'Brien, "A Brief Appreciation," *Gentlemen's Quarterly*, September 2007, 158.

92. Dan Shaw, "Unmentionables? No More," *New York Times*/NYTimes.com, August 14, 1994.

93. Cooper, "Robes Gallery," December 1984, 223.

94. Christine McParland, "Practical Matters: How to Buy a Hat," *Esquire*, September 1984, 36.

95. Nelson, "The Ten Commandments of Style," May 2006, 167.

96. Ibid., "Is Your Tie Too Wide?" August 2004, 156.

97. Omelianuk, "Seventh Avenue," September 1996, 216.

98. Omelianuk, "Seventh Avenue," December 1993, 178; Nelson, "Is Your Tie Too Wide?" August 2004, 156.

99. Haber, "The Strides of March," March 1982, 192.

100. Jim Moore, "Twenty Things the Well-Dressed Man Needs to Know Right Now," *Gentlemen's Quarterly*, August 2004, 54.

101. John Fleming, "Pain in the Back Leads Innovative Businessman to Create a New Wallet Design," *Men's Workout*, June 2008, 88.

102. Nelson, "The Ten Commandments of Style," 168.

103. Nieman-Marcus ad: *Gentlemen's Quarterly*, November 1983, 39.

104. Susan Ferraro, "O Come, Let Us Adorn Him," *Gentlemen's Quarterly*, July 1988, 102.

105. Lucy Kaylin, "I Love You, Man," *Gentlemen's Quarterly*, November 1996, 224.

106. Rebecca Johnson, "Hoop Screams," *Gentlemen's Quarterly*, April 1997, 84.

107. Ferraro, 105.

108. Nelson, "The Ten Commandments of Style," 165.

109. Jack Smith, "Golly, Gekko, The Wet Look is Back," *Gentlemen's Quarterly*, June 1988, 258.

110. David Friedman, "Hirsute It Is," *Gentlemen's Quarterly*, March 1988, 321.

111. Roger Streitmatter, *Sex Sells!* (Cambridge, MA: Westview, 2004), 119.

112. O'Brien, "Glenn O'Brien Solves Your Sartorial Conundrums," March 2003, 164.

113. Robert Moritz, "Botox Nation," *Gentlemen's Quarterly*, October 2004, 164.

114. L'Oréal ad: *GQ Style*, Spring 2006, 143.

115. Chris Rovny, "Stylish Tattoos," AskMen.com, January 29, 2009.

116. Will Welch, "Kids! Be the First on Your Block NOT to Get a Tattoo," *Gentlemen's Quarterly*, September 2009, 122.

117. Aaron Hicklin, ed., "The Line of Beauty," *Out*, June/July 2009, 109.

118. John Sedgwick, "The Foreskin Saga," *Gentlemen's Quarterly*, February 2000, 156–61.

119. Blechman, "Circumcision Does Not Decrease Sensitivity," 58.

120. Sedgwick, 161.

121. Miller, "English Youth Has Its Say," 175.

122. Elizabeth Wilson, 157.

Adams, James. *Dandies and Desert Saints: Styles of Victorian Manhood.* Ithaca, NY: Cornell, 1995.

Agins, Teri. *The End of Fashion: The Mass Marketing of the Clothing Business.* New York: William Morrow, 1999.

Allen, Frederick Lewis. *Only Yesterday: An Informal History of the Nineteen-Twenties.* New York: Harper and Brothers, 1931.

Alvarez, Erick. *Muscle Boys: Gay Gym Culture.* New York: Routledge, 2008.

Armstrong, Nancy. *Victorian Jewelry.* New York: Macmillan, 1976.

Ashdown, Emily. *British Costume During XIX Centuries.* London: T. C. and E .C. Jack, 1910.

Ashelford, Jane. *The Art of Dress: Clothes and Society 1500-1914.* London, National Trust, 1996.

Avedon, Richard, and Doon Arbus. *The Sixties.* New York: Random House, 1999.

Baclawski, Karen. *The Guide to Historic Costume.* New York: Drama, 1995.

Bailey, Adrian. *The Passion for Fashion: Three Centuries of Changing Styles.* Limpsfield, UK: Dragon's World, 1988.

Bailey, Perkins, ed. *Men's Wear: History of the Men's Wear Industry 1890-1950.* New York: Fairchild, 1950.

Baines, Barbara. *Fashion Revivals from the Elizabethan Age to the Present Day.* London: B. T. Batsford, 1981.

Baker, Patricia. *Fashions of a Decade: The 1950s.* New York: Facts on File, 1991.

———. *Fashions of a Decade: The 1940s.* New York: Facts on File, 1992.

Barfoot, Audrey. *Discovering Costume.* London: University of London Press, 1959.

Barnard, Malcolm. *Fashion as Communication.* London: Routledge, 1996.

Batterberry, Michael, and Ariane Batterberry. *Mirror, Mirror, A Social History of Fashion.* New York: Holt, Rinehart and Winston, 1977.

Baudot, Francois. *Fashion: The Twentieth Century.* New York: Universe, 1999.

———. *The Allure of Men.* New York: Assouline, 2000.

Bell, Quentin. *On Human Finery.* New York: Schocken, 1976.

Benson, Elaine, and John Esten. *Unmentionables: A Brief History of Underwear.* New York: Simon and Schuster, 1996.

Berendt, John. *Esquire Fashions for Men.* New York: Harper and Row, 1957.

———. *Esquire Fashions for Men.* Rev. ed. New York: Harper and Row, 1966.

Bergler, Edmund. *Fashion and the Unconscious.* Madison, CT: International Universities Press, 1987.

Biddle, Julian. *What Was Hot: A Rollercoaster Ride through Six Decades of Pop Culture in America.* New York: MJF, 2001.

Bigelow, Marybelle. *Fashion in History: Western Dress, Prehistoric to Present.* Minneapolis, MN: Burgess, 1979.

Binder, Pearl. *The Peacock's Tail.* London: Harrap, 1958.

Black, J. Anderson, and Madge Garland. *A History of Fashion.* New York: William Morrow, 1981.

Blackman, Cally. *One Hundred Years of Menswear.* London: Laurence King, 2009.

Blanchard, Tamsin. *Antonio Berardi: Sex and Sensibility.* New York: Watson-Guptill, 1999.

Block, David. *Carnaby Street.* London: Lord Kitchener, 1967.

Bolton, Andrew. *Bravehearts: Men in Skirts.* London: V&A, 2003.

Bonner, Paul, ed. *The World in Vogue.* New York: Viking, 1963.

Bordo, Susan. *The Male Body: A New Look at Men in Public and in Private.* New York: Farrar, Straus and Giroux, 1999.

Bosker, Gideon, and Lena Lencek. *Making Waves: Swimsuits and the Undressing of America.* San Francisco: Chronicle, 1988.

Boston, Lloyd. *Men of Color: Fashion, History, Fundamentals.* New York: Artisan, 1998.

Boucher, Francois. *A History of Costume in the West.* London: Thames and Hudson, 1967.

Bowman, Sara, and Michel Molinare. *A Fashion for Extravagance: Art Deco Fabrics and Fashions.* New York: E. P. Dutton, 1985.

Bradfield, Nancy. *Costume in Detail 1730-1930.* Boston: Plays, 1968.

Bradley, Carolyn, G. *Western World Costume.* New York: Dover, 2001.

Bradley, Dennis, ed. *The Man of Today.* London: Pope and Bradley, 1914.

Braun-Ronsdorf, Margarete. *Mirror of Fashion: A History of European Costume 1789-1929.* New York: McGraw-Hill, 1964.

Breward, Christopher. *The Culture of Fashion.* Manchester, UK: Manchester University Press, 1995.

———. *The Hidden Consumer: Masculinities, Fashion, and City Life 1860-1914.* Manchester, UK: Manchester University Press, 1999.

Brooke, Iris. *English Costume 1900-1950.* London: Methuen, 1951.

Brown, William. *American Men's Shirts 1750-1900.* Gettysburg, PA: Thomas, 1999.

Bryan, Robert. *American Fashion Menswear.* New York: Assouline, 2009.

Buck, Anne. *Victorian Costume and Costume Accessories.* New York: Thomas Nelson, 1961.

Butterfield, Roger. *The American Past.* New York: Simon and Schuster, 1947.

Buttolph, Angela, et al. *The Fashion Book.* London: Phaidon, 1998.

Buxbaum, Gerda. *Icons of Fashion of the Twentieth Century.* Munich: Prestel Verlag, 1999.

Buzzaccarini, Vittoria de. *Elegance and Style: Two Hundred Years of Men's Fashions.* Milan: Lupetti, 1992.

Byrde, Penelope. *Nineteenth Century Fashion.* London: B. T. Batsford, 1992.

Calasibetta, Charlotte. *Essential Terms of Fashion.* New York: Fairchild, 1986.

Campbell, Emily, et al. *Inside Out: Underwear and Style in the UK.* London: Black Dog, 2000.

Carlyle, Thomas. *Sartor Resartus.* New York: Macmillan, 1927.

Carnegy, Vicky. *Fashions of a Decade: The 1980s.* New York: Facts on File, 1990.

Carroll, Bret, ed. *American Masculinities: A Historical Encyclopedia.* Thousand Oaks, CA: Sage, 2003.

Carter, Ernestine. *The Changing World of Fashion.* New York: G. P. Putnam's Sons, 1977.

———. *With Tongue in Chic.* London: Michael Joseph, 1977.

Cassin-Scott, Jack. *The Illustrated Encyclopedia of Costume and Fashion from 1066 to the Present.* London: Studio Vista, 1998.

———. *Costume and Fashion in Color 1760-1920.* New York: Macmillan, 1971.

Celant, Germano, and Harold Koda. *Giorgio Armani.* New York: Guggenheim Museum, 2001.

Chenoune, Farid. *A History of Men's Fashion.* Trans. Deke Dusinberre. Paris: Flammarion, 1993.

Chic Simple Partners. *Men's Wardrobe.* New York: Knopf, 1993.

Claudon, C. David. *Beefcake Beachwear: A Brief History.* New York: Lulu, 2008.

Cobbett, William. *Advice to Young Men.* 1830. Reprint, London: Oxford University Press, 1980.

Cobrin, Harry. *The Men's Clothing Industry: Colonial Times Through Modern Times.* New York: Fairchild, 1970.

Cohan, Steven, and Ina Rae Hark , ed. *Screening the Male: Exploring Masculinities in the Hollywood Cinema.* London: Routledge, 1993.

Cole, Shaun. *Don We Now Our Gay Apparel.* Oxford: Berg, 2000.

Coleman, Elizabeth. *Changing Fashions 1800-1970.* Brooklyn: Brooklyn Museum, 1972.

———. *Of Men Only: A Review of Men's and Boy's Fashions 1750-1975.* Brooklyn: Brooklyn Museum, 1975.

Coleridge, Nicholas. *The Fashion Conspiracy.* London: Heinemann, 1989.

Connell, R. W. *Masculinities.* 2nd ed. Berkeley: University of California Press, 2005.

———. *The Men and the Boys.* Berkeley: University of California Press, 2001.

Connickie, Yvonne. *Fashions of a Decade: The 1960s.* New York: Facts on File, 1991.

Connolly, Joseph. *All Shook Up: A Flash of the Fifties.* London: Cassell, 2000.

Contini, Mila. *Fashion from Ancient Egypt to the Present Day.* New York: Odyssey, 1965.

Cooper, Wendy. *Hair: Sex, Society, Symbolism.* New York: Stein and Day, 1971.

Corbin, Harry. *The Men's Clothing Industry: Colonial Through Modern Times.* New York: Fairchild, 1970.

Cosgrave, Bronwyn. *The Complete History of Costume and Fashion from Ancient Egypt to the Present Day.* New York: Checkmark, 2000.

Costantino, Maria. *Fashions of a Decade: The 1930s.* New York: Facts on File, 1992.

———. *Men's Fashion in the Twentieth Century: From Frock Coats to Intelligent Fibres.* London: B. T. Batsford, 1997.

Craik, Jennifer. *The Face of Fashion.* London: Routledge, 1994.

Crawford, M. D. C. *One World of Fashion.* New York: Fairchild, 1947.

Cremers-Van de Does, Eline. *The Agony of Fashion.* Trans. Leo Van Witsen. Poole, UK: Blandford, 1980.

Cumming, Valerie. *Understanding Fashion History.* New York: Costume and Fashion Press, 2004.

Cunningham, Patricia, ed. *Dress in American Culture.* Bowling Green, OH: Bowling Green State University Press, 1990.

Cunnington, C. Willett, and Phillis Cunnington. *The History of Underclothes.* London: Michael Joseph, 1951.

Curtis, George. *Clothes and the Man.* London: Jonathan Cape, 1926.

D'Assailly, Gisele. *Ages of Elegance, Five Thousand Years of Fashion and Frivolity.* London: MacDonald, 1968.

Davenport, Millia. *The Book of Costume.* New York: Crown, 1948.

Daves, Jessica. *Ready-made Miracle.* New York: G. P. Putnam's Sons, 1967.

Deloffre, Claude, ed. *Thierry Mugler: Fashion, Fetish, Fantasy.* Los Angeles: General, 1998.

Devlin, Polly. *Vogue Book of Fashion Photography 1919-1979.* New York: Simon and Schuster, 1979.

Diamonstein, Barbaralee. *Fashion: The Inside Story.* New York: Rizzoli, 1988.

Doran, John. *Habits and Men with Remnants of Record Touching the Makers of Both.* New York: Widdleton, 1865.

Dorner, Jane. *Fashion in the Forties and Fifties.* New Rochelle, NY: Arlington House, 1975.

———. *Fashion: the Changing Shape of Fashion through the Years.* London: Octopus, 1974.

Dotson, Edisol. *Behold the Man: The Hype and Selling of Male Beauty in Media and Culture.* New York: Harrington Park Press, 1999.

Downey, Lynn, et al. *This is a Pair of Levi's Jeans: The Official History of the Levi's Brand.* San Francisco: Levi Strauss, 1995.

Drake, Nicholas, ed. *The Sixties: A Decade in Vogue.* New York: Prentice Hall, 1988.

Drake, Nicholas. *The Fifties in Vogue.* New York: Henry Holt, 1987.

Duffey, Eliza Bisbee. *The Ladies' and Gentlemen's Etiquette: A Complete Manual of the Manners and Dress of American Society.* Philadelphia: Porter and Coates, 1877.

Earle, Alice. *Customs and Fashions in Old New England.* New York: Charles Scribner's Sons, 1893.

———. *Two Centuries of Costume in America 1620-1820.* New York: Macmillan, 1903.

Edwards, Tim. *Men in the Mirror: Men's Fashion, Masculinity and Consumer Society.* London: Cassell, 1997.

Eicher, Joanne B., and Ruth Barnes, eds. *Dress and Gender: Making and Meaning.* Oxford: Berg, 1992.

Eichler, Lillian. *The Customs of Mankind.* New York: Doubleday, 1924.

Ellis, Havelock. *Studies in the Psychology of Sex.* New York: Random House, 1942.

Evans, Caroline. *Fashion at the Edge: Spectacle, Modernity, and Deathliness.* New Haven: Yale University Press, 2003.

Evans, Mary. *Story of Textiles.* Boston: Little, Brown, 1942.

Evans, Mike, ed. *Key Moments in Fashion.* New York: Hamlyn, 1998.

Ewing, Elizabeth. *History of Twentieth Century Fashion.* Lanham, MD: Barnes and Noble, 1992.

———. *Dress and Undress.* New York: Drama, 1978.

Feirstein, Bruce. *Real Men Don't Eat Quiche: A Guidebook to All That Is Truly Masculine.* New York: Pocket Books, 1982.

Feldman, Egal. *Fit for Men: A Study of New York's Clothing Trade.* New York: Public Affairs, 1960.

Feldman, Elane. *Fashions of a Decade: The 1990s.* New York: Facts on File, 1992.

Finlayson, Iain. *Denim: The American Legend.* New York: Fireside, 1990.

Flocker, Michael. *The Metrosexual Guide to Style: A Handbook for the Modern Man.* Cambridge, MA: Da Capo, 2003.

Flugel, J. C. *The Psychology of Clothes.* London: Hogarth, 1950.

Flusser, Alan. *Clothes and the Man.* New York: Villard, 1985.

———. *Dressing the Man: Mastering the Art of Permanent Fashion.* New York: Harper Collins, 2002.

Foster, Vanda. *A Visual History of Costume in the Nineteenth Century.* London: B. T. Batsford, 1982.

Foucault, Michel. *The History of Sexuality: An Introduction.* Vol. 1. Robert Hurley, trans. New York: Vintage, 1978.

Fowler, Orson. *Creative and Sexual Science: Manhood, Womanhood and Their Mutual Inter-Relations.* New York: Physical Culture, 1870.

Fox, George. *Fashion: The Power That Influences the World.* 3rd ed. New York: Sheldon, 1872.

Fraser, Kennedy. *The Fashionable Mind.* New York: Knopf, 1981.

Friedan, Betty. *The Feminine Mystique.* New York: Laurel, 1983.

Fujii, Satoru, ed. *Vision: George Stavrinos.* Tokyo: Tokyo Designers Gakuin College, 1984.

Fukai, Akiko, et al. *Fashion: A History from the Eighteenth to the Twentieth Century.* Los Angeles: Taschen America, 2005.

Galbraith, John. *The Affluent Society.* Boston: Mentor, 1956.

Gale, Bill. *Esquire's Fashions for Today.* New York: Harper and Row, 1969.

Gan, Stephen. *Visionaire's Fashion 2000: Designers at the Turn of the Millennium.* New York: Universe, 1997.

———. *Visionaire's Fashion 2001: Designers of the New Avant-Garde.* New York: Universe, 1999.

Garland, Madge, et al. *Fashion 1900-1939.* London: Idea, 1975.

Geijer, Agnes. *A History of Textile Art.* London: Phillip Wilson, 1982.

Gere, Charlotte. *European and American Jewellery 1830-1914.* London: Heinemann, 1975.

Gernsheim, Alison. *Fashion and Reality.* London: Faber and Faber, 1963.

———. *Victorian and Edwardian Fashion.* New York: Dover, 1981.

Gillow, John. *World Textiles: A Visual Guide to Traditional Techniques.* Boston: Bulfinch, 1999.

Gilmore, David. *Manhood in the Making: Cultural Concepts of Masculinity.* New Haven, CT: Yale University Press, 1991.

Glynn, Prudence. *In Fashion: Dress in the Twentieth Century.* London: George Allen and Unwin, 1978.

———. *Skin to Skin: Exoticism in Dress.* New York: Oxford University Press, 1982.

Gold, Annalee. *One World of Fashion.* New York: Fairchild, 1987.

Gorsline, Douglas. *What People Wore.* New York: Viking, 1952.

Graham, Nicolas. *A Brief History of Shorts: The Ultimate Guide to Understanding Your Underwear.* San Francisco: Chronicle, 1995.

Grappa, Carol Di. *Fashion: Theory.* New York: Lustrum, 1980.

Grass, Milton. *History of Hosiery: From the Piloi of Ancient Greece to the Nylons of Modern America.* New York: Fairchild, 1955.

Graveline, Noel. *Jeans: Levi's Story*. Paris: Minerva, 1990.

Greeley, Horace, et al. *Great Industries of the United States*. Hartford: Burr and Hyde, 1872.

Greenwood, Kathryn, and Mary Murphy. *Fashion Innovation and Marketing*. New York: Macmillan, 1978.

Griffin, Gary. *History of Men's Underwear from Union Suits to Bikini Briefs*. Los Angeles: Added Dimensions, 1991.

Gross, Kim. *Chic, Simple Men's Wardrobe*. New York: Alfred A. Knopf, 1998.

Hall, Carolyn. *The Forties in Vogue*. New York: Harmony, 1985.

———. *The Thirties in Vogue*. New York: Harmony, 1985.

———. *The Twenties in Vogue*. New York: Harmony, 1983.

Hall, Lee. *Common Threads: A Parade of American Clothing*. Boston: Bulfinch, 1992.

Hannah, Barry, et al. *Men without Ties*. New York: Abbeville, 1994.

Hardy, Karen. *Not Just Another Pretty Face: An Intimate Look at America's Top Male Models*. New York: Plume, 1983.

Harris, Alice. *The White T*. New York: Harper Style, 1996.

Harris, Jennifer, ed. *Textiles: Five Thousand Years*. New York: Harry N. Abrams, 1993.

Hart, Avril. *Ties*. New York: Costume and Fashion, 1998.

Harvey, John. *Men in Black*. Chicago: University of Chicago Press, 1995.

Hawes, Elizabeth. *Fashion Is Spinach*. New York: Random House, 1938.

Haye, Amy de la, and Cathie Dingwall. *Surfers, Soulies, Skinheads, and Skaters: Subcultural Style from the Forties to the Nineties*. Woodstock, NY: Overlook, 1996.

Haye, Amy de la, and Elizabeth Wilson, ed. *Defining Dress: Dress as Object, Meaning and Identity*. Manchester, UK: Manchester University Press, 1999.

Haye, Amy de la, ed. *The Cutting Edge: Fifty Years of British Fashion, 1947-1997*. Woodstock, N.Y.: Overlook, 1997.

———. *Fashion Source Book: A Visual Reference to Twentieth Century Fashion*. Secaucus, NJ: Wellfleet, 1988.

Heard, Gerald. *Narcissus: An Anatomy of Clothes*. New York: E. P. Dutton, 1924.

Hecht, Ann. *The Art of the Loom: Weaving, Spinning, and Dyeing across the World*. New York: Rizzoli, 1990.

Henley, Clark. *The Butch Manual: The Current Drag and How to Do It*. New York: New American Library, 1982.

Herald, Jacqueline. *Fashions of a Decade: The 1920s*. New York: Facts on File, 1991.

———. *Fashions of a Decade: The 1970s*. New York: Facts on File, 1991.

Hill, Daniel Delis. *Advertising to the American Woman 1900-1999*. Columbus: Ohio State University Press, 2002.

———. *As Seen in Vogue: A Century of American Fashion in Advertising*. Lubbock: Texas Tech University, 2004.

———. *History of World Costume and Fashion*. Columbus: Prentice Hall, 2010.

———. *Fashion from Victoria to the New Millennium*. Columbus: Prentice Hall, 2010.

———. *History of Men's Underwear and Swimwear*. San Antonio: Daniel Delis Hill, 2010.

Hill, Margot, and Peter Bucknell. *The Evolution of Fashion: Pattern and Cut from 1066-1930*. London: B. T. Batsford, 1967.

Hix, Charles. *Dressing Right: A Guide For Men*. New York: St. Martin's, 1978.

———. *Looking Good: A Guide for Men*. New York: Hawthorn, 1977.

———. *Man Alive: Dressing the Free Way*. New York: Simon and Schuster, 1984.

Hollander, Anne. *Seeing through Clothes*. New York: Avon, 1978.

———. *Sex and Suits: The Evolution of Modern Dress*. New York: Alfred A. Knopf, 1994.

Horrocks, Roger. *Masculinity in Crisis: Myths, Fantasies and Realities*. New York: St. Martin's Press, 1994.

Hunt, Marsha. *The Way We Wore: Styles of the 1930s and '40s*. Fallbrook, CA: Fallbrook, 1993.

Hurlock, Elizabeth. *The Psychology of Dress: An Analysis of Fashion and Its Motives*. New York: Ronald Press, 1929.

Hyde, Jack, ed. *Generation of Change: A History of Male Fashion Trends, 1956–1980, on the Occasion of the Twenty-Fifth Anniversary of the Founding of the Men's Fashion Association*. New York: Men's Wear, 1980.

Hyman, Peter. *The Reluctant Metrosexual*. New York: Villard Books, 2004.

James McCabe, James. *The Illustrated History of the Centennial Exhibition*. Philadelphia: National Publishing, 1876.

Janson, H. W., and Anthony Janson. *History of Art*. 6th ed. Upper Saddle River, NJ: Prentice-Hall, 2001.

Jennings, Peter, and Todd Brewster. *The Century*. New York: Doubleday, 1998.

Jobling, Paul. *Man Appeal: Advertising, Modernism, and Menswear*. Oxford, UK: Berg, 2005.

Joselit, Jenna Weissman. *A Perfect Fit: Clothes, Character, and the Promise of America*. New York: Metropolitan, 2001.

Kaiser, Susan. *The Social Psychology of Clothing*. New York: Macmillan, 1990.

Karpinski, Kenneth. *Red Socks Don't Work: Messages from the Real World about Men's Clothing*. Manassas Park, VA: Inpact, 1994.

Kasson, John. *Houdini, Tarzan, and the Perfect Man: The White Male Body and the Challenge of Modernity in America*. New York: Hill and Wang, 2001.

Keen, Sam. *Fire in the Belly: On Being a Man*. New York: Bantam Books, 1991.

Kemper, Rachel. *Costume*. New York: Newsweek, 1977.

Kerr, Rose. *One Hundred Years of Costumes in America*. Worcester, MA: Davis, 1981.

Kimbrell, Andrew. *The Masculine Mystique: The Politics of Masculinity*. New York: Ballantine, 1995.

Kimmel, Michael. *Manhood in America: A Cultural History*.

New York: Free Press, 1996.

———. *Guyland: The Perilous World Where Boys Become Men.* New York: HarperCollins, 2008.

Klein, Bernat. *Design Matters.* London: Secker and Warburg, 1976.

Klein, Kelly. *Underworld.* New York: Alfred A. Knopf, 1995.

Koda, Harold. *Extreme Beauty: The Body Transformed.* New York: Metropolitan Museum of Art, 2001.

Kohler, Carl. *A History of Costume.* Trans. Alexander Dallas. New York: Dover, 1963.

Kunzle, David. *Fashion and Fetishism.* Totowa, NJ: Rowman and Littlefield, 1992.

Kurella, Elizabeth. *The Complete Guide to Vintage Textiles.* Iola, WI: Krause, 1999.

Kutchta, David. *The Three-Piece Suit and Modern Masculinity: England 1550-1850.* Berkeley: University of California Press, 2002.

Kybalova, Ludmila. *The Pictorial Encyclopedia of Fashion.* Trans. Claudia Rosoux. London: Hamlyn, 1968.

Lakoff, Robin Tolmach, and Rachel L. Sherr. *Face Value: The Politics of Beauty.* London: Routledge and Kegan Paul, 1984.

Langner, Lawrence. *The Importance of Wearing Clothes.* New York: Hastings House, 1959.

Laver, James. *Clothes.* London: Burke, 1952.

———. *A Concise History of Costume and Fashion.* London: Thames and Hudson, 1979.

———. *Costume and Fashion.* London: Thames and Hudson, 1995.

———. *Dandies.* London: Weidenfeld and Nicolson, 1968

———. *Dress: How and Why Fashions in Men's and Women's Clothes Have Changed During the Past Two Hundred Years.* London: John Murray, 1950.

———. *Edwardian Promenade.* Boston: Houghton Mifflin, 1958.

———. *Fashion and Fashion Plates 1800-1900.* London: King Penguin, 1943.

———. *Victorian Vista.* Boston: Houghton Mifflin, 1955.

———. *Victoriana.* New York: Hawthorne, 1967.

Lee, Sarah, ed. *American Fashion.* New York: Fashion Institute, 1975.

Lees, Elizabeth. *Costume Design in the Movies.* London: BCW, 1976.

Lehnert, Gertrud. *Fashion: A Concise History.* London: Laurence King, 1998.

———. *A History of Fashion in the Twentieth Century.* Cologne: Konemann, 2000.

Lester, Katherine, and Rose Kerr. *Historic Costume.* Peoria, IL: Charles A. Bennett, 1977.

Levin, Phyllis. *The Wheels of Fashion.* Garden City, NY: Doubleday, 1965.

Levine, Martin. *Gay Macho: The Life and Death of the Homosexual Clone.* Ed. Michael Kimmel. New York: New York University Press, 1998.

Levitt, Sarah. *Victorians Unbuttoned.* Boston: Allen and Unwin, 1986.

Ley, Sandra. *Fashion for Everyone: The Story of Ready-to-Wear 1870s-1970s.* New York: Charles Scribner's Sons, 1975.

Lipovetsky, Gilles. *The Empire of Fashion.* Trans. Catherine Porter. Princeton, NJ: Princeton University Press, 1994.

Lobenthal, Joel. *Radical Rags: Fashions of the Sixties.* New York: Abbeville, 1990.

Loughery, John. *The Other Side of Silence.* New York: Henry Holt, 1998.

Lurie, Alison. *The Language of Clothes.* New York: Henry Holt, 2000.

Lussier, Suzanne. *Art Deco Fashion.* New York: Bulfinch, 2003.

Lynam, Ruth, ed. *Couture.* Garden City, NY: Doubleday, 1972.

Lynd, Robert, and Helen Lynd. *Middletown: A Study in Contemporary American Culture.* New York: Harcourt, Brace, 1929.

———. *Middletown in Transition: A Study in Cultural Conflicts.* New York: Harcourt, Brace, 1937.

Machett, W.J. *The Tailor's Compass.* Baltimore: n.p., 1829.

Mackrell, Alice. *Art and Fashion: The Impact of Art on Fashion and Fashion on Art.* London: B. T. Batsford, 2005.

Maeder, Edward. *Hollywood and History: Costume Design in Film.* London: Thames and Hudson, 1987.

———. *Salvatore Ferragamo: Art of the Shoe 1896-1960.* New York: Rizzoli, 1992.

Malossi, Giannino, ed. *Material Man: Masculinity, Sexuality, Style.* New York: Harry N. Abrams, 2000.

Mansour, David. *From Abba to Zoom: A Pop Culture Encyclopedia of the Late 20th Century.* Kansas City, MO: Andrews McMeel, 2005.

Marchand, Roland. *Advertising the American Dream: Making Way for Modernity 1920–1940.* Berkeley: University of California Press, 1985.

Marcus, Stanley. *Minding the Store.* New York: Little Brown, 1974.

Marly, Diana de. *Fashion for Men: An Illustrated History.* New York: Holmes and Meier, 1989.

Martin, Richard, and Harold Koda. *Cubism and Fashion.* New Haven: Yale University Press, 1999.

———. *Giorgio Armani: Images of Man.* New York: Rizzoli, 1990.

———. *Jocks and Nerds: Men's Style in the Twentieth Century.* New York: Rizzoli, 1989.

———. *Orientalism: Visions of the East in Western Dress.* New York: Metropolitan Museum of Art, 1994.

———. *Splash! A History of Swimwear.* New York: Rizzoli, 1990.

Martin, Richard. *American Ingenuity: Sportswear 1930s-1970s.* New York: Metropolitan Museum of Art, 1998.

———. *Fashion and Surrealism.* New York: Rizzoli, 1996.

———. *Versace.* New York: Universe, 1997.

McClellan, Elisabeth. *History of American Costume 1607-1870.* New York: Tudor, 1969.

McDowell, Colin. *Fashion Today.* New York: Phaidon, 2000.
———. *The Man of Fashion.* London: Thames and Hudson, 1997.
———. *McDowell's Directory of Twentieth Century Fashion.* Englewood Cliffs, NJ: 1985.
McNabb, Nan. *Body Bizarre, Body Beautiful.* New York: Fireside, 1999.
McNeil, Peter, and Vicki Karaminas, eds. *The Men's Fashion Reader.* London: Berg, 2009.
Meller, Susan, and Joost Elffers. *Textile Designs: Two Hundred Years of European and American Patterns.* New York: Harry N. Abrams, 1991.
Mendes, Valerie, and Amy de la Haye. *Twentieth-Century Fashion.* London: Thames and Hudson, 1999.
Metzner, Sheila. *Form and Fashion.* Sante Fe, NM: Arena, 2001.
Milbank, Caroline. *New York Fashion.* New York: Harry N. Abrams, 1996.
Mo, Charles. *Evening Elegance: One Hundred Fifty Years of Formal Fashions.* Charlotte, NC: Mint Museum of Art, 1998.
Moffitt, Phillip, et al. *The American Man 1946-1986.* New York: Esquire, 1986.
Montgomery, Florence. *Textiles in America 1650-1870.* New York: W. W. Norton, 1983.
Moore, Doris. *Fashion through Fashion Plates 1771-1970.* New York: Clarkson Potter, 1971.
Morris, Bernadine. *The Fashion Makers.* New York: Randon House, 1978.
Morris, Bob, and Ben Widdicombe. *The Blue Jean.* New York: Powerhouse, 2002.
Mosconi, Davide, and Riccardo Villarosa. *Getting Knotted.* Trans. Clive Foster. Milan: Ratti, 1985.
Mosse, George. *The Image of Man: The Creation of Modern Masculinity.* New York: Oxford University Press, 1996.
Muir, Robin. *Clifford Coffin: Photographs from Vogue 1945 to 1955.* New York: Stewart, Tabori, and Chang, 1997.
Musgrave, Eric. *Sharp Suits.* Brighton, UK: Pavilion, 2010.
Nixon, Sean. *Hard Looks: Masculinities, Spectatorship and Contemporary Consumption.* New York: St. Martin's, 1996.
Norris, Herbert. *Nineteenth-Century Costume and Fashion.* Mineola, NY: Dover, 1999.
Nunn, Joan. *Fashion in Costume 1200-1980.* New York: Schocken, 1984.
Nystrom, Paul. *Economics of Fashion.* New York: Ronald, 1928.
Odenwald, Robert. *The Disappearing Sexes.* New York: Random House, 1965.
O'Hara, Georgina. *The Encyclopaedia of Fashion.* New York: Harry N. Abrams, 1986.
Olian, Joanne. *Authentic French Fashions of the Twenties.* New York: Dover, 1990.
Omelianuk, Scott, and Ted Allen. *Esquire's Things a Man Should Know About Style.* New York: Riverhead, 1999.
Panati, Charles. *Panati's Extraordinary Origins of Everyday Things.* New York: Perennial Library, 1987.

Parsons, Frank. *The Psychology of Dress.* Garden City, NY: Doubleday, Page, 1921.
Pascoe, C. J. *Dude, You're a Fag: Masculinity and Sexuality in High School.* Berkeley: University of California Press, 2007.
Peacock, John. *The Chronicle of Western Fashion from Ancient Times to the Present Day.* New York: Harry N. Abrams, 1991.
———. *Fashion Accessories: The Complete Twentieth-Century Sourcebook.* New York: Thames and Hudson, 2000.
———. *Fashion Source: the 1920s.* New York: Thames and Hudson, 1997.
———. *Fashion Source: the 1930s.* New York: Thames and Hudson, 1997.
———. *Fashion Source: the 1940s.* New York: Thames and Hudson, 1998.
———. *Fashion Source: the 1950s.* New York: Thames and Hudson, 1997.
———. *Fashion Source: the 1960s.* New York: Thames and Hudson, 1998.
———. *Fashion Source: the 1970s.* New York: Thames and Hudson, 1997.
———. *Fashion Source: The 1980s.* New York: Thames and Hudson, 1998.
———. *Men's Fashion: the Complete Sourcebook.* London: Thames and Hudson, 1996.
Pearson, Henry. *Crude Rubber and Compounding Ingredients: A Textbook of Rubber Manufacture.* New York: India Rubber, 1909.
Perrot, Philippe. *Fashioning the Bourgeoisie: A History of Clothing in the Nineteenth Century.* Trans. Richard Bienvenu. Princeton, NJ: Princeton University Press, 1987.
Polhemus, Ted. *Street Style: From Sidewalk to Catwalk.* London: Thames and Hudson, 1994.
———. *Style Surfing: What to Wear in the Third Millennium.* New York: Thames and Hudson, 1996.
Pope, Harrison, et al. *The Adonis Complex: The Secret Crisis of Male Body Obsession.* New York: Free Press, 2000.
Pronger, Brian. *The Arena of Masculinity: Sports, Homosexuality, and the Meaning of Sex.* New York: St. Martin's, 1990.
Reuter, Donald. *Heartthrob: A Hundred Years of Beautiful Men.* New York: Universe, 1998.
Ribeiro, Aileen, and Valerie Cumming. *The Visual History of Costume.* London: B. T. Batsford, 1989.
———. *Dress and Morality.* New York: Holmes and Meier, 1986.
Riesman, David. *The Lonely Crowd: A Study of the Changing American Character.* New Haven: Yale University Press, 1950.
Robinson, Julian. *The Fine Art of Fashion: An Illustrated History.* New York: Bartley and Jensen, 1989.
———. *Body Packaging: A Guide to Human Sexual Display.* Los Angeles: Elysium Growth, 1988.
Robinson, Julian. *The Fine Art of Fashion: An Illustrated*

History. New York: Bartley and Jensen, 1989.

Roetzel, Berhard. *Gentlemen: A Timeless Fashion.* Cologne: Konemann Verlagsgesellschaft, 1999.

Rotundo, Anthony. *American Manhood: Transformations in Masculinity from the Revolution to the Modern Era.* New York: Basic Books, 1990.

Ruby, Jennifer. *Costume in Context: The 1920s and 1930s.* London: B. T. Batsford, 1988.

———. *Costume in Context 1930-1945.* London: B. T. Batsford, 1995.

———. *Costume in Context: The 1960s and 1970s.* London: B. T. Batsford, 1989.

———. *People in Costume: The 1970s and 1980s.* London: Chrysalis, 1988.

———. *Costume in Context: The Edwardians and the First World War.* London: B. T. Batsford, 1988.

———. *Costume in Context: Underwear.* London: B. T. Batsford, 1996.

———. *Costume in Context: The Victorians.* London: B. T. Batsford, 1994.

Rudofsky, Bernard. *Are Clothes Modern?* Chicago: Paul Theobald, 1947.

Russell, Douglas. *Costume History and Style.* Englewood Cliffs, N.J.: Prentice Hall, 1983.

Ruttenber, Edward. *The American Male: His Fashions and Foibles.* New York: Fairchild, 1948.

Schnurnberger, Lynn. *Let There Be Clothes: 40,000 Years of Fashion.* New York: Workman, 1991.

Schoeffler, O. E., and William Gale. *Esquire's Encyclopedia of Twentieth-Century Men's Fashions.* New York, McGraw-Hill, 1973.

Selbie, Robert. *The Anatomy of Costume.* New York: Crescent, 1977.

Shau, Michael. *J. C. Leyendecker.* New York: Watson-Guptill, 1974.

Shaw, William. *American Men's Wear 1861-1982.* Baton Rouge: Oracle, 1982.

Shover, Edna. *Art in Costume Design.* Springfield, MA: Milton Bradley, 1920.

Sichel, Marion. *Costume Reference: Regency. Vol. 5.* New York: Chelsea House, 1978.

———. *Costume Reference: 1918-1939. Vol. 8.* Boston: Plays, 1978.

———. *Costume Reference: 1939-1950. Vol. 9.* London: B. T. Batsford, 1987.

———. *Costume Reference: Victorians. Vol. 6.* New York: Chelsea House, 1986.

———. *History of Men's Costume, Roman to 1930s.* London: B. T. Batsford, 1984.

Spignesi, Stephen. *American Firsts: Innovations, Discoveries, and Gadgets Born in the USA.* New York: Barnes and Noble, 2004.

Squire, Geoffrey. *Dress and Society 1560-1970.* New York: Viking, 1974.

———. *Dress, Art and Society.* London: Studio Vista, 1974.

Steele, Valerie. *Fetish: Fashion, Sex and Power.* New York: Oxford University Press, 1996.

———. *Fifty Years of Fashion: New Look to Now.* New Haven: Yale University Press, 1997.

———. *Men and Women, Dressing the Part.* Washington, D.C.: Smithsonian Institution, 1989.

Steinberg, Warren. *Masculinity: Identity, Conflict, and Transformation.* Boston: Shambhala, 1993.

Strong, Roy. *Gianni Versace: Do Not Disturb.* New York: Abbeville, 1996.

Sullivan, Mark. *Our Times 1900–1925.* New York: Charles Scribner's Sons, 1936.

Swenson, Marge, and Gerri Pinckney. *New Image for Men: Color and Wardrobe.* Costa Mesa, CA: Fashion Academy, 1983.

Tasker, Yvonne. *Spectacular Bodies: Gender, Genre and the Action Cinema.* London: Routledge, 1993.

Taylor. Lou. *The Study of Dress History.* Manchester, UK: Manchester University Press, 2002.

Thieme, Otto Charles. *Simply Stunning: Two Hundred Years of Fashion from the Cincinnati Art Museum.* Cincinnati, OH: Cincinnati Art Museum, 1988.

Thieme, Otto, et al. *With Grace and Favor: Victorian and Edwardian Fashion in America.* Cincinnati, OH: Cincinnati Art Museum, 1993.

Thomas, David. *Not Guilty: The Case and Defense of Men.* New York: William Morrow, 1993.

Tortora, Phyllis, and Keith Eubank. *Survey of Historic Costume.* 3rd ed. New York: Fairchild, 2000.

Tozer, Jane, and Sarah Levitt. *Fabric of Society: A Century of People and Their Clothes 1770-1870.* Manchester, UK: Laura Ashley, 1983.

Truman, Nevil. *Historic Costuming.* London: Isaac Pitman, 1936.

Tucker, Andrew. *London Fashion Book.* London: Thames and Hudson, 1998.

U.S. Bureau of the Census. *Historical Statistics of the United States: Colonial Times to 1970.* Washington, D.C.: U.S. Department of Commerce, 1975.

Van Bree, Marc. *The Metrosexual Defined: Narcissism and Masculinity in Popular Culture.* N.p., 2004.

Versace, Gianni. *Rock and Royalty.* New York: Abbeville, 1996.

Versace, Gianni. *Signatures.* New York: Abbeville, 1992.

Vreeland, Diana. *Allure.* Boston: Bulfinch, 2002.

Walkley, Christina. *Dressed to Impress 1840-1914.* London: B. T. Batsford, 1989.

Warwick, Edward, et al. *Early American Dress.* New York: Benjamin Blom, 1965.

Wenzell, A.B. *The Passing Show.* New York: Collier, 1913.

Wheeler, R. E. M. *Costume 1558-1933.* London: Lancaster House, 1934.

Wilcox, Claire. *Radical Fashion.* London: Victoria and Albert Museum, 2001.

Winters, Peggy, et al. *What Works in Fashion Advertising.* New York: Retail Reporting, 1996.

Worrell, Estelle. *American Costume 1840-1920.* Harrisburg, PA: Stackpole, 1979.

Yarwood, Doreen. *Encyclopedia of World Costume.* New York: Bonanza, 1978.

———. *Fashion in the Western World 1500-1990.* New York: Drama, 1992.

Zahm, Volker. *The Art of Creating Fashion.* Pocking, Germany: Mondi, 1991.

Periodicals Cited in Notes

Adweek

After Dark

American Mercury

California Men's and Boy's Stylist

Collier's

Cosmopolitan

Details

Dress

DNA

Esquire

Esquire Gentleman

Fashion Inc

Fitness RX for Men

Genre

Gentry

Gentlemen's Journal

Gentlemen's Quarterly

Godey's Lady's Book

Good Housekeeping

GQ Campus and Career Annual

GQ Scene

GQ Style

Harper's Bazar

History Workshop Journal

Jet

Ladies' Home Journal

Lady's World

Life

Literary Digest

Look

Men's Wear

Men's Workout

Motion Picture

Ms.

Nation

New York Times

New York Times Magazine

Newsweek

Out

Peterson's

Physical Culture

Printers' Ink

Quest

Rolling Stone

Sartorial Art Journal

Saturday Evening Post

Vanity Fair

Vogue

Vogue Hommes International

Washington Post

Woman's Day

Youth's Companion

Acknowledgments

The author would like to thank Phyllis Specht of the Costume Society of America and Judith Keeling of Texas Tech University Press for suggesting this study. Special thanks to Joanne Vickers for her insightful copyediting and to Rob Schorman, Miami University, Ohio, for his thorough reviews and feedback. A gold star also goes to the production, editing, and marketing teams of Texas Tech University Press for helping ensure the success of *American Menswear from the Civil War to the Twenty-First Century.*

Feedback and corrections are welcomed. Please contact the author at DanielDelisHill.com.

Riviera, 144, 145, 187, 189, 191
rockabilly look, 303, 305
rock-and-roll, 209, 211, 241, 243, 246, 305
Rockne, Knute, 139
Rococo suits, 40
Rogaine, 335
Rogers, Roy, 185
Rogue Wallet, 330
roll neck sweaters. *See* turtlenecks
roller skating, 267
Rolling Stone, 304
Rolling Stones, ix, 246
Romania, 209, 290
Rome, 217
Romijn, Rebecca, 319
Ronson ad, *202*
Roosevelt, Franklin Delano, 162
Roosevelt, Teddy, viii, 77–78, *77,* 83, 99, 128, 290
Rooster butterfly bowties, *Color Plate 22*
Rose, Axl, 320
Rosie the Riveter, 170
Rotary Club, 125
Rough Riders, 77
Royal Ascot shirts, 183, *183*
Royal Household Guard, 130
rubber (cause) bracelets, 331
Rudolfsky, Bernard, 280
Russia, 115, 117, 123, 126, 195, 209, 290
Ruth, Babe, 139
Ruttenber, Edward, 127

S. Buchsbaum ads, *200*
sack coat, vi–vii, viii; Edwardian styles, 84–85; interwar
    years styles, 128–3, 137; nineteenth-century origins, 43;
    Victorian styles, 48–49, *48,* 53. *See also* tuxedo
saddle oxfords. *See* footwear
safari (hunter) jacket, 189, 257, 272–73
safety bicycle, 26; cycling craze 1890s, 27
safety razor, invention of, 110
Saks Fifth Avenue tail coat, *313*
sandals. *See* footwear
Sanders, Deion, 332
Sands, Tommy, 235
Sanger, Margaret, 121
Sanitary Woolen System, 63, *63*
Sartor Resartus (Carlyle), 33
Sartorial Art Journal, The, 88, 95
Saturday Evening Post, The, cartoon, 1936, *166*
Saturday Night Fever, 249, 250, 179
Savile Row, 29, 84, 123, 174, 249, 276
S-bend silhouette, *79,* 84
Scarlet Pimpernell, The, 34
Schick Styling Dryer ad, *283*
Schick, Jacob, 203
Schoeffler, Oscar, v; *Esquire's Encyclopedia of Twentieth
    Century Men's Fashion,* v
Scholte, Frederick, 130, 173, 174, 192
Schwartzman Tiger Suit, *253*

Scotchgard fabric treatment, 272
Scotland Baratta sport jackets, *Color Plate 14*
Scribner's, 15; illustration from, 1897, *58*
Seaflame swim brief, *226*
Sears, Roebuck and Company, 5, 12, 26, 90, 94, 147, 148,
    182–83, 198, 273; army field jacket, *194;* Beta VCR, *292;*
    catalog, 1907, *13,* 100, 110; cigarette lighters, *155;* coats,
    146; Correcto suits, *85;* hats, 151, *151;* dining suite,
    1907, *79;* jeans, *223;* jewelry, 1903, *109;* living room
    suite, 1937, *164;* neckwear, *152;* overalls, 185; overcoats,
    193, *193;* robes, *150, 196;* roll neck sweaters, 93; shirts,
    183, *183,* 184, *184, 224;* shoes, 106; teddy bear, 1912, *79;*
    underwear, 229; women's pantsuit, *242;* work trousers,
    137
Secessionists, 123
Second Feminist Movement. See feminism
Second Industrial Revolution, vi, 14, 24, 26, 35, 56, 243
seersucker, 177
Selective Service Act, 212
separate spheres, 82, 83, 168–69, 171; men's roles, 32, 34,
    35, 36, 82, 171, 214; women's roles, 35, 36, 39, 82, 214,
    282
serge de Nimes. See denim; nineteenth century
servant's livery, 41
sewing machine, vi, 28; compared with hand sewing, 8;
    introduction of, vi, 4, 7–8; *Ladies' Home Journal* treadle
    sewing machine, *7;* Wilson shuttle sewing machine, *7*
Sex Pistols, 304
sex-sell advertising, 325–26
Sexual Inversion, 38
Sexual Psychopathy, 38
sexual revolution: 1920s, 120–21; 1960s, 241, 247
Shaft (movie), 250
shag hair cut. *See* grooming
shaving cream. *See* grooming
Shaw, William Harlan, v; *American Men's Wear 1861–1982,*
    v
Shields silk pocket accessories, *279*
shirts: banded collar revivals, 263; Bold Look, 221–22; coat
    cut, 53, *53,* 89, *89;* Edwardian styles, 88; first short sleeve
    styles, 92, 141; interwar years styles of, 135–36, *136,*
    182–83; locker loops, 260; mod styles, *Color Plate 15;*
    nineteenth century, 51–53, *52, 53;* nylon acetate, 263,
    263; permanent press, 250–60; rayon, 183; short-sleeved
    business shirts introduced, 223; silk, 183; soft collar
    popularization, 136, 141; sports shirts, 92, *92;* 224, *224;*
    tennis shirt, 92, *92;* Trubenized collars, 182–83, *183;*
    work shirts, 90, *90;* 137, *137;* WWII styles, 183
shiruschakar. See seersucker
shoes. *See* footwear
shorts: bermuda, 220, 225; bike, 320, 321, *321;* cargo, 316;
    suit, 219–20, *219;* tennis, 189; walking, 187
shoulder bag, 280, *280,* 329–30, *330*
Shu-Lok fastener. *See* footwear
Sid Vicious, 304
sideburns. *See* grooming
signet rings. *See* jewelry
Silent Generation, 210, 216, 239

403729